THE WORLD TODAY SERIES®

Africa
1995

PIERRE ETIENNE DOSTERT, J.D.

30TH EDITION

STRYKER–POST PUBLICATIONS
HARPERS FERRY
WEST VIRGINIA
NEXT EDITION—
AUGUST 1996

Pierre Etienne Dostert . . .

Former Circuit Judge, State of West Virginia. American University (B.A., 1957), Political Science, Georgetown University (J.D., 1959). The retired jurist has long been one of the closest observers of world trends and developments, particularly in contemporary Africa and Latin America. He is widely traveled and speaks a number of languages. As editor of the World Today Series®, he has energetically encouraged the production of accurate, but challenging, texts for a generation of students.

Some portions of this book are the result of contributions of others. When they are significant, they are acknowledged.

First appearing as *Africa 1966*, this annually revised book is published by

Stryker–Post Publications
P.O. Drawer 1200
Harpers Ferry, WV. 25425
Telephones: 1–800–995–1400
   From outside U.S.A.: 1–304–535–2593
   Fax: 1–304–535–6513

International Standard Book Number: 0–943448–89–1

International Standard Serial Number: 0084–2281

Library of Congress Catalog Number 67–11537

Cover design by Susan Bodde

Chief Bibliographer: Robert V. Gross

Printed in the United States of America by Braun–Brumfield, Inc., Ann Arbor, Michigan

Typography and design by Stryker–Post Publications and Braun–Brumfield, Inc.

Photographs used to illustrate *The World Today Series* come from many sources, a great number from friends who travel worldwide. If you have taken any which you believe would enhance the visual impact and attractiveness of our books, do let us hear from you.

CONTENTS

Africa Today   iv
Understanding the Tropical African
    Environment and Ways of Life   2
Maps: *Africa 1905* and *Africa Today*   9

Historical Background (pre-Colonial period)   10
Prehistoric Africa   10
Early Civilizations of the Nile Valley and
    Mediterranean Sea   11
Early Christian Era Movements   11
The Hamitic Kingdom of Ethiopia   12
The Spread of Islam   12
Arabs in East Africa   13
The Early Empires of West Africa   13
European Discovery and Exploration   14
Early Ethiopian and European Contact   15
The Arabs and Ottoman Turks in North Africa   15
European Settlers in South Africa   16

The Colonial Period   18
The Portuguese (about 1550)   19
The British (about 1660)   19
The French (about 1830)   27
The Americans (1835, see Liberia)   32
King Leopold II and the Belgians (1885)   32
The Spanish (1885)   33
The Germans (1885)   34
The South African mandate (1919)   35
The Italians (1927)   35

Coastal West Africa
Benin   38
Cape Verde Islands   236
Côte d'Ivoire (Ivory Coast)   41
The Gambia   44
Ghana   46
Guinea   49
Guinea-Bissau   52
Liberia   54
Senegal   59
Sierra Leone   62
Togo   64

Central West Africa
Cameroon   66
Central African Republic   69
Equatorial Guinea   72
Nigeria   74

Equatorial West Africa
Angola   80
Burundi   86
Rwanda   89
Congo   92
Gabon   94
São Tomé and Príncipe   236
Zaïre   96

Southern Africa
Botswana   104
Lesotho   106
Malawi   108
Mozambique   110
Namibia   114
South Africa   118
Swaziland   150
Zambia   152
Zimbabwe   155

East African Island Nations
Comoros   236
Madagascar   160
Mauritius   162
Seychelles   236

Eastern Africa
Djibouti   165
Eritrea   166
Ethiopia   168
Kenya   174
Somalia   178
Tanzania   182
Uganda   186

South Sahara Africa
Burkina Faso   190
Chad   193
Mali   196
Niger   200
Sudan   202

North Africa
Algeria   208
Egypt   214
Libya   222
Mauritania   226
Morocco—(Western Sahara)   228
Tunisia   232

Selected Bibliography   237

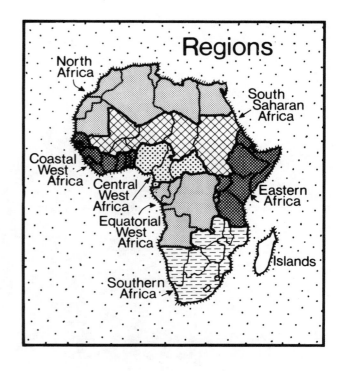

A young Sudanese farmer

Africa Today

Geography and History . . .

Africa is not a land mass divided into easily understood geographical and political features. National boundaries are no more than arbitrary lines drawn by the European powers in the 19th and 20th centuries which do not reflect ethnic or natural land divisions. This book is organized into regional areas to give a clearer understanding of the problems and prospects of people living close to each other on this vast continent.

Democracy and "Freedom" . . .

Only a few nations in Africa have been governed "democratically" as we understand that word—with openly competing political parties and total freedom of the press. In some others, such as Nigeria, there have been frequently–stalled plans by the military to turn the government over to civilian rule with no tangible results. In the remainder, if there is an "election," the winner gets a majority usually exceeding 95%. The leadership heads the major, or only political party, and therefore is the choice of "the people." Nevertheless, although such systems prevail, the people of many of these other nations are governed democratically in the ultimate sense of the word. The leaders must show a responsibility and concern for the welfare and wishes of the people in order to remain in office. Such a state of affairs has been the exception rather than the rule in far too many African nations since independence from colonial rule began more than a generation ago.

It is regrettable that democracy is being equated in many African minds with economic improvement. This is not the case—the key is modernization with outside technical assistance, if economic progress is to be speeded up.

Some countries are run by military men, many of whom have changed their uniform to a business suit or regional garb. Others are civilians, but maintain their power only through the muscle of the armed forces. In either case, without military backing, African heads of state may be turned out of office in one day. Such a move is a *coup d'etat*, ("seizure of the state) and usually means that a military government will be supreme until "free elections" can be held, or, indefinitely.

Recent World Changes . . .

One of the cruelest hoaxes ever visited upon mankind commenced in the former Soviet Union in 1917 when revolutionaries who were nominally communist came to power. Although they, over the years, devised elaborate and painstaking theories of government disguised as jingoes and slogans, communist practice, as envisioned by its founding father, Karl Marx, never existed anywhere in the world.

Marx had concluded that profits of enterprises were wrongfully appropriated by capitalists, depriving their workers and creating a wide disparity of income. He envisioned a "dictatorship of the proletariat" (the workers) in which the workers would receive their share in the profits of an enterprise. The state, no longer needed, would "wither away."

He was partially correct. Even in this day and age, an employer hires a worker *in order to make a profit* from his labors. It is because of this that capital is attracted to an enterprise and there is seldom any need for government assistance in spite of contrary sentiments by a burgeoning bureaucracy. The law of supply and demand and the cost of the goods manufactured determine profit and the construction and maintenance of newer facilities. Under communism, all workers were supposed to share in the profits of the enterprise and, further, with prosperity, there was hope of climbing the ladder within the enterprise because of increased knowledge and skills. In theory, because profits were distributed to workers, there was supposed to be no need for capital investment to provide for tomorrow's needs.

In Russia, the theory of communism sounded good, but overlooked one factor: following the revolution of 1917, no one knew what he or she was supposed to do. The dictatorship of the proletariat did not spontaneously spring forth, but rather, a substitute quickly filled the gap. A huge bureaucracy grew almost overnight (it took the U.S. a century after the civil war to "achieve" the same result). Profits, where such occurred, were diverted not to finance development or to satisfy the needs of the workers, but to feed and clothe the bureaucrats in the comparatively luxurious style to which they had increasingly become accustomed.

Without fanfare, the capitalist system of the U.S. and other nations fulfilled the shortcomings of 18th–19th century England objected to by Marx. Owners shouldered nominally unpleasant duties as providing for sickness, lack of work, accident and disease arising out of employment, and, ultimately, pensions when a worker is ready for retirement. Although profits were diminished by these expenses to a degree, they became available for future development and research, as well as for investors. Workers, through direct and indirect investment, often became owners.

The post–World War II era ushered in the rivalry of the Cold War, which continued from the late 1950's intil it cracked in 1985 and was demolished by events within the former Soviet Union in 1989–1991. The Cold War furnished excellent opportunities for underdeveloped nations such as those newly independent ones of Africa, to exploit differences between the superpowers, resulting in gain which would not otherwise have been available. Money was dispatched with few, if any, strings attached other than nominal allegiance to the worldwide ambitions of communism (Russian imperialism) and the efforts of the capitalist nations to preserve the *status quo*.

Numerous African nations experimented with what was supposed to be communism with the same result: dicta-

torship of the elite. In schemes, capitalist assistance, with strings attached, was regarded as exploitation of the workers. A pattern developed in which foreign aid was subjected to the hamstrings of bureaucratic regulation and corruption which made it impossible for borrowing nations and enterprises to repay loans on time or at all. This, ingrained for more than a generation since independence, may well have become permanent. There also has been a lingering fear of nationalization with which many African nations experimented following independence.

Since 1989, with competition ended between rival superpowers, there is consequently, a greater desire to attach conditions and regulations to continued loans for Africa. One observer in sub–Sahara Africa commented that the Soviet Union had deserted Africa economically, leaving it to the vicious wolves of western economic imperialism. Not only is the former Soviet Union penniless, but the capitalist nations of Europe and the Western Hemisphere are hard–pressed to find funds to continue the largesse of the past.

This has led to tremendous pressures for change in Africa caused by international economic forces. It is no longer possible to "play" capitalist nations against communist forces. Increasingly, in order to attract external aid and capital, it is necessary to present opportunities

based upon economic and social attractiveness. If a proposal amounts to little more than pouring more money into dubious projects and enterprises, it will not be found.

The International Monetary Fund . . .

For the past decade and a half, increased emphasis has been on the International Monetary Fund and the World Bank as conduits of economic aid and investment. The funds available through these bodies, however, carry with them responsibilities—the obligation to insure that the money accomplishes what is intended without diversion and/or corruption, in addition to the soundness of a given project. Further, there are far, far more needs than there are funds available, so even then many worthy plans may frequently have to be overlooked. Even with control measures, a substantial portion of loans are "skimmed" by bureaucracies which tend to discuss everything possible in the passive tense: "it happened," instead of "I did it."

Corruption in Africa and Elsewhere

The more economically wealthy nations from which African nations have sought aid directly and indirectly have since about 1990 required as a condition of loans and grants something called "good governance." This embodies some form of representative government and

The homemade guitar—Zambia

v

minimal corruption. But in reality, two standards have been applied.

Inept and corrupt management left American taxpayers with the burden of paying more than $500 billion to shore up savings and loan institutions and banks. Personnel of and attorneys for the Resolution Trust Company turned out to be hardly more trustworthy than the bankers. Hungry lawyers, accountants and others fed on its assets created with taxpayer money. "Leveraged buyouts" of the 1980s were nothing more than a means of creating money which did not exist ("junk bonds"). "Inside trading" on stock exchanges has been rampant. Members of Congress, with their political action committee donations, insured their own reelection with dubious and illegal contributions, a pattern which may finally have been changed in the 1994 elections.

The Black mayor of Washington D.C., videotaped using drugs but convicted only of a minor offense with a minimal jail sentence by making racial appeals to a jury with a majority of Blacks, is now back in the saddle again. Largely due to his prior tenure as mayor, the nation's capital is flat, stone broke. Efforts are now underway to figure out how to bail out the city with taxpayer's money without taking control away from the mayor!

A former Black U.S. District judge was impeached and convicted of accepting a bribe while judge. The U.S. Constitution mandates that no person who has been impeached shall be permitted to hold an office of trust in the government. Yet when he was later elected to the House of Representatives, the same people who impeached him welcomed him with open arms, lest persons of his color in their home districts turn on them in the next election.

A decade ago it was discovered that the Speaker of the House of Representatives had been engaging in scandalous conduct. The "establishment" persuaded him to leave, lest its image be tarnished by a public exposé of disgraceful actions. A senior member of the House, charged with fraud, embezzlement and witness tampering based on events occurring in the House Post Office, was defeated in 1994 after his defense of "it happened while I was a member of Congress and I am immune" was rejected by a judge.

Achievements Since Independence . . .

It is necessary to use generalizations in this section, all of which have one or more exceptions depending upon the nation involved. But the exception is just that, not the rule generally found in experience and history.

Prosperity: This is generally measured by increased income, expressed in the figure for per capita gross domestic profit, or in median income of the people of a nation. In dealing with Africa, these figures are misleading. Local goods and labor is always valued at a lower price than international imports. With the exception of some oil–producing nations and a small elite in most African nations, the rate of change has been negative. Lest there be any doubt about this, a March 1994 report, *Adjustment in Africa: Reforms, Results and the Road Ahead* issued by the World Bank states very plainly that unless there is change, it will take 40 years (2034) for sub–Sahara Africa *to return* to its pre–1973 per capita income! Since that year, sub–Saharan output has declined by 20%. The report made an embarrassing comparison between African and Asian nations, both of which had little growth from 1930 to 1960. It termed Asian growth since 1960 "stunning," but said African governments had followed policies which have been ruinous, and urged them to "give markets a chance to breathe." The need is for less intervention, less regulation, fewer subsidies, freer flows of trade and of money.

Education: Expressed by average levels of achievement, the results have been minimal at best and dismal in all too many cases. Even more regrettable are those who were and are, at state expense, educated abroad and who fail to return to serve the people from where they came. Further, the educational process is retarded by a lingering racist outlook which looks inward instead of toward the sunshine of achievement based upon international standards and usages.

When revolution beckons, school doors close. Where strife has gripped nations, such as Angola, Mozambique, Liberia, Somalia, Guinea, Zaire, South Africa and others, progress, particularly among Black people, has been *none*.

Health: Foreign assistance notwithstanding, general health levels in sub–Sahara Africa have fallen sharply. *AIDS* has claimed countless victims, most of whom don't know what they are dying of. The progress in health care: *none*.

Communication: Technical improvement has occurred in television broadcasting via satellite. However, the number of TV sets remains small, and programming is difficult since so much of it originates among predominantly White western sources which appeal little to the people. Political broadcasting, direct and indirect is too common (a statement true of the U.S.). The verdict: *none*.

Housing: Much of Africa remains in traditional housing in rural areas, punctuated by teeming shanty–filled slums in urban regions. Few governments have any housing policy or program and those, such as South Africa, which do, sponsor far less than needed by the general population. Progress in this respect has been *none*.

Political Progress: This is hotly disputed, since that which is progress to one is regression to another. Even though a ruler be chosen by a majority of the people in honest elections, if he does not have the support of the army, the bureaucracy and the small elite, he cannot last in office. Even if a ruler comes to power in an undemocratic manner, if he is skilled and is responsive to the needs of the great majority of the people, that is all that can be expected.

One of the tragedies of the African move toward a multi–party system is the promises that are made as to its meaning. Democracy is equated with wealth, which just isn't true, particularly in Africa. Wealth is a product of a combination of effort expended and brainpower used, both intended to make life easier by providing more items of comfort and convenience. Democracy, specifically a multi–party system, carries no guarantee that wealth will follow. All too often, it appears that those who are making extravagant promises are interested in achieving power in order to have an easier time stealing.

Progress in this respect should not be judged in the light of American experience (and lack thereof) over two centuries. One observer recently termed the U.S. governmental process as being one of "institutionalized thievery." To the extent that this is valid, little that is favorable can be said . . . either for it, or against African regimes. It is well known that U.S. Members of Congress start running for reelection the day they are sworn in; this tends also to occur in Africa where multi–party systems exist.

There is in all too many cases, evidence that two flaws exist in the efforts to achieve democracy. Faced with the inevitable, some one–party regimes have, silently or actively, encouraged the emergence of multiple political parties. The theory, which works in reality, is that a strong political organization has little to fear from a multitude of rivals which divide discontent among themselves so carefully it becomes diluted and powerless. The second shortcoming lies in election fraud. This may take the form of a simple requirement that voters line up for balloting, identifying themselves with a picture of the candidate they support. There is an implicit threat that they will be dealt with by the party in power in the months and years after the election if that picture is not the right one.

Or, cruder methods may be employed: stuffing ballot boxes, voting the graveyard, transporting the faithful to several precincts to vote, cutting off voter registration at an early date, thereby catching the opposition off–balance, advancing the date for balloting to accomplish the same result and a multitude of other means to defeat the genuine will of the people. Progress: *none*, with a refreshing

Firewood

exception to that statement found in South Africa.

Tribalism: Although this was one of the most difficult problems in sub–Sahara Africa prior to independence, increased inter–ethnic contacts and communication have lowered the seriousness of this age–old heritage. Few Africans harbor ill will or hostility toward one another based upon tribal affiliation. It only becomes a problem when unprincipled leaders fan the flame of hatred in the name of tribalism. Thus, President Arap–moi of Kenya complained that a multi–party system would not work in his nation because of tribalism. But when there were multi–party elections in 1992, he exploited tribal differences without shame to secure his own reelection.

If there can be increased emphasis on education, this will go a long way toward reducing this possibility. The most direct measure of progress in this area is a lowered death rate associated with tribalism. Except in remote areas with little exposure to the world such as Burundi and Rwanda (where overcrowding, not tribalism, is the root cause of strife) progress in lowering tribal tensions has been *satisfactory*.

Racism: Because the concept of racism arouses the passions and prejudices of mankind so acutely, it is hard for all to discuss in this day and age. No matter how carefully a thought is expressed, there now is a lingering fear that it will be construed as a racist remark. Even more tragic is the tendency of those with little knowledge to toss off something which is not understood with an accusation of racism. If there can be no statement regarding racism, there can be no objective study of Africa.

There is abroad in the U.S. the idea that somehow Black people (or even half–Black people) are somehow more knowledgeable about things concerning Black people. That is nonsense which need not be dignified, but very popular nonsense.

Racism is the conscious or subconscious classification of a person's ability and behavior based solely upon the color of his or her skin and other associated physical characteristics. A social corollary is blind allegiance based upon race, rooted in lack of education and political awareness on both continents. Thus, it would be unthinkable in the small mind of many for a White person to lead in an overwhelmingly Black nation of Africa. That would carry a connotation that Black people are unable to manage their own affairs.

The Russians faced a similar problem in the 9th century A.D. They were plagued by inter–clan rivalry, poverty and had very little self–esteem. Wanting to do something about their problems and aware of Norse Vikings (Varangian) who had established trade routes through Russia to the Black Sea, and considering them superior to local talent, they invited the *Varangian Russes* to rule over the restless and hostile people. Not much is known of this period, but with prosperity that followed under the Varangians, things calmed down.

Good sense indicates that outside help would be of assistance in Black Africa. Insistence of Black leadership is crude racism and willingness to accept untalented leadership in preference to economic progress. The idea that White people don't understand the problems of Black people is silly. It is derived from decades of narrow, parochial beliefs which acquire the dignity of fact. This, however, has no roots in present realities.

Racism is most visibly rooted in stereotypes as stated above. Non–Blacks are regarded as exploitive, conniving, unscrupled and greedy people who, using a language and education system foreign to Africa, want to *use* the Black people. Black people are thought of as lazy, indolent, uneducated and untalented, to be relegated to only the most simple and demeaning tasks. Factually, these fixations are thankfully *the exception* rather than the rule in most cases. But, nevertheless, they all too often widely persist.

The author of this book has been accused of racism because he has unhesitatingly been willing to report the shortcomings of Black societies and governments in Africa to the same extent he is willing to do so in cases involving Whites. Such an accusation reflects the talent of persons with racist outlooks to examine only the facts which support their already formed conclusions. A detailed description of years of legal and social work on behalf of Black persons by the author is tempting, but inappropriate in this space.

The Reverend Dr. Martin Luther King, Jr., widely respected in the U.S. and the world, is selectively remembered by many. To the militant Black his message "We shall overcome" has strong appeal. But basic to his teachings was the concept of a non–racial society in which all will be treated equally *based upon their own achievement* ("I have a dream"). The message of the militants has strong appeal to uneducated and untalented people. Their idea of overcoming connotes overwhelming the imagined oppressors by brute force. Violence, however, was not Dr. King's teaching or practice. On the contrary, he urged that adversity be overcome by achievement. Two columnists in a Washington liberal newspaper, disturbed by recent apparently lowered achievement of their fellow Blacks, have concluded that efforts of Blacks to overcome this should be undertaken without delay—that people should begin *now*.

Interestingly, inner cities of the U.S. are witnessing an exodus to the suburbs of responsible Black families fed up with the high crime rate experienced where they have lived; this includes the nation's capital, Washington, D.C., where 55% of all male Black youths are now in one stage or another of being a criminal defendant following arrest.

The writer is concerned that both in the United States and Africa the teachings of the militants have been and are encouraging Blacks, linguistically and otherwise, to *relegate themselves* to poverty, disease, crime, under–achievement and general ordinariness. They appear secure in a vague promise that all shall be overcome by *someone,* for them, and are not very specific as to how this shall be achieved. Even middle and upper class African Americans appear to have forgotten their African brethren, as shown by the reluctance of many of such persons to contibute to the *African National Congress* during appearances of Nelson Mandela in Washington for inaugural festivites in January 1993.

It is well known that a person cannot think unless he can verbalize an idea or concept. The languages of the U.S. ghetto and native African societies are simply inadequate for this task in today's world. Thus, languages of thought, preferably English, correctly spoken and written, should be the universal vehicle of education. This goal has been diminished in the name of racism in the U.S. and Africa. Why would anyone approve in this modern world of the teaching of Swahili, utterly useless outside of East Africa, in preference to correct English? What can be done with the ghetto "rap" talk idolized on MTV? The answer is obvious: nothing.

There is a need in post–independence Africa to import non–African people of skill and goodwill *now* to assist in planning and administration. To the extent that lingering racism prevents this from alleviated present shortcomings, Africa will remain in the grip of racism.

Islamic Fundamentalism

The "back to Islam" movement has bloomed in all northern African countries to one degree or another. It is in reality not in favor of anything, including Islam, but rather the guise under which anti–westernism has acquired respectability. It spreads across national boundaries and openly courts the worst sort of terrorism as a tool to reach its goals. Islamic fundamentalism has become so threatening a movement that a conference of 16 North African and Middle East countries was

A "private" school in the highlands of Ethiopia. A teacher holds classes outside his home and is paid the equivalent of $0.20 a month by students. WORLD BANK PHOTO by Kay Muldoon

convened in Tunisia at the beginning of 1993.

It served only to focus attention on this serious problem. Action was not possible because unanimity could not be obtained, particularly from Sudan, the military government of which is flirting with fundamentalists in order to exert at least minimal influence among them. Libya, under the unpredictable Qadhafi, has its own style of Islamic fundamentalism.

Those favoring the movement point out how well the traditional approach has worked in Saudi Arabia and the successes it has seemingly had in Iran (which finances much of the fundamentalist movement in other nations). Both are wealthy, it is observed; this overlooks that the wealth came from oil, not Islamic fundamentalism.

Some scholars fear that if the fundamentalists succeed in Algeria, all of North Africa will be swept into a "tide." This overlooks the fact that the extremists are split into hundreds of factions, each claiming to be the only "genuine" contemporary representative of *Allah*.

The Organization of African Unity . . .

After more than three decades as a not very unified body the Organization of African Unity will most probably close its doors shortly. The only visible purpose it had was an annual condemnation of Israel for aggression against the Palestinians and South Africa for the evils of its *apartheid* system.

Of the 53 member nations, only 15 have paid their dues in full. Twenty–eight nations are several years in arrears; the total of unpaid dues is $70 million. Threats to withdraw voting rights of delinquent nations will not cure the situation.

Devaluation of the CFA Franc

In early 1994, France devalued the CFA Franc *(Commaunité Financiére Africain)*, a currency used by most of its former possessions in Africa which it had supported since the independence of these nations. The reason was simple: it was vastly overvalued (U.S. $1 = 295 CFA Francs) because of profiteering by wealthy Blacks in Africa. Further, this currency was allowed to "float" by France—its value now is determined by its actual worth.

Almost overnight, the prices of imported goods more than doubled on store shelves. Those who suffered the most from this drastic alteration were the poor of Africa. The move also resulted in numerous strikes for higher wages to offset the increase in prices. Although the move was condemned by many African leaders, it was no more than a move to prevent the rich from getting richer at France's expense.

Foreign Debt . . .

Although staggering, Africa's foreign debt ($240 billion), is modest compared to Latin American obligations. No radical measures were taken to unilaterally reduce payments to creditor nations. The problem is extremely serious—about one–third of the earnings of most African nations go to pay foreign debt. A UNICEF official commented that "as a result of our inability to put Africa economics back on track" 1,000 children are dying each day (the figure is now probably 5,000). Following the lead of France, European creditor nations and the U.S. have written off one–third of the external debt of some 30 of the poorest African nations.

In sub–Sahara Africa, foreign investment virtually dried up from 1980 to 1986 and now is only making a very hesitant comeback. Trade restrictions abound and

Street scene in the older part of Marrakech

Courtesy: Mr. & Mrs. Schuyler Lowe

dealing with local bureaucracies is all but impossible. Even when foreign enterprises show a profit, the act of getting it out of Africa to pay the sources of investment can prove to be all but impossible.

At the 1989 OAU conference, a message was sent to European and American creditors that a ten–year moratorium on repayment of principal and interest was urgently needed. Although sympathetic to the plight of the African nations, the creditors did nothing, lest any action be interpreted as a signal to Latin America.

But the latest development is an offer of the U.S. to forgive 50% of the debt owed it.

The Killer Climate . . .

Although Africa is no stranger to drought, in early 1983 the climate turned "killer" with a savagery unknown in recent history. This time it was not just the Sahelian countries which were Nature's target—the drought spread its fiery fingers across most of the continent. Thousands died each day from malnutrition and continue to die. More than 240 million Africans live in the afflicted areas. Although tons of relief food continue to pour in from all over the world, officials have a difficult time with distribution. They are hampered by civil wars, poor roads and a shortage of trucks, as well as internal corruption of politicians. This catastrophe eased by 1985 particularly in southern Africa, but made an ominous reappearance since 1987.

Favorable rain conditions in sub–Sahara Africa boded well for the nations of the region, but this blessing was minimized when the same rains created ideal breeding conditions for countless hordes of a second generation of locusts in 1988–1989. The UN had spent more than a $40 million dollars to fight the insects, a threat to the crops on 50,000 square miles of land. A project is now underway in northern Nigeria with Japanese supervision and financing to farm lands in the Sahel (the belt of land just below the Sahara) in 250 acre tracts, intended to replace the traditional family plots of about five acres. A belt of trees (as in Algeria) designed to contain the expanding desert land is at the heart of the program. This will foster surpluses of food, hopefully, replacing subsistence farming traditional to the area and it is hoped to extend it all the way to Senegal.

The savage climate again revisited in 1992, and in the year 1993 the highest levels of starvation were seen in Africa in the absence of energetic foreign assistance. There will be no improvement until modern agricultural techniques overcome social and political backwardness, permitting the farming of large, economical tracts of land. Education will, of course, have to come first. In the 1890s in the U.S., about one of six workers labored to pro-

A pocketbook production line, Mahajanga, Madagascar

duce food; in the 1990s the figure is 1 of 98. In sub–Sahara Africa in the 1990s, the number is one out of every two.

In the meantime, if all the money spent on becoming obese in wealthy nations was combined with the money spent on weight reducing videos, diets, pills, machines, costumes, spas, doctors, clinics etc. and dispatched via CARE, immediate relief could be obtained.

"Privatization" . . .

The years 1985–86 saw the introduction of the concept of "privatization" in many nations of Africa. This simply means dissolving state–run farms and businesses by selling them back to private ownership from where they came. Although only a tiny beginning has been made in this direction, it is highly significant. It is a good move, particularly for food production. Collective or state ownership means no individual motivation, opportunity or ambition. All of these

ideas are traditional elements of African life.

Even the Republic of South Africa has embarked on a vigorous program of privatization within the past three years.

AIDS and Family Planning . . .

The lack of family planning in Africa has traditionally been countered by a tremendous infant mortality rate. In spite of this, there has been widespread starvation in sub–Sahara Africa and children are the first to suffer. U.S. policy forbade provision of foreign assistance for family planning and has been totally unrealistic in this respect. If a human life is not conceived, obviously there will be no starvation or suffering.

In Africa, a life of want and misery is the rule, not the exception. The question facing world and African leadership is not whether suffering and hunger will occur, but when. Stated otherwise, how soon after birth will this happen? Most

African societies do not have the technical or social wisdom to deal with the problem of overpopulation and they need help. Feeding starving children is humanitarian. Having fewer starving children is more humanitarian. Having no starving children is an ideal to be sought within reasonable and moral limits.

A cloud looms over sub–Sahara Africa (which may well invade North Africa): the rapid rise in the disease of Acquired Immune Deficiency Syndrome (AIDS). In the areas most afflicted (cities) the toll among technical and professional citizens is alarming. Women have an average of almost seven children. The disease is spread through sexual intercourse, but is also transmitted at birth. Professionals estimate that as many as 50 million Africans will perish by the year 2000. Uganda and Tanzania are particularly affected, where the disease is known as "slim," or "he/she get thin and die." By late 1987 the scourge reached into the highest political circles—President Kounché of Niger died in Paris and President Kaunda of Zambia publicly admitted that his son had been struck down by the disease. The World Health Organization recently noted that although Africa has only 2% of the world's population, it has 60% of worldwide AIDS victims.

The disease is the leading cause now of death in the sprawling city of Abidjan, Côte d'Ivoire. It is rampant in the Central African Republic where widespread sexual activity is socially acceptable. Unless a vaccine is developed, the disease will double the death rate among African women and wipe out about a third of able–bodied men by 2015. Millions of orphans will result. In just 25 short years, African life expectancy will be reduced by an appalling 19 years. Today in Tanzania one in three children are exposed to the deadly HIV virus at birth, almost always resulting in infection. South Africa is expected to lose 60% of its male workforce by 2004. Even if a vaccine is developed, which probably will occur, Africa will face the problem of a lack of coordinated family planning.

U.S. Policy in Southern Africa

There is only one word to describe accurately U.S. policy in southern Africa since 1975: hairbrained. It was uneven, meandering and produced nothing that wouldn't have happened anyway, often at a cost of millions of dollars. Idealists in the highest positions of the U.S. decided that somehow it was the responsibility of the U.S. to end *apartheid* (separation of the races) in the Republic of South Africa and bring an end to White minority rule in that nation.

Much attention was paid to the *African National Congress* and to Anglican Archbishop Desmond Tutu. This was focused by and through TransAfrica, an organization headed by Randall Robinson in the U.S. The problem was that the *ANC* and allied organizations, were communist–backed, and Archbishop Tutu represented only a small minority of Blacks in the Republic of South Africa.

In 1976, the *ANC* drifted toward revolutionary violence, proclaiming a slogan of "Independence *before* Education." Admittedly, the educational opportunities afforded Blacks in South Africa were often unsatisfactory. But the slogan failed to recognize that *some* education is better than none. The result has been that by the late 1980's, a large number of Black persons existed in South Africa with little or no education, capable of offering only menial jobs with low wages; widespread unemployment resulted from an oversupply of untalented persons. Younger people are now enthusiastically returning to increasingly integrated schools, but the 1976–1994 period left a generation of illiterates.

The U.S. utterly failed to recognize the existence of an equally substantial number of Black Zulus and others led by Chief Mangosuthu Buthelezi (Mang–goe–*su*too Boot–el–*leh*–zee) who advocated a South Africa devoid of *apartheid* with no consideration of color, only equal opportunity for all according to abilities and education.

The result in 1985–1992 was a state of virtual warfare between the "comrades" of the *ANC* (primarily Xhosa, Sotho and other Black groups) and Zulus led by Chief Buthelezi. Rather than trying to assist in a peace effort involving the three contesting elements in South Africa, pressures in the U.S., principally from militant Black organizations, resulted in a program of "disinvestment" calculated to punish Whites and further *ANC* ambitions to topple the government. Initially, the White South African government resisted this, but since 1990 it worked toward arrival at compromise rooted in practicality accommodating all factions. A new constitution will hopefully settle differences *on the surface*, but the reality of economic *apartheid* will remain. By partisanship and vacillation, the U.S. substantially forfeited any power to influence the future of South Africa.

Culture, Languages, Usages and Pronunciation . . .

Because of severe space limitations, this book cannot more than touch upon a few of the multitude of fascinating cultural aspects of the people of this continent. Phonetic pronunciations follow most proper names to assist the reader.

The term *Negro* became unfashionable about two decades ago and the word *black* took its place. This was later modified by some to capitalize the word: *Black*. This further modification was adopted, but, in the interest of equality, the word White was also capitalized. Both were initially used in this book to indicate the word was a noun as opposed to an adjective. This then was changed to make the capitalization standard, rather than have students wonder whether they were confronted with a noun or an adjective. Now it is urged *African American* is an appropriate combination. That may perhaps be true, but is not what this book is about. Interestingly, the descendants of freed slaves in Africa refer to themselves as Americo Liberians.

Modern usages can be curious and troublesome. If material is military, then it becomes materiel. People don't use drugs anymore— they "do" drugs, in an apparent effort to get away from the idea that they are a user, with all of the negative connotations of that word. Such smokescreens are illusory and temporary.

Maps . . .

Designed to assist in understanding the text, the maps often omit cities, railroads, locations and rivers not covered in the text. Other more detailed maps are widely available, and at the *gentle* insistence of our geographer friends, all of the maps have been upgraded.

With the advent of the 1985 edition, we underwent a change in technology. I have been personally able to compose the typography on a computer, which is instantly reduced to magnetic symbols on "floppy disks." They are transmitted to the capable hands of the personnel at Braun–Brumfield, Inc. in Ann Arbor, where they are the basis for the finished product. To this advance has been added another in technique: computerized page layout. In but one generation the art of producing a book has undergone a profound change difficult to imagine. When it is time to revise this book for the next edition, last–minute changes can be made simply by "calling up" the appropriate section onto a computer screen and making deletions, additions and alterations. If such speed and flexibility had been available to classical authors, the result would have been beyond imagination.

P.E.D.

Harpers Ferry, WV
June 1995

Understanding the Tropical African Environment and Ways of Life

by Louis J. Mihalyi

Africa is a very large continent, some 2 million square miles greater than North and Central America combined, with an estimated population of 522 million in 1992. The landmass shows a very considerable diversity of the physical and cultural environments which, in a simplified approach, may be divided into two broad regions: North Africa, including the Sahara, and tropical Africa, including the Republic of South Africa.

In the North African region, aside from the mountains of the Atlas, Ahaggar and Tibesti ranges, the terrain is characterized by a low topography in the Sahara, often appearing as an "endless" desert landscape. Part of the Sahara is covered with sand while in other areas it has large expanses of exposed gravel and rock. Due to the prevalent trade winds from the northeast, the finer sand and surface soil is generally carried westward and south–westward; this accounts partly for the advance of the desert into

the zone of the *Sahel*, greatly affecting life and livelihood in that region.

The climate of North Africa ranges from semi–aridity to aridity with only a narrow strip of Mediterranean climate north and northwest of the Atlas ranges. The environment imposes considerable limits on cultural activities. Below the Mediterranean coastal zone all agriculture requires irrigation; the arable area is limited due to the presence of a single river—the Nile—with a sufficient volume of water year round, although parts of the northern Sahara do contain significant amounts of water in deep–lying bodies which occasionally surface as oases in the otherwise bone–dry landscape.

Dependence on irrigation is aggravated by the ever present danger of soil salinization due to high evaporation and the use of improper irrigation techniques. In addition, the slowly moving waters provide favorable conditions for the spread of *bilharzia*; this disease is transmitted by the miroscopic larvae from fresh water snails which penetrate the body while a person may be either

bathing or simply wading in a river or stream. Its effect is to sap human energy permanently, since proper treatment seldom reaches the poor and the isolated who are its principal victims. In the delta of the Nile, this disease affects at least 60% of the rural population with no medicine or vaccine available.

In the Sahara proper, the livelihood aside from the few oases is limited to the practice of nomadic pastoralism by tribes like the Tuareg, formerly a feared group preying on the caravans crossing the desert. The major income earned for the countries is limited to few resources: oil and natural gas in Algeria and Libya, phosphates in Morocco, and tourism—especially in Egypt, in addition to tolls derived from the Suez Canal.

Historically, North Africa was closely associated with the Mediterranean region and the Middle East—not with tropical Africa, due to the barrier of the vast Sahara. This alignment is reinforced by two major unifying cultural factors of the region: the religion of Islam and the Arabic language. Since Greek and Roman times, people from North Africa worked and moved around the Mediterranean basin; presently well over a million Algerians are located in France. These trends are projected to be continued in the future.

The tropical African region, as defined earlier, includes about 8.5 million square miles, with a population of about 390 million in 1985. Topographically, the simplest division would indicate two major parts: "low" Africa in the west, including the Congo basin, then northward from Lake Albert (Lake Mobutu) along the watershed of the White Nile to the Red Sea, and "high" Africa containing the rest of the continent and the island of Madagascar, with an average elevation of 3,000 feet or above. On the average, temperatures decrease 3.3°F. per 1,000 feet of elevation. In both areas, volcanic peaks and ranges rise to great heights like the Cameroon mountains, the Mitumba mountains along the west side of the great African lakes, Mt. Elgon in Uganda and Mt. Kilimanjaro in Tanzania.

The Great Rift Valley, an immense fault more than 3,000 miles long, runs from the Dead Sea through the Red Sea and Ethiopia to the mouth of the Zambesi River. It has actually two branches in East Africa, with the western branch occupied partly by the immense lakes of several thousand feet deep. Lake Victoria, the largest of them, is not part of the Rift system, but it received great attention in the early exploration of East Africa by Europeans searching for the source of the Nile.

The low, humid coast of West Africa, the extensive swamps of the Niger delta, the marshy areas along the river, and the "inland delta" of the Niger, are ideal environments for the spread of many diseases like malaria, yellow fever and river blindness. As the early European expeditions often attempted to use the rivers as "highways" to the interior, numerous attempts were made to penetrate West Africa along the Niger. Losing most, if not all their explorers, the European powers gave up the idea of establishing settlers in West Africa. Conversely, the cooler highlands of East and South Africa were favorable to European settlement; partly through government support the lands were seized from native holdings with little, if any compensation. All over tropical Africa the cities were founded by European invaders. Cities on the coast were generally established for easy access, trade or partly military considerations; those founded inland were along a railroad or in a mining area for the most part.

The climate of tropical Africa across the region has basically two traits in common: warm temperatures and a marked seasonality of rainfall, aside from the areas covered by tropical rainforests. Outside the areas with high elevations where the temperatures are lower, the indigenous people are able to survive without constructing substantial, permanent dwellings or producing heavy clothing. The year–round warm temperatures also make it possible to pursue agricultural activities accordingly, *provided there is sufficient rainfall for the crops.* The diverse physical setting supports a great variety of natural vegetation and provides the opportunity for gathering native plants for food during much of the year.

The rainfall pattern in tropical Africa deserves special attention—it is the underlying cause of many of the problems affecting daily life and livelihood. Every day is warm or hot with little exception; but not every night is rainy, even in the most humid regions. The striking features of the rains are the great seasonal differences, their intensity and poor reliability.

The savanna region, an extensive area of grassy woodland, is the largest climatic area in tropical Africa, with a very distinct wet and dry season. The rainfall controls the responses of plants and animals and influences greatly human activities. Where the yearly rainfall is below 25 inches or so, the rains can be very erratic in both arrival and total amount. The areas of Africa affected by famine, the extent of which increased greatly in 1984–1985, are heavily concentrated in the low rainfall regions, like the Sahel zone south of the Sahara, where crop and animal losses can be devastating in any particular year.

Even when the rains come on schedule, they may cause severe problems. Tropical rains often arrive as very heavy showers or thunderstorms. Up to 4 inches of rain *per hour* may fall, causing swift run–off and erosion. Temperatures in the rainforest region are not excessive, practically never over 90° F. Water cannot evaporate rapidly due to the saturation of the air with its vapor; that is the reason for the great discomfort in humid tropical or subtropical climates. In tropical Africa a minimum of 60 inches of rainfall annually is necessary for thick forests; in the high latitudes of the temperate zone, the forests of the "taiga" exist with a precipitation of only 15 inches.

The ecology of the African savanna is remarkable. This area was in the past unexcelled for immense numbers of game which made Africa famous, and due to the favorable habitat, may well have been the location of emergence for *homo sapiens,* suggested by the large number of pre–human remains found in East and South Africa. However, the long dry season promotes the spread of fires, and for centuries the savannas have been burned by accident or design; the existing vegetation is characterized as a "fire climax."

A problem of immense proportions has emerged in the late 1980's in the East African savanna. Game poachers are killing the rhinos and elephants for their horn and tusks, respectively, at unbelievable rates. The 17,000 elephants of Kenya in 1970 now number fewer than 5,000. Uganda, seized by lawlessness, is a poachers paradise. Of all the Black African nations, only Tanzania has a reasonable anti–poaching program, but it is being swiftly undermined by desperately impoverished Zambian poachers. These game thieves have become so bold they assault game wardens sent to protect animals.

In 1989 there was a world pact to end all trade in ivory. Nevertheless, the activities of the poachers continued. In spite of their activity, present estimates of the African elephant population are 573,000–598,000. Zimbabwe, South Africa, Namibia, Botswana and Malawi have asked that the restrictions be relaxed, but there is wide resistance to the move. The argument they use is increased human population needs. The argument used by their opponents is that (1) the population should naturally be controlled and (2) there are a number of other substances which can be suitably substituted for ivory. This item will remain very controversial.

Another continuing problem is that of the chimpanzees. Monkey flesh is regarded as a delicacy in most parts of Africa. The slain animals are singed to remove the hair and then roasted. This is regarded as virtual cannibalism in other parts of the world, where the similarity of the chimpanzee to humans is recognized. Perhaps the worst part is the sale of their young children as pets. Young chimps are cute and adorable. When they pass maturity, they are not. Raucous, generally quarrelsome and wanting to live in their own society, they become very combative and frustrated.

Many "pet" chimpanzees wind up chained to a tree, spending the rest of their lives in misery. They bite (yes, people) and are tremendously strong. It takes four strong men to hold an adult down in laboratories where they are used for testing. (Their genes are about 99% comparable to those of humans.) The old *Tarzan* movies, with their amusing "Cheetah" were not realistic. Ten times as much film as was used in them was thrown in the wastebasket—the female, the more docile of the species, simply would not behave. As adults, they defecate and fling the results with dreadful accuracy. If one goes to Africa and is offered a cuddly youngster, forget it.

The savanna landscapes located in the proximity of the cities and large settlements show a considerable decline due to extensive deforestation. Aside from the small middle and upper class residential

3

areas, the vast majority of Africans use wood or charcoal for cooking. The method used for converting the wood to charcoal is especially wasteful; only about 8% of the total wood piled into the "clamp," i.e. kiln, will actually end up as charcoal.

The environment of the savanna presents a number of hazards to humans and animals. The foremost among them is the presence of the tsetse fly, which excludes the raising of good quality domestic animals in the affected regions. Game animals are immune to the disease *trypanosomiasis* carried by the insect, but domestic animals are generally killed by the "nagana," and humans fall victim to the "sleeping sickness."

Getting rid of the fly permanently requires both the killing of the game which is resistant to the "nagana," but still is host to the disease and the cutting of the brush and other vegetation for the conversion of the area to permanent, intensive farming to prevent natural revegetation and return of the game. Presently, perhaps 1/3 to 1/4 of the entire savanna area may be infected by the tsetse.

Of the biological dangers affecting the crops are the presence of a large variety of ants and insects, the occasional flight of hordes of locusts and many grain–eating birds. Due to poverty and the low level of technology, the African farmers have no defense against these enemies. In addition, poor storage techniques result in a yearly crop loss estimated to be from 15% to 30%.

In the semi–arid grasslands of tropical Africa the pastures are reasonably good for animal husbandry and the tsetse fly is seldom a problem. But the prolonged dry season causes great hardships, especially in terms of the water supply. Overall, the wildlife, cattle and other livestock walk long distances for grass and water under the hot sun and show only a small weight gain during the year. In addition, ticks spread a variety of diseases, some of them fatal. However, perhaps the main handicap to proper animal raising lies in the traditions and customs of the pastoral people, especially those of East Africa. The monetary value of cattle is not as important as the *social* one; the prime consideration is to increase numbers for *status*, prestige or dowry. Little concern is given to the carrying capacity of the range; this overgrazing is one important factor in the spread of the desert in the Sahel region.

In tropical Africa good soils are the exception. The fast growth of the rainforest is based not so much on the soils but the rapid recycling of the nutrients from the plants' fast decomposition. The year round warm temperatures provide a perfect setting for the rapid decay of organic material and, with the warm waters carrying dissolved chemicals, essential ele-

Child leading victim of river blindness

WORLD BANK photo

4

ments for growth penetrate the soil deeply. The minerals carried downward can be reached by the long roots of the large, long–lived plants; but when these are replaced by short–cycle, 3–5 month crops, plant growth is stunted. This factor, among others, led to the practices of shifting, slash–and– burn cultivation with the ashes from the burned vegetation providing reasonable fertility for a period of 2–4 years.

In the savanna region, coarse sand, rock and clay particles remain after the soluble materials have been carried away by waters rapidly leaching the soil; this gives rise to a hard, unyielding surface, often forming laterite—reddish in color and generally hard enough to be used for road surfacing. Applying mechanized farming techniques to any part of tropical Africa requires a careful approach and study of the existing conditions to avoid failures such as occurred in Tanzania after World War II.

Often called the "peanut scheme," the British government attempted to raise peanuts on a large scale (for edible oil). The area selected had an erratic rainfall of 6 to 25 inches each year, and the dry soil was extremely hard. The machinery used was mainly war–worn bulldozers and caterpillar tractors from U.S. surplus in the Philippines; they broke down rapidly. The project folded in a few years with a loss of millions of dollars. However, in some parts of tropical Africa, such as on the highlands of Kenya, in Zambia and Zimbabwe, properly established modern farming techniques have proved to be successful.

African cultivation is of two types: (1) permanent, or (2) shifting—slash and burn. The first appears in areas generally limited to good soils, near cities and in parts of the coastal strip. Aside from crops, a variety of fruit trees are also planted.

Far more widespread is the second approach; shifting cultivation developed hundreds of years ago when land was free and plentiful—and there was a relatively low population density. Farming is simple; the major tools are the axe and the hoe. The trees and brush are cut, then burned, and the seeds are sown in the ashes. Animal power is very seldom used, so these farmers, in general, are at the stage which existed in Europe about the time of the Roman conquests. Upgrading such farming techniques is a very difficult task; great leaps forward into mechanized farming have generally resulted in a disaster.

One percent of sub–Saharan African farming is mechanized, draft animals are used in another 10%, but human labor accounts for 89%. Although the men occasionally help out with the heaviest tasks, the burden falls almost exclusively on women to produce food. Yields are

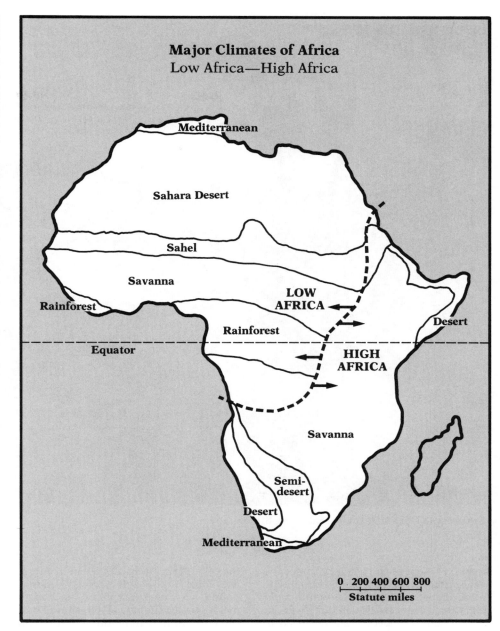

Major Climates of Africa
Low Africa—High Africa

Mediterranean
Sahara Desert
Sahel
Savanna
Rainforest
LOW AFRICA
Desert
Rainforest
Equator
HIGH AFRICA
Savanna
Semi-desert
Desert
Mediterranean

0 200 400 600 800
Statute miles

modest, being the product of a hoe and hour upon hour of grueling labor. Surpluses are seldom produced and there are large losses due to insufficient storage facilities. However, Africans are very talented farmers, using local plants for food or medicine, and are able to survive even in spite of crop failures.

Partly to overcome the numerous biological hazards, the average family may cultivate several plots at scattered locations. However, in spite of these efforts, food is often in short supply before the harvest of the major staple crop; the children are the first to suffer.

The diet of the African population is usually inadequate. Carbohydrates represent most of the food supply while meat consumption—of very poor qual-

ity—is at most about 6% of that in the average American's diet. Malnutrition is widespread, especially among the children, and heavily affects women during pregnancy. The majority of families is limited to one daily meal—in the evening. Even in the cities, the drinking water is polluted by a variety of organisms, but little is done to tackle the problem.

Ideally, western, and in particular American, mechanized agriculturural techniques should be supplied to Africa, particularly legumes (peas, beans, particularly soybean growing should be taught) to raise the bulk, adequacy and protein of the African diet. But this is impossible because of present conditions. National, state, tribal and local leaders usually de-

Spraying to kill small snails that cause Bilharzia

WORLD BANK photo

mand a "piece of the action." Under the circumstances, no capitalist from the more industrially advanced world could be attracted to participate in such an effort. Thus, the people are relegated to their routine, starch–laden diets.

The Republic of South Africa possesses the capacity to change things, and is making efforts in this direction. Western economic measures directed against that nation in the name of racial righteousness, have hampered it in its efforts, as well as deprived thousands of Black South Africans of something even faintly resembling a decent standard of living.

Because of widespread poverty and the absence of electricity in all but the urban areas, refrigeration equipment is extremely limited. Leftover food spoils rapidly. Where food preservation is practiced, like in the case of fisheries along the lakes and streams, it is a common sight to see fish cut up and laid out to dry in the open—covered with flies and dust. The same is true with animal carcasses after slaughtering, especially in the rural areas. In Lake Victoria man introduced the Nile Perch—a fish that can grow six feet long and weigh several hundred pounds. It ate almost all of the native, much smaller Tilapia fish which was preserved by drying in the sun. Oily and too large for sun–drying, the Nile Perch has to be smoked to preserve it. Thus, forests in the region are suffering from excessive wood loss. Further, the Tilapia ate algae and the snails that transmit *bilharzia*—both are multiplying at an alarming rate.

The recent spread of "modernization" led to the availability of Coca–Cola and other soft drinks popular among the younger generation, but with "empty" calories in terms of proper nutrition. Africans in general consume a considerable amount of beer, originally produced from some staple foods—millet, maize or bananas—although bottled, manufactured beer is gaining increased popularity and prestige. "Kat" is a widely–used opiate (excitant) in Ethiopia, and "dagga" (bhang) is smoked by adults on occasion.

The tropical African environment, especially that of the savanna region, harbors a large variety of diseases affecting the human population. Aside from *bilharzia*, which is estimated to affect at least 80 million Africans, amoebic and bacillary dysentery are very widespread and are a major factor in high childhood mortality. Malaria is spreading again, especially in the more humid areas—mosquitos having increased resistance to sprays. *Filariasis,* a disease due to parasites, often causing swelling in the limbs, is commonly found in mosquito–prone areas. Hookworm affects many children who generally go barefoot. *Yaws* and *leishmaniasis* (carried by the parasite which forms ulcers on the skin) are frequently encountered in the region of the equator. *Onchocerciasis* ("river blindness"), spread by black fly eggs, is prevalent along streams in West Africa.

Fortunately this will become a problem of the past. An American pharmaceutical company has developed a serum which, if made widely available, will eliminate the disease. The company has agreed to furnish the medicine at no cost.

To the list must be added Guinea

Worm Disease which exists in a belt of the Savanna–Sahel stretching clear across Africa. It is spread by contaminated water. The ovum of the worm is consumed by drinking and locates itself within the human body, most usually in the legs. It grows to a length up to three inches and immediately seeks exit from its victim, a process that is excruciatingly painful, taking several weeks. Seeking relief from the pain of a worm half in and half out of the body, infected persons soak in nearby ponds and streams. The worm exits and starts the cycle again by producing more eggs. This causes substantial loss of work and productivity.

Overall, much of the population and especially the children suffer from widespread incidence of multiple vitamin deficiency. *Kwashiokor*, an almost always fatal disease among youngsters, is caused by a protein–deficient diet and . . . starvation. Ironically, improved vaccination availability against measles and other childhood diseases in the last decade have led to lowered infant and child mortality, resulting in even more mouths to feed with an inadequate food supply.

Because of inadequate medical reporting, it is impossible to estimate the number of cases of AIDS in Africa. Frequently the disease is not identified, or the victim does not seek medical treatment. No relief in the form of a vaccine is now in sight. In the coming years until the turn of the century, it has the potential to infect more than 50 million people on the continent. It knows no class distinctions and is claiming the lives of sorely needed technicians and professionals.

Medical services and facilities, aside from the urban areas, are very simple and utterly inadequate over tropical Africa. Even when the people are "cured," re-infection occurs very frequently, and some diseases—like *bilharzia*—have *no* dependable cure unless the person receives prolonged treatment in Europe. Sanitary and hygienic facilities across the continent are all but absent, and even the hospitals have great problems with proper staffing. Many African doctors trained at considerable expense leave the continent to advance their fortunes; those who remain practice mainly in the urban areas. Communication with patients is very difficult due to the *over 700 indigenous languages* with few competant interpreters.

The social fabric of tropical African life is characterized by a large number of tribes, at least 700, living within closely defined kinship obligations of the "extended family" system. This does not include the "de–tribalized" Africans who left their homelands particularly during and after the World War II period, to live, often in squalor, in urban areas to which they were attracted by industrial or mining employment. The tribal organization provides for relative security of the individual within the tribal area, but makes cooperation difficult on the national level. The dependence on relatives is the main reason for the widespread practice of nepotism (favoritism shown to a relative), with the problems caused by inefficiency and inexperience greatly aggravated by corruption. Other problems in tropical Africa are related to the conquest by European powers and are part of the colonial legacy.

From the start of European domination, education for Africans was left generally in the hands of the missionary societies until well after World War I. The student body had a large majority of boys, with subject matters concentrated on reading, writing and religious instruction—in addition to some training in trades such as carpentry and bricklaying so that the Africans would be "useful workers."

"Higher" education always used the language of the colonial power, which then became the official language of the country once it achieved independence. Few Africans received advanced training, and then almost always overseas in the respective "mother" country. Their education was primarily in the liberal arts and humanities. As a result, at the time they became independent, illiteracy in

tropical African countries ranged from 80% to 90% of the total population with only a handful of graduates in engineering and sciences. For these reasons, the newly independent countries have had to rely on foreigners to handle many of the technological and administrative tasks until these can be replaced by sometimes hastily–trained Africans. This has had a detrimental effect on efficiency, and that is the characteristic situation across much of tropical Africa at the present time. On the other hand, where the government maintained the existing foreign personnel and production methods such as in the mines and agriculture, operations were hardly disrupted at all.

The political situation in tropical Africa has had many facets since the arrival of independence. Divergent vested interests of more than 700 tribes and clans, in addition to the selfish motives of the existing elite, have severely limited development. Populations with a high rate of illiteracy cannot possibly decide on the relative merits of any candidate running for election even if there *are* elections. Social, political and economic policies are simply beyond their understanding.

Dictatorial policies and monetary dishonesty of several African leaders have resulted in almost perpetual turmoil and financial crises. Relief efforts to avert starvation in areas such as Ethiopia and Sudan should be via recognized international agencies. Another example of needless economic hardship has been found in Liberia, where three crops of paddy rice can be harvested each year with proper cultivation. Yet this staple food was imported for lack of local supplies. To this has been added the spectre of widespread hunger and malnutrition associated with revolution accompanied by virtual anarchy in that nation for more than two years.

Although foreign investment is desirable, sometimes it results in exploitation. Because of low living standards, cheap labor is available to assemble parts made elsewhere into products at wages as low as $5.00 a week. It is highly unlikely that tropical Africa will enter the stage of the Industrial Revolution within the 21st century without there first occurring basic changes. Subsistence agriculture, disease, and power shortages constitute the only future that one can see for the Black–ruled nations of sub–Sahara Africa, unless capital and technological skills can be attracted for improvement.

Gathering wood, Burkina Faso   WORLD BANK photo

AFRICA 1905

AFRICA TODAY

9

HISTORICAL BACKGROUND

Sunrise over the Niger River

WORLD BANK photo

PREHISTORIC AFRICA

As is true in most of the world, evidence in Africa of prehistoric man is very scanty, although some of the most significant archeological findings have been made on this vast continent. Primitive paintings and frescoes in the caves of the Tibesti Mountains of southern Algeria, remnants of skeletons and prehistoric men found in Zimbabwe, Tanzania and Kenya and stone weapons and implements scattered throughout the continent have no definite relationship to each other. Among recent discoveries was part of a skull that is approximately 4 million years old! Early *homo sapiens* was short in stature, had a small brain in comparison to modern man and did not walk in a completely erect position. He had a wider mouth and a somewhat low–hanging brow. He had two features which distinguished him from animals—

the power of reasoning and language ability.

In 1984 there was discovered the skeleton of a teenage boy 1–1/2 million years old representative of *homo erectus* who would have reached an adult height of six feet. This African discovery indicates the continent was indeed the place of origin of modern man.

These discoveries are not inconsistent with the teachings of the first book of the *Torah* and Bible—Genesis—the purpose of which was to relate the origin of the concepts of good and evil which are an essential part of the life of man on earth.

Small numbers of dark–skinned people—pygmies and negrillos—evolved and emerged in the central areas of Africa, slowly gathering together into groups which began to use primitive hunting techniques and later learned how to domesticate animals. There is a

theory that as early as about 30,000 B.C. a migration of people from another land in the equatorial Indian Ocean to the continent of Africa occurred. Mixed with the negrillos and possibly to a lesser extent with the pygmies, the primary combination of ancestry of the Bantu people evolved and stabilized over a period of about 20,000 years, bringing agriculture and iron techniques to the continent. Another group emerged in the Mediterranean area with ancestry similar to that of the people of the Middle East.

There probably was some intermixture of these northerners of so–called Semitic ancestry with the Negrillo–Bantu people, stabilizing into a people referred to as Sudanic (Hamitic, Nilo–Hamitic and Cushitic) in the area of east Africa now part of the Sudan, Ethiopia and the Somali Republic. These people, taller and somewhat fairer skinned than the pure Negrillo–Bantu, were to slowly spread westward to the area of what is now Senegal, occupying the immense semi-arid regions south of the Sahara Desert. They also expanded to a more limited extent southward through the highlands of the Great Rift Valley to the shores of Lake Tanganyika and the high mountains of south–central Africa.

EARLY CIVILIZATIONS
OF THE NILE VALLEY
AND MEDITERRANEAN SEA

The people from the Middle East who settled in the Nile Valley area began to develop agricultural skills about 5,000 B.C. and were able to form one of the first centrally organized societies of the western world by about 3,000 B.C., the beginning of the Egyptian dynasties. Under the control of the succession of kings (Pharaohs), the social organization of the people permitted rapid evolution and development of writing, architecture, religion and the beginning of scientific thought.

The Egyptians' early religious efforts were varied; they conceived of a god represented by a variety of animal forms. Under the rule of the dynasties, these individual symbols were gradually discarded in favor of the obelisk (a tall, usually pointed four–sided structure with ornate carvings and frescoes which was used as a symbol of *Re*. It is probable that *Re* was associated with local gods which the people were accustomed to worship, but this concept of God led to the development of the first-known

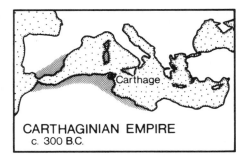

CARTHAGINIAN EMPIRE
c. 300 B.C.

beliefs in life after death. The development of writing, first in hieroglyphics (illustrations portraying a variety of thoughts and concepts) and later in abstract symbols (an early "alphabet") in turn enabled the development of a highly stylized literature. A calendar of 365 days was adopted. The religious concept of life after death led in turn to invention of enbalming methods to preserve the human body after death. This further resulted in the combination of early geometry with architecture, which permitted the construction of obelisks and elaborate and immense pyramids, the burial tombs of the pharaohs.

The Egyptians under the pharaohs reached their period of greatest power in the 2nd millenium before the Christian era, and gradually declined in strength and organization until they were invaded by a succession of other Mediterranean powers—the Assyrians in the 7th century B.C., the Persians and finally the Greeks under Alexander in the 4th century, B.C.

Phoenician traders on the northern coastline of the African continent combined over many centuries with the small number of other people of Middle East origin, emerging into a unified society known as Carthage in the 9th century B.C. in what is now Tunisia and part of Algeria. These aggressive people fought with the inhabitants of Sicily and

Sardinia for about four hundred years, eventually winning control of the two islands after many changes in the fortunes of war in the 2nd century B.C. Carthaginian control was brief—the powerful Roman Empire was able to completely conquer Carthage by 122 B.C.

EARLY CHRISTIAN ERA
MOVEMENTS

There was a second but smaller immigration of people to Africa from some other land of the equatorial Indian Ocean and Far East–Indonesian area which probably occurred during the first millenium of the Christian era. These people, known as the Hovas, settled in the highlands of the island of Madagascar and to a much lesser extent in east central

The Zimbabwe Ruins

11

Africa, now Kenya and Uganda. There is no way to estimate the numbers of people arriving, nor is there any indication as to the method by which they reached the continent other than that the movement was by sea rather than overland. They remained cohesive on the island of Madagascar, but combined with the Negrillo–Bantu people of the mainland to some degree, becoming part of the stabilized Bantu people.

The Bantu and Sudanic groups expanded at a relatively rapid rate during the first millenium of the Christian era. The Negrillo people who were not absorbed into the Bantu population were gradually pushed northward and westward, eventually to West Africa, where they in turn split into many local groups, now collectively identified as West African Negro. The numbers of Bantu grew, occupying the Congo River region from what is now Gabon southward to Angola.

There was initially rapid expansion of the Bantu in the eastern regions of Africa into what is now Tanzania, Zambia and Zimbabwe.

The imposing circular stone walls of the Zimbabwe ruins, located in the southwestern part of that nation now bearing the name (formerly *Rhodesia*), are huge granite slabs fitted together without mortar. Rising some thirty feet and about 800 feet around, they were probably constructed by Shona tribesmen in about the 3rd century A.D., although there is considerable disagreement among scholars concerning this sole remnant of early architecture south of the Sahara.

Zimbabwe is the Anglicized version of the Shona word *Dzimbahwe*, meaning stone houses—later understood as graves, or dwellings, of chiefs. The significance must run far deeper. Built in a gentle valley, it is believed that this was a sacred place where a person could communicate with his ancestors. Stone huts attached to portions of the ruins indicate that it later became a home for the living. Zimbabwe was abandoned in the early 19th century when fierce Zulu warriors destroyed the Shone confederation. The rituals which took place here are forever shrouded by the mists of time.

In succeeding centuries, the Bantu people emerged into rather powerful societies in what is now Uganda and the Zaïre (Congo) River Basin. A king of a Bantu state in Uganda who was deposed in 1966 claimed to be the 37th monarch in an uninterrupted rule of a single family. Religious life of the Bantus evolved over the centuries into countless varieties of animistic, traditional tribal beliefs—faith in many gods represented by animal, vegetable, mineral and astronomic symbols, each possessing a degree of power in the daily life and future of mankind.

Since there was a lack of the written word during these early centuries, there is no chronicle of the Bantu people as is found in those parts of the world where writing skills had been developed. History was recorded dimly by spoken words preserved by numerous folk tales passed from generation to generation, usually altered at will by the imagination of the tellers. There was no calendar except that provided by nature in the form of the slight changes of season during the year. The passage of years was recorded by the chronology of the important events such as drought, famine, war or disease, and by occurrences relating to the almost continuous quarrels and intertribal battles of these restless people. Although possessing a high degree of similarity, the language and dialects of the Bantu split into hundreds of groupings in the same pattern that the people became divided.

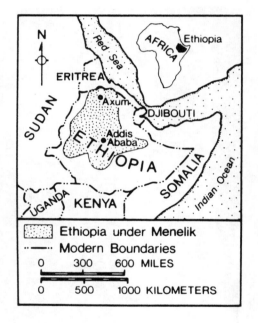

Ethiopia under Menelik
···· Modern Boundaries
0   300   600 MILES
0   500   1000 KILOMETERS

The Bantu expansion southward continued at a very slow rate. Most of the few remaining Negrillo–type people in south–central Africa were pushed into what is now South Africa, Botswana, Lesotho, Swaziland and Namibia (South–West Africa) and Zambia. In the area of Botswana there is a small group of Bushmen who bear a striking resemblance to the "aborigines" of Australia. The relationship of the two groups if any, is shrouded in the mists of time. The primitive pygmy people, probably the oldest inhabitants of the continent, were driven in dwindling numbers into remote forests and jungle areas of central Africa. Bantu expansion finally reached what is now South Africa in the mid–17th century at the time that Dutch

pioneers were pushing inland from the Cape of Good Hope.

THE HAMITIC KINGDOM OF ETHIOPIA

By tradition, the Ethiopian kingdom dated back to a visit by the Queen of Sheba (a city in Yemen also known as Saba or Sabah) at the court of Solomon. Menelik I, son of Solomon and the Queen, founded the Ethiopian monarchy. There are other indications that the Ethiopians had progressed at a relatively early date in African history. Herodotus, a Greek writer of the 5th century B.C. described Ethiopia; Homer refers to the Ethiopians as a "blameless race" in his writing of about 800 B.C. There are numerous references to Ethiopia in the Bible.

Not much is known of the history of Ethiopia at the beginning of the Christian era. The capital was moved from the ancient city of Axum to Addis Ababa and the distinctive Amharic language of the Ethiopians slowly evolved. By tradition, Christianity came to Ethiopia in the 4th century A.D. when Frumentius and another young member of the Coptic (Egyptian) Christians converted the King and his court. The Christian Church in Ethiopia was established as a branch of the Coptic Christian Church headed by the Patriarch of Alexandria in Egypt. Contact with other Christians was later severed by the Islamic–Arab conquest of North Africa in the mid–10th century.

THE SPREAD OF ISLAM

The teachings of Mohammed, a religious prophet of the neighboring Arabian peninsula, were the basis for the religion known as *Islam*, sometimes incorrectly referred to as *Mohammedanism*. The writings of Mohammed, together with his teachings, are gathered together in a book known as the Koran. He envisioned his prophecy to be supplemental, or in addition to the other revelations, including those of Judaism and Christianity of a single God. Preaching a belief in *Allah*, a single, all–powerful God, Mohammed was supposed to be the last prophet of God. He thought that there is a Last Judgment, a duty to donate to the poor, and, most important, there is an obligation to engage in a daily system of prayer.

The faith of Islam was initially a great unifying force among its Arab believers, who began a rapid expansion at the close of the 7th century. A line of Islamic rulers established themselves at what is now Damascus in Syria, and from that base other Moslem leaders conquered all of Africa within a century, even going further to seize most of Spain.

Islam spread southward from the 8th century A.D.; most of the Nilotic, Nilo–Hamitic and Hamitic people of the semi–arid regions south of the sands of the Sahara Desert were converted. Their adoption of Islam in the south Sahara resulted in the formation of a succession of empires of substantial strength and advanced development. Because of this contact with the Islamic Arabs, who brought the art of writing, much more is known of the history of this region of the African continent.

ARABS IN EAST AFRICA

From the 8th to the 10th centuries A.D. the Arabs penetrated the shoreline of East Africa in increasing numbers, establishing trading posts at Mogadishu (Somali Republic) and Mombasa (Kenya) and in what is now Mozambique. Ivory and African slaves were the basis of a brisk trade, as well as gold, shipped primarily to India. This continued in one form or another until control of the area was seized by European colonial powers in the last part of the 19th century.

THE EARLY EMPIRES OF WEST AFRICA

A segment of Hamitic–Negro people living in the area south of the Sahara gathered together in the first "empire" of West Africa in the 4th century A.D., eventually controlling a large area which is now part of Burkina Faso (Upper Volta), southern Mali and eastern Senegal. The basis of this early group of people was a lively trade in gold and slaves with the nomadic people to the north. *Ghana*, as this empire is historically known, should not be confused with the modern state bearing that name. Its existence continued until it was conquered by the Islamic Berbers from the north in 1076, who converted the local people to their faith.

West Africa's history after Islam arrived in the sub–Sahara dry regions is one of conflict between various Hamitic–Negro tribes and kingdoms, all located within the same general area described above. The Songhai Empire in western Niger, which had controlled the region since the 7th century, adopted Islam, as did the Mandingo Empire which arose in Mali. Initially, most of West Africa from about 1000 to 1200 A.D. was divided between the Songhai and Mandingo rulers, with the exception of areas closer to the coast in what are now parts of Guinea, Ivory Coast, Ghana and Burkina Faso.

Trade with the Arabs to the north and east was lively for several centuries, with caravans linking Timbuktu, Gao (Mali), Kano (Nigeria) and the Lake Chad region with the Middle East by way of the Sudan and Egypt. The more affluent Islamic people journeyed on traditional pilgrimages to Mecca from this area of West Africa. Other trading was conducted with the Arab–Berber people of the North where Morocco, Algeria, Tunisia and Libya are now located.

The Mandingo rulers gradually acquired more territory at the expense of the neighboring ethnic groups after 1200 A.D. A brief domination by the Soso people from Guinea, led by Sundiata, was ended by the Mandingos in 1235, and there followed a period of rapid expansion which eventually engulfed the Songhai empire in 1325. Timbuktu, located in a remote part of what is now Mali, became a center of culture and progress fabled throughout West Africa, and was visited by many Arab merchants and travelers.

The Mandingo Empire disintegrated in the 15th century when Timbuktu was invaded and sacked by Tuaregs (a darker–skinned Berber people from the desert to the north). A generation later, in 1468, the Songhai rulers were able in turn to expel the Tuaregs. The Songhai reached their greatest power in the following six decades, at a time when the first Portuguese explorers began to penetrate the area.

Several initially non–Moslem kingdoms arose along the southern coast of West Africa at about the same time the Islamic empires of the upper Niger River were powerful. The Fulani, also known as Peulh, established several states from what is now Senegal to Nigeria, occupying an area between the Moslem empires and the coastal lands, and gradually were converted to Islam. Closer to the coastline, the Mossi created two distinct states within what is now southern Burkina Faso (Upper Volta) and Ghana, also adopting Islam.

The Ashanti became established in what is now central Ghana, as did the Soso in Guinea, the Yorubas in Dahomey and southwestern Nigeria and the Ibos in southeastern Nigeria. All of these states were populated by persons of West African Negro heritage, and occupied the more humid coastal region with countless numbers of sub–groups and local tribes, each having its own animist beliefs. Further southeast, a Bantu kingdom arose in the area of the Congo River, which occupied a large expanse of territory from Gabon to Angola by the time of European colonization of Africa.

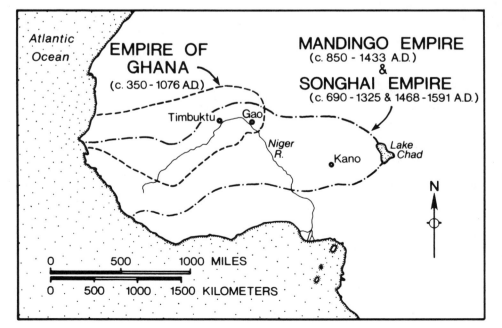

EMPIRE OF GHANA (c. 350 - 1076 A.D.)

MANDINGO EMPIRE (c. 850 - 1433 A.D.) & SONGHAI EMPIRE (c. 690 - 1325 & 1468 - 1591 A.D.)

Atlantic Ocean

Timbuktu Gao

Niger R. Kano

Lake Chad

N

0   500   1000 MILES
0   500   1000   1500 KILOMETERS

acy in the eastern coastal area of the continent.

In spite of this rather rapid navigational discovery, there was to be almost no penetration inland by the Europeans for more than three hundred years. With the exception of a Dutch settlement at the Cape of Good Hope, the sub–Sahara inland African regions remained the same dark, forbidding land that was first seen by the Portuguese. Following the precedent of the Arabs of East Africa, the Europeans started a lively West African trade in human cargo—slaves to perform the tasks of labor needed to colonize other parts of the world.

It was an easy task, with little exception, to acquire slaves along the so–called Gold and Ivory coasts of West Africa. Anchoring their slave ships in natural harbors, the Europeans negotiated with the chiefs of the more powerful ethnic groups or tribes that lived inland. When a suitable price (in terms of value, almost nothing) was agreed upon, the men and sometimes the women of a weaker neighboring tribe would be brought to the coast in bondage after a brief skirmish. They were delivered as promised to the slave traders. It was in this manner that Black Africans, tempted by their desires for the wealth offered by the White slave traders, sold the bodies of other Black Africans into slavery.

The Africans had no reluctance in this trade—they were doing no more than disposing of people that were a real or imagined threat to them, their families and their tribe. Further, their traditional tribal beliefs in a multitude of gods associated with animals and the forces of nature almost without exception encouraged and gave them the strength to deal with such real or imagined threats. Without the moral judgments of Christianity, the ability to deliver slaves at the coastline was actually a measure of ability, stature and superiority among the tribal groups.

Packed shoulder to shoulder in quarters on the slave ships that were so cramped no one could stand, the cargo of humans, regarded as animals, was transported across the sea, usually to the Western Hemisphere. Those unable to survive were dumped overboard at suitable intervals following their death. The remaining survivors were sold at a handsome profit compared to the sum paid for them along the African coastline—a profit possible even if more than one–half of the ship's cargo died during the trip to the "new world." The fact that an individual slave had survived this journey was testimony to his hardiness and stamina as compared to his less fortunate brethren who had perished.

Arriving at a particular destination in the Western Hemisphere where he was sold, the slave was to begin a new and

EUROPEAN DISCOVERY AND EXPLORATION

The first exploration of the African coastline started early in the 15th century when Portuguese navigators reached Senegal, Guinea and the islands lying adjacent to the West African coast. By 1492 Fernao Poo reached the island off the coast of Cameroon which bore his name, translated into Spanish—Fernando Poo. Fifteen years later, Bartolomeu Dias, usually referred to in English as Bartholomew Diaz, was blown by a storm in a southerly direction to the bottom of the continent. Turning eastward, he became the first European to navigate around the Cape of Good Hope.

In 1497, shortly after Columbus' sec-

ond voyage to America, Vasco da Gama sailed around the African cape in search of a way to India., using the primitive navigation information supplied by Diaz. He stopped at Mozambique, Mombasa and Malinda on the east coast of Africa, and was able to obtain the information necessary to proceed onward to India from the Arabs who were already established along the African coast.

With the arrival of increasing numbers of Portuguese vessels, quarrels with the Arab traders intensified. Francisco de Almeida was sent with a squadron to control Arab interference with Portuguese shipping; he took Mombasa in 1505 and ultimately demolished the Arab fleet in 1509, establishing Portuguese suprem-

incredibly difficult life in a totally strange surrounding where he would be judged by his physical ability to perform long, long hours of hard manual labor. A new language had to be learned and a new "family" created; the slave of the Western Hemisphere quickly became estranged from his African homeland and brethren—a tie, which having been severed, has not and probably will not be reestablished other than in the form of a basic friendship and allegiance.

EARLY ETHIOPIAN–EUROPEAN CONTACT

In the late dark ages of Europe, a letter from a supposed Christian king of Africa received widespread acclaim as possibly being from an unknown people dating from Biblical times. Inspired by this, a Roman Catholic Pope dispatched several Dominican brothers in the 14th century to locate this Christian kingdom. The results of these efforts are not clear, but an Ethiopian emissary did reach Venice in 1402, arriving later at Lisbon and Rome. In turn, European kings and the Pope sent emissaries to Ethiopia, hoping to enlist help in the continuing "crusades" against the Islamic people of the Middle East and North Africa. This diplomatic effort continued unevenly for four centuries, and there was no other significant contact between this region of Africa and

Europe during the passage of those years.

Increased penetration of Ethiopia by Europeans occurred in the 19th century. Although Ethiopia was not formally colonized by any European power, it became subject to a variety of "spheres of influence" of the British, French and Italians in the latter part of the century. The succession to the Ethiopian throne was irregular—every time a king died there was usually a two or three way contest for the throne. The somewhat weak char-

acter of the nation was further complicated by periodic skirmishes and quarrels over territory with the neighboring Sudanese who were led by fanatic religious–political figures with the title *Mahdi*. The Somalis to the east, who were Islamic, also claimed Ethiopian territory, sometimes with the assistance of the French or the Italians. The borders of the kingdom changed countless times during this period.

The modern history of the country begins with the reign of Emperor Menelik II, the first monarch to choose that name since the reign of the son of Solomon and Sheba. It was under the second Menelik that Ethiopia began to have regular contact with the outside world.

Although he was at first forced to acknowledge an Italian protectorate over Ethiopia, by 1896 he had consolidated his power sufficiently to send a military force which decisively defeated the Italians.

Lidj Yassu, the grandson of Menelik II succeeded to the throne in 1913, but was deposed in 1916. Zauditu, Menelik's daughter, was installed as Empress. Her cousin, Ras Tafari Makonnen ascended the throne in 1930, taking the name *Haile Selassie*, which means "the power of the Trinity" in Amharic.

THE ARABS AND OTTOMAN TURKS IN NORTH AFRICA

The Arab–Berber rulers of North Africa who came to power with the spread of Islam were known first as the Almavorid and subsequently the Almohad dynasty. Initially these Moslem kingdoms were characterized by a centralized power, but in the 13th to the 16th centuries there was gradual division into countless numbers of local rulers. Just as Christianity had split into numberless sects, so also had Islam been divided. Although the internal unity of the Arabs diminished, they were usually able to unite against non–Arabs on the infrequent occasions when outsiders threatened their territory.

The Moslem rulers of the Turkish Ottoman Empire gained control of most of Egypt and Libya at the beginning of the 16th century; their power in this area was not absolute since both regions quickly became no more than tribute–paying vassal states of the Empire. The Ottoman rulers were almost continuously occupied in wars with Europe and had insufficient resources to bring North Africa directly within the Empire as was done in Syria and Iraq. It was not long before most of North Africa was within the Ottoman sphere.

With the exception of Egypt, the remainder of North Africa continued under the loose control of the Ottoman Empire until World War I. Egypt remained under the Ottomans until the invasion by Napoleon in 1798. The Turks sent Moham-

The Imperial Family of Ethiopia, 1930

15

med Ali from an Ottoman military family (probably of Albanian origin) as commander of forces opposing the French; together with the British under Lord Nelson, they were finally able to expel the invaders in the summer of 1799.

Mohammed Ali quickly established his personal rule in Egypt as an Ottoman *Pasha.* Although he and his successors were able to avoid absolute domination by the Ottoman rulers, in reality Egypt continued to be a tributary vassal of the Empire for about 75 years until the British influence became paramount.

Khedive Ismail, grandson of Mohammed Ali, ruled as king but under the authority of the Sultan and Caliphs of the Empire; he had received a European education for several years. The Suez Canal was under construction principally in order to provide the British with a shorter route to their possessions in India and the Far East, although the construction effort was in the name of a cooperative effort of most of the European nations and Egypt. In anticipation of the revenues expected from the canal which opened in 1869, Ismail borrowed large sums of money at extremely high interest rates from European banks. When he was unable to repay the loans on schedule, the British used this as a pretext to assert their authority in Egypt, initially with Egyptian cooperation, in order to bring areas bordering the Red Sea waterway and in the Sudan under control.

By 1876 Khedive Ismail had been forced to sell all Egyptian shares in the Suez Canal, and Egypt was placed under the supervision of British and French financial controllers. This is considered the start of the colonial period in Egypt; although the Khedives continued to be the nominal power, they were little more than the instrumentality through which the British ruled.

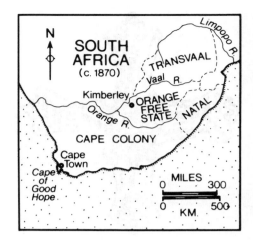

EUROPEAN SETTLERS IN SOUTH AFRICA
The Dutch at the Cape of Good Hope

Holland, seeking a food and fuel station for its ships sailing to the Dutch East Indies, established a small station on the Cape in 1652. A fort was constructed to guard against the Hottentots and Bushmen found in small numbers in the area. This outpost developed rapidly, with the outlying farms worked by slaves brought from the East.

There was a slow expansion of this Dutch community into the interior, though such was not actively pursued by the Dutch East India Company. A substantial number of Huguenot religious refugees from France arrived in 1688, adopting the Dutch social patterns. Further settlement of the interior by the Dutch *Burghers* continued for the next hundred years, since there was little opposition to their desire for additional farmland. It was not until the Dutch had

penetrated 200 miles to the northeast that they first encountered the Bantu people who were then in a process of migration from the southeast lake region of Africa. Bitter frontier warfare between the two groups of migratory people continued for the next seventy–five years, with large numbers of casualties on both sides.

The British took possession of Cape Town in 1795 in the name of the Prince of Orange, who then reigned in Holland and in England when his nation was overrun by the French. The British handed the area over to the Batavian Republic, a puppet state of France, in 1803 (all of this was a product of shifting alliances in Europe involving Napoleon's activities). But in 1806 the British returned; the Cape Colony was officially ceded to it in 1814 and it became a Crown Colony. A substantial migration of British settlers arrived in the succeeding 30 years, which by 1834 caused widespread unrest among the Dutch farmers of the Eastern Cape, who resented British rule.

Led by men of courage like Andries Pretorius, for whom Pretoria is named, the *Voortrekkers,* or pioneers, journeyed in covered wagons to the northeast, overcoming severe hardships and fighting the fierce Bantu tribesmen. In 1839 they founded a new republic called Natal, but were later pushed even further into the interior by the arrival of British military forces. Crossing the Drakensburg (Dragon Mountains), they went into the Orange Free State and Transvaal. In each area, a *Boer* republic was proclaimed. Thus, toward the end of the 19th century, there were two *Boer* republics and two British colonies in what is now the Republic of South Africa. A mammoth deposit of diamonds was discovered at Kimberly in 1891, attracting fortune hunters from all over the world.

Opening of the Suez Canal, 1869

THE COLONIAL PERIOD

Nigeria dances for Queen Elizabeth and Prince Philip, 1956

THE PORTUGUESE
Coastal West Africa: Portuguese Guinea

Although the Portuguese explored the coastline of Guinea as early as 1446, the area remained a slave trading coastal region for about the next 450 years. Portuguese control of the area occurred only because it was permitted by the other, more aggressive colonial powers. This was somewhat poor territory and literally what was left after the French and British had colonized West Africa.

The final boundaries were delineated in 1905, after both Britain and France had appropriated parts of Portuguese Guinea. Penetration into the interior was negligible until about 1912; in recent years the Portuguese had only sporadic control of the region, which was still theoretically a part of European Portugal. It was declared independent on September 10, 1974.

Equatorial West Africa: Angola, Cabinda, São Tomé, Príncipe

Angola was first explored in 1482 by Diego Cao of Portugal, who found this region of Africa controlled by the Bacongo people, led by a mighty King of the Congo. A scattering of Portuguese immigrants arrived during the following decades, but they were restricted to the coastal areas by the native Africans as a result of a series of bloody clashes. The King was overthrown, but later reestablished by the Portuguese in 1570.

During the 17th and 18th centuries, Angola was the prime source for slaves deported to Brazil to work the huge coffee plantations in that Portuguese Latin American colony. Also, an infamous penal colony was established in Angola.

During the late 19th and early 20th centuries, a multitude of treaties between Portugal and the British, French, Belgians and Germans gradually fixed the boundaries of Angola and Cabinda. The colony was given a form of internal autonomy in 1914, but this was strictly under White minority rule.

There were periodic uprisings in the 20th century, and in general, Portugal had almost exclusively favored the Portuguese immigrants and their descendants. In a flurry of civil war, accompanied by Cuban assistance for a Soviet–backed group, Angola, after formally being granted independence, became a Marxist state (see Angola).

Economic development under the Portuguese consisted of agriculture in the form of coffee and cotton production and mineral extraction based on diamonds in northeast Angola.

Cabinda is a part of Angola; it is a small enclave north of the Zaïre River. São Tomé is a tropical island devoted to cocoa production; it is inhabited by a uniform group of people of mixed, but predominantly African ancestry. There also was a small commercial element of Portuguese immigrants, most of whom left following the wars after independence. Príncipe is a small and poor island barely supporting the handful of descendants of freed slaves. These islands became independent on July 5, 1975 as *The Democratic Republic of São Tomé and Príncipe.*

Southern Africa: Mozambique (Moçambique)

The Portuguese presence along the coast of Mozambique dates back to the voyage of Vasco da Gama in 1498. He found a number of trading posts that had been established by the Arabs, who offered little resistance to Portuguese construction of settlements and forts during the next century. These stations were intended more as an aid to Portuguese efforts in India and the Far East and were little more than stopping places for commercial vessels bound to and coming from those areas.

Shortly after Africa was partitioned at the Berlin Conference of 1885, both the French and Germans recognized Portuguese supremacy in Mozambique and elsewhere; Britain, preoccupied with its own colonial ambitions, ignored the Portuguese. Five years later, after expanding into neighboring Nyasaland (now Malawi), the British reached an agreement recognizing Portuguese claims. At the same time, the Mozambique Company was chartered to manage and invest in the colony, backed by substantial amounts of British capital. A massive uprising of Africans at the close of the 19th century hampered economic development in Mozambique. An early attempt was made in 1907 to establish a legislative council with membership restricted to White settlers in the colony.

As a result of the German defeat in World War II, the Portuguese added a small piece of German East Africa to Mozambique. The colonial period was relatively eventless between the two world wars. Railroad lines were extended initially from Beira to Nyasaland (Malawi), Southern Rhodesia (Zimbabwe), Northern Rhodesia (Zambia) and as far as the southeastern province of Katanga (Shaba) in the Belgian Congo, now Zaïre.

Portugal resisted attempts on the part of the native African majority to obtain independence during the postwar period. Following a liberal–army revolution in Portugal itself, this colony was granted independence in mid–1975 (see Mozambique).

THE BRITISH
Coastal West Africa: (The) Gambia

The claimant to the throne of Portugal granted English merchants, in exchange for an undisclosed sum of money, the

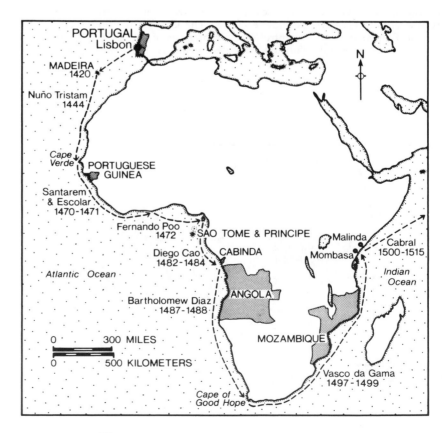

19

exclusive right to trade with the people along the Gambia River.

Queen Elizabeth I confirmed this sale by granting letters patent to English businessmen, and in 1618 James I granted a charter to the Royal Adventurers of England, giving the company trade franchises in Gambia and in the Gold Coast.

At the same time the British merchants were developing trade in the river area, French interests were expanding in Senegal, and the Gambia River was the best route to the interior of Senegal. Hence, an intense rivalry arose between the two nations in this area of colonial Africa. Their disputes were partially resolved by the Treaty of Versailles in 1783 which granted Gambia to the British, but reserved for the French a small enclave across the water from Bathurst.

There had been little exploration or penetration up the river to the interior until after 1860 when British explorers went inland and negotiated treaties with the local chief to obtain additional territory. The city of Bathurst remained a separate entity for the next two decades, sometimes administered from Sierra Leone, otherwise governed as a separate colony.

The present boundaries of The Gambia were delineated by a British–French agreement in 1889. Although the exportation of slaves had been prohibited, it was not until 1906 that the local practice of slavery within Gambia was abolished by British decree.

From the turn of the century until after World War II, there were few significant historical events in Gambia. Periodic efforts of the French to acquire control of the area were unsuccessful. With the ex-

ception of Bathurst, no Europeans lived in Gambia.

During World War II, Gambia not only served as an important naval base for military convoys, but contributed soldiers who fought valiantly in the Burma campaign of General Stilwell against the Japanese. The postwar period saw the birth of nationalist sentiment in Gambia. The Governor–General granted increasing powers of self government to the Africans of the country and established an advisory council.

In the late 1950's, Gambian leadership gathered into four political parties: the *Progressive Peoples Party*; the *United Party*; the *Democratic Congress Alliance*; and the *Gambian Congress Party*. The leaders of these groups actually had few differences, except with regard to possible association or federation with Senegal.

In general elections held in 1962, the *Progressive Peoples Party* gained 18 of the 32 popularly elected seats of Parliament. Prior to that time, Pierre Sarr N'jie, leader of the *United Party*, had been Chief Minister. David K. Jawara was selected Premier when his *Progressive Peoples Party* received support from the single delegate of the *Gambia Congress Party*.

Through subsequent defections, the *United Party* of N'jie lost five members to the organization of Jawara. An assembly of tribal leaders were selected by the Governor–General with the advice of the Prime Minister, but they had no vote. Thus, the National Assembly's membership totaled 38.

Internal self–government was granted to The Gambia in 1963, followed by explorations of the possibility of union with Senegal. A U.N. recommendation for

unity between the two was turned down.

Coastal West Africa: Sierra Leone

The people of the European mercantile powers, particularly in England, had felt increasing antipathy toward the principle of slavery by the end of the 18th century after the American Revolution. A Society for the Abolition of Slavery was formed under the leadership of Granville Sharp, which planned to establish a colony in Sierra Leone for the slaves that were to be set free. In 1788, the Temne King, Naimbana and his subordinate chiefs, sold a portion of the coastal area of Sierra Leone to the Society, which was then settled initially by a group of 300 Africans freed as a reward for their service in the British armed forces in the battles of the American Revolution, joined by some former Jamaican slaves. The diminutive settlement was administered by the Sierra Leone Company and was immediately burdened by the task of fending off attacks from neighboring groups and French warships.

There was little growth—the burden of defense, development and settlement proved to be severe for the Company, and in 1808 Sierra Leone was taken over by the British as a Crown Colony. The English Parliament had abolished slave trade in 1807. Freetown, the name of the Company settlement, became a base for a squadron of ships which sailed the shores of West Africa searching for and intercepting the privateer slave ships. The first slave ship found was quickly condemned in 1808; its human cargo, so recently abducted from other African areas, was released at Freetown. As further slave ships were captured in the succeeding years, thousands of Africans of great diversity in origin were released, most of whom elected to remain in Sierra Leone, settling largely in the areas closest to the coast.

The period of the 19th century was one of gradual development by the British in Sierra Leone, with the establishment of a flourishing trade, schools, a college and Christian church missions. The former slaves, called *Creoles*, isolated from their native peoples and traditions, adopted many English customs which prevail today among their descendants, now numbering more than 125,000. In 1896 a British protectorate was established over the territory, which by then had definite boundaries with the adjacent French territories as a result of treaties signed in 1861.

The roads to democracy and independence were ones of peaceful development of responsibility and unity among the Creoles and the inland groups, with the first elections for local office being held in 1924. Sir Milton Margai, a Creole leader, was appointed to successive

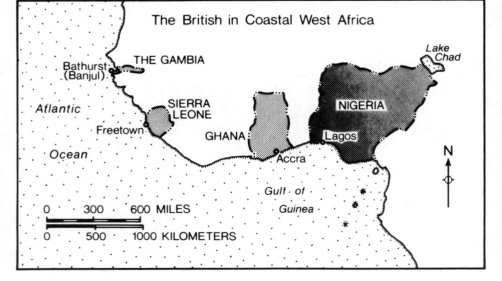

The British in Coastal West Africa

offices in 1954 and the following years, becoming the first Prime Minister in 1960.

Coastal West Africa: Ghana (Gold Coast)

The Portuguese intially landed in Ghana as early as 1470; they were followed in 1553 by an English arrival on the shores of what was then known as the Gold Coast. Seeking gold, ivory and spices, the Portuguese built a castle which now stands in ruins on the coast. English, Danish, Dutch, German and Portuguese commercial interests controlled ports on the Gulf of Guinea during the next 250 years. By 1750, only the English, Dutch and Danes remained.

Great Britain assumed control of English commercial settlements in 1821, negotiating treaties with the local chiefs in the southern areas in 1844. Shortly thereafter, the Danes and Dutch ceded their interests to the British.

It was necessary for the English forces to fight a long series of battles against the Ashantis of the interior; there were four major campaigns in which the British subdued them: 1824–27, 1873–74, 1893–94 and 1895–96. It was only in 1901 that colonial authority spread through the entire country. After seizing Togoland (Togo) from the Germans during World War I, the British administered it from Accra. With the exception of the commercial activity in the south coastal area, there was little economic development during the colonial period.

Following World War II, there was a sharp rise of nationalism among the Africans of higher education in Gold Coast, as the colony was called. The *United Gold Coast Convention*, led by J.B. Danquah, exerted continuous pressure for autonomy and independence.

Political developments quickly came to revolve around one person: Kwame Nkrumah. After receiving college educations in the United States and Great Britain, obtaining several degrees in advanced courses of study, he returned to the Gold Coast from England in 1947. As Secretary of the *UGCC*, he assisted in promoting riots and strikes in early 1948. Both he and Danquah were exiled to a remote northern village by the British Governor. The British accused Nkrumah of being a communist.

Under continuing pressure, the British in 1949 promulgated a new constitution and released the exiled leaders. Nkrumah, restless under the leadership of Danquah, formed his own political party, the *Convention Peoples Party (CPP)*. Further civil disobedience under Nkrumah's leadership resulted in his arrest, conviction and sentence to a two–year jail term. Constitutional reforms in 1951 provided for election of a greater number of Africans to a legislative council

Kwame Nkrumah

and Nkrumah was freed from prison to head the new government.

A new constitution of 1954 established a cabinet composed entirely of African representatives. The subsequent elections again resulted in a majority for the *CPP*. Two years later, Nkrumah, as Prime Minister, demanded independence. The British, not convinced that this was the will of the people, held new elections in 1956, which perpetuated the majority of the *CPP* (71 out of 104 seats). Independence was declared in 1957.

Central West Africa: Nigeria

The Portuguese were also the first explorers to land at Nigeria in 1472. For the next 300 years, traders from all nations called briefly in Nigeria, but there was no settlement. The principal purpose of their visits was to obtain human cargo to work in the colonies of the Western Hemisphere. The hundreds of Nigerian tribes periodically attacked each other, and the victor carried off the defeated to be sold into slavery for never more than $10.00 each. Transported across the ocean, they brought prices of up to $300.00. Close to 70% died in the slave ships. Slavery was not outlawed internally in Nigeria until 1901. There was a slow penetration of the British into the interior of Nigeria following the Napoleonic wars. The colony of Lagos was founded in 1862. Twenty–three years later, the Niger River Delta was established as a British Protectorate and British influence in Nigeria was formally recognized at the conference of European powers at Berlin in 1885. The British continued to expand in Nigeria through the Royal Niger Company, but in 1900 the territory came under the control of the British Colonial Office.

The people of northern Nigeria were believers in Islam; the Hausa and Fulani, as they are known, were feudally governed by a variety of monarchs known as Emirs (also spelled Amirs).

Even after penetrating into areas of Nigeria, the British had difficulty in controlling the people; there were widespread disturbances and revolts in southern Nigeria in 1904 and an uprising in the Sokoto region of northern Nigeria in 1906.

It was not until 1914 that northern Nigeria was fully brought under control, at which time the Colony and Protectorate of Nigeria was formally established. Shortly after World War I, African legislators were included in the Council governing Lagos and southern Nigeria. The British enlarged tin mines on the Jos Plateau and improved the roads, schools and port facilities of Nigeria during the succeeding decades. Following World War II, the Colonial Office adopted successive constitutions which expanded African participation in Nigerian administration on a representative, federal basis. Three political parties evolved on a regional basis: the *Nigerian Peoples Congress* (North), the *National Convention of Nigerian Citizens* (Southeast) and the *Nigerian National Democratic Party* (Southwest). The latter two of these parties pressed energetically for full independence, but the *Nigerian Peoples Congress* advocated a lesser nationalistic outlook because it feared domination by a combination of the other two parties.

Discussions were held in London in 1957, at which time there were demands by 15 ethnic groups that they become individual and independent nations within the territory of Nigeria. The British resisted these demands and established a central parliamentary government with many powers reserved to the individual provinces; independence was granted in 1960.

Central West Africa: Cameroons

The British had early colonial ambitions in Cameroon and dispatched an emissary to negotiate treaties with the local chieftain in 1884. He arrived on the coast five days too late—the German representative had already concluded agreements with

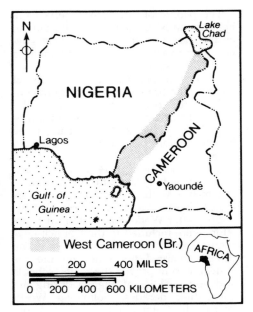

West Cameroon (Br.)

0   200   400 MILES

0   200   400   600 KILOMETERS

the coastal people, and Cameroon was to remain a German colony until 1916.

An extensive campaign was waged by the British and French against the German forces in Cameroon during the first world war. The fighting ended with the surrender of the Germans in 1916 (in Cameroon) and under the Treaty of Versailles Britain was awarded the smaller West Cameroon territory and France obtained East Cameroon. The fact that there were two colonies where there had been one gave rise to the plural name *Cameroons* for the area, creating confusion which persists even after they were again joined together in 1961.

The British held a mandate over its part from the League of Nations and subsequently under a trusteeship from the United Nations. Because of the language difference between the colonial powers of the two countries, there was wide divergence of opinion among the people of West Cameroon as to the political future of the territory in the late 1950's. The British conducted a plebiscite under UN supervision in 1961 to determine whether the people of West Cameroon desired to become a part of the English–speaking Nigeria to the northwest, or to join the French–speaking East Cameroon in a federation.

Rather than conduct the plebiscite on the basis of all votes cast in the entire territory, it was decided to count the votes of the northern and southern portions separately. The people of the North voted to become part of Nigeria, which was effected, and the people in the South voted for the federation with the former French Cameroon. The voting procedure was strongly opposed by East Cameroon, considerable opinion existing to the effect

that the vote should have been counted as a whole. Had this been done, no part of West Cameroon would have become a part of Nigeria.

———— • ————

The difference in language brought to West Africa by the British and the French has been the basis of post–independence problems. Almost uniformly, the official and commercial language of each area is that of its former colonial ruler. English–speaking Gambia should logically be a part of Senegal where French is spoken; Ghana is an English language nation surrounded by French–speaking nations, and many Ghanians, in the ethnic sense of the word, live in neighboring former French areas.

There also remains an economic pattern which is based on former colonial status; almost every nation of West Africa is economically tied to either France or Britain. Fluctuations and devaluations in currency, trade restrictions and the political problems associated with the European Common Market have all served to prevent a genuinely free flow of commerce among the present–day African nations.

South Africa

Since the period of partial British control of what is now the Republic of South Africa was brief and hotly contested by the *Afrikaaners* of Dutch ancestry, the history of the colonial period appears in the section on South Africa. There were, however, three territories in the area over which exclusive British control was continuous: Botswana (called Bechuanaland), pronounced Beh–*kwa*–na–land), Lesotho (called Basutoland, pronounced Ba–*soo*–toe–land) and Swaziland (pronounced *Swah*–zee–land). During the colonial period, which ended in 1967–1968, all three were economically dependent upon what is now the Republic of South Africa even though they were colonies of Great Britain.

Southern Africa: Botswana (formerly Bechuanaland)

The Tswana, as the majority of the people of Botswana are called, remained split into hundreds of tribes and communities until Khama I, Chief of the powerful Bamangwato tribe, consolidated them into a loosely constituted group in the last half of the 19th century.

As the *Boers* of South Africa were pushed northward from the Cape by the British, they attempted to penetrate into what is now Botswana, and battles

erupted between the two peoples. Khama I, a Christianized native, appealed to the British for assistance, and the country was proclaimed to be under British protection.

Khama I reigned over the loosely united country until his death at the age of 93 in 1923, and was succeeded by his son, Sekgoma, who died three years later in 1926.

The British did little more than maintain peace in Bechuanaland during the period of the protectorate, although in later years they provided an annual grant to assist the colony's economy. In 1920 they set up two advisory councils—one for the native African people and one for the European settlers and their descendants who had come in small number to the area. Later, in 1934, they established a constitution which granted authority to the local chieftains and native courts.

The native rule of the Bamangwato passed to Seretse Khama, then the four–year–old son of Sekgoma, under the regency of Tshekedi Khama, brother of the dead ruler. The British had difficulty in controlling Tshekedi—at one time he was deposed as regent for a short time after having had a Britisher flogged.

Seretse Khama left for England in 1945 to pursue higher education; while studying law he met a young English woman, Ruth Williams, and married her. This interracial marriage of 1949 infuriated the white population of South Africa, and the embarrassed British Government removed Seretse Khama from office and forced him to remain in England until 1956.

After obtaining a renunciation of his chieftainship, the British permitted him to return to Bechuanaland in 1956 as "Mr. Khama." Many of the lesser chiefs opposed his return, as did his uncle, Tshekedi. The British established a Legislative Council in 1958 composed of 35 members equally divided between the races to advise and consent to the acts of the British High Commissioner, who was also executive authority in Swaziland, Basutoland and Ambassador of Great Britain to South Africa. Tshekedi was removed as Regent–Chief in 1959; the avowed purpose of establishing the Council was to prepare Bechuanaland for independence.

Political parties emerged rapidly after the first Council meetings—K.T. Motsete formed the *Bechuanaland People's Party* in 1960, demanding immediate independence and removal of political power from the White settlers. The British tacitly permitted Seretse Khama to enter politics because of his popularity, which had grown since his return from exile. He formed the *Bechuanaland Democratic Party*, with membership from both races, and advocated a policy of non–racism in government, a move toward internal

22

self–government by 1965 and independence as soon thereafter as possible.

The British reviewed the status of Bechuanaland in 1963 and established a new constitution in consultation with the representatives of the political parties. The first elections in 1965 under the new system were won by Khama's *Democratic Party* and he was named Prime Minister. Further negotiations led to an agreement for full independence which became effective on September 20, 1966; Bechuanaland took the name *Botswana*—land of the Tswana.

Southern Africa: Lesotho (formerly Basutoland)

The people of what is now Lesotho, although composed almost of what are now referred to as South Sotho people, were organized in a multitude of subgroups and tribes in the early 19th century. Raids from neighboring Zulus and Matabeles had depleted their number, and the remainder were gathered together in a loosely united kingdom by Moshoeshoe I, a chieftain from the northern region of Lesotho. The land was mountainous, hilly and generally regarded as unsuited for farming by *Boer* descendants of the original settlers of South Africa who had been driven from the Cape region into the interior of South Africa by British pressures.

But pressures for more land led to a twelve year war between the Whites of the Orange Free State and the Sothos between 1856 and 1868 which weakened the latter; they lost a substantial portion of their territory, still referred to as the "Conquered Territory." Facing total defeat, the Sothos appealed to the British for protection in 1868. The land area of the protectorate was poorly defined; the British resisted further *Boer* expansion, but had difficulty establishing control in what was considered a remote (from the Cape) land.

Basutoland, as it was then called, was annexed to the British Cape Colony in 1871, an act which was resented by the Basutos at the time because the English were just as eager for expansion in southern Africa as were the *Boers*. The unstable union was plagued by disturbances within Basutoland; the British, faced with a state of near–anarchy among the people, placed the colony directly under the control of Her Majesty's Government in 1884.

The British High Commissioners spent most of their time in Basutoland settling tribal differences and determining who was Paramount Chief—since the reign of Moshoeshoe I the land had been governed by about twenty–two lesser chiefs, who were in turn superior to approximately 2,000 minor chieftains. Little was done to improve and modernize the lives

Seretse Khama and his wife shortly before independence

of the people living in the remote wilderness of the highlands.

The Basutoland Council was informally constituted in 1903 to provide direction in internal matters, and it was recognized officially by the British in 1910 as a legislative body to be consulted on internal affairs of the colony. The Council requested further reform in 1955 in order that its decisions might be conclusive on all internal questions. After a period of negotiation a revised constitution was adopted in 1959, to take effect the following year, which granted the wishes of the Legislative Council.

Pressures for total independence slowly gathered momentum, and Britain decided on a course of action in early 1965. Elections were held in April of that year to determine the popular will with respect to leadership of the colony. The *Basutoland National Party* of then–moderate Chief Leabua Jonathan gained 31 of the 60 parliamentary seats. The opposition party, the *Panafricanist Congress Party*, led by Ntsu Mokhele, a leftist, received 25 seats, and the right–wing *Maramatlou Freedom Party*, which supported the aspirations for power of Moshoeshoe II, hereditary Paramount Chieftain, won 4 seats. One delegate from the *Maramatlou* party defected to

the *National Party* shortly after the election.

Although Chief Leabua Jonathan, who conducted his campaign from a helicopter provided by the Republic of South Africa, had received a minority of 44% of the popular vote, he negotiated for independence with the British in London.

An independence agreement was reached on June 18, 1966 whereby Basutoland was to become independent and was to be called *Lesotho*, indicating the lowlands of the Sotho—the area they traditionally occupied.

Southern Africa: Swaziland

The Swazis came to their present territory during one of the many Bantu migrations. In the 18th century, Zulu raids into their country forced the tribal chieftain of Mawati to seek British assistance through the Agent General in Natal, who mediated a peaceful relationship between the two groups. For a time, the Transvaal Republic (now a province of South Africa) protected and administered Swaziland. After the *Boer War* (see the Republic of South Africa), control of the territory passed to the British.

In 1907, administration of Swaziland

23

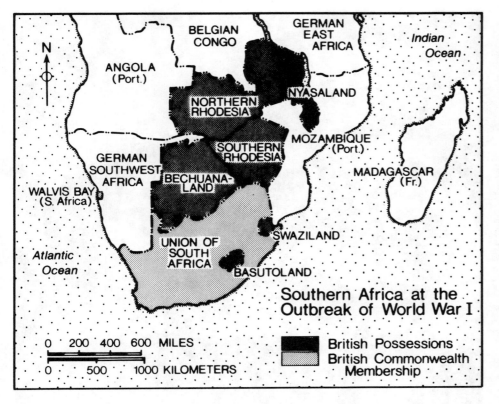

Southern Africa at the Outbreak of World War I

```
0   200  400  600 MILES
0      500      1000 KILOMETERS
```

British Possessions
British Commonwealth Membership

was charged to the British High Commissioner for South Africa. A proclamation was issued in 1944 by the Commissioner which recognized the Paramount Chief and Council as native authority for internal matters.

The British agreed in 1967 that Swaziland was to be independent after September 6, 1968. Internal self–government was established in April 1967 and elections were held shortly thereafter. The *Imbokodvo National Movement* (also known as *The Grindstone Movement*), led by Prince Makhosini Dlamini, won all 24 seats in the National Assembly. King Sobhuza II ascended the throne at the time of independence. Dr. Ambrose Zwane, leader of the opposition *Ngwane National Liberation Council*, pressed charges that the elections were rigged before the Organization of African United and in the UN. Both organizations listened, but did nothing.

Southern Africa: Rhodesia, Zambia, Malawi

A steady, but small procession of traders and missionaries of many European nations established themselves in Mozambique after the Portuguese in the 16th century. Actually, there was no colonial effort until almost four hundred years later. Diamonds and gold had been discovered in the former *Boer* states of South Africa, Transvaal and Orange Free State, both of which were coveted by the British. Transvaal had been successful in maintaining its independence. In an effort to surround the people of Dutch ancestry, the British commissioned the British South Africa Company in 1889, giving it all rights to an area north of Transvaal without limit.

Under the leadership of Cecil Rhodes, Salisbury was founded in 1890 in what was then known as Mashonaland, inhabited by Matabele (Bantu) people. Leander Jameson, a close friend of Rhodes, was appointed administrator of the thinly–settled area which included what is now Zambia and the name *Rhodesia* was adopted in 1895.

Since the most valuable of the natural resources of this part of Africa were then believed to be only in South Africa, the settlement of Rhodesia was slow. For decades, Salisbury was a rural town with wooden sidewalks and was the only urban settlement in what was a vast agricultural area. In the early 20th century, Zambia was recognized as a distinct state called *Northern Rhodesia*; both areas were granted full internal autonomy in 1923, when Rhodesia was declared to be a Crown Colony instead of the property of the British South Africa Company.

The White Rhodesians were few in number, but steadily grew into an industrious, conservative society. The African people, with the exception of a few missionary efforts, were largely ignored, and restricted to the poorer lands in the ensuing decades. Salisbury emerged as a cosmopolitan and large city by the end of World War II, which was the beginning of a period of migration of more thousands of White Europeans—principally British—to Rhodesia.

The African people of Rhodesia became increasingly restless after 1960 as many colonies of Africa were granted independence under African leadership, but the resulting limited political effort was unsuccessful because of the power of the White minority which was firmly established. Southern Rhodesia was joined with Northern Rhodesia (Zambia) and Nyasaland (Malawi) into the Federation of Rhodesia and Nyasaland in 1953, but this crumbled because of the overwhelming opposition of the African majorities in what are now Zambia and Malawi. Although there were earlier visits by traders and missionaries, the first significant penetration of Malawi was by the intrepid Scotch missionary, Dr. David Livingstone, on September 15, 1859. For almost 15 years he devoted his life to exploration of southeastern Africa and teaching Christianity to the native people. Formal annexation of the area occurred in 1883 when a representative of the British government accredited to the kings and chief of central Africa appeared and negotiated treaties with them. In reality, this was no more than an effort to exclude Portugal and Germany from the area. The British energetically and successfully ended slave trade of Arab raiders.

During the colonial period, particularly after the discovery of gold and diamonds in South Africa and copper in Rhodesia (Northern), the men usually spent several years working in the mines of those territories, bringing their limited wages back home to Nyasaland, as the area was then called. Because of this, and the prevalence of the Christian faith among the people, there was no rapid surge of nationalism. This changed in 1953 when Nyasaland was joined into the Federation of Rhodesia and Nyasaland—the Nyasas greatly feared the White supremacy movements that were strong in the other two members of the Federation. In an effort to suppress opposition, the British tried to arrest the chief of the Angoni tribe who advocated a passive resistance to the Federation. The attempted arrest was unsuccessful, but was the source of an even higher level of mistrust of the British and other White people by the Nyasas. There was a gradual transition to internal autonomy from 1961 to 1963 based upon elections in which the *Malawi Congress Party* of Dr. Hastings Kamuzu Banda won an overwhelming victory. The despised Federation was dissolved in 1963 and independence was granted the following year.

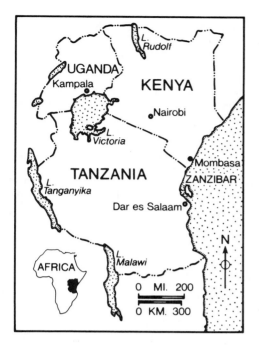

Jomo Kenyatta

East Africa: Kenya, Uganda and Tanzania (Tanganyika and Zanzibar)

The first British efforts in East Africa occurred in 1823 when Admiral William Owen entered the coastal area, supposedly in an attempt to end the Arab slave trade that had been going on for centuries along the coast. In theory, the Sultan of Muscat on the Arabian coast was the ruler of the region, and his authority was exercised by a viceroy (Sayyid) on the island of Zanzibar. The British, using a combination of threats and treaties, gradually established their control about the turn of the century.

German exploration and annexation of Tanganyika and part of southern Uganda from 1878 to 1885, in turn, aroused the interest of the British in Kenya and Uganda. The Sultan of Zanzibar granted the British East Africa Company a 50–year lease of what is now Kenya in 1887; this in turn was changed to the East Africa Protectorate, governed by a Commissioner, by the British government in 1895.

The last quarter of the 19th century in the eastern region of Africa was turbulent. There were efforts by both the British and Germans to enter Uganda, which was divided into four semi–autonomous kingdoms—Buganda, Busoga, Butoro and Bunyoro, of which Buganda was the most powerful. King Mwanga of Buganda, who reigned from 1884 until he was captured and exiled in 1899, tried to play the British off against the Germans by alternating his allegiance. In addition to this swirl of activity on behalf of Germany and Great Britain, there were roving remnants of Arab slave traders and religious conflicts involving and between Catholic and Protestant missionaries and believers, as well as those of Islamic faith.

The borders of this region were adjusted countless times, and not generally along the lines of actual colonial power. By a process of bargaining and trading, accompanied by line–drawing, particularly in Berlin in 1885, the eventual boundaries of the German, British and Portuguese territories, as well as those of King Leopold of Belgium were fixed. The almost straight line that now separates Kenya and Tanzania cuts almost through the center of the territory inhabited historically by the Masai people.

The British encouraged immigration of White settlers to Kenya after the turn of the century, and they established immense plantations in the most select parts of the colony. The tribespeople of Kenya, particularly large numbers of the Kikuyu (referred to as "kooks" by the British) were relegated to the poorer, tsetse–fly infested farmlands. White immigrants entered Uganda only in very small numbers.

At the start of World War I, 300,000 British, South African and colonial Indian troops invaded German East Africa, renamed Tanganyika following the establishment of British control after the war. A force of slightly more than 200 German officers, commanding native troops numbering between 2,500 and 4,000 fended off the massive force for four years under the brilliant leadership of General Paul Von Lettow–Vorbeck.

After the war, the British sent the German settlers from Tanganyika, confiscating their lands; a small number were permitted to return within a few years. Kenya was completely dominated by the White farmers and a substantial number of Indians who were descendants of workers brought in to complete a railroad between Nairobi and Mombasa which had opened in 1895. Uganda was governed through the local kings, and the cultivation of cotton and coffee quickly rose to be the source of the leading exports, permitting Uganda to become the richest British colony in Africa.

Government in Kenya was through a variety of commissioners sent from Britain; it was at a relatively late date that local councils were permitted, and initially even these consisted of people appointed by the commissioners. The White farmers of Kenya requested a regional council for Kenya, Uganda and Tanganyika as early as 1926, but were turned down since it was felt that this was merely an effort of theirs to preserve and extend their power which excluded the African majority from sharing in government.

Following World War II, the ability of the British to rule effectively in Kenya and Uganda sharply decreased. The population of Kenya was stratified into three groups: the rich, landowning White (a small minority), the Indian and Arab merchant class, and (at the bottom) the huge majority of Africans. The African population had doubled in 25 years, creating tremendous pressure for expansion into the lands exclusively held by White farmers. The White population, instead of recognizing the needs of the Africans, instituted progressively more strict and severe laws directed against the majority.

The restive Africans formed a terrorist organization, the *Mau Mau*, to achieve their goals. Dreadful brutality became commonplace. Not only did the *Mau Mau* seek the lives of the Whites, they mercilessly slaughtered those of their own people who were servile to and worked for the Whites. White retaliation was equally brutal. Jomo Kenyatta, the political leader of the majority of African people, educated in Europe, was arrested, tried and convicted for participating in the *Mau Mau* conspiracy. He was sentenced to seven years in jail. In 1957 Kenya erupted in a total state of civil anarchy. *Mau Mau* terrorism had spread into almost every area of the country. Africans suspected of participating in this secret society were shot on the spot by Whites. Even long–trusted house servants had by this time joined the secret organization.

It became increasingly apparent that in order to bring stability to Kenya, the British would have to accede to the demands of the *Mau Mau*. Most of the British farmers departed, and in 1960 an agreement was reached in London which gave the Africans a majority in the Legislative Council.

Dissension and political quarrels among the Africans in Kenya retarded the goal of full independence. Kenyatta, released from jail, headed the *Kenya–African National Union (KANU)*, which represented the larger tribes of the country. The *Kenya African Democratic Union* drew its support from the many smaller tribes. After prolonged discussion in London, a complicated constitution was adopted providing for a loose, federal system of government.

The election conducted in May 1963 resulted in an overwhelming victory for *KANU*. Under pressure from the majority, the constitution was amended to strengthen the authority of the central government. The British recognized the independence of Kenya in December 1963.

Uganda was not without disturbance during the postwar period, although not as bloody as that in Kenya. In 1953, with the intent of establishing a central government, the British Commissioner informed the Kabaka (King) of Buganda that there were to be reforms in administration which would undermine his authority. Edward Mutesa II, the Kabaka, adamantly refused to accept these regulations and he forthwith was dismissed as King and put on a plane for London. The Buganda people regarded this as nothing short of an outrage. The British had to constitute a form of martial law to control the people throughout Uganda, and the economy suffered a steep decline.

The British attempted to solve this state of affairs by proposing that the *Lukiko*, the Ugandan tribal assembly, be permitted to vote on whether a new king should be chosen; the Assembly would not listen to the proposal. Kabaka Edward Mutesa was subsequently returned and the British set up a ministerial system of government, increasing African membership in the Legislative Council. The United Kingdom of Uganda was granted full independence in October 1962.

The movement toward independence was relatively tranquil in Tanzania (Tanganyika). The British had received a mandate from the League of Nations to administer the former German colony. This continued under a U.N. trusteeship. A gradual development of internal self–government was undertaken by the British, starting with a Legislative Council appointed by the government in 1926. Subsequent elections were held in 1958 and again in 1960, the latter of which was won by the *Tanganyikan African National Union* of Julius Nyerere, who was President of Tanzania until 1985. He retired in that year, but is still a figure of power in the country. Full independence was granted in December 1961.

Northeast Africa: Egypt and the Sudan

During the first half of the 19th century, interest in European technology and education grew rapidly in Egypt, ruled by the Khedives (kings) nominally subject to the control of the Turkish Ottoman Empire's sultan. The basis for the construction of the Suez Canal lay in this interest, coupled with British and French desires for a shorter route to India and the Far East.

After negotiation with Khedive Ismail, European powers, working through their financial institutions, began construction of the canal, which was completed and opened amid great fanfare in 1869 with a multitude of European royalty present; they later heard the first performance of the opera *Aida*, by Giuseppe Verdi, erroneously said to have been written for the occasion. Egypt had been enriched by the demand for cotton created by the United States Civil War, but had also heavily borrowed at high interest rates to help finance the construction of the canal. From 1870 to 1883, the British succeeded in conquering most of the Sudan, penetrating as far as Uganda, supposedly in partnership with Egypt. The prime interest initially in this area was to end the oppressive slave trade that was firmly entrenched.

There was a financial crisis which compelled the Khedive to sell all of the Egyptian shares in the Suez Canal to Great Britain in 1876, giving the British a majority interest in the canal. Further financial deficits and inability to repay European loans were the basis of increasing British control of Egypt. The Khedives rapidly became figurehead kings, totally subject to British control, which led to an early rise of Egyptian nationalist desires. An

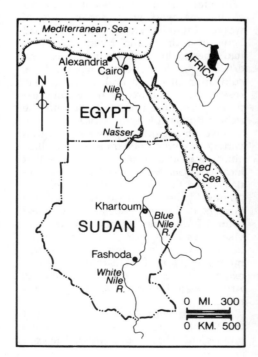

army revolt, coupled with a popular nationalist uprising was the excuse used to invade Egypt, and absolute British control of the region resulted.

Although the Khedives were retained as the nominal rulers, their power quickly became almost nonexistent in the face of growing pressures of the nationalist leaders. Eventually, a scheme of rule was devised under the so–called *Organic Law* which included a legislative council and cabinet with advisory powers. The Khedive was controlled by a "Resident and Consul–General" of the British; all high Egyptian ministers had a British "advisor."

In the Sudan, Mohammed Ahmed, a leader known as *Mahdi*, quickly achieved wide popularity following 1880—in addition to his political military support, he was regarded by his followers, the *dervishes*, as a modern–day prophet of Islam. By 1884, he had all but completely demolished British and Egyptian forces within the territory. An expedition sent by the British offered the *Mahdi* some concessions which were flatly rejected; the Mahdi immediately laid siege to Khartoum where General Charles Gordon and his forces were located.

After several months, the Mahdi entered the city and the British were slaughtered; General Gordon was impaled by a dervish spear. A relief force sent to help arrived in Khartoum three days later, but was greeted only by smoking rubble and the silent stench of death. Fearful of also being wiped out by the fanatical Sudanese, the rescue force beat a hasty retreat. The control of the Sudan remained with the Mahdi and his successor for ten years. The British, faced with the growing French expansion on the western side of the Nile River in the Sudan, sent a large force under General Sir Horatio Hubert Kitchener to reconquer the territory in 1896–1898. The Mahdi had died and the dervishes were disorganized; in the ensuing battle almost 10,000 Sudanese lost their lives and were only able to claim that of 50 British and Egyptians in return. One of the young lieutenants in the British force was none other than Winston Churchill, destined to lead Britain through World War II.

Kitchener was later entitled Lord Kitchener of Khartoum in recognition of his leadership. Entering Khartoum, he emptied the revered tomb of the original Mahdi and dumped the corpse into the river, and then quickly captured and killed the *Khalifa*, successor of the Mahdi.

Kitchener marched rapidly southward, meeting the French at Fashoda (now Kodak) in an effort to reassert British power. The result was the Fashoda Crisis (discussed under *The French in Africa*) that was finally ended by agreement on areas of control which roughly defined the boundaries between what is now the

King Farouk at 16 in 1936

Sudan, Central African Republic and Chad.

Great Britain and Egypt set up a joint administration of the Sudan; although they were nominally equal partners, the British were in fact the dominant power.

After World War I, the British had to institute increasingly harsh measures to maintain their control in Egypt and the so–called Anglo–Egyptian Sudan. At the start of World War I, the Ottomans in Turkey demonstrated sympathy for the German cause, and as a result, the British declared war against them. Although the Ottoman control in Egypt was little more than imaginary, the British used the war as a pretext to proclaim a protectorate status over Egypt, which aroused a great deal of local opposition. The *Nationalist,* or *Wafd Party,* quickly became dominant, opposing both the British and the Khedives.

A multitude of administrations under a semi–democratic constitution ruled following World War I. Ahmed Fuad, the Khedive, repeatedly dissolved nationalist governments and announced new elections, in all of which the nationalists scored tremendous victories and returned to power. The nationalist movement was not genuinely popular, however; its primary support came from the wealthy, land–owning *pashas* who had become established during the Ottoman era. The Protectorate status was withdrawn in 1922 and Egypt achieved internal autonomy as a result of *Wafd* efforts.

There were some efforts at economic development during the period between the two World Wars based upon the opening of dams along the Nile to partially control the age–old flood and drought cycle of the river. Constitutional reforms gave increasing power to the Egyptian *pashas.* The worldwide depres-

King Farouk at 32 in 1952

sion of the 1930's further lessened British control, and upon the death of King Fuad I in 1936, his handsome 16–year–old son, Farouk, came to power. Colorful and pleasure seeking, he was at first very popular. With the consent of the British and other European powers, Egypt became nominally independent in 1936 and was admitted to the League of Nations a year later. British military control was limited to the Suez Canal area.

The King dissolved the *Wafd* government in 1938, and the election that followed was a complete victory for the new pro–King party. Initially arming itself for World War II, Egypt maintained a passive neutrality during the conflict, although it was the scene of battles between the Allied and Axis powers.

Following World War II, the Egyptians sought to end the last vestiges of British domination. Weakened by the war, England was in no position to offer opposition to this demand. The picture was further complicated by the presence of the newly–born Jewish state of Israel, carved out of a portion of Palestine, opposed by the Arabs, which led to a brief Egyptian–Israeli battle in 1948, won by the Israelis.

The *Wafd Party* again returned to power in 1950 after several changes of government reflecting the desires of the nationalists and unrest among the army leadership. Egypt demanded withdrawal

of British troops from the Canal Zone and from the Sudan. Great Britain immediately retaliated with a plan for Sudanese independence; this appeared realistic in view of the traditional hatred for and distrust of Egyptians by the Sudanese. Events moved swiftly—the U.N. requested that Egypt lift its embargo forbidding use of the Suez Canal by ships bound for or coming from Israel. Egypt replied by abrogating its treaties with the British of 1899 and 1936 and the British navy attacked Port Said and landed forces in the area. Riots erupted in Cairo and there were two rapid changes of government. King Farouk, having grown fat and dissipated at the age of 32, was overthrown and exiled by the military in July 1952; a new era began in Egypt which is now generally thought of as the beginning of true independence in the modern age.

Prior to the defeat of Farouk, the British offered the Sudan a plan of internal self–government which was condemned by Egypt. The colonial government was able to work out a compromise arrangement with the military *junta* that succeeded Farouk, which provided that the Sudanese should decide whether they were to be independent or part of a federation with Egypt. In 1953 an overwhelming number of the Sudanese voted for independence, which was granted in 1956.

THE FRENCH IN AFRICA
North Africa: Algeria, Morocco and Tunisia

With the exception of Morocco, all of Arabic–speaking North Africa was at the turn of the 18th century in theory a part of the vast Ottoman Empire; the area consisted of a number of small principalities ruled by Turkish military men who had titles of *Bey* or *Dey,* depending upon the location. Commerce consisted of trade with regions to the south, and piracy of European shipping in the Mediterranean Sea.

The booty seized from the vessels consisted not only of cargo, but the crew as well, which was sold into slavery. After other nations had sent expeditionary forces against the Arab raiders, France sent a force into Algiers in 1830, deposing the Dey and seizing a few of the coastal towns. Another Dey was selected by the local people, who promptly marshaled attacks upon the French. Eventually the occupying forces had to recognize the new Dey, Abd el–Kader. He engaged in sporadic warfare for fifteen years against the French, who relinquished to him their claim to interior lands initially, but later drove him into Morocco where other French forces invaded and captured him in 1847.

Although the French presence in the area now known as Algeria was initially military, efforts were made to settle colonists from France in the 1860's and 1870's

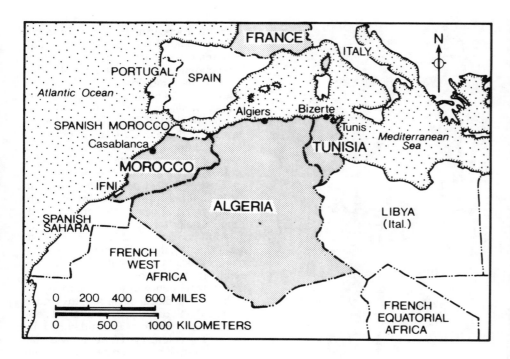

in constant rebellion. Riff tribesmen of the Moroccan mountains and the Berber and Tuareg horsemen of southern Algeria never did accept French control. Arab unrest also came from the Moslem *Senussi* sect in neighboring Libya that spilled over into Tunisia which was populated by Italians as well as French immigrants.

Further complicating the peaceful colonization of North Africa, the immigrants to the area from France were principally military personnel and their families—they quickly developed a militant and conservative attitude as evidenced by their armed opposition to French efforts in the 1870's to placate the restless Arabs. Substantial numbers of Arabs went to France during the colonial period, but both in Africa and in France the two ethnic groups—French and Arab—resisted integration with vigor.

The French colonists assumed the dominant position in North Africa, both economically and in terms of status derived from education. Lower schools were provided for those of French ancestry, but with little exception, no comparable effort was made on behalf of the Arabs. The local rulers were allowed to retain nominal powers, since it was actually easier to rule through them rather than try to depose them.

The earliest signs of Arab nationalism in the region occurred in Morocco in the 1930's, partially because of the world economic depression which had a severe

when most of what is now Algeria was gradually brought under colonial control. In Tunisia, the French had economic competition from England and Italy. In return for control of Cyprus, the British acknowledged France's authority in Tunisia. Because of an outbreak of violence, a naval force seized Bizerte in 1881 and forced the *Bey* of Tunis to accept the status of a French protectorate over the area. The British, Italians, and Turks all protested, but France had the support of Germany in the move, given in exchange for French support of German colonial ambitions elsewhere in Africa.

Morocco initially escaped domination by a colonial nation, although the major powers had forced a treaty in 1880 which protected the rights of foreigners within the country. After a 13–year–old boy succeeded as Sultan in 1894, the internal conditions deteriorated, reducing Morocco to virtual anarchy by the turn of the century. In exchange for concessions in Libya, Italy relinquished any claim it might have had in Morocco and the British later also acknowledged French supremacy in 1904. A nominal French–Spanish control was established in 1906 after a visit to Morocco by German Kaiser Wilhelm II as evidence of a German interest; negotiations led to an acknowledgment of French domination of the country in 1909. This was given by Germany in exchange for some economic guarantees and a section of the French Congo, which became part of Germany's colony of Kameroun (now Cameroon).

As was true with most colonial efforts, the French purpose in North Africa was primarily to enrich France. Although legally recognized as being in control of the area by 1910, actual control was much less than complete. During the entire colonial period from the 19th century until about 1960, the Arabs were almost

Habib Bourguiba celebrates Tunisian independence

28

effect on the economy of all North Africa which was based almost entirely on the agricultural production on farms of European immigrants and their descendants. This effort was the basis of continuing anti–French sentiment among the Arabs to which was added growing worldwide liberal–nationalistic ideals that were temporarily interrupted by World War II before making any progress.

Upon installation of a pro–German government under Marshal Henri–Phillipe Petain in France following the German invasion of that country in World War II, Algeria, Morocco and Tunisia were brought under the nominal authority of the *Vichy (Vee–shee)* government which he headed, named after a town in central France from which part of France was administered by his regime in 1940–1944. Although only a relatively insignificant number of French troops loyal to the Axis powers were stationed in the area, the Allies felt that it was necessary to establish Free French control in the area prior to invading Italy.

A combined American–British force invaded Morocco and Algeria on November 8, 1942, and three days later a cease-fire arranged with Admiral Jean François Darlan, the *Vichy* commander, led to Allied control of French North Africa within a short time, with Admiral Darlan achieving the post of Chief of State with Allied approval. Following his assassination shortly afterward, the Anglo–American command tried to install the aging General Henri Giraud as commander of French forces outside France in spite of the more energetic anti–Axis, anti–*Vichy* activities of the Free French led by the younger General Charles de Gaulle. His forces had conducted assaults in and from Brazzaville, French Congo. A brief German offensive in North Africa was repulsed by the Allies in May 1943.

The French were restored to continued colonial control of North Africa following World War II. Their rule was no more effective than the unstable and numerous French governments of mainland France. In Algeria, the conservative colonists (*colons*) of French ancestry completely dominated all phases of government, although Algeria was legally supposed to be an integral part of France. The Communist Party had been outlawed in Morocco, a colony, but this could not be done in Algeria since the communists were not outlawed within France. The *National Liberation Front* quickly rose in power and spearheaded a revolt which started in late 1954 and lasted for seven years. This group was a leftist–socialist–communist Arab party, united in opposition to French colonial rule.

A last ditch effort of the *Secret Army Organization (OAS)*, composed for the most part of French–descended Europeans, failed to stem the overwhelming tide of revolution in spite of cruel and terroristic anti–Arab measures in 1961. A cease–fire was finally negotiated in March 1962 and President Charles de Gaulle, who had promised the French to end the bloody conflict, recognized Algerian independence on July 3 of that year.

At the close of World War II, the *Istiqlal Independence Party* was formed in Morocco; it promptly issued a demand for independence which was refused. The party quickly gathered momentum with the tacit consent of the Alouite monarch, Sultan Mohammed V.

The willingness of this ruler to permit existence of the independence movement created great dissatisfaction among the French administrators. The French deposed him in 1953, sending him into exile, first on Corsica and then to Madagascar. Assisted by the Berber *Glaoui* (Sheikh) of Marakesh, the French placed Mohammed VI on the throne—a colorless, subservient member of the ruling family who was generally disliked by Moroccans.

Growing resentment led to severe rioting; terrorists struck swiftly, retreating to the safety of the hills and mountains to regather their forces, in the same manner as the formerly rebellious Riff tribesmen. The United States indicated great dissatisfaction with French policy, and in 1955, because of internal and external pressures, the French returned Mohammed V to the throne. Under the overwhelming influence of a strong and popular king and the independence party, Morocco ended its colonial status in 1956.

In Tunisia there was also a postwar surge of nationalism. A large middle class of well–educated people had emerged and backed this movement, led by an Arab lawyer educated in France, Habib Bourguiba. His *New Constitution Party* succeeded the older *Constitution Party*. Bourguiba's life during the French colonial period alternated between periods of exile and/or imprisonment and periods of nationalistic leadership. Exiled in 1934, he returned in 1936, was rearrested in 1938 and later was freed by the Germans in 1942. He again was arrested when the French returned, but escaped and went into exile. When he returned in 1952, he was arrested, and in 1954 was banished into exile.

By this time Tunisia was in a full state of insurrection requiring the presence of 70,000 French troops to attempt to control the colony. France granted internal autonomy to Tunisia in 1955 which also provided amnesty for all freedom fighters. Bourguiba was permitted to return, and full independence was achieved on July 20, 1956.

The South Sahara: Mauritania, Mali, Upper Volta (Burkina Faso), Niger, Chad.

Colonization of the southern Sahara region of Africa was a much slower process than in other areas of the continent because the almost uniformly arid land held little importance to the French, other than strategic. The only reasons for colonization were in order to connect other

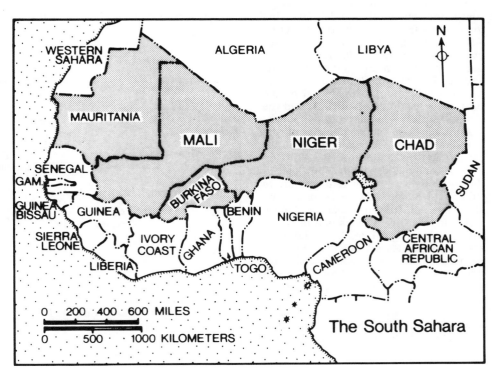

The South Sahara

more valuable colonies together and to exclude other foreign colonial effort in the region.

At a meeting known as the Berlin Conference, arranged by Otto von Bismarck of Germany and the French foreign minister in 1884–1885, the major world and colonial powers officially decreed that African slavery was to be abolished and that there was to be free navigation of the major rivers of the continent. It was further decreed that colonial power in the area was to be based on presence and actual control. Unofficially, and more important, the representatives took a map of the continent and drew lines indicating areas of interest of the respective powers.

The maps of the continent at that time were uncertain—boundaries differed sometimes more than a thousand miles, depending on the map and the nationality of the cartographer. In their effort to connect the West African and Equatorial African colonies, the French, in 1896–98 sent an expedition under Jean Baptiste Marchand that pushed rapidly northeastward as far as Fashoda (later named Kodak) on the Nile River. At the same time, having defeated the Sudanese, supposedly on behalf of Egypt, British Lord Horatio Herbert Kitchener was leading his forces southward along the Nile from Omdurman, and a second British expedition was pushing north on the river from Uganda. Further complicating the picture was the imminent arrival of an Ethiopian army on the right bank of the Nile at Fashoda, accompanied by another group of French forces.

The result was the Fashoda Crisis in which the British and French were eyeball-to-eyeball on the brink of total war. However, France was preoccupied with a complicated political scandal involving top military figures in Paris (the Dreyfuss Affair) which had political and religious overtones. The French blinked first, ending the crisis with an agreement on the lines of French and British authority in the area, which approximately fixed the present eastern borders of Chad and the Central African Republic with the Sudan.

Although the major powers of the world recognized French authority in this barren land by the end of the 19th century, the nomadic people who lived in the south Sahara region refused fully to submit to foreign rule for several years afterwards. In the final analysis, France was compelled to rule this part of Africa through local tribal leaders who possessed a large measure of autonomy. This permitted nominal French control without large-scale military forces which would have been necessary for direct rule.

The region was administered as a whole; it was part of French West Africa. Mali, Niger, Chad and southern Algeria were also known as French Sudan, the French spelling of which was Soudan.

The lives of the people were hardly disturbed by colonial rule. There was virtually no immigration of Europeans such as occurred in North Africa; the only French presence was essentially military. Occasional revolts occurred which were contained, rather than defeated by the French.

Although there was some sporadic German penetration in World War II during the North African campaigns of 1942–43 in the Mali, Niger and Chad regions, the local people were not involved in the battles. Free French forces under General Jean LeClerc fought several engagements with the Germans in the northern Chad area. With little exception, there was no political movement toward independence from France following World War II in the south Sahara. Niger shared in the development of the *Democratic African Rally Party*, but in this respect was dominated by the members from the Ivory Coast under Félix Houphouet–Boigny. As a result of unrest of the Moslem Mossi people in what was then called Upper Coast, the area now constituting Upper Volta (Burkina Faso) was separated after World War II from Ivory Coast, taking the French name *Haute Volta*.

Following the election of Charles de Gaulle as President of France, the *French Community* was established in 1958—a plan whereby France's colonies in Africa were granted internal autonomy. This was an effort to satisfy independence movements in areas of French Africa outside the south Sahara. It proved to be unsatisfactory in many respects, not the least of which was continued opposition to French authority over foreign relations by a multitude of African nationalists within the *Community*. Because of this, France granted independence to the remaining south Sahara and West African colonies, numbering thirteen, in 1960. Thus, without any substantial internal effort to promote independence, the south Sahara region was freed of French authority (which in reality had never been firmly established).

Coastal West and Equatorial Africa: Senegal, Guinea, Ivory Coast, Togo, Dahomey, East Cameroon, Central African Republic, Gabon, Congo.

France initially had no colonial ambitions along coastal Africa—scattered missionary stations were established in the 17th and 18th centuries and slave trade was also prevalent at the time. Following the abolition of slave trade in 1815, France maintained very small "factories" (trading posts) along the various parts of the coast.

Colonial interest quickened during the mid–19th century when the major European powers feared that one or another of them would obtain some valuable territory available to all nations, with a potential discovery of valuable metal ores and gems. In reality, with the exception of widely scattered and exaggerated tales brought to Europe by occasional explorers, almost nothing was known of the interior coastal lands of West and Equatorial Africa.

Senegal was the first area of increased French activity—General Louis Faidherbe headed an armed force in 1854 that was immediately resisted by the natives and their Tukuler ruler, Hajk Omar, but it was gradually able to subdue most of the area. The most commercially important region of Senegal—the Gambia River Basin—

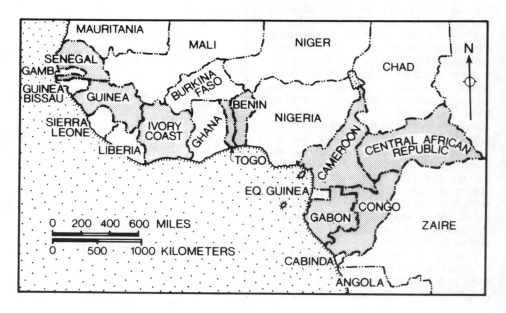

Marketplace vendor, Mali

had been seized by the British decades prior to the arrival of the French.

At about the same time a military mission was sent to Guinea, but because of the fierce resistance of the people of the region, penetration into the interior was slow. The Mandingo chieftain, Samory Toure, intially signed a treaty which permitted him to claim additional territory to the northwest. This peace was short–lived; further French military efforts were necessary in 1885–6, and a dire threat to the French was mounted when Toure united with the Tukuler people previously driven from Senegal into Mali.

The French offensive was on two fronts—north and east in Guinea and north and west in Ivory Coast, which finally resulted in the defeat of Toure in 1898. He was exiled to Gabon after his capture, where he died two years later. Penetration from southern Ivory Coast had also been slow. Although treaties were signed with the coastal chieftains of the Grand–Bassam and Assime regions, the Agnis and Baoules, two groups closely related to the warlike Ashanti people of Ghana to the west, offered fierce resistance to drives into the interior. Further north, the Mandingo people of Samory Toure and the Tukuler Africans prevented progress; Ivory Coast was not fully conquered by the French until about 1915.

As a result of a treaty signed with the French in 1851 by Ghezo, ruler of Abomey (Dahomey) a small commercial effort was initiated in that country. Coutonou was ceded as a trading post in 1868. The colonization of Dahomey was not uncontested—the Portuguese and British attempted to encourage inter-tribal rivalries in order to unseat the French from the coastal area, but without success.

Dahomey, with the exception of its narrow coastal strip, was left virtually untouched until 1890 when Benhazin, the last powerful king of Abomey, refused to sign additional treaties with France. Military occupation of Coutonou was ordered, swiftly followed by a violent uprising which continued with periodic interruptions until 1894, when Benhazin surrendered. The interior of Dahomey was slowly subdued during the following decades.

Togo was not gained by the French until World War I. The larger part of this former German colony was occupied by French troops in 1916; this control was converted into a mandate by the League of Nations, which divided the colony between France (East) and Britain (West). The British area was joined with the Gold Coast (Ghana). The East Cameroon region was also acquired from Germany in a similar fashion in 1916, also resulting in a League of Nations mandate.

Count Pierre Savorgnan De Brazza of France entered the northern side of the Congo River region of coastal Africa at about the same time that the British–American explorer Henry Stanley was claiming the southern side of the river region on behalf of King Leopold of Belgium in the first part of the 1880's. Both followed the same procedure of entering into so–called "treaties" with the various sub–chiefs of the once–mighty Kingdom of the Congo, a Bantu empire which once had extended from Gabon to Angola including an area several hundred miles inland from the coast. After exploring most of Congo (Brazzaville), De Brazza went into Gabon and established a small coastal outpost.

The area which now is the Central African Republic was not penetrated by the French until about 1889, when an outpost was established at Bangui, the present capital. The French named this territory *Ubangi–Shari* after its two principal rivers. It was not until after the turn of the century that effective French control was imposed on Congo, Gabon and the Central African Republic, all of which were combined in 1910 to form French Equatorial Africa, a distinctive administrative area. Upon receiving a mandate from the League of Nations over East Cameroon, a section of the former German colony (Kameroun) was made a part of French Equatorial Africa.

Mauritania, Senegal, Guinea, Ivory Coast, Dahomey, Mali, Upper Volta and Niger had been joined together as French West Africa in 1904; the entire territory was administered from Dakar, Senegal. The part of former German Togoland acquired after World War I was joined into this vast colony.

A variety of local councils were permitted by the French, giving the Africans a limited voice in their local affairs during the colonial period. European–style education was introduced, but never achieved widespread enrollment due to a shortage of trained teachers willing to live in Africa. Small numbers who did obtain secondary education usually went to France if they desired higher level studies.

Roads and railroads were constructed to the extent necessary to commercially develop this area of the continent, such as in Ivory Coast to permit export of agricultural products and in Gabon to support wood production.

After obtaining the necessary medical education, Dr. Albert Schweitzer, a world–renowned German philosopher and musician, received permission to establish a Protestant Christian medical mission and hospital at Lamborene in the interior of Gabon. He labored among the people, relieving the illness and misery of Africans regarded as little more than savages by the rest of the world—but whom he considered priceless human beings—

from 1913 until his death in 1965. He adapted medical methods to harmonize with the customs of the Africans. The mission continues its work under the leadership of his daughter, who engages in fund–raising to support its activities.

Other than medical facilities provided principally for Europeans living in West and Equatorial Africa, almost none were established for the benefit of the African people during the colonial years, but there was some improvement in the post–World War II period. Boundaries were stabilized over a number of years by agreements with the British, Belgians and Liberians; the map of colonial Africa underwent no substantial change in West Africa after 1920.

The World Depression of 1929 and the following years had great impact in the coastal colonies of French West and Equatorial Africa, where agricultural products usually were the sole exports. The sharp drop in prices paid for foodstuffs meant a corresponding decrease of income, and accompanying lower living standards which had not really been much more than marginal.

When France fell to the overwhelming might of the German Nazi military machine, a puppet, pro–German administration was established in France—the *Vichy* government (1940), named for its location in central France. It quickly dispatched administrators and personnel to take control of French Africa; they were generally disliked by the French living in the colonies. Their policies tended in many cases to be openly racist and repressive. French General Charles de Gaulle led a force aided by British vessels which attempted to seize Dakar, Senegal in 1940, but it was repulsed. A month later, he was able to capture Douala, Cameroon; Brazzaville was also occupied and a powerful transmitter was erected in order to make daily Free French broadcasts which were received in distant areas.

Following World War II, colonial rule continued, but there was a rapid upsurge of nationalism among native Africans. France itself had been economically devastated by the war and only slowly recovered with great amounts of foreign assistance provided by the United States. Political extremism, both rightist and leftist (communist) was rampant, making orderly French government all but impossible. Félix Houphouet–Boigny, a nationalist leader in Ivory Coast, organized the *Democratic African Rally (RDA)* with associated parties in most of France's West African colonies; the allied party succeeded in electing almost all of the area's deputies to the Assembly in Paris between 1947 and 1950. The relatively small number of African delegates allowed by the constitution allied themselves with the communist deputies during this period in an effort to gain support

for their nationalist viewpoint, but that allegiance was discontinued in 1950.

France was severely drained by the communist rebellion within its Indochinese colonies, including Vietnam, during the postwar period which ended in a military disaster for the French in 1954. Immediately, a second total rebellion was mounted by the Algerian *National Liberation Front* which resulted in devastating warfare within that colony for seven more years, with accompanying additional strain upon the French economy. Principally for those reasons, the French were in no position effectively to oppose nationalist demands of their African colonies.

The Overseas Reform Act (*Loi Cadre*) of 1956 gave the African colonies internal autonomy, leaving matters of defense and foreign policy to France in an effort to quiet the demands for total independence. After Charles de Gaulle assumed almost absolute powers in France in 1958, he announced the creation of the *French Community*, the first step towards granting total independence to the colonies. Guinea, led by Sékou Touré, rejected the plan and that colony gained immediate independence.

Senegal and Mali were joined into the Federation of Mali in 1959 and France made some other minor changes, but granted full independence to all its remaining colonies in West and Equatorial Africa in 1960.

East Africa: Madagascar, French Somaliland

The immense island of Madagascar was known to navigators since the 15th century, but there was no attempt at colonization. The Hindu Merina (Hova) people of Indonesian and Malaysian descent lived in the central highlands; persons of Arab and African heritage inhabited the coastal areas. There was only a brief period when the island was under single control during the 16th century, established by Sakalava (Arab) rulers.

The Merina kingdom became dominant in the 18th century under King Andrianampoinamerina (1787–1810); he and his successors alternately encouraged the French and British in their tentative efforts at colonization so that neither would gain the upper hand. Between 1775 and 1824, the island was a stronghold of marauding pirates, including John Avery, Captain Mission and William Kidd. The pirates even formed a republic called *Libertalia*, which was of brief duration.

Other nations of the world later established commercial relations with the Malagasy people; a treaty of peace, friendship and commerce between the United States and Madagascar was signed in 1881. During this period, British influence in the interior became strong. In 1869, Merina Queen Ranavolona I and

her Court were converted to the English Protestant faith. French interests continued to dominate the coastline.

At the Berlin Conference of 1885, as a result of concession by the French to the British in other parts of Africa, Great Britain supported the establishment of a French Protectorate over Madagascar. This status led to the end of the Merina Kingdom. General Joseph Simon Galliene, the first French Governor, with the aid of French troops, unified the entire island.

The people—particularly the Merinas—had little use for French rule. In 1916 they rose unsuccessfully in bloody rebellion. The differences between the pro–French coastal inhabitants and those of the interior was expressed in this movement for independence which was limited to the people of the highlands. After the fall of France in World War II, Madagascar, first administered by the *Vichy* (pro–Nazi) government of France, was occupied in 1942 by the British to prevent possible Japanese seizure of the strategic island. The Free French gained control in 1943. By 1947, an independence movement had become overwhelming and there was a national uprising suppressed only after months of bitter fighting which resulted in the death of more than 10,000 people of the island.

Subsequent constitutional reform in France lessened the tensions in Madagascar, and led to the establishment of the Malagasy Republic within the French Community in 1958. The Republic became fully independent in 1960.

The tiny, sun–blistered colony of French Somaliland came into existence when treaties were signed with local chieftains in 1862. This colonization, as well as that of the British and Italians in the area, was to secure the regions south of the Suez Canal, then under construction, in order to prevent any disruption of shipping. The only asset of the territory was a deep, natural harbor facing the Gulf of Aden. At the turn of the century, a railroad from Addis Ababa, Ethiopia to Djibouti was completed and was thereafter the prime source of revenue. This colony achieved independence from France in June 1977 and is now known as the Republic of Djibouti.

THE UNITED STATES OF AMERICA IN AFRICA
See Liberia: History.

KING LEOPOLD AND THE BELGIANS IN AFRICA

Zaïre (formerly known as Congo, Kinshasa, and earlier, Congo (Leopoldville), or The Belgian Congo.

The Belgian efforts at colonization in the Congo region of West Africa call to mind the name of one man: Henry

Leopold II of Belgium

Stanley. Following his birth in Wales, he migrated to the United States where he became an author, soldier and adventurer, fighting on both sides in the American Civil War. Seeking new adventure, he turned to Africa and went to locate the Scottish missionary, Dr. David Livingstone, who had disappeared while exploring central Africa. After locating Dr. Livingstone on the shores of Lake Tanganyika in 1871, he explored the lake regions of the continent and then proceeded westward to the Congo River region. It took him three years to traverse the length of the river; he arrived on the Atlantic coast in 1877 and departed for Europe.

Stanley was immediately summoned by King Leopold II of Belgium, who saw in this explorer a means to compete in the scramble for colonial territory in Africa. Stanley accepted the offer of employment and returned to the Congo, entering into treaties on behalf of King Leopold with the native chieftains. The curious thing about this colonization is that it was not on behalf of the Belgian nation— this was Leopold's personal project.

At the Berlin Conference of 1885 when great portions of Africa were divided between the European colonial powers, King Leopold had personally been awarded the area south of the Congo River as far as Portuguese possessions in the Angola region.

Although the area was referred to as "The Congo Free State," the years which followed were harsh. King Leopold desired wealth from the Congo and all policies in the territory were used toward that desire. Forced labor and torture were used to compel production of wealth; it is estimated that up to 8 million Africans lost their lives during the 23 years of Leopold's exploitation. By 1904, knowledge of these repressive conditions had become known in Europe and the United States; in response to pressure from Britain, Germany and the U.S., King Leopold sent a commission to investigate conditions. The report of the commission, issued in late 1905, indicated that the actions of Leopold's administrators were scandalously cruel and improper. Bowing to continued international pressure, the Belgian parliament passed an act in 1908 annexing the Congo State of Belgium.

During the period at the turn of the century, there was friction between the British, French and King Leopold over control of the upper (southern) Nile area in the region near Lake Albert. As a result of a compromise, the Congo Free State received a small portion of territory known as the Lado enclave, which reverted to the Sudan (Anglo–Egyptian Sudan) at the death of Leopold in 1910. There were a variety of treaties between the several colonial powers that gradually and firmly demarcated the borders of the Congo region.

Under Leopold, the copper–rich Katanga (now Shaba) area had been opened up, and economic development based on that region's wealth proceeded forward under Belgian administrators. The general approach was that the native Africans should not be given too many privileges lest they become restless. Due to efficient administration, however, the per capita income rose to be one of the highest in colonial Africa.

Belgian forces moved to occupy the northwestern part of German East Africa at the start of World War I. This region, consisting of what is now Rwanda and Burundi, was then called Ruanda–Urundi and became a mandated territory assigned to Belgium in 1923; it was joined administratively with the Congo, which was given a wide degree of autonomy at the same time. Between the two world wars, Belgium made substantial capital investments in the Congo, including construction of railways connecting Kinshasa (then called Leopoldville) to the mineral wealth of Shaba (then called Katanga).

Nationalist pressures on the part of the native Africans mushroomed after World War II. Belgium, prostrated by the battles and German occupation of the war, was actually in no position to resist this movement. In a completely unexpected change, Belgium announced in January 1960 that it would grant independence to the Congo as of June 30th of the same year. It is highly probable that the Belgians hoped that a quick grant of independence would result in chaos to a degree that would justify continued colonial control. This hope, motivated by the desire for further wealth, was almost realized.

THE SPANISH IN AFRICA
Spanish Sahara, Spanish Guinea, Ifni, Ceuta, Melilla

The colonization and division of Africa between the major powers in the 19th century was during a period when Spain, having formerly been a powerful colonial nation, was in a state of decline. The result was that Spain succeeded in claiming Spanish Sahara (also called Spanish Morocco, Rio de Oro), a barren desert area, and Spanish Guinea, a small section of oppressive jungle on the west coast at the Equator which included the island of Fernando Poo. The enclaves of Ifni, Ceuta and Melilla along the coast of Morocco were holdovers from the time when both Morocco and Spain were controlled by Moorish Arabs. The areas in which Spain was able to lay claim were available largely because of lack of interest in them on the part of other stronger colonial nations.

Although Spain was technically supposed to be in partnership with the French in Morocco during the colonial period, the actual control was by the French. Spain ceded its theoretical protectorate right to Morocco in 1956 when the French granted it independence; a small part of southern Morocco was relinquished in 1958. The enclave of Ifni was returned to Morocco in 1968; Ceuta and Melilla, coastal cities along the coast where Spain and Morocco are closest, remain under Spanish control with the tacit consent of the King of Morocco.

Wind–swept and arid, Spanish Sahara is inhabited by a handful of nomadic Berber–Bedouin tribesmen who had been left to themselves by the Spanish. There had been almost no interest in this area on the part of the rest of the world prior to 1966 when extensive and rich deposits of phosphate were located. After withstanding pressures from the UN, Morocco and Mauritania for a decade, Spain vacated the territory in 1976 (see Western Sahara).

Spanish Guinea, now the mainland portion of Equatorial Guinea, consisted of an undesirable, oppressively hot and humid area acquired at the Berlin Conference in 1885, which was joined administratively to form a single colony with Fernando Poo, an island ceded to Spain by Portugal in 1778. There was no significant nationalist movement reported during the postwar period and no effort was made to prepare the colony for independence.

In the mid 1960's, Spain began to bring increasing pressure on the British to cede the Gibralter peninsula on the ground

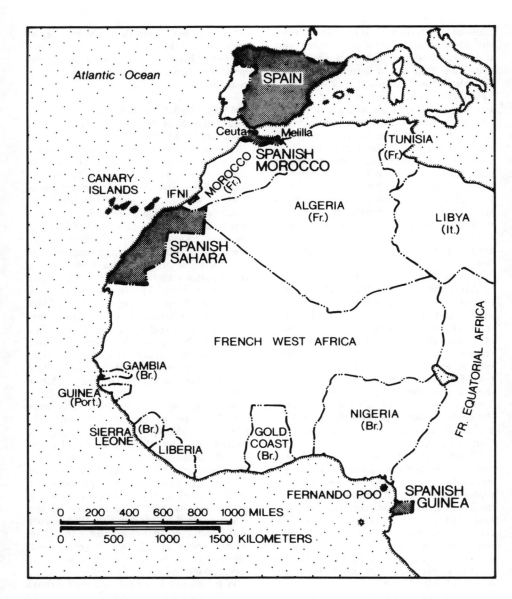

(Fernando Po in Spanish) had explored the coast of Cameroon in 1472; the prolific shrimp in the River Wouri inspired the sailors to christen the river *Rio dos Cameroes*, meaning "River of Shrimp" in Portuguese. There was a variety of commercial activity during the 19th century pre–colonial period, a time when no single European nation dominated Cameroon. The British decided in 1884 to annex Cameroon and sent an emissary to sign treaties with the local inhabitants. He arrived five days too late—spurred by the rush for colonies, a German Consul had already visited Douala, the seaport, and obtained the signatures of the chieftains on treaties annexing Cameroon to Germany; the area was named Kameroun, a Germanization of the original Portuguese name.

The colonial rule of the Germans was similar to that in Togo—exploitive and often cruel. There was some penetration into the interior but control was not established in the northern regions by the Germans. Throughout the colony it became difficult to locate the tribal chieftains, who went into hiding to avoid possible punishment or being held hostage by the colonial administrators. In exchange for support of French claims in Morocco, Germany was granted about 100,000 square miles of Congo (Brazzaville).

Cameroon was the scene of an extensive campaign early in World War I. British and French forces wrested control from Germany, and by the terms of the Treaty of Versailles, Cameroon was split between the two powers. The land previously acquired from Congo (Brazzaville) was rejoined with that territory.

that it, lying at the entrance to the Mediterranean Sea, belonged to Spain by virtue of natural geography. In order to reinforce its arguments, Spain granted Spanish Guinea independence in 1968, giving little prior indication of its intention to do so.

THE GERMANS IN AFRICA
West Africa: Togo, Cameroon

Although there was some German missionary and trading activity on the coasts of Togo and Cameroon from 1845 onward, these areas also were open to religious and commercial efforts of the remaining European nations. In the rush to acquire colonies during the 1880's, Gustav Nachtigal negotiated treaties with the Ewe chiefs of the region at Togoville, located on the banks of Lake Togo. The most powerful of these was King Mlapa III.

During the thirty years that followed the announcement of a German protectorate in Togo, there was slow penetration into the interior. The borders with the surrounding colonies were adjusted several times by treaty. The rule of the German administrators was harsh and exploitive; there was no effort to provide any benefit to the people of the region, since the only interest was commercial. Large numbers of Togolese were jailed and forced to labor for the Germans. There was little regret when the British and French arrived early in World War I.

The territory was jointly administered for five years, but was then split into two areas with the British in a smaller, western portion and the remainder controlled by the French. The British area became part of what is now Ghana, formerly known as Gold Coast.

The Portuguese navigator, Fernao Poo

Kaiser Wilhelm II of Germany

South Africa: South–West Africa

The Germans first entered the region of South–West Africa in the 1840's in a strictly missionary effort, similar to British efforts in South Africa among the native Africans. This outpost, called the Bethany Mission, slowly expanded during the following decades, and numbers of Germans went into the interior from Walfish (Walvis, Walvisch) Bay. The German missionaries twice asked for the British to assume protection of the Bay area, and in 1877 this request was granted.

There was substantial German migration into South–West Africa during the last quarter of the 19th century. After quarreling with the British for several months, the Germans proclaimed a protectorate over the area in 1884; administration initially was by the German Colonial Company, but in 1892 South–West Africa came under the control of the German government.

The migrants to the area were principally farmers and herdsmen who occupied the scarce and choice lands suitable for cultivation and grazing. Discovery of mineral wealth led to further measures designed to exploit the wealth of the land for the benefit of the Germans. The Bantu Hereros, also known as Damaras, rose in bloody revolt from 1904 to 1908, requiring 20,000 German troops to finally defeat them. Several thousand of these people fled to neighboring Botswana (then Bechuanaland) during the revolt.

Within a year of the start of World War I, a combined British and South African *Boer* army was able to defeat the German force of about 3,500 stationed in South–West Africa. The territory was assigned to the British–*Boer* Union of South Africa as a mandate by the Allied Council and later by the League of Nations.

East Africa: Tanzania (German East Africa)

Initial exploration of the East African coast area occurred in 1860–1865 when Karl von der Decken entered the region, but it was not until 1884, when Karl Peters signed a series of treaties with native kings that the colonial effort actually started. The agreements provided for a sale of land to the Germans for a very small fraction of its probable value. The German status in the area was recognized at the Berlin Conference of 1885, and the German East Africa Company was created to administer the colony.

In the early colonial period, the Germans also acquired lands in adjacent Uganda and coastal Kenya by signing treaties in the former, and coercing the Arab viceroy in Zanzibar to surrender lands in the latter. These were given up by treaties to the British in exchange for a somewhat worthless island in the North Sea and other minor concessions; treaties were also entered into with King Leopold of Belgium and the Portuguese which fixed the border of German East Africa. Penetration into the interior was slow and difficult. The native Africans resisted the German movement; there was a violent uprising of the Moslem Arabs along the coast (1888–90), a revolt of the Wahehe (Wahaya) people (1891–93) and a combined Moslem–Angoni rebellion (1903–1905). The Angonis, a Bantu group related to the warlike Zulus of South Africa, were all but exterminated during this conflict, known as the Maji–Maji Rebellion, in which the Germans ruthlessly destroyed crops and villages, rendering a large area completely desolate.

In 1914, 300,000 British, South African *Boer* and Indian troops invaded German East Africa. A force of slightly more than 200 German officers, commanding native troops numbering between 2,500 and 4,000 fended off the massive attack for four years under the spirited and brilliant leadership of General Paul Von Lettow–Vorbeck.

With great effort, the allies slowly pushed Lettow–Vorbeck from German East Africa into Mozambique and Rhodesia. The Germans refused to stop fighting, and the battles ceased only when their commander was informed that the Armistice of November 11, 1918 had been signed, ending World War I, and providing for the evacuation of Germans from German East Africa.

The British received a mandate from the League of Nations to administer the former German colony, which was renamed Tanganyika. Substantial numbers of German immigrants who had established large, prosperous farms and plantations, were deported to Germany; a few were later permitted to return to the British colony.

A small, northwestern part of German East Africa which had been occupied by Belgian troops at the start of the war was mandated to Belgium in 1923; initially called Ruanda–Urundi, following independence it became the two nations of Rwanda and Burundi.

THE SOUTH AFRICAN "MANDATE" Namibia (German South–West Africa, South–West Africa)

The Union of South Africa received a mandate from the League of Nations in 1919 over what had been German South–West Africa. After The UN came into existence, it exerted pressures to grant the people of *Namibia* their independence. Finally, on March 21, 1990, that goal was achieved (see Namibia, p. 114).

THE ITALIANS IN AFRICA
The Eastern Horn; Somalia, Ethiopia

In comparison to other European nations, Italian colonial efforts were relatively weak and delayed because of the fact that Italy itself was not closely united as a nation. Following agreement among the stronger powers in 1885, the Italians signed treaties during the next four years with the three Moslem sultans in the "horn" region of East Africa. Although Italian Somaliland was acquired as a colony, full control was not established in the area until as late as 1927. The bleak, uniformly hot and dry region was considered to be valueless as a colony and the nomadic Cushites and Somalis who lived in the region, including part of Kenya and Ethiopia, were difficult to control.

British and French Somaliland, both areas somewhat more desirable, separated Somaliland from Eritrea, a semi–arid expanse given to the Italians by a lack of interest on the part of more powerful colonial nations. Benito Mussolini, the fascist dictator, came to power in Italy in 1922. He began to flex colonial muscles, eyeing with envy the vast territories taken without resistance by the rest of Europe in Africa and elsewhere.

From bases in Eritrea, Italian forces invaded ancient Ethiopia in 1936; Emperor Haile Selassie begged for assistance at the League of Nations, but his plea fell on deaf ears. The fate of Ethiopia had been decided earlier in Paris, when the British and French gave the Italians wide authority over Ethiopia in an effort to appease Mussolini. The figurehead King of Italy proclaimed himself Emperor of Ethiopia, a title recognized at once by Austria and Germany and in 1938 by Great Britain and France.

Ethiopia was joined with Somaliland and Eritrea to form Italian East Africa; initially there was some effort at economic development and road building.

Benito Mussolini

Haile Selassie enters Addis Ababa in 1941

However, an attempt was made to assassinate the Italian governor at Addis Ababa in 1937. A reign of terror followed, with widespread arrests and summary executions in an attempt to terrorize the population. Further unrest became intense, and by 1940 the Italians were besieged from within by Ethiopian terrorists and from without by British forces. Exactly five years after the first entry of Italian troops, Haile Selassie entered Addis Ababa at the head of a British–Ethiopian force and Italian rule was ended.

During the postwar period, a plan whereby Eritrea was to become a part of Ethiopia was promulgated at the UN; following its acceptance, the two were joined. The UN granted a trusteeship over Somalia to Italy in 1949; this area had been occupied by the British since the early years of World War II. The trusteeship provided for complete independence within ten years, which was achieved in 1960.

North Africa: Libya

Although many Italian immigrants had settled in North Africa, particularly in Libya and Tunisia, there was no effort to colonize the area until the 20th century. The ambition had then been present for decades—when the British and French settled the Fashoda Crisis (see *The French in Africa*), the Italians protested since they did not share in the division of the Sahara region of the African continent. Using a short–term ultimatum to provoke a conflict, Italian forces invaded Libya in 1911 in an attempt to seize control from the Ottoman Turks. After taking a few coastal towns, a protectorate status was proclaimed by the Italians.

The Moslem *Sanusi* sect immediately organized a revolt that continued until about 1931 at various places within Libya. Because the Arab–Berber people were given only the poorest parts of the land in which to live, the people of Libya, through eventually subdued, continued to have a smoldering hatred for the Italians.

Italian rule was ended in the two years following 1940. Extensive campaigns were waged by the Allies throughout the land against the Nazis who had gained control of North Africa when it became apparent that Italy could not act with military authority in the area. The country, historically divided into three provinces of Cyrenaica, Tripolitania and Fezzan, was split between Allied powers at the end of World War II. Fezzan was occupied by the French, and the remaining two provinces were under British administration.

The question of Libya's status was submitted to the United Nations, which adopted a resolution providing for Libyan independence by the end of 1951.

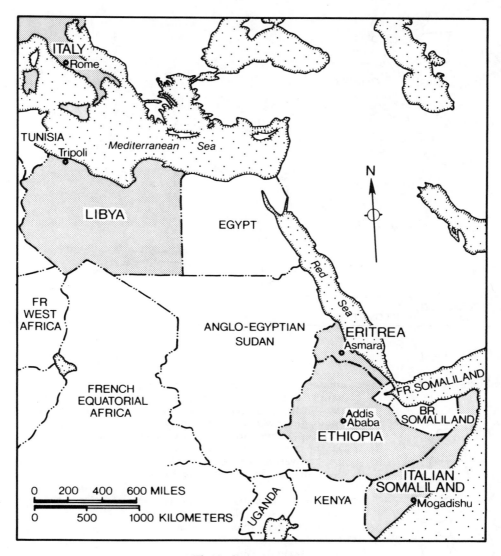

The Italians in Africa

COASTAL WEST AFRICA

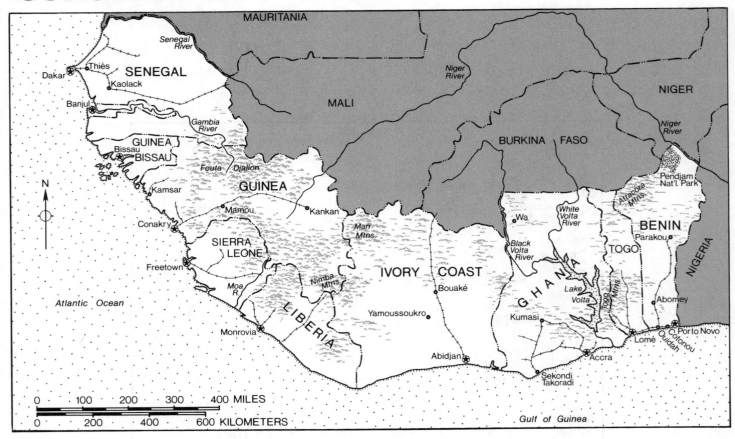

Benin (formerly Dahomey)

(pronounced beh–*neen*)

Area: 115,773 sq. km. = 44,483 sq. mi. (slightly larger than Tennessee).

Population: 5.25 million (estimated).

Capital City: Porto Novo (Pop. 228,000, estimated; The main port is nearby Cotonou with a population of 335,000, estimated).

Climate: Hot and humid in the South tempered by sea breezes; tropical in the North, with wet seasons in the South (mid–March to mid–July and mid–September to mid–November. Northern Benin historically had a single wet season (June–October) but has been afflicted by drought for the last decade.

Neighboring Countries: Togo (West); Burkina Faso (Northwest); Niger (North); Nigeria (North, East).

Official Language: French.

Other Principal Tongues: Fon, Adja, Yoruba, Bariba.

Ethnic Background: There are 42 distinct ethnic groups in Benin, all of West African heritage. The Fons, Adjas, Yorubas and Baribas are the largest, constituting more than half of the population.

Principal Religions: Traditional beliefs (about 77%), Christianity (about 15%), Islam (about 8%).

Chief Commercial Products: Cocoa, cotton, palm products, coffee, peanuts, kapok, tobacco.

Per Capital Annual Income: About U.S. $440.

Currency CFA Franc (African Financial Community).

Former Colonial Status: French Protectorate (1892–1960).

Independence Date: August 1, 1960.

Chief of State: Nicéphore Soglo, President, since April 1991 (pronounced Nih–*ceh*–pho–reh *Soh*–gloh).

National Flag: A green field with a red star in the upper left–hand corner.

Benin lies in a small belt of land stretching from the warm waters of the Atlantic Ocean to a distance of 450 miles inland. The coastline is 78 miles wide, but in the North the width increases to over 200 miles.

The coastal area, with palm trees waving gently in the breezes from the ocean, is a region of picturesque lagoons and inlets. A narrow sandbar lies close to the entire coastline; the lagoons open to the sea in only two places.

A series of clay plateaus extend further inland for a distance of about 50 miles, terminating at the rocky foothills of the stretch of mountains which divides the North from the South. There usually has been abundant rainfall in this region, as

38

well as along the coast, supporting dense vegetation in the areas not under cultivation.

Immediately south of the Attacora Mountains, which rise to a height of 2,300 feet, there is a swampy depression. From these mountains to the north, the land gently descends in a patchy forest with very little undergrowth, to the plains of the Niger River valley. Temperatures north of the mountains have a wider variation than is found in the rest of the country. The dry season from November to May has in recent years been transformed to a year–long drought, creating severe conditions for the people located in the area.

The Pendjam National Park, next to the borders of Burkina Faso and Niger, is a reserve to protect the country's dwindling numbers of wild game. It extends across the boundary into the two neighboring countries. Although hunting is not permitted within its limits, hunters pursue animals in the surrounding areas.

History: The record of shifting tides of migrant people in Benin extends back to the late 16th century. A group of people traveled west from the Mono River and settled near what is now the city of Allada, establishing a kingdom. After a war of succession to the throne in 1610, a young contender named Dacko went to Cana, near the present city of Abomey, and founded the Kingdom of Abomey,

becoming its first ruler. This monarchy expanded gradually; Dacko's son conquered the lands belonging to a neighboring king named Dan. Angry with the aggressive invader, Dan is reported to have said "If I don't surrender, you will go so far as to kill me and build over my corpse." Dan was beheaded, buried and a building was erected over his body. The former name of the country, Dahomey, comes from the two words *Dan Home* which literally means "on the belly of Dan." The Abomey Kingdom quickly became paramount over all other tribal rulers in the southern region. Their superior position continued for 350 years until the French abolished the monarchy.

Ghezo, the ruler of Abomey from 1818 to 1858 signed a treaty of friendship and commerce with the French in 1851. His son, Glele, ceded the commercial city of Cotonou to the French 17 years later. For details of the colonial period, see *The French in Africa.*

Shortly before independence in 1960, three major political parties united and brought pressure against a fourth to disband. The combined organization, the *Dahomey Unity Party,* captured all 60 seats in the unicameral National Assembly. There followed a period of behind–the–scene activity by the three prominent leaders, Hubert Maga, Souran Migan Apithy and Justin F. Ahomadegbe.

A rapid succession of governments followed:

1963: Military *coup* led by Col. Christophe Soglo ousted the government; President Maga went into exile in Paris.

1964: Elections were held, Apithy became President, Ahomadegbe became Vice–President.

1965: The leadership resigned under pressure; Soglo again assumed power and sent both in exile to Paris.

1967: A *coup* by young army officers ousted Soglo and sent *him* to Parisian exile. The top military command, after four days of house arrest, picked Chief of Staff Alphonse Alley as head of state.

A new constitution forbade any ex-president, ex–vice–president or other ex-ruler to run for office. The Supreme Court held this action to be illegal, but it was adopted. The Parisian exiles urged a boycott of the elections and the military responded by throwing out the results and naming Dr. Emile Zinsou president. He lasted until the end of 1969.

A military *junta* wielded power as a result of political violence, ruling through a Presidential Council of military members. The last military *coup* occurred on October 26, 1972 (although there have been at least five known attempted ones since then). The then Major Mathieu Kerekou announced "that authority of the State has disappeared everywhere." Many politicians were arrested and some were put to death. In an effort to widen his support, Kerekou established the *National Council of the Revolution* in late 1973;

Water dwellers, Ganvie, Benin. The more elaborate house at left is that of the Chief of the Fons.

President Nicéphore Soglo

a year later he announced the transformation of Benin into a Marxist, one-party state.

Foreign interests were nationalized. Although ties were established with the U.S.S.R., China, Cuba and North Korea, little assistance was forthcoming from those nations, except endless quantities of advice. These moves alienated western goodwill and resulted in lowered financial assistance.

It was in 1975 that General Kerekou declared the country's name would be changed from Dahomey ("imposed upon us by the colonialists") to the People's Republic of Benin (in 1989, to simply Benin). The *Benin People's Revolutionary Party* was the only legal political group, and the 196–member Revolutionary Assembly has been its rubber stamp. First elected (officially) to a three–year term as president in early 1980, Kerekou was re-elected to an extended five–year term in mid–1984 and again in 1989. After 1984, the country veered sharply toward a "marxist" style of government.

Because Benin's economic condition was disastrous, President Kerekou visited Western European nations in late 1986, stressing the nation's moves toward economic liberalization as opposed to rigid central control and "privatization," a subject he had downplayed when he went on to the Soviet Union, which promised (but didn't deliver) economic assistance. Matters proceeded unevenly in 1987–1990. There was serious unrest in 1989, but nevertheless, Kerekou was re-elected by a huge majority. But pressures mounted in 1990 as the economy remained stagnant. Late in the year a constitutional document was approved which called for elections in March 1991.

They were held, with five coalition groups vying for the support of the people. Since no candidate won a majority, there was a runoff in April.

The winner was Nicéphore Soglo, a French–educated econimist with respected experience at the World Bank in Washington. Several former ministers of the old regime were prosecuted in 1992.

The National Assembly was split until 1993 between five factions with many sub-groups; they accused the president of ruling by decree. But late in the year, three of them joined in a coalition, the *Benin Renaissance Party*, with the avowed purpose of supporting Soglo and ending the divisiveness which had impeded progress in Benin for years. The president assumed leadership of the party in mid–1994.

Culture: This is a country of rich diversity in customs and language. Education, which prior to 1976 was largely in church schools, was taken over by the state in 1976, when Islamic learning institutions were also seized. Although a majority of the children attend school for at least four grades, the estimated literacy rate is 20%.

While Porto Novo is the official capital of the nation, most government offices and embassies are found twenty miles to the west at the port city of Cotonou (*Coo–toe–new*). This is Benin's chief commercial center and has magnificent beaches. It has in the past been a weekend resort for many foreigners, with excellent seafood.

The Abomey Museum contains a fascinating display of ancient and modern works by Beninese artists and craftsmen, especially hand–cast bronze artifacts and beautifully dyed tapestries. The first fort built by the Portuguese during their earliest exploration of the region is located at Ouidah (*Wee–*dah), also on the coast, as well as the Temple of the Serpents, where enormous living pythons are sheltered.

The only newspaper printed in Benin was the semi–official *Ehuzu*, a word from the Fon language meaning "all has changed." When Benin veered to Marxism, the lives of the people changed drastically. State–run radio stations broadcast a steady, tedious stream of propaganda which had to be played loudly in each town square. Life has changed for the better in Benin. The people appear to have hope, and the economic climate is slowly coming back to life. There is finally a sense of freedom in a land which for so many years was under the iron fist of dictatorship.

Economy: The only significant Benin exports are cocoa, cotton, and palm products. A small amount of coffee is also produced. Following independence, France supplemented the economy with $8 million per year. The economy is now

in utter disarray and the people of the North are starving because of drought and invasion of the Sahara desert into lands which once at least supported grazing, but now are filled with dust and sand. Floods in the northeast and central areas in September 1988 forced the government to issue an urgent appeal for food aid. The average per–capita income of small–tract farmers is less than $100 per year. Too much land is collectively and inefficiently farmed; diversion into other crops is a number one priority. Graft and corruption at all levels of government sap the economic strength of Benin.

Benin is struggling to keep its economic nose above water; energetic efforts to obtain funds from the International Monetary Fund were finally successful after several years, when the country veered from Marxism to a more free market economy. Sixty percent of the people are engaged in agriculture, usually using primitive methods. Life expectancy is only 50 years because of poor sanitary conditions, lack of adequate health care facilities and a very high infant mortality rate.

France ended its support of the CFA Franc in early 1994; the result was hoarding and a jolt of rapid inflation which particularly harmed the poor.

The Future: Soglo's government was strengthened by the addition of yet another party to the *PBR*, making the outcome of February 1995 elections a foregone conclusion.

The Republic of Côte d'Ivoire

The government established the French form of *Ivory Coast* as the country's official designation, pronounced *Coat deev-whar*.

St. Paul Cathedral, Abidjan

AP Wide World Photo

Area: 323,750 sq. km. = 125,000 sq. mi. (somewhat larger than New Mexico).

Population: 13.5 million (estimated).

Capital City: Yamoussoukro (Pop. 230,000, estimated, birthplace of the president. Adidjan, Pop. 3.7 million, estimated, is regarded as the capital by the U.S.).

Climate: Tropically hot and humid in the South, with two wet seasons (March–July and October–November). Warm and less humid in the North with a single wet season (May–October).

Neighboring Countries: Liberia, Guinea (West); Mali, Burkina Faso (Upper Volta–North); Ghana (East).

Official Language: French.

Other Principal Tongues: Akan, Dru, Dioula, Mandinka, Wolo and others.

Ethnic Background: There are more than 60 distinct tribal groups, predominantly of West African Negro origin. Principal groupings include the Agnis–Ashantis–Baoules, Kroumen, Mandingo, Senoufo, Dans–Gouros and Koua. There are about 65,000 French and 32,000 Lebanese.

Principal Religions: Traditional tribal beliefs (about 55%), Christianity (about 28%) Islam (about 17%).

Chief Commercial Products: Cocoa, coffee, instant coffee, rubber, timber, cotton and food products, including bananas, pineapples, palm products.

Per Capita Annual Income: About U.S. $900.

Currency: CFA Franc (African Financial Community).

Former Colonial Status: French Colony (1839–1960).

Independence Date: December 7, 1960.

Chief of State: Henri Konan Bédié, President (since Dec. 9, 1993).

Head of Government: Allassane Quattare, Prime Minister (1990).

National Flag: Three vertical stripes of orange, white and green.

The Republic of Côte d'Ivoire occupies an area in the center of the south coast of the west African bulge. The coast, warmed by the waters of the Gulf of Guinea, is 340 miles long; from the border of Ghana for a distance of 185 miles to the west, it is flat and sandy, with many inland lagoons. The remainder of the coast towards Liberia has numerous sharp rocks and is higher. The surf along the entire shore line is quite heavy, steadily pounding the sand and boulders. Dense forests and jungles spread their green foliage further inland, covering almost 40% of the country. Tall niagou, samba and mahogany trees struggle against each other for precious sunlight, crowding smaller trees and undergrowth.

Approximately midway to the north, the trees gradually become thinner and are succeeded by low scrub trees, grasses and brush vegetation. This in turn gives way in the extreme northern area to a semi–arid (recently *arid*) climate, which has in the past supported grasslands, occasionally interrupted by taller growth. With the African drought of the past decade, this northern region has become increasingly desolate.

The country is almost entirely level—only the Man Mountains in the area closest to Mali and Guinea relieve the monotony of the plains.

The southern and central portions of the country have traditionally received ample rainfall and have a high humidity. Temperatures are warm in the North, with less (or hardly any) rainfall.

History: Artifacts discovered in Côte d'Ivoire suggest that a Neolithic civilization flourished there in prehistoric ages. Not much is known of the history of this country prior to the 14th century.

At the time of the arrival of the first Europeans, there were three strong kingdoms, the Krinjabo and Bettie in the North and the Boundoukou in the East. There were, besides the three major kingdoms, more than 50 other small tribal groups which had little contact with each other.

The severity of the surf and the forbidding appearance of the land discouraged early European exploration. For greater detail on early history and the colonial period, see Historical Background and *The French in Africa*. When full independence was gained by Côte d'Ivoire on August 7, 1960, Félix Houphouet–Boigny (*Fay*–lix *Who*–fway *Bwa*–nyee) became its first president. He was well–prepared for the tasks which faced him.

One of the Baoulé people, with ancestors including a line of chiefs, he attended a colonial school in Dakar, Senegal. He

became a paramedic in 1925; his skill led to extensive travel throughout Côte d'Ivoire, enabling him to establish good relations with many tribal chiefs and elders. Houphouet–Boigny inherited large, coffee–producing tracts of land in 1940. Using modern techniques, he was able to expand their output, becoming a wealthy man in a relatively short time. He emerged as leader of the African Agricultural Trade Union, an organization which fought trade policies that favored French coffee growers, and worked to end forced labor of Africans on white–owned plantations.

He formed the *Côte d'Ivoire Democratic Party* in 1945 into which several ethnic groups were attracted. He was a natural choice for the country's seat in the French Assembly where he pushed through a law forbidding forced labor, making him a hero.

He was the architect and builder of Côte d'Ivoire's rise from a backward French colony to its present status as an industrious, comparatively wealthy republic. One of his biggest contributions was success in avoiding tribalism which tore at the heels of so many newly–independent African countries. He was stern, shy, shrewd, retiring, highly idealistic and capable of resorting to dictatorial means to obtain his desires.

The government since independence has consisted of a single–chamber National Assembly of 120 members elected by national suffrage for a period of five years; all candidates so far have been nominated by the party's 70–member Political Bureau. The president also has a five year term, and a wide range of powers within the framework of separation of the executive, legislative and judicial branches. Legislation may be presented to the legislature by the president or to the people via referendum.

The *Côte d'Ivoire Democratic Party (PDCI)* was for 30 years after independence the sole political party. This system made possible a high degree of stability under the firm leadership of the late president.

During more than three decades after independence, Côte d'Ivoire built itself into the most prosperous agriculturally–based Black African nation on the continent, with a per capita annual income now approaching $1,000. The bubble of prosperity has periodically been dampened by decreases in world prices of cocoa and coffee. This nation is the world's leading cocoa producer and number 3 coffee source. Compounding the effect of dropping prices for these commodities was a severe drought in the 1980s with accompanying fires which were said to have destroyed 60% of productive plants (some said this figure was exaggerated to cover up official corruption). The government does not permit much media discussion of alleged

corrupt practices of officials, particularly when the president was reported to have been a participant.

If Houphouet–Boigny had not been such a popular, talented and effective president, he would have been regarded as just another African dictator. When economic austerity measures led to strikes by students, teachers and professionals in 1982–3, the president responded energetically. He ordered teachers moved out of their state–owned homes and suspended them; he closed the schools and announced that he was considering using his powers of military draft against college professors, physicians and pharmacists that were striking. The measure was ef-

President Henri Konan Bedie

fective—the objects of his wrath evaporated and quietly returned to work—and everything returned to normal—a la Houphouet–Boigny. He said the source of discontent was one of his favorite targets: Gadhafi of Libya.

Unlike other African leaders, Houphouet–Boigny could (and did) freely travel abroad without fear of being overthrown. Most Black African leaders grumbled privately that he was an "Uncle Tom," accepting the continued presence of thousands of former French colonists. But in international affairs, in which he maintained a consistent pro–western stance on Cold War matters, he was thoroughly respected. His advocacy of dialogue with South Africa during the years that nation was avidly devoted to racial separation did result in some bitter criticism by African heads of state, which he simply ignored. One accomplishment for which he was criticized was the removal of the capital city from crowded Abidjan to the president's home city of Yamoussoukro, about 166 miles to the north. The

vote in favor of that measure was considered to be a means of thanking him for his tireless devotion to Côte d'Ivoire following independence.

The waves of sentiment for multi–party democracy were felt as the 1990 elections approached; in response to popular demand as well as pressure from the World Bank, free formation of political parties was allowed for the first time. The result in this nation of 60 ethnic groups was predictable: 17 of 25 opposition parties fielded candidates and the *PCDI* won 163 of the 175 seats in the National Assembly.

After suffering for months from incurable cancer, Houphouet–Boigny died on December 7, 1993 when, shortly after dawn, he ordered life–supporting medical treatment discontinued—on the day of the 33rd anniversary of his nation's independence. The people of the nation were prepared for this—rumors of his death had been circulating for months. Prime Minister Alassane Ouattare wept as he announced the death, but wasted no time in declaring, contrary to law, that he was the successor of the late president.

The constitutional successor to the presidency, Henri Konan Bédié, President of the National Assembly and a Baoulé, quickly and successfully moved to assume the office; he was unanimously chosen head of the *PCDI* in 1994. But a fringe number of deputies formed a group to support Quattare in the 1995 contest. He, however, went to Washington to work for the IMF. In December 1994, an election law was pushed through the legislature decreeing that in order to be eligible to run for president, one had to be *continuously* in Côte d'Ivoire for five years preceding the election. This assured the reelection of the president, despite inconsequential talk of civil war by Quattare supporters.

Culture: The many different ethnic groups contribute to the diversity of customs among the people of Côte d'Ivoire. Each group has its own style in works of art and to a lesser degree, in loose–fitting clothing styles. Sculptors using the talents passed on by their forefathers, render articles from wood, clay and gold, possessing a rough, almost abstract realism, which are valued throughout the world. Bronze, ivory and leather are also favored mediums of artistic expression.

Music and dancing, accompanied by a variety of instruments, perpetuate folklore and legend which originated in unknown times. The traditional tribal beliefs of the majority of the people center around songs and dances, providing not only a spirit to their beliefs, but also a source of unique entertainment.

Abidjan, the former capital city, is located on lagoons inland from the coast. Hot and humid, it brings to mind Paris with its friendly sidewalk cafes, and it boasts architectural structures as modern as any city in the world—its skyline could be that of New York City. A small community of 20,000 people 50 years ago, Abidjan is now more than 150 times that size; traffic jams are common on its wide, palm-lined boulevards. Many have come from the interior to work at the large port and in the manufacturing plants of this cosmopolitan city. As part of his efforts to move the capital to his native town of Yamoussoukro, the late president announced the construction of the largest Roman Catholic basilica in the world there in 1987. It is a gift from his family to the Church, built on land donated by him. The completed structure, subject of much criticism, was dedicated by the Pope in 1990.

Color television is available several hours a day; there are more than a half million sets in the nation to receive the lively programming.

Economy: Côte d'Ivoire has one of the most flourishing economies on the continent. An easy mixture of state-controlled enterprises blending with capitalism, it encourages overseas investors, most recently from the United States, which held two trade fairs there during the 1980's. While its neighbors rushed to build industries following independence, Côte d'Ivoire concentrated on improving its agricultural base and expanded its cocoa and coffee plantations. This paid off handsomely until the 1980's, when austerity measures had to be adopted at the insistence of international monetary powers. A drop in cocoa prices had a strong adverse effect on the nation—formerly selling for $3,800 per ton, the price has been as low as $700 a ton since 1980; even though it leveled off at about $1,500 this was still less than the price guaranteed to growers by the government. In a controversial move, the government decreed a ban on all cocoa exports in mid-1988; the purpose was plainly announced: to force world prices higher. With the exception of a large amount exported to France, the unrealistic ban accomplished its purpose. Its actual result was the storage of immense quantities of the product.

Commerce is largely in the hands of French and Lebanese businessmen which has caused some internal grumbling. French officials in high-paying positions are resented by Ivorian college graduates who wish to replace them, but the government is thus far reluctant to use its relatively inexperienced citizens in the managerial jobs—especially in the face of economic adversity. The growth rate of the gross national product has slowed from 7% per year to about 3.4% between 1980 and 1988. Côte d'Ivoire has been able to attract cheap labor from its less fortunate neighbors. Roads and communica-

tions are first rate, and electricity is widely available as a dependable source of energy.

Debt repayment ($8.6 billion) was successfully renegotiated in 1986 and again in 1988, giving the country some leeway badly needed. Among other things, western industrial nations agreed to postpone payment of principal and interest on about $2 billion until 1993–2002. Until Côte d'Ivoire can cease having a two crop economy, dependence on the prices of coffee and cocoa will create uncertainties. A continuing worldwide coffee surplus adversely affects the country and will do so in the immediate future. At IMF insistence, Côte d'Ivoire reduced the price paid to farmers for the commodities to 66 for a 16 ounce pound. The same pound is traded in New York at about 84 for a full pound, but it somehow shrinks to 13 ounces before it reaches the supermarket shelf. The price: $2.00–$4.70 "lb." for

good to excellent coffee, and much more— $25.00 lb.—for luxury class coffee beans. Low coffee prices have resulted in severe hardships on both large and small farms in Côte d'Ivoire.

An epidemic of AIDS in crowded Abidjan is frightening; it is now the leading cause of death and is a dead weight limiting economic growth.

The Future: The quick settlement of the succession question indicates that President Konan Bédié will have no serious challenger in the 1995 elections.

Increased mechanization of agriculture, organization of cooperatives and crop diversification all will be needed to make the import of food unnecessary. These measures will, if pursued, reduce the dependence on world prices for just two agricultural commodities. The nation will continue its slow movement away from agriculture as a means of foreign earnings.

Dome of "Our Lady of Peace" basilica, Yamoussoukro   AP/Wide World Photo

The Republic of The Gambia

Mothers lined up for food

Area: 10,463 sq. km. = 4,005 sq. mi. (Connecticut is 1/5 larger).
Population: 1.4 million (estimated).
Capital City: Banjul (Pop. 96,000, estimated).
Climate: Subtropically warm with a wet summer (May–October) and a dry and somewhat cooler season (November–April).
Neighboring Countries: The Gambia is enclosed on three sides by Senegal.
Official Language: English.
Other Principal Tongues: Malinke, Wolo and others.
Ethnic Background: Most groups are a mixture of West African Negro and Sudanic ancestry, including Mandingo (41%), Fulani (14%), Wolof (13%), Serahuli (10%), Jola (8%) and others (14%), divided into many small groups; figures are approximate.

Principal Religions: Islam (95%), Christianity (about 4%), traditional beliefs.
Chief Commercial Products: Peanuts and peanut products, fish, tourism, hides, cotton lint, beeswax.
Per Capita Annual Income: About U.S. $225.
Currency: Dalasi.
Former Colonial Status: British Colony (1816–1965).
Independence Date: February 18, 1965.
Chief of State: Capt. Yahya Jameh, President (1994).
National Flag: Three horizontal stripes of red, purple and green; thin white lines separate the stripes.

The Gambia has the smallest area of any independent nation on the African mainland. Slicing thinly into the northwest coast of Africa and facing the tropi-

cal waters of the Atlantic Ocean, this country lies within an area smaller than Jamaica. It was named *The* Gambia by the government to avoid confusion with Zambia.

The Gambia is a finger–like projection into the territory of southern Senegal by which, except for the seacoast, it is surrounded. The wide Gambia is one of the larger and more navigable rivers of northwest Africa—it is possible for ocean–going vessels to travel 150 miles inland and for smaller ships to traverse its entire length. The estuary contains one of the finest natural harbors in Africa.

The entire territory is low–lying, never exceeding a height of 120 feet. On each side of the broad river, thick swamps contain mangrove trees which reach heights of up to 100 feet. Further inland from the river is a region of swamps and river flats. These are often flooded, sometimes by salt water during the wet season. This swampy belt is succeeded by round hills and rolling plateaus with thick growths of grass and periodic clumps of trees. There is ample rainfall for cultivation in this long and narrow nation, seldom more than 20 miles in width.

History: Between the 10th and 15th centuries there was a migration of Hamitic–Sudanic people from the Nile River Valley westward. They arrived in The Gambia and Senegal, settled and intermingled with the West African Negro people already living there. The various waves of migration evolved into distinct tribal patterns, many of which are evident today. The first Europeans to visit The Gambia, about the same time Columbus reached the West Indies, were from Portugal. By 1500 the lower river area had become a regular port of call for traders seeking slaves and gold. For details of early and colonial history, see *The British in Africa* and *The French in Africa*.

Conferences between the British colonial rulers and The Gambia in 1964 led to full independence on February 18, 1965; David K. Jawara was installed as the first Prime Minister. He was knighted by Queen Elizabeth in 1966. The Gambia elected to become a republic within the British Commonwealth in 1970 at which time Prime Minister Jawara became President. Continued British annual aid makes it possible for The Gambia to function.

Elections held in April 1977 (the first in ten years) resulted in a continuation of control by the *People's Progressive Party* led by President Jawara, who was elected to a five–year term. The principal opposition parties are the *United Party* headed by

44

Pierre N'Jie and the *National Convention Party* of Sherrif Dibba.

The head of state was converted to Christianity in 1955 and took the Christian name David; in 1965 he reverted to his original Islamic faith, resuming use of his Moslem name, Dawda Kairaba Jawara (*Daw*–dah Care–*abah* Jah–*wah*–rah). In mid–1981, while he was in London attending the wedding of Prince Charles, a force of leftists attempted to overthrow the government. Help was asked of pbxSenegal, and the week–long uprising ended as the rebel force fled into the bush country hotly pursued by 1,500 Senegalese soldiers. Most were caught, tried and sentenced to death, but President Jawara commuted the sentences (estimated to be 50) to life imprisonment. Elections held in May 1982, prior to the attempt resulted in a legislature with 27 *PPP* members, 3 from the *NCP* and 5 independents.

Elections in 1987 were contested by two other parties competing with the *PPP*, the *NCP* and the *Gambian People's Party*. In spite of this, President Jawara was re-elected by a comfortable 59% of the vote, although this was lower than the 72.4% in the prior election.

Trials of three charged with attempting a *coup* in April–June 1988 resulted in stiff sentences. President Jawara charged that Libya's Gadhafi was the source of the move to recruit dissidents and foment revolution. The three were said to be part of the same group that made the same effort in 1981. President Jawara initially announced in late 1991 that he would not stand for reelection, but in early 1992 he changed his mind, and moved the elections from March to February. The outcome was not unexpected—he won 59% of the vote; his party elected 25 of the 36 members in the legislature.

A small beginning toward cooperation with Senegal was marked in 1982 by the establishment of the Senegambian Confederation (official name: The Senegambian confederal Council of Ministers). Little resulted except meetings of cabinet officials from each nation to discuss problems of mutual interest. It was dissolved in September 1989 after Senegalese troops, which had entered the country to counter another threatened *coup* against Jawara, peacefully departed.

Unrest which had been bubbling below the surface in The Gambia erupted in mid–1994 when a group of junior military officers, led by Lt. Yahya Jameh, staged a *coup*; President Jawara fled to a visiting U.S. Naval vessel which transported him to Senegal.

The basic problem was that army personnel had not been paid while rampant government corruption was obvious. Within weeks, Jameh proclaimed himself president and promised an end to government irresponsibility. Senior officers (who had been paid) attempted a counter–*coup* in November 1994 which failed.

Culture: Traditions and customs in The Gambia are derived from the same sources as those of Senegal. The people wear colorful, loose–fitting clothing of elaborate style which consumes large amounts of material, particularly in their dress for formal occasions. There are few Christians in The Gambia—Islam was established for many centuries prior to the arrival of Europeans.

Almost all people live a rural, isolated life in which the family unit is primary. The Gambia achieved fame in 1976 as being the reported place of origin of Kunta Kinte, a remote ancestor (possibly fictional) in the best–seller *Roots*.

The only "newspaper" is the *Gambia News Bulletin*, an official government publication appearing three times a week. Several independent mimeographed news sheets are printed once or twice a week.

Economy: The Gambia has historically had a dependent economy. After independence, grants from the United Kingdom were necessary to enable government services to function. The income level of the people is less than an average of $225 per year; less than 35% of the people are employed in the "money" economy. Peanuts constitute about 75% of the value of all exports; the principal source of government revenue is tariffs on exports. Drought, which periodically envelops neighboring Senegal, also affects The Gambia, causing further strain on the debt–gripped economy. It receives annual assistance from the European Community (EC) and about $7 million from the U.S. Hotel and resort construction has result in increased tourism from Europe, but this source of income is underdeveloped. There is the usual amount of corruption, thievery and bribery, but very little violence. A terribly low literacy rate (12%) is an economic ball and chain attached to this nation's economy.

The Future: The situation in The Gambia is extremely fluid. The self–proclaimed president has said civilian rule will not return to The Gambia until 1998 at the earliest. Until then, tourism, upon which this country is largely dependent, will decline sharply. The U.S. has suspended all but humanitarian aid.

Capt. Yahya Jameh

The Republic of Ghana

A farmer clears his land for planting.

Area: 238,537 sq. km = 92,100 sq. mi. (Oregon is slightly larger).

Population: 16 million (estimated).

Capital City: Accra (Pop. 1.7 million, estimated; pronounced Ah–*Krah*).

Climate: Hot and humid in the southwest; warm and less humid in the north. Ghana has a wet season (May–September) and a dry season (October–April).

Neighboring Countries: Ivory Coast (West); Burkina Faso (Upper Volta—West, North); Togo (East).

Official Language: English.

Other Principal Tongues: Akan, Twi, Mole–Daghani, Ewe, Ga–Adangbe.

Ethnic Background: Ashanti, Fante, Ewe, Fanti, Hausa, Nzima and many other smaller groups.

Principal Religions: Traditional tribal beliefs (45%), Christian (43%), Islam (12%).

Chief Commercial Products: Cocoa, timber, gold, diamonds, manganese, bauxite and aluminum.

Per Capita Annual Income: About U.S. $440 (still below $540 in 1970).

Currency: Cedi.

Former Colonial Status: British Colony (1821–1957).

Independence Date: March 6, 1957.

Chief of State: Jerry Rawlings, President (b. 1947).

National Flag: Three horizontal stripes of red, yellow and green with a five-pointed black star in the center of the yellow stripe.

Ghana is situated in the center of the Gold–Ivory Coast of Africa and has a 334–mile–long shore washed by the warm waters of the Gulf of Guinea. The coastline is an irregular pattern interrupted by streams and lagoons covered with strand and mangrove growth. The plant cover is not continuous, but gathers in tufted and erect green patches of grass and low vegetation. In the eastern inland coastal area, the terrain consists of a stretch of scrub and grassland, interrupted by clumps of bushes and small trees. Inland from the western coast there is an area of jungle, which receives ample rainfall, supporting dense growths of trees towering to heights of 200 feet.

The dense vegetation gives way 175 miles north from the sea to a somewhat smooth grassland area with less rainfall. The trees of this region are widely spaced among grasses which attain heights of 12 feet. The *harmattan*, a dry wind from the Sahara, penetrates from November to April. The humidity drops during this dry season and both the grasses and trees turn yellow; the trees lose their foliage within a few weeks. Temperatures in this region are high since there is no cooling breeze from the sea. In the extreme North, rainfall rapidly diminishes and becomes nonexistent. Northern Ghana has all but become totally arid during the

46

last decade and faces invasion by the expanding Sahara Desert. There are no true mountains in Ghana—the highest elevation is 2,900 feet in the part closest to the eastern boundary.

History: The folklore of the people of Ghana refers to migrations from the North, and it is probable that these legends relate to the travels of Sudanese people from the Nile River in the 10th–15th centuries A.D. The name Ghana is derived from a powerful kingdom believed to have been centered some 200 miles north of Bamako (now the capital of Mali) as shown on p. 13. For earlier history, see also p. 21.

After independence, President Kwame Nkrumah (*Kwah*–mi N–*kroo*–mah) rapidly transformed the government into a dictatorship patterned after various communist nations. His *Convention People's Party* became the instrument of all political thought, and the government was supposed to be the servant of the party. Nkrumah acquired the power to jail people for ten years without trial; the press was rigidly censored. But in spite of these measures, he initially was an immensely popular figure.

Establishing close ties with Russian and Chinese communists, Nkrumah accused the Western nations of "neo–colonialism" with tedious regularity. He bolstered his ego with titles such as the "lion," "giant" and "prophet" of Africa. He was inconsistent, argumentative and stubborn; although there was an appearance of prosperity in Ghana under Nkrumah, this was only on the surface. He borrowed huge sums of money from abroad and spent them on lavish projects, such as the then modern Accra Stadium adjacent to Black Star Square, home of an able soccer team which has won international awards. Agricultural improvement and industrial development were largely ignored. The economic situation became increasingly difficult, but Nkrumah did give the Ghanaians pride, however imaginary it might have been. When he was deposed, it became apparent that he left Ghana in an economic shambles.

A group of army officers seized power while Nkrumah was visiting China and North Vietnam in early 1966. A *Liberation Council* was formed, Nkrumah sympathizers were arrested and almost 1,200 political prisoners were released from jails. Communist technical and political personnel were quickly expelled. Nkrumah went to Guinea, where his personal friend, Sékou Touré, bestowed on him the honor of titular head of state.

There followed a succession of governments, military and civilian, none of them able to solve the problems of soaring inflation, dishonesty in government, unemployment and all the ills accompanying a nation deep in debt. Twelve years later, with the military in power, elections were scheduled, but many people knew that the outcome was prearranged; extra ballots had been printed to assure victory for the chosen candidates. At this point, Flight Lt. Jerry Rawlings, with a group of young officers, took over the government. This group of idealistic men went forward with the elections which were held in September 1979. The winner was a highly respected former foreign service officer, Dr. Hilla Limann, who declared his intention to bind up the nation's economic wounds and set Ghana on a solid economic course.

The Limann government lasted only until New Year's Eve, 1981, when Lt. Rawlings again appeared on the scene and deposed the elected chief executive. He was disgusted. Corruption, an ingrained tradition in Ghana, had not abated. Ghana still teetered on the edge of economic collapse. The new military leaders pledged to reverse that trend and to provide stable democracy. Rawlings, head of a 7–man Council, suspended the constitution, abolished all of Ghana's six political parties, accused the Limann government of failing to provide for the needs of the people, and called upon the citizens to become actively involved in "the decision–making process" (whatever that meant).

The new government, on the surface, appeared to have turned radical—Rawlings was an unabashed admirer of Libya's Colonel Gadhafi. Plans were afoot to install "popular committees" which would, in theory, manage *all* aspects of the lives of Ghanaians. "People's Defense Committees" briefly mushroomed in city neighborhoods, in rural villages and industry. They were supposed to serve as watchdogs against corruption and black market dealings.

There were many incidents of violence involving various military elements in Ghana during the years after 1982, accompanied by a disturbing lack of military discipline. Churches were both burned and vandalized and officers were murdered. Ghana was in a state of regional rampant vigilantism with little central government control.

Three senior judges of the nation's highest court were kidnapped and murdered in mid–1982. The administration denied involvement, charging that anti–government elements, of which there have been an abundance, were behind accusations of official involvement. In response to external and internal pressure, an investigative commission was convened to look into the matter. It indeed turned out that a high party official was responsible; he and three others were executed for their deed. Still dissatisfied by the judicial system's failure to deal with corruption, the Rawlings government announced a system of people's and military tribunals. The outcry against this measure caused it to be quickly rescinded. The government was "reorganized" in late 1983, but no substantial change was made.

Further changes in late 1984 were more in name than in substance. Continued dissatisfaction was evidenced in an early 1985 attempted *coup* against Rawlings; five members of the military were summarily executed after being held responsible. Yet another attempted *coup* was reported in mid–1987, with resulting arrest of several persons. "Dissidents and mercenaries" from an unnamed Middle East country were blamed. Finally, there were allegations of an attempted *coup* in September 1989 which are doubtful.

Economic hardships added fuel to the fires of dissent which present a continuing threat to the regime. It was this that led to an about–face by Rawlings and his regime in 1987–88. About 45,000 civil servants were fired, foreign investment policy was reversed and a less revolutionary style was adopted. It was announced that elections for 110 district assemblies would be held in late 1988,

President Jerry Rawlings

and almost 90% of the population registered to vote. Political parties, however, remain banned.

Encouraged by these and other moves to put Ghana's economy in order, the International Monetary Fund and the World Bank, as well as several western nations, extended credits to the country that had been withheld. Foreigners were invited to use modern techniques in the gold mines, producing favorable results.

Bowing to international pressures, Lt.

Rawlings allowed a multiple party system to develop in the early 1990's preparatory to elections scheduled for November 1992. He resigned from the air force (as required by new election laws) and ran as a civilian. Rawlings won with 60% of the vote, but there was substantial tampering in the contest without which he probably would have won anyway. Opposition parties have become less strident and are disposed to give his government a chance. Unrest in the North was ethnic and concerned tribal area disputes during the first half of 1994. The military had little difficulty bringing it to at least a temporary halt.

Culture: The people of Ghana have a unique culture—a combination of British conservatism, traditional local customs and an energetic desire for knowledge and economic progress which was led astray during the Nkrumah years. The dress of the people is colorful, using unique prints and designs which are copied in Paris, London and New York. Accra nightclubs resound with the most modern rap, hip–hop and "high–life" music which transfixes dancers and listeners until dawn.

The Market Women of Ghana are not mere salespeople—they are a respected institution. Noisy, sometimes quarrelsome, but brilliantly arrayed, they vend their wares in the town and city markets, often occupying the same space for years. They highly resent price "freezes" adopted in recent years, being firm believers in the traditional bargaining method of selling their wares.

Improvement in education has occurred since the Nkrumah years; college and youth organizations are among the most vocal critics of Rawlings' government. About 1 million students attend primary and secondary schools and more than 40,000 are studying in high schools, training colleges and academic universities, including the University of Ghana. The literacy rate is admirably high—over 60%—in dramatic contrast to 30% one short generation ago.

Economy: At the time of independence, Ghana was the world's leading cocoa exporter. Production of 570,000 tons in 1957 fell to less than 124,000 tons. After 1977 the price fell to $840.00 from a former level of $3,600 per ton; it has since rebounded, but not enough to compensate for inflation now running about 11% a year. Ghana, as did many other African nations, fell behind in repayment of foreign loans, all of which were rescheduled in the late 1980's. The total is now about $4.3 billion. Regrettably, a great deal of fertile land is being under–used or left totally idle.

The Limann government not only proved corrupt, but was simply unable to put Ghana's economic house in order. The Black Market is still evident under the Rawlings government, albeit to a slightly lower degree. The increase in world oil prices (since abated) hit Ghana as well as other African nations. Fuel was continuously in short supply and is still somewhat scarce.

A 1982 government decree which directed investigation of all bank accounts in excess of $50,000 Cedis met with some success. Excess funds were confiscated. Unemployment and inflation rose greatly in 1983–4 as Nigeria, faced with dwindling foreign reserves, expelled foreign workers, included an estimated one million Ghanaians. International efforts to resettle these workers within Ghana had minimal success.

Ghana is slowly climbing from its deepest economic trouble since independence. Once a greatly literate and rich nation in Western Africa, it was slowly reduced to a bare, minimal sustinence state. Its educated professionals largely left in order to survive, and Ghana's farmers refused to grow crops for worthless paper money. At the same time, international sources demanded currency reform. Measures were taken in 1985–6 to devalue the currency and institute measures to increase cocoa production, which persuaded the International Monetary Fund to grant additional credits in late 1986. The effect of this became readily apparent.

Unable to secure assistance from the communist bloc, Rawlings not only called a halt to nationalization and other radical measures in order to enable Ghana simply to survive, he did an abrupt about–face. Although a strong privatization of state–owned enterprises was announced, it has been painfully slow, weighted down by bureaucratic inertia. After years in the economic doldrums, Ghana is now moving upward, with an annual growth rate of about 5% which could be doubled with effort.

Although it has the potential to become self–supporting in food production, poor management has made this impossible. There have been *too many* managers—the government bureaucracy formerly sapped almost two–thirds of the national budget. Diamond, gold and agricultural production reached all time lows, but now are dramatically increasing. U.S. aid was suspended in 1985 after Ghana expelled four Americans alleged to be spies. It since has been resumed.

Important economic developments occurred in 1988–89—West Germany and Libya made large concessions on debts owed them by Ghana, and other sources became available as a result of currency reforms under which foreign currencies are legal in Ghana.

In order to help service the foreign debt, which has been eating up more than 60% of export earnings, Rawlings in 1990 decreed increased sales taxes on fuel, cars, fruit and some beverages. Cocoa production doubled in 1989 to 300,000 tons, offset by falling world prices. Inflationary pressures which diminished real income have substantially lessened,

The Future: Ghana's potentially positive future will continue to be limited by minor, but persistent ethnic conflicts. The civil rights record of this nation was and is uneven. Economic growth is now underway because of a clearly unified and coherent economic policy. Private foreign investment is returning, but very slowly; additional time will be needed to mute memories of the Nkrumah disaster years.

The Central Library, Accra

The Republic of Guinea

(pronounced *Gih*–nee)

Guinean mother and children outside traditional conical roof thatch hut.

Area: 245,857 sq.km. = 95,000 sq. mi. (about the size of Oregon).

Population: 7.9 million (estimated).

Capital City: Conakry (Pop. 1 million, estimated).

Climate: In the extreme Southeast and Southwest there are small hot and humid areas of jungle with two rainy seasons (May–July and September–November). The climate gradually changes the terrain to a warm, semi-arid region in the North with a single rainy season (April–October).

Neighboring Countries: Guinea Bissau (West); Senegal, Mali (North); Ivory Coast (East); Liberia, Sierra Leone (Southeast).

Official Language: French.

Other Principal Tongues: Malinke, Fula, Sussa and 15 other tribal dialects.

Ethnic Background: Most people are an admixture of West African Negro and Hamitic–Sudanic ancestry, the most prominent groups include the Malinke, Fulani, Mandingo, Soussou and Kissi people.

Principal Religions: Islam (about 85%), traditional beliefs (about 15%); there is a small handful of Christians.

Chief Commercial Products: Alumina, bauxite, diamonds, coffee, tropical fruits.

Per Capita Annual Income: About U.S. $490.

Currency: Guinea Franc.

Former Colonial Status: French Colony (1894–1958).

Independence Date: October 2, 1958.

Chief of State: Col. Lansana Conté, President.

National Flag: Vertical stripes of red, yellow and green.

Facing to the southwest on the Atlantic Ocean in the western extension of Africa, Guinea has an irregular, but level coast line. Immediately inland there is a gently rolling area, covered with dense vegetation in the more southern coastal area. Grassy plains, interspersed with trees, are found in the north coastal region.

Further inland the landscape slowly rises in a series of flat plains and table mountains. The Fouta Djallon mountains rise to heights of 6,000 feet in central Guinea and are the source of three large West African rivers: the Niger, the Gambia and the Senegal.

Further to the northeast, the land slowly descends to a flat grassland which has greater variation in temperatures than the more humid coastal area. These grasslands attain a rich, green color towards the end of March and the vegetation grows rapidly in the ensuing rainy season which lasts until November.

In southeast Guinea the terrain becomes somewhat higher, containing dense forests with a pattern of rain quite similar to that of the plains land. As the dry season commences in the latter part of November, the leaves of the trees turn into a panorama of brilliant colors, not because of cold weather, but because of the lack of moisture. This is the equivalent of "winter" in Guinea, and it is not until April that the landscape is again green.

History: Guinea was dominated in early times from the 10th to the 15th centuries by kingdoms overlapping from neighboring countries. The vast empires of Ghana, Mali and Songhai successively occupied the country during the period. Earlier migrations of people to Guinea remained during the period of these kingdoms. The nomadic Fulani (also known as Peulhs), the agricultural Mandingos, Malinkes and Soussous had become established in times unknown and today inhabit this area of West Africa. For details of early and colonial history, see Historical Background and *The French in Africa.*

Under pressure for independence from its African colonies, France enacted the *Loi Cadre* in 1958, extending to the colonies the choice of full independence or autonomy within the *French Community.* Guinea quickly elected to become fully independent—the only French colony to make that choice— and it was proclaimed a nation on October 2, 1958.

Following independence, Guinea was actually a total dictatorship under the iron rule of its first president, Ahmed Sékou Touré. There were trappings of democratic government, i.e. elections for the president every seven years and for seats in the National Assembly every five years. However, the *Democratic Party of Guinea* was the sole political force in the country. Sékou Touré was its Secretary–General. Membership in the party was said to be as many as 2 million, organized into thousands of local committees. Therefore, elections were a mere formality. The president went from left to right in his foreign political leanings, first wooing the Soviet bloc and then turning to Western nations when the country's economy predictably soured. His regime was filled with convictions, executions, long imprisonments and over 2 million Guineans fled into exile. Terror was the main theme of government.

Sékou Touré's one–man rule ended very swiftly in a Cleveland hospital when he died on March 26, 1984 during an operation to correct a blood vessel defect. His closest confidante, Prime Minister Louis Lansana Beavogui immediately took control of the government. A 40 day period of mourning for the late "hero" was proclaimed. The party's 14–member political bureau was scheduled to meet in order to select the successor of Touré.

Early in the morning of April 3, 1984, junior military officers, disgusted with prior civilian rule, took over the country, proclaiming that Touré's rule was no more than a "bloody and ruthless dictatorship." This undoubtedly had something to do with the fact that Touré regularly "purged" the military to insure his own seat of power. A Military Committee was established which assured all foreign nations that Guinea would live up to its commitments; it immediately began to release some political prisoners from Conakry's notorious Camp Boiro, a barracks where many atrocities were said to have taken place. At least 10,000 political prisoners had been seized during Sékou Touré's regime, of whom some 2,500 simply "disappeared."

The *Democratic Party of Guinea* and the constitution were suspended. Political prisoners surviving Touré's holocaust, numbering 250, were given radio time to relate their experiences to the people. The new regime was initially led by Col. Lansana Conté, President and Col. Diarra Traoré, Prime Minister; rivalry led to the latter's demotion in December 1984.

Dissatisfied, Traoré and others attempted a *coup* in July 1985 while President Conté was in Lomé (Togo) at a conference. The President returned to Guinea after giving a speech at the conference and had no difficulty in restoring control. Some 30 people involved in the attempt were summarily executed, including Traoré. The whole affair had tribal overtones.

Since the death of Touré, Guinea has embarked on a new course. A $2.3 million loan was negotiated with France and the International Monetary Fund soon granted a line of credit to begin the refurbishing of a potentially wealthy African nation. The Soviet bloc belatedly came forward with promises (not money) of future assistance. Programs were undertaken to cut the government bureaucracy (87,000) drastically and to sell several government–owned enterprises to the private sector.

Human rights conditions did not immediately improve in Guinea. The results of military trials in 1986–7 of about 200 officials of Touré's regime resulted in 60 death sentences, 21 of them *in absentia*. Some of the accused were presumed to be already dead. The purpose was to instill fear, particularly in urban areas, where the government popularity had plunged because of severe economic conditions. Stokely Carmichael, a former U.S. civil rights activist unwisely living under the name Kwame Touré in Guinea, was held for three days without official explanation (he was suspected of revolutionary activities). Newspaper publishers were pointedly reminded not to confuse freedom with "libertinism."

Things have improved after 1987. The widow and son of Traoré were released together with several dozen others associated with the 1985 *coup* attempt; life

French President Mitterrand greets Guinean President Conté in Paris, 1987

AP/Wide World photo

The Guinean coastline

sentences were commuted. However, riots erupted in early 1988 because of price increases for food staples and gasoline. Prices were frozen at their prior levels; the president accused speculators of sabotaging the regime's liberalization program.

The president elaborated in 1989 on a prior plan for a new constitution which may possibly provide for a political government; parties were legalized in 1992 and there are now 7 of them, squabbling endlessly over things of little import. The "legislature" has been the *Transitionional Committee for National Recovery (CTRN)* picked by Conté and his clique of insiders. The first multi–party elections held since independence were marked by confusion, violence, and threats of boycott by the opposition. Because there was no opportunity for "preparation" for the contest, the opposition does not recognize the "victory" of Conté (51% of the vote) and his cohorts.

Culture: More than 80% of the people of Guinea live a rural life on small farms that provide their basic needs. Artistic and literary expressions, formerly limited by the single political party and its leader, are re–emerging. About 10,000 people who fled the nation during the Touré years have returned and are being resettled with international assistance. There are more than 16 distinct ethnic groups within the country, the great majority of which profess Islam as religion. When splinter groups of Islam began to appear, the gov-

ernment banned them and established the *National Islamic League,* the only group authorized in Guinea. In spite of the efforts of the former ruling party, basic values have been retained. Observers from the western world were severely limited in Guinea for a generation. This has been replaced by free cultural and informational exchanges, impossible in the past.

Economy: When you think of Guinea, think of bauxite, the principal ore used for making aluminum. Guinea has about one third of the world's known reserves! Diamonds are now being recovered from river bank areas, as well as gold. A single diamond of 103 carats fetched $1.6 million in early 1987. Although blessed with natural resources, Guinea remains a relatively poor nation because of the Touré years of mismanagement from which it is still recovering. The misguided government of Touré, unhappy with the rate of expansion of mineral production, turned things over to Eastern European technicians. Governmental corruption had much to do with an unnecessary slowdown in exports.

Even Touré realized the root of Guinea's problems, and turned to the west for help in his waning years. Failing to become a full economic partner in the Soviet bloc, Guinea turned once again to France and the West for development capital and expertise. The latest bauxite mining has resulted in the rapid growth of Guinea's external income—but it has been matched by the temptation to borrow. The foreign

debt is $2.6 million, much of which is owed to the Soviet Union and its former European clients and to China. The Soviets also received bauxite at well below world prices, a practice that no longer prevails. Farmers were forced to raise crops for less than their costs, leading to a healthy black market. In spite of the fact that much rich land is available, Guinea still imports foodstuffs.

Economic decentralization is now virtually complete—a healthy departure from a centrally planned economy. The influx of surplus Soviet military hardware has all but ceased. France remains Guinea's principle external benefactor in amount of $100–$140 million. The best economic news is the start of mining of iron deposits adjacent to Liberia. The ore is fantastically rich: 70–75% pure iron. Nevertheless, an influx of tens of thousands of Liberian refugees during the 1990 civil war in that country created severe problems. The economy has made little progress since 1984.

The Future: Slow, but steady economic progress is being made in Guinea, which probably would not be possible in an atmosphere of political instability. Both France and the IMF made loans in 1994 and will continue to do so in the future, boosting a modestly high per capita income.

The Republic of Guinea–Bissau

A quiet area near Bissau

Area: 36,260 sq. km. = 14,000 sq. mi. (the size of Connecticut and Massachusetts; includes the Bijago Archipelago).

Population: 1.3 million (estimated).

Capital City: Bissau (Pop. 170,000, estimated (pronounced Bee–*sow*).

Climate: Very warm and humid with a wet season from May to October and a drier period from November to June.

Neighboring Countries: Senegal (North); Guinea (Southeast).

Official Language: Portuguese. A local variation of this, *Crioulo* (Creole) is frequently heard.

Other Principal Tongues: Balante, Malinke and Fulani sub–dialects.

Ethnic Background: West African Negro (Balante, 30%), Negroid–Sudanic (Fulani 20%, Mandyako 14%, Malinke 13%, others 23%); figures are approximate.

Principal Religions: Traditional tribal beliefs (66%), Islam (30%), Christianity (4%). Figures are approximate.

Chief Commercial Products: Cashew nets, palm kernels and oil, peanuts, rice.

Per Capita Annual Income: About U.S. $170.

Currency: Guinea–Bissau Peso.

Former Colonial Status: Portuguese Colony (1885–1974). During this period, the area was considered by the Portuguese to be an integral part of European Portugal.

Independence Date: September 10, 1974 (The date on which Portugal recognized independence; unilateral declaration of independence was on September 24, 1973).

Chief of State: João Bernardo "Nino" Vieira, President (1980).

National Flag: Three stripes—red, vertical nearest the staff upon which there is a centered, black star and two horizontal stripes of yellow (top) and green (bottom).

Bordering on the waters of the Atlantic, most of Guinea–Bissau is a swampy coastal lowland with about sixty small islands lying close to the shoreline. On its eastern and southern borders it is protected by the Foutah Djallon mountains

52

of Guinea. The level land, coupled with more than adequate rainfall, contributes large quantities of produce with less labor than is found in most areas of Africa.

History: The Balante people are probably the oldest inhabitants of Guinea–Bissau, joined only during the last millenium by the Mandingo and pastoral Fulani (Peulh) people. For details of earlier history, see Historical Background, *The Portuguese in Africa*.

Nationalist guerrilla warfare was unevenly conducted from the dense interior jungles beginning in 1961; as a result of this rebellion, Portugal had to maintain up to 26,000 troops, half of whom were African, stationed within the territory to oppose some 7,000 rebels. The colonial forces controlled only the coastal areas, and the interior was dominated by the rebels, who established basic schools and government services. Occasional Portuguese raids into the interior were made, but little more than temporary control resulted. The time of day or night was often the determining factor in deciding which force controlled what territory.

Initially there were two resistance movements, but one, the *African Independence Party of Guinea and Cape Verde (PAIGC)* initially led by Amilcar Cabral emerged as the sole effort. By the early 1970's the rebels held one–half of the country and threatened one–fourth. They were able to bombard Bissau periodically. Their support came from Soviet and Chinese arms and Cuban trainers all located in neighboring Guinea. Portugal retaliated by transporting Guinean rebels from Bissau to Conakry in late 1970 to raid *PAIGC* headquarters there, as well as other installations.

Fighting between the mulatto Cape Verde troops and the Black African soldiers marred the struggle for independence; the army of Guinea had to intervene to stop the strife. Cabral was assassinated in early 1973 and was succeeded as head of *PAIGC* by his brother, Luis. The revolution was successful because of a governmental change in Portugal; liberal military officers there realized it was futile to hold on to the rebellious colony. Independence was recognized on Sept. 10, 1974 and the Portuguese were gone within a month.

Cabral rose to the office of President by common consent and was "reelected" in March 1977. Economic conditions took a sharp turn for the worse; this led to Cabral's ouster in 1980 in a bloodless *coup* led by General João Bernardo Vieira. President Pereira of Cape Verde was accused of being a part of the whole problem. Although the quest for independence united the two territories, what little unity they had dissolved in the early 1980's.

Although a return to constitutional rule was supposed to occur in 1984, the government still had all the trappings of a communist–style regime—a Central Committee, Politburo and single party. There were attempted *coups* in 1984 and late 1985; as a result of the latter, six were executed (including the vice president) and six others died suspiciously while in detention from very imaginative causes—"blood pressure complication," "a clot on the lungs," "heart trouble" and "[he] succumbed to a long illness which suddenly worsened."

General Veira was elected to a term of five years as President in 1984 and again in 1989. Communist rhetoric all but vanished, but until 1992 there remained only one political party, when opposition was permitted in response to international and local pressures. Elections scheduled for 1992 were repeatedly postponed, attracting considerable criticism, and were finally held in July 1994. The president and his party were elected in a multi–party contest (but not without accusations of election fraud). International observers termed the contest a fair one.

Culture: The Balantes live in a subsistence agricultural manner in the coastal lowlands; the Mandingos (Mandyakos) and Fulani people of the interior place greater emphasis on the ownership of livestock. Contact between the Portuguese and the Africans was minimal during the colonial period; almost no educational facilities were provided for the Black people. A tiny handful of Africans lived as *assimilados*, speaking Portuguese and adopting European customs. They are now the civil servants in government. The civil strife displaced an estimated 200,000 people, 150,000 of whom went into exile in Senegal and Guinea. With the assistance of grants from Western European nations and the United States, these people were resettled in 1975–1976.

The Cape Verdians (of mixed blood) long dominated the business scene in Bissau and always assumed a higher position on the social scale than their darker–skinned brethren. This was the cause of smoldering resentment, among others.

Bissau is a bustling provincial town of stucco houses with orange–tiled roofs, a capital city whose people are warm and hospitable—and where no building stands above three stories.

Economy: Portuguese investment in Guinea–Bissau during the colonial period was minimal. There are known bauxite and other mineral deposits, but they have not yet been developed. Agriculture sustains the population, but barely. Since independence, the government has regularly sought, and received, assistance from Portugal and other sources; aid from the USSR has been minimal. Steps to de-

velop its resources are in the early stages.

The World Bank has recently been active in road–building efforts in order to open up the interior. As of 1983, fishing produced only 6,000 metric tons, but there is a development in this area, a venture undertaken with Russia, Algeria and France. Most of the product goes to those nations—especially shrimp. Efforts are being made to reclaim rice paddies, abandoned since the revolutionary strife.

In spite of foreign assistance, which had been rescheduled in 1987 on very generous terms and partially "forgiven" in 1988, Guinea–Bissau remains one of the poorest nations on earth. In 1989 it was beset by a plague of locusts, necessitating imports of large quantities of grain, much of which was donated.

The Future: Little will change in this poorest of West African nations. Periodic dissatisfaction with the Central Bank will be voiced by creditors; it is a beehive of *PAIGC* stalwarts.

President João Bernardo Vieira

The Republic of Liberia

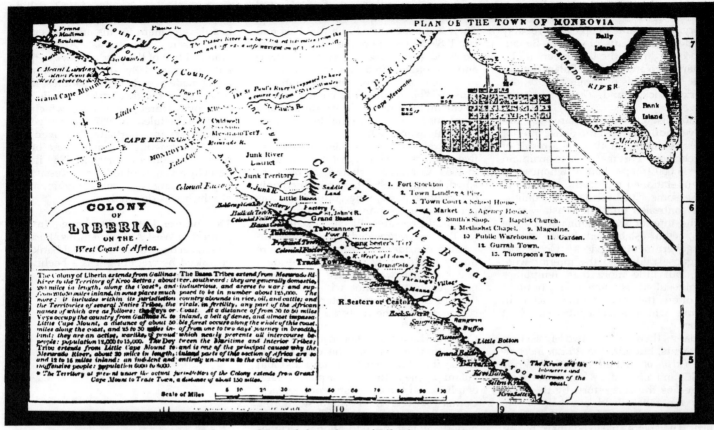

Map of the colony of Liberia, ca. 1827

Area: 111,370 sq. km = 43,000 sq. mi. (Pennsylvania is slightly larger).

Population: 2.6 million (estimated).

Capital City: Monrovia (Pop. 400,000, swelled by about 125,000 refugees in 1992–93).

Climate: Warm and humid, with a wet season (April–November) and a drier season (December–May).

Neighboring Countries: Sierra Leone (West); Guinea (North); Ivory Coast (Northeast, East).

Official Language: English.

Other Principal Tongues: About 20% of the people speak *Creole*, a combination of English and many dialects. Native dialects are spoken by about 90%, including Kru, Mandingo and Gola. There are about 25 sub–dialects within these three groups.

Ethnic Background: West African Negro, including sub–groups of Kru, Mandingo and Gola. There are about 60,000 Americo–Liberians, descendants of freed slaves.

Principal Religions: Christianity (about 65%), traditional beliefs (about 20%), Islam (about 15%).

Chief Commercial Products: Iron ore, rubber, diamonds, timber, coffee, cocoa.

Per Capita Annual Income: About U.S. $400.

Currency: Liberian Dollar.

Former Colonial Status: Liberia has traditionally been an area of United States development.

Independence Date: July 26, 1847.

Chief of State *(de facto)*:Charles Taylor, title not determined, leader of guerrilla groups since severe anarchy gripped the nation in late 1989. Four others claim the title.

National Flag: Eleven horizontal stripes of red and white, with a single white star on a blue rectangle in the upper left–hand corner.

Liberia is located on the southern part of the west coast of Africa, facing the warm equatorial waters of the Gulf of Guinea. It is within the tropical region of Africa and as such, has a warm, humid climate. Its jungle areas are thickly carpeted with roots, dead leaves and debris, which are quickly made a part of the earth by the rapid rate of decay. From the floor of the jungle, shrubs and small trees entangled with vines, rise from 40 to more than 100 feet. Interspersed with this thick growth are the so–called

crown trees which bear foliage only at immense heights, having trunks up to twelve feet in width. The coastal area of Liberia, receiving the most rainfall, is dotted with lagoons, tidal creeks and marshes. Further inland the terrain rises slowly to a level of 1000 feet in a series of plateaus obscured by the dense undergrowth. Low mountains rise occasionally throughout the country, seldom reaching a height of more than 3,000 feet, with the exception of the Nimba and Wale mountains, which are 4,500 feet high.

Six rivers flow from the interior southwest to the Gulf of Guinea; they are not navigable for more than a few miles inland and are bounded by level land suitable for cultivation.

During the 8–month rainy season, hardly a day passes without an inch or more of rainfall, including sharp thunderstorms intermingled with a steady, tedious downpour.

History: In all the world, Liberia's birth as a nation was unique. The Kru, Mandingo and Gola ethnic groups had lived for countless centuries in Liberia prior to the arrival of the white man. Easily

reached by the ships of slave traders plying the south Atlantic, local chiefs greedily sold conquered peoples to them. The market for field labor on the plantations of the southern colonies of America and in the West Indies was immense. Often, the traders took only the men for heavy work, leaving the women and children to fend for themselves.

The origins of Liberia took vague shape as early as 1691 when the Virginia legislature passed a law requiring slave owners who granted freedom to any to arrange for their passage out of the colony within half a year. Where they went was not spelled out, but a feeling was growing that danger lurked if both slaves and freed Blacks mingled. But Blacks who were born free could remain.

More than a century passed before Virginia lawmakers once again considered the problems caused by slavery. An idea was put forth to establish a penal colony for any Blacks (in the judgment of their masters) fomenting rebellion. The 1789 slave revolt in Haiti had sent a chill through plantation owners. Thomas Jefferson had openly expressed the view that there should be a plan for colonizing Blacks; he advocated a separation of the races, and that appeared to be the only reasonable way to accomplish this.

Finally the Virginia legislature, in the forefront of the movement, requested President James Monroe to obtain land outside the United States, preferably in Africa for this purpose. Voices were being raised against the slave trade (but not always *slavery*), and the idea of a colonization project developed. The African slave trade had been outlawed by the U.S. Constitution as of 1808.

Robert Finley, a New Jersey Presbyterian minister, spurred into action by British efforts to initiate a freed slave colony on Africa's west coast, felt that an American–sponsored colony could right a wrong continued by labor–starved plantation owners. Such an African colony

would be built upon the framework of Black Christian settlers and would remove a "servant class" from American shores. Finley decided to launch such a movement right in the nation's capital.

Just before Christmas in 1816, with the support of clergymen from many denominations and with the backing of such influential friends as U.S. Speaker of the House Henry Clay, he helped to organize the *American Society for Colonizing the Free People of Color in the United States*. This group targeted two classes—originally, Blacks *born* free, and subsequently *freedmen* (those who had been slaves). The plan was designed strictly for those who wanted to be resettled, and the Society had no intention to interefere with the institution of slavery. The intended communities would be established in Africa in the pattern of American society.

However noble these efforts might have appeared at the time, an underlying reason for the action might be found in Clay's own words in which he counseled that such colonization would "draw . . . off" free Blacks. The Reverend Finley's calculating comment was: "We shall be clear of them." But getting Congress to

sponsor and finance such a venture proved to be a major hurdle.

Northerners emphasized the missionary nature of the plan and the uplifting from bondage of an exploited and oppressed people. Southerners, on the other hand, stressed the possibility that free blacks might incite a slave rebellion; remote Africa offered an ideal place to send such potential troublemakers.

Finally a sum was allotted by Congress to transport Africans rescued from illegal slave ships and resettle them on their home continent, but that sum was *not* for the purchase of land. The American Colonization Society (as it had come to be known) pressured the government for a portion of the money to be used for land purchase.

In 1820 a small expedition of 86 landed on a small island off the west coast of Africa, just south of Britain's earlier–established colony of Sierra Leone. The two government–appointed agents died within a few weeks from yellow fever or malaria which had no known cure at the time. Others in the party also died and the remaining settlers sought British protection in the nearby colony.

Sketch of first settlement

Sample of currency made available by Maryland

The following year another expedition suffered the same fate, but in 1822 a third group of colonists arrived about 240 miles south of Sierra Leone. The land had finally been purchased by the U.S. from local chieftains for about $300, but it was left to the Society to raise money for the maintenance of the colony. Chapters were formed in many states and funds were solicited. Subsequently, in 1827, the Maryland legislature passed a law—never fully enforced—that no Blacks could remain within the state. Each year $1.000 was earmarked for the state chapter of the Society to be used in the colony, and special currency was even printed for the purpose.

By 1830 the tiny colonization effort had grown to a thousand people. This new "land of liberty" was named Liberia, and the colony continued to expand; trade increased because the settlers preferred American food which had to be brought in by ship.

The people united in 1839 to form the Commonwealth of Liberia under a governor appointed by the American Colonization Society, and in 1847 the Free and Independent Republic of Liberia was proclaimed. The new nation was recognized within a short time by the European powers, but not by the United States until 1862.

In the 1850's several U.S. states had become vocal in advocating the abolition of slavery altogether, infuriating the Southern states which then withdrew what had been lukewarm support for the colonization effort. By 1857 the movement was all but dead as tensions mounted between North and South in America. Nevertheless, the Republic of Liberia was able to exist as an independent country, albeit under extremely harsh conditions.

The territorial area of Liberia was poorly defined. Lack of transportation to the interior prevented effective surveys of the land and in the succeeding decades

M/Sgt. Samuel K. Doe

Assassinated President Tolbert in a "swearing-in suit"

there were many adjustments of the boundaries which resulted in a loss of substantial territory to other neighboring colonies.

The life of the descendants of the freed slaves was harsh. This was a hostile land—a difficult place in which to survive, though the tribes of the interior were not aggressive people. It was not until the 1930's that there was any real penetration of the interior by the Americo–Liberians via routes hacked through the dense jungle.

Shortly after World War I there were rumors that the Americo–Liberians were engaging in slavery, using people from the tribes of the interior. A commission was established in 1929 to investigate the charges. The findings indicated that there was widespread shipment of so–called "contract labor" to neighboring colonies. There was evidence of involvement of government officials in this activity; the report also indicated that a custom of pawning people for terms of years to pay off debts existed.

Under pressure of other nations as a result of the report, the government resigned and some officials were prosecuted. The U.S. withheld recognition of the succeeding regime until it was clear that these practices had ended.

William V.S. Tubman was elected to a four–year term of office as president in 1944 and again in 1948. The constitution was amended in 1952 to permit him to serve another term of office. In later years, this formal and conservative executive accepted a "draft" election to office at the call of the *True Whig Party*.

Both President Tubman and Vice–President William R. Tolbert were reelected to four year terms of office in 1967 and 1971, but Tubman died suddenly in mid-1971. Tolbert was inaugurated the 10th presi-

dent of Liberia in 1972 in ceremonies attended by a multitude of world dignitaries. He was reelected in 1975 and at the same time a constitutional amendment was adopted providing for an eight–year term of office which he strongly supported; the president may no longer run for a second term. Tolbert was the first Liberian president to speak an interior tribal dialect.

The True Whig Party, named for a political party in the U.S. which was dominant in days before the Civil War, had for over a hundred years been run by the Americo–Liberians who had carefully excluded from "the club" all but their own, except in the 1970's when a few "safe" outsiders were invited to join. In efforts to promote reforms for more press freedom, expand educational opportunities and bring people from the interior into the elitist government, President Tolbert was said to have "let peasants into the kitchen."

Signs of trouble surfaced in 1979. When rice supplies dropped as inefficient and often lazy growers found it more profitable to work as laborers on the large rubber plantations, the government proposed that the price per hundred pounds be raised from $22 to $26 to encourage greater production. Since rice is the staple food of the people, the plan touched off populist riots in Monrovia; there was widespread looting. About 50 people were killed and another 500 injured.

Ninety percent of the businesses in the capital were either partially or totally destroyed, with damage said to be about $50 million. President Tolbert imposed a curfew on the city and the Congress granted him emergency powers. These measures proved to be too late to stem the tide of rebellion—enemies of the establishment surfaced and on April 12, 1980, soldiers led by Master Sergeant Samuel K. Doe forced their way into the Executive Mansion, killed the president and by the end of the takeover, many hundreds of government officials had been gunned down and crudely buried in a mass grave. This was the first time any Liberian government had been overthrown.

Doe installed himself as Commander-in–Chief and Chairman of the *People's Redemption Council*, charging (truthfully) that there was widespread corruption. The first year after the revolution, things were turbulent. Soldiers roamed the streets attempting to settle old scores against the ousted Americo–Liberians. This took the form of harassing businessmen, confiscation of property and extortion of money.

The decade 1980–1990 was grim in Liberia. Doe raised himself by degrees to the rank of general. Although semi–literate, he arranged to have the degree of Doctor bestowed on him by the University of Liberia. Citizens were summarily executed and thievery by government officials was open and notorious. But Doe was also very shrewd. He repeatedly "conned" the United States out of countless millions of dollars. He rigged elections, the constitution, and even the date of his own birth so he could retain the presidency. There were at least ten known *coups*, and probably several others. Coming from the small Krahn tribe of the northeast, he stuffed the government and army with his fellow clansmen and created a very talented presidential guard (trained by Israelis).

He completely cowed the Americo–Liberians, including Winston Tubman, nephew of the late president, who joined the government. Corruption and counter–corruption were rampant; typical Liberian methods were used to steal. Charles Taylor, a minister of the government with a U.S. education, ordered $1 million worth of bulldozers which never arrived, he stashed the money in American bank accounts.

When his arrest appeared imminent, he escaped to the U.S., where he was arrested and, represented by ex–Attorney General Ramsey Clark, was held awaiting trial in an old Plymouth, Mass., jail. Hacksawing the window bars on the second floor, he escaped and made his way back to Africa, where he successfully enlisted the support of Moamar Qadhafi of Libya as well as from neighboring Côte d'Ivoire. With a force of more than 750 Liberians (which quickly grew to 5,000+) who were disgusted with Samuel Doe, he overran Liberia. One of his principal aides, Prince Yormie Johnson, suspected of secret rivalry, formed a second rebel group with about 1,000 members in 1990.

The U.S. evacuated personnel and Liberia descended into chaos. At the urging of the U.S. and others, under the aegis of the United Nations, the assistance of the Economic Community of West African States (ECOWAS) was asked to provide a force to maintain stability in Liberia. Refugees fled the countryside for the "safety" of Monrovia while citizens of that city headed for refuge in the countryside. By April 1994 more than 150,000 were dead, mostly from malnutrition, another name for starvation. Ships from around the world bearing food had refused to unload because of a genuine threat of violence.

Doe had been seized at a peace meeting (September 1990) between the factions; he was taken by a force dispatched by Prince Johnson and was slowly mutilated and tortured to death while his captors videotaped the grisly scene. What had started as a rebellion quickly degenerated into a seedbed of horror which continued until the first part of 1994. Remnants of Doe's forces initially occupied the presidential palace and parts of Monrovia, supported by a newly–arrived peacekeeping force.

Charles Taylor's *National Patriotic Front of Liberia* controlled the rest of the country and briefly established a capital at Garanga, 135 miles northeast of Monrovia. The rebel force was largely one of lawless adolescents and teenagers, most of whom wandered about stoned on marijuana which grows wild in Liberia.

The "peacekeeping" force was undisciplined, poorly paid, and subject to the command of various national commanders from West Africa. Not have any genuine stake in the outcome of the fighting, the troops were reluctant to expose themselves to gunfire or even minimal risks. The *ECOWAS* officials, evidently not caring that the strife was another rerun of the Monrovia "elite" of Americo–Liberians vs. the native Africans of the interior, appointed Amos Sawyer as interim President, ignoring the fact that Charles Taylor controlled about 95% of the land and people until his decline in 1993.

The swirl of events between the opposed forces were and are unimportant. The important thing was the incredible amount of suffering inflicted on innocent lives which were snuffed out less fre-

Mother and child, Liberia WORLD BANK Photo by Pamela Johnson

quently by bullets than they were consumed by starvation. The dread *kwashiokor*—protein starvation—was common among children of tender years, with their characteristic orange hair, distended bellies and sunken eyes.

Using smuggled diamonds as an economic base, Taylor's forces were able to mount a sustained effort until early 1993, occupying even Monrovia with the exception of the presidential palace. His sources gradually dried up by mid–1993, and as they were driven slightly into the interior, they ran out of arms and ammunition. At about the same time, Nigeria, principal provider of the *ECOWAS* forces, with immense domestic political problems, decided it could no longer sustain the Liberian effort; its withdrawal effective April 1, 1994, was announced.

An interim government nominally put in charge in April 1994 got absolutely nowhere in bringing strife to a halt in Liberia. Charles Taylor was "deposed" as head of the *NPFL*. The result: there are now two *NPFLs*. The Krahn–Mandingo force is split into two factions. Indiscriminate slaughters and atrocities take place on a daily basis, even in Monrovia, nominally under the control of the *ECOWAS*

forces. People have taken to the streets chanting "We are tired of the killing."

The chances of getting six battling factions to agree on anything are less than 10%. As in Somalia, there are too many arms and munitions which can be easily obtained. Liberia now is a wasteland.

Culture: There has been a basic divergence of cultural traditions in Liberia. The descendants of freed slaves living in the coastal regions were for the most part urban, Christian people. English is the language of choice and they prefer American styles in dress. They particularly valued formal attire, including, until lately, tuxedos and top hats notwithstanding the close, tropical climate. Now, all are considered fortunate if they are able to get any kind of clothing.

The people of the interior were relegated to a rural life based on subsistence agriculture. Clothed in the manner of West Africans, with flowing styles and brilliant colors, all had a high rate of literacy. But schools have been wrecked and plundered during the strife of the last years and few remain.

Missionaries have plied their efforts endlessly for the last half–century in the

interior, but the majority of people retain their traditional beliefs passed on to them by their forefathers. There have been a few conversions to Islam.

Until the strife, foreigners lived in Monrovia, engaging in professional occupations. They have left—the city was turned into utter devastation, with no water, no sewage system, no garbage collection, only intermittent electricity, very little food, no banks, no hospitals . . . nothing. Like a badly wounded fighter, it and the rest of Liberia are just barely beginning to recover a small fraction of what was.

Economy: As of 1995, Liberia's economy doesn't exist. It traditionally was an economic dependent of the United States, which periodically advanced loans since its founding to provide basic necessities and to overcome periodic financial crises. U.S. economic investment had a high price tag, since it was calculated to extract more from Liberia than was put into it. This economic oppressiveness abated slightly after the depression of the 1930s.

Post World War II investment by the U.S., Germany (west) and Sweden in iron ore development and steel production gave Liberia a genuine boost. But upon the rise of Samuel Doe and his seizure of power, an element of uncertainty was associated with the Liberian economy and foreign enthusiasm all but dried up. Now, after years of conflict, only foreign aid is available to Liberia. Investment will not resume in the forseeable future.

Exploration for offshore oil was successful, but profits evaporated into the pockets of the elite in power; this resource never was a source of wealth or convenience for average Liberians.

The Future: *De facto* anarchy will prevail indefinitely.

Rural gas station   World Bank Photo

The Republic of Senegal

Independence Plaza, central Dakar

Courtesy: Embassy of Senegal

Area: 196,840 sq.km. = 76,000 sq. mi. (about the size of Nebraska).

Population: 8 million (estimated).

Capital City: Dakar (Pop. 1.8 million estimated).

Climate: Warm and dry in the North; warmer and more humid in the South, with usually a wet season (July–October) and a dry season (November–June).

Neighboring Countries: The Gambia is a finger–like projection extending eastward from the Atlantic coast to the interior; Mauritania (North); Mali (East); Guinea–Bissau, Guinea (South).

Official Language: French.

Other Principal Tongues: Wolof (spoken by about 75% of the people), Peulh, or Fulani, Serere, Tukuler, Diola, Sarakole, Mandingo.

Ethnic Background: Wolof (36%), Fulani (17.5%), Serere (16.5%), Tukuler (9%). Diola (9%) other small groups (12%). (Figures are approximate).

Principal Religions: Islam (89%), Christianity (primarily Roman Catholic 10%), traditional tribal beliefs (1%).

Chief Commercial Products: Peanuts, peanut products, phosphate, canned fish.

Per Capita Annual Income: About U.S. $760.

Currency: CFA Franc, no longer tied to the French Franc.

Former Colonial Status: French Colony, a part of French West Africa (1895–1960). French commercial interests were active in Senegal prior to the formation of French West Africa.

Independence Date: June 20, 1960.

Chief of State: Abdou Diouf, President.

National Flag: Three vertical stripes of green, yellow and red, with a green star on the middle yellow stripe.

The Republic of Senegal, the westernmost portion of Africa, lies in a transitional zone between the steaming jungles of the Gold–Ivory Coast to the south and the endless, dry Sahara to the north. Its unique position has made it a true "crossroads" of the world—between Europe and Latin America, the United States and the Near and Far East, and finally, between South Africa and the European and American continents.

This is a flat, rolling plains country with characteristic grasslands and low tree vegetation. In the Southwest there is a small area of jungle and the coastline is often marsh or swampland. There are no high mountains in Senegal, but there are four large rivers flowing in parallel courses from east to west. These rivers are navigable to a substantial distance inland from the Atlantic, particularly during the wet season.

The hot breath of strong winds from the Sahara ushers in the traditional dry season each November. This wind of dry months, call the *harmattan* by the people, occasionally rises to almost torrential velocity, producing severe dust and sand-storms. In the last decade, all too frequently the wind is year–around, creating severe drought problems and intrusion of the Sahara at the rate of about four miles per year.

History: From the characteristics of the people who today live in Senegal, it is apparent that many centuries ago there was a migration of Hamitic–Sudanic groups from the Sudan area of the Nile River, but it is impossible to pinpoint the period of these migrations. These groups were well–established in approximately twenty distinct parts of the country at the time of the first European explorations. For details of early and colonial history see Historical Background and *The French in Africa.*

For a brief period in 1959 Senegal and the former French Soudan were joined to form the Mali Federation, which was ultimately dissolved when Senegal withdrew and proclaimed itself a republic. France had, prior to this move, granted full independence to the federation.

The constitution of Senegal first provided for a President with a seven–year term of office and a Prime Minister chosen by the legislature. The first president was Leopold Sedar Senghor, a well–known educator and literary figure, apart from his political stature, who had been a respected statesman not only in Senegal, but throughout the former French West Africa. The largest political party, the *Progressive Senegalese Union,* now the *Socialist Party,* was led by him. Political rivalry between the president and Prime Minister Mamadou Dia, led to an attempt by Dia to seize control of the government in 1962. This was quelled without bloodshed, but caused Dia's imprisonment and the adoption of a new constitution replacing the former parliamentary system with a presidential government for a period of time.

The *Socialist Party (PS)* won all 100 seats in the National Assembly in elections held in January 1973; all were selected from a single–party list. President Senghor was reelected to a five–year term.

Constitutional amendments provided for additional political parties and indefinite eligibility of the president to be reelected. Further provision was made for succession to the presidency by the prime minister after that office was reestablished. The additional political parties had little success; President Senghor was overwhelmingly reelected in 1978 to another five–year term.

In perhaps the most orderly transfer of power seen in post–independent present–day Africa, the aging president resigned his office on December 31, 1980, and turned it over to his able prime minister, Abdou Diouf, who completed his predecessor's term of office.

In February 1983 President Diouf rolled up an impressive victory in democratic elections; both he and the *PS* received more than 80% of the vote. Seven other parties competed in the contest. The candidates for president included Mamadou Dia.

Although there was protest before the nation's Supreme Court that the elections were not properly conducted, the charges, unsupported, were rejected. The *Senegalese Democratic Party,* however, did elect eight members to the National Assembly. Apparently recognizing that they could not conquer while divided, seven opposition parties gathered in 1985 under the name *Senegalese Democratic Union.* All had two things in common: they were leftist and wanted *rapid* changes from the old order. When the new coalition created a Central Committee and a Politburo, this, however, was too much for the government, which proceeded to outlaw the organization on the ground that parties were prohibited from grouping together. The various elements have since split anew.

Diouf initiated a law which allows unlimited democracy; Senegal now has 16 political parties. Seven of them participated in February 1988 elections for the National Assembly.

Democracy prevails in Senegal, but within limitations. Opposition to the administrations of Diouf centered around Abdoulaye Wade's *Senegalese Democratic Party (PDS),* the principal non–government in 1983 and 1988 elections. The result of these contests was heavily weighted in favor of Diouf's supporters. After brief bitter opposition following the 1988 elections, Wade and three other opposition leaders joined in a coalition government with the socialists; this lasted until late 1992 when they resigned, com-

President Abdou Diouf

plaining that they had been influential on only minor and trivial decisions.

The real reason for the resignations was the desire to freely compete in elections held in February 1993. Due to splintered and divided opposition, President Diouf won reelection handily.

Senegal has a multitude of tensions in addition to those based on competitive politics. The government is composed of Islamic moderates who dress in western styles. As in other regions of Africa in the 1990s, Fundamentalist Islamics are a very significant group that engenders more than a little instability and unpredictability.

In 1989 Mauritania, gripped by a fundamentalist "Back to Islam" movement, expelled more than 1,000 people southward to Senegal—Wolof, Fulani and Tukuler—on the ground that they were not Mauritanian. Armed conflict over the issue between the two nations was barely avoided; the ousted people are still living within Senegal as refugees. A second problem is a separatist revolt which has simmered in the southern province of Casamance for a generation. Originally caused by ethnic and religious differences, the rebellion has emerged as a movement seeking independence based on little more than greed. A cease–fire agreement in 1994 was effective for only a few days; sporadic violence continues.

Adverse economic conditions in 1993–4 led to cuts in the civil service and general wage reductions, both of which were unpopular. When students went on strike in 1994, the academic year was voided—everyone will have to repeat the work. Three opposition parties have gathered into the *Bokk Sopi Senegal* ("Unity to Change Senegal"); it is led by Abdoulaye Wade, Landing Savane and Mamadou Dia.

Senegal's first president, Hon. Leopold Sedar Senghor

Culture: The gleaming beauty of Dakar, the busy seaport and capital of Senegal, is almost unique among the cities of Africa. The city has grown by leaps and bounds and is peopled by modern, urban dwellers of many cultures. There are, of course, inevitable slum areas, which have grown dramatically in recent years when the eastern part of Senegal has been gripped by drought.

The younger generation tends toward European clothing styles, but the traditional long, flowing *Sabador* and *Grand Boubou* for formal occasions and the traditionally less elaborate, loose fitting costumes, are resplendent with brilliant colors and prints. The port facilities at Dakar are almost constantly filled by a procession of ships from every nation of the world, particularly when the Suez Canal was closed in 1967. The modern airport, capable of handling the largest jets, is a stopping point for almost every transcontinental airline.

Wielding great influence in this largely Islamic nation are "the brotherhoods." The clout of these conservative societies is through their religious hold on the peo-

A small industry: military arm patches   World Bank photo

The Caliph of Murid

The Caliph of Tijanis

ple. Their opinions strongly influence the political, commercial and social life of the country.

The most numerous of these is the *Tijanis* (Tea–*jan*–is), although the *Murid* (Moo–reed) owns the largest peanut plantations and is considered the most influential. The *Hadria* (Hod–ria) is the third. Each has its own spiritual leader, or *Caliph General* (pronounced *Hah*–leaf). The power of this high office is passed down through the family.

The life of the people of the interior revolves around the cultivation of peanuts, produced in tremendous quantities. Rural folk, with rich traditions of Moslem–Sudanic origin, they have relatively fair skin and are proud and tall, with classic features.

Economy: Senegal's economy has been totally dependent upon the production of peanuts for the past three decades; production now exceeds well over one million metric tons a year, made possible by improved methods of cultivation and development of plantations to replace smaller farms. France supported peanut prices until 1967. Production has been uneven since then because of adverse weather conditions. Other problems have included what the government has termed "peasant malaise." This actually was a boycott consisting of a refusal to (1) grow peanuts and (2) to market them through the national monopoly. Higher prices and immediate payment led to widespread smuggling of the crop into The Gambia. (The direction reversed periodically when prices were higher in Senegal than in The Gambia.)

The state–run monopoly pays only half of the export price to the farmer; the re-mainder is supposed to be held against the threat of low yields in future years. In reality, it is used for government support and ordinary expenses, and a small part simply disappears into the teeming bureaucracy of Dakar.

The dependence on peanuts has been markedly reduced since the early 1980s. A drought parched the land for more than a decade, forcing the abandonment of marginal land and decreased peanut crops. The price of this primary export took a tumble (but has risen since the late 1980s). One of the largest obstacles to higher Senegalese prosperity is U.S. protection of its own peanut farmers (paid for by U.S. consumers). A switch to other crops has been steadily underway, but with limited success. In spite of being agriculturally–based, the per capita annual income of Senegal is relatively high for West Africa.

Periodic loans from the International Monetary Fund have enabled Senegal economically to survive. The conditions for these loans have been difficult: austerity and more austerity. This has included disposing of several government monopolies and reduced salaries for government workers, as well as the "final" solution: elimination of government jobs.

Almost a million Europeans are annually attracted to Senegal's beautiful beaches and warm sun during northern winter months.

The Future: Adverse economic conditions will fuel fires of discontent in Senegal. The government will continue to limit any alternative to its control.

The Republic of Sierra Leone (pronounced See–*air*–uh Lee–*own*)

The old commercial district in Freetown.

AP/Wide World Photo

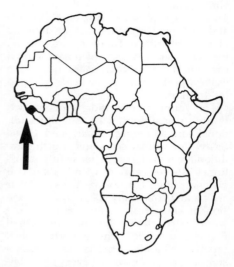

Area: 72,326 sq. km. = 27,900 sq. mi. (slightly larger than West Virginia)

Population: 4.4 million (estimated).

Capital City: Freetown (Pop. 530,000, estimated).

Climate: Equatorial, very warm and humid.

Neighboring Countries: Guinea (North and Northwest); Liberia (Southeast).

Official Language: English.

Other Principal Tongues: Krio (a widely spoken "pidgin English" dialect), Mende, Limba, and Temne.

Ethnic Background: Mende (South); Temne (North); Creole (descendents of freed slaves from almost every part of Africa) and 18 smaller groups.

Principal Religions: Traditional tribal beliefs (45%); Islam (30%); Christianity (25%)—figures are approximate.

Chief Commercial Products: Resources include diamonds (industrial), iron ore, palm products, cocoa coffee. All of this is virtually unavailable through legitimate commercial means, but is abundant through "unofficial sources"—i.e. thieves.

Per Capita Annual Income: About U.S. $285.

Currency: Leone.

Former Colonial Status: British Colony (1808–1961)

Independence Date: April 19, 1961.

Chief of State: Capt. Valentine E.M. Strasser, Chairman, *National Provisional Ruling Council* (April 1992).

National Flag: Three equal horizontal stripes of green, white and blue.

Sierra Leone lies on the legendary Gold Coast of the immense portion of Africa that extends westward into the Atlantic above the equator. Its climate is almost identical with that of the Zaïre (Congo) River Basin to the southeast—hot, rainy and oppressively humid. The Freetown area along the seacoast receives 150 inches of rain each year, and the relative humidity seldom drops below 80%. The coastal belt, averaging sixty miles in width, is a region of dense mangrove swamps quite similar to the Florida Everglades.

Stretches of wooded hill country rise from the coastal belt to gently rolling plateaus in the North. Mountains tower to heights of 6,000 feet in the southeast area near the Moa River. Although there is a nominally dry season from November to April, heavy rains, especially in July, August and September, contribute to the dense, jungle growth characteristic of portions of Sierra Leone. This compact green vegetation contains the many species of the rain forest, but few of the hoofed animals of the African plains.

History: Sierra Leone was thinly populated by the Mende and Temne people, who date back to unknown times when the Portuguese explorer Pedro de Cintra visited the coastal area in 1460. Impressed by the beauty of the mountains of the southeast, he name the territory *Sierra Leone*—"Lion Mountains." For details of earlier and colonial history, see Historical Background and *The British in Africa*.

Following achievement of independence in 1961, the constitutional parliamentary government was controlled by the *Sierra Leone People's Party (SLPP)*, led initially by Sir Milton Margai, and, after his death in 1964, by his brother, Sir Albert Margai. Elections held in 1967 were hotly contested by a rival party, the *All People's Congress*, led by Siaka Stevens. The Mende and Temne people of the interior supported the *SLPP* and the coastal Creoles favored the *APC*. A pre–election attempt of Margai to outlaw the *APC* failed. Early returns indicated that the *APC* had captured 32 seats in the parliament to 28 for the *SLPP*. Governor General Sir Henry Josiah Lightfoot Boston (a Creole) quickly gave the oath of office to Siaka Stevens, making him Prime Minister. The military arrested both Stevens and Boston ten minutes later.

The National Reformation Council, established by the officers, continued in power until April 1968. Both Margai and Stevens were imprisoned and later exiled— Margai died in 1980 near Washington, D.C.

A group of non–commissioned officers ousted the *National Reformation Council* in 1968 and brought Siaka Stevens from exile in Guinea to be Prime Minister. He ruled during the following years with increasing repression, subduing rioting of Margai supporters in the interior with army troops. A state of emergency was proclaimed in late 1970 because of continued agitation against Stevens.

Fearful because a loss of respect for him was evident by late 1970, Stevens went to Guinea in 1971 and signed a "defense" treaty with the leftist regime of Sékou Touré in that country. He established ties with the communist bloc nations. Stevens introduced into Parliament a bill in 1971 empowering him to proclaim Sierra Leone a republic; the bill was quickly approved and Stevens was unanimously elected president. "Elections" in 1973 resulted in a resounding Stevens victory.

In 1978 a referendum was held to decide on a one–party state; not surprisingly, 97.1% voted "Yes." In one northern province, out of almost 1 million votes, not one brave soul voted "no." Stevens was sworn in for a 7–year term under the new constitution, the sole party being his *APC*. He rejoiced in the rejection by the voters of ". . . the worn–out, multi–party (system) . . . inherited from our colonial master, Britain."

Affairs in Sierra Leone were very quiet under Stevens' rule. Occasional cabinet shuffles and political unrest were only sporadic. Economic adversities common to this area of Africa were present, and the International Monetary Fund periodically granted "standby" loans to help cover deficits. External debt repayments amounting to $400 million were rescheduled.

As Stevens' term was coming to a close in 1985, elections were postponed for six months. Army chief Maj. General Joseph Momoh was designated by the elderly leader as his successor, and proceeded to campaign on promises of "discipline" and "political accountability." Receiving 90% of the votes cast, he was installed in office in December 1985. Of mixed, northern tribal heritage, he received his training in England. He was reelected (unopposed) in early 1988.

President Momoh has made some efforts to bring order to the chaos which had gripped the economy. Subsidies on both rice and gasoline were gradually reduced, but the effect of this was modified by falling world oil prices. Stricter controls were placed on diamond and gold marketing in order to reduce smuggling. Nevertheless, the company buying and exporting diamonds closed its operations in 1988 because of continued economic instability.

Momoh's austerity measures, insisted upon by the International Monetary Fund, lowered the standard of living and had met with mounting opposition. Government corruption has been so deeply rooted that it is difficult to know where to begin to rid Sierra Leone of this plague. When a measure was taken to require all civil servants to appear personally and collect their pay in cash, it was discovered that in one agency 75% of the listed workers *did not exist!*

Under considerable pressure to permit multi-party reforms, Momoh had promised free presidential elections by November 1992, but he did not move quickly enough, and after a *coup* in April 1992 fled to Guinea.

Captain Valentine E.M. Strasser led the *coup* which brought the National Provisional Ruling Council to power, later changed to the *Supreme Council of State* in July. It promised to end all evils in Sierra Leone within a short time. The *coup* simply put a swollen army of 12,000 in power; Strasser is reported to be increasingly isolated and unable to control his troops. Discontent is heightened by the sight of young troops careening around in sporty 4x4 vehicles.

Culture: The Mende of the North and the Temne of the South constitute 60% of the population, largely rural people dwelling in the interior regions. There are 18 smaller groups each with its own language and cultural traditions in the inland area. Krio, the "pidgin English" dialect of the coastal Creoles, is widely spoken among all of the ethnic groups of the nation, a language perpetuated by many folk tales and proverbs. The loose–fitting clothing worn by the people is similar to that of other West African nations—colorful and flowing.

The Fourah Bay College, founded in 1827 at Freetown, is the oldest seat of education in western Africa. This institution and Njala University College are parts of the University of Sierra Leone, with a present enrollment of more than 3,000. Primary and secondary education, well–established in the coastal towns and cities, is gradually being instituted in the remote

Captain Valentine E.M. Strasser, Chairman and Head of State, National Provisional Ruling Council (NPRC)

interior. In spite of this, literacy remains at about 20%.

Sierra Leone has a very distinct cultural heritage different from any other area of Africa, established and developed as the country became a melting pot for freed slaves and their descendants. Freetown, a busy seaport and the capital, is a comparatively modern city, although somewhat uncomfortable because of the heat and humidity. The urban dwellers reflect the diversity of origin, containing a substantial community of Europeans.

Economy: There has been not only a total lack of economic progress in Sierra Leone, but actually a steep decline in income. Increased population and decreased production have taken a terrible toll. Under Margai, several initially attractive light manufacturing ventures were undertaken, but were doomed to failure. Government mismanagement has never crept out of the basement insofar as basic skills and talents are concerned. The result: per capita real income is now about 15% of what it was in 1961.

Mining had replaced agriculture are the prime source of income by 1951, based on diamonds, iron ore and bauxite. But these products have made little real progress. The country's oil import bill has more than trebled since 1978, but exports declined during the same period. The reason for this terrible state of affairs: theft. Sierra Leone has been described by some as a kleptocracy, and indeed, theft is a national pastime. Diamond smuggling is a finely polished art.

The economy is 97% underground in order to make it easier to evade taxes, and even better yet, to avoid the payment of ordinary debts. No nation or company does business here without first obtaining payment in advance in hard, western currencies. Of course, the result is a shortage of everything. Inventories of essentials and spare parts are impossible to maintain. The dreadful and huge bureaucracy is periodically trimmed back, but is like a hydra: for every head that is lopped off, two (or more) appear to take its place.

The Future: Sierra Leone, in its present state, has no future. It will be a paradise for thieves, taken seriously only by thieves. Even if something is nailed down behind closed, locked doors in the evening, chances are it will be missing in the morning, particularly if it is portable. But even bulldozers disappear. Look for change(s) of government and/or disorganized strife in Sierra Leone. The U.S. will continue to feed 1.5 million people at an annual cost of $18 million.

The Republic of Togo

A balanced converstion in Lomé

AP/Wide World Photo

Area: 56,950 sq. km. = 21,988 sq. mi. (Half of Mississippi, vertically).

Population: 4 million (estimated).

Capital City: Lomé (Pop. 421,000, estimated).

Climate: Warm, humid and tropical.

Neighboring Countries: Ghana (West); Burkina Faso (Upper Volta, North); Benin (East).

Official Languages: French, Kabiye, Ewe.

Other Principal Tongues: Mina, Cotocoli, Konkomba.

Ethnic Background: Ewe, Kabrais, Mina, Ghen, Konkomba, Bassari, Akposso, Bedere, Bogo–Ahlon and six other smaller groups of West African Negro and Sudanic origin.

Principal Religions: Traditional beliefs (about 50%), Christianity (Roman Catholic, about 35%), Islam (about 15%).

Chief Commercial Products: Phosphates, cocoa, coffee, cotton, kapok, peanuts, palm oil.

Per Capita Annual Income: About U.S. $370.

Currency: CFA Franc (no longer tied to the French franc).

Former Colonial Status: German Colony (1885–1916), French Colony (1916–1960).

Independence Date: April 27, 1960.

Chief of State: General Gnassingbé Eyadema, President, b. 1930. (Pronounced Nah–sing–*bay* Aye–ah–*day*–mah)

Head of Government (in theory): Kokou Koffigoh, Interim Prime Minister (since August 1991).

National Flag: Green, yellow and red horizontal stripes with a white star in the red portion.

Lying almost in the center of the Gold and Ivory coasts, Togo is a long, narrow country stretching 360 miles from the blue Atlantic into the interior. This small nation is only thirty–one miles wide at the coast and 100 miles in width at its broadest point. As is common to this region of Africa, the climate of Togo is predominantly hot and humid on the coast with a drier and slightly cooler region in the North. Picturesque Lake Togo, with quiet, fresh water, is located in the central coast region, a center of modern recreational facilities. The central section is traversed by the Togo Mountains and is succeeded in the North by a level territory of farms.

History: Not much is known of the pre–colonial history of this region of Africa. That which is known is based on tradition passed on verbally through many generations of people living in Togo at the time of the first European explorations. From the ethnic background of the people, it is certain that the majority of the population, of West African Negro origin, had lived there for countless centuries. A smaller group, of Sudanic ancestry, settled in northern Togo during the period of their migration westward from the Sudan–Nile region in the 10th–13th centuries. For details of early and colonial history, see Historical Background and *The Germans in Africa* and *The French in Africa*.

Pre–independence elections installed Nicholas Grunitzky of the *Togo Progressive Party* as president. The *Togo Unity Party* subsequently gained in popularity and membership under the leadership of Sylvanus Olympio. This well–educated man spoke many foreign languages as well as the native Ewe dialect. Olympio was not a native of Togo, having been brought to Africa from Brazil by his father when he was a small child. Ostensibly a moderate, after becoming president in 1960, he disqualified the *Togo Progressive Party* from participating in 1961 elections; the *Togo Unity Party* won 90% of the vote and all 51 seats in the assembly. Grunitzky, who was Olympio's brother–in–law, went to Benin in semi–exile.

Shortly after a state visit to the United States, Olympio was assassinated in early

1963 outside the U.S. Embassy in Lomé where he had been seeking refuge. Grunitzky returned later and was named Prime Minister by Sgt. Etienne Eyadema who was in the group that killed Olympio. A new constitution was adopted and four political parties participated in elections held in 1963 which were officially won by Grunitzky's *Togo Progressive Party*; he became president.

The followers of Olympio attempted a *coup* in 1966, but Eyadema, by then a Lt. Colonel, assisted in resisting the move successfully.

Dissatisfied with a general lack of progress which he attributed to the time–consuming bickering of politicians, Etienne Eyadema seized power in 1967, abolishing all parties. He later formed the *Togo Popular Rally* and ran in 1972 as the sole candidate for president, receiving about 90% of the vote in a "yes" or "no" contest.

Although Eyadema accused a French phosphate firm of attempting to arrange his death in 1973, retaliating by seizing the firm's assets, agreements were reached with the French in 1976 for extended economic and cultural ties between the two nations.

There have been repeated assassination attempts against Eyadema's life. It cannot be ascertained whether these attempts were real or were announced for public consumption. All—in 1977, 1979, 1983 and 1986—were alleged to be backed by Olympio sympathizers or by his sons. The last two were supposed to be the work of Gilchrist Olympio. After his inauguration for another term in late 1987, Eyadema, in response to growing criticism from human rights organizations, released 526 political prisoners and commuted the death sentences of eleven more. Reports persist of continued detentions under his iron rule.

General Eyadema is a rather tall, athletic man, extremely conscious of the dignity of his high office. He works long hours at his desk, but he has good reason to be nervous about the many plots constantly brewing against him. Modesty is not one of his virtues. A few years ago a small plane in which he was flying crashed in northern Togo. The pilot and co–pilot were killed, yet the president survived without injury—*miraculously!* Soon after, a modernistic circular monument was erected on the spot, with the ruins of the plane enshrined therein. A huge, heroic statue of the president presides over the scene, and a ceremony is held each year to celebrate his escape.

General Eyadema visited Washington in October 1983 in order to encourage U.S. investment . . . with very limited success. A visit to France in 1985 was more successful. The IMF had extended Togo further credits based on its performance in 1984–5 and again in 1989.

Assassination and torture have been used routinely by Eyadema and the military in Togo for almost three decades. Educated Togolese regard the president as crude and low–class. In 1991 it briefly appeared that Eyadema's strangle–hold on Togo might be broken when the presidency was stripped of almost all power. However, Eyadema's support by the military remained steadfast. His chosen prime minister, Kokou Koffigoh quickly became subservient to his wishes.

The only potential rival in 1992 elections was disposed of when Gilchrist Olympio, the son of the assassinated Sylvanus, was almost killed in an assassination attempt. He underwent many

President Eyadema

months of medical treatment in France because of his severe injuries. He refused to return to Togo for medical examination, justifiably fearing that the Togolese doctors would murder him.

Eyadema waffled on elections until a law was passed allowing him to run even though he is a member of the military. Finally held in mid–1993, they were a sham—as many dead people as live ones voted. Eyadema reportedly won by 95%. Legislative elections in 1994 were just as silly. In late 1994 the legislature decreed a halt to all legal proceedings against those who opposed the presidential and legislative balloting—including Gilchrist Olympio.

Two journalists who reported that Eyadema had acquired a *rocket*–proof Mercedes luxury car for more than $500,000 were summarily jailed.

Culture: The people of the populous southern coast area are better educated and economically better off than those of the sparsely settled North—a pattern common to many countries in this area of Africa. The Ewe people have dominated the cultural life in Togo and extend be-

yond its borders well into Ghana to the west. There are few communities that lack educational facilities within the Ewe country. Although a few of this group continue the animist and pagan customs of their past, most are Christians, widely employed and leading modern, urban lives. In spite of this, the literacy rate of Togo as a whole is about 20%.

The lives of the people further inland are based upon small family holdings of farmland, and they have little daily contact with the larger cities of the South. The brilliantly–colored costumes of these people, with their lengths of shining beads and elaborate headdresses, are distinctive.

Economy: Small family–type farms which grow cocoa and coffee are the basis of the predominantly agricultural economy of Togo. Income dropped sharply when the price of cocoa descended from $3,700 a ton in 1977 to $700 a ton in 1981. Although the price is now back to $1,500, the exchange rate of the dollar against European currencies and the CFA Franc has had the effect of deflating the actual price.

A large phosphate deposit, having a production of more than 1–1/2 million tons a year, is being mined at Kpeme, near Lomé. Phosphate exports constitute the number one source of income, but 90% of the people are employed in agriculture and stock raising. Foreign aid has been instrumental in improving the prosperity of Togo, which has achieved a moderate rate of economic growth, interrupted temporarily by the recession of 1980–1982. A large harbor at Lomé boosts the economy by facilitating exports from and through Togo. An annual subsidy provided by France to make up for the annual deficit of Togo was withdrawn in early 1993, and virtually all other sources of aid have dried up. All prior foreign debts of Togo are meaningless—there is no hope whatsoever they will be paid. Togo has joined the ranks of nations on a C.O.D. trade basis; ships won't even go there unless their cargo has been paid for in advance in hard, western currency.

The Future: Togo will remain politically stifled until Eyadema is disposed of and army control is ended. At least 48 were summarily executed after a January 1994 attempted *coup* in Lomé. Most adults have lived all of their life under Eyadema and know very little about genuine democracy.

CENTRAL WEST AFRICA

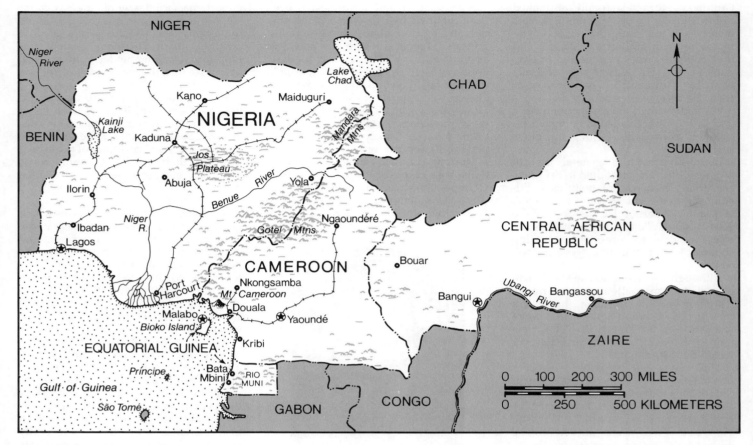

The Republic of Cameroon

Area: 475,400 sq. km = 183,552 sq. mi. (The size of California and 1/4 of Oregon).

Population: 12.5 million (estimated).

Capital City: Yaoundé (Pop. 470,000, estimated; pronounced Yah–oon–*deh*).

Climate: Hot and humid in the South, progressively becoming drier to the inland north; arid in the Lake Chad area.

Neighboring Countries: Nigeria (Northwest); Chad (Northeast); Central African Republic (East); Congo, Gabon, Equatorial Guinea (South).

Official Languages: French (East Cameroon) and English (West Cameroon).

Other Principal Tongues: There are twenty–four major native languages, most of which are Bantu dialects.

Ethnic Background: There are 200 ethnic groups in Cameroon; Cameroon Highlanders (31%), Equatorial Bantu (19%), Kirdi (11%), Fulani (10%), Northwestern Bantu (8%), Eastern Sudanic (7%), other African (13%). Figures are approximate.

Principal Religions: Christianity (about 53%), traditional beliefs (about 25%), Islam (about 22%).

Chief Commercial Products: Crude Oil, Refined Petroleum, Cocoa, coffee, bananas, timber, aluminum, cotton, palm products, peanut oil, rubber, tobacco and tea.

Per Capita Annual Income: About U.S. $1,100.

Currency: CFA Franc (no longer tied to the French franc).

Former Colonial Status: German Colony (1884–1916), British Colony in West Cameroon (1916–1961); French Colony is East Cameroon (1916–1960).

Independence Date: January 1, 1960 (East Cameroon); October 1, 1961 (West Cameroon independence and federation with East Cameroon).

Chief of State: Paul Biya, President (1982).

National Flag: Three vertical stripes of green, yellow and red with two golden stars on the green.

This land of contrasts, containing almost every species of flora and fauna of tropical Africa and numerous varieties of wild game, stretches north from the Atlantic in a "hinge" position between West and Central Africa. From the Polynesian–like beaches, washed by the waters of the Bight of Biafra, there rise towering mountains which proceed directly north into West Cameroon. Mount Cameroon, the tallest peak in western Africa, towering almost 14,000 feet high, is presently an active volcano located close to the seacoast. Reportedly christened *Chariot of the Gods* by Hannon, a Carthaginian chief of the 6th century B.C., this volcano, with a base of about 700 square miles, erupted as recently as 1959. The southern part of Cameroon, extending eastward in a horizontal line, is characterized by a low coastal basin with equatorial jungles. In the more north–central part of the country there is a series of grassy plateaus whose heights reach 4,500 feet, but in the extreme northern Lake Chad region, the dry climate supports only seasonal grazing and nomadic herding, culminating in a marshland. This area has been gripped for the last decade in the drought of the *Sahel*, with disastrous results, causing inhabitants to flee southward in order to live.

History: Cameroon has been inhabited since early times, containing relics of prehistoric societies in the North. Commerce with the Mediterranean region was active, with trade routes across the Sahara Desert used to transport ivory, panther skins, ostrich feathers, bronze and salt to Egypt and other early civilizations. Originally populated by pygmies, who are now found only in small numbers along the southern border, Cameroon was successively dominated by other native groups. The Bantus arrived in substantial numbers in the 15th century, settling in the central plateau region. In 1472, a Portuguese explorer, Fernão do Poo (Fernando Po in Spanish) arrived on the coast of what is now Cameroon. For details of early and colonial history, see Historical Background, *The British in Africa*, *The Germans in Africa* and *The French in Africa*.

France granted independence to East Cameroon on January 1, 1960; the British relinquished West Cameroon on October 1, 1961, and there was a reunification of the two Cameroons. A Federation Constitution was adopted and a single–party system emerged, based upon the *Cameroon National Unity Party (UNC)*. President Ahmadou Ahidjo (from East Cameroon) and Vice–President John Foncha (from West Cameroon) received 97.5% of the vote in 1970 elections. Constitutional reforms in 1972 eliminated the state government of the two regions, but guaranteed the continuation of the French language in the East and English in the West. Subsequent reforms in 1984 simply reaffirmed that Cameroon is a bilingual nation.

Ahmadou Ahidjo, possessing a high school education, was a master politician in his ability to pull about 200 tribes together under a single government. Legislative elections were held in 1978 and presidential elections in 1980 at which time President Ahidjo was elected to a fifth five–year term. All candidates were from the *Cameroon National Union (UNC)*.

Coming as a complete surprise, President Ahidjo resigned on November 6, 1982, handing over power to the Prime Minister, Paul Biya, who completed Ahidjo's term of office. The former president was said to be exhausted. There was a supposed attempted *coup* against Biya in August 1983 by two former aides of Ahi-

President Paul Biya

djo. After a "trial" of the two in February 1984 they, and Ahidjo (in absentia, living in France) were sentenced to death; the sentences were commuted by Biya to "detention." In January 1984 elections, President Biya, a Christian from the south, was elected in his own right to a five–year term of office by a margin of 99.98% Although it was technically possible for persons to run against him, in reality, legal obstacles made this impossible and practicality made it unwise.

In an effort to consolidate his power and eliminate potential competition, President Biya saw to it that the constitution was amended to eliminate the office of Prime Minister. The name of the nation was changed from the "United Republic of Cameroon" to simply the "Republic of Cameroon.

In early April 1984 there was another attempted *coup*. Fierce fighting erupted in Yaoundé—mutinous members of the Republican Guard, which was supposed to *protect* the president, composed mostly of Islamic northerners, waged a pitched battle with regular army units. Biya, after the rebellion was snuffed out, announced that it was on behalf of Ahidjo, who still was in Paris. The official number of deaths was "about 70," but the actual number was probably close to 1,500. Within weeks, 35 were tried and summarily executed. Almost 1,000 others who had been detained were released.

Five members of the *Cameroon Times* staff, an English weekly published in West Cameroon, were arrested and held briefly for publishing articles critical of President Biya and alleging corruption in the government. It is well known that revenues from oil production are diverted in part into secret accounts.

In order to demonstrate his "New

Deal" policies, President Biya changed the name of the sole legal party in 1985 to the *Cameroon Democratic Rally (RDPC)*. This was done at a convention in Bamenda, the capital of the English–speaking portion of Cameroon; in 1986 party balloting (secret) resulted in the ouster of several officials who had served under Ahidjo—a consolidation of power by the president.

Tragedy struck Cameroon in mid–1986 in the regions surrounding Lake Nyos when the lake belched forth a cloud of deadly carbon dioxide and hydrogen sulphide. Since these gases are heavier than air and were trapped by the surrounding hills, more than two thousand people were fatally suffocated within a few minutes; thousands of cattle and animals were killed.

French and Cameroonian scientists began an experiment in April 1992 in order to see whether it is possible to pump water saturated with carbon dioxide and sulphur from the bottom of the 600–foot–deep lake in the hopes of reducing the possibility of another frightening gas release.

President Biya advanced elections scheduled for early 1989 to April 24, 1988. The *RDPC* approved 324 candidates to contest 180 seats; the result was a National Assembly with younger members. The president was reelected with a 98.75% majority. Having received the mandate he sought, Biya announced wide–ranging programs to pare the size of the bureaucracy and cut government expenditures. The result was a positive response to requests for foreign aid.

Summary arrests of journalists and widespread unrest followed the approval of a multi–party system in 1990. Regrettably, the opposition was divided into 48 parties, none very strong. But this was translated into reality in legislative elections in March 1992; the *RDCP* received 88 of the 180 seats. Principal opponents were the *National Union for Democracy and Progress (UNDP)* which elected 68 members and the *Union of Peoples of Cameroon (UPC)* which won 18. There were boycotts of the balloting by 16 of the opposition parties, including that of popular English–speaker John Fru Ndi's *Social Democratic Front*.

Presidential balloting was advanced from the spring of 1993 to October 1992 in order to catch the divided opposition unprepared, and was marred by massive fraud and irregularities. The state–owned television gave 2–1/2 hours of time to Biya, but only 16 minutes to the opposition.

The opposition has refused to meaningfully participate in government, and Biya has responded with harsh measures. In late 1993 a police water cannon truck rammed Fru Ndi's auto to prevent his attendance at a press conference. Insulting the president by the press is a crime causing immediate imprisonment. Opposition activists are frequently detained. Despite political turmoil, France, the IMF and the World Bank continue to extend credits to Cameroon.

Culture: The great majority of the people in Cameroon live in the simple, rural tribal life of their ancestors. There is a great diversity which is clarified by the religious grouping in the nation with Christians in the Southwest. Animists (half the people) live in the central interior and a substantial community of Islamic people are located in the North. The many ethnic groups which make up the population each have a distinct heritage of art, music and folklore.

Yaoundé, the capital, is a modern city with good hotels, fine French restaurants and other modern facilities. The bustling commercial center of Cameroon is attractive Douala, which has an excellent museum and colorful markets.

Educational facilities in Cameroon are limited, but compare very favorably with most Black African nations. The literacy rate in the South is more than 40%. Enrollment at the University in Yaoundé is increasing. Four fifths of the urban population is French–speaking while the remainder uses English. School children are required to study both languages from age 11, and all business in the National Assembly is done in the two languages simultaneously. (The author is proud to note that his late father, Professor Leon E. Dostert, was the pioneer and developer of simultaneous translation, first used at the Nurnberg War Crimes Tribunal and later at the UN—a system still favored in that world body.) Bilingual programs are provided on the government–run radio. The *Cameroon Tribune*, the leading government–owned newspaper comes out daily in French; its companion *Cameroon Times* in English is a weekly. But it is clear that undercurrents of antipathy between the two language groups still exist.

Radio broadcasts are available in both languages as well as in ten regional ones. Television made its debut in 1987, broadcasting Thursday to Sunday.

Economy: The backbone of Cameroon's trade traditionally has been its cacao and coffee crops. Because Cameroon was too dependent on these two commodities, when world prices dropped, there was a severe shock to the economy. For this reason the government began a ''green revolution'' in 1972, investing heavily into large farming operations for growing cotton, tobacco, tea and rubber. This diversification of crops is now paying off. Oil production is now the number one source of foreign earnings, both in the form of crude oil and refined products. In spite of this, 70% of the people make their living from the land—farmers producing about one–third of the country's income. Aluminum production now exceeds a level of 50,000 metric tons a year due to additional hydroelectric facilities.

In highly ambitious and visible projects, substantial sums are being invested to wipe out the slums which surround Yaoundé and Douala.

Skillful management has resulted in a trade surplus and a government which spends less than it takes in. Mechanization in agriculture offers distinct possibilities to significantly raise the income of Cameroon. This moderately prosperous African nation has been in the past a relatively good place for investment.

The Future: The major question facing Cameroon is whether the degree of political and human rights repression now being applied is justified by built–in division and differences of the people. The answer is no, it is not. It is an image of French colonial techniques and is distasteful. A total of 16 groups have joined together in a populist coalition led by Fru which does not bode well for the president.

The old way of cultivation, Cameroon

The Central African Republic

Area: 626,780 sq. km. = 242,000 sq. mi. (the size of Texas and New Mexico).

Population: 3.3 million (estimated).

Capital City: Bangui (Pop 640,000, estimated; pronounced Ban–*ghe*).

Climate: Temperate, with a rainy season (June to October) and a dry season (November to May).

Neighboring Countries: Congo and Zaïre (South); Cameroon (West); Chad (Northwest); The Sudan (Northeast and East).

Official Language: French.

Other Principal Tongues: Sangho (national, widely used language).

Ethnic Background: Banda (47% and Banda–Mandjia (27%) other (26%). Figures are approximate.

Principal Religions: Protestant (40%), Roman Catholic (24%), Islam (8%); traditional tribal beliefs are intermingled with the religious beliefs of the Christians.

Chief Commercial Products: Cotton, coffee, diamonds, lumber.

Per Capita Annual Income: About U.S. $450.

Currency: CFA Franc (no longer tied to the French franc).

Former Colonial Status: French Colony (1894–1960).

Independence Date: August 11, 1960.

Chief of State: Ange-Felix Patasse, President.

National Flag: Four horizontal stripes (from top to bottom) of blue, white, green and yellow, divided by a red stripe down the middle, with a yellow star on the left hand side of the blue stripe.

Located in almost the exact center of Africa, the Central African Republic is a vast, rolling plateau rising 2,000 to 2,500 feet above sea level. Lying more than 300 miles from the sea, this sun–drenched land of agricultural and forest products found its original wealth in ivory from its once large herds of massive elephants. Prolific groups of wild animals roam the land today, making it one of the most zoologically interesting areas of Africa.

There is a small area of jungle in the southwest which is rapidly succeeded by the rolling plateaus of the plains, rising gently to the mountains of the northeast. Heavy rainstorms occur almost daily during the wet season from June to October, seldom permitting the ground to become dry. The shift of the sun to the south in November is the start of the dry season when the leaves of the trees turn to brilliant hues because of lack of moisture.

In the following weeks the leaves fall, and the grass, having grown to the height of more than five feet, changes its lush green color to a tinder–dry yellow. Fire becomes a great danger as the drought continues. This grassy highland, shared with other countries by the Central African Republic, extends more than three thousand miles westward to the coast of Guinea on the Atlantic Ocean.

The Ubangi River flows along a good portion of the southern border, then plunges south to join the water of the mighty Zaïre (Congo).

History: Little is known of the early history of this remote area of Africa. The Central African Republic shared the numerous migrations of different ethnic groups, most of which are of Bantu origin. For details of earlier and colonial history, see Historical Background and *The French in Africa.*

The country gained independence on August 11, 1960, taking the name Central African Republic. The constitution initially provided for a unicameral National Assembly with 50 members elected for a five–year term by universal suffrage. David Dacko's *African Social Evolution Party* immediately won a majority in the assembly, and banned all other parties. He became the first president and was reelected in 1964 by a majority of 99.4%. Dacko established close relations with the communist Chinese; the influx of Chinese technical and diplomatic personnel aroused the resentment of the military, which ousted Dacko in 1966. General Jean–Bedel Bokassa assumed power and abolished the constitution, dissolved the legislature and transferred administrative duties to his appointed cabinet.

There were constant Cabinet changes during Bokassa's rule and several attempts on his life. In early 1976, one resulted in death sentences for alleged conspirators, including the President's son–in–law.

Bokassa proclaimed himself president for life in 1972 through the country's sole political party, the *Movement for Social Evolution of Black Africa,* but that was not nearly enough for the short Field Marshal. In late 1976 a new constitution brought into being the Central African *Empire.* In late 1977 in sweltering Bangui, a crowd of over 3,000 guests witnessed Jean–Bedel Bokassa place a 2,000–diamond encrusted crown on his head and proclaim himself Emperor Bokassa I. The spectacle was said to have cost well over $22 million in this land–locked country where the average per capita annual income was $120. The Emperor was outraged by some of the tongue–in–cheek news stories of his coronation. An admirer of Napoleon, Bokassa tried to give the colorful pageant as much pomp as had the one in 1804. But, muggy Bangui is no Paris.

Former Emperor Bokassa I

Student riots broke out in early 1979 following an order by the Emperor that they should wear school uniforms. The demonstrations quickly spread and assumed an anti–imperial tone. They were brutally suppressed by the Emperor's forces. Agitation continued, however, until April when the Emperor had several hundred students arrested and over one hundred killed in a Bangui prison. The commission of African jurists investigating reported that Bokassa had taken an active part in the slayings; the atrocities created outrage in world public opinion. Opposition to Bokassa continued to harden in the country and abroad.

While the the Emperor was visiting Libya, he was overthrown by his cousin and advisor, David Dacko (from whom Bokassa had seized power in 1966). With the support of French armed forces, Dacko reestablished the Republic; Bokassa was given asylum in Côte d'I-

voire. But the CAR continued to be plagued by corrupt, inept government swollen by useless insiders and relatives of the elite. Elections held in 1981 were clouded by accurate charges of fraud. When Army Chief of Staff General André Kolingba demanded President Dacko's resignation four months later, he quickly received it.

Food shortages, student unrest and general unrest marked the ensuing years. In a referendum in late 1986 a new constitution was approved which provided for only a single political party; President Kolingba, having changed from his uniform to a tuxedo, was sworn in for a six–year term. He duped former Emperor Bokassa into leaving his luxurious chateau in France and returning to the CAR, promising a hero's welcome for the witless monarch. (Although France desired his departure, it denied having anything to do with his exit.)

Bokassa was tried for multiple murders and embezzlement, but cannibalism charges were dropped. His defense was that he didn't know what his underlings had been doing. Found guilty, he was sentenced to death in 1987. This was later lowered to life imprisonment which was reduced in separate acts (all by Kolingba) to 20 years, 10 years and he was released in early September 1993. He was immediately welcomed as a guest in the presidential palace. In full regalia, he compared himself to Jesus Christ in a speech. It reasonably may be assumed that each instance of leniency was fully supported by a suitable bribe with the money he had ripped off during his years in power.

General Kolingba

President Patasse

mented by French nationals and American Peace Corps volunteers.

Elè Songo, the government (and only) newspaper is, by Western standards, very unsophisticated. It is issued daily, runs 8 pages, gives the government line, with the back page devoted to sports.

Economy: Agriculture, centered on the production of cotton and coffee, has traditionally dominated the economy—which has been in a shambles for several years. Farmers have little incentive to produce above their needs. Exports have fallen by one–third during the last two decades, and during Bokassa's 13–year rule, traditional marketing patterns were broken. Wood exports, basic to the CAR's need for foreign exchange, are sluggish. Diamond production, a vital part of the economy, has fallen 50% since 1960. It was thought that exports would be up in 1981 once Bokassa's regime had passed into history, but instead they fell. President Kolingba promised drastic measures to pull the country out of economic disas-

ter, including freezing of government salaries, but only tentative moves in that direction were taken.

Fully one–third of the country's budget is financed with external aid, principally from France, which maintains a sizable garrison of troops which basically prevents a descent into anarchy. There have unverified, but probably true, rumors of toxic waste being shipped to the CAR from France, paid for with French francs.

The limited economy will not improve until the bloated bureaucracy is reduced, which would permit business to be transacted without customary bribes.

The Future: The Central African Republic will not enter the 20th century until the 21st century has started. The country's leadership will be a "good old boys" club functioning within limitations set by Paris.

In response to pressures for multi–party democracy that increased in the early 1990s, resulted in Kolingba summoning a "Grand National Debate." Fourteen parties opposed to Kolingba's *Central African Democratic Rally (RDC)* boycotted the session. He then advanced the date of elections from 1993 to October 1992 in order to catch the opposition off balance; this strategy failed in the face of unrest and Kolingba ruled by decree. Due to the large number of presidential candidates, the contest was finally held in two rounds on September 19 and 27, 1993; Kolingba was eliminated in the first.

Ange–Felix Patasse *(Central African People's Liberation Party)* won with 52% of the vote in the second round of apparently fair elections. He formerly had been prime minister under Emperor Bokassa, but was jailed and exiled by the erratic self–styled monarch. His Prime Minister, Jean–Luc Mandaba served in the Kolingba regime before being imprisoned.

The toll from *AIDS* in the Central African Republic during the 1990s has been very high—indiscriminate sexual contact is an accepted form of entertainment.

Culture: Within this vast, thinly populated nation, nine out of ten people live in rural isolation, cultivating traditional subsistence crops on small farms, raising livestock as well as engaging in hunting and fishing. There is little contact with the central government. Elementary schools are located in most parts of the country and secondary education is found in more than 25 villages. In spite of this, the literacy rate is about 20%. The teaching staffs of the schools are supple-

BANGUI ABRITE L'ATELIER INTERNATIONAL SUR LA SANTE ANIMALE DE BASE. (Page 3)

ECONOMIE
LA BANQUE MONDIALE FAIT LE POINT SUR LE PROBLEME DE LA DETTE

OUVERTURE DES TRAVAUX D'UN ATELIER DE CONCEPTION DES COURS EN TELECOMMUNICATIONS (Page 6)

TOURNOI DE FOOT-BALL : LE CLUB UNIVERSITAIRE BANGUI (C.U.B.)... FINALISTE INATTENDU. (Page 8)

The Republic of Equatorial Guinea

A catch off Rio Muni

of the region. The mainland, formerly Rio Muni, became Mbini but is now generally again called Rio Muni.

On the protected shoreline of mainland Equatorial Guinea, hot and humid Rio Muni, the narrow white sandy beach quickly gives way to thick growth of interior jungle, where immense ebony, mahogany and oak trees crowd each other to bask in the sun. It is uniformly hot and oppressive. Few roads penetrate into the interior, but the land is thick with streams which are the home of giant frogs (as long as three feet and weighing up to six pounds!) which perch motionless on the spray–drenched rocks, their tongues darting out to catch unwary insects. Here in the steaming jungle back in the mid–1960's was found a baby gorilla which, through a genetic quirk, had a pink face and white fur.

The scenic Island of Bioko is large and was productive until the 1970's, being the source of one of the best qualities of cocoa in the world. Production was on large plantations; contract help from Nigeria was imported, but almost all fled when brutality entered the nation under the hand of the demented former ruler, Ma-cías Nguema. Ships from many nations called at the port, and the international airport was the base from which relief supplies were flown into strife–torn Nigeria in the early 1970's.

History: Almost nothing is known of the pre-colonial period of this remote part of Africa; the Fang and other Bantu people settled thinly in Rio Muni and the Bubis settled on Bioko. For details of early and colonial history, see Historical Background and *The Spanish in Africa*.

Spain granted independence to Equatorial Guinea in 1968; the territory had been internally self–governing since

Area: 28,051 sq. km = 10,830 sq. mi. (slightly larger than Vermont).

Population: 470,000 (estimated).

Capital City: Malabo (on Bioko Island, pop. 25,000, projected).

Climate: Tropically hot and humid.

Neighboring Countries: Cameroon (North); Gabon (East and South). The island portion of the country lies some twenty miles off the west coast of Cameroon.

Official Language: Spanish.

Other Principal Tongues: Fang, Bubi, Ibo.

Ethnic Background: Fang (Rio Muni), Bubi (Bioko).

Principal Religions: Most people are nominally Roman Catholic; traditional tribal beliefs are intermingled with their Christian faith.

Chief Commercial Products: Cocoa, coffee, bananas, timber.

Currency: CFA Franc (no longer tied to the French franc).

Former Colonial Status: Spanish Colony (island, 1778–1968, mainland 1885–1968).

Independence Date: October 12, 1968.

Chief of State: Col. Teodoro Obiang Nguema Mbasogo, President, Supreme Military Council (Pronounced Tay–oh–*dor*–oh *Oh*–be–ang N–*gway*–mah M–bah–*so*–go).

National Flag: Three horizontal stripes of green, white and red, with a blunt aquamarine triangle next to the staff.

Per Capita Income: About $400 (this is a very rough estimate).

Note: Between 1974 and the present, geographic place names have been changed from Spanish to African and then to *other* African designations and back to Spanish. The island, first known as Fernando Poo, was renamed by the late president in his own honor. It then was designated *Bioko* after an early king

72

1964. Elections held in 1968 under UN supervision resulted in a plurality of votes for Francisco Macías Nguema; in the run–off ballot he won a majority and was installed in office.

Disputes between the remaining Spanish people and the government of Macías in 1969 led to a demand that all Spaniards and troops be withdrawn from the country. This was not done immediately and violence erupted that threatened thousands of lives.

Almost immediately following independence Macías Nguema arranged for the arrest and execution of political figures on the ground that they were plotting his overthrow. He rapidly installed members of his family in key government posts—but he even kept a close eye on *them*. Conditions steadily worsened until by early 1969 the country was in a state of anarchy and there was widespread starvation.

Life became increasingly grim in this two–part nation. In 1972 Macías Nguema's hand–picked National Assembly named him "president for life."

His mental condition worsened by leaps and bounds; in 1974 he had a high wall built around the palace in Malabo. A report sent to the UN states that by 1974 two–thirds of the members of the 1968 National Assembly had just *disappeared*. Stories increased about imprisonment, torture and execution of anyone who so much as lifted an eyebrow against the government, and rumors of forced labor were proven to be correct. All boys between 7 and 14 were forced to receive military training or their families would suffer the consequences—generally meaning death.

Macías Nguema used the youth organization *Youth Marching with Macías* to accomplish his more grisly missions. After more than 25,000 Nigerian laborers fled the country to save their lives, arriving home penniless because their labor contracts had not been paid for, Macías Nguema expelled all the rest—there had been about 45,000 Nigerians working on the cacao plantations; he then ordered the arrest of 25,000 people on the mainland, Rio Muni, to be used as slave labor to replace them.

His madness increased. After an attempt to overthrow him in 1976, he decided to abandon Malabo on the island and set up shop in his home village of Mongomo, near the easternmost mainland border of Equatorial Guinea. In closing down government operations, he saw to it that some $60 million left in the national treasury was moved to a wooden hut in the village. Day–to–day government affairs were placed in the hands of his nephew and deputy defense minister, Lt. Col. Teodoro Obiang Nguema Mbasogo.

The nation fell into a state of abandon-

ment; journalists were barred for many years. The national currency, formerly the Ekoule, disappeared from circulation; primitive bartering was the only salvation of the people. Most of the fishermen's boats had been destroyed so that no more citizens could escape the terrorized nation. Civil servants went unpaid and the gates of the finance ministry were shut with a huge padlock. There was no electricity; the capital's generator had blown up in the summer of 1978 and there was no money to repair it. Malabo dwindled from a city of 60,000 to 20,000. Shops were shuttered since there was nothing to sell—no fish, no meat, clothing, medical supplies. It literally became a ghost town where the people went out of their homes only when absolutely necessary because of thieves. The provincial capital of Rio Muni, Bata, was even worse. It is estimated that a third of the population fled and about 40,000 were used as forced labor; the same amount were executed.

In the summer of 1979 Macías Nguema was suddenly overthrown by his nephew, Teodoro. He was captured hiding in the bush at Mongomo; he and six close associates were executed by firing squad within weeks.

Church bells rang and photographs of the new president were put up everywhere. But most Equatorial Guineans living abroad waited. Was the new president a professional soldier whose conscience had forced him to act? The answer turned out to be no. He is just another of the Nguema dynasty and almost, but not quite, another edition of his infamous uncle. But government did start functioning again with increasing effectiveness.

"Elections" were held in 1983 and again in mid–1988 for candidates hand–picked by the president. The basic problem continues to be ethnic. The Fang of Rio Muni are less cultured and educated than are the Bubi of Bioko. The latter are effectively excluded from government; there was no legislature until 1994. It now consists of members produced by massive election fraud.

The *Democratic Party of Equatorial Guinea (PDGE)* of the Nguema clan was the only political party after independence until 1993. Elections in that year were no more than a farce; opposition candidates had been murdered or jailed for years, leading to a boycott of the contest by any meaningful opponents. Conditions were so bad that voters fled into the jungle rather than register to vote at the point of a gun. After the U.S. denounced the elections, the security chief of Equatorial Guinea (Capt. Manuel Nguema Mba) accused the U.S. ambassador of taking medicine from the opposition, administered by a witch doctor, in order "to make the vote come out badly."

Needless to say, the Nguema family won the elections. Because of their quality, Spain now provides only medicines and other humanitarian aid to Equatorial Guinea.

Culture: The people in Rio Muni live in rural solitude, surviving on limited forestry and primitive agriculture. Those on the island of Bioko have more contact with the world and are more sophisticated. Education, severely limited in former years, is again found on the island, but remains virtually nonexistant in Rio Muni. The literacy rate is estimated to be no more than 20%.

Economy: The export of cacao and coffee were the backbone of the nation's economy; since independence production has dropped to less than 5,000 tons per year. The economy was starting to creep back into existence with the help of the IMF, Spain and France, but now that has ended. Business is utterly impossible to transact in Equatorial Guinea because Nguema family/clan members have to be paid members of the board of anything remotely wealthy or important.

When the CFA franc was first devalued and later had its ties with the French franc severed, the very limited economy of Equatorial Guinea, which uses that currency, suffered tremendously. In real dollars, production is less than 20% of what it was prior to independence.

The Future: If the clock had been turned back a century, it would be far easier to understand the feudal, savage tactics of the Nguema family/clan, which has been reliably reported to engage in cannibalism. There is no means presently inside or outside of this country to change its ways.

President Obiang Nguema Mbasogo

The Federal Republic of Nigeria

Tire advertisement does not help this traffic jam in Lagos

AP/Wide World Photo

Area: 924,630 sq. km. = 357,000 sq. mi. (the size of the traditional southern states east of the Mississippi River, omitting Florida).

Population: 116.5–120 million (estimated).

Capital City: Abuja (Pop. 850,000, estimated).

Climate: Hot and humid in the coastal belt and southern interior; hot and less humid in the central plains regions; semi–arid to arid and hot in the extreme north.

Neighboring Countries: Benin (West); Niger, Chad (North); Cameroon (East).

Official Language: English.

Other Principal Tongues: Hausa, Fulani, Yoruba, Edo.

Ethnic Background: There are over 250 identifiable ethnic communities in Nigeria. They are of West African Negro and Sudanic–Hamitic origin and there are intermixtures of the two, including the Hausa and Fulani of the north, the Yorubas of the south and the Ibos of the east.

Principal Religions: Islam (47%), Christian (34%), traditional tribal beliefs (19%). Figures are approximate.

Chief Commercial Products: Oil, petroleum products, cocoa, peanuts, palm products, cotton, rubber, timber, tin.

Per Capita Annual Income: About U.S. $375.

Currency: Naira.

Former Colonial Status: British Colony (1914–1960).

Independence Date: October 1, 1960.

Chief of State: General Sani (Sanni) Abacha, Commander–in–Chief of the Armed Forces, Chairman, Provisional Ruling Council and Chairman, Federal Executive Council (cabinet).

National Flag: Three vertical stripes of green, white and green.

Nigeria, the fourteenth largest country on the African continent with the largest population of any African nation, lies facing the Gulf of Guinea on the southern coast of West Africa. From the warm waters of the ocean the land has a flat appearance; there is a belt of dense swamp and towering mangrove trees 10 to 15 miles wide. This marshy coastal area resembles the bayous of Louisiana, particularly in the delta of the Niger River.

Further inland, there is a region 50 to 100 miles wide where the vegetation is thick green jungle rising from more stable ground. The trees of this warm and humid area reach heights of 200 feet where vines entwine all growth. This jungle area and the coast receive up to 150 inches of rainfall per year.

The land rises slowly in a series of foothills to the Jos Plateau, reaching altitudes up to 1,000 feet. Tall grasses grow rapidly between widely spaced trees. The dry season, from October to April, evaporates moisture from the ground, hardening the earth so that when the spring rains come, the soil erodes into the rivers.

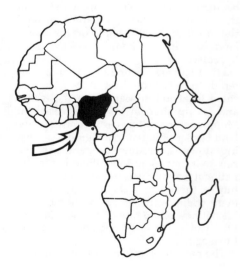

74

There is a semi–arid to arid region in the extreme north, close of Lake Chad and Niger. This is the transition zone lying between the Sahara Desert and the green forests and jungles of the South, receiving 25 inches or less of rain per year. In the last decade, the "or less" has been the rule. This area is threatened by the expansion southward of the great desert.

During the dry season, particularly in December and January, the *harmattan*, the hot wind blowing from the desert, penetrates to the Gulf of Guinea, lowering the humidity and raising dust storms in the interior.

History: The early history of Nigeria is traced through the people by their poetry and legends. The Yoruba tribes were established between the 11th and 14th centuries in the southern coastal region. The Hausa kingdoms were gradually established after the 12th century in the North; the people, of Sudanic–Hamitic descent, were converted to Islam in the 14th century. The Fulani (Peulh) nomadic cattle herdsmen became rulers in the Hausa regions of the North in the late 19th century. The Ibo occupied the southeast region for many centuries before the arrival of the first Europeans, organizing themselves into family units. For details of early and colonial history, see Historical Background and *The British in Africa*.

Following its independence granted in October 1960, Nigeria became a part of the British Commonwealth, but altered its status to that of a Republic within the Commonwealth in 1962. President Nnamdi Azikwe replaced Queen Elizabeth II as titular chief of state with this change.

Regional differences were inevitable; Nigeria was at that time divided into three regions: the largest, the North, inhabited predominantly by Islamic believers, and two smaller states in the South. Of these latter, the Eastern Region was dominated by the progressive, Christian Ibo people and the Western Region was controlled by the religiously mixed, but predominantly Christian Yorubas. Each of the three groups was split into innumerable factions, tribes and groups, and none of them constituted a unified factor in Nigerian politics. At the top of government was the Federal Prime Minister, Sir Abubakar Tafewa Balewa.

There were four short years of apparent harmony, but this was true only on the surface. Elections in 1965 provided a scenario in which corruption and ethnic strife has continued at higher and lower levels since that year. With the exception of a few brief periods, the leadership of Nigeria was determined by *coup* and assassination. Widespread lawlessness accompanied the confusion.

The basis for this virtual anarchy was the more numerous Islamic Northerners dominating either of the two main southern groups, and the inability of the latter two to cooperate with each other. Conditions worsened in 1965–66, leading to an attempted *coup* by Ibo army officers. Ibos had settled throughout Nigeria, with occupations such as technicians, clerks and civil servants. There ensued an effort by the Hausas and other groups of the North to eradicate as many Ibos as possible. Conferences to settle the conflict were fruitless.

Colonel Odumegwu Ojukwu, an Ibo, assumed control of the Eastern Region and proclaimed independence of the area, naming it *Biafra*. Strife immediately intensified, continuing until early 1970. The innocent suffered the most. The bellies of Biafran children became swollen and their black hair turned orange by the dreaded *Kwashiokior*—the Ghanaian word for protein starvation. Collected into orphanages, they became too tired to eat, sat down—and died. Burial, when possible, was usually in mass graves. The conflict abruptly ended when Ojukwu fled and the Ibos surrendered.

Based upon the 1967 performance of the Northerners, widespread genocide and starvation was generally expected, but thankfully averted. A military government emerged in firm control. Recovery from the civil war was rapid, but uneven. During the latter 1960s and the years succeeding, a mass migration to the cities occurred in Nigeria, severely straining the ability of the government to provide essential services.

Starting in the 1970s, petroleum production burgeoned (exported principally to the U.S.) and contributed an additional basis for dispute. One in five barrels simply evaporated and the money from its sale went directly into the pockets of one or more Nigerians in a position to steal, either in or out of government.

Adopting a new constitution in 1979, Nigeria made an attempt at democratic government until 1983. The constitution, however, only presented a theater for a replay of ethnic differences. Oil revenues, which peaked in 1980, provided prosperity that drew attention away from them. More than 1 million Africans from neighboring nations (principally Ghana) were allowed in to work in positions related to oil production. This changed in the 1990s when they were summarily expelled in order that Nigerians could claim the same jobs.

With its candidate reelected in 1983, the northern *National Party* pressed for installation of its stalwarts in office. It was not long before they were in office, shipping money to foreign accounts while the good days lasted. But they didn't. By 1983 income from oil had dropped in half. The military, disgusted with rampant corruption, seized control. Mismanagement

**President Shehu Shagari
(from 1979 through 1983)**

and corruption were everywhere. It instituted military tribunals for officials suspected of corruption and placed strict controls on currency to lower all forms of thievery. Public executions of violent criminals became commonplace.

The construction of the new federal capital city at Abuja was a classic example of Nigerian corruption. By the mid–1980s half–completed government buildings and luxury hotels were everywhere, replete with poor quality, design, workmanship and materials. Transfer of governmental bureaus from overcrowded Lagos to Abuja is still underway, although the official goal for completion of this was 1992. The new buildings are not stable because of the moist heat typical of the area.

When in 1985 oil prices plummeted to less than $10 per barrel, chaos in the Nigerian economy resulted. The military regime imposed yet another round of austerity measures, including pay cuts for the military which were most unpopular.

External and internal pressures led to planning for a return of multi–party civilian government by the beginning of the 1990s. The military chief of state was charged with having a secret goal: maintenance of military control over Nigeria. This was untrue; he sought to prevent the total collapse of his country. Legislative elections were held in 1992, but the victors were put on "hold" awaiting further developments. The promised legislature simply evaporated. The military dictated that there be only *two* parties in order to coerce the population into making political sense. One, the *Social Democratic Party* was to be "a little" to the left; the other, the *National Republican Convention*, was to be "a little" to the right.

After three postponements, elections were finally held in mid–1993. Moshood K.O. Abiola, a billionaire Yoruba Moslem of the *Social Democratic Party*, promised instant paradise for all if elected (prosper-

Northern Nigeria's ancient Moslem city of Kano at the edge of the Sahara

AP/Wide World Photo

Moshood K.O. Abiola

ity within six months!) Both he and his *Republican* opponent were close friends of the military leader, Ibrahim Babangida. Only about 30% of the disbelieving Nigerians voted, but they apparently chose Abiola, who is an astute politican, a conniving thief or an *Uncle Tom* (or a combination of all three) depending on who is relied upon.

Babangida and the military, correctly sensing Nigeria was heading for disaster, arranged the filing of a series of pre-arranged lawsuits alleging the election was riddled with irregularities (there weren't that many by Nigerian standards). While the cases were pending in court, the military nullified the election "to save our judiciary . . . " (!)

Promising elections in August 1993, Babangida instead stepped down. An insignificant tribal chief was briefly president until the real power behind the military stepped forward in November to personally attend to the leadership of Nigeria: General Sani (Sanni) Abacha.

Political parties were outlawed, their candidates were silenced and labor strikes were promptly abolished; state, local and federal government offices were seized. The usual internal and external protest was loud, and the response was that civilian government "had not been abandoned."

A promise that is perennial in Nigeria was heard. There must be a constitutional convention to bring about reconciliation. To mute criticism at home and abroad, General Abacha decreed that the 1979 Nigerian constitution be restored. His cabinet contains several former supporters of Abiola, who has termed the military takeover an act of God. The military rules a fragmented Nigeria which just barely avoided disintegration and anarchy. The composition of the members of and date of a constitutional convention remained unannounced as of mid–1994, although an inconclusive meeting of prominent persons was held in February. The U.S. and other western nations grumbled about the latest military takeover. The U.S., opposition to military rule and insistence on a return to the civilian president, has been almost totally absent, compared to Haiti. The reason: Nigeria has oil and Haiti doesn't. It is most predictably and efficiently extracted and exported to the U.S. under military rule.

Moshood Abiola addressed popular anti–military rallies in 1994 and was arrested on charges of treason in mid–year. Legal proceedings against him (which the British described as being "irregular" but are more properly termed a serial farce) are not yet complete, yet he is confined to jail and is reported to be ill. The latest wrinkle came when the trial judge walked out of the courtroom because he felt "threatened," most certainly true.

A pro–democracy oil workers strike was broken in late 1994; the workers demanded the installation of Abiola as president. But economic necessity forced the workers to return to their labors. The government responded by publishing decrees granting itself "absolute power."

The U.S. under President Clinton decided to become active in Nigerian affairs. It dispatched Rev. Jesse Jackson in late 1994 to that country for an unspecified "preemptive strike." And in early 1995, having "solved" the problems of South Africa and Haiti, Trans–Africa (a Washington–based, self–serving Black group) has decided to take on the lack of democracy in Nigeria. General Abacha responded to all of this by issuing a decree that he would rule indefinitely; no talk of political democracy would be given consideration.

Contemporary Problems

As Nigeria entered the 1990's it was faced with enormous problems which have no immediate solution or even medicine to lessen painful awareness of them. Unless checked, its population of 118? million will triple to more than 300 million in a generation. Birth control programs have been greeted with hostility, particularly by Christians who practice monogamy in contrast to Islamic polygamy. Annual per capita income has sagged from about $800 in 1984 to about $250 in 1993. People complain bitterly about having to eat casava meal, formerly regarded as peasant food, but now in short supply.

Armed robbery, murder and thievery are growth industries in southern Nigeria. In Lagos, hardly any taxis will operate at night and simply run red lights in the daytime lest they be seized by outlaws if they stop. There are shortages of everything (unless one has the right price), even of basics such as medical supplies. A thriving black market now deals in such commodities. Nigerians have been regularly used as "mules"—couriers of drugs to Europe and the United States. The favored method is to swallow condoms filled with heroin, with sometimes fatal consequences. Attempts to intercept such carriers has resulted in more than a few indignities visited upon professional Nigerians. When a "mule" (or any innocent person) has the effrontery to tender cash for an airline ticket, he immediately is classified as a high risk drug courier and treated accordingly.

Religious tensions have been running high. With about 235 ethnic groups, sometimes divided into Moslem and Christian sub–groups, there have been repeated incidents of sporadic street fighting throughout the country. A "brain drain" has been going on for almost two decades. Seeing only hardship and shortages with no future, many medical doctors, educators, scholars and scientists are leaving for places as far away as Alaska.

Nigerian thievery is open and notorious; no one there is ashamed of it—the talent with which it is executed is regarded as a virtue. When entering Lagos, one is confronted with signs advertising a number of talents, principally forgery, all calculated to advance some sort of thievery. Documents can be obtained in 48 hours that look so genuine they cannot be identified as less by experts. Stolen credit cards are perfectly duplicated. Documents purporting to be

Gen. Sani Abacha

A farmer feeds his livestock.

of government origin are beautifully done.

These talents have not been limited to Nigeria, but have been exported to foreign countries, including the U.S. A large forgery ring of Nigerians in suburban Washington, D.C. was recently reported to have stolen successfully more than $3 million using forged credit cards. Another Nigerian convinced top–flight brokerage houses that he was licensed to deal in U.S. Treasury notes, using only a telephone and fax machine in his home. The estimated loss: $85 million.

Other operations which never left Nigeria have bilked unsuspecting U.S. churches for uncounted amounts by promising astronomical returns on investments. These efforts use forgeries of government documents.

Who or what is to blame for the current state of affairs. By and large, it is *Nigerians*. One observer termed the nation "a garden of Eden in decay." He further noted that during the oil glut days one out of every five barrels was stolen—within Nigeria. The efforts of the present government have been labeled "a war against indiscipline." The behavior of the people is said to be rooted in their lack of respect for foreign powers during the colonial period. This viewpoint, however tempting, is not quite accurate. Social disorganization is rooted in Nigerian competitiveness, which simply has few, if any, scruples. If it works and is profitable, it is done, no matter what it may happen to be. Although keenly desiring the comforts of modern life, the average Nigerian will not hesitate to act contrary to the interests of the community and nation in general if by doing so it is possible to climb another rung on the ladder to success, an elusive and slippery goal that is constantly changing.

Culture: In almost no other nation of Africa is there so much diversity as is found in Nigeria. Colorful clothing, worn by the women, consists of a blouse, a wrap–around skirt, which sometimes covers the blouse, and an elaborate headdress to match. The men wear trousers and a shirt, covered by a long, flowing robe.

The Fulani and Hausa of the North are organized under local monarchs called Emirs, but the family is the social unit among the Ibos. Throughout Nigeria the songs and dances, performed in great varieties, provide entertainment and are part of religious rituals. The complex rhythm of drums predominates in the accompaniments.

English is the language of instruction in all high schools and universities. There are more than four million pupils in primary schools, a substantial number in courses through junior college and many are enrolled in the technical colleges and 12 universities. In spite of sometimes ineffective efforts in education, the literacy rate is high—in many cases the result of self–education. The Nigerians have enjoyed sports and for many years were the first Black African nation to participate in the Olympic Games. There are widespread organizations of Boy and Girl Scouts.

Lagos on the coast, Kano in the North and Ibadan in the West are the three largest cities, containing up–to–date architecture, and modern conveniences. Television and radio programming is varied and of high quality. A campaign to reduce the number of accidents on the highways has fizzled; driving in Nigeria was traditionally spirited at minimum and more often simply wild, harrowing and dangerous. The oil glut proved an indirect blessing to the large cities, particularly Lagos. When the government withdrew fuel subsidies, increasing the price of gasoline, traffic jams which lasted a full day diminished to only two to three hours. But ambushes from thieves have added to the danger. Living conditions in Lagos were accurately summed up by one observer: bad government, bad weather and the world's worst drivers, (and more expensive than New York City).

Economy: Nigeria is Africa's most populous country. As such, it is an enormous market for foreign goods and services. Although the officially recognized population figure is 92 million, experts say that a proper census would easily find that it exceeds 100 million; a more realistic figure is 118 million. A 1990 census (the results were announced in 1992) was inconclusive although officially accurate. It did show that the Islamic north is more populous than the southern region. This, too, must be considered with caution as to its accuracy.

A host of foreign companies do business in Nigeria, paying innumerable government officials "dash" (bribes) to perform even ordinary services. Substantial foreign investment supports the oil industry, which produces about 80% of Nigeria's foreign income, principally from the U.S. But trade with this nation has been increasingly difficult since 1992 because of economic disorganization and inflation (now about 70% annually). The central bank has contributed to rather than helped economic problems.

At the insistence of the IMF, subsidies of local gasoline were ended; the price rose from 3¢ a gallon to 27¢, still the cheapest available in the world. But nevertheless there were strikes and protests against the move. Foreign debts were rescheduled in 1992 with little success; Nigeria is barely able to pay only the interest due on more than U.S. $31 billion. Additional rescheduling was necessary by early 1994, but the adoption of a national budget that amounted to an economic fairy tale made this impossible.

Final withdrawal in March 1994 of troops from peace-keeping forces in Liberia, of which Nigeria was the largest supporter, was an absolute economic necessity. Even with this measure, military expenditures still are high and will remain elevated indefinitely.

The periodic need of foreign nations to write off Nigeria's debt has made credit very limited; the limited sums available have strict conditions and high interest rates which compound the economic problems of this country. Economic conditions cause a constant shortage of foreign goods and even basic foodstuffs. This, and the ever-expanding population, are the basic causes of roving bands of youths in Lagos who steal and extort money from passersby.

The Future: It is difficult to imagine any democratic system that can be devised to govern and foster unity in Nigeria. This is particularly true because the popular image of a government job is an opportunity to get "a piece of the action." The human rights record of the military indicates a limited responsiveness to the needs of the people, which will continue. The matter of what constitutes a "right" will be debated—endlessly.

Abuja—National Mosque (upper left), National Ecumenical Center (upper right), International Conference Center (center)

Photo by Tony Azogu

EQUATORIAL WEST AFRICA

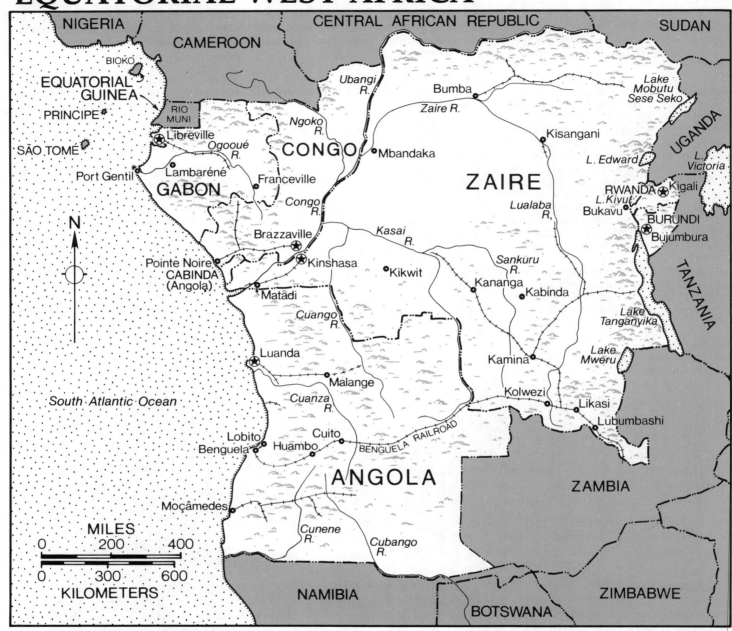

The People's Republic of Angola

Area: 1,245,790 sq. km. = 481,000 sq. mi. (about four times the size of New Mexico).

Population: 10.5 million (estimated).

Capital City: Luanda (Pop. 480,000, estimated).

Climate: Moist and warm in the North, dryer and hot in the large, central plateau area; arid, semi–desert in the South.

Neighboring Countries: Zaïre (North); Namibia (South); Zambia (Southeast).

Official Language: Portuguese.

Other Principal Tongues: There are about 55 dialects of Bantu origin, in- cluding Ovimbundu, Kimbundu, Ba- kongo and Chokwe; a small number of Bushmen in the southern desert use a unique "click" language symbolized by use of a "!".

Ethnic Background: Bantu, including the major groups—Ovimbundu (38%); Kimbundu (23%), Bakongo (13%), other, (24%), mestizo (mixed black and European, (2%).

Principal Religions: Traditional tribal be- liefs (84%), Christianity (16%); figures are approximate).

Chief Commercial Products: Oil, petro- leum products, coffee, diamonds, sugar, peanuts, sisal, fish and fish prod- ucts, iron ore, corn, cotton, palm oil.

Per Capita Income: About U.S. $450; the oil income is used to maintain defenses of the central government against a large guerrilla opposition movement, not for the benefit of the people in general.

Currency: Kwanza.

Former Colonial Status: Portuguese Col- ony until November 11, 1975; actual control passed in early 1975.

Independence Date: November 11, 1975.

Chief of State: José Eduardo dos Santos, President.

National Flag: Two horizontal stripes of equal width, red and black, upon which is centered a 5–pointed yellow star, halfway surrounded by a wheel and crossed by a machete.

For most of its sprawling area, Angola is a high, grassy plateauland ranging from 3,000 to 4,000 feet above sea level, dotted by occasional trees and brush hardy enough to withstand the scorching heat of the day. The coastal belt, home to about 20% of the population, is from 15 to 60 miles wide, stretching from the tropical mouth of the mighty Zaïre (Congo) River, down to the palm–lined central beaches, and then on to the reddish sands of the Namib Desert in the extreme south.

Lofty mountains drive eastward, splitting the country in half until the terrain gradually levels out, dipping first northeast into the hot, steaming jungles of Zaïre's river basin and then southeast to isolated, semi–arid land. The mountains are the source of rivers which fan out in all directions.

The Cuanza River, Angola's largest, twists north for 600 miles in a wavering half–circle and then drains into the Atlantic below cosmopolitan Luanda. The Cunene's cold waters gush south down the mountains, slow as they pass through the plains, become sluggish in the silent desert, then lazily turn westward and are caught by the huge Cunene Dam, which regulates its flow as it forms the 175–mile border with Namibia to the ocean. Another river, in the northeast, offers unique drama.

Meandering aimlessly across the sun–parched grasslands, the Lucala unexpectedly reaches a wide, curved rock shelf where the placid waters suddenly plunge into a 350–foot gorge, sending up a heavy spray–mist which transforms the immediate area into a lush oasis, rich with dark mosses and tropical foliage— the Duque de Bragança Falls—a truly spectacular sight. Again docile, the river moves across the flat land and joins the waters of the larger Cuanza.

Cutting across otherwise unspoiled country teeming with wildlife is the Benguela Railroad. Its tracks have clattered to the tune of millions of tons of rich copper ore shipped from the vast mines in Zaïre and Zambia to coastal Benguela and then to Lobito, Angola's principal port. Due to guerrilla activities, the line has not been in regular use since 1975 except in the coastal region.

History: The Bushmen were probably the first inhabitants of Angola during the late Stone Age; they were driven southward by a Bantu migration which was to occupy most of Africa below the Sahara Desert. This region constituted the southernmost part of the once–mighty

Portuguese troops fighting in Angola, 1971

Kingdom of the Congo—a loose confederation of Bantu tribes dominated by the Bakongo prior to the arrival of European explorers. For details of early and colonial history, see Historical Background and *The Portuguese in Africa*.

Nationalism arrived in Angola at about the same time that Belgium hurriedly gave Zaïre (Belgian Congo) its independence in 1960. Following the revolt of the army in the former Belgian colony to the northeast, strife seized Angola, particularly in the regions bordering Zaïre. Black Angolans slaughtered about 1,500 Portuguese settlers and swift reprisal was mounted against the rebels, resulting in the death of thousands.

During the late 1960's and early 1970's there were conflicting reports concerning the casualties from the continuing rebellion. The rebels claimed well over 1,000 Portuguese troops killed each year along with dozens of aircraft and motor vehicles destroyed. The Portuguese denied the figures, making counterclaims concerning rebel manpower losses and belittling the strength of the rebels.

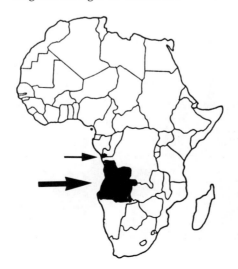

The governments of Zaïre and Zambia acted with restraint in supporting the rebellion, since the Benguela Railroad, affording transport for the products of both countries, went through Angola and Mozambique on the east coast of Africa.

Angola's birth as a nation came hard— and the strong impact of the period preceding independence still scars and weakens the large, sparsely populated and potentially rich country. Angola's march toward independence centered around three rival military–political groups, each claiming to be the only "legitimate" representative of the Angolan people. The exact title of each in Portuguese is not important; they all called for independence of Angola from Portuguese colonialism; their initials are sufficient.

The oldest group was *FNLA* led by Holden Roberto, drawing principal support from the Bakongo people of the northern provinces. The next in terms of age was the Soviet–backed *MPLA* headed by Dr. Agostinho Neto, based on the Kimbundu people of the capital and corridor extending to Malange in the east. The newest group was *UNITA* championed by its learned president, Dr. Jonas Savimbi; its major support came from the Ovimbundu people and smaller tribes of the South and East.

In the 14 years preceding independence the three groups had a common enemy—Portugal—but as independence approached, they began to fight among themselves. A military takeover by liberals in Portugal opposed to rebel activities in Angola set the stage for the end of hundreds of years of Portuguese exploitation in Africa. By October 1974, all three groups had signed cease–fires, ending the anti–colonial war.

Some Angolan Whites, afraid of losing their colonial privileges, fled the country.

In the new situation, racial incidents became common. Portuguese plans to grant independence after a two year interim period under a coalition was rejected by the Black Angolan political groups. However, when the cease–fires took effect, all three groups were free to form political parties, establish headquarters in Luanda and in cities and towns elsewhere in the country and to start recruiting membership for the upcoming elections, which did not take place. It is widely believed that if they had been held, *UNITA* candidates would have won a solid majority in the legislature.

Portugal, under considerable pressure from within Angola and from neighboring African nations, finally agreed in January 1975 to grant independence to the country on November 11, 1975, the 400th anniversary of the founding of Luanda. A scheme of government was devised whereby each of the three groups would have a Prime Minister who would rotate each month as chief executive. They were required to have a secretary of state from a rival power. The major flaw was that government officials were not responsible to the Prime Minister, but to separate political movements.

By March 1975 heavy fighting broke out between *MPLA* and *FNLA* forces. *UNITA* drew back to avoid conflict with the two, but it was impossible to remain uninvolved; by June *UNITA* party offices throughout Angola were attacked by *MPLA* supporters. Fighting reached a high pitch of intensity—mortars and bazookas belched; the Soviet Union supplied *MPLA* troops with the latest in weaponry. The United States began to supply *UNITA* and *FNLA* with arms in order to retain some military balance, amid cries in the U.S. Senate that another Vietnam was at hand.

Arrival of Cuban Mercenaries

When it appeared that *MPLA* was not faring well in the fray, new players emerged on the scene: 3,000 Cuban troops who arrived to fight beside *MPLA* soldiers. Events moved quickly. About 500 South African troops entered southern Angola to protect the Cunene Dam and its hydroelectric facilities which provide southern Angola and northern Namibia power; another 1,000 South Africans joined in what had become an invasion of Angola. Six provincial capitals were occupied, not so much in support of *UNITA*, but rather to back a small, White–dominated group which had fled Angola. Later these troops fought along side *UNITA* forces against the *MPLA*–Cuban forces. Savimbi called for additional help from Western nations and received some—from the United States—too little and too late.

Two separate "republics" were proclaimed on November 11–12, 1975. Troops of the *FNLA* held large portions of the North and *UNITA* forces were strong in the South and eastern portions of the country. The two groups formed a coalition government which did not work. In late 1975, South Africa called for greater U.S. assistance to support the anti–Soviet forces opposing the puppet government. The United States Senate, usurping the powers of the U.S. president, voted to withdraw support for *UNITA* and *FNLA*. It wanted no more foreign wars fought against communist regimes, even if only with U.S. arms.

The Organization of African Unity met in early 1976 to attempt settlement of the division in Angola, but was divided—22 members voted to recognize the *MPLA* government and 22 insisted that all foreign troops had to be withdrawn and a government of national unity had to be established. Cuban troops by then numbered 14,000 and were later to grow to 25,000 and then 55,000. South Africa, discouraged by the lack of support from Western nations, withdrew its troops. *UNITA* and *FNLA* held out in the central cities for three weeks but then retreated to the countryside where they had broad support among the people. The *MPLA* claimed control over most of Angola. The United States vetoed Angola's admission to the UN in 1976 because Cuban troops were fighting there, but its application was finally accepted in 1977.

The years following 1976 were bitter—continuing guerrilla warfare against the *MPLA* government was quite effective, in spite of the fact that the government maintained an army of 100,000, (poorly trained), augmented by 25,000–55,000 Cubans. The *FNLA* all but disappeared.

Agostinho Neto was caught in a crossfire. Although the Soviets paid him "lip service," they apparently never really trusted him. Neto refused to allow USSR bases in Angola and made tentative moves to draw closer to Zaïre and to the Western nations, the capital and expertise of which was badly needed in Angola. Neto flew to Moscow in September 1979 to discuss mutual problems with the Soviets and for medical treatment. Following an operation, he died on September 10—some believe under suspicious circumstances. The presidency passed to José Eduardo dos Santos, who also since that time has been caught in crossfire.

His primary problem continued to be Dr. Jonas Savimbi and *UNITA*. The bearded, barrel–chested leader was and is shrewd, charismatic and very intelligent. He received his doctorate in law and political science at the University of Lausanne and is fluent in English, Portuguese and French in addition to speaking five of the principal languages of Angola. Although most African nations maintained relations with the *MPLA* government, he visited more than 21 of them prior to 1994; many quietly supported him. Kenya, Morocco and Senegal openly endorsed him as leader of the Angolan people. He received financial support from innumerable foreign nations, particularly South Africa and China (which opposed *anything* supported by the Soviets).

Dos Santos' second problem was the Soviet desire to support via Angola *SWAPO*, the formerly leftist–communist group claiming leadership in Namibia to the south. Opposing this group was White South Africa, which periodically

Dr. Jonas Savimbi of *UNITA*

Jason Lauré, Woodfin Camp

sent troops into Angola to further that position; they frequently assaulted Cuban and *MPLA* forces. Criticized for its actions, South Africa announced it would withdraw from Angola when Cuban troops were withdrawn, paving the way for defeat of the Luanda government. Angola was justifiably accused of being a puppet of the Soviet Union, which financed the Cuban troops.

During the late 1980s, in spite of increased Cuban troop presence, things went badly for Angolan and Cuban forces. The Soviet economy was no longer able to sustain the expense of Cuban troops and Castro was told to bring them home. The collapse of the Soviet Union in August 1991 made the communist allegiance to the dos Santos regime irrelevant. It found itself a relic of the past consisting of mixed Black and White ancestry with no compelling reason for its continued existence. Savimbi's backing was and is primarily of Ovimbundu heritage, traditionally occupying the lower rungs of Angola's social ladder.

U.S. policy in the late 1980s was two-faced and useless. The State Department tried for eight years to obtain some sort of peace agreement in southern Africa which included Angola. At the same time, the Central Intelligence Agency was providing substantial assistance to Savimbi's forces, including modern weaponry such as Stinger hand-launched PBX missiles which had proved so effective against the Soviets in Afghanistan. Savimbi was received in 1989 in Washington by President Bush, who assured him that U.S. aid would not be discontinued. The Luanda regime was purchasing chemical warfare supplies from the Soviets with its oil money.

Peace Agreement No. 1

An accord was signed in late 1988 between Angola, Cuba and South Africa intended to end the Angolan strife and grant Namibia independence. It provided for South African withdrawal of troops from Angola and similar Cuban removal of forces, but over a period of 27 months. Savimbi, however, did not sign the pact. This gave Mobutu of neighboring Zaïre the excuse to convene a subsequent conference in mid–1989. It resulted in nothing, and Angolan strife, which had ebbed, resumed.

In 1990, to try to save just a little face, Cuba staged an offensive which failed, leaving disabled Soviet military equipment scattered widely. When it tried to suspend its withdrawal, Russia intervened, and it was quickly resumed. Angola sank into a lull in which mass starvation was threatened in the central and southern areas because of *MPLA* government insistence on receiving relief supplies.

Peace Agreement No. 2

Amid tensions, political change and mistrust, a carefully prepared peace agreement was signed in Lisbon (the Bicesse Agreement) in May 1991 by both *MPLA* and *UNITA*. Sweeping and startling changes were called for, including a multi–party system and separation of party from national government and the military. More than a half–dozen parties were recognized, none of which were significant compared to the two major ones.

Change slowly was evident—roads into the interior were reopened, a free press blossomed and elections were set for September 1992. The seeds of destruction, however were saved: although a single army was supposed to be formed,

José Eduardo dos Santos

both *UNITA* and *MPLA* withheld troops from the organization—more than joined it. As the elections neared, the level of discord rose. *UNITA* became almost exclusively Ovimbundu; the government in Luanda was dominated by persons of mixed Black–White ancestry (mulattos) who had embraced communism as a convenient means to retain their traditionally preferred status.

Any objective evaluation of the elections was impossible under the conditions prevailing in Angola. The results: dos Santos 49 + % and Savimbi 40 + %. The result was pronounced "relatively honest and fair" by about UN observers, who saw the contest through rose-colored glasses for reasons that are not clear.

Jonas Savimbi denounced the election results, claiming that the contest had been rigged by the *MPLA*. Savage fighting resumed in October 1992. By the close of the year, *UNITA* irregularly controlled as much as 80% of Angola. The year 1993 was one in which death by armaments and by starvation vied with each other as the top cause of fatalities.

In an abrupt about–face, the U.S. announced its opposition to *UNITA* and its recognition of the *MPLA* government. This occurred because of pressure from Black African nations which had long ago recognized the dos Santos regime; the pressure was brought to bear on Black members of the U.S. Congress. They in turn turned the pressure on President Clinton, who desperately needed their votes on controversial economic, health care and other disputes pending in Congress. Thus, the foreign policy of the U.S. was for the first time, based indirectly on considerations rooted in racism.

The UN adopted a resolution called for a total embargo on shipments to *UNITA*, which initially was of little import. It was ignored by Mobutu of neighboring Zaïre, and others. But Zaïre was in the process of sinking into an economic mess and its contributions steadily decreased. With few resources upon which to draw, Savimbi decided to return to the negotiating table to salvage as much as possible.

Peace Agreement No. 3

Peace negotiations proceeded in Lusaka, Zambia, unevenly during the first part of 1994. The stumbling block was in the form of demands of *UNITA* that it be granted control of certain ministries in the government, and control of government in several states. *MPLA* agreed to a few of these demands and a date of November 15, 1994 was set for the signing of the final agreement. But at the same time, sensing a military weakness of *UNITA* it mounted an offensive against rebels in general and the city of Huambo, controlled by its adversary since being seized in 1993. *MPLA* forces were joined by 500 South African mercenaries.

This so overwhelmed Savimbi that he initially refused to appear for the signing of the agreement, justifiably fearing for his own safety. But it was ultimately adopted in early 1995 over the objection of *UNITA* generals who initially opposed the party's congress. It provides for the seating of *UNITA* delegates in the legislature, and for a second stage of the elections of 1992 to be held at the start of 1996.

Angola is shell–shocked, confused and starving. A half million lives were sacrificed on the altars of exterior forces and interior personalities since 1975. Angola became an experimentation place for the latest techniques in land mine technology. The result: there are more amputees than in any other nation in the world. The disgrace of this is that their devastation was not directed at soldiers, but at *anyone* having the misfortune to be walking over them.

The present legislature in Luanda has been unrepresentative and totally riddled with corruption; it is considered a joke in

View of Luanda from its harbor

poor taste by the people of the capital city. Members are quickly identified by their luxury automobiles. This opulence was occurring at the same time cannibalism was evident elsewhere in Angola on the part of people that preferred it to death.

Culture: Until 1974 there were two cultures in Angola—the approximately 300,000 Europeans, mostly Portuguese, who were the businessmen and farmers, and that of the original inhabitants of the land. The latter lived a marginal existence in the cities and in the hinterland, working as laborers in the factories and fields of Angola. A small group of these lived as *assimilados*—they adopted European customs, the Portuguese language and passed an educational test. They now are the leadership of *MPLA*.

Since independence, all this has changed. All but a few of the Portuguese have left, although some did return to offer their managerial skills to the nation.

The capital, Luanda, a modern city once bustling with life and commerce, is now depressing—its people are discouraged by the lack of food, unemployment, the lack of city services and shortages of just about everything. Huambo, Angola's second largest city, is devastated; it formerly was a thriving agricultural center whose markets once rang with the voices of vendors. Stalls were heaped high with fruits and vegetables. All this is gone. Lobito was a very modern port protected from

the Atlantic by a 3–1/2 mile sandbank. It may again become the main export terminal for copper from Zaïre and Zambia if the Benguela railroad is restored. But copper mining in those countries is uneconomical.

About 40% of the people live on the central plateau and the Huambo area, about 20% along the coastal strip and the rest are found along the Luanda–Malange railroad. Many have migrated to the cities, particularly Luanda, to avoid the strife that gripped the nation following independence.

Economy: Angola's economy prior to World War II was agricultural, centered mainly on coffee and sugar exports. This changed when the first oil deposits were discovered, resulting in a tremendous growth of income. Extensive offshore oil resources in the region of Cabinda boosted production to more than 300,000 barrels a day.

The civil war has ravaged the economy. Coffee was exported at the rate of 200,000 tons per year, but production is now about 12%–15% of that amount. Agricultural production has also been dealt a severe blow by the unsettled conditions, now at one–third of the normal yield. Diamond mining dropped 80%, and is climbing back only very slowly. A large iron ore deposit in the southern area was mined, with a production of more than 7 million metric tons a year, but the operation has come to a

standstill. A well–developed fishing industry has all but collapsed.

Angola is very important to the entire region, and can become a rich country if peace is restored and the Benguela Railroad begins to function again. Angola's potential natural resources are tremendous. Fluctuating world oil prices have made dependence on this one source of hard currency undependable; oil earns 75% of export earnings.

In the last two years, marked changes have occurred in the economy. There is a two–level market system. The official state–owned markets have no stock since they deal at the official exchange rate (30 K = $1.00 U.S.) The black market rate, from 2,000 to 6,500 K = $1.00, was the basis of a lively traffic between Angola, Lisbon and Rio de Janeiro by market women. This diminished as the Kwanza sank in value to virtual infinity in 1994–5.

The economic questions facing Angola are whether sufficient external aid can be obtained and whether the government will start spending money used to keep it in power for the benefit of the people.

The Future: Peace Agreement No. 3 is extremely fragile. Angolans are no more prepared for self–government now than they were in 1975. Savimbi's charisma has not departed, as has the reason for his rise to influence and power. The situation will remain murky for at least the coming year.

CABINDA

Tiny Cabinda, until 1950 a Portuguese colony distinct from Angola, fronts the Atlantic for 80 miles, north of the Zaïre (Congo) River. Separated from the rest of Angola by a 25–mile strip of land giving Zaïre access to the sea, it is bounded by Congo–Brazzaville to the north and Zaïre to the east and south. It is home to about 95,000, many of whom lack tribal, political and cultural ties with the rest of Angola.

Cabinda is important to Angola and the rest of the world primarily because of major off–shore oil reserves. Oil companies such as Chevron, Gulf, Elf Aquitaine (French parastatal) and others pay the formerly communist *MPLA* government $2–3 billion per year for rights to pump crude. During the years of strife in Angola, these revenues were the chief means of paying Cuba for its troops and the Soviets for military materiel to use against the *UNITA* rebels. Following a ceasefire, the money was used to influence elections in 1992.

Although *UNITA* blew up a pipeline in 1984, no further substantial damage occurred because of the Angolan war. There is an independence movement, *FLEC* which demands self–determination. U.S. and French oil companies view an independent Cabinda as a potential for added profits from its oil.

About 15,000 Angolan troops have occupied Cabinda to safeguard its production facilities. In view of the negotiated end to warfare in Angola, the future of Cabinda is uncertain. Angola will try to raise its earnings from oil here, which will be resisted by western oil companies. This may well result in some sort of effort to separate Cabinda into an independent nation or part of another nation.

The Republic of Burundi

Aerial view of Bujumbura and the northernmost extent of Lake Tanganyika

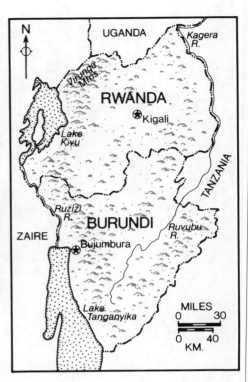

Area: 28,490 sq. km. = 11,000 sq. mi. (slightly larger than Maryland).

Population: 5.9 million (estimated).

Capital City: Bujumbura (Pop. 186,000, estimated).

Climate: Temperate, with an alternating wet season (October–April) and dry season (May–December).

Neighboring Countries: Rwanda (North); Tanzania (East): Zaïre (West).

Official Languages: French KiRundi.

Other Principal Tongues: KiSwahili.

Ethnic Background: Hutu, sometimes incorrectly called Buhutu (85%), Tutsi (sometimes incorrectly called Watusi (14%), Twa, or Pygmies (1%). Figures are approximate.

Principal Religions: Christianity (60%), Traditional tribal beliefs (38%), Islam (2%). Figures are approximate.

Chief Commercial Products: Coffee, tea, cotton, hides.

Annual Per Capita Income: Less than U.S. $100.

Currency: Burundi Franc.

Former Colonial Status: Part of German East Africa (1899–1917); occupied by Belgian troops (1916), Belgian trust territory under League of Nations and United Nations (1923–1962).

Independence Date: July 1, 1962.

Chief of State: Sylvestre Ntibantunganya, President, 1994. (Hutu)

Head of Government: Anatole Kanyenkiko, Prime Minister, 1994 (Tutsi).

National Flag: Two diagonal white stripes meet in a large white circle centered upon which are three six–pointed red stars outlined in green; the remaining top and bottom fields are red, the left and right hand fields are green.

A cool, pleasant land of mountains and plateaus, the Republic of Burundi was known as Urundi before its independence; it was the southern portion of Ruanda–Urundi. Burundi is situated in the highlands of central Africa, and though only two degrees below the Equator, the climate is tempered by altitude. Fabled Lake Tanganyika, the longest fresh water lake in the world, separates Burundi and Zaïre. This amazing body of water is more than 2,500 feet above sea level on the surface, yet its floor reaches a depth of about 2,000 feet below sea level. The lake abounds in fish, hippopotami, crocodiles and other native species.

Countless eons ago a great strip of land between parallel faults in the earth sank to great depths, forming the basin of the Red Sea and continuing into the land mass of east and central Africa. This

unique land feature is known as the Great Rift Valley, an area of grassy, upland plains. The wet season has characteristic daily downpours with intermittent clear, sunny weather. Almost no rain falls during the five–month dry season.

History: The old Kingdom of Burundi dates back to the 15th century; tradition indicates that the Twa (Pygmies) were the first inhabitants, a few of whom are found in the remotest parts of Burundi today. They were succeeded by the Hutu, a peaceful Bantu agricultural group, who in turn were subdued by the extremely tall Tutsi, who reduced the Hutu to serfdom. For details of early and colonial history, see Historical Background, *The Germans in Africa* and *The Belgians in Africa*.

Following independence in 1962, it appeared that Burundi would emerge as a stable nation. It seemed that the Tutsi and Hutu people had been able to work together in government with representation from both groups.

The Kingdom of Burundi was established as a constitutional monarchy with Mwami (King) Mwambutsa IV as ruler. The legislature, or National Assembly, was dominated by the *Burundi National Party of Unity and Progress (UPRONA).* This was a coalition of Tutsi and Hutu leaders, but was dominated by the upper class Tutsi nobles known as the *Ganwa.* The coalition underwent a severe setback in 1965 when a group of Hutu leaders attempted a *coup.* Prime Minister Biha was seriously wounded by gunfire,

President Sylvestre Ntibantunganya

Rural Tutsi tribesmen in a ritual ceremony

Mwambutsa departed for Switzerland, 76 Hutu leaders were executed and the defense minister, Michel Micombero, was given absolute power.

Mwambutsa made a half–hearted effort to return to his kingdom, but was ousted by his son, Ntare in 1966. When the youthful King was out of the country, Micombero proclaimed himself president of the *Republic* of Burundi. He had the support of the *Bahima* clan of the Tutsi, who traditionally were jealous of *Ganwa* power.

Restless Hutus living in exile in Tanzania plotted a revolution with the aid of that country in mid–1972. Emboldened by drugs and assurances of invincibility from local folk priests, they mounted a swift campaign. The plot involved Ntare, but after being put under house arrest, he was later killed "while escaping."

About 2,000 Tutsis were mercilessly slaughtered; they responded with a blood bath that took the lives of more than 200,000 Hutus within six weeks. Worst of all, this vengeance was directed against educated Hutus needed to perform a multitude of important tasks. A second wave of Hutus poured over the Tanzanian border in May 1973, creating further strife. Unconfirmed reports give totals up to and exceeding a half million people who were casualties of the inter–tribal strife.

The first constitution was adopted in 1974 and contained some unusual features. The head of the sole party, *UPRONA*, was both President and Premier. Micombero's tenure was extended for seven years. Then came the inevitable. Rivalries between army groups within the Tutsi tribe flared, and Col. Jean–Baptiste Bagaza led a bloodless *coup* in 1976. *UPRONA* was dissolved; a military council was formed which selected Bagaza to lead the country.

In 1980, Bagaza commenced anti–Catholic Church measures which led by 1987 to the expulsion of more than 450 foreign priests. He viewed the Church as an instrument of potential Hutu rebellion. He was ousted in 1987 by a military–backed fellow clansman, Pierre Buyoya. The new leader welcomed back the expelled Catholics in spite of suspicions of right–wing Tutsis. Leftist Hutus based in Rwanda (where they are the majority) convinced northern Hutu Burundians that the Tutsi were plotting their annihilation. Attempting to strike preemptively, the Hutus slaughtered about 500 Tutsis. The army (Tutsi) responded by slaughtering an estimated 20,000 Hutus; many more fled to Rwanda, most of whom have returned.

Pierre Buyoya demonstrated himself to be a mature capable leader, and established a government that crossed ethnic lines. Nevertheless, Burundi was ripe for pressures leading to multi–party democracy which were blooming all over Africa. They were scheduled and held June 1, 1993 and, predictably, Melchior Nda-

daye, a respected Hutu banker and candidate of the opposition *Front for Democracy in Burundi (FRODIBU)* won by two to one over Buyoya. He had served as Prime Minister under Buyoya. But this election of the first Hutu head of state caused a great deal of unrest among Tutsi students and government workers. Burundi's present troubles, however, were only beginning.

Even though he appointed a Tutsi as prime minister (Sylvie Kinigi, a female) there was an attempted *coup* by Buyoya supporters before the presidential inauguration in July. The next attempt in October resulted in the death of Ndadaye; waves of civil strife ensued in which about 150,000 people of both groups were mercilessly slaughtered. More than a million Burundians fled from the terror, initially to neighboring Rwanda. But when intense strife also erupted in that nation in April 1994, they joined Rwandans fleeing to Tanzania and Zaïre. Refugees from both nations began to die of starvation at the rate of thousands each day (see Rwanda).

Anarchy reigned in Burundi at the beginning of 1994. Rivalry between the Tutsi and Hutu was a factor, but even more serious, the army was out of control, and youths, joining in gangs, murdered indiscriminately, using the violence as an opportunity for thievery and grisly "joy" killing. Particularly during the last two generations, intermarriage between urban Hutus and Tutsis had become more common, and the resulting children cannot be accurately termed as belonging to either group.

Quickly amending the constitution in spite of *UPRONA* opposition, the National Assembly's Hutu *FRODIBU* elected one of their number as President, but *he* was killed in early April. A plane carrying both he and Rwanda President Juvenal Habyarimana (also a Hutu) crashed after being fired upon while landing at Kigali airport. The two had been at a conference to discuss ethnic strife in their countries.

During the first months of 1994, periodic massacres along tribal lines occurred frequently in Burundi. It remained adrift until October 1994 when a compromise government was selected. But the violence did not end, and still continues.

The principal leaders include a conciliatory Hutu President Ntibantunganya, and an equallly conciliatory Tutsi Prime Minister Kanyenkiko. Of equal importance are conservative Tutsi *UPRONA* leader Charles Mukasi, former Hutu president Pierre Buyoya, and Tutsi and Hutu gangs which fight endlessly in and around Bujumbura. The capital city has a curfew commencing at 7 P.M. Further complicating the picture are the armed forces, under Tutsi nominal control, undisciplined and capable of random violence directed against Hutus.

The hapless victims of this horror are usually innocent bystanders—they are sought out and summarily murdered because of what they are, not because of what they did. Neither Tutsis nor Hutus have any abiding interest in accomodating each other—even a little bit.

Culture: In terms of its rich African heritage, the customs of the people of Burundi are unique and beautiful. The Tutsi are unbelievably tall, reaching heights of seven feet, and possess a high degree of unity based on social order, with the *Ganwa* traditionally at the top and the *Bahima* somewhat lower. A great variety of dance accompaniments with highly stylized rhythms have been among the most intricate to be found on the continent. Rural Tutsi dancing is breathtakingly graceful—the unison movements of the men are accented by headdresses ornamented frequently with monkey hair. Due to the massive ethnic warfare of 1993–4, these customs are now difficult to find.

European night life had invaded Bujumbura before the strife, with several nightclubs featuring the latest western clothing styles and music—very popular among urban residents. A substantial number of people are now of both Hutu and Tutsi ancestry as a result of intermarriage between the two groups. Radio, widely available for years, both government and clandestine, was used with vigor to incite people to violence in recent months by use of the worst sort of insults possible. Television, with western programming, arrived via satellite in 1984.

Social disorganization is now rampant and will take years to abate, if it does at all. Virtually all foreigners, including a small UN force, have departed.

Economy: With an extremely dense population and a rural social system based upon the ownership of cattle, the economy of Burundi after independence was hard to find. In years of drought, thousands died of famine. Government programs to boost food production were resisted by the traditions of the Tutsi overlords.

Important loans were necessary and were received from several sources, this kept Burundi temporarily afloat. The economy has been directly tied to the fluctuating international prices of coffee and fuel oil. Progress in tea production has been virtually wiped out by warfare in 1993–4 with the attendant displacement of large numbers fleeing the strife. The limited economy of Burundi has evaporated. No crops are being planted or tilled; the closing half of the 1990s will see no harvests are a result.

The Future: Indefinite foreign aid will be required. The result, sadly, will be continued genocide in Burundi.

The Republic of Rwanda   (pronounced Rh–*wahn*–dah)

Typical rural Rwandan dwelling near Kigali, with a woman working her garden plot.   AP/Wide World photo

Area: 28,900 sq. km. = 11,158 sq. mi. (slightly smaller than Maryland).

Population: 7.9 million (estimated).

Capital City: Kigali (Pop. 40,000, estimated, down from 350,000 in 1994).

Climate: Temperate, with dry seasons (January–February, June–September) and wet seasons (March–May, October–December).

Neighboring Countries: Zaïre (Northwest); Uganda (Northeast); Tanzania (East); Burundi (South).

Official Languages: KiNyarwanda, French.

Other Principal Tongues: KiSwahili, English.

Ethnic Background: Hutu (about 90%), Tutsi (about 9%), Twa, or pygmy (1%).

Principal Religions: Christianity (55%) traditional tribal beliefs (44%), Islam (1%). Figures are approximate.

Chief Commercial Products: Coffee, tea, cassiterite (tin ore) wolfram, pyrethrum.

Annual Per Capita Income: Less than U.S. $100.

Currency: Rwanda Franc.

Former Colonial Status: Part of German East Africa (1899–1916); occupied by Belgian troops (1916); Belgian trust territory under the League of Nations and the United Nations (1923–1962).

Independence Date: July 1, 1962.

Chief of State: Pasteur Bizimungu, President.

Head of Government: Faustin Twagiramungu, Prime Minister.

National Flag: Three vertical stripes of equal width, red, yellow and green, with a large "R" on the yellow stripe.

Rwanda, often called the "African Switzerland," is a land lying in the eastern lake region of Africa, composed for the most part of a gently rolling plateau land. Sharp volcanic peaks rise to towering heights in the West on the border of Lake Kivu, generally considered one of the most beautiful of the unspoiled great lakes in Africa. Another mountain range lies to the northwest, topped by Mt. Karisimbi at a height of 13,520 feet.

Rwanda has a mild and temperate climate—the temperature seldom rises above 80°F. during the daytime and the nights are always cool, with frost in the highlands and the mountains.

Many centuries ago, the Virunga volcanoes, some of which are still active, dammed up a section of the Great Western Rift Valley, creating Lake Kivu, with fjord–like bays and inlets. This lake, now the site of resort towns, with swimming, boating and fishing, drains into Lake Tanganyika to the south through the waters of the Ruzizi River. The volcanic activity thus diverted water which flowed upward to the Nile River, forcing it to flow westward to the Atlantic through the immense Zaïre River (Congo), since Lake Tanganyika drains westward to the Zaïre through the Lukuga Creek.

History: As is true in Burundi to the south, the original inhabitants of Rwanda were dimunitive pygmies who seldom reached a height of more than five feet. The Twa were succeeded in turn by the Hutu, sometimes called Buhutu, an industrious people of hunters and farmers having Bantu ancestry. About four centuries ago, a warrior tribe of Hamitic origin, the Tutsi, sometimes called the Watusi, invaded Rwanda from the north. The Hutu were unable to defend themselves against the Tutsi, who were seldom less than six feet tall! The Hutu were reduced to serfdom, each choosing a Tutsi lord protector who gave them the use (but not ownership) of cattle, the most important status symbol and source of wealth among the Tutsi. For early and colonial history, see Historical Background, *The Germans in Africa* and *King Leopold and the Belgians in Africa*.

At the close of the colonial period, the restless Hutu, weary of their serfdom, rose in revolt in 1959 and the years following. They sought equality for all groups in Rwanda, acting through the *National Party of Hutu Emancipation*. Civil war broke out after the death of a Hutu leader and the Mwami, or Tutsi king, and his advisors departed from the country hastily—this was a period when the Tutsi justifiably feared for their lives.

Under Belgian supervision, communal elections were ordered in 1960, resulting in a landslide victory for the more numerous Hutus. Gregoire Kayibanda was selected to head the first government. After a republic was proclaimed in 1961, Kayibanda was appointed Prime Minister. General elections under the supervision of the UN were held in 1961; independence was recommended for Rwanda, which was granted in 1962.

Led by Kayibanda, the *Parmehutu Party* of the Hutus had controlled the government since independence, electing all 47 members of the single–chamber assembly. Alternate members of the party were usually provided as candidates for each seat.

The period 1967–1969 was marked by tension with nearby Zaïre arising out of the continuing struggles within that country. Kayibanda and the *Parmehutu Party* were routinely returned to office in 1969.

Renewed strife between the Hutus and the Tutsi minority occurred in March 1973. Kayibanda was criticized for being too lenient with the Tutsi, who were slaughtering thousands of Hutus in neighboring Burundi. Kayibanda had hoped to change the constitution to permit his return to office for a fourth term in 1973.

Suspecting his Defense Minister Juvenal Habyarimana—the lone northerner in the Cabinet—of disloyalty, Kayibanda ordered him arrested. The attempt triggered a takeover by the army and General Habyarimana was named the new president. A death sentence against Kayibanda was later commuted to life

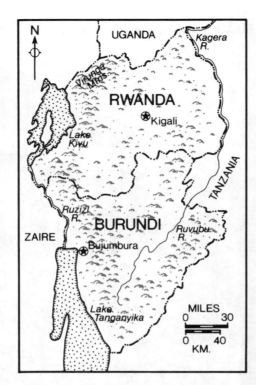

imprisonment. After the 1973 *coup* the government pushed economic reforms vigorously, with limited success because of the ever–swelling population.

The constitution of 1973 effectively limited the presidency to a Hutu, but in the presence of pressure for multi–party government, it was amended in the early 1990s and the restriction was ended. Multi–party elections were scheduled, but postponed because of political unrest and a festering rebellion in the North by Tutsi who fled Rwanda when the Hutu took over the reigns of government. As the contest drew nearer in early 1994, the revolt continued, and Habyarimana was faced with growing pressure from within his own party and the military, both of which thought he was being "too soft" generally in dealing with Tutsis. This feeling had been heightened when Habyarimana agreed in 1992 to an interim government in which power was shared with the rebel Tutsis.

Fighting that erupted in late 1993 in neighboring Burundi largely between the two ethnic groups, proved to be a major factor in igniting warfare in Rwanda in April 1994. Tutsis from Burundi poured into Rwanda by the tens of thousands. Clandestine and government radio stations in both nations fueled the flames of sheer hatred ("You [Tutsis] are cockroaches! . . . We will kill you!"). The Rwanda fighting started in early April 1994 when a plane carrying President Habyarimana (and the Hutu president of Burundi) was shot down while landing at Kigali airport. The enraged presidential guard embarked on the merciless, barbaric killing of any Tutsi found, believing

that persons from that group had downed the aircraft. It is most probable that disgruntled Hutu military personnel were the perpetrators. Habyarimana had been quietly arranging the eradication of his Hutu opponents for several weeks.

Unleashed by a political vacuum and lack of central government, conservative Hutus, particularly the national army, set out to annihilate Tutsis. Barbaric cruelty and genocide ensued in which 1.5 million perished, mostly Tutsi. Their bodies floated downriver into Uganda and Tanzania, creating a nightmare of health problems as they rotted in the hot sun. Civilian Hutus, aware of a 400–year–old tradition of Tutsi vengeance, massively fled to Tanzania and Zaïre to avoid what was certain to be a total Tutsi revenge which would surely spare no Hutu.

The devastation of Rwanda during 1994 continued and no force, internal or external, was able to contain it. Tutsi women who were not slaughtered were raped repeatedly, and in 1995 are bearing children they refuse; they regard their infants as criminals.

The Tutsi *Rwandan Patriotic Front* (FPR) which proclaimed itself the leader of Rwanda in July 1994 after taking Kigali, announced the formation of a coalition government. It is headed by Faustin Twagiramungu, a Hutu. The remainder of Habyarimana's government fled to Zaïre (Goma) from whence it has since attempted to foment a counter–revolution in Rwanda. France had taken an area in southwest Rwanda under its control during the heat of fighting for which it is now under criticism. The *RPF* charges that Hutu forces are being sheltered there. France says it wished to return to the "logic" of "power sharing." The *FPR* government does share power.

Former President Habyarimana

Rebels with the Rwanda Patriotic Front patrol Kigali, June 1994　　　　　　　　AP/Wide World Photo

Culture: More than 90% of the people of Rwanda are agricultural, rural folk, densely crowded (708 per square mile) on the large, grassy plateaus. Although most are Christian, particularly among the Hutus, almost half retain traditional beliefs. Western style clothing has made a slight appearance in the capital and towns, but the traditional *pagne*, tied at the waist over a blouse, with another *pagne* draped about the shoulders is seen widely in the overwhelmingly rural areas. The people are well–known for folk songs and dances, similar to those of the Hutu in Burundi.

Contemporary culture is dominated by savagery described above. It will take decades to revert to normalcy.

Economy: Subsistence agriculture on four million acres of land is overwhelmingly the means of production in Rwanda. Some coffee and tea have been sources of meager amounts of foreign earnings. Rwanda has good hydroelectric potential; there have been several dams in operation before strife enveloped the nation.

Modest economic progress since independence has been wiped out in a few weeks by ethnic strife in 1994 which still continues. No crops have been planted and there will not, therefore, be any significant harvests now. Humanitarian efforts, particularly in food supplies for the people and refugees are only marginally sufficient. Economic activity that was

modest in 1993 disappeared and will not appear until after the turn of the century.

The Future: A very, very fragile stability is now present in Rwanda. Warfare and genocide can erupt without notice, particularly with huge numbers of disgruntled Hutus lurking in Zaïre and Tanzania, waiting for an opportunity for vengeance. The Tutsis are trying to disperse Hutus who remain in refugee camps and are afraid to return to their homes. Ominously, the government has an announced it will conduct "war crimes trials," which in Rwanda simply means more genocide.

The Republic of Congo

Area: 349,650 sq. km = 135,000 sq. mi. (twice the size of Missouri).

Population: 2.55 million (estimated).

Capital City: Brazzaville (Pop. 850,000, estimated).

Climate: Tropically hot and humid.

Neighboring Countries: Gabon (West); Cameroon (Northwest); Central African Republic (North); Zaïre (East, South).

Official Language: French.

Other Principal Tongues: Bantu dialects, principally Lingala, KiKongo, Munoko-toba and KiBougo.

Ethnic Background: There are about 50 identifiable subgroups of Bantu origin, with the following major groups: BaKongo (48%), Brazzaville, South;

Songha (20%) and M'Bochi (12%), North; Teke (17%), central area.

Principal Religions: Christian (sometimes with mixture of local beliefs (50%), traditional tribal beliefs (49%); figures are approximate.

Chief Commercial Products: Oil, wood products and timber, potash, palm oil, cocoa, bananas, peanuts.

Annual Per Capita Income: About U.S. $1400.

Currency: CFA Franc (no longer tied to the French franc).

Former Colonial Status: French Congo (1883–1910); one of the four territories of French Equatorial Africa (1910–1960).

Independence Date: August 15, 1960.

Chief of State: Pascal Lissouba, President (b. 1930).

Head of Government: Jacques–Joachim Yhombi–Opango, Prime Minister.

National Flag: Red, with the national emblem in the upper lefthand corner which includes a yellow star above a crossed hoe and hammer flanked by two green palm branches.

This lush, green land of ancient tradition lies immediately to the north of the great Zaïre (Congo) River. Formerly a part of French Equatorial Africa, the country has the same general geographical features as the Republic of Zaïre to the south.

As early as the fifteenth and sixteenth centuries, this land was part of the great native Kingdom of the Congo. Its present day boundaries, as is so often the case in Africa, are based upon arbitrary determinations of the 19th century European powers rather than on cultural and physical reality.

A low–lying, treeless plain extends forty miles from the coast to the interior, succeeded by a mountainous region parallel to the coastline known as the Mayombe Escarpment. This is a region of sharply rising mountain ridges covered with jungle and dense growth. Continuing further, the Niari River Valley, an important agricultural area, extends to the east, and to the north lies The Pool, a region of treeless hills and a succession of grassy plains, covering some 50,000 square miles. Part of the Zaïre River Basin lies in the extreme northeast, a region of dense jungle and all but impassable plains. The climate is uniform and equatorial—hot and humid all year.

History: As in the neighboring country of Zaïre, legend common to this region conveys the story of the mighty Kingdom of the Congo, said to have been founded by Wene, also known as Nimi Loukemi, the first king, who reigned more than 400 years ago. For details of early and colonial history, see Historical Background and *The French in Africa*.

Following independence, Fulbert Youlou, who had been instrumental in charting the course toward independence, was installed as president in 1960. A single–chamber assembly of 55 members was established under the constitution, which had the power to remove the president.

There was an uprising in 1963 which removed Youlou from office, and the military established a provisional government; following constitutional reform and adoption, Alphonse Mossambat–Debat was elected to a five–year term of office as president.

From 1966 to 1968, Cubans replaced advisors from all other nations, but since that time their influence has waned. Chinese influence was prevalent for a period, and substantial loans were made by the Soviet Union.

Mossambat–Debat was ousted from office in late 1968 after the army leadership rebelled. A *National Revolutionary Council* initially selected Alfred Raoul to lead the nation, but he was soon replaced by Marien Ngouabi. It was announced that the country would be known as the "People's Republic of the Congo" and the sole party was to be the *Congolese Labor Party*. He insisted that although Marxism is a "universal science," nevertheless it has different application in each country. He refused to take sides in the ongoing Soviet–Chinese war of words, and he was one of the few African leaders to state openly that a single–party system is necessary to prevent tribal warfare.

For over a decade, relations between the United States and Congo were frozen. Normal ties were restored between the two in 1977.

Ngouabi was assassinated in March 1977; a military tribunal was hastily convened which quickly accused and convicted Mossambat–Debat of being behind the killing. He was executed and an 11 man military committee took control. Ngouabi's military successor lasted two years, and was ousted in 1979; Colonel Denis Sassou–Nguesso took over as "caretaker" president—and was confirmed in that office in late March. Sassou–Nguesso tried to deal with traditional North/South tribal divisions within Congo and took a number of steps to correct economic problems, such as adoption of austerity measures, agreements with the International Monetary Fund to improve the balance of payments, and a complete reorganization of state–run enterprises. Congo became a more attractive place for western investment, especially in the areas of forestry and petroleum exploration. His governments included former critics. He was popular enough to capture 1989 elections, winning a third 5–year term.

Required membership of government officials in the communist party was dropped in 1990, and an interim government was given the task of writing a new constitution to establish a multi–party system. Scheduled elections were postponed until mid–1992 after 14 political parties emerged. The elections were held in two rounds; the first eliminated Sassou–Nguesso and in the second round Pascal Lissouba, of the then–opposition *Pan African Union for Social Democracy (UPADS)* was chosen president by a majority of 61%. The former president was granted amnesty as to any acts committed during his years in office.

Legislative elections were inconclusive and a coalition government lasted only until late 1992. Elections, that should have been held within 45 days after the fall of the government, were postponed because of violence, which although low–level, was almost continuous. The opposition coalition, the *Union for Democratic Renewal–Congolese Workers Party (URD-PCT)* charged there were irregularities in several contests. It took months of negotiations in Libreville (Gabon) followed by more elections to resolve the disputes by further elections in October 1993. Pascal Lissouba was victor in the contest for the presidency; his party and its allies control 65 out of the 125 seats in the National Assembly. Private militias persist, including that of Sassou–Nguesso who still claims the 1993 election was invalid; there is periodic violence in Brazzaville because of them.

Culture: The tribal patterns of the Bantu people dominate the social life of the Republic of Congo. Their music and dance has a singular beauty identical with that of the people to the south in Zaïre. One–sixth of the population lives in the two principal cities, Brazzaville and Pointe–Noire, both of which have modern architecture and up–to–date

Former President Sassou–Nguesso

President Pascal Lissouba

medical and educational facilities. The country has the highest literacy rates in Black Africa, estimated at over 75%.

In the countryside, social life centers around the family, tribe and clan, living together in small, isolated towns having little contact with each other. Although there is extensive farm industry in the Nairi Valley, most of the remaining interior is still the wild, mysterious, hot and sparsely populated region of yesteryear.

Economy: Traditionally tied to agriculture, Congo has gradually been able to broaden its economic base to include oil production, now accounting for more than 50% of its foreign exchange. Chief agricultural products are coffee, cacao and tobacco. Many fine hardwoods such as okoumé and limba are in much demand in foreign markets, while tin and lead are among the principal mined minerals.

Congo had a temporary romance with the communist bloc nations, but now is firmly interrelated with the western nations economically. As one government figure put it, "We are not *too* red." External debts were renegotiated in the late 1980s and again in 1994 to permit payment of past due wages to government employees and the military. One condition of continued external credit is lower salaries paid to government workers.

The Future: Political rivalry will remain at a high level despite the fact that almost all politicians were members of the old communist party.

The Republic of Gabon (pronounced Gah–*bonh*)

Gabonese mechanics replace an outboard motor on the Ogooue River

World Bank photo

Area: 264,180 sq. km. = 102,000 sq. mi. (about the size of Colorado).

Population: 1.28 million (estimated).

Capital City: Libreville (Pop. 137,000, estimated).

Climate: Hot and humid. Although there is almost no rain from June to September, the humidity remains quite high. Rainfall in the remaining months totals more than 100 inches per year.

Neighboring Countries: Equatorial Guinea (Northwest); Cameroon (North); Congo (East, South).

Official Language: French.

Other Principal Tongues: Bantu dialects, including Fang (a widely used *lingua franca*), Eshira, Adouma, Okanda.

Ethnic Background: Almost all Gabonese are of Bantu origin. There are 40 tribal groups; major groups are the Fang, Eshira, Mbade, Adouma and Okanda. There are 20,000 resident French nationals.

Principal Religions: Christianity (60%) sometimes with intermingled traditional tribal beliefs, the remaining people worship according to traditional tribal beliefs.

Chief Commercial Products: Petroleum, timber, manganese, uranium, gold.

Annual Per Capita Income: About U.S. $4,000.

Currency: CFA Franc (no longer tied to the French franc).

Former Colonial Status: French Colony (1903–1960).

Independence Date: August 17, 1960.

Chief of State: Omar Bongo, President.

National Flag: A tri–color, with horizontal stripes of green, golden yellow and royal blue.

Lying astride the Equator on the west coast of Africa, Gabon is a land of hot and humid jungle with a heavy rainfall. The coastal lowlands from 20 to 120 miles in depth receive up to 150 inches of rain per year. A series of plateaus rise further inland, spreading from the northeast to the southeast of the country with altitudes from 1,000 to 2,000 feet. They are densely packed with lush green vegetation. The remainder of the land is covered by gentle, round mountains extending to heights of 5,200 feet.

The jungle is filled with the sounds of animal life—the roar of mammoth gorillas, the cough of night–roaming leopards, the screech of treetop monkeys and a symphony of tropical bird calls. The land,

although somewhat inhospitable to man, is an animal paradise.

The ground, choked by vines and dense brush, is dimly lit during the day—very little light penetrates through the thick crowns of the tallest trees. Wind may blow overhead, but it cannot pass through the tall foliage to relieve the high temperatures and moist air close to the ground.

History: For countless generations, the Bantu tribes, divided into many distinct groups, lived undisturbed by explorers and adventurers. For details of earlier and colonial history, see Historical Background and *The French in Africa*.

At the time of independence there were two major political parties—*The Gabon Democratic Bloc* and the *Social Democratic Union of Gabon*. The parties, led respectively by Leon Mbá and J.H. Aubame, were evenly divided in the first election; neither captured a majority of the 40–seat Assembly, but Mbá's party, joined by four independent representatives, selected him as the first Prime Minister. Through a series of measures, Mbá was able to get rid of the opposition party and then he dissolved the Assembly in 1964 to hold elections under rules excluding his opponents. The army revolted, but French troops intervened the next day and reinstated Mbá's government. It later won an overwhelming majority in the Assembly; since 1964 *The Gabon Democratic Party* became the sole party, winning all seats in each election. When Mbá died in 1967, he was succeeded by Vice–President Albert Bongo.

Bongo announced in 1973 that he was renouncing Roman Catholicism and adopting Islam, changing his name from Albert–Bernard to *El–Hadj* Omar. He ran a tight ship and was "reelected" to three seven–year terms. Even hints of dissent were put down. He threatened to exile resident French nationals (about 2,000) who meddled in Gabon's internal affairs. Corruption in government is rampant; a reduction in salaries had little meaning because of this. The impressive wealth from oil fuels political restiveness.

In spite of pressures, a multi–party system was rejected by the president in 1990, but he quickly reversed his position. He was re–elected in a contest in December 1993 by a 51% majority. His principal opponent was Paul Mba Abessole of the *National Rally of Woodcutters (RNB)*, but there were ten more candidates who effectively diluted opposition voting. Unrest for two months followed the election, which although officially proclaimed to be untainted, was most probably riddled with irregularities. The radio station of the woodcutters in Libreville was seized by presidential forces in early 1993 after Abessole had proclaimed

President Omar Bongo

himself president of a "parallel" government.

At the firm suggestion of the French, Bongo appointed six members of the opposition to the cabinet; they took office in late 1994 after some initial resistance to the move. Whether this will lessen tensions remains to be seen.

Culture: The majority of Gabon's people live in the cities and larger towns. Much of the interior land has not been settled except by a few pygmies dwelling in the dense rain forest. Literacy is rapidly advancing under the influence of universal education. The government claims a literacy rate of 80% but a more accurate figure would be about 50%. Most students are in the primary grades, but several thousand pursue advanced courses of study, some of whom attend colleges and universities in other countries.

The dress, language and customs of the people are as varied as the number of ethnic groups. There is a high percentage of

Christians, predominantly Roman Catholic, most of whom live in the coastal region. With the exception of a few thousand Islamic believers, the rest of the people cling to their traditional tribal beliefs. One interesting variation is *Christianisme Cëleste*, which originated in Nigeria and other nearby countries.

Libreville, the capital city, strategically situated on a peninsula, contains an irregular pattern of modern buildings and small, tin–roofed dwellings. Port Gentil, at the mouth of the Ogooue River, in which life centers around trade and commerce, is the second largest city.

Economy: Gabon is the richest Black nation of Africa because of oil production and export of minerals and tropical woods. Manganese ore, with uranium and gold content, is an important resource. Wood products, principally Okoumé, a moderately soft wood suitable for plywood is the largest non–oil export.

The trans–Gabon railway links Libreville to the southeastern border, opening the interior's resources. Fluctuations in world oil prices have made budgeting difficult in this nation which is so dependent upon the revenues produced. The price has been more stable in the 1990s. As might be expected, Gabon has borrowed substantially ($2 billion) against future oil earnings and has had to seek renegotiation of the terms of repayment.

The Future: Political rivalries are actually contests over access to the national treasury. It will be safe to oppose the government in Gabon, as long as there is not too much discord.

Gabonese boxers

The Republic of Zaïre (pronounced Zah–*ear*)

Downtown Kinshasa

AP/Wide World Photo

Note: Throughout this chapter the country is referred to as Zaïre, but was designated the *Belgian Congo* before independence, then the *Democratic Republic of the Congo* in 1967. President Mobutu had it renamed Zaïre in 1971.

Area: 2,343,950 sq. km = 905,000 sq. mi. (one–third the size of the U.S.).

Population: 38 million (estimated).

Capital City: Kinshasa (Pop. 3.9 million, estimated).

Climate: Warm and humid tropical weather in the western and central areas, temperate in the eastern highlands.

Neighboring Countries: Congo (North, West); Central African Republic, Sudan (North); Uganda, Rwanda, Burundi and Tanzania (East); Zambia and Angola (South).

Official Language: French.

Other Principal Tongues: Lingala (Northeastern Zaïre River basin); KiNgwana (Northeastern, Eastern and Southern areas); KiKongo (Kinshasa coastal area); Tshiluba (Southeastern area); KiSwahili is widely used.

Ethnic Background: There are about 200 identifiable tribes in Zaïre, with the following major groupings: Bantu—Bakongo, Bangala, Bamongo, Batetela, Lulua (Bavalulua), Baluba, Balamba and Bakomba, about 70%; Sudanic, about 20%, Pygmy, about 7%; Nilotic–Hamitic, about 3%.

Principal Religions: Christianity (90% +, often with local beliefs and practices intermingled), traditional beliefs (7%), Islam (1%); figures are approximate.

Chief Commercial Products: Diamonds, cobalt, petroleum, coffee. Very little economic activity remains after years of mismanagement and corruption.

Annual Per Capita Income: Less than $100 U.S. except in diamond mining areas.

Currency: Zaïre (worthless).

Former Colonial Status: Personal possession of King Leopold II of Belgium (1885–1907); Belgian Colony (1907–1960).

Independence Date: June 30, 1960.

Chief of State: General Mobutu Sese Seko, President (b. 1930); he formerly used his baptismal name, Joseph Dèsirè Mobutu.

National Flag: Green, with a yellow circle surrounding a red torch.

The deep green region of Zaïre has intrigued explorers, adventurers and writers for centuries, becoming one of the popular stereotypes of Africa in the western mind. Dark jungles and rain forests abounding in game, and almost as unknown today as at the time of Stanley's explorations, adjoin huge mining developments and vast plantations, some of which have been broken down into smaller farms. The very size of Zaïre is one of its most distinctive features. Even more interesting, this huge nation has only a 25–mile–long coastline which allows it to "breathe" on the South Atlantic Ocean.

There are three distinctive features of this land mass: the immense river basin of the Zaïre and its tributaries, tropically hot and humid; the rich mining areas are

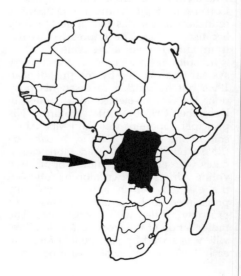

located in the eastern sector and the upland plains in the northeast and southeast with tall, rippling grasses and snow-capped mountains rising to almost 17,000 feet in the East near the Equator. The eastern lake region, which includes Lake Kivu and the western shores of Lakes Tanganyika, Mweru, Albert and Edward, is unsurpassed in scenic beauty and abounds in wildlife.

Tributaries of the great Zaïre River flow from these lakes into the Lualaba River, which in turn becomes the Zaïre after it reaches 4° south latitude. From this point, the Zaïre surges in a wide, island-dotted course through the jungles, joined by its other tributaries. Three hundred miles inland from the Atlantic, at Malebo Pool (near bustling Kisangani), the river widens into a lake, continuing on to the sea with a width of up to ten miles. The river is navigable for the most part and widely used in commerce, interrupted only by cataracts at Malebo Falls (formerly Stanley Falls) and below Kinshasa. Railway by-passes have been constructed at these cataracts to maintain the continuity of commerce.

History: Before the arrival of European explorers, the mighty Kingdom of the Congo, with an age-old way of life, included not only the present-day Republic of Zaïre, but what is now Angola and west equatorial Africa. Until the middle of the 19th century, this area was virtually unknown to the western world. Earlier, Portuguese penetration was not sig-nificant, though it did result indirectly in the consecration of the first Black bishop by the Roman Catholic Church in 1520. For details of early and colonial history, see Historical Background and *King Leopold and the Belgians in Africa.*

There was little effort made prior to independence to prepare the Black people of Zaïre for self-rule, although the Belgians did establish primary and secondary schools which would have eventually served as a basis for higher education. Much of this effort was through Catholic missionaries. In the middle 1950's, two leaders became prominent when political activity was first permitted. Joseph Kasavubu led *ABAKO*, an organization composed of Bakongo people. Patrice Lumumba, a Batetela from the interior, headed the *MNC*, which had almost no tribal identity and was composed of memberships of a number of smaller ethnic groups.

Belgium proposed in 1956 that The Congo (Zaïre) become independent in 30 years, but Kasavubu demanded freedom in "much less than 30 years." For the first time, elections were scheduled in 1957 in which Africans were to participate; they were limited to lesser municipal offices. When French Congo, across the river, was offered independence by French President Charles de Gaulle in 1958, there was renewed pressure brought on Belgium to grant independence to its colony. An impending threat of independence, coupled with tumbling world copper prices, led to a withdrawal of foreign capital from Zaïre in the late 1950's, making a shambles of the economy and creating widespread unemployment.

In this turbulent atmosphere, Belgium summoned the African leaders to Brussels in early 1960 and announced that independence would become effective on June 30th. The Belgian government (and the industrial giants who had large investments in Zaïre) promoted this swift move in the anticipation that conditions would deteriorate within Zaïre, justifying a resumption of control by Belgium. This was a gamble they came close to winning.

The African politicians hurried home to Zaïre to gain support; the people were tantalized by a multitude of promises of good things to come with independence (under the "right" leadership, of course). A multitude of new parties sprang up, almost overnight. The intense political and tribal activity served as a forewarning to thousands of Europeans, who began to leave Zaïre in droves.

Although pre-independence elections were relatively calm, the result was an impossible splintering of representation. Lumumba's *MNC* won the greatest number of seats—33 out of 137 in the House and 24 in the 84-seat Senate. After ten days of bargaining behind closed doors, Lumumba announced a coalition with a 37-member cabinet containing officials from no less than 16 parties. Amid pomp and ceremony, but with overtones of bitterness, independence was declared on the chosen date with Kasavubu as president and Lumumba as premier.

President Kasavubu (center) and Premier Lumumba confer with Belgian army chief, 1960

Premier Moise Tshombe greeted by spear-carrying warriors in Kivu Province, August 1964.

The situation in Zaïre quickly deteriorated into lawlessness, rebellion, anarchy, revolt and secession. It started when the *Force Publique,* consisting of 1,000 White officers and 24,000 African soldiers, disintegrated into open mutiny. The Black soldiers seized arms in the major cities and embarked upon sheer terrorism against their officers in particular and against *all* White people in general. Hundreds of Whites were mercilessly slaughtered and thousands of others were beaten and tortured; within a week there was a renewed mass exodus of White people. A refugee airlift had to be instituted when commercial flights were cancelled. The events taking place over the succeeding five years consisted of unrestrained violence in a nation where there was literally no central government.

The turmoil which had almost immediately engulfed the new nation brought a new and ambitious actor to the scene. Moise Tshombe, Premier of the copper–rich southeastern province of Shaba (then called *Katanga),* announced that the area would be a separate nation; a neighboring province, South Kasai, also seceded from Zaïre. With President Kasavubu and Premier Lumumba literally at each other's political throats, Belgium flew in paratroopers to put down the civil war which it quickly realized could not be handled by the central government, but troops in Shaba fought them tooth and nail. In the meantime, a UN peace–keeping force was sent into Zaïre to help maintain some semblance of stability.

Two months after Shaba had announced its severance from Zaïre, President Kasavubu decided to eliminate his rival, Lumumba, once and for all—he had the army seize power and hand Lumumba over to the self–proclaimed President of Katanga (Shaba), Moise Tshombe. Kasavubu's plan worked— Lumumba was promptly killed.

A year later, the country was still caught up in civil war, and UN Secretary General Dag Hammerskjold was killed in a plane crash on his way to try to talk peace with the tough Tshombe.

The fierce fighting continued into August 1962 when the UN submitted a plan for peaceful settlement of the civil war. Tshombe was riding high and would have no part of it; Katangan troops even fired upon UN forces in late 1962 to show their scorn for the world organization's interference in their independence movement. But it was a losing battle against too many outside forces, and Tshombe gave in to the central government in early 1963. Under these conditions, UN troops withdrew from Zaïre in mid year.

Another rebellion of rival factions began to take shape. In a move made out of desperation—and urgently needing a strong individual to take charge—President Kasavubu appointed Tshombe to become premier. The defeated leader used foreign mercenaries and Belgian paratroopers to put down the rebellion.

He got no word of thanks from President Kasavubu, who, frightened and envious of Tshombe's growing popularity, fired him as premier. Then General Joseph Dèsirè Mobutu took center stage and ousted *the president* in late 1965.

Army Chief of Staff before his decision to take power, Mobutu immediately nationalized the huge Belgian mining operation which had controlled Zaïre's copper production since colonial times. He also took precautions with Tshombe—he was ordered to leave Zaïre nine months after Mobutu had seized the government. In some way which has never been explained, Tshombe's plane was hijacked by a French mercenary pilot and he was held under arrest in Algeria until his death of a heart attack two years later.

By juggling bureaucrats and sewing the seeds of suspicion to pit one tribe against another (at which Mobutu has been a master), he all but eliminated opposition in the 1970 elections and won a 7–year term as president.

Basic Change From the Past

Mobutu clashed head–on with the Roman Catholic Church of which he was a member, in 1971. He decreed Africanization of all names, including his own, trying to force Catholic priests to stop using Christian names at baptism. When the Church publicly opposed the policy, his newly–formed party, the *Popular Movement for the Revolution (MPR)* sought indictment of the Cardinal for an unspecified crime. The Catholic press in the country was shut down. Mobutu replaced the name of Congo (Kinshasa) with *Zaïre,* the Portuguese transliteration of the native name "Big River." The Cardinal left for Rome and Mobutu told the Pope to keep him there. Tensions increased, and some 5,000 foreigners were expelled for trivial reasons.

The Cardinal returned in mid–1972; Mobutu had increased his demands to include allowance of the youth wing of the *MPR* to work in Catholic schools, which had been closed. The Zaïrese bishops acceded and the schools reopened.

Mass nationalization began in late 1973; Zaïre took total control over the copper industry. All ore was to be refined within the country. All plantations and farms owned by foreigners became Zaïrese property, to be paid for by fair compensation over a period of ten years. Every foreign private company had to have a Zaïrese chairman or general manager; competence was not a consideration—friendship or relationship with Mobutu was what counted.

The country's constitution was revised in 1974, establishing the *MPR's* doctrine of "Mobutism" which embodied the "thought, teaching and actions" of the president. Zaïre would become neutral towards religion. Religious instruction in the primary and secondary schools was replaced by courses in civics and politics *a la* Mobutu. He justified this by saying that the children should first know the man who "sacrifices himself for them day and night before they know of the Pope . . ." (He is reliably reported to have sacrificed $6 *billion* of the public treasury to himself in foreign bank accounts while the people live in abject poverty).

By 1977, foreign pressures forced Mobutu to hold scheduled elections (which he would have liked to avoid) for president and for a 270–member legislature. The elections were remarkably free, but the legislature has been little more than a debating society—President Mobutu makes the decisions.

During the Angolan war of 1975–1977, Mobutu backed the *FNLA* guerrillas, whose leader, Holden Roberto, was a relative by marriage; he opposed the Soviet–backed *MPLA*.

Mobutu made some drastic changes in 1975. He nationalized most of the economy which had not been, barred religious instruction in schools and Africanized all names, beginning with his own.

Southern Zaïre was attacked from Angola in 1977 by a group calling themselves the *Congolese National Liberation Front* which pushed into Shaba Province and came close to the hub of the mining operations in the area, the bustling town of Kolwezi. France and Belgium immediately supplied weapons—but not troops—when Mobutu appealed for help. Shortly thereafter, France flew in 1,500 Moroccan soldiers who defeated the invaders and drove them back into Angola. The following year there was another onslaught from Angola; this time it was better organized. Kolwezi fell to the rebels and over 100 Whites and 300 Blacks were killed in fierce fighting. This time France and Belgium sent men, not just arms. Over 1,000 Foreign Legion paratroopers drove the rebels back into Angola and 1,700 Belgians helped evacuate the 2,000 frightened Europeans from the area. The United States sent in cargo planes to help airlift out the civilians—there was general agreement that this second invasion was the work of the Soviets and their Cuban underlings operating within Angola.

General Mobutu Sese Seko Kuru Ngebendu Wa Za Banga, once just a salaried army officer, is now one of the world's wealthiest men. A proud, secretive man, he has avoided all public rallies as his popularity rating has diminished. His family and friends have also reaped large fortunes—it has been said in the past that almost 40% of revenues find their way into the pockets of Zaïrian bureaucrats.

There has been a pattern of corruption and mismanagement of business which is unmistakable. The army, police and a network of informers, have made Zaïrese suspicious of each other—and of all outsiders. Government and military officials are carefully screened. To lessen any threat of secession from Shaba Province, hub of the copper and cobalt operations, Mobutu in 1984 appointed Ditenje Tshombe, son of the late Moise

An earth mover deep in the Kolwezi Copper Pit, formerly the biggest in the world   AP/Wide World Photo

President Mobutu Sese Seko

Tshombe, Secretary of State for Mines and Energy.

Belgian and French personnel struggled to make the army into a strong, disciplined unit after the Shaba invasions, with limited success. After talks with Israeli officials, Mobutu announced in 1982 the formation of an elite guard trained by that country's military personnel. The purpose: protection of the president, which it has done well.

Mobutu's rule has been charitably called "very tight." An economy plagued by corruption and mismangement lagged badly, necessitating repeated devaluations of the Zaïre. Accompanying food shortages have been acute and inflation always out of hand. He came to the U.S. in 1981 to seek aid (the currect deficit in foreign loans exceeds $5 billion). When he and his entourage of almost 100 spent $2 million on parties in New York and Florida, the U.S. budget for Zaïrian aid was pared substantially, causing President Mobutu to renounce U.S. aid, terming a demanded investigation into Zaïrian official corruption and the reduction "insulting."

Relations with Belgium for the last decade have been tempestuous. That country's leadership resented the widespread and open corruption of Zaïre's leadership, particularly insofar as it involved the disappearance of all or part of substantial loans made to its former colony. Mobutu hinted at establishing close ties with the French. Belgium capitulated, forgiving substantial loans and rescheduling others.

Zaïre now is in a state of virtual anarchy. The events leading up to this started in 1991 and a chronicle of them is not as important as is an understanding of the forces (and lack thereof) which have led to this state of affairs. They are discussed in order of current importance:

(Joseph) Mobutu Sese Seko—Generally disliked except by those he finan-cially supports and favors, this despot regards Zaïre and all that is within it as his own property in the same manner that King Leopold II regarded the former Belgian Free State (see p. 33) as his personal property. He has accumulated immense wealth ($6 billion) in foreign bank accounts. During 1992–3 diamonds were his source of wealth, but thievery at the mines and processing centers has reduced the amount received by what is left of the government to less than 10% of what it formerly had been.

In order to preserve his own power, Mobutu has actually promoted anarchy in Zaïre, most probably on the theory that it is easier to maintain authority over nothing rather than something. The presence of 200 tribal groups and an absence of a legislature with continuity in Zaïre has meant that it has not been possible for anyone to become an actual rival of Mobutu. Calling off scheduled elections in 1991, he simply proclaimed himself president for a fourth term.

The Presidential Guard—This exceptionally well–trained elite unit is the force that keeps Mobutu in power. It has a high degree of loyalty to him and regards itself as superior to ordinary military personnel. It is paid regularly and well in hard currency rather than in the usually worthless Zaïre. Estimates of its strength vary from 1,800 to 4,500.

The Army—Numbering about 50,000, the army personnel are also regularly paid, but with Zaïres which diminish in value so rapidly they are spent while they are worth at least something. Mobutu avoids a repetition of non–payment of the army; this quickly leads to disobedience, mutiny and activities resembling resistance such as occurred in 1993 when payment was made in "new" Zaïres. The basic loyalty of the army is to a regular paycheck, not to Mobutu. Few other government workers have been paid since 1991 and exist by thievery and corruption in a wide variety of forms.

But veterans are not paid and there is an abundance of them. To survive, they usually group into

Militias—These well–armed groups have no relation to the army and no allegiance toward Mobutu. They are the loose cannon on Zaïre's deck. Travelling about usually in appropriated vehicles, they plunder and murder randomly, sometimes seizing entire towns to extract anything of value. The army is reluctant to exercise any control over these groups. In 1992 these groups engaged in rioting in which the French Ambassador was murdered by machine gun. Foreign troops removed the small number of non–Zaïrese, ferrying them across the river to Brazzaville. These militias are widely feared.

Etienne Tschisekedi wa Malumba—This leader of the *Sacred Union*, an anti–Mobutu coalition, is not widely respected; the reason, among other things, has been his ineffective opposition. From Kasai province, he was arrested in 1988 and tried (after being "treated" for a mental disorder supposedly arising out of his political activism). Nevertheless, Mobutu selected him as Prime Minister in late 1991, in an attempt to preempt the opposition. The arrangement lasted three weeks before he was fired, but he still refuses to be fired and has the support of the High Council of the Republic (HRC) (see below). He has some (but little) power there, but *it* has none. Thus, in reality he is nothing but a politician which the army and presidential guard harass more often than other members of the (HRC).

The National Conference—Stalling for time, Mobutu in 1991 called for the convening of *The National Conference*, consisting of more than 2,000 delegates. He stacked the membership with his own people; for this reason it appeared to be purposeless when it convened on July 31, 1991. Nevertheless, before it adjourned permanently on December 6, 1992, it abolished the old legislature (National Legislative Council) and established the 435–member High Council of the Republic (HRC). It "elected" Tchisekedi Prime Minister; Mobutu dismissed the moves, saying it had no powers and that he, alone, possessed sovereign powers.

The High Council of the Republic—This was and is a "transitional" legislature established by the National Conference (above). It is treated with utter contempt by Mobutu, and it confirmed the "election" of Tshisekedi as Prime Minister in retaliation. In 1993 Mobutu dismissed the Prime Minister because of his "inability" to form a government. After leaving to receive dental treatment in France, he had troops surround the People's Palace where the HCR met.

A trench was dug around the building, and food and water were cut off. The announced purpose was to force the legislature to endorse the new Z 5 million currency bill which had been repudiated by Tchisekedi. It had been printed in such large quantities that it was worthless. In response to howls of protest from the U.S., the blockade was ended but the army affirmed its duty to assume its "responsibilities."

Another controversial move by the HCR was repudiation of the name *Zaïre* and reversion to the name "Congo;" this infuriated Mobutu and the matter has just been left hanging.

The Sacred Union—This is a loose coalition of no less that 130 political parties and is active as the majority in the HCR. It's anti–Mobutu outlook is just about the only glue that holds it together.

Zaïre has descended into *de facto* anarchy. There is only sporadic electricity, almost no telephone service, no public transport, no wares in the stores, no police protection, no functioning sanitation facilities or personnel, very little money of value, no employment, no salaries . . . nothing. Few government employees even appear at work except to collect a bribe. The people blame Mobutu, but the politicians in the HCR run a close second.

An example of the disintegration of Zaïre occurred in December 1993 when Shaba Province in the South declared itself to be totally autonomous, reverting to its former name Katanga. The gesture was meaningless since most evidence of the central government's authority had already evaporated.

Zaïre is theoretically operating under a new constitution which failed to recognize Tchisekedi's position as Prime Minister. The National Assembly, Zaïre's currency, the new Prime Minister and his cabinet are all simply irrelevant. At the close of 1994 there was U.S. $2,000 and a few Swiss franks in the national bank. The nation of *Zaïre is non–existent in fact—it is a void where there is no government or meaningful organization.*

Relief efforts to support a half million Rwandan refugees are by the UN and are tenuous. Although the death rate in camps located in eastern Zaïre has been lowered, efforts have been hindered by Rwandan army (Hutu) corruption in distribution of food. Further, return of Rwandans to their homeland is blocked by those troops. The collapse of Zaïre's public health institutions poses an immediate threat.

Culture: The social structure of Zaïre is almost unchanged from what it was prior to the arrival of Europeans. Family, clan and tribe are the units of organization. Tribes are usually names for a distant ancestor or a nearby river. Dance is associated with every important event from birth to death, accentuated by the clapping of hands and the accompaniment of varieties of drums, bells, horns and locally–fashioned flutes.

The three largest cities, Kinshasa, the capital (west), Lubumbashi (south) and Kisangani (north) have dominated the cultural and commercial activities in Zaïre, but are now little more than centers of anarchy. Public schools rapidly replaced the religious schools, but they have evaporated. Teacher salaries have remained unpaid since 1992, so pupils bring the salary of their instructors to school with them.

Virtually no foreigners are present in Zaïre because of impending chaos. They formerly were present to train Zaïrian nationals in technical and educational skills intended to reduce dependence on "outsiders."

Although Mobutu likes to be called *The Guide* and appear as a father–figure to the Zaïrese, this posture deceives few people, who are more concerned with the harsh reality of eking out a living.

Economy: There is no economy in the present–day sense of that word. Almost all activity is by a primitive barter system that inadequately serves the needs of the people, if at all. The currency, gripped in an inflation rate of 9,000% annually, is all but worthless, even in its new form. The Zaïre technically trades at $2.00 with the U.S. dollar, but it is luck when it fetches two cents.

At the time of independence, this was one of the potentially richest nations in the world, with vast deposits of copper, cobalt and diamonds. But government corruption, mismanagement and thievery was a ball and chain around the economic leg of Zaïre through the 1980s. A political class emerged with varying labels, usually identified with one side or the other of the Cold War, or neutrality. But, regardless of category, the political class was fervently devoted to ordinary thievery, and was like an arid blotter placed on a moisture–laden table.

This state of affairs was possible since 1965 largely because of the Cold War. Mobutu was staunchly anti–communist and seemed to be an angel among devils on the African continent in the eyes of the U.S. and western Europe. When the Cold War evaporated in the late 1980s, the justification for Mobutu's continued presence left. But he stays on, dragging Zaïre into an economic pit with dogged determination.

The immense copper mines of Shaba province are now flooded and unworked. About 30% of the diamonds mined *are not stolen* but of the money they produce, about 50% reaches a "legitimate" destina-

tion: the corrupt army. Diamond mining towns resemble their equivalent in the U.S. west in the 19th century—fortunes come and go and many perish in the quest for primarily industrial quality stones. Illegal miners ("clandestines") infest government mines and are dealt with ruthlessly when apprehended.

At the time of independence there were about 80,000 miles of good to fair roads in this huge country; most have been swallowed up by jungle growth, leaving few passable by vehicles larger than a jeep. Transportation in the interior is by primitive river barge on the Zaïre River, the avenue of almost all internal trade.

Until the 1990s the government bought all farm crops at prices set by it; this depressed output by imposing a layer of thieving bureaucrats between the farmers and their markets. Well over 1,000 businesses were taken from their owners and distributed to Mobutu's friends. Not possessing the skills and motivation to run them, the new owners let them simply rot away. Only a few former owners returned, but since have left Zaïre.

External debts are now just being ignored by Zaïre; the result is that only humanitarian supplies trickle into the country.

The Future: Utterly nothing can happen which is constructive in Zaïre until Mobutu and his presidential guard are no longer part of the scene. But even such a change does not mean things will improve because there are just too many people of little ability and no sense of humanitarian service available to lead Zaïre out of its chaos. Only 25 years of luck and hard work will return this country to its pre–independence economic level.

Presidents Mobutu and Bush discuss a peace plan for Angola   AP/Wide World Photo

101

SOUTHERN AFRICA

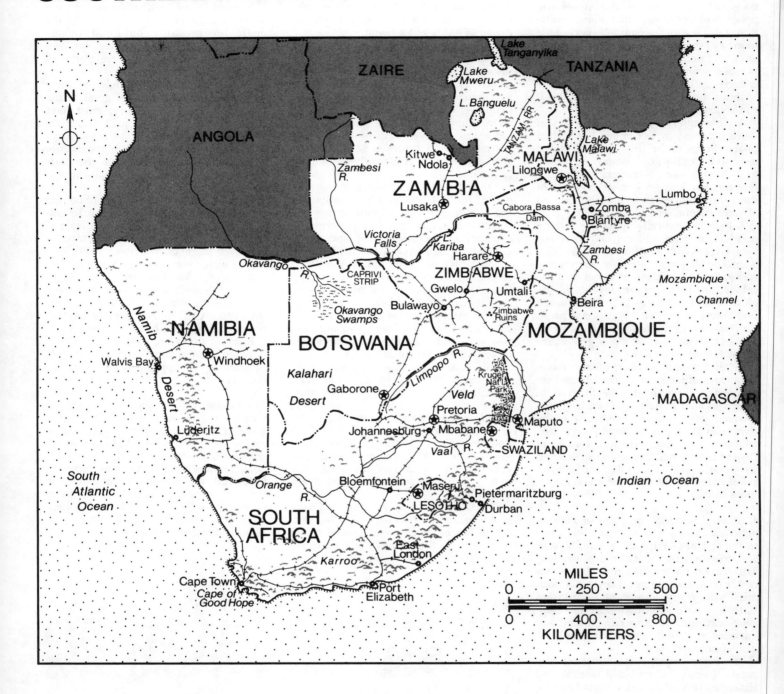

THE CITIZEN

INCORPORATING THE FINANCIAL GAZETTE

Johannesburg Tuesday 10 May 1994

Cover price: 90c

HISTORIC DAY FOR SA, MANKIND

Says US Vice-President Gore

UNITED States Vice-President Al Gore, heading a 65-strong US delegation, the most senior to visit South Africa, for the inauguration of President Nelson Mandela today said the moment was historic not only for South Africa but for all mankind.

The inauguration of Mr Mandela marked a tran- sition in the history of the world, he said.

He spoke on a day in which British Foreign Secretary Douglas Hurd, Cuban President Fidel Castro, Palestinian Liber- ation Organisation chair- man Yasser Arafat, Tan- zanian founding President Julius Nyerere and more than 80 other leaders ar- rived to heap praise on South Africa and its people.

Vice-President Gore said the US civil rights movement and the strug- gle for democracy in South Africa were histori- cally intertwined with both countries sharing the spirit of the fight for full democracy.

"And so the people of the United States rejoice with the people of South Africa. We look forward

TO PAGE 2

President-elect NELSON MANDELA and President DE KLERK stand at attention as they listen to the country's two national anthems outside Parliament in Cape Town yesterday after Mr Mandela was elected President by the National Assembly.
● *Picture by Greg English, Associated Press*

Surprise move
FW names Pik as Minister

By Brian Stuart

CAPE TOWN. — In a surprise move, Mr F W de Klerk yesterday named Mr Pik Botha, veteran Minister of Foreign Affairs, as Minister of Mine- ral and Energy Affairs in the new "national unity" Cabinet.

He will nominate the present Minister of Jus- tice, Mr Kobie Coetsee, as President of the Sen- ate, which is to be consti- tuted in Cape Town on May 20, moving Mr Coet- see out of the running for a Cabinet post.

It appears that Presi- dent-elect Nelson Mande- la may concede the Sen- ate presidency to the Nat- ional Party, instead of according it one of the se- curity posts in the Cabi- net.

Mr De Klerk is known to have been unhappy that all the security posts were given to ANC mem- bers, particularly because of SA Communist Party links among them. He wanted at least one post,

so as to bring the NP into the National Security Council.

The naming by Mr De Klerk of the NP's six Mi- nisters in the new Cabinet yesterday indicated that Mr Mandela had not given way on this issue.

Nor has Mr Mandela agreed to retain Mr Pik Botha in Foreign Affairs, instead of the ANC's Mr Alfred Nzo.

In terms of the Consti- tution, Mr Mandela will name 18 members of the Cabinet from the ANC, and there will be six from the National Party and three from the Inkatha Freedom Party.

TO PAGE 2

Mandela election pictures, Pages

Mandela snubs Winnie

CAPE TOWN. — Mr Nelson Mandela snubbed his estranged wife, Winnie, during the first sitting of the multiracial Parliament yesterday, and the personal divide between them seemed as big as ever.

Moments after Mr Mandela was chosen as President, he refused to acknowledge Mrs Man- dela when she sat briefly beside him to nominate a fellow women's rights activist, Dr Frene Gin- wala, as the country's first woman Speaker.

When Mrs Mandela got up to announce the nomination, she was re- quired to walk over to where her husband was seated on a brown leather bench.

Sitting less than an

ahead as the woman once known as "Mother of the nation" read out Dr Ginwala's name, then returned to her seat.

Mr Mandela's reac- tion showed the extent of his aloofness toward Mrs Mandela since their separation in 1992. She was convicted a year earlier on kidnapping charges.

Wearing a black suit with a green blouse, Mrs Mandela was seat- ed three rows behind

United States Vice-President AL GORE addresses the media with First

The Republic of Botswana

Area: 569,800 sq. km = 220,000 sq. mi. (slightly larger than France).

Population: 1.38 million (estimated).

Capital City: Gaborone (Pop. 90,000, estimated).

Climate: Subtropical, with temperatures as high as 100°F. in the summer (November–April) and as low as 20°F. in winter (May–October). Rainfall varies from 25 inches per year in the North to 9 inches or less in the southern Kalahari Desert.

Neighboring Countries: Namibia, or South–West Africa (West and North); Zambia ((North); Zimbabwe (Northeast); South Africa (South).

Official Languages: English, seTswana.

Other Principal Tongues: siNdebele, Afrikaans, siKalanga, otjiHerrero, Chimbukushu and other Bushman dialects.

Ethnic Background: Tswana subgroups (94%), Bushman (5%), other (1%); Figures are approximate.

Principal Religions: Christianity, about 60%, traditional tribal beliefs.

Chief Commercial Products: Diamonds, cattle, copper, nickel, asbestos.

Annual Per Capita Income: About U.S. $2,800.

Currency: Pula.

Former Colonial Status: British Protectorate (1885–1966).

Independence Date: September 30, 1966.

Chief of State: Sir Ketumile Masire, President.

National Flag: Five horizontal stripes of blue, white, black, white and blue.

Botswana is a large, landlocked country which lies in the transition zone between the dry deserts of South Africa and the jungles of Angola. In the South, a vast area is covered by the shifting red sands of the Kalahari Desert, occasionally interrupted by limestone rock formations and clumps of grass and scrub brush at the few places where water is close to the land surface.

The change from desert to grassland is so gradual that it is hard to see where the first ceases and the latter begins. The growth becomes increasingly thicker and there are frequent patches of trees. Annual rainfall slowly increases until it reaches a level required to support farmland where the food and cattle of the nation are produced in non–drought years.

Vegetation becomes dense in the North and the land turns into the dismal marshland in the Okavango Swamp, fed by the Okavango River, which drains northward into Angola.

The country's elevation, averaging 3,300 feet, modifies its subtropical climate.

History: The original inhabitants of Botswana were tribes of primitive Bushmen who lived for untold centuries in isolation from the world. The Bantu tribes of central and east Africa migrated into the area in the 16th century; during the following centuries, intermarriage and population growth of the Bantus reduced the number of pure Bushmen to a handful.

The Tswana remained split into hundreds of tribes and clans until they gathered together under Khama III, Chief of the powerful Bamangwato tribe; this was a loose federation which emerged in the last half of the 19th century. For details of pre–independence history, see Historical Background, *The British in Africa* and *The Republic of South Africa*.

After gaining independence on September 30, 1966, the pre–independence government continued in office. Elections since then have resulted in substantial majorities in the 36–seat Legislative Assembly for the *Botswana Democratic Party*. There are three other small political parties which actively compete in the free elections, but their following is not significant.

The chiefs of the eight largest tribes are permanent members of the House of Chiefs, and are joined by seven other sub–chiefs. the Legislative Assembly consists of 36 representatives, 4 of whom are appointed by the government, but it can-

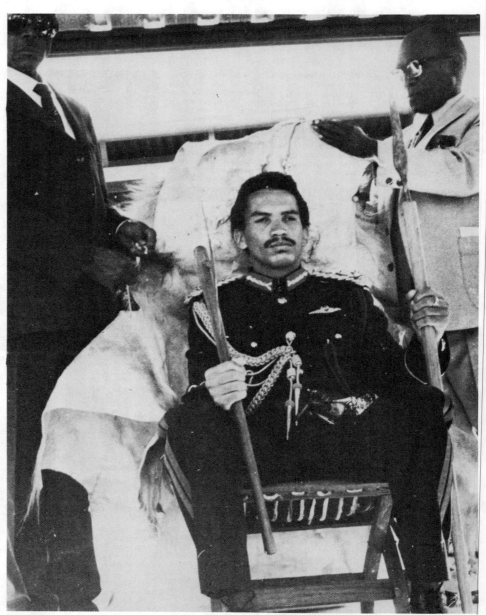

Brigadier Ian Seretse Khama having draped over his shoulders the traditional lion skin on his installation of Chief of the Bamangwato

not act upon matters concerning internal tribal affairs without first submitting a draft to the House of Chiefs.

Elections in October 1979 resulted in a resounding victory for President Sir Seretse Khama (who had been reelected chief executive since independence), with almost 60% of the voters turning out at the polls. He was to have served for another five years, but the President died in June 1980; Vice–President Quett K.J. Masire was installed to fill out his term and was reelected in September 1984. Khama's eldest son, Ian Seretse Khama, was installed in May 1979 as Chief of the Bamangwato Tribe; he was also Deputy Commander of the Botswana Defense Force numbering about 3,500 men.

Botswana has been the victim of strife in neighboring nations. During the Black–White struggles in Zimbabwe, it was briefly invaded in 1977 by a White–controlled security force seeking Black revolutionaries. South African forces conducted a commando raid in 1985 and an air raid in 1986 against houses occupied by members of the formerly outlawed *African National Congress* of that country. Incidents involving South African racial policies sharply declined after legalization of the *ANC* by South Africa and subsequent moves (1990–93) toward a multi–racial basis of government in that nation.

The *BDP* and the president, who changed his first name from Quett to Ketumile, won resounding victories in October 1989 elections. This is due largely to economic prosperity which has generally prevailed since the mid 1980's. A land scandal in 1992 led to demonstrations against the government in Gaborone which were deemed by the president to be a "gross overraction." But he had to force the resignation of the vice–president and two cabinet ministers because of the affair.

Culture: Less than 40% are now work in agriculture, a dramatic reduction of the 80% figure of the 1960s. Many of the Tswana men work in South African mines and industry. Several towns of this underpopulated nation now exceed 40,000 in population. Most rural building consists of hardened mud walls with thatch roofs.

It is a custom of the Tswana that every person should belong to a central village, even though he tills land and raises cattle elsewhere. When the summer rains start in November, part of each family moves out to their lands to plough and plant, remaining until the harvest in April and May, and then returning to their towns. Further distant from the settlements are cattle posts, grouped around waterholes, to where another part of the family journeys to tend their beasts throughout the year. In recent years the people have begun to move permanently to their farmland, creating a number of very small groups of houses which dot the countryside.

About 15% of the people of Botswana are practicing Christians, although estimates of the number of believers in that faith run as high as 60%. Tribal healers still play an important part in religious life, particularly in the more remote areas.

Educational programs have raised literacy levels in Botswana to averages of more than 89% (seTswana) and 40% (English). All villages of more than 600 have a primary school.

Economy: Cattle raising, the traditional source of income, has been surpassed by mining. A nickel–copper production facility at Selebi–Pikwe and a diamond mine at Orapa—both started in the 1970's— are now in full production. Not only mineral wealth, but hydroelectric potential have been discovered in the northern part of the country which hold promise for the future.

Botswana received a substantial economic setback in 1982 when drought caused failure of the maize and sorghum crops. Because of lowered availability of food, cattle had to be slaughtered. Smuggling activities involving diamonds in Angola and Zaïre glutted the world market to the extent that Botswana has only been able to sell half of its production in recent years.

Drought conditions resulted in substantially reduced agricultural and livestock production in 1983–1986, causing loss of income.

In neighboring homeland Bophuthatswana within the Republic of South Africa, it was announced in early 1987 that train crews entering the territory would have to obtain visas. Since the rail line carries half to almost all of the export and import trade of the "front line" nations abutting South Africa, this was viewed by some as an attempt to force those countries to recognize the South African homelands. The matter was settled when it was agreed that South African crews would take over at the border of the homeland. A more accurate analysis is that the move was a successful attempt of South Africa to remind the bordering nations that their southern neighbor could put an economic squeeze on them at will.

A socio-economic problem associated with the earlier drought, particularly in the Kalahari Game Reserve, revolves around about 1,000 Bushmen remaining in the reserve. Although powerful cattle ranchers have been encroaching into the reserve, putting up fences which have disrupted migration and caused numerous deaths of native game species, the government has blamed the adverse conditions on the Bushmen and is proceeding with a resettlement program. Left to their own, the Bushmen are subsistence

President Masire

hunters and gatherers, although they are regarded as subhuman by Bantu Tswanas. When they are resettled or work under inhuman conditions for cattle ranchers, they become apathetic and disorganized.

The drought which has hit southern Africa has not spared Botswana, although not so severely as nearby countries. A controversial plan was developed for impounding and redirecting the flow of waters in the Okavango river delta, the largest inland water system in the world. The purpose was to make more water available for towns, farming and diamond mining. Due to adverse effects on the environment, particularly of native wildlife, the plan was quietly discarded in 1992 in recognition of the fact that it is impossible to create more water by redirecting and impounding this all–important resource.

The Future: Elections are to be held this year and will be virtually uncontested. Economic association with, rather than dependence on, the Republic of South Africa now looms on the horizon. The diamond industry will remain depressed because of worldwide smuggling.

The Kingdom of Lesotho (pronounced (Leh–*su*–tu)

A home in the style of a Basotho hat, Maseru.

AP/World Wide Photo

Area: 30,303 sq. km. = 11,700 sq. mi. (somewhat larger than Maryland).
Population: 1.88 million (estimated).
Capital City: Maseru (Pop. 120,000, estimated).
Climate: Temperate. The western lowlands, about one–quarter of the country, have temperatures ranging from a high of 90°F. in the summer to 20°F. in the winter. The remaining area of highlands has a wider range of temperatures, with readings below zero on the snow–capped peaks of the Drakensburg Mountains.
Neighboring Countries: Lesotho is completely surrounded by the Republic of South Africa.
Official Languages: Sesotho, English.
Other Principal Tongues: Various tribal dialects derived from the Bantu heritage of the people.
Ethnic Background: South Sotho (Basotho, Basoto) 99.7%.
Principal Religions: Christianity (frequently with overlays of local customs, about 90%) local beliefs (about 10%).
Chief Commercial Products: Wool, diamonds, small manufactured goods, and mohair.
Per Capita Annual Income: About U.S. $480.
Currency: Maloti, at par with the South African Rand.
Former Colonial Status: British Protectorate (1868–1966).
Chief of State: King Moshoeshoe II. (Moe-*shway*-shway)
Head of Government: Ntsu Mokhele, Prime Minister (since April 1993).
Independence Date: October 4, 1966.
National Flag: The Basotho Shield on a background of white, blue and green stripes.

Lying deep within the lofty peaks of the Drakensburg Mountains, Lesotho is the only nation of the world which is completely surrounded by another country. One–fourth of the land is relatively low—from five to six thousand feet above sea level. The warm sun of Africa raises the temperatures in this agricultural region during the summer. The rest of the nation is made up of scenic highlands from 6,000 to 9,000 feet, with some peaks rising as high as 11,000 feet above sea level.

The snow–capped Drakensburg Mountains form a natural boundary between Lesotho and Natal Province of the Republic of South Africa; they also provide water for the neighboring country. The mountain snows melt, and, augmented by gentle and usually uniform rainfall, the water flows into the small streams which unite to form the Orange and Tugela rivers, which flow into an otherwise somewhat dry South Africa.

The mountain scenery of Lesotho is comparable to the pastoral setting of Malawi and the mountainous parts of Kenya. Remote and unchanged by modern civilization, it is one of the truly virgin areas remaining in the world.

History: In times immemorial the Bushmen established a thinly populated primitive society high in the mountains of Lesotho. The waves of Bantu migration from east and central Africa of the 17th century reached the country as did the Bafokeng, Maphetia and Baphuthi tribes, which settled among the Bushmen. The two ethnic groups intermarried during succeeding generations and their descendants are a somewhat uniform people known as Basutos, or Basothos. For details of early and colonial history, see Historical Background, *The British in Africa* and *The Republic of South Africa*.

An independence agreement was reached in 1966 whereby the colony, called Basutoland, would become independent under Chief Leabua Jonathan. The royalists and left–wing representatives had walked out of the independence conference, and Jonathan signed the treaty. The Union Jack was finally lowered at Maseru on October 4, 1966, and was replaced during the ceremonies by the unusual flag of Lesotho.

Chief Jonathan visited South Africa and was received by the then Prime Minister Hendrik Verwoerd in late 1966. Recognizing the need of each nation for the other, mutual cooperation and respect was pledged. The meeting only lasted a few hours so Jonathan could return to Lesotho rather than spend the night in South Africa, racially separated by the doctrine of *apartheid*.

Friction between Leabua Jonathan and King Moshoeshoe (pronounced Mo-*shway*-shway), the hereditary monarch, developed rapidly after independence. The King was placed under house arrest and several left–wing leaders who had participated in Maseru riots were jailed in 1966. Elections held in early 1970 were contested between Chief Jonathan's *Basotho National Party* and the leftist *Basotho Congress Party*, led by Ntsu Mokhele. When Jonathan realized he was being defeated, he announced a state of emergency, arrested the opposition and took steps which led to the exile of the King. (After agreeing to stay out of politics, the King returned the following year.)

Jonathan rescinded the emergency orders in 1973; Mokhele had been released from prison in mid–1971 after 17 months in jail. In late 1973, the *BNP* and Jonathan

106

announced plans to make Lesotho a one–party state. Mokhele and his followers attempted a *coup* in early 1974 which failed. Reprisals were taken not only against the leadership (some of whom escaped to South Africa and Botswana) and members of the *BCP,* but villages suspected of harboring *BCP* followers were destroyed.

A four–way struggle commenced in 1982. South Africa, charging that Lesotho was harboring members of the *African National Congress (ANC),* outlawed in South Africa, which advocated Black rule within that country, raided Maseru and other parts of the country in 1982–1983. Leabua Jonathan hotly denounced the move, charging that it was an effort on behalf of the Lesotho Liberation Army, the military wing of the *BCP.* South Africa countered with a charge that Jonathan was simply trying to divert attention from his own internal troubles. Jonathan denied granting a haven to members of the *ANC.* Further complicating things, Jonathan visited communist China, North Korea, Yugoslavia, Romania and Bulgaria in mid–1983 to establish diplomatic and economic ties. This infuriated both the South Africans and the Catholic clergy, who in prior times gave strong support to the government (Jonathan was Roman Catholic). A cabinet minister resigned, denouncing the communists as apostles of atheism. South Africa charged that the communist embassies would be made into bases for the *ANC.*

Lesotho was invaded by terrorism. There was no question as to the presence of *ANC* members in Maseru and elsewhere; more than 50 were deported to Tanzania in 1984 and about 100 to Zambia in 1986. However, machine guns and terrorist bombs became common. No faction or nation admitted responsibility for attacks in both Lesotho and South Africa (or denied it). Elections were not held after 1970 and there was no indication whether or when they would be held until November 1984 at a Congress of the *BNP.* On July 31, 1985, Chief Jonathan announced that balloting would take place on September 17–18. He later stated that since no opposition candidates had registered to run for seats in the National Assembly as of the August 14 deadline there would be no need for an election. The move was denounced as a farce. Jonathan went two steps further. He formed *Youth League of Chief Jonathan's Basotho National Party* and imported about 14 North Korean "advisers." This set the conservative element within the military on edge, since the orientation of the Youth League was clearly radical, if not communist.

South Africa continued to charge that Lesotho was harboring members of the *ANC* in 1983–1986 and periodically closed the borders and conducted raids in Ma-

seru to root out the rebels. Jonathan claimed they were "refugees" from South Africa, not members of the *ANC.* The White South African government closed the border in late 1985 which made conditions impossible because of drought which made food imports absolutely necessary. Finally, on January 20, 1986 the Lesotho military acted, ousting Chief Jonathan. A Military Council was installed, headed by Major General Metsing Lekhanya. The border was promptly opened as South Africa hailed the move. The Pretoria government denied having anything to do with the *coup.*

The military government announced amnesty for all opposition leaders, including Ntsu Mokhele. The King, however, decreed that all political activity would cease for two years. From 1987

King Moshoeshoe II

increasing powers were wielded by the King—too many for the comfort of General Lekhanya; the King was sent into exile in the spring of 1990 and was said to be studying toward his Ph.D. in Britain.

In an effort to bestow legitimacy upon itself, the military promoted a royal *coup,* installing the eldest son of the king, Prince Mohato Sereng Seeisa (King Letsie III) as monarch in late 1990. Military control was tenuous, and under pressure, parliamentary elections were held in 1993 after being postponed. The result gave the *BCP* all 65 seats in the National Assembly, and Ntsu Mokhele, now a centrist rather than a leftist, became Prime Minister. Lekhanya was forced from office, and a civilian government was re-

portedly fairly elected; Moshoeshoe II was restored to the throne in January 1995.

Culture: The people of Lesotho have a very high rate of literacy—70%—in spite of the fact that they live, for the most part, in rural isolation. Sheep and cattle raising occupy their daily lives among the scenic peaks and plateaus. The people have divided themselves into many local tribal groups, each with its own distinctive customs, albeit similar to that of all Basothos. English is the language of commerce and government. Intermarriage has erased the primitive culture of the Bushman, and Christianity has replaced much of the traditional tribal beliefs of the Basothos. Roman Catholicism predominates.

Economy: Small quantities of wool and mohair are the only major exports of this small nation; there is some limited diamond mining. There is otherwise no significant known mineral wealth.

Prior to independence, Great Britain had to supply a substantial amount each year to overcome the deficit of the country. The economy is not self–sufficient; centered on agriculture, it cannot produce as much as the people consume each year. Foreign aid has been received from many nations, including the United States.

There is limited transportation—there are but a few miles of paved road; only 1.6 km. of railroad is owned by South Africa. Demonstrating Lesotho's dependence on South Africa, about one–half of the work force is employed in that nation, primarily in its mines.

Drought conditions from 1981 to 1985 brought hard times. It was necessary to import substantial quantities of grain and foodstuffs to make up for poor harvests. Entry of such imports, even when provided by international relief agencies was, of necessity, via South Africa. It appears that the dry conditions have considerably lessened. The vital treaty on the Highlands Water Project was signed with South Africa in 1986. This remarkable engineering feat, involving dams, tunnels and canals to pump the headwaters of the Orange River in Lesotho to the dry industrial area of South Africa will provide half of the country's income. Further, electric turbines are planned for the tunnels, which will make Lesotho self– supporting in electricity.

The Future: The election of a Black–controlled government in South Africa is a positive event; the source of friction and needless expense caused by it has gone. If political and economic calm continues to prevail in a somewhat wobbly South Africa, it might be to Lesotho's advantage to join with it, particularly if prosperity can be gained from such a union.

The Republic of Malawi

A village chief examines his corn near Lilongwe.

spersed with large, sparkling lakes and fertile plateaus. Situated on the western edge of the Rift Valley, Lake Nyasa (also known as Lake Malawi) spreads its long, deep waters over three–fourths of the eastern boundary of Malawi. The surface of this body of water is 1,500 feet above sea level; the water extends to a depth of 2,300, thus the floor of Lake Nyasa is over 700 feet below sea level. The lake pours into the River Shire, which flows southward to join the Zambesi River 250 miles away.

The countryside of Malawi has characteristic plateaus in the middle and on the top of steep mountains. For the most part, these are 3,000 to 4,000 feet above sea level, but rise as high as 8,000 feet in the North. Immediately south of Lake Nyasa are the Shire Highlands, gently rolling plateau country which is 3,000 feet high. From this green, almost level land, the mountain peaks of Zomba and Mlanje tower to heights of 7,000 and 10,000 feet, respectively.

The altitude modifies an otherwise equatorial climate for the most part. The summer, from November to April, is pleasantly warm with equatorial rains and sudden thunderstorms. Towards the end of March, the storms reach their peak, after which the rainfall rapidly diminishes. During the winter from May to September, wet mists float down from the highlands, invading the cool and dry reaches of the plateaus. There is almost no rainfall during these months.

For strikingly beautiful scenery, Malawi is almost unexcelled by any other nation on the African continent.

History: Before the waves of Bantu migration arrived many centuries ago, Malawi was probably very scantily settled. The restive Bantu tribes from the north expanded slowly southward from about

Area: 95,053 sq. km. = 36,700 sq. mi. (the size of Indiana).

Population: 9.4 million (estimated, including refugees from Mozambique).

Capital City: Lilongwe (Pop. 340,000, estimated).

Climate: Hot in the low–lying extreme South; cool and temperate in the highlands with heavy rains (November–April); the amount of rainfall is related to the altitude.

Neighboring Countries: Mozambique (South, Southwest, Southeast); Zambia (Northwest); Tanzania (Northeast).

Official Language: English and Chichewa.

Other Principal Tongues: Tombuka, Yao, Tonga, Nkhonde, Lomwe, Sena, Chichewe.

Ethnic Background: There are several tribal groups all of Bantu heritage, including the Nyanja, Yao, Cewa, Angoni, Tonga, Ankhonde and Lomwe.

Principal Religions: Christianity (about 50%), Traditional beliefs (about 35%) Islam (about 10%), other.

Chief Commercial Products: Tobacco, tea, sugar, cotton, peanuts, corn.

Annual Per Capita Income: About U.S. $200.

Currency: Kwacha.

Former Colonial Status: British Colony (1883–1964).

Independence Date: July 6, 1964.

Chief of State: Bakili Muluzi, President (since May 1994).

National Flag: Three horizontal stripes of black, red and green with a rising sun in the center of the black stripe.

Malawi, formerly known as Nyasaland, is a country of high mountains covered with lush, green foliage, inter-

the 10th century onward, sending successive waves of transients through this country on their journey to the south. Some stayed as permanent settlers, forming into distinct tribes based on common ancestry. There is no written record of these people; legend must be relied upon. For details of early and colonial history, see Historical Background and *The British in Africa*..

During the latter part of the period when Malawi was part of the Federation of Rhodesia and Nyasaland (1953–1962) the British devised a constitution which for the first time provided for legislative members directly elected by native Africans. In 1961 and in elections held thereafter, the *Malawi Congress Party* led by Dr. Hastings Kamuzu Banda claimed all 50 seats in the assembly; three additional members were selected from a list limited to White voters.

After independence was granted in 1964, Dr. Banda served first as Prime Minister and then as President when Nyasaland, renamed Malawi, was proclaimed to be a republic. The only disturbance in the system occurred in 1965 when there was a minor revolt within the party which resulted in the exile of a few persons.

In a series of moves that were vehemently criticized by Nyerere of Tanzania and Kaunda of Zambia, Dr. Banda entered into trade and aid agreements with White–controlled South Africa, establishing diplomatic relations with that country in 1968. Opposition to this move in Tanzania was so adamant that rebel groups opposed to Dr. Banda were based in that nation during the ensuing years. This external threat lessened, however, and by 1985 diplomatic relations between the two nations were established.

All 85 members of the National Assembly were returned to office through nomination by the government in 1976; however, in 1978 elections for as many as two–thirds of the seats were contested, including those of prominent political figures. Two ministers were defeated. This election, which marked a genuine democratic trend in the political process, also initiated the secret ballot.

Confiscation of the holdings of a small number of resident Asians was undertaken in 1975–76; they were permitted to live in only three Malawian cities—Blantyre, Zomba and Lilongwe.

Dr. Banda was made "Life President" in 1970. During his time in office he was an intellectual, dynamic and demanding person, a reflection of his early years as the only Black student at the University of Chicago in 1931 when he received a Ph.D. and completed his medical education in 1937. He was critical of what he considered emotional responses of Black African leaders to post–independence problems. Many of them, in turn, derided him as an "Uncle Tom" in dealing with Whites, particularly those controlling the Republic of South Africa.

During the 1980s, elections only involved the *MCP* candidates selected by Banda. Opposition figures died under very suspicious circumstances. His rigid rule was typified in the 1990s by accusations of human rights violations, particularly those involving the *Malawi Young Pioneers* which emerged as a paramilitary organization and personality cult devoted to Banda. Strife in neighboring Mozambique closed rail lines vital to Malawi's exports, forcing the use of South African facilities.

Under external and internal pressures, the life president grudgingly agreed to a referendum which was held in 1993. He was stunned when 67% voted for multi–party democracy. Illness overtook the

Former President Banda

president in late 1993 when he had to go to Johannesburg for brain surgery. During his absence a presidential council was formed and the life presidency was abolished; the grip of the *MCP* was ended; the youth group was officially disbanded and a new constitution was adopted.

Banda was defeated in May 1994 elections when Bakili Muluzi of the *United Democratic Front (UDF)* received 47% of the vote over Banda's 34%. The government, however, had to be one consisting of a coalition with two other small parties because the president refused to negotiate with the *MCP* or the *Alliance for Democracy (AFORD)*. The result is unclear, since the *UDF* does not have a majority in the National Assembly. There were charges of intimidation during the elections which were probably true.

The government is staging a publicity trial of Banda and his former police minister for the 1983 murders of opposition leaders. Well into his 90s, he is totally deaf, senile and too ill to attend.

Culture: The Malawis are modern, religious, industrious and thrifty people, known for their advanced culture throughout southeastern Africa. As in the past decades, thousands of men go each year to find work in other countries, returning sometimes only after many years of economic exile. The tribal life strongly resembles that of neighboring Zambia. Education is common through the eighth grade, but rare above that level. With the assistance of a loan from South Africa, the capital was moved from Zomba to Lilongwe in 1975.

One of the most vocal Christian sects is the Jehovah's Witnesses, who engaged in conversion efforts with such vigor in the 1970s they had to flee persecution. They are now back, after agreeing to cease trying to convert other Malawians.

Economy: Despite Malawi's high population density, the careful development of agricultural resources has in the past enabled the population to both support itself and produce export products. Plantations produce the tobacco, tea and cotton. However, in 1983–84, the drought which gripped most of southern Africa invaded the country, lowering production rates. International Monetary Fund loans were necessary to maintain the economy. Drought again invaded Malawi in 1994 and persists into 1995.

The Future: With age, Banda became increasingly convinced that he was infallible. His genuine contribution was sound organization of agricultural production and marketing. The new president was dismissed from the Banda government in 1982 for stealing. The probability of sustained agricultural production now is low, and the new government has yet to show any genuine administrative talent. Sheer political ambition without a hint of altruism will dominate Malawi's future.

The Republic of Mozambique (pronounced Moe–zam–*beek*)

View of central Maputo

Area: 786,762 sq. km. = 303,769 sq. mi. (twice the size of California).

Population: 16 million (estimated, including about 2 million living as refugees in neighboring areas).

Capital City: Maputo (Pop. 800,000, estimated).

Climate: Tropically hot and humid, modified somewhat in the mountain areas close to Lake Nyasa, the uplands bordering Zimbabwe and in coastline, cooled by ocean breezes.

Neighboring Countries: Tanzania (North); Malawi, Zambia (Northwest); Zimbabwe (West); South Africa, Swaziland (Southwest); Madagascar lies 300 to 600 miles off the coast.

Official Language: Portuguese.

Other Principal Tongues: Ronga, Tonga, Shangaan, Muchope, Byasa, Nyanja, Yao and other Bantu dialects.

Ethnic Background: All of the many African groups of Mozambique are of Bantu ancestry; the Macoua, located in the coastal area show traces of Arab and Indian blood.

Principal Religions: Christianity (50% +), traditional beliefs (45%), Islam (5%); figures are approximate.

Chief Commercial Products: Shrimp, cotton, cashews, copra, tea, sisal, and other agricultural products.

Annual Per Capita Income: Negligible.

Currency: Metical.

Former Colonial Status: Portugal claimed that Mozambique was an integral part of Portugal until September 7, 1974; a provisional government was decreed to wield power until formal independence.

Independence Date: June 25, 1975.

Chief of State: Joaquim Chissano, President. Elections are scheduled in October 1994.

National Flag: Beginning at upper left hand corner, and flaring out therefrom, stripes of green, red, black and yellow, each triangular–type stripe separated by thin white stripes; a white gear at the upper left contains an open book crossed by a machine–gun and a hoe.

The flat terrain of the coastline of Mozambique, filled with dense, tropical jungle in areas which are not cleared, gives way gradually to a series of plateaus and highlands which gently rise toward high mountains in the part closest to the western borders. Towering green peaks are located in the Lake Nyasa area, and the temperature is moderated by the altitude. Most of the intense agricultural production takes place in the coastal lowlands and surrounding plateaus.

History: Prior to the arrival of European explorers, Arab traders had established

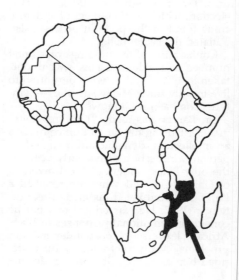

110

active trading posts along the coast of Mozambique, dealing in the notorious slave trade, principally, and in commerce involving agriculture to a much lesser degree. For details of earlier periods and colonial history, see Historical Background and *The Portuguese in Africa.*

There was little development of nationalism among the African people of Mozambique such as occurred in most other colonies on the continent after World War II. The movement did not actually commence within the colony; in 1964 it was started in the two neighboring nations of Tanzania and Zambia.

Guerrillas received training and weapons, usually of Soviet or Chinese communist manufacture starting in late 1963, and commenced armed resistance within Mozambique in 1964. Two competing leadership factions were based in Dar es Salaam, Tanzania: *Frelimo,* the abbreviated form of the *Mozambique Liberation Front,* was led until early 1969 by American–educated Dr. Eduardo Mondlane, who was assassinated at that time. The other and much smaller rival group was called *Coremo.*

Frelimo received support from Tanzania, Algeria, the Soviet Union, Communist China and lesser amounts from several European nations, a few foundations and U.S. church organizations. It was often torn by dissension based on tribal and regional differences within Mozambique, and on Soviet–Chinese lines among its participants and leaders, who all classify themselves loosely as *Marxists.* During the late 1960's, *Frelimo* was able to mount offensives which required 40,000 Portuguese troops in Mozambique; by 1973 the number had increased to 65,000—more than half were Black Mozambicans. Efforts centered on the creation of *aldeamentos*—fortified hamlets and towns in districts where the rebels were active. The revolutionaries frequently employed techniques of sabotage and disruption; the Portuguese maintained a secret police organization and jailed suspects without trial.

From 1972 to 1974 there was almost a total lack of objective reporting within Mozambique. The White minority played down the importance of the revolutionaries and their deeds; at the same time *Frelimo* personnel distributed exaggerated stories of rebel successes from Dar–es– Salaam, Tanzania. It was not so much the efforts of the revolutionaries as the internal events in Portugal that led to basic changes in Mozambique. Marcelo Caetano, dictator of Portugal, was determined to hold on to African possessions, but was ousted by a *coup* in the spring of 1974. The military officer who succeeded him, General António de Spínola, announced a basic change in policy toward granting independence to the colonies. The financial drain caused by colonial wars was overwhelming. Spínola was in turn overthrown by a more radical group of officers who in mid–1974 hastened progress toward independence.

The revolution more or less ground to a halt under the terms of an unwritten cease–fire. *Frelimo's* Samora Machel met with Portuguese emissaries, and in September 1974 the Lusaka Agreement was signed in neighboring Zambia. It provided for an interim government until formal independence on June 25, 1975.

The White minority, fearful of a Marxist–style Black government, took up arms and several weeks of disorder followed. The White reaction was short–lived, and thousands fled to South Africa as Black control was asserted within the country. Sporadic violence continued for several weeks. After gaining full independence, Samora Machel, who had only recently entered the country from neighboring Tanzania, became Provisional President. His initial policy statements were to the effect that Mozambique would become ruled by principles of "African Marxism."

Events since independence have been turbulent and radical; a purge of Portuguese–trained officers in the army led to an unsuccessful *coup* in late 1975. The military units of *Frelimo* were transformed into a national police with the power to arrest and detain persons without judicial proceedings. The president declared his opposition to the Roman Catholic Church and announced nationalization of just about everything, including schools and colleges.

Although President Machel and ex–U.S. President Carter met in New York in October 1977, there was no substantial thaw in U.S.–Mozambique relations; aid

A precarious road deep within Mozambique

111

President Machel (left) and Vice President Chissano shake hands with President Botha of South Africa at Nkomati, March 1984

from the U.S. was blocked by a prohibition tacked to the appropriations bill in the Congress.

Mozambique and South Africa signed an agreement in 1979 providing for cooperation in maintenance of the railroad systems. However, there were three factors which caused relations between the two nations to slowly deteriorate. First, Mozambique provided sanctuary for Black guerrillas led by Robert Mugabe who were attempting the overthrow of the White–dominated government of Zimbabwe, then known as Rhodesia; needless to say, South Africa backed the Rhodesian government. Second, Mozambique became a haven for the *African National Congress (ANC)* seeking overthrow of the White government in South Africa. South Africa responded initially by backing the *Mozambican National Resistance Movement (MNR)*, which has been active since 1979, engaging in terrorist actions and general warfare against the Maputo government. Rhodesian raids into Mozambique were frequent. Although Mugabe's "freedom fighters" left, returning to Black–ruled Zimbabwe. *Renamo*, as the rebel movement is known, resorted to terrorist activities at varying levels until 1992.

South Africa, in retaliation for an alleged *ANC* terrorist attact, bombed several houses in Maputo which sheltered *ANC* members. This led President Machel to meet with then President Botha of South Africa; the session at Nkomati on the border resulted in an agreement which provided that neither nation would be a haven or support for rebel forces opposing the government of the other.

About 800 *ANC* members were sent out of Mozambique to Zambia and Zimbabwe. The *Renamo* forces were even more active within Mozambique, attacking all provinces and even threatening the capital city. There was a tentative move towards a cease–fire in 1984 which fizzled.

The reason: about 700,000 persons of Portuguese descent and others with anti–communist sentiments lived in the Republic of South Africa and supported the rebels, taking the place of the former White conservatives of Rhodesia. South Africa, notwithstanding its pledge, supported the rebels, and yet additional aid came from Brazilian and West German conservatives.

The rebels succeeded in disrupting electrical distribution to the extent that South Africa itself was denied electricity from the Cabora Bassa Dam generators.

While flying to Maputo in a Soviet aircraft in late 1986, Machel was killed in a crash that few survived. He was succeeded by Joaquin Chissano, former vice president. Claims that South Africa arranged the crash were untrue.

By 1987 the rebels had free control of most of Mozambique except Maputo and a few larger cities. Their force of about 25,000 easily outmatched the 90,000+ government troops by employing age–old practices of jungle and bush warfare. Widespread malnutrition became an apparently permanent part of Mozambique in the late 1980's, reaching devastating proportions by 1992. *Renamo* troops destroyed more than 50% of the crops before harvest; pervasive drought conditions almost finished off what was left.

U.S. measures preventing assistance were removed in order that humanitarian aid could reach Mozambique. But at the same time, the Soviet Union apparently became bored with Mozambique after Gorbachëv came to power in that former nation. What little food was left disappeared from stores. Conservative elements in the U.S. were even more shocked when it was revealed that clandestine military aid had been provided to the *Frelimo* government since 1982.

With an ample share of its own domestic problems, the years 1988–90 marked the end of Soviet interest in settling

Mozambique's continuing internal conflict. All references to communism were dropped from documents introduced at a Mozambican party congress in 1989. With some encouragement, there could have been a negotiated settlement between *Renamo* and *Frelimo* in 1989–90. This was particularly true as South Africa became increasingly embroiled in its own domestic problems. Both sides took the first steps toward peace in 1989, but *Frelimo* demanded command of the nation, quickly rejected by *Renamo*.

As the drought tightened its grip in 1990, conditions became deplorable—people resorted to eating roots, berries, nuts and leaves. Even the despised cassava meal was in short supply. The two groups waging warfare were accurately likened to two punch–drunk prizefighters determined to outlast each other. In spite of the horrible conditions, the fighting went on as peace efforts met with but limited success. Negotiations between the two in Rome, however, showed promise for the future. A multi–party system was adopted in preparation for elections scheduled for 1991, but *Renamo*, denying the validity of the congress, rejected the measure.

Afonso Dhlakama emerged as the chief spokesman for *Renamo*. He and President Joaquim Chissano signed a forward–looking cease–fire in October 1992 in Rome, Italy. It called for about 8,000 UN peacekeeping troops and personnel (UNOMOZ) which slowly arrived in the country as funds became available.

With the demise of the Soviet Union, communism became irrelevant in Mozambique; the contest became no more than a rivalry between two men each of whom wanted to preside over the shambles that Mozambique had become. The cease–fire was followed by extended negotiations on demilitarization of the rebels and the government army which took place in 1993 while the people, particularly in rural areas, starved. One issue was familiar: what can be done with revolutionaries and the army after the revolution is over?

The problems with refugees (1.7 million), food and clothing was staggering. When aircraft flew into remote locations, incredibly thin people clustered around them shouting "Mealie!"—their word for relatively high–protein American corn meal, much preferred over the native cassava meal that fills the belly but leaves a person hungry.

Genuine progress toward reconciliation of the two sides stalled until the Chissano regime discovered a means to include the *Renamo* leadership into a process that at least appeared democratic. Dhlakama was provided a luxurious home with swimming pool and servants. His hitherto sharp criticism of the former communists became muted and negotia-

President Chissano

tions picked up in tempo; *Renamo* agreed to participate in 1994 elections. But the situation still remained unstable as both sides jockeyed for position before the October electoral contest.

The outcome indicated that the elections were probably fair despite a high rate of illiteracy. Opposition to Chissano was not only by *Renamo,* and Dhlakama, but by no less than ten other presidential candidates. *Frelimo* was popular in the southern, more populated areas, and Chissano won slightly more than half of the votes for president. Dhlakama won 34%. *Frelimo* holds 129 of the 250 seats in parliament; *Renamo* has 112.

This indicates that Mozambique is ascending from the pit of warfare as a basis for government. But it has been so weakened that at least two decades will be required for it to reach its potential prosperity, which should have happened two decades ago. UN–sponsored efforts to teach contemporary agricultural methods are underway. White farmers from Zimbabwe, disgusted with the land appropriation policies and utter mismanagement by Robert Mugabe, are showing increasing interest in Mozambique as a place where they can acquire land and produce food in tremendous quantities compared with that now gleaned from small, family–held plots.

Culture: The European minority was located almost exclusively on the coastline and larger interior plantations of Mozambique. Although most left before and after independence, there are about 30,000 Portuguese in Mozambique, principally in Maputo. Other Europeans assist in furnishing technical services not otherwise available. It is not unusual to see Black and White Mozambicans mix-

ing together in restaurants and even at private parties, although such events are becoming rarer with a lack of luxury items. Mozambique needs doctors, teachers, civil servants, and technicians, and in an about–face has been actively seeking White Europeans for such positions. This need was one of the factors leading to an attempt at agreement with the guerrillas; few persons wished to live where terrorism was rampant. With jobs scarce in Portugal, many are interested in returning, but not to a civil war.

Immigration of rural people to the cities continues to be a headache in Mozambique and other African nations; crop failures due to drought led to a sharp increase of this movement starting in 1983–84.

Economy: The formerly thriving economy of Mozambique was based on agricultural production with only a small amount of light industry. The exodus of the White population resulted in sharply lowered production. The rebel movement exacted a cruel toll in fifteen years of activity. Starvation associated with irregular drought conditions since 1983 forced presidents Machel and Chissano to issue urgent pleas for external humane assistance. The years of sufficient rainfall did not furnish a basis for badly needed food production, particularly in the presence of continuous warfare.

Although formerly a client state of the communist bloc, Mozambique reversed this direction. Cooperation with South Africa became possible as the government orientation shifted away from communism. In reality, during the years when Mozambique was "esteemed" by the Soviet Union and its associates, assistance was frequently minimal—in 1983 $13 mil-

lion in consumer goods (poorly made) were furnished this nation of then 13 million people, a total of about $1 per person. U.S. assistance even during the communist years was more than $75 million of record, and much more that was not of record. The price paid was terribly steep: loss of western investment which would have meant so much for Mozambique.

The Cabora Bassa Dam, a huge complex on the Zambezi River, was completed in 1980, but seldom has operated more than one turbine for electrical power, far below capacity. The rebels severed almost all power distribution lines. These are now being rebuilt by South Africa, which badly needs the long–delayed electrical capacity of the dam. Actual transmission of power to that country will not commence until 1996.

The Limpopo River, almost dried up to little more than a sandy trench during the conflict, is gradually being brought back to its former flow. It can, under favorable conditions, provide thousands of peasant farmers with adequate water.

The Future: Power relationships are largely settled, but it is clear the people realize the years of communist–style government brought hardship to Mozambique. If Chissano and Company are to remain in power, concrete, positive results will have to soon appear, just as in South Africa. If this country is managed correctly, in a manner different from other nations of sub–Sahara Africa, it might, after another five years, prove to be a tempting place for foreign investment. In the meantime, external assistance in monumental amounts will be necessary for survival.

View of the Cabora Bassa Dam   AP/Wide World Photo

The Republic of Namibia

Herero women in their finery

Courtesy: CALTEX

Area: 823,620 sq. km. = 318,000 sq. mi. (twice the size of California).

Population: 1.85 million (estimated).

Capital City: Windhoek (Pop. 115,000, estimated).

Climate: Hot and dry except in the Caprivi Strip, which has more rainfall.

Neighboring Countries: Angola (North); South Africa (South); Botswana (East); Zambia (Northeast).

Official Language: English.

Other Principal Tongues: Several Bantu dialects, including Ovambo, Herero, Damara, Nama and Kavanga, plus other smaller group dialects; Afrikaans, German.

Ethnic Background: Bantu subgroups, including Ovambo, (52%), Herero, Damara, Nama, Kavango, mixtures of African Black and White, including Coloureds and Basters; Bushmen.

Principal Religions: Christianity (about 90%), traditional beliefs and other (about 10%).

Chief Commercial Products: Diamonds, gold, tin, zinc, copper, lead, uranium, vanadium, wool, karakul lamb skins.

Annual Per Capita Income: About U.S. $1,300.

Currency: Namibian Dollar (at par with the South African Rand).

Former Colonial Status: The Republic of South Africa asserted control of the territory (as South–West Africa), claiming a mandate under the League of Nations continued since the formation of the United Nations. The UN passed a resolution in 1966 declaring South–West Africa to be under direct UN control and designated the area *Namibia* in 1968.

Independence Date: March 21, 1990.

Chief of State: Sam Nujoma, President (pronounced Noo–*yome*–ah).

Head of Government: Hage Geingob, Prime Minister.

National Flag: Diagonal stripes of blue, red and green separated by thin white stripes. On the blue stripe, near the pole, is a golden sunburst.

Per Capita Income: About US $2,300

The narrow white beach of Namibia is quickly replaced by a 60–mile–wide stretch of red–colored Namib Desert which runs the entire length of the coastline. The barren Kalahari Desert stretches along the north and eastern borders of the territory, occasionally interrupted by harsh formations of gray rock and thin scrub vegetation. The only rain in this region comes from torrential storms which occasionally gather—their rapid downpour is swallowed up quickly without leaving a trace of moisture.

The central area of Namibia is a vast plateau suited to pastoral raising of sheep and cattle. Here, there is somewhat more rain, which permits a thin forage to cover the soil. This region produces thousands of karakul sheep, the lambs of which are treasured for their shiny black, curly pelts used in fur coats. The mineral wealth of the region lies in the northeast sector adjacent to the Kalahari Desert.

History: In times unknown, the Bushmen commenced living in what is now Namibia, followed by several Bantu tribes. The Ovambos and Damara–Hereros became the most numerous groups. For details of early and pre–World War II colonial history, see Historical Background and *The British in Africa, The Germans in Africa* and *The South African Mandate*.

South Africa controlled this territory under a mandate from the League of Nations after having occupied the area in 1915. When the United Nations came into being, its Charter provided that all previously mandated dependent territories came under its supervision. In most cases, the mandates were transformed into *trusteeships*, but with the requirement that annual reports be presented to the UN concerning the development of the territories and their progress towards eventual independence.

South Africa applied for "permission" to make South–West Africa part of that nation in 1946. The UN rejected the proposal, but offered South Africa a trusteeship. South Africa rejected that offer (undoubtedly on the ground that what was given could be taken away) and made moves to incorporate the land within its national boundaries regardless of UN protests. By 1949, certain laws had been extended to South–West Africa and its White representatives sat in the South African parliament. The League of Nations mandate was, it insisted, still in force. Over the next sixteen years there were many legal proceedings designed to have South Africa withdraw from the territory. Each year the UN passed a

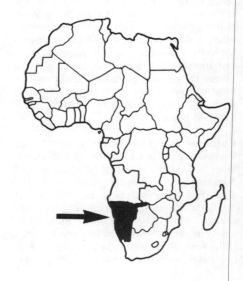

114

resolution condemning South Africa for its failure to live up to the terms of the UN Charter, but this meant nothing in substance in the absence of force.

During the 1960's, a political group took shape in South–West Africa. It called itself the *South–West African People's Organization*, or *SWAPO* for short. *SWAPO's* aim was to gain independence for the territory with majority rule. Although its headquarters was actually in Dar es Salaam, Tanzania, the guerrilla fighters it sponsored roamed the land, recruiting volunteers, terrorizing Black and White farmers, sabotaging public utilities and ambushing army patrols. South African punishment came quickly; hundreds of guerrillas were rounded up and jailed, including the group's leader, Herman Toivo ja Toivo; he was sentenced to 20 years imprisonment on dreaded Robben Island, South Africa, after being convicted of "crimes against state security" (1968). The fighting escalated, backed by surrounding Black African nations, which, like Angola and Zambia, provided refuge for *SWAPO* forces.

Finally the UN had enough. It decided in 1966 once and for all to terminate the South African "mandate." South Africa did not budge—and had the military force to back up its resistance to the organization's resolution. It then set up a constitution for the territory intended to assure continued White control.

The UN renamed the territory *Namibia* (derived from the name of the Namib Desert) and established a *Council for Namibia* as a temporary, transitional government, but the Council operated in New York, not in Namibia; this move failed to affect the South African government, except to harden its resistance to what it considered outside interference in its affairs by elements without knowledge of the true state of affairs. In another landmark decision, the UN recognized *SWAPO* as the "representative" of the Namibian *people*. This was the first time in its history that the organization officially recognized a group of revolutionaries.

The years passed without change. *SWAPO* guerrillas and South African troops engaged in bloody skirmishes. In 1974 the UN tried again. It *required* South Africa to begin an orderly transfer of power to Namibia (i.e. *SWAPO)* by May 1975 *or face UN action*. No one (except South Africa) really knew whether it was just a bluff or not. Shortly before the deadline, the then Prime Minister Vorster of South Africa rejected UN supervision of South–West Africa, but stated he was prepared to negotiate independence for the territory, but definitely not with *SWAPO*. The reason for this on the surface was *SWAPO's* rigid espousal of communism, but ran much deeper: it basically represented a distaste of having a

hostile regime govern a neighboring nation called Namibia.

As a further concession, the all–White South–West Africa legislature eased the hated *apartheid* laws (see South Africa) which separated the races *in public places* only. White voters endorsed a new constitution in 1977 which organized an interim government for the territory, but still was based on racial separation. After considerable diplomatic pressure from the U.S., Canada, Britain, France and West Germany, South Africa gave in to a plan for peace discussions which would include *SWAPO* representatives. With *SWAPO* approval, Justice Marthinus Steyn (Mar–*tee*–nus Stain) was appointed by South Africa to administer the area during its transition to independence.

Three major events occurred at about the same time. Justice Steyn ended all laws which separated the races. South–Western representation in South Africa's parliament ended and South Africa announced that it would keep Walvis Bay after independence. This is the only deep water port of the territory. It was reasoned that it had never been part of the former German colony, but had always been a possession of Britain. *SWAPO* would have no part of the proposal.

The first talks in early 1978 ended in failure when *SWAPO* representatives demanded that half of South Africa's 3,000 troops must be withdrawn before UN–supervised elections could be held. The Foreign Minister of South Africa walked out angrily, declaring that the ultimatum called for would be handing over of the territory to marxist terrorists (an accurate statement). The five western nations

which had for months been trying to work out a peaceful solution to the problem continued negotiating with both sides, but with little success. By March 1978 the political situation worsened. Clemens Kapuuo, respected chief of the Damara–Herero people, was gunned down outside his general store in a Black suburb of Windhoek. This was soon followed by a South African raid on *SWAPO* bases in Angola, which drew loud protests from the UN.

South Africa made another move to find an "internal" alternative to *SWAPO* government in late 1978. It promoted mid–1979 elections in Namibia which were won handily by the *Democratic Turnhalle Alliance (DTA)*, a multi–racial coalition of conservatives with White leadership. *SWAPO* boycotted the contest and did what it could to disrupt the elections even though there were 18,000 South African troops stationed within the territory to protect the voters.

The *DTA* insisted that the United Nations back down on its recognition of *SWAPO* as the sole "representative" of the Namibian people, but that organization was, in the eyes of the UN, the only "strong entity" which existed.

Negotiations dragged on and on. The situation was further complicated by Angola's Marxist regime, its endorsement and support of *SWAPO* and the presence of about 50,000 Cuban troops, necessary to ensure continued communist control of that country (see Angola). A strong South African force invaded Angola in 1982–1984 to clean out *SWAPO* rebels. Angola accused South Africa of assisting *UNITA* rebels in *that* country (probably

Bustling Windhoek

Courtesy: CALTEX

115

true, although denied by South Africa). Clashes between South African forces and Cubans were inevitable.

Western efforts to "solve" the problem were constant and, unfortunately, until 1988, a failure. South Africa declared a "linkage" policy in 1983: South African troops in Angola would not be withdrawn until Cuban troops were first withdrawn. Angola and Cuba responded with a firm declaration that Cuban troops would not depart unless South African forces were first withdrawn. The hands of the United States were literally tied by an amendment tacked onto the U.S. budget by a Democratic–controlled Congress, paralyzed by a "no more Vietnams" fear which forbade any aid to *UNITA* forces in Angola. The extent of U.S. involvement was diplomatic efforts by the Department of State which got nowhere.

Talks continued in 1985 with very little results. *SWAPO's* original leader, Herman Toive ja Toive, was released in 1984 by South Africa in order to splinter the group. This did not occur; he was named Secretary–General and Sam Nujoma continued as head of the movement. In a bold move, President P.W. Botha of South Africa offered South–West Africa to any of the five western nations who would take over and see that a genuinely representative government was installed. None wanted that headache, however, since it came with an annual cost of administering the territory of $1 billion.

South Africa posed a legitimate question. Why did Angola object to the withdrawal of Cuban troops from Angola prior to Namibian independence? Was it because *SWAPO* and the Angolan regime could not exist without the Cuban military? If the answer to these questions was "yes," then the South African accusation that *SWAPO* was nothing more than a gang of Marxist guerrillas indeed had some substance. Some hints were made that Angola and Cuba were willing to

restrict the Cubans to the north of the 16th parallel. The probable reason for this is related to the expense to the Soviet Union of maintaining Cuban presence in Angola. Further, the U.S. budget amendment was dropped in election year 1986 and *UNITA's* leadership had a highly successful visit to the United States.

South Africa nominally reinstated legislative and executive powers in Namibia in 1985, while retaining control over external affairs and the legal status of the territory. A transitional government consisting of a 62–member National Assembly selected from nominees of established political parties was provided for. Twenty–two members were from the *DTA* (composed of 11 ethnic groups) and eight each were from *The Labour Party*, the *SWAPO–Democrats*, the *South–West Africa National Union (SWANU)*, the *Rehoboth Free Democratic Party (RFDP)* and the *National Party of South West Africa (NP–SWA)*, the latter group being a White organization. *SWAPO*, infuriated, said it would refuse to participate in any such government. Some 3,500 *SWAPO*–supporting demonstrators marched in protest when the new government was installed in mid 1985.

Declaring that South African Defense Forces could not longer guarantee the safety of the people of South–West Africa, it was announced by South Africa that compulsory military service would be instituted in Namibia.

During the last half of the 1980s *SWAPO* forces waned from a high of about 12,000 to 3,000; many joined the South–West Africa Defense Force. The organization did not in reality represent all Black people within Namibia—its leadership was and is overwhelmingly Ovambo. It could not have accomplished its goals without external assistance. UN support of *SWAPO* was denounced by South Africa, which accused the organization of espousing tribalism in Africa.

As the Namibian armed forces grew,

SWAPO increasingly resorted to terrorist tactics within Namibia which contributed to its lowered popularity. Government forces included the infamous *Koevoet* ("Crowbar") units which in turn engaged more frequently in widespread atrocities, to the disgust of many. Further complicating the total picture were about 1,000 Namibians held by *SWAPO* in crude prisons located in Angola because of accusations they spied for South Africa.

By 1988 the Soviet Union's Gorbachëv decided that the expensive Cuban presence in Angola had to come to an end. At about the same time, former President Botha of South Africa decided that continued participation in Angola's civil war and guardianship of Namibia were counter–productive. For these reasons (not because of eight years of diplomatic efforts by the U.S.), agreement was reached in December 1988 for a regional settlement which was far–reaching.

Among other things, it provided free elections would be held in Namibia after which a national assembly would draft a constitution leading to independence by April 1990. South Africa would retain Walvis Bay and be limited to 1,500 troops within Namibia until independence under the agreement. Because of the overpowering economic position of South Africa this in reality meant very little change.

Nor was the result peace. *SWAPO* woke up to face the fact that it would not be the "sole representative" of Namibia, a title with which the UN had exalted it. Events leading up to the election were lively and often violent. In order to establish a single–party state, it would have to muster a two–thirds majority at the polls. The precarious peace plan was nearly evaporated by *SWAPO* leader Sam Nujoma, who wanted to have the appearance of a conquering hero. He dispatched about 1,600 *SWAPO* guerrillas into Namibia the day South African troops started leaving; at the insistence of the UN they were withdrawn.

Sam Nujoma was and is immensely popular among the Ovambos but had little following elsewhere. His revolution–oriented speech offered little reassurance to anyone. But after independence ceremonies held March 21, 1990, he predictably dropped talk of nationalism and made strenuous efforts to assure White investors and businessmen of an orderly continuation of economic policies.

Elections held the prior November mirrored both the dominance of the Ovambos and the diversity of Namibia. *SWAPO,* with 57% of the vote, won 41 seats in the 78–seat constituent assembly. Even when combined with two smaller parties holding a total of five seats, this was and is not sufficient to dictate a new constitution, which was drafted and adopted in just 80 days. The principal opposition, the *Democratic Turnhalle Alliance* is multi–racial; it received 28% of the vote (21 seats).

The constitution which was adopted created one of Africa's most free democracies. President Sam Nujoma (elected unanimously by the legislature) and Hage Geingob, the prime minister, have left behind decades of rebel radicalism and communist rhetoric and have discharged their responsibilities well.

Demonstrating its continuing popularity, *SWAPO* won all 26 seats of the National Council, an upper chamber of the legislature with very limited powers, in 1993. Among other successes the turnover of control of Walvis Bay was notable on March 1, 1994, which even when held by South Africa was freely accessible for Namibia's trade and use. It is Namibia's only deep water port.

As December 1994 elections neared, President Nujoma admitted that the toughest thing to deal with since independence was the high expectations of the Black majority. He promised that after the elections there would be "no excuse for lagging behind in further uplifting the standard of living of our people." *SWAPO* has 53 seats in parliament to 15 for the *Democratic Turnhalle Alliance* which is now led by Mishake Muyonga. The opposition leader claimed Namibia was poorer than it was at independence.

Culture: A small minority—some 115,000 Whites—have enjoyed the wealth of Namibia and the vast majority has been living, for the most part, in backward poverty, engaging in herding livestock to support themselves. The White Afrikaaners and others have completely dominated all facets of education and the mass media. This is destined to change under the new constitution. Compulsory education to the age of 16 will be a significant undertaking.

One of the obstacles to a genuine political settlement of the issues surrounding independence was the illiteracy and resulting political disinterest of the huge majority of Black persons, 16% of whom are literate. They distrusted politicians (as do many literate persons in the world) and often sense that *someone* is trying to get *something* from them. With increased education, hopefully this will change.

Windhoek is a pleasant city with marked German architectural styles dating back to that country's prior colonial period. These buildings are now side–

President Sam Nujoma

by–side with tall structures possessing the latest styles in design and appearance. The city is neat and well–kept. On weekdays, the Damara–Herero women wear ordinary clothing, but on formal occasions and Sundays for Christians, they dress in ankle–length ornate dresses reminiscent of the Victorian era, together with large hats, even when the temperatures are high—a throwback to the dress of the German colonial era.

West Germany withdrew Lutheran pastors from the territory until the approximately 30,000 Lutherans agreed to have a single church for both Whites and Blacks; they have reopened.

An unusual group of people live in about 6,000 square miles of pastoral land south of Windhoek. Calling themselves *Basters,* they are the descendants of mixed European–Qanama Bushman ancestry. They have lived on their land, called the *Rehoboth Gebiet,* for more than a hundred years and now number about 28,000. In response to efforts in 1969 to establish the territory as a part of the Republic of South Africa, leaders of this group appeared before the International Court. Conservative and clannish, they just want to be left alone . . .

Economy: Exports of diamonds (now more than 1 million carats a year) and metals provide most of Namibia's income, earning some $500 million per year. Karakul lamb pelts are the chief agricultural product and are higher priced since Iranian production fell victim to the confusion of the Ayatollah in that nation. A recently–opened gold mine is adding to the wealth of Namibia. Drought conditions, which are nothing new to Namibia, were especially severe in 1989 and 1993, causing severe hardship among the Ovambo and Damara people, who were left with almost no crops to harvest.

One problem was not solved by independence and remains outstanding: the wide disparity in income of Black and White people. This may not change for another generation.

More than 100 boats operate out of Luderitz, which harvest tons of lobsters from the sea—the waters are chilled by the Benguela current originating in the South Pole region, flowing northward along the west coast of Africa. South African "rock lobster tails" are frozen and exported to the world. Seals and penguins are found in this most unusual area.

The Future: It will be hard to "turn things around" in Namibia because of (1) a 40% unemployment rate among adults causing (2) a rising crime rate and, finally, (3) the uncertainty of the economic future of the Republic of South Africa. But a clock will tick until 1999 when a vital question will again be posed: how much better off are we now than in 1990?

The Republic of South Africa

Modern, sophisticated Johannesburg at night

Area: 1,222,470 sq. km. = 472,000 sq. mi. (three times the size of California).

Population: 40 million (estimated).

Capital Cities: Pretoria (administrative, Pop. 989,000); Cape Town (legislative, Pop. 2 million, projected); Bloemfontein (judicial, Pop. 170,000, projected).

Climate: Temperate and sunny. The eastern coastal belt is hot and humid, the western areas are dry and hot. Only high mountain peaks are covered with snow during winter.

Neighboring Countries: Namibia (Northwest); Botswana, Zimbabwe (North); Mozambique, Swaziland (Northeast); Lesotho is enclosed by South Africa.

Official Languages: Afrikaans (derived from Dutch and understood by 60% of Whites and 80% of Coloureds), English.

Other Principal Tongues: Four major groups, including (1) Nguni (Xhosa), Zulu, Transvaal Ndebele, Nrevhele, Swati or Swazi, Mbayi or Pai and Phut-

shi; (2) Sotho (South Sotho, Qwaqwa. Pedi or North Sotho, Tswana or Western Sotho); (3) Tsonga or Shangana and

(4) Venda. Zulu is rapidly becoming a *lingua franca* used by other Black groups.

Ethnic Background: Primarily Bantu Black Africans, with some Hamitic admixture; White, including descendants of Dutch, British, German, French, Portuguese, Greeks and Italians, Coloureds (mixed Black, White and Asian), Asian (primarily from India).

Principal Religions: Methodist and other Protestant Christians, (10.2 million), Afrikaaner Dutch Reformed, split into three sects (5.2 million), Roman Catholic (1.2 million), Anglican, split into two sects (1.1 million), traditional tribal beliefs, Hindu, Islam. The above figures are of nominal allegiance rather than persons active in religion.

Chief Commercial Products: Gold, diamonds, uranium, platinum, chrome, vanadium, manganese, asbestos, copper, iron, coal, corn, sugar, processed foodstuffs, textiles, fertilizers, fruits, hides, fish products.

118

Annual Per Capita Income: About U.S. $2,750.

Currency: Rand.

Former Colonial Status: Member of the British Commonwealth as the Union of South Africa (1910–1961). Previously, British authority in a colonial sense was sporadic in the Orange Free State and Transvaal.

Independence Date: May 31, 1961 (The Union of South Africa became The Republic of South Africa).

Chief of State: Nelson Mandela, President (May 10, 1994). —First Deputy Executive President: Thabo Mbeki (Mm–*beh*–kee). —Second Deputy Executive President: Frederik W. de Klerk.

National Flag: From the pole, a black triangle separated by a thin gold stripe from thick green stripes which join to extend horizontally across the flag; there is a white stripe on either side of it separating the green from a field of red at the top and one of blue at the bottom.

Washed on the west by the South Atlantic and on the east by the Indian Ocean, the Republic of South Africa occupies the southernmost part of the continent. This land of bright, sunny days and cool nights has a consistently uniform climate year around, with a mean annual temperature of slightly less than 60°F.

In the extreme southern Cape area, there is a period of rain between April and September, but the summer (December–May) is warm and dry. The western coast is washed by the cool Benguela Current originating in Antarctica, which produces a climate that supports a large colony of penguins on the shore line. Further inland to the north, after the interruptions of the Cedarburg, Swartberg and Louga Mountains, the land stretches forth in a vast, semi–arid region known as the Karroo Desert. This is not a true desert as encountered in the central Sahara, since the periodic light rainfall supports vegetation which provides food for many species of wildlife. Occasional sharp projections of volcanic rock stand prominently in an otherwise flat land.

The eastern coast along the warm Indian Ocean is hot and humid, supporting almost every type of wild game known to southern Africa. In modern times, this climate has fostered the growth of high intensity agriculture similar to that found in southern California. Multi–colored coral formations are prominantly displayed by the brilliant white sands of the beaches. The northwestern central territory, covering the Orange Free State and most of Transvaal, is a high plains land (veldt), stretching to the north from the scenic peaks of the Drakensburg Mountains. Receiving ample rainfall for the most part, its temperate climate supports rich farmland; the land also contains huge gold and diamond deposits.

The northern part of Transvaal province is lower than the high veldt to the

A busy shopping area in Cape Town

119

In Kruger National Park

south. Kruger National Park, on the eastern border, is visited by tourists from all over the world. Here, all game is preserved, and visitors are not permitted to get out of their autos, which proceed slowly along the road to enable their occupants to see and photograph the many species.

Actually, two–thirds of South Africa is desert, semi–desert, marginal cropland or urban. Altogether, only 12% is ideally suited for intensive cultivation.

History: Before the arrival of Dutch East India Company employees in 1652, South Africa was thinly populated by Bushmen (Hottentots) and a very few pygmies. Bartholomew Diaz had reached the southern cape in 1486, six years before Columbus touched the West Indies. The rough, inhospitable appearance of the cape region attracted only free Dutch burghers, sent to grow grain and make wine to supply ships bound to and from Dutch East India possessions.

Settlement

They were joined by French Huguenot refugee settlers at the close of the century, who were accepted by the Dutch as equals; the two peoples gradually melded into a single society. Expansion of the Dutch–French was slow and generally in a northeastly direction; cattle–raising was their principal undertaking. Because of the need for farm labor, slaves were introduced from West Africa and later from Asia. They were added to modest numbers of Hottentots working under conditions of virtual slavery. Large families were common among the pioneers living in the equivalent of the

American West at the time, and children were born of frequent non–marital unions of settlers and slaves, becoming the ancestors of today's Coloured (Cape Coloured, mulatto) population of South Africa.

It was not until the swirl of events in Europe surrounding intense rivalry and competition between the British and French at the turn of the 18th–19th centuries that non–Dutch persons began to enter the Cape Colony. Slave trade was abolished, creating labor shortages. The British initially acted under color of the authority of the exiled Dutch Prince of Orange, but later discarded that fiction and in 1814 came into legal possession of the Cape. This heralded the arrival of substantial numbers of British colonists who had been preceded by numerous missionaries determined to make the lives of natives better, much to the consternation of the *White* natives.

When slavery was abolished in 1834, about 35,000 people were emancipated; there were many protests about the inadequacy of compensation to the former owners.

The Dutch chafed under British authority, and many went northeastward into what is now Orange Free State and Natal. At the same time, the area was being occupied by numerous Bantu tribes from points further north. Conflicts with the settlers were inevitable as the rivalry sharpened and as White settlers became more numerous. Their numbers grew substantially during the period of the Great Trek which penetrated north and east of the Orange River in 1835–42. Just as Americans are fascinated by tales of

the western frontier during the 19th century, *Boer* South Africans never tire of retelling life during the treks.

The conflicts of this period and the years which followed are said to involve *Kaffirs* (i.e. Black people). This is a misnomer the remnants of which exist to this day. *Kaffir* is a word borrowed from Arab slave traders used to refer to East African natives sought by them. It is defined in the dictionary as "a member of Bantu–speaking people," which further confuses matters. There is no Bantu language; there are uncounted Bantu languages. There was no Bantu tribe; there were many of them. History books tend to give a distorted view of a unified Black people struggling against White settlers. Almost identically, today the cause of South Africa's Black people was not a unified one under the *African National Congress* as many believe from misleading media accounts.

At the time of White expansion into northeast South Africa, Black warriors opposing them were as busy killing each other as they were occupied with trying to get rid of the settlers. This pattern was repeated in the 1980s and in the 1990s (but on a smaller scale). As early as 1837 what was Zululand and Natal were virtually depopulated by the ravages of Chaka Zulu, military chief of the Zulus. Two decades later the Zulus, believing a promise by their prophets that heroes of old would reappear and drive the White man out, killed almost all of Zulu–owned cattle; the starvation which ensued caused their population to shrink by about two–thirds.

Kaffir today is a racial insult in South Africa, equivalent to the use of *nigger* in the United States. Yet, further compounding the confusion, the British in South Africa founded *Kaffraria* in 1847, a mini–state, later incorporating it into the Cape Colony in 1866. This was but one of many British efforts to legally establish and perpetuate Black "homelands" promoting racial segregation in South Africa, an aim usually associated with the *Boer* population. Other British measures later included the establishment of property ownership and educational requirements for voters in the Cape Colony.

Boer–Anglo Disputes

The *Boers*, Dutch–descended people, were not the only ones on the move. Ostensibly under pressure from missionary zealots to protect Black populations, the British fought many skirmishes, battles and wars of words with the *Boers*. Their zeal was not entirely innocent, however, since they were, as in other colonies, seeking means of wealth to add to what became the Commonwealth (which by the last half of the 20th century turned out to be neither common nor wealthy). British problems were compounded by the fact that many of the people who they nominally sought to protect hated them as much as they did the *Boers*. At an early time (1846) the British initiated the ancestor of racial separation *(apartheid)* when they established a Location Commission in Natal.

Over a period of years, various forms of government were tried by the British the success of which was directly related to their ability to leave the *Boers* alone. Self–government was tried in Natal, Transvaal and the Orange Free State. Discovery of immense sources of wealth in diamonds (1867) and gold (1886) proved to be a lure which was virtually irresistable to fortune seekers, not dissimilar to the California and Alaska gold rushes of the United States. The *Boers* actively disliked the new people, calling them *outlanders*.

One of these opportunists, Cecil Rhodes, an energetic Welshman, accumulated a vast fortune by wheeling and dealing. His treaties with Black chieftains in particular were heavily weighted in Rhodes' favor. He belatedly tried to salvage what was left of his reputation by establishing the Rhodes Scholarship program which provides the cost of a period of education in England to aspiring students.

Towns sprang up virtually overnight as a result of the wealth. Johannesburg, laid out in 1886, soon had a population of more than 100,000, about half of whom were Black. Rhodes evidently satisfied both the *Boers* and the British, since he became Prime Minister of Cape Colony in 1890, nominally functioning under President Paul Kruger from Transvaal. The latter is generally thought of as the founding father of South Africa, affectionately referred to as *Oom* ("Uncle") Paul Kruger.

President Kruger correctly concluded that Rhodes, in order to advance his own interests and, secondarily, to maintain the appearance of British supremacy in South Africa, was financing an anti–*Boer* movement among the *outlanders*. The first tangible act was the aborted Jamison Raid (1895) which led to the ouster of Rhodes as prime minister. In the remaining years of the century, relations between the British and the *Boers* soured. Kruger was elected to a third term as president at the same time the British high commissioner was promoting war between the two societies.

A minor dispute over voting rights of immigrants was a pretext for the Boer War of 1899–1902. By the end of the conflict the British were hopelessly mired down. They had to build concentration camps for *Boer* women and children, several thousand of whom died of disease and neglect. Some 300,000 British troops were required to barely "win" over about 75,000 *Boers*, who then took up guerrilla

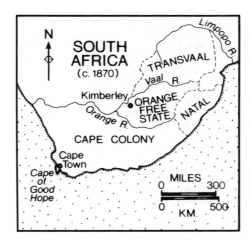

warfare. The weary British woke up to the fact that the riches of South Africa were being squandered on a meaningless quarrel and offered $113 million and self–government "when possible" to the *Boers* if they would stop fighting. The offer was accepted and the money was used in part to rebuild *Boer* farms which had been ruthlessly destroyed.

The Union of South Africa

Principally in response to the pleas of General Jan Christiaan Smuts (*Boer* commander–in–chief of the Republican forces in the Cape Colony during the final months of the war), the British established the *Union of South Africa* in 1910, thereby granting self–government in Transvaal and Orange Free State. The constitution bound together the two former *Boer* republics with the British Cape Colony and Natal. An administrative capital was established at Pretoria (Transvaal), a legislative capital at Cape Town (Cape Colony) and a judicial seat at Bloemfontein (Orange Free State), an arrangement that prevails to this date. Thus the two groups—the descendants of the Dutch and the British—were encouraged to form a closer bond and still retain the dignity of being important parts of the whole union.

At the same time, a political party was founded by General Louis Botha and James Hertzog, the *South African Party*. It was moderate, encompassing both English and *Afrikaans* speakers stressing the equality of both and pressing for independent status within the British Empire. Within a short time, however, Hertzog and the rural, conservative *Boers* split off to form the *Nationalist Party*.

A basic law was drafted and passed in 1912 which included provisions limiting the areas in which Black persons could own or purchase land and further restricting the movement of Asiatics. The latter caused severe unrest among the Indian population, then led by Mohandas K. (Mahatma) Gandhi, which widely demonstrated against its provisions. This law was the beginning of legal separation

of the races—*apartheid*—which would be more fully enacted into law after World War II.

World Wars and the Interwar Period

South Africa joined in World War I, fighting the Germans in their possessions in Africa (German S.W. Africa, German East Africa, now Namibia and Tanzania). Hertzog appeared at the Paris peace conference at the close of the conflict to demand independence for South Africa, which was ignored. Because no other logical power was in the region, South Africa was given a League of Nations mandate to control the former German colony of South West Africa. This continued without interruption until 1990 when South Africa became convinced that communism no longer posed a threat in what is now Namibia. Countless international protests over its continued control of the territory and annual United Nations resolutions were ignored (see Namibia). The British did, however, recognize the Union of South Africa as an independent nation within the British Commonwealth in 1931.

Until 1934 government power was exercised by either or both the South *African Party* (Smuts) and the *Nationalist Party* (Hertzog). When the two united, adopting the name *United South African Nationalist Party*, the conservative members of Hertzog's party re–formed under the old party name with the leadership of Daniel F. Malan. Since the turn of the century, anti–Black sentiments had been slowly crystallizing. Initially they were not matters of law, but a product of social organization. Just as the U.S. "Pennsylvania Dutch" (Amish) needed no laws to regulate the bahavior of their people, social pressures were used in South Africa by common consent.

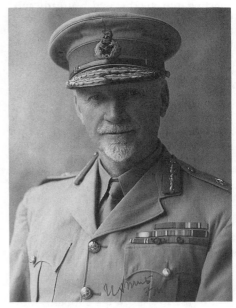

General Jan Christiaan Smuts

Problems were settled in the church forum and enforced by practices such as shunning those held in disrepute. An informal system of informants existed, particularly in rural areas, and little that went on escaped the notice of church elders. In the pulpits, elaborate Biblical justifications were developed to explain the need for the races to stay apart, thus justifying segregation (the theories were largely discarded in the 1980s).

The sentiment for racial segregation was by no means limited to the *Boers*. English–speaking conservatives accepted the notion readily and supported it politically. A very small number of *Boer* liberals did not support segregation, joining with a minority of English–speakers politically. However, liberalism was unfashionable in South Africa among Whites, who were largely able to withstand the ravages of the worldwide depression of the 1930s by virtue of the country's vast mineral wealth.

Black persons were allowed to vote, but on a special ballot whereby three White persons represented them in the Union parliament.

South Africa declared war on the Axis Powers of World War II, but its participation was minimal because of its distant location from the fighting. Further, there was a sizable *Boer* element in the parliament which had no use for liberal English–speakers. During the opening years of World War II, this group expressed little regret at a possible defeat of England by Germany. The end of the conflict was the end of the Hertzog–Smuts coalition which had been in power since 1934. As 1948 elections approached, the *National Party*, then led by Daniel F. Malan, campaigned on an openly racist platform, advocating that White South Africans insure their moral and financial future by enacting into law that which already substantially existed by virtue of social customs and economic patterns: *apartheid*, the Dutch Boer word for "separate" (pronounced A–*par*–tate).

End of "The Generals Era"

The *National Party* won 1948 elections by a narrow margin. If the issue of communism within the *African National Congress* had been fully developed at the time, its margin would have been greater. By the turn of the decade it came into full bloom as the Cold War gripped international attention. During World War II an improbable Jewish refugee from Lithuania made his way to South Africa. Joining with fellow Jews who controlled the *South African Communist Party (SACP)*, in spite of the ravages visited upon Jews by Joseph Stalin in the Soviet Union, Joe Slovo became a dedicated communist. He identified readily with the concept of oppression of the masses in his adopted country; these were, in his mind, Black people

in general and the *African National Congress* in particular. His eloquent messages of violent overthrow of the White man's government sounded like manna from heaven to his listeners.

As the post–World War II threat of communism grew internationally and its tenets became more and more a part of the *ANC* leadership's agenda, the organization itself came to represent a threat to the security of White South Africa. In actuality, it also posed a threat to Black South Africa, since if its aims had been realized—violent overthrow of the government—a new class of exploiters would have replaced the White leadership. The lot of Black South Africans would undoubtedly have been comparable to those unfortunate animals that believed in the pigs which heroically took over George Orwell's *Animal Farm* only to exploit their innocent supporters.

Since the threat of international communism largely evaporated with the collapse of the Soviet Union, it is easy to forget the reality of its former threat. It must not be forgotten that in the 1950s the Communist Party was outlawed in the United States and that Julius and Ethel Rosenberg were executed for espionage committed on behalf of their Soviet masters. This was the era of the Un–American Activities Committee of the U.S. House of Representatives. Nor is it easy to overlook Nikita Khrushchëv at the UN, pounding his shoe on a table and screaming "We will bury you!" The reaction to this perceived threat in South Africa was, therefore, no more abnormal than elsewhere, particularly the United States.

Because of the *ANC* under the tutelage of Joe Slovo, anti–communism acquired a distinct anti–Black aspect since most Black militants were communists at the time. This has not disappeared even though the international threat of communism has abated. As late as 1992 when *ANC* militants marched on Bisho, in Ciskei, there was an outbreak of Black–on–Black violence which President de Klerk blamed on communists within the *ANC*, particularly the leader of the march, the late Chris Hani, a dedicated communist.

The 1950s through the 1970s: Prosperity and Repression

In the postwar period, South Africa bloomed as an industrial nation, underpinned by continued export of gold and diamonds. Increasing numbers of Blacks were needed to support the burgeoning economy; many migrated to urban areas, taking up residence in what were initially squatter areas. As in the United States, South African Blacks began to chafe under what many considered to be inferior conditions at all levels—economic, social and governmental. Sporadic protests

were easily put down by the South African police. This period of relative prosperity in South African history was marked by the leaderships of D.F. Malan, J.G. Strydom, Hendrik P. Verwoerd (*Ferverd*), who was assassinated in 1966, and John Vorster.

All were inflexible stalwarts of the *National Party*, determined to maintain the *status quo*. In addition to stringent laws regulating the races, South Africa had a police surveillance system and "voluntary" press censorship law which kept close tabs on liberals in general and subversives (i.e. communists) in particular. This period of relative prosperity lasted through the late 1970s, when the *National Party* leadership was rocked by scandal.

The schemes which were involved included illegal funding of a variety of undertakings calculated to shore up support for South Africa abroad; they included campaign contributions to U.S. political figures and an aborted attempt to buy control of *The Washington Star*, a moderate newspaper which later discontinued publication for unrelated reasons. Events flowed swiftly, forcing the then President John Vorster to resign. Leadership was assumed by Pieter W. Botha, former defense minister, who was exonerated from participation in the scandals.

A detailed chronologically arranged history of South Africa would not adequately focus on the multitude of forces which have played a role in the recent emergence of a multi–racial nation, and would be somewhat confusing since all of these forces were to a great degree working at the same time and interacting. This problem is made worse by the amount of disinformation which became very popular folklore in the U.S.

Although some Black leaders were coming to the fore during the 1950's, it was not until the 1960's that Black South Africans began to press vigorously for reform—greater freedom of movement was particularly desired, together with wages equal to those of White workers, social benefits and participation in government at all levels. No longer was South Africa faced with isolated tribal groups scattered here and there about the vastness of the country, but countless thousands of Blacks surrounding the cities as a result of rural–urban migration. They sought employment and greater opportunity which often simply did not exist. The government responded in some instances with increased housing and educational opportunities, but found it all but impossible to keep up with the ever–expanding needs of the Black population.

Until the 1950's there were some rights reserved to Blacks which were legally protected and blunted the harshness of the *apartheid* system to a degree. They, however, were all but eliminated in a series of measures enacted in 1953 by the *National Party* in its efforts to more rigidly preserve the power of the White minority. These were a response to communist and radical elements which had infiltrated the Black equality movement during the late 1940s and 1950s.

Apartheid

Prime Minister Malan and the *National Party* wasted no time in their efforts to deliver the promises made during the 1948 campaign. Within a year citizenship and other important rights were curtailed or eliminated. A person who took up residence in South Africa, no matter what his origin, was able to claim South African and Commonwealth citizenship almost immediately. A five–year waiting period was enacted and enforced which had the effect of limiting access to the voting booth. Mixed race marriages were banned by law (they had not been widespread before it was passed).

Perhaps the most fundamental law calculated to change the face of South Africa was the *Group Areas Act* of 1950. Combined with the land acts of 1912 and 1936,

it strictly limited the area in which a person was allowed to live based on race. Under it, together with enabling regulations, an estimated 3.5 million Black people were removed from lands they occupied.

One respected source has described this as "their" land, which is misleading. That term indicates ownership, but in fact most of the property was occupied by Blacks who had no indicia of ownership. Under laws common to Britain, South Africa and U.S. law it was and is possible to become an owner of land by simply occupying it, but that has to be done in a certain way to be valid. The occupation must be exclusive (excluding all others), open (not secret), notorious (known by people in the community) continuous and under a "color of right" (usually a deed) for a given period, usually ten years. If each and every condition is met, a person becomes the legal owner of the land and it cannot be taken from him without compensation.

The condition that people who don't know the law slip up on most often is "color of right," even though it isn't

difficult. It need be no more than a *quit–claim* deed from another. It simply indicates a sale of "all my right, title and interest" in the real estate, and it doesn't matter that the person "selling" it doesn't own it. It is important that the deed be written and recorded in the local land records. Such "quit–claim" deeds were the basis of ownership of countless thousands of tracts of land in the U.S., particularly during the settlement of the West.

The *Group Areas Act* and associated laws had the effect of denying Blacks any possibility of ownership based on occupation of land. Thus, if a given tract was within a "White only" area, all that was necessary to oust a Black person was proof that he wasn't White and therefore it was illegal for him to occupy the tract by living on it.

The *Population Registration Act* classified everyone by race at the time of their birth: Black, White, Asiatic, Coloured, Other. This determination controlled almost every aspect of a person's future—where he lived, worked, went to school, wages, voting (if any), property ownership, etc., and became a foundation for the laws

Part of Durban as seen from the harbor

requiring that everyone have a passbook. In many cases, it was illegal for a person to merely *be* in a given area.

The *Internal Security Act* of 1982 granted virtual dictatorial powers to the government and abolished any semblance of civil rights which remained. It provided for the banning of organizations opposed to the state, made it illegal for individuals to belong to them, imposed involuntary censorship on the press, allowed detention without trial of persons suspected of terrorism, and imprisonment of anyone for 10 days without any charges.

To carry out the aims of the *apartheid* laws, the police ("South African Defense Force, SADF") developed a highly intensive system of espionage, informants and control calculated to strike fear into the hearts of all. In particular, the use of informants was widespread, enabling police to arrest would–be criminals before their crime could even be attempted. Prison facilities were designed as tools of the police and to further the ends of justice under *apartheid*. If the degree of proof of the guilt of an individual was dubious or flawed, he or she might well die in prison awaiting trial . . . "slipped on the soap while taking a shower" . . . "fell downstairs" . . . "was assaulted" . . . "died while trying to escape" were all heard with frequency in South Africa if, indeed, anything was heard at all.

Before the days of compulsory censorship, newspapers were guided by the principles of "voluntary" censorship. In its most fundamental regard, this simply meant that anything embarrassing to the state should not be published. If a newspaper violated this imperative too seriously or too often (elusive quantities), paper supplies, bank credit and often telephone service evaporated. Worst of all, no official at whom a finger could be pointed ever did anything illegal. Things just happened.

The *Publication Bill* unashamedly was directed at reporting of Black activities in the press. It demanded that the media exercise "due care and responsibility concerning matters which can have the effect of stirring up feelings of hostility between different racial, ethnic, religious or cultural groups" in South Africa. True to the form of the Dutch–descended *Boers* it professed to "avoid the spirit of permissiveness and moral decay sweeping the world and communications media in the country."

How was it possible for a Black person, and to a much lesser extent, non–Black persons, to live in such a stifling society? It was just as easy as it was in 1950 and preceding years to live in the U.S. where schools, universities and colleges, theatres, restaurants, recreational centers and a host of other facilities and institutions were segregated by law, regulation, custom or a combination of the three.

Apartheid at the beach in Durban

There was no *Group Areas Act* because there was no need for one. Economic forces relegated Black Americans to the least desirable housing with few exceptions. Those who were able to rise above racial limitations found limited acceptance among Whites—tolerance which could be revoked without notice at any time.

No detention act was then in force in the U.S., but arrests for a crime called "investigation" were a daily occurrence. Newspapers would blunt their reporting of such events by using language as "held for questioning," or "being investigated," rather than hint at an illegal detention. And if one journeys back to the days of the city political party bosses of the U.S., conditions bordered on the unbelievable. People survived by following the advice of the late Sam Rayburn, Speaker of the U.S. House of Representatives: "In order to get along, you gotta go along."

In South Africa, the *Suppression of Communism Act* was used as a vital tool to impose state interests over individuals and organizations. The U.S. equivalent, purporting to ban the communist party, actually was virtually unheard of; communism was terribly unpopular and party membership was, almost without exception, harmless. Simple exposure in the press was sufficient to ruin a person financially and socially. In contrast, because Black militancy was closely tied to communism in South Africa, it became the equivalent of illegal communism and was prosecuted.

The African National Congress

The *African National Congress* was initially formed in response to the enactment of a 1912 *Basic Law* which regulated the areas in which Black people were allowed to own land. Passage of the act resulted in the expulsion of some people without adequate compensation from lands they and their ancestors had occupied for generations. The organization had little mass appeal prior to 1948 because of a general lack of political awareness of Blacks, and their limited economic condition. The leadership was generally conservative, hoping to deal with the White–dominated government to seek redress of land seizures. Its outlook was not unlike that of the NAACP in the U.S. during the initial years of its existence.

With the advent of Joe Slovo, who purportedly received a legal education in Lithuania, the *African National Congress* underwent a fundamental change. It had been more or less committed to furthering the welfare of South Africa's Black population by working *within* the system of laws for change. After 1948, with the advent of *apartheid* it became a militant, openly communist organization determined to oust the White minority from power with a commitment to seizing the economic wealth of the nation in the name of Black power.

By the early 1960s, South Africa's government was gripped with an obsessive fear of militant Black leaders. It outlawed not only the *Communist Party* but also the *ANC*, whose leaders without exception were dedicated communists. In 1962 both organizations went underground and warrants were issued for the party leadership of each. Militant Blacks countered with the *Umkhonto we Sizwe* ("Spear of the Nation") in 1961, the militant branch of the *ANC*. Its purpose: guerrilla warfare to replace mass popular demonstrations which had been made illegal.

After a year and a half as a fugitive, Nelson Mandela (45) and Walter Sisulu were tried in 1964 (the Rivonia trial) and found guilty. The sentence: life imprisonment without possibility of parole. The leadership that was not arrested remained underground, taking refuge in neighboring and nearby nations such as Zambia (the location of its headquarters), Mozambique, Tanzania and Botswana. From these exile posts they directed the affairs of the *ANC*. Nelson Mandela was sent to Robben Island prison, noted for its harsh conditions.

The late Oliver Tambo, with whom Mandela had established South Africa's first Black legal firm in 1953, became leader of the *ANC*, remaining in that position until he suffered a major stroke in 1988. The real head of the organization was Joe Slovo, also Secretary General of the *South African Communist Party*. A virtual personality cult of staggering proportions evolved around this man. Videotapes have been shown in the U.S. showing Black men dancing while chanting hypnotically "We are Joe Slovo's boys."

During the 25 years after the trial of Mandela and Sisulu, the *ANC* grew steadily as the rigid separation and denial based solely on the basis of race became far more onerous. Ironically, it helped to found the *Inkatha Freedom Party* of the Zulus in 1974, feeling that the anti–apartheid movement ought to have some lawful (i.e. non–communist) presence in South Africa.

ANC Lobbying in the U.S.

The Black Caucus of the U.S. Congress, overwhelmingly Democrat, proposed in 1976 that there be established in the United States a "foreign policy lobby" of and for Black nations of Africa, particularly, and worldwide, generally. Within a year, TransAfrica was incorporated. It followed a pattern well–known in Washington, enlisting an Executive Director who has a pleasing TV appearance and securing as many prominent people as possible in the Black community to serve as directors. Their names are listed on the stationery to assist in the organization's efforts, particularly in fund raising. Its activities have been based on the questionable idea that only those with a black skin may properly evaluate matters concerning African and Caribbean Blacks and bring about the "right" influence over U.S. foreign policy.

Technically, it was formed to lobby on behalf of African Black people in general, but its actual purpose was to promote the cause of the *African National Congress* within the U.S., minimizing the communist connections of that organization. Since it wasn't lobbying for a foreign nation, it did not have to register as a lobbyist or foreign agent, and since it is nominally non–profit, it could collect and use funds without any substantial disclosure which might prove embarrassing.

The purposes of the organization were carried out in a four–pronged fashion. First, numerous public appearances and press releases furthered the cause of Black Africans in general and of the *ANC* in particular. Secondly, of even greater effect has been its program in cooperation with the Black Caucus of the Congress. Computer profiles are developed on all congressmen and senators with emphasis on those in "sensitive" districts and states. This is defined as a congressman or senator who is elected or reelected by a slim majority in a district or state where there is a significant number of Black voters; he is pressured to vote the "right" way on a given bill or measure. Not–so–subtle hints of retaliation at the polls are made to persuade him or her of the wisdom of TransAfrica's position on a matter.

The third approach was to persuade and threaten U.S. firms "doing business" with or in South Africa with Black retribution if the firm did not withdraw. This effort also was all–inclusive: boards of directors and treasurers of universities and colleges, pension funds, state and municipal legislators and treasurers and other organizations with large funds, were lobbied in the name of "political

correctness" to withdraw their investments in firms "doing business" in or with South Africa. Withdrawal of investments by stock and bondholders, required by law or otherwise, came to be known as "disinvestment," intended to cause security sales that would drive the price of a company's stocks or bonds downward. "Sanctions" were the result of various laws, federal, state and local which forbade doing business in South Africa and/or imposed various embargos on trade with South Africa. The purpose of sanctions was to secure departure from the South African market; this was included in "disinvestment" and "sanctions," laws, both intended to continue so long as *apartheid* existed in South Africa.

Fourth, picketing of the South African Embassy was widely promoted, again in the name of "political correctness." Although the embassy under international law is considered an integral part of South Africa and picketing of it is illegal except under rigid conditions, these organized efforts became the "in" thing to do. Liberals, including prominent people, both White and Black, joined in the effort. Reporters and photographers were called and innumerable pictures of the famous being arrested appeared on a regular basis in the media.

Dissatisfied with the slow pace of these efforts to produce results, yet another approach was agreed upon: obtain the presence of a well–spoken Black South African to come to the U.S. for a much–publicized visit to promote the anti–*apartheid* cause. This resulted in the choice of Anglican Bishop (now Archbishop) Desmond Tutu of Cape Town. Although the

Xhosa farmers in the Eastern Cape

diminutive cleric had not been particularly active against *apartheid* and its associated evils, he is an eloquent speaker. Arrangements were made for the visit in 1984 which included an address before a joint session of Congress, an honor customarily limited among foreigners to chiefs of state.

The press widely touted Tutu as a visionary leader of "12 million Black people of South Africa," a description he knew to be utterly false, yet he remained silent. Within South Africa, the Anglican Church, as elsewhere, is traditionally the bastion of upper class English–speaking White people; relatively few Black South Africans list themselves as Anglicans. Bishop Tutu generally avoided the subject of the *ANC*, since it included the potential liability of its communist connection. Bishop Tutu, among other things, came to symbolize the militant Black attitude in South Africa, urging that Black employees poison the coffee of their White employers and that there should be violence, revolution and starvation in South Africa, where Black peo-

ple, according to him, preferred communism over *apartheid*.

An unemployed Black person in South Africa later made a significant remark concerning the efforts of Bishop Tutu, the *ANC* and others to direct economic sanctions against South Africa. He complained that they had ruined the economy while flying around the world in luxury, eating sumptuously and "running their mouths." He said that he not only lacked freedom, he was hungry.

The efforts of the *ANC* and the Black Caucus–TransAfrica visionaries in the U.S. to promote sanctions reached their peak in 1986. A bill was introduced and passed in Congress enacting several measures virtually identical to those proposed by the *ANC*.

American policy in South Africa after 1984 was somewhat unbelievable. The area had been virtually ignored during the Nixon, Ford and Carter presidencies. Initially, the Reagan administration undertook a policy of "constructive engagement" whereby a State Department official tried to work out some means of

establishing communications between Black South Africans and the government—unsuccessfully. A sanctions measure adopted by Congress was equally unbelievable, leading the South African Foreign Minister to correctly charge that "[I]t is impossible to deal with the United States. It has 535 Secretaries of State."

The sanctions enacted in September 1986 included (1) a ban on all investments and loans in South Africa, (2) a ban in the import of iron, steel and agricultural products as well as uranium, coal and textiles, (3) termination of South African airlines landing rights in the U.S., (4) exclusion of all South African bank deposits in the U.S., (5) a continued ban on the export of U.S. oil, arms or equipment connected with nuclear power, (6) approval of $40 million in aid to disadvantaged South Africans (technically, regardless of race) and finally a "request" that the *ANC* end its ties to the *South African Communist Party*, suspend its terrorist activity, and commit itself to a free and democratic future.

126

The final provision was necessary because the *ANC* had, in 1984 at the time of Bishop Tutu's tour, embarked upon a very well publicized program of violence and terrorism. Almost every day or week the U.S. media included tales of atrocities without specifying the source. Only careful inquiry revealed that it was Black on Black violence, which had to be condemned by the U.S. Congress.

President Reagan vetoed the measure and TransAfrica redoubled its efforts. Pressure was mounted upon members of Congress from "sensitive" districts and states which resulted in the override of the veto. Notwithstanding this, Oliver Tambo, was given a welcome in Washington (1987) usually reserved for a head of state. While in the U.S. he carefully forgot all communist and terrorist rhetoric; the matters were not raised during talks with administration officials.

Other informal lobbying efforts in the name of "political correctness" occurred within the halls of the United Nations in New York. Using its overweighted majority in the General Assembly, the Black nations of Africa, joined by a great many "Third World" nations, ramroded through a measure whereby the credentials of the delegation from White–dominated South Africa were rejected and it was not seated. This marked the first time in the organization's history that a member nation was denied participation because of disapproval of its internal racial policies and practices. Since there are countless other nations of the UN with a tarnished record on racial relations and human rights, respect for the UN understandably declined. The South African delegation was re–seated in 1994 shortly after election of a Black–dominated government.

Urban Overcrowding and Resulting Unrest

During the 1960s and onward, there was a continual influx into Black townships which were located on the edge of every major and smaller city of South Africa; this was caused by starkly primitive conditions prevailing in rural areas and an influx of immigrants from surrounding African nations. These urban areas became quickly known as off–limits to White people after dark since one of the results of overcrowding was lawlessness.

A UN report indicated that migration to "third world" cities was a problem common to the whole African continent. In reality it is a worldwide phenomenon—cities are frequently surrounded by shacks where people live in the most degrading squalor. South Africa tried to limit expansion of these urban slums by adopting an identity card (pass book) system intended to protect employed workers around the cities from competition by illegal immigrants. By and large, urban Blacks accepted the identity card system.

When the same system was adopted in Tanzania in 1984 no one paid any attention. But in the case of South Africa, a worldwide howl of protest was heard about this being a horrible violation of human rights. In order to understand how silly the protesters were, it should be realized that most U.S. states offer an identity card bearing a picture for use by those without a driver's license.

The misery of *Crossroads* and the new town, *Khayalitsha*

The pass laws were, among other measures, repealed in 1986 because of the clamor coming from mindless people anxious to condemn South Africa in any way possible.

The government established "homelands" in order to take the pressure off of Black townships to reduce its burden to provide decent housing and services. It also sought to neutralize Black political power. Technically, all township residents were required to vote in the homeland from which they or their ancestors had come, or to which they had been assigned. To further encourage migration to the homelands, and in spite of their continuous growth, the government also decreed that no new high school facilities could be built in them.

Soweto

It had, back in 1953, been ordered that instruction in all high schools be 50% in *Afrikaans* and 50% in English, but not in the native language of the pupils which was used during the first six years of schooling.

Soweto, outside of the large city of Johannesburg, was one of the early Black townships, and thus had a great many four–room houses built by the government which on the surface appeared reasonably presentable. But only about 15% of them had inside running water and toilet facilities. The great majority of the homes had 6 to 8 people crowded in very limited space with no heat.

As early as 1960 (Sharpeville) there had been demonstrated the capability and willingness of Black citizens to use firearms against the White police (which had a substantial number of Black officers also). The disturbance which is remembered most widely, occurred in Soweto in mid–1976. The cause is traditionally remembered as a directive that all school education be in *Afrikaans*. That is not an accurate statement.

The 1953 agreement on 50–50 use of English and Afrikaans had gradually been ignored in Black high schools in favor of English only. This was a sensible move—*Afrikaans* was and is an outdated, parochial language compared to English. The *Boer* members of the parliament, led by the arch–conservative, Dr. Andries Treurnicht, insisted on 50% *Afrikaans* in high school classrooms, and the announcement was made by the then education minister Pieter Botha.

The teachers in Soweto undoubtedly spread the word of this occurrence, using words of polarity, and they were repeated by the students at home. Within hours on June 16th a disturbance that turned into a riot started that lasted until the 24th; before it was over, 174 Blacks were killed (compared to 2 Whites). There were 1,222 Black casualties, contrasting sharply with 6 Whites wounded.

The disturbance–riot was suppressed with excessive force. Botha retracted the demand for the use of *Afrikaans*.

The event is memorable because it was the first time Black people were more than could be readily controlled by Whites in South Africa. Its anniversary is celebrated to this day. Many Black youth in the U.S. are inspired by the symbolism of Soweto and enjoy telling others of it, even though the facts have not been reported accurately. (There is a lingering notion that there was a refusal to use *any* White language, which is not true.) Another counter–productive program emerged following the Soweto riot: a boycott of schools. The slogan "liberation before education" became a watchword which has proved to be costly. As Black majority rule approached in 1994, it became evident that 18 years of school boycotts had left a generation of young illiterates in South Africa.

As the years rolled forward into the 1980s, Blacks in South Africa became more assertive, a trend which later would be transformed into a resolve to be ungovernable. Disturbances became more common. The government did relax a few of the minor *apartheid* laws, but it tripled its security budget "for more rapid local control and to combat insurgencies."

Black Homelands

A "solution" to racial problems for the government was adopted under President Vorster in the form of a Black Homelands Act. This consisted of granting internal self–government to ten areas either traditionally associated with or assigned to a tribal group. When each requested independence, it was to be granted. The states would be given special treatment, such as low trade barriers and tax exemptions. The first to take the plunge was the Xhosa area in southeast South Africa, *Transkei*, with then about 3 million inhabitants (1976). The next occurred the following year when Bophuthatswana ("homeland of the Tswanas"), a nation in six separated areas with 2.1 million people, was granted self–rule; most of its parts lay to the north, bordering Botswana. Venda, with almost a half million, became independent in 1979 and Ciskei in 1981.

Although the new homeland republics did not receive diplomatic recognition except by South Africa, they maintained offices in major foreign capitals. Neighboring African nations were strongly op-

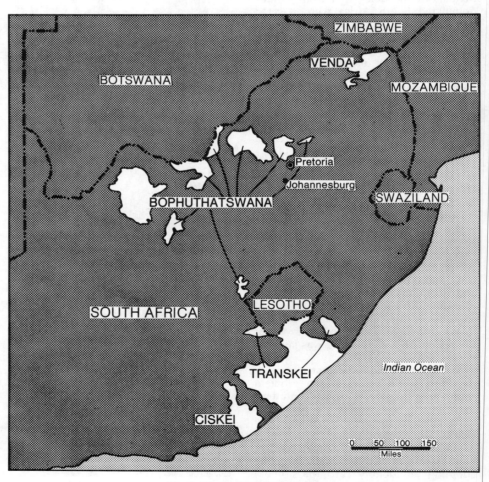

Black "homeland" republics

posed to what they saw as a plan to keep White South Africa in control of the most productive and desirable land, and to retain economic and political strength.

Of equal concern during the early 1980s was a move to relocate thousands of Black South Africans living in rural areas who had acquired their land legally in "White only" areas before the 1912 *Group Areas Act* was adopted. Strong adverse reaction in the foreign press brought a halt to this attempt at forced moving, although the government denied being influenced by such expressions.

The Black Homelands solution addressed only a portion of a social and economic impasse. More than 14 million Black people lived in townships adjacent to the largest cities and industrial areas of South Africa; even the government classified them as "detribalized." But to express themselves politically, they were *required* to vote in the homeland to which they had been assigned (which had no role or vote in the government of South Africa) whether or not they had ever been physically present. The system of identity cards was used, in part, to determine who could live outside his or her "homeland."

Viewing the homelands as potential rivals in the quest for Black supporters, both the *ANC* and the *UDC* vigorously opposed the homeland concept, which actually was in large part a move to accommodate the more right–wing conservatives.

Not all urban Black settlements had bad news during the 1970s and early 1980s. A shantytown close to Cape Town called Crossroads had grown to more than 50,000. The government found it impossible to provide vitally needed services because of overcrowding, so it began a housing project several miles away in 1984—the new town of Khayalitsha. By mid–1985 almost 20,000 had accepted the offer to live in new homes which had water, light, sanitation facilities, playgrounds, schools and stores, all of which were lacking in Crossroads.

The new residents were not required to have work papers for 18 months in the hope that they would by then have secured work. New units cost about $2,000. But unfortunately, the 1980s was a period of increasing financial pressures on the South African government, including widespread rent strikes sponsored by the *ANC* that limited the ability of township, state and federal agencies to provide even minimal municipal services. They also prevented the construction of new units.

Attempted Reforms

Former President Botha, as early as 1980, saw the need for additional reform and embarked on a wide–ranging series of measures, stating that revolution was not just a remote possibility. He proposed elimination of the *Group Areas Act,* the *Slums Act* and the *Community Development Act;* the names sounded innocent, but the laws were tools of *apartheid.* But the conservative element of the National Party, led by the intractable Andries Treurnicht resisted any reform whatsoever. They persuaded the usually astute president to embark on a "new" approach that would lead to violence and change in South Africa.

Dr. Andries Treurnicht

The plan was an attempt to placate both international opinion and internal resistance by Blacks to White rule. It was supposed to be the answer to the exclusion of Blacks from *any* participation in government. Sometime in the mid–1970s a scheme had been devised to constitutionally create

A Three–House National Assembly . . . . . . (With No Blacks).

The plan was first promulgated during the term of office of John Vorster, but met with little enthusiasm in South Africa or abroad. Vorster's tenure ended in mid–1979 amid various scandals involving use of public money for not–so–secret projects calculated to sustain *apartheid* and the White–ruled Republic of South Africa. He was ultimately succeeded by Pieter W. Botha. But as unrest slowly and steadily escalated from 1979 to 1984, the plan began to look more and more attractive.

The heart of the "solution" as of 1984 was obvious to the conservative government: *include* Blacks in *some* level of government, but nothing of importance to the *Boers.* If the test at limited self–gov-

ernment failed, that could be cited as a reason to continue denial of full participation in the important levels of government.

To appear to be as democratic as possible, a scheme was devised to create a three–house National Assembly with a large body restricted to White membership, two smaller units to represent Coloureds and Indians, and no Blacks. The latter were to be given control of the townships in which they were a majority.

In this way, it was felt, Black leadership could be used to contain increasing unrest in the townships and, at the same time, satisfy the hunger for self–rule. The *Boer* leadership actually convinced themselves that something was being given to the Blacks of South Africa. The *ANC* leadership felt it was no more than just another chapter in the book of *apartheid.*

The National Assembly had a 185–seat White parliament, a 92–seat one for Coloureds and a third for Asians (46 seats). The smaller houses had no powers except with respect to matters of concern to the minority they represented. The larger White parliament could veto any act of the other two. This three–tiered system of parliament, coupled with Black "home rule" proved to be White South Africa's most costly and serious mistake; it was instrumental in the downfall of White–controlled government.

The plan itself was unworkable, and quickly gave way to a government by oligarchy: the Presidential Council of about 60 members proposed all laws and the parliament became a rubber stamp. But even worse was Black reaction: instead of seeing a half full glass, they saw only a half empty one. A fundamental decision was made in response to the measure—*make South Africa ungovernable!*

The *ANC* devised a two–pronged agenda to accomplish its aim of seizing control of South Africa (it did not envision doing its will through the ballot box until the early 1990s). First, using violence as a tool against non–Zulu Black South Africans, an effort was made to make all persons, particularly within the townships, either members of *ANC* or sympathizers with the cause it espoused. This was accomplished by making it dangerous *not* to fall within one of the two categories. Second, the *ANC* leadership recognized that *Inkatha,* led by Mangosuthu Gatsha Buthelezi, was a potential rival that had to be eliminated or at least controlled in the struggle for power that was to come. Both of these programs unleashed terrible violence, which immediately increased tremendously; the police were virtually helpless to deal with it because of sheer quantity.

In most cases, well–meaning Blacks ran for township office—mayor and council—and with an *ANC* led boycott of elections, they were voted in by a small

RACIAL COMPOSITION

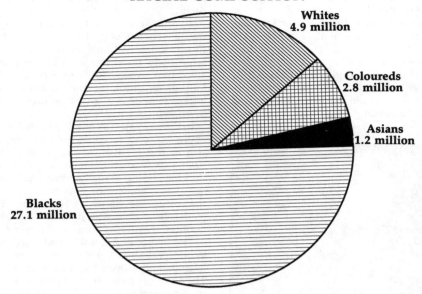

Whites
4.9 million

Coloureds
2.8 million

Asians
1.2 million

Blacks
27.1 million

MAJOR BLACK GROUPS

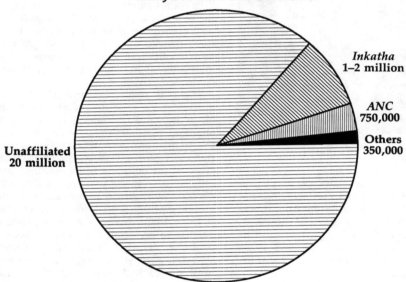

Inkatha
1–2 million

ANC
750,000

Others
350,000

Unaffiliated
20 million

minority of the electorate. Interestingly, Zulus did not run for these offices, as will be explained. The ones chosen were treated dreadfully—they were regarded as subservient Uncle Toms, cooperating with the despised White–controlled government. They, and anyone cooperating with, talking with, being seen with or simply not opposing them with suitable enthusiasm, became acceptable targets of *ANC* and *MK* violence.

After violence rose to the level hoped for, the *ANC* and those in sympathy with its aims began to use the turmoil as the greatest reason for economic disinvestment and sanction programs directed against South Africa by foreign businesses. It was implied that investment in or doing business with South Africa would be helping Whites to kill Blacks

there. Such misinformation effectively disguised what was actually going on in South Africa for a decade following 1984: *Black vs. Black* violence.

In the decade 1984–1994, a grand total of over 20,000 Blacks were killed in South Africa; of these, about 11,000 were murdered after 1990 when Nelson Mandela was released from prison by the White government. Of the total, about 1,500 were killed by the South African Defense Forces of the White government. Those who perished included common criminals who resisted arrest or attempted violence on the police or others and could not be restrained without the loss of life. The significant figure is that 94% of the murders were of *Blacks by Blacks*.

The commission which developed those figures also concluded that of the

Black on Black homicies, those killed were about 85% *ANC* members or supporters, or lived in *ANC*–controlled areas.

Neighboring Conflicts, Foreign Affairs

When Portugal granted independence to both Angola and Mozambique in 1975, the stage was set for South African involvement in the affairs of both nations because of what was perceived to be a threat of a communist take–over in each of the countries.

In Mozambique, the communist rebel movement quickly took over the government and was in turn beset by a counter–revolutionary, conservative group. Fighting continued unevenly from 1975 until 1992 and the result was twofold: the government never really controlled a substantial portion of the countryside, and the people starved to death in massive numbers. South African involvement was not direct; only one instance occurred which involved a South African air raid on what were believed to be subversive *ANC* units based in Mozambique. As a result of the raid, the units departed to Zimbabwe and Zambia.

The question of indirect involvement in the activities of the conservative *Renamo* is elusive. It is known that it received support from conservative Portuguese–speaking individuals living outside Mozambique. No satisfactory proof exists indicating South African support, but such would have been entirely logical. But even if such support is assumed, it is known that South Africa kept communications channels with the communist regime open, resulting in cooperation with it concerning several areas of mutual concern. For greater detail on this, see Mozambique.

As the decline of the Soviets set in (1989) and was finalized (1991), their influence over all client states rapidly dwindled. In Mozambique, they never had much influence to begin with. When the situation was clear as of 1991, there was no longer anything to arouse continued South African opposition in Mozambique. The regime had quietly discarded communist trappings and was attempting energetically to open contacts with the U.S. and other Western sources in a desperate attempt to receive badly-needed aid and assistance.

Angola was another case, however. Three factions contested the control of the country at independence. When the communist one appeared to be losing ground, under Soviet pressure, 3,000 Cuban mercenaries arrived to assist. After 1975, the number quickly grew to more than 50,000; they were backed up by Soviet "advisers" numbering in the thousands.

South Africa reacted by dispatching troops to Angola, determined that communists not be permitted to seize the state by force. The conflict which ensued was uneven and the venture proved to be dreadfully costly to the Cubans and Soviets. Cubans had no direct stake in the outcome of the conflict and thus had no enthusiasm for exposing themselves to hostile gunfire by fighting on the front lines. In the few instances when they were ordered into battle, their effectiveness was extremely poor. This attitude carried over to and became evident among Angolan troops loyal to the communists.

One factor which led South Africa to act was Angola's sheltering the communist rebel movement (SWAPO) of South–West Africa (Namibia) within its borders, providing what was considered a subversive organization sanctuary.

Another complication was the fact that the communist leadership in Luanda consisted primarily of mulattos who under the Portuguese were considered to be the upper class of Black people in Angola. The darker troops of the communist army as well as the UNITA rebels resented the positions of power and prestige held by top members of the regime.

An economically weakened Soviet Union under Gorbachëv concluded correctly in 1987 that the Angolan venture could never be more than a loss. A phased withdrawal of Cuban troops was agreed to which was acceptable to South Africa. Nevertheless, the Cubans, in order to save face, attempted one final offensive in 1989 which proved to be a disaster.

An example of the conflict occurred at Cuito Cuanavale, where a force of 3,000 South Africans and UNITA forces faced an army of almost 30,000 Cubans and communist Angolans. Losing thirty–one, the South Africans inflicted seven to ten thousand casualties on their enemies; the fighting was so fierce there was no time to count bodies. The communists lost equipment valued at $1 billion U.S. The last South Africans (and Cubans) withdrew from Angola in 1990. For greater detail and the current status of the strife, see Angola.

A third area involving potential communist domination was Namibia, formerly South–West Africa, administered by South Africa since the end of World War I. Pressures for its independence mounted steadily during the 1980s, which was refused by South Africa, since it would have meant turning over the administration of the territory to the communist rebel organization, the South–West Africa People's Organization (SWAPO). This, South Africa steadfastly refused to do, in spite of annual UN resolutions condemning its actions and widespread international criticism.

Here again, the outcome was hastened by the decline and fall of the Soviet com-

munists. This led the SWAPO organization to become more conciliatory and to agree to genuinely free elections as a basis for independence. South Africa agreed, and all was done according to the agreement. Although the communists won the elections, they did not win sufficiently to control constitutional negotiations. Even more important, they became far less communist, dropping all of the trappings and rhetoric from their agenda. For greater detail, see Namibia.

This resistance to communism in neighboring territories and internal apartheid policies resulted in widespread international criticism and ostracism of South Africa, particularly within the UN. This barrage was withstood, however, and abated after the release of Nelson Mandela and the repeal of most of apartheid. South Africa did not resist the temptation of periodically tweaking the noses of righteous nations and individuals offering gratuitous condemnation; it pointed out the miserable human rights records and acts of aggression of world nations about which utterly nothing was heard.

Inkatha Freedom Party and Chief Buthelezi

By the early 1970s the ANC had been all but eliminated as an imminent threat by the White–controlled government of South Africa, and the organization was somewhat demoralized. The system of spies and informants which was developed by the South African Defense Forces made it dangerous to belong to the underground organization or to be a communist comrade–in–arms. In order to try to maintain some form of legal pressure against apartheid, the ANC leadership rec-

Chief Mangosuthu Buthelezi

ognized the need to have a Zulu–based organization to bring pressure on the White government.

The Zulus live primarily in Natal province, surrounding areas and homelands, and have traditionally never been friendly with the Xhosas, who are the core of the ANC, together with the Sothos and Tswanas. Thus, although they had no particular affinity for potential rivals, it was a matter of practicality for the ANC to enourage and assist in the founding of the Inkatha Freedom Party in 1974. Its leader was and is Chief Mangosuthu Gatsha Buthelezi (Man–go–soo–too Gat–sha Boo–teh–lay–zee), a well–spoken moderate leader, known for his ability to communicate with the White leadership, in spite of Inkatha's staunch opposition to apartheid.

Buthelezi firmly believed that change in South Africa was possible, but also steadfastly believed that if basic changes occurred in such a manner as to impoverish the country, they would be worthless. His attitudes largely reflected the lifestyles of most of the members of Inkatha, as well as most Zulu non–members.

The Xhosas and Sothos tended to cluster with their families in shantytowns around the large industrial and mining centers of South Africa, where children were raised in poverty and hardship. The Zulus, on the other hand, were the chief clientele of hostels—shelters for male workers with a minimum of comfort and convenience—where they lived for usually 27 out of 30 days. In the period of respite from work, they went back home (where they had been sending their wages after expenses) to their wives and children. Living in this manner, their needs are minimal, their wages are comparatively high and family tensions and quarrels are usually at a low level since they didn't have time to escalate. Of equal importance, their wives and children weren't exposed to the crime, violence and deprivations of the townships, where living is harsh and often unruly.

Buthelezi and Inkatha enjoyed immense popularity among the Zulus—reports of dues—paying membership went as high as 2 million, but slightly more than 1 million was a more realistic figure. This was in contrast to the ANC which charged no membership dues and was estimated at 750,000 members and sympathizers. In 1994 it was predicted by the U.S. media that 90% of the younger Zulus would vote for the ANC, an estimate which was greatly inflated.

After 1984 during the campaign to discredit Inkatha and Chief Buthelezi, actions of the MK wing of the ANC soon were out of control. Instead of mere words, violence was directed against Zulus, a poor choice which backfired.

When the National Party leadership perceived that the ANC was attempting to

cans, words are *indeed* a justification for violence since they assault a precious commodity: honor. Members of the *MK* had been using belittling words with tedious regularity directed at the Zulus, and the only possible result could have been violent which was viewed as self-defense by them. They termed the language used by the *ANC* "killing words."

This is not meant to imply that the Zulus had only nasty words inflicted upon them by the *MK*; that organization quickly came to be associated with the Zulu's arch-rival tribe, the Xhosas, and violent acts of cruelty, torture and death became commonplace, directed at Zulus individually and at the hostels in which the men resided while employed. Countless hundreds died as a result, and thousands more predictably sought revenge.

Thus, when the *ANC* successfully demanded the government to ban the Zulu weapons, the government's acceptance was viewed as a basic betrayal by Zulus in general and *Inkatha* in particular. The Xhosas and the *ANC* had won a concession at the conference table which had not been possible in battle. The ban was largely ignored, but it effectively alienated a source of Black moderation in South Africa.

Chief Buthelezi and *Inkatha* leaders particularly had difficulty with the position of the government in view of the fact that the organization had received financial support over a period of years from the White government.

ANC Recruitment Techniques
Many non-Zulus are known to have

destabilize South Africa with violence, the conservatives and military of the government sought and obtained an informal alliance with *Inkatha* to combat the rise in violence. There is a substantial body of evidence, all unproven, however, that the Zulus were armed and trained by members of the South African Defense Force and the armed forces. As this became evident to the *MK* leadership, efforts against Zulus were redoubled.

A commission report of the percentage of those killed by tribal affiliation showed that about 15% were Zulus or their sympathizers. Based upon knowledge of these offenses, it can be stated that in cases of violence when Zulus killed, they usually had been provoked directly by *ANC* followers or were resisting conscription into *ANC* ranks.

Among Zulu customs, the carrying of traditional weapons, referred to also as *cultural weapons*, is important. They are uniquely associated with the passage from boyhood to manhood. Although not universally carried at all times, their presence certainly marks the bearer as a Zulu for all to see, a fact in which not a small amount of pride is held. For reasons that are not clear, an obscure South African judge in 1989 ruled that they were dangerous weapons in the eyes of the law, and therefore could not be carried in public. Making a bad mistake, the government agreed, and told the Zulus they could not carry spears and axes as was their right in the past, even though the Zulus, when resorting to violence (usually considered by them to be defensive) used *modern* weaponry.

Chief Buthelezi and his followers, as well as Zulus in general, were shocked at the decision. Within limits, they had remained loyal to the concept of change as produced by law, not violence. It appeared that in the name of appeasement the government was caving into the whims of the *ANC*, which had been complaining bitterly about the weapons. *Inkatha*, and the Zulus appeared to have become in a sense the sacrificial lamb at the altar of injustice.

Chief Buthelezi, and Goodwill Zwelethini, King of the Zulus, denounced the measure in no uncertain terms, widely supported by Zulus in Natal and elsewhere. Together with conservative White South Africans, the chief began to speak with regularity of a Black state seceding from South Africa under his leadership. In the alternative, in the event that agreement could be reached on a non-racial government, a system of strong federalism was favored, creating the equivalent of states' rights. This attracted favorable interest among many White conservatives, who sought to establish a "White homeland" in the event of a Black-dominated government in South Africa.

In order to understand the importance of banning traditional weapons, it is necessary to realize differences in law which exist in South Africa and in the U.S. Here, mere words will never justify the slightest physical violence, let alone a fatal assault or action purportedly in self-defense. The law imposes the burden upon the recipient of such words to simply walk away. Among Black South Afri-

King Goodwill Zwelethini

132

lost their lives either within South Africa, or in the vicious concentration camps maintained in neighboring nations sympathic to the *ANC* cause.

The late Oliver Tambo, Chris Hani, and Joe Slovo, as well as Cyril Ramaphosa, have all been directly implicated in these infamous camps which were created for punishment, extinction and "attitude adjustment" of those considered to be disloyal to the *ANC* cause. Conditions in them were unspeakably horrible and compared to Hitler's operation in style (but not numbers) during World War II.

Most carried off to these camps were murdered after being tortured for the amusement of their captors. A few were allowed to return to their townships in order to spread the word of *ANC* prowess in dealing with those who failed to support its agenda. They spread the word to others. Those not removed to the camps were usually murdered, more often than not by being "necklaced."

Who was most likely to be chosen by *MK* for fatal treatment? A profile slowly emerged—he or she would have one or more of the following traits or characteristics:

1. Employment,
2. in a White–owned business or firm,
3. receiving a relatively moderate to high income,
4. well–dressed,
5. educated,
6. possibly elected as mayor or councilman in a township,
7. failed or refused to get involved in *ANC*–led demonstrations or protests,
8. failed to contribute money to the *ANC*,
9. even worse, was critical of the *ANC*,
10. was suspected of being an informant of the South African Defense Force,
11. was seen voluntarily having a conversation with a member of the SADF,
12. was simply disliked.

This does not include Zulu workers living in hostels. Since they were fair game at any time, they usually went about in groups for their own protection.

The Black–on–Black violence came to be so pervasive that the police, demoralized, simply stopped responding to calls for assistance in the Black townships, fearing that their presence would be a catalyst which might cause an eruption of violence on a larger scale. For this reason, it is impossible to give precise figures of fatalities in South Africa during the last decade.

Exit President Botha, Enter President de Klerk

Nelson Mandela wrote to the then President Pieter W. Botha in 1988, urgently stating that the two should confer about matters vital to the future of the nation. Although it was not publicized, the conservative president met with Mandela.

The two discussed the apparent need for serious negotiations to seek some way to end South Africa's violence which had become rampant. Although President Botha favored development of some pathway to negotiations, he was limited in what he could do by the presence of the *Conservative Party* within the halls of parliament. Futher, the rigid communist approach devoted to Black seizure of the nation so dear to the *ANC* made a quick move toward negotiations impossible.

A generally astute leader, President Botha suffered a stroke in January 1989. After a brief recuperation, he announced in March 1989 he would resume his duties as president, but there was immediate opposition from the party leadership, which secured the nomination of Frederik W. de Klerk to run in September elections.

Three weeks before the elections, an angry and frustrated Botha made a television broadcast denouncing de Klerk, the *ANC* and all others perceived by him to be hostile, and resigned as president. From the rambling content of his speech, it was obvious that his time to leave the scene had come, but he definitely had left his mark on his country's history: the seeds of basic change. In his own way, the "old crocodile," as he was affectionately referred to, provided astuteness and judgment, realizing what was desirable and possible to an amazing degree, and compromising when necessary (but usually on his own terms). His successor showed a generally more conciliatory approach and was able to ignore the White conservatives who were a continuous source of aggravation in South Africa.

State visit of former President Botha to Transkei

133

President de Klerk and Mr. Nelson Mandela (February 1990)   AP/Wide World Photo

Nelson Mandela

Nelson Mandela, born in Umtata (later within the homeland of *Transkei*) in 1918, turned 77 in July 1995. When the *ANC* was banned in 1962 he went underground, as did many others among its leadership. Apprehended, he was charged under the anti–communist and anti–terrorism laws in force in South Africa and was sentenced to life imprisonment without hope of parole. This received almost no attention in the U.S. because he was at the time just another communist revolutionary.

While in prison, he kept abreast of current matters in South Africa, including the turn to violence and terrorism in 1984.

It was not until F.W. de Klerk became president in 1989 and had a chance to solidify his power base that further contact was established with Mandela leading to his release from prison. At about the same time, others, including Walter Sisulu, were released.

President de Klerk correctly concluded that continued detention of Mandela would be counter–productive and his chances of meaningful negotiations would be more possible if they were with the older leaders of the *ANC*. Oliver Tambo had suffered a major stroke and had been largely neutralized by it.

Thus, in February 1990 de Klerk ordered the release of Nelson Mandela, whose name by that time was a legend among the Black people of South Africa. There was dancing and widespread celebrating in the townships. He was almost immediately made Deputy President of the *ANC* effectively being transformed overnight from the status of prisoner to head of the organization from which he had been removed almost 27 years past when seized.

Although he made some mistakes following his release, he was quite astute in walking a tightwire, engaging in negotiations with President de Klerk, traveling abroad in search of desperately needed funding, and acknowledging that the anti–*apartheid* rival *Inkatha* movement of South Africa had to be given some sort of recognition. His conduct, however, infuriated the more radical members of the *ANC* who for so many painful years cherished the visions of Black power, confrontation, seizure of the state and bloody revolution.

He had not been adequately informed of the fact that communism had been rapidly crumbling in the Soviet Union and Eastern Europe nor could he be expected to foresee the utter collapse of the doctrines he had come to cherish. His initial statements, made in a large stadium in Soweto, shocked White South Africans:

> "We have waited too long for our freedom. We can no longer wait. Now is the time to intensify the struggle on all fronts. To relax our efforts now would be a mistake which generations to come will not be able to forgive."

In the speech, he saluted the *MK*, the *South African Communist Party*, and several members of that organization, including Secretary General Joe Slovo ("one of our finest patriots"), regarded by most Whites as little more than a shabby opportunist.

A hammer and sickle flag was displayed (but not on U.S. television) immediately below the platform from which he spoke. What was not realized is that those words were for (1) home consumption and (2) more importantly, to assure Mandela of an undisputed claim as leader of the *ANC* as opposed to the militant wing of the organization. His strategy worked, for it was not long before he was proclaimed Commander of the *Umkhonto we Sizwe* (an honorary title). But within a day he was saying: "Whites are fellow South Africans and we want them to feel safe and [to know] that we appreciate the contribution they have made towards the development of the country."

The major mistake he made then and after the speech was to insist upon nationalization of South African industries, in particular, the immense Anglo–American Mining Company, a multi-national consortium with worldwide interests as well as its diamond and gold mines of South Africa. When in 1992 Mandela had concluded that his advocacy of sanctions and disinvestment was the wrong policy, to his remorse, he found that trying to turn away from these policies in order to attract investment to South Africa was far harder than he had imagined. His earlier position had laid the foundation for an atmosphere of suspicion and distrust.

Even in 1993, as multi–party talks hopefully leading to a stable, racially peaceful South Africa seemed to be a closer possibility, no serious international investor would consider placing funds there in view of instability and turbulence for the past decade, particularly when coupled with nationalization pronouncements. That speech sent shudders throughout the South African financial community.

Mandela had been expected by many, including this writer, to be a dedicated, violent revolutionary gripped by the misjudgments of an uninformed old age. To the contrary, he has shown great astuteness and flexibility, walking tightwires where there often was no visible wire. The pressures under which he has survived have been immense. He had to risk the disfavor of the militant wing of the ANC when he, after months of pondering what to do about his wife, finally opted to part ways.

She had accompanied him on foreign tours in 1991, including the United States,

Nelson Mandela

helping to raise funds for the ANC. In reality he had no choice: he would not be taken seriously as a present or future leader of Black South Africa with her at his side. Other pressures came from 1992 "massacres" of ANC followers in and near Natal province, at Boipatong, and Bisho in the Ciskei "homeland." Withdrawing from negotiations with the White government, he accused it of complicity with Zulu members of *Inkatha* and with Ciskeian defense forces who did the actual shooting at these occurrences.

In June 1992 and months following of the same year came the revelation of information that was generally known, but not capitalized on: the White South Africans had been aiding, abetting and subsidizing *Inkatha* probably since its founding in 1974, in varying degrees and manners.

How could he negotiate with the White oppressors who had for so long made his life and the lives of Blacks in South Africa so miserable? The instinct and teaching imbedded in the Black people was to wreak vengeance on their enemies and oppressors. To sit and talk peace and harmony with them simply went against the grain of ANC doctrine of violent seizure of power which, embraced for so long, had been virtually carved in stone.

On the other hand, how could he, after negotiating with de Klerk's government, scarcely wait to utter the worst insults imaginable at the Whites in general and, to a greater degree, de Klerk? They were accompanied by countless ultimatums with often impossible terms, all calculated to satisfy the disappointed desires of the militants and fanatics of the ANC.

The two discussed the apparent need for serious negotiations to seek some way to end South Africa's violence which had become rampant. Although President Botha favored development of some pathway to negotiations, he was limited in what he could do by the presence of the *Conservative Party* within the halls of parliament. Further, the rigid communist approach devoted to Black seizure of the nation so dear to the ANC made a quick move toward negotiations impossible.

With her husband in prison and being far from the "action" in South Africa, Winnie Mandela was bored. Violating her exile in 1986, she worked her way to Soweto, a Black township outside of Johannesburg. A luxurious home, complete with swimming pool had been built for her amid the two–room tar paper and tin shanties of the town. There was a minor uproar of protest, so she did not immediately move in.

When she did, she formed "The Winnie Mandela Soccer Team," a gang of young thugs which proceeded to terror-

Winnie Mandela

ize Soweto and other nearby Black townships. Trials of real and imagined offenders took place in her home, where she often "presided." Sentences of beating and death were meted out. When members of the team raped a young girl in an adjacent township, residents gathered in anger and proceeded to the house, setting it on fire. Sowetans stood around, mutely watching the blaze; when the fire engines finally arrived, they had no water.

The structure was rebuilt and the terrorism was resumed. A very damaging event occured in 1988 when a 13–year-old boy was kidnapped from a Soweto Methodist Church shelter by the "team" and taken to the house. He was accused of being a police informer and was beaten severely, reportedly partly by her. Taken to a nearby field by the "team," he was murdered. In the storm which ensued, Winnie tried to counter the charge of her involvement in the slaying with a hasty allegation that he had been abused at the Methodist home (untrue).

Acting through his lawyer from prison, Nelson Mandela ordered her to release three other kidnapped youths and to disband the "team." She was ousted from the ANC, losing her informal title "Mother of the Nation." A trial was held sporadically because radical members of the ANC kept threatening and actually kidnapped co-defendants and state witnesses, removing them from the country. After listening to her testimony the judge (there is yet no jury trial in South Africa) called her a "calm, composed, deliberate and unblushing liar." She was sentenced to six years in jail; an appeals court sustained the conviction in early June 1993 but, in a political decision which was wise, vacated the prison sentence.

Winnie Mandela is sixteen years

younger than her estranged husband; she had a marriage prior to their union. When he was convicted and sentenced, she was directed to keep herself in an isolated, rural location in Natal.

The trial was held after the release of Nelson Mandela from prison; neither he nor the *ANC* leadership directly rallied to Winnie's defense. She was rebuffed in an effort to rejoin the *ANC* leadership when Walter Sisulu's wife withdrew from the race for president of the Women's Auxiliary and threw her support to an opponent. While her husband was trying to engage in meaningful negotiations with the White government, Winnie appealed to the militant sector of the *ANC*; they remembered her for her famous 1987 statement: ''With our matchboxes and our necklaces, we shall liberate!''

''Necklacing'' occurs when an old tire is jammed down over the shoulders of the victim. Filled with gasoline, it is ignited. As the victim writhes in abject agony, the crowd gathered for the occasion yells and cheers with excitement usually associated with a holiday gathering. Who got this treatment? Anyone disapproved of by *MK* leaders was chosen, including a woman past the age of 80 suspected of being a witch. It was used time after time against Blacks believed to be unsympathetic to the aims of the *ANC*, including township mayors, councilmen and police.

In the spring of 1992 Nelson Mandela decided to divorce Winnie because of ''tensions'' of an unspecified nature.

The last was not heard of Winnie, however. Acting in the tradition of a woman scorned, she lashed out at the *ANC* leadership, including her estranged husband, saying:

> ''The *NP* [National Party] elite is getting into bed with the *ANC* in order to preserve its silken sheets, and the leadership elite in the *ANC* is getting into bed with the *NP* to enjoy this new–found luxury.''

Needless to say, this was immensely appealing to the militants of the *ANC*, including the late Chris Hani, then head of *Umkhonto we Sizwe*. When he was assassinated in April 1993, she showed up at his home near Johannesburg, dressed in guerrilla camoflage, and gave several inflammatory statements to the press.

Having won the elections of April 1994, Nelson Mandela and the *ANC* faced a genuine dilemma: Winnie was a highly loaded loose cannon on the new ship of state which could go off without notice. In a wink she was rehabilitated to her old prestigious stature with the title Mother of the Nation restored. It didn't matter that she had been having an open, torrid relationship with a man to whom she is not married. But she did poll No. 5 in popularity among *ANC* voters and she was elected to the legislature.

Aerial view of bustling Cape Town

To keep her quiet, the leadership appointed her to be Deputy Minister of Arts, Culture, Science and Technology. One of the requirements of the job was silence. After taking office, she went about acting like a messenger from God when she spoke of her husband, referring to him and herself in the collective ''we.''

But in the months following she reverted to the old Winnie. She became involved in activities that resulted in accusations of influence–peddling and shady business deals. As president of the Woman's Auxiliary, she did things her way, failing to consult the directors, 11 of whom resigned in protest. Worst of all, she repeated her criticism of the government (i.e. her husband) and accused it of failing to deliver on election promises while squandering money. Furious, Nelson Mandela demanded a written apology which Thabo Mbeki wrote for her, but in late March 1995 fired her from her post. She still remains, for the time being, head of the Auxiliary. She filed a court suit questioning the propriety of her discharge in which she was supported by Mangosuthu Buthelezi. She was ''unfired'' so that constitutional requirements could be met (consultation with heads of parties by the president) before she is again dismissed.

Even more serious, a stepped up inquiry involving new evidence is underway regarding Winnie Mandela's involvement in deaths and disappearances in 1989 arranged by her football club. Nevertheless, she remains tremendously popular among the young, radical segment of the *ANC* and there is serious talk of her running for president in 1999.

The Repeal of Apartheid

President de Klerk and the *National Party* wasted no time in 1990–1 to repeal *apartheid* laws in South Africa. After they were repealed, nothing happened. What then, was the purpose of even being anti–apartheid? Many who fought hard to end the oppressive system failed to realize that even though it was abolished, the economic inequalities arising out of *apartheid* were not changed. The *ANC* leadership complained that the 3.5 million people dispossessed of ''their'' land were not compensated for it, and therefore were entitled to receive it back. The problem was they had no proof that they had indeed been owners of the land from which they were moved. Further, repeal of the *apartheid* laws had no effect

136

on the Black homelands, which remained just what they had been.

Black people in South Africa did not realize that *apartheid* was much more than a set of laws. It had become a way of economic life and reality in South Africa. The only way to satisfy Black demands and expectations would be to repeal the law of property in the nation, which would mean economic collapse. The problem was postponed and is still outstanding. In reality it has no answer that will satisfy everyone.

Although many Blacks cherish the idea of owning a small family farm in South Africa, that would mean tremendous problems. A family living on 40 acres using outdated farming techniques can raise just about enough to feed itself when the weather is right. If 400 families are living and cultivating 4000 acres with modern equipment, the members of 300 families can go to work in nearby industries or even in distant ones, leaving those of 100 to do the farm work. The people of the 100 families will have more time for recreation and self–improvement, and those of the 300 families will hopefully be bringing home wages. Thus, the standard of living is vastly higher, particularly since the large farm produces a surplus which is sold.

The family farm is a thing of the past in the U.S. and in most of South Africa. Vast holdings there produce tremendous crops of vegetables in the winter to ship to Europe.

VIOLENCE OF THE 1990s

Repeal of *apartheid* meant that it was legal for Black people to be in any area they wish at any time. If this newfound privilege was used legitimately, no harm would have resulted. But it wasn't; the effect was obvious in the larger cities and in *ANC–Inkatha–*Zulu clashes.

Large City Violence

Detention laws and states of emergency had been used to control Johannesburg and other large cities in South Africa under *apartheid.* Thus, if a Black person was in the traditionally White areas of Johannesburg, he or she would be picked up and jailed. In most cases, he or she was released from jail without being charged. This procedure, by its existence, discouraged Blacks from entering forbidden areas.

Criminal opportunists used the changes in the law to "do their thing" both in Johannesburg and in the Black townships with virtual impunity. If accosted by the police, they claimed to be part of *ANC*'s effort to throw off the chains of *apartheid.* The police, fearing an "incident" with attendant publicity, did nothing even under the most suspicious of circumstances.

Compounding the situation was *ANC* insistence that criminals in prison for offenses related to resistance of *apartheid* were entitled to immediate freedom. This led to release of a "political prisoner" who in 1986 had planted a pipe bomb which killed three White women and injured 87 others.

At night there was almost no one on the streets of the formerly bustling city of Johannesburg. Luxury hotels closed, re-opening several months later at bargain prices to attract customers. Fences and walls around homes in White suburbs grew higher and higher. Prison bars at the windows, together with elaborate security systems became the order of the day. Purse snatching and petty thievery were common.

Conditions in Johannesburg and Washington D.C. were comparable. People have been warned against driving with open car windows. Hordes of beggars (homeless people in the U.S.) sometimes become "confrontational" with autos and pedestrians. The central police placed a special unit on duty to protect tourists from abroad who are a target favored especially by the lawless in Johannesburg (and in Miami, Florida).

Rivalry between jitney ("taxi") drivers got to the shooting stage in the large cities. They traditionally vie for regular routes to the townships and serve Black workers commuting to the cities. It was impossible, particularly in the townships, to predict when a group of youthful *ANC*

"comrades" would get hyper and go on a crime rampage.

In the rural areas and small towns it was no better. White people were brutally assaulted and killed without cause or for robbery. One elderly, retired farmer rigged his house with booby–trapped shotguns actuated by almost invisible nylon fishing line. He explained that his wife was bedridden and helpless and "the police don't come any more."

Morale of the South African Defense Force and local police organizations descended to an all–time low. Turnover in personnel was high, resulting in a training period of only six weeks. Recruits had to be constantly reminded they were a "legal" target for just about any gun–toting person, criminal or otherwise, who bore a grudge against the police in general or simply wanted to escape criminal responsibility for an act.

The *ANC* decided in 1986 on a basic shift in strategy. Instead of limited terrorism to victims in the Black townships, military and industrial targets, they began to concentrate on "soft spots"—places where there were large crowds. Planted bombs invaded the downtown areas of South Africa. One continuing source of violence was the press corps, particularly those pursuing "advocacy journalism." This element was avidly looking forward to reporting violence on the tenth anniversary of the Soweto uprising. Howls of disap-

Flea Market at Pretoria

pointment were heard because the government imposed a press "blackout." The move probably saved hundreds, possibly thousands of lives. Since violence had been popularized among *ANC* youths, if left to itself, the press would have become the producer, not the reporter of violence, since such persons love to "show off." The government correctly concluded that South African misfortune was going to be used to sell foreign newspapers.

A self–censorship rule against reporting violence (on pain of expulsion from South Africa) led to a dramatic drop of violence and terrorism within the country.

An act of violence gained worldwide attention in 1993 involving youthful members of the extremist Black organizations, *Pan African Congress–Azanian People's Front*. A young White female foreign student in Cape Town went to an outlying Black township, escorting her boyfriend to his home. Several youths dragged her from the vehicle and proceeded to stab and hack her to death, shouting "one settler, one bullet!" All Whites are settlers according to the party principles. At court hearings, the accused youths wore tee shirts with emblems of their party affiliation on them and were contemptuous of the proceedings, laughing and joking in the courtroom.

ANC–Zulu Violence

The campaign against *Inkatha* and Zulus in general was a poor choice. Reprisals were thorough—Zulus are more fearless and better fighters than the uneducated youth of the *ANC* and their vengeance was often directed against any Blacks who weren't Zulu.

It would be impossible to describe in this limited space all of the clashes between these two principal organizations and tribal groups during the 1990s, which occurred virtually on a daily basis. In general, the *ANC* and its members, particularly those with poor judgment, generally provoked violence. It must be remembered that provocation occurred in the minds of the Zulus when only verbal insults were made. Zulu men are intensely proud and despise anyone belittling them as was the custom of those associated with the *ANC*. Historically, they were and are generally regarded as clannish and backward by other Blacks in South Africa, an attitude which justified vengeance in the rationale of the Zulus.

Why?

From 1984 until 1990, murders of Black people in South Africa averaged 1,000 per year, the majority of which were committed by other Blacks. But from 1990 thru 1993 there were 5,000+ every year. Why was there an increase?

The answer is clear. Release of Nelson Mandela provided a figure around whom people could unite and do all necessary

for Black majority rule. The leadership of the *ANC* had been weak in the 1980s and at the end of the decade was lethargic and uninspiring. Nelson Mandela, after his release, confined himself to generalities when he spoke, all of which were well–received. But the *ANC* leadership and bureaucracy knew why Mandela had been released: to enable the Whites and the *National Party* to escape the continuing dilemma of minority rule. This slowly galvanized the *ANC* and *MK* into the acts of violence, directed against the rival Zulus.

The means of peaceful accord were twofold—the Whites could make some sort of arrangement with the *ANC* or they could seek an accommodation with Chief Buthelezi and the Zulus. As late as mid–1993 it appeared that the latter course might well be taken. The thought of this terrified the *ANC* leadership and raised the level of murderous fighting to an even higher degree, with the *ANC* almost always on the losing side when it challenged the Zulus.

The drift of things became quite apparent when the White government banned traditional weapons (i.e. Zulu spears and axes). Chief Buthelezi and his followers were disgusted, but continued the struggle. How could the White government give arms and support to the Zulus to battle the *ANC* and then turn its back on them so coldly?

The answer to that question is the Whites were also sorely divided among themselves. The *ANC* demanded that the Zulus give up their traditional weapons in a symbolic gesture of humiliation and defeat. Dared the Whites refuse? If they did, was it not possible that bridges would be burned which would forever prevent any sort of accommodation with the *ANC*?

The *ANC* prevailed in mid–1992, but the Zulus continued their fighting with even renewed vigor. So the question remained open through mid–1993 as to with which Black faction the Whites

would negotiate. The *ANC* boycotted meetings because of alleged injustices by the South African Defense Force; they were actually defeats at the hands of the Zulus. It later made itself grudgingly available, but the Zulus snubbed all meetings, which quickly raised another dilemma. If peace and the future of South Africa was settled between the White *National Party* and the *ANC* in the absence of the Zulus, would it be legitimate? In an effort to break the impasse, the *ANC* tried to make a deal with King Zwelithini of the Zulus behind the back of Chief Buthelezi; it was refused.

Both sides knew the answer to the above question was "no," so in late 1993 they began energetic efforts to include the Zulus in the negotiations, which continued through into 1994. Chief Buthelezi continued the Zulu boycott, and plans for elections went ahead anyway.

As the elections neared, the question of the status of Black homelands arose; under the agreement reached by the *ANC* and the *National Party* they were to be integrated into the whole of South Africa. Balloting was to take place under the plan for national elections within the homelands. The people of Bophuthatswana were impatient with their ruler, Lucas Mangope, and there were riots which included criminal activity, causing him to flee in spite of efforts by conservative Whites to shore up his leadership. Local governments in the other homelands except KwaZulu evaporated quickly.

Constitutional Negotiations

In 1991 the competing elements in South Africa began meeting informally and later in conferences of *CODESA*,—"Congress for a Democratic South Africa." The White leadership met demands of the *ANC* when possible and refused them when impossible. Prior to negotiations, *apartheid* laws had been repealed and political exiles (often common criminals, numbering 50,000) were allowed to return to South Africa with amnesty from

---

Summary of *ANC* Activites, 1990–1994

1990–1: *ANC* engaged in fund–raising in U.S. and other overseas locations. There was a readjustment and evaluation of possibilities and alternatives. The result was an encouragement of *ANC* and *MK* aggression against *Inkatha–Zulus*.

1991–2: Fund raising abroad, consolidation at home. Continued aggression directed against Zulus. Preliminary conferences with Whites via CODESA, with posturing, walk–outs and ultimatums, some of which were impossible.

1992–3: Continued confrontation, but greater emphasis on cooperation, all without surrender of goals. Constitutional negotiations held with *Inkatha* absent, a preempt by virtue of numbers.

1993–4: After 23 months, a negotiated settlement on constitution and elections, to be held if necessary without *Inkatha–Zulu* participation. *ANC* went to the brink of disaster without the Zulus, but retreated at the last moment in 1994 in order to include them in the elections.

April 26–30, 1994: Elections (the voting period was extended).

charges that they left the country illegally (but not from other charges).

The talks were interrupted periodically by rising tides of violence, but settled down in May 1993 with a renewed sense of purpose. Political sniping from the conservatives had led de Klerk to have a national referendum on the direction desired in the talks by White South Africans. His efforts were supported by 70% of Whites, who thus for the first time voted to share power peacefully with the Black majority.

The *ANC* had to be careful of what was said because Blacks distrusted the idea that Whites would genuinely negotiate away their control of South Africa. In statements outside of the conference room, Mandela was careful to level gross insults at de Klerk calculated to reassure his own supporters that he wasn't giving in to White pressures.

Inside the room, there was a concensus: (1) an interim government had to be elected to draw a permanent constitution and to govern, and it (2) would have to see to minority (i.e. White) protection. Black power without limit was quietly discarded by the *ANC* senior leadership (but not its membership). Why?

The White negotiators tried to instill in Mandela & Company the need for continuity if anything resembling the declining wealth of South Africa was to be preserved for the future. Visions of a dramatic inaugural were undoubtedly related to him, e.g.:

"Congratulations, Nelson Mandela. You won. Here are the keys to the office. By the way, don't forget to feed 20 million people tonight. They are hungry and you have promised this to them. Don't forget."

The approach of White negotiators brought home to the *ANC* the idea that revolutionary skills are not productive of administrative ability needed to run a large nation. This had to be presented to the Black people in a manner that did not offend them, however.

A New Constitution

Ink was signed on an interim constitution on November 17, 1993, which was the result of months of painstaking negotiations. The substance of the document was a fundamental victory for the *ANC* and a radical departure from the most widely accepted principles of democratic government. This was necessary, in the opinion of *ANC* leadership, to prevent regionalism and factionalism in the government which would come into being in 1994.

The constitution provided for elections and specified that the 400–member National Assembly members *would not* represent any specific constituency. They were to be chosen from lists prepared by

The magnificent forests of northern Transvaal

each national party and from their state units, selected from popularity polls. The number of seats for each party is based on the party's percentage of the total (national) vote. A Senate of 90 members consists of 10 members selected by each of the nine states made up from the previous four provinces and 10 Black homelands.

This in effect places all power in the hands of the national parties. Most important was the fact that it is an interim constitution—the new legislature is charged with the responsibility to draft and enact a new one within five years. At the time it was adopted, there was a reasonable expectation that the *ANC*, particularly in the absence of *Inkatha*–Zulu voting, would win more than two–thirds of the popular vote. If that happened, the party would be in a position to dictate the language of a new constitution.

The document made a coalition cabinet mandatory, giving portfolios to each party in proportion to the vote it received.

After its adoption, plans proceeded forward toward elections on April 26, 1994. The *ANC*, in anticipation of the elections, had started a registration drive the previous March (1993). Thorny questions remained to be settled—who was a voter, what were the requirements or lack thereof, where and how would he or she vote?

One of the things which had to be prevented at the ballot box was voter intimidation. Although this can be so casual and subtle it is difficult to detect, avoidance of intimidation was generally successful in the contest of April 1994.

A Last Minute Accord

Because of increased political violence and apprehension over the imminent elections, President de Klerk declared a state of emergency in KwaZulu–Natal on March 31, 1994, which infuriated Chief Buthelezi and made him even more adamant. According to statements, he demanded the constitution be amended to secure the position of King Goodwill Zwelithini and the historic Zulu kingdom. As part of the state of emergency, 3,000 members of the SADF were dispatched to enforce it, all to no avail. On April 5, 15,000 Zulus armed with spears and clubs marched through the town of Empangeni; the SADF forces considered them too dangerous to disarm.

The election commission said balloting in KwaZulu would have to be postponed. Mandela rejected this, and the possibility of a constitutional violation because of delay was raised. International mediators, including Henry Kissinger from the U.S., failed to budge the parties who continued their intense negotiations. Finally there was a breakthrough on April 19th after two days of talks. The Zulus

A group of Zulu women at market

would, after all, participate in the balloting, abandoning demands for amendment of the constitution. But there were guarantees as to the continued status of the monarchy and the kingdom of Kwa-Zulu–Natal.

The real nature of the settlement was not apparent until almost a month after the elections. More than a million acres of KwaZulu–Natal land was promised to Zwelithini. Buthelezi (jobless after the elections) would become Minister of Home Affairs in the expected new government lead by Mandela. A quiet session of the KwaZulu legislative assembly approved the land deal on April 22, 1994. And thus Zulu participation in the election came to pass. One further matter is important: the Chief and the King were aware of increasing Zulu impatience with the idea that they would not be participating in the first elections in modern South African history.

The Elections

Elaborate and painstaking preparations were made for the first popular balloting including all races in South Africa. The biggest problem to overcome was fear of the unknown. So many possessed the notion that voting was a process to help

someone do something against them or steal something from them. Local witch doctors (faith healers, etc.) didn't help at all. Many were convinced that the *sangomas* would know what was done inside the voting booth regardless of precautions, and that the wrong people would be told.

The problem of illiteracy was immense—50%—so it was decided that the pictures of the leaders of each party would be listed above that choice on the ballot. But Clarence Makwetu, leader of the *Pan Africanist Congress*, who resembles Mandela closely, wound up in the number one position on the ballot. People were told to look down the list carefully for the true Mandela. Some White employers told Black employees the only way to vote *against* de Klerk was to put an "X" by his picture!

Overcoming well–grounded fears, and waiting in line for hours on end, more than 70% voted. The time for voting was extended for 24 hours because it took longer than expected. Another several days were used to tally the result, which was announced on May 10, 1994.

A secret ballot for individual protection was an unknown in a society where things traditionally were accomplished

on a communal basis. It also presented problems for voters in precincts where just voting was the same as a death sentence. The voting started two days early for the elderly and ill, who reported in large numbers.

Other Political Parties and Groups

The *Freedom Front (FF)* was formed in March 1994 after conservatives made tactical errors in (1) refusing to register as a political party and (2) getting involved in a debacle concerning continued power of an unpopular Black leader of Bophuthatswana which they lost. The *Freedom Front* is headed by former defense chief General Constand Viljoen whose less than right–wing approach appealed to many conservatives.

White conservatives formerly belonged exclusively to the *Conservative Party (CP)*, which is led by the Dr. Ferdi Hartzenberg, successor of Andries Treurnicht. Its principal efforts in 1993 were directed at derailing the talks between the *ANC*, the *National Party* and *Inkatha* using many tactics, and it almost succeeded in its ambition. Its principal objective was the creation of an all–White state by the interim constitution, a proposition that was never taken seri-

140

Party	Votes	Percent	National Assembly
African National Congress	12,237,655	62.6	252
National Party	3,983,690	20.4	82
Inkatha Freedom Party	2,058,294	10.5	43
Freedom Front		2.2	9
Democratic Party		1.7	7
Pan Africanist Congress		1.2	5
Afr. Chr. Democratic Party		.5	2
Others		.9	–

The fact that the *ANC* did not receive a majority of more than two–thirds is the most important aspect of the results; had it done so it could have dictated the constitution which will be written by the National Assembly. The document will be the result of consensus, which in the long run is important—it will not be the result of dictation by the *ANC*.

ously. It refused to register as a political party for the elections.

The *Afrikaner Resistance Movement (ARM)* is a right–wing militant group which also refused to participate in elections. It is led by Eugene TerreBlanche, who was recently sentenced to prison for his anti–state activities.

The *Democratic Party (DP)* is the successor of two liberal parties popular among English speakers which opposed *apartheid*. It is headed by Tony Leon.

The *Pan Africanist Congress (PAC)* and its militant wing, the *Azanian Peoples Army)* is a radical Black party led by Clarence Makwetu; it is a fringe party which adopted a slogan "one settler [a White], one bullet." It has done the Black cause in South Africa great harm by ruthless armed attacks on innocent, overwhelmingly White people.

The results, awaited with great suspense, were predicted before announced. The *ANC* did well in areas where it was expected to as did the *National Party* and the *Inkatha Freedom Party*. The *National Party* did well among Coloured and Asiatic Indian voters. The *Freedom Front* of the right did well in areas dominated by rural Whites.

ANC Victory

Nelson Mandela worked hard for the victory at the polls. The campaign started only after 23 months of irregular negotiations in which his patience was severely tried and he in turn tried the patience of his counterparts. During the campaign he had worked at least 18 hours a day, seemingly without tiring. But his efforts showed in his temper, which fortunately did not reveal itself in public. He is always thought of as the smiling Mandela because of the many pictures of him in that manner, but he hated smiling; he thought it made him look like a fool. Actually he has a vitriolic temper which has frequently been directled with full force at F.W. de Klerk in the 1990s. Great forbearance on the part of de Klerk has been necessary to ensure progress in the ongoing changes.

Small wonder at the victory celebration that he spontaneously broke into an elderly version of the *toyi–toyi*, a dance–march of Black people expressing dissatisfaction and defiance joined with expectation, joy and triumph.

The victory celebrations of the *ANC* followed closely by the inauguration of Nelson Mandela, were momentous occasions. Celebrities, "wannabe" celebrities and hangers–on from around the globe were present. Vice–President Albert Gore from the U.S. was present, but Jesse Jackson and Coretta King felt they had to be there also, prominently pictured with Mandela. At the inauguration, Winnie Mandela looked out of joint and out of place; her estranged husband looked like an icicle when she was near him.

The oratory was expansive. Archbishop Tutu used the words "After 300 years . . ." and they were enlarged in the western press to 352 years [of White oppression], totally ignoring the fact that the beginning of *apartheid* was not until 1912. The next item on the agenda was

Cabinet Appointments

President Mandela hastened to name his cabinet publicly which irritated some persons involved who thought they would have a chance to haggle over who got what. They claimed that the announcement should not have been made prior to legislative approval of the appointments.

Cyril Ramaphosa, Mandela's heir–apparent, was refused the post of Deputy President probably because he was considered too young by the president. Thabo Mbeki who was chosen is a long–time communist and *ANC* idealogue who has lofty thoughts that occasionally make listeners think he is down to earth. In accord with the agreement of the parties, de Klerk was appointed as the other Deputy President. His capacity for practical matters is well–known, and within a short time he assumed day–to–day management of the government bureaucracy. Ramaphosa was, however, later appointed to head the assembly charged

with the duty of drafting a permanent constitution.

Excellent appointments were made from the *National Party*. Former Foreign Minister Roelof ("Pik") Botha heads the Mineral and Energy Department, a concession to Anglo–American mining interests, the strength of which is vital to South Africa. Roelf Meyer is over Provincial Affairs and Constitutional Development; he was the master behind the temporary constitution which made the present appearance of stability possible. He will be of great importance in developing the permanent constitution. Chris Fisner is top man is the Justice Department, known for his even–handed approach to matters in this area.

Joe Slovo, having shed his communist convictions (but not his membership), if he ever really had them, headed the Department of Housing until his death caused by cancer in late 1994. During his time in office, he replaced his former idealism with pragmatism. Chief Buthelezi was appointed Housing Minister, a dubious honor since there won't be adequate housing in South Africa for a generation under any circumstances. Alfred Nzo, appointed Foreign Minister, an old–line *ANC* friend of Mandela, is not qualified for the position. He depends on his Deputy Minister, Aziz Pahad, for guidance.

Winnie Mandela was appointed Deputy Minister of Arts, Culture, Science and Technology. Since a loyalty oath to the government was required, she took it, but didn't take it seriously, and resumed her old controversial ways resulting in her ouster. Ironically, her boss was Ben Ngubane from *Inkatha*.

Joe Modise, appointed Defense Minister, won the trust of the White military commanders but has had only partial succcess in combining former Black revolutionaries into the SADF. A vast bureaucracy of underlings has been running South Africa in the year following the elections, much in the manner it had been.

Initial Statements of the New Government

The Budget . . .

Following pre–election announced intentions, the budget was prepared and submitted to the Legislative Assembly in June. Those who expected radical change were disappointed; it was basically conservative and realistic. It's content made it appear to be written by a White bureaucracy, which it was. It basically provides for a million new housing units and a million new jobs, but over a five–year period. It was proudly noted that no new taxes will be required for these goals.

Critics pointed out that it will indeed cost more than the estimates provide for, and it does not deliver enough soon enough to deprived Black South Africans. Both of these objections are valid, but the budget itself is a document of compromise between two irreconcilable realities.

The document is otherwise unremarkable. No change was included which will affect the mining of gold and diamonds, so vital to the economic survival of South Africa.

However, Derek Keys, the respected Finance Minister responsible for the budget, resigned within days after it was presented "for personal reasons." The South African Rand dropped sharply in value and the key bond rate fell 50%. Mandela quickly appointed Christo Liebenburg to the position and Keys agreed to stay on and assist for several months, reassuring the domestic and international business community.

Agriculture, Land Use . . .

A small amount is allocated to restoration of Blacks to lands from which their ancestors were driven during *apartheid*.

This goal will fade as other means of restitution are explored. Particularly with lands taken without adequate compensation pursuant to the 1913 act, it is unrealistic to attempt restoration of great–grandfather's land to great–grandson, or even the value of the land. What figure should be used? Its worth in 1912 or 1994+? If it is now part of an industrial farm producing commercial crops, economically speaking it should be left that way. And payment of any sum of money would assume that if great–grandfather had received adequate compensation he would have carefully set it aside for great–grandson. That doesn't happen in South Africa or anywhere in the world.

A far more realistic measure would be a tax on that produced by industrial farms (but not so burdensome as to make it uncompetitive) to be used for training in modern agricultural techniques used in reclaiming marginal lands. Only 18% of South Africa is cultivated, but another 5% could probably be brought into economical production.

The Minister of Agriculture has clearly stated that South Africa will pursue a policy of market economics in agriculture, rather than artificial crop supports and subsidies paid to poorer people. It is probable that a food stamp system will come into being in South Africa before long.

The Restitution of Land Rights Act, a very controversial measure, was adopted in late 1994 establishing a Land Claims Commission and a Land Claims Court. The act directs "balancing the desirability of remedying past human rights violations against . . . the need to avoid major social disruption." The act was vehemently opposed by South Africa's 60,000 White commercial farmers; it's language is so vague it will probably result in an argumentative, overloaded bureaucracy producing little, if any, change.

Arms Manufacture . . .

This industry, the number one manufacturing enterprise in South Africa, is the product of sanctions, which included

A ship docks at Cape Town, the parliamentary capital of the country

142

Part of a huge multiracial crowd attending a Pop Music Festival

the export of arms to South Africa. In the absence of a foreign supply, it developed its own, and started turning out light and heavy arms manufactures of a very superior quality esteemed in many parts of the world. This money–maker will not be downgraded in spite of the hopes of liberals around the world. Somehow, exports will be limited to nations using the arms for legitimate purposes and not for human rights violations. How that will be accomplished is not clear.

Education . . .

The boycott of schools is over and hordes of children are packing schools again, eager for knowledge, including many of the street "comrades" of the *MK* (unlike similar youths in the U.S.). Available schools are still funded at about 1976 levels which urgently must be increased while there it yet time to do so. New school construction is a declared priority of the government.

One very thorny problem will take a minimum of three years, and more probably a decade, to unravel: textbook content. It is scheduled to change, but, using outmoded systems, it will take at least three years to get texts off the press. Reflecting the state of the country as a whole, their basic content will be debated

for at least a decade during which there will be avid axe–grinding. Even though the strife is apparently over, the ill–will that caused it abounds. The process has already started, and includes questions about the the difference between a "settler," "someone who just appeared," and an "oppressionist." In this effort, few will be persuaded to avoid words of extreme polarity. On the other hand, the use of neutral words can be boring and uninformative. Hopefully, common sense will prevail.

Foreign Investment . . .

The government energetically announced its receptiveness to foreign investment—the more the better, and as soon as possible. The IMF approved substantial credit for South Africa which had been denied prior to 1994 as part of UN–imposed sanctions. Although sanctions had been dropped by the U.S. government in 1991–2, literally nothing happened.

Even though investment was again permitted, there has been little time in which to overcome institutional paralysis. States, counties and cities of the U.S. all enacted a myriad of anti–investment statutes forbidding investment of public funds in any company "doing business"

with or in South Africa. Repeal of these measures is cumbersome, time consuming and often overlooked.

Even worse, in the U.S. liberals could not readily reverse signals. Negotiations had resumed between the parties in South Africa in March 1993 and it was reasonably clear that some sort of agreement would be reached for a settlement. Yet the following month, a group of shareholders introduced the sixth unsuccessful resolution calling for sanctions and disinvestment by IBM at its annual shareholders meeting, which stated,

—"Government–instigated violence, including assassinations of anti–apartheid activists, massacres of freedom marchers, and brutal attacks in [Black] neighborhoods has destroyed hopes for a peaceful transition to democracy . . . More than 7000 South Africans have been killed since Nelson Mandela was released from prison. Ruthless, violent apartheid rule remains in place . . . Sales to South Africa's military industry make IBM's decision–makers complicit with the violence in Southern Africa . . ."

Because the *ANC* and *MK* were not heeding Mandela's pleas for an end to killing, there indeed was violence in

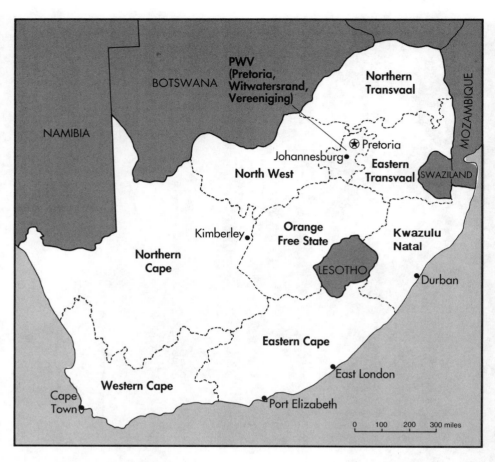

South Africa. It earned a response of vengeance from *Inkatha* members. Had the resolution passed, it would have required IBM to ignore South Africa until a repeal of the resolution was passed. The majority of stockholders decided to reject the measure. But it is an example of what obstacles now face South Africa's search for foreign capital.

Those who espoused sanctions and disinvestment did not understand that it is not easy to change such a posture. Even if the policy is altered, a decade of disinvestment leaves a stain in the minds of potential sources. Investment is a voluntary decision taken to make money from spare money with a prime objective of safety. In the absence of safety or doubt as to its future, either interest rates are dreadfully high, or capital seeks a safer alternative for investment, even at a lower rate. Having no history of safety from 1984–94, and beset with many economic problems after that decade, adequate foreign capital will not soon be available to South Africa. However, Ford Motor Company has announced plans to reacquire its former automotive holdings in South Africa and Mercedes–Benz of Germany is making substantial investment.

President Mandela made a trip to the U.S. to raise capital in early 1995 and though well–received, made little progress. The Congressional Black Caucus had been severely weakened in November 1994 elections and could do little to help. President Clinton pledged U.S. $600 million in aid—the same money he had pledged after the South African elections. When he got back to South Africa, Mandela denounced the offer as "peanuts."

AN UNSTEADY BEGINNING

Since President Mandela took office, South Africa's progress toward democracy has been unsteady; it has created as many or more problems than it solved. This was to be expected and actually was quite natural because a well–known process was and is underway: the determination of power relationships. The equation involves not just two forces, however, but multiple, intertwined forces as well as personalities.

Privatization

A Reconstruction and Development Plan started in 1994, and one of its first announcements was a privatization program. This was an about–face for the *ANC* and a change that reflected economic reality. Included are transportation, electrical generation, telephone service. Some members of the cabinet and the *COSATU* labor unions sharply criticized the plans; the dispute was settled by Mandela, who decided this was necessary in order to reassure the international business community.

The Military

The SADF was renamed the *South African National Defense Force* in a plan in mid–1994 intended to integrate former *MK* guerrillas into government units. This was a task that could not be accomplished rapidly enough, and several hundred demonstrated on the lawns of Mandela's Pretoria office in September 1994, demanding equal rights and pay. He said he would investigate.

The matter escalated in October when about 7,500 of the 27,000 former guerrillas were absent without leave. President Mandela decreed that they had seven days to return and failure to do so would result in dismissal. More than 4,000 returned; the defense minister announced the dismissal of 2,221. When their leader threatened a return to armed struggle, Mandela warned against a "suicidal plot." The matter has not been fully resolved. The basic problem is economic; the fledgling state just does not have enough to support the ex–guerrillas in the luxurious style of which they had dreamed.

"Truth and Reconciliation" Commission

This mild–sounding name was given to a group with the responsibility of investigating murders and other human rights abuses under the former White government. It nominally will include unlawful acts by liberation groups, including the *ANC*. In making the announcement of formation of this body, however, Justice Minister Dullah Omar said in mid–1994 the commission would "not equate those who fought in the struggle against apartheid with those who participated in all kinds of activities in order to keep apartheid in place." This ominous statement certainly indicates some form of systematic, unequal justice may well be underway in South Africa.

This move calls into question a blanket amnesty granted to the commanders and members of the 3,500 man SADF just prior to the 1994 elections. Dullah Omar says it was illegal; Mandela favors reconciliation; the commission is opposed by the *Inkatha Freedom Party* and the *National Party*, who see it as a device to open old wounds and prevent reconciliation.

Housing

In 1986 the *ANC* urged as part of its program of destabilization a refusal to pay rents and mortgages. The rents for land in the Black townships financed in part the limited services that were provided. Defaults on mortgages left the lender helpless, since seizure of the land would be meaningless. The *ANC* announced the end of the rent strike in early 1994, intending to finance the construction of 1 million houses in a five–year

Ndebele women

Former South African President F.W. de Klerk (left) and African National Congress foreign policy specialist Thabo Mbeki (right) are deputy presidents in President Nelson Mandela's first Cabinet.

period with the proceeds of the resumed payments. But living rent free had become a pleasant habit and only about 30% resumed payment. The Housing Minister threatened evictions for non–payment; this did not result in any substantial improvement.

A scheme was developed with South African banks to provide mortgage money for housing, but only for those with a minimum annual income of about $3,500. This effectively excludes three out of four Blacks from the housing market.

Education

Integration is the official education policy of the government. This noble ideal does not take into consideration practical difficulties that are insurmountable for at least 20 years. It is reasonably possible to integrate a first year school class. It is impossible to integrate a 6th, 8th or 10th year class. Black students who had been boycotting schools are not prepared to perform at the level which White students who had been attending school are capable. Language diversity and illiteracy are in themselves tremendous barriers. Progress toward this goal is uneven.

Justice

The 1993 interim constitution provided for a high court (The Constitutional Court) and South Africa's first Bill of Rights. The latter replaced the supremacy of the legislature and executive council, guaranteeing all citizens basic rights.

The initial Constitutional Court took the oath of office in February 1995. Seven of the eleven judges are White, three are Black and there is one Indian. Of the eleven, three are women. The oaths of office were administered in English, Afrikaans, Zulu, Sotho and Xhosa. The president, Arthur Chaskalson, assisted in Mandela's defense in 1964 and the others were noted opponents of *apartheid*. One of its first cases is expected to outlaw the death penalty. One question to be answered is how firmly the new system of justice can permeate the Black communities and towns, where "street justice" is meted out by the people.

Zulu Rumblings

After the April 1994 elections, control over Zulu King Goodwill Zwelithini's royal purse and security guard passed to the *ANC*–dominated government, weakening the influence of his uncle, Chief Mangosuthu Buthelezi, over the monarchy. A celebration commemorating 19th–century warrior–king Shaka Zulu in September touched off a vitriolic quarrel between the two, particularly because at the same time, the king was seeking to replace Buthelezi with Prince Mcwayizeni Israel Zulu, a member of the executive committee of the *ANC*.

Late in the month, things were so bitter an open brawl erupted in front of live TV cameras—Buthelezi and his bodyguard attacked a member of the king's council who was being interviewed.

Buthelezi apologized "to the Cabinet and to the nation" (but not to the king) after being censured. Zwelithini promptly severed all ties with his uncle.

Buthelezi in turn used his support in the Kwazulu–Natal legislature to establish a *House of Traditional Leaders* consisting of all the Zulu kings, princes and chiefs in which Zwelithini would be no more than an equal. *ANC* opposed the move; tensions remain high.

Social Discontent

Tensions are running high among South Africa's Black population. During the election campaign they were promised far, far more than could be realistically delivered. As the months wore on after the contest, their lives have not changed. Symptoms of this malaise include a high crime rate, near–anarchy, corruption, squatting on land, moving into nearby homes after ousting the occupants, illegal strikes. As in the U.S., some in South Africa have viewed unrest, particularly in the form of protest marches, as an opportunity to loot business areas, particularly retail stores.

All of this was strongly condemned by President Nelson Mandela in his February 1995 speech opening parliament. He criticized what he termed "a culture of entitlement," and accused Blacks who "misread freedom to mean license." He condemned those guilty of murder of police officers, taking hostages, riots, looting and other crimes.

Mandela still maintains a high degree of respect bordering on reverence among the majority of Black people, but there is a significant number that wish his time would somehow end as soon as possible. They view his restraint as an obstacle to their own progress. He has announced he will not run for election in 1999, and no other Black has anything remotely resembling his charisma.

Culture: The *Boer* people, who ruled through their *National Party* and sympathizing to a degree with the *Conservative Party*, reasoned that because their ancestors were in some areas of South Africa before the arrival of Bantu and Indian people, they were the rightful successors to *exclusive* control of the government. Conservative by nature, and clinging to their language and traditions, they have a strong desire to pass their way of life on to their descendants. *Apartheid* controlled daily life in Africa for 35 years; historically its roots were in the bitter conflicts between the *Voortrekkers* and the then savage Zulus, Xhosas, Sothos and Tsonga people during the 18th and 19th centuries. Interracial marriage and love affairs were strictly prohibited for generations until 1985.

The Bantu–descended people together with other non–Whites outnumber Whites by about five to one; combined with the Indians and Coloureds, the figure is about six to one. Political awareness among non–Whites increased dramatically since 1960 and led to resentment of rule by a minority under rigid conditions. The growth of nationalism and independence in Africa was bound to contribute heavily to changed thinking among this majority.

The program to place all Black, non–urbanized persons in "Black Homelands" was a separate and not very equal concept designed to enable the Whites to continue their control, particularly over the wealth, of South Africa. When shortly before and after the 1994 elections the homelands simply evaporated into the whole of South Africa indicates that they were, at best, an artificial creation which could not last. Unfortunately, in some, near anarchy conditions existed when puppet regimes disappeared.

Christian clerics developed elaborate arguments based on quotations from the Old Testament to justify *apartheid* before 1984, but these concepts were rejected. When some started to denounce *apartheid* from their pulpits, they were warned by the government to keep politics out of the church. Denunciation of *apartheid* led to the arrest, trial and conviction of a prominent Anglican bishop. *Apartheid* was rejected by the Reformed Church in 1986 and denounced as a sin in 1989, but there were many who preferred bland sentiments favoring an absence of politics in the pulpit. The controversy lingers to this day.

Apartheid and its many evils has disappeared from the law books in South Africa. Even though the races are not legally separated, they are in fact. In this respect, conditions are analogous to those in the U.S., although in the latter, Black people have opportunities to climb the economic ladder which have been rare in South Africa. Substantial numbers of White people opposed *apartheid*, but this does not necessarily mean they favored integration. Even among educated liberals, the idea of a Black family on the same block is not accepted—"Not in my neighborhood" is the typical reaction. Even among otherwise understanding Whites, tensions can mount swiftly to the point where the word *kaffir* is shouted in anger, the equivalent to the ugly expression "nigger" in the U.S.

Widespread burning and looting after the death of Chris Hani in April 1993 did the Black cause great harm. The *ANC's* image descended to a stereotype: given the opportunity provided by civil strife, Black people will loot and burn.

With the exception of Johannesburg, urban life has until recently been pleasant and modern. In "Jburg," or simply "JB," the streets are owned by street vendors in the daytime and a lawless element which, although constantly a threat, is most commonly encountered at night. There is a substantial motion picture industry, large symphonies, well–performed opera and ballet productions. An immense quantity of *Boermusiek* tells the traditions of the pioneers to the accompaniment of the guitar, accordion and concertina. Art and literature play a major role in the nation's cultural heritage.

There are several excellent Black performing groups whose music and dance are known worldwide. But entertainment is a luxury few Black people can afford. Life in the townships is hard. Few homes have electrical lines, water pipes or sewer service. With burgeoning populations and widespread unemployment, metal shacks are almost always the only possible housing *if they can be obtained*. Education is generally poor among Blacks, partly because of their own actions. After riots in Soweto, it became fashionable, particularly among followers of the *ANC*, to boycott schools. The result is a generation of illiterate people lacking basic skills which would make them employable—they can't even read the simplest directions or instructions.

Regrettably, *ANC* comrades not only boycotted schools, they actively discouraged others from going to classes. Many of the dropouts insisted on hanging out in and around the schools, disrupting them with outbursts of violence and anti–social behavior. The result: unemployment is well over 50% among young, Black males. Even a prized high school diploma is no guarantee of employment because the upheaval of the last decade has produced economic depression.

Ridding the country of racism in education will not be easy. A decision in 1991 to allow three empty formerly White schools to become "nonracial and open"

Orchestral practice

was thought to be a breakthrough, but the result was 99% Black enrollment. The problem became one of how to attract White students to voluntarily attend "nonracial" schools—a problem now often encountered throughout the U.S.

Nearly every Black person who works rises at 4:30 A.M. to get to a job in a nearby city via an intricate system of taxis which run regular routes—an informal public transit system. Many households supplement their income with a small store of basics on hand to sell to neighbors at tremendously inflated prices. Coca–Cola is a favorite, as is beer. Rhythmic music at small night clubs is a delight to hear, but only if you are Black and in the right company.

Television has become widely available in South Africa; it formerly was used partially to extol the virtues of *apartheid*. There are more than 70 transmitters and 24 repeating stations operating on three channels. The first provides Afrikaans and English programming, the second carries Nguni (Zulu and Xhosa) and the third Sotho (South Sotho, North Sotho and Tswana) broadcasts. About half of the programming is produced in South Africa, but a substantial amount from the U.S. also appears. Reruns of *Miami Vice* ("Misdaad in Miami") are popular, but the actors' voices are dubbed in and speak with a low–pitched, rhythmic Afrikaans rather than in hippy Americanese. Other popular shows include "The Bill Cosby Show" and "Dallas." A license fee of about $50 per year is assessed for each television receiver; the amount charged the elderly is about half. This enables elimination of endless, irritating commercials.

In July 1991, after three decades of being barred from the Olympics, sanctions were lifted against South Africa, enabling the first racially mixed teams to compete at the games in Barcelona, Spain, in 1992.

South Africa's leading novelist as well as one of *apartheid's* severest critics has been Nadine Gordimer, author of 10 novels and several hundred short stories, who was awarded the Nobel Prize for Literature in 1991. Former president de Klerk and President Mandela were jointly awarded the Nobel Peace Prize in 1993.

Kruger National Park on the border with Mozambique is the best–kept game preserve in the world. It offers unexcelled opportunities to photograph game in a natural setting from one's car. If a pride of lions settles on the road because of its warmth, visitors simply steer around the animals or wait until they move. Tourism at this park and other areas of South Africa is quickly rising, but visitors must discreetly avoid areas where tensions are high. When it is cold winter in Europe, South Africa is experiencing a warm, sunny summer.

In the rural areas there has been little change. Tribal customs abound among the Black people. The singular clothing is quite interesting, and people are generally more open than those living in the townships.

Traditional doctors administer what passes for treatment among the people, who rarely see a medical practitioner. The *Sangomas* also give endless advice on just about anything. This lack of professional medical treatment presents many unnecessary problems. For instance, the Xhosas and about 4 other tribes cling to the tradition of circumcision after puberty rather than at birth. The unsterile "operations" with no anesthetic result in a multitude of deaths a year from infection. Nelson Mandela, writing in his book "Long Walk to Freedom," vividly recalls the pain and humiliation of his experience with this rite. Educational efforts have been largely ineffective.

Economy: South Africa's economy has been the strongest and most diversified on the African continent. But investment, output, employment and consumption have been falling for the past few years. The reason: basic instability. Capital generated within South Africa has been removed to foreign locations which offered greater security and investment opportunity. This is where the communist rhetoric of the *ANC* has hurt the most.

The prospect of having property nationalized without compensation, or inadequate compensation at best, simply has never attracted investors and, in fact, has insured that capital which otherwise would be available will be withdrawn. Sanctions and disinvestment initially had a minimal effect, but as racial tensions increased, the result has been much more noticeable. It also has caused an outflow of domestic capital and a rise in emigration. To stem this, rigid rules limiting transfer of funds out of the country were enacted. If a citizen wishes to emigrate, a maximum of $60,000 can be taken out of South Africa to his new homeland.

Until 1987, standards of living had been improving in all sectors of South Africa. It has substantially declined among wage–earning Blacks and Whites since that time. The formerly agricultural economy of the mid–1800s quickly gave way to one based on diamond and gold mining. By 1945, manufacturing became the most important segment of the gross domestic product. Sanctions dried up imports of military materiel by the mid–1980s and in response, South Africa developed an armaments industry which now is the leading source of exports, as well as one of criticism abroad from the "politically correct" element. The reason the arms industry has been so successful is quality. Bullet proof personnel carriers from South Africa, for example, are strong favorites among the undeveloped and underdeveloped nations of the world. They can be found in Sri Lanka, where they are used to control the restive Tamil population.

With the advent of drought conditions in 1990, food production in South Africa and surrounding nations dropped substantially. It appears to be holding its own in 1994, however. One of the things the *ANC* is pressing for, if it comes about, would be a disaster: settlement of countless Black people on small holdings of land from which they or their ancestors were alleged to have been removed will cause the agricultural potential of the nation, limited by natural conditions, to plummet. By analogy, the U.S. production figures illustrate this. In the 1890s, a single farm worker generated enough food to feed almost 6 people using the machinery then widely available. By the 1990s, this figure had risen to 98 people. Comparable figures for South Africa are not available, but certainly follow this pattern, made possible by large land holdings, automation and modern agricultural techniques. Placing valuable farmland in the hands of unskilled, uneducated Blacks farming ten acre allotments with hoes would make South Africa a food importer instead of exporter.

Labor unions, formerly compelled to be racially segregated by law, are now allowed full integration, which was accomplished rapidly. The labor movement, centered around the *Congress of South African Trade Unions (COSATU)* is quite strong. Its upper echelons are completely dominated by old–line communists. In spite of energetic efforts, wages of Black workers generally still do not equal those of Whites for the same work, and promotion of Blacks to managerial positions remains the exception to the rule.

When international sanctions threatened to lead to fuel shortages, *SASOL* was formed and erected the world's largest facility for synthetic fuels from South Africa's immense quantities of coal. Thus, there is no dependence on world oil prices or OPEC. Other nations are now studying these techniques. If and when the price of oil rises to $40 a barrel (as it almost did during the Persian Gulf crisis and war of 1991), this will become an economically viable alternative to the world oil market.

In late 1989 South Africa succeeded in renegotiating its external debt ($12 billion) much to the frustration of those favoring sanctions and disinvestment. South Africa, without external interference, is a solvent nation.

One potential source of income which has been in the doldrums for several years is tourism. As a result, prices for accommodations have fallen and are now among the most reasonable to be found. The scenery in most areas is spectacular

The SASOL Refinery

and inviting. A properly planned vacation in South Africa has little chance of being interrupted by racial violence—no more than in Washington D.C.

Economic sanctions against Africa have now been officially lifted throughout the world. Nelson Mandela and the government are avidly pursuing foreign investment with a modest degree of success. It will, however, take at least another five years to overcome the hardships produced by the evaporation of foreign investments and loans.

In order to attract foreign capital, a global issue of five–year bonds was launched in late 1994. It was so enthusiastically received that the offering was increased from US $500 million to $750 million. The World Bank and the International Monetary Fund are again extending credit to South Africa.

The Future: The Black people of South Africa have lived in extreme poverty for decades and believed that with the advent of democracy their poverty would be over. But they are genuinely disappointed and frustrated over what they perceive as a lack of progress since the 1994 elections. That which was promised them is a potential future time bomb now ticking.

The problem of what to do with the revolutionaries now faces South Africa. They have no talent for anything but revolution, which is not needed now. If neglected, they will be a potential for trouble.

Nelson Mandela, now 77, is tired and frustrated. This clearly shows when he periodically boils over in temper rages directed at F.W. de Klerk, in which the worst insults are hurled, causing threats of resignation from the deputy president. He will not run in 1999 and his troublesome estranged wife, Winnie, probably will. She will have the backing of the radical segment of the *ANC*, even though she is actually a shallow opportunist. Nelson Mandela has started to groom his successor, Thabo Mbeki, but will have to do much more than he has to get Mbeki into the limelight.

Permanent constitutional drafting is now underway in an assembly headed by Cyril Ramaphosa. The principal issue is a strong central government vs. regional powers. Buthelezi has announced he and the Zulus will sit in the assembly but will boycott all proceedings. Favoring strong regional power, this position will not profit *Inkatha* or the Zulus, but will result in a document dictated by the *ANC*.

The experiences of the past year show how practicality can overcome all problems, even if at the moment that practicality seems hollow and against all principle. It certainly is preferable to terrorism and violence, and hopefully will avidly be pursued.

The Kingdom of Swaziland

King Mswati III

Area: 17,364 sq. km. = 6,705 sq. mi. (about the size of Hawaii).

Population: 864,000 (estimated).

Capital Cities: Mbabane (Pop. 40,000, estimated—administrative); Lobamba (Pop. 23,500, estimated—legislative).

Climate: Temperate, with chilly nights during the winter months.

Neighboring Countries: Mozambique (Northeast); Republic of South Africa (North, West, South).

Official Languages: siSwati, English.

Other Principal Tongues: Afrikaans.

Ethnic Background: Swazi, a small number of other Bantu ethnic groups, European, mulatto.

Principal Religions: Christianity (57%), Traditional tribal beliefs.

Chief Commercial Products: Sugar, asbestos, wood and forest products, citrus, cotton, iron ore.

Annual Per Capita Income: About U.S. $1,200.

Currency: Emalangeni (at par with the South African Rand).

Former Colonial Status: Under South African protection (1894–1906); British Protectorate (1906–1968).

Chief of State: King Mswati III (b. 1966).

Head of Government: Prince Jameson Mbilini Dlamini, Prime Minister.

Independence Date: September 6, 1968.

National Flag: Horizontal stripes of dark blue, red and dark blue, divided by thin yellow bands. A shield and spear design is in the center of the red stripe.

High plateaus with groups of forested mountains are found in western Swaziland which gradually descend from a maximum of 4,500 feet to a central region with a 2,800 average height. This gives way to a lowland in the East, and the Lubombo Mountains rise at the easternmost border. The temperate climate is warm enough to permit large quantities of sugar cane to grow, but at the same time it is ideally suited for forest growth of excellent hardwoods. The rolling landscape closely resembles the Appalachian mountain region of the United States.

History: Swaziland was thinly inhabited by a variety of Bantu groups in the 18th century. The Swazis (Emaswati) migrated to the area from what is now Mozambique about 1750. The British–*Boer* competition in the last two decades of the 19th century resulted in Swaziland becoming a British protectorate. For details of early and colonial history, see Historical Background and *The British in Africa.*

The British agreed in 1967 to grant independence to Swaziland on September 6, 1968, which was done in formal ceremonies in Mbabane. Many foreign representatives were present, including high officials from the Republic of South Africa. King Sobhuza's 112 wives were also included among the spectators.

All 24 seats of the National Assembly were held initially by King Sobhuza's *National Movement.* Reigning since 1921 until his death in 1982, he was the oldest ruling monarch on earth. Elections in 1972 reduced the party to 21 seats; Dr. Ambrose Zwane's *National Liberatory Congress Party* won three seats and six additional members were appointed by the King. However, within weeks the King abolished the constitution, dismissed the Assembly and announced he would rule the old–fashioned way—by decree. Later, in 1979, a new bicameral parliament was opened consisting of a 50–member lower house and a 20–member upper house. Ten of each were chosen directly by the King.

King Sobhuza died in August 1982. Intrigue and plotting among the wives and 70 sons of the dead monarch began before he was buried. The numerous persons involved are not now important. The struggles revolved around (1) The

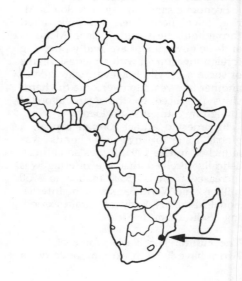

150

Queen Regent, (2) the *Liqoqo* (National Council), (3) the "Authorized Person" (4) The Prime Minister and (5) The House of Assembly and the Senate.

The young Crown Prince, the second–youngest son of the late king, studied in Britain until 1986, when he reached the age of 18; his coronation was held on April 25, 1986. Three days of celebration were attended by numerous heads of state in southern Africa, including President Botha of South Africa. The young king quickly moved to assert his power, reshuffling the cabinet, dismissing the *Liqoqo*, and replacing the Prime Minister.

Swaziland cooperated with South Africa in limiting the presence of the *African National Congress*, the formerly communist–dominated Black group seeking the overthrow of the White–controlled South African government. The latter made raids into Swaziland in 1986 seeking members of the outlawed organization; Swaziland deported members to Lusaka, Zambia in the same year. Further raids in 1987–8 resulted in seizures of large quantities of Soviet manufactured arms, arrests and deportations.

King Mswati III dissolved the parliament in late 1987; an electoral college based on tribal allegiance selected a new legislature. which has limited powers. The new cabinet was chosen by the king from among his loyal followers and at the same time about a dozen princes of the royal family were arrested and subjected to secret trials which ended with prison sentences in 1988. The king thus further solidified his position and power.

The king dissolved parliament in late 1992 when he received a report from *Vusela–2*, a commission formed to investigate political conditions and recommend a new constitution. Elections were postponed in 1992 and finally were held in late 1993. The electoral process was non–partisan; the selection was limited to members of the *Tinkhundla* (traditional assemblies). The membership of both the 55–member House of Assembly and the Senate (20) are generally conservative and loyal to the king and his extended family. A constitution has yet to be framed and adopted.

Culture: Approximately 35% of the Swazis are literate; government schools are provided through the primary level to all children, and several high schools are spread throughout the country. Swazi customs completely dominate the cultural life of the people and are the source for a substantial quantity of the laws and court system (which has refused to get involved in the power struggles of the monarchial family).

The Swazi's are related to the Zulu and Xhosa people, have a highly developed warrior system and were historically regarded as a fierce enemy by the early White settlers and pioneers in South Africa.

When in 1985–1986 it appeared that *ANC* elements had infiltrated the university, it was closed. When it reopened, re–registration was required and "foreign" enrollment (i.e. from South Africa) was limited to 5% of the student body. A student strike was very brief.

Economy: Of all the former British South African colonies, Swaziland is modestly endowed with limited resources which provide a modest level of prosperity. This has been supplemented and made possible by substantial capital investment of Great Britain during the post–World War II years, totaling $100 million. The annual British subsidy has been ended, however. Iron ore is now exported, principally to Japan.

One problem from the colonial period remains—ownership of land. The kings leased land to White settlers and this ripened into White ownership of the land. The King decreed that the Justice Minister would have control over the sale of all land. The decree was withdrawn in 1988 because of strenuous protests from the banks, which still have substantial interests in the involved lands.

Tourism plays a major part in the economy. There are several large hotels outside of Mbabane (with gambling casinos) which serve as a magnet for vacationing South Africans.

The "disinvestment" sanctions imposed on South Africa to destabilize that country and thereby end its *apartheid* system of racial segregation proved to be a boon for Swaziland. Products formerly made within South Africa were either made in or imported through Swaziland. Partially assembled manufactures of the same nation were finished in Swaziland and labeled "Made in Swaziland" for export to European countries. There were no tariffs on such goods inasmuch as Swaziland is a member of the Lomé Convention intended to benefit former French colonies in Africa. Three times as many oranges as can be grown in Swaziland were exported with domestic labels.

The Future: Conservative Swaziland will avoid any involvement in power struggles now underway in South Africa. Its economy will continue to be closely connected to that of its larger neighbor which is struggling to recover from years of embargo and disinvestment.

Mbabane, Swaziland's capital in the Mdimba mountains

The Republic of Zambia

Victoria Falls

Area: 745,920 sq. km. = 288,000 sq. mi. (The size of Nebraska, South Dakota, Iowa and Minnesota combined.)

Population: 8.9 million (estimated).

Capital City: Lusaka (Pop. 1.2 million, estimated).

Climate: Temperate, because of its altitude, although Zambia lies close to the Equator. There is a wet season (October–April) and a dry season (May–September).

Neighboring Countries: Angola (West); Zaïre (Northwest); Tanzania (Northeast); Malawi (East); Mozambique (Southeast); Zimbabwe and Botswana (South).

Official Languages: English, Tonga, Kaonde, Lunda, Luvale.

Other Principal Tongues: Bembe, Lozi, Nyanja.

Ethnic Background: Bantu subgroups, including Barotse, Tonga, Ila, Lozi, Bemba, Makishi. There is a substantial European community in the copper mining area.

Principal Religions: Christianity (75%) traditional tribal beliefs (23%) Islam, Hinduism.

Chief Commercial Products: Copper, zinc, cobalt, lead, tobacco.

Annual Per Capita Income: About U.S. $380.

Currency: Kwacha.

Former Colonial Status: British South Africa Company administration (1895–1923); British Colony (1924–1964).

Independence Date: October 24, 1964.

Chief of State: Frederick Chiluba, President (since November 1991).

National Flag: Green, with an orange eagle in flight over a square block of three vertical stripes, red, black and red, on the right side.

The Republic of Zambia is located in south central Africa, stretching 750 miles west from the mountains of the great Western Rift. This is a high plateau country with an average elevation of 3,500 feet above sea level, which modifies its otherwise equatorial climate. It is only in the low river valleys that any oppressive heat and humidity are encountered.

The gently rolling country alternates between the waving grasses of the plains and forests of widely spaced trees. Great numbers of wildlife are supported by the vegetation which grows rapidly during the rainy season of the year. The country is drained by two major river systems: the tributaries flowing north to the Congo (Zaïre) River, and the Zambezi River, which flows southeast through Mozambique to the Indian Ocean. One of the greatest sheets of flowing water in the world is found at incomparable Victoria Falls, near Livingstone in the South.

Swampy Lake Banguelu spreads its great width in the north–central part of the country; the deep blue sparkling waters of Lake Mweru and Lake Tanganyika are found in the North.

History: Like many of the adjacent countries, Zambia was probably inhabited in early times by primitive pygmies and other groups. The great wave of Bantu migration over a period of several centuries virtually took over this country, and very few indications remain of earlier civilizations. For details of early and colonial history, see Historical Background and *The British in Africa*.

Northern Rhodesia became fully independent in 1964, taking the name Zambia from the Zambezi River. A republic form of government was established with a single legislative house initially composed of 75 members, but increased to the present 125. Until 1969, ten seats were reserved for White voters. The president is chosen by direct election; Kenneth Kaunda was selected as the first (and only) president in 1964 and his latest reelection was in 1983 by an overwhelming majority.

Initially there were two major parties— the *United National Independence Party (UNIP)*, led by Kaunda and the *African National Congress (ANC)*, led by Harry Nkumbula (who died in 1984 in neighbor-

152

ing Zimbabwe). After winning a large majority in 1968, Kaunda abolished the opposition party in the name of "national unity."

Racial, religious and tribal frictions have been frequent in Zambia since independence. Political repression and suppression has added to dissatisfaction with Kaunda by many. A dramatic program of nationalization of every major enterprise was started in late 1970. A system of state–owned and managed enterprises and marketing facilities was instituted. Because of poor planning and lack of technical skills, the economy, particularly in the agricultural sector, suffered. Production levels have risen, but not fast enough to keep pace with the growing population.

In the early 1970's, Kaunda silenced all organized political opposition by jailing Simon Kapwepwe, a former vice president and boyhood friend who had formed an opposition party. The party was banned and in addition to Kapwepwe, 123 leaders were imprisoned. Although Kapwepwe was released in 1973, Kaunda had made several changes to get rid of opposition permanently.

Zambia was officially made a one–party state, with *UNIP* the sole party. The Assembly was dissolved in 1973 and new elections were set. A "primary" election was first held; before a successful candidate could run in the general election he had to have the approval of the *UNIP* Central Committee; several who won in the primary were eliminated in this way. Twenty candidates were announced as "official candidates" of the party, insuring their election.

Kaunda exhibited qualities of statesmanship during his tenure. Until 1976, he worked long hours to assist in resolving the Rhodesia conflict revolving around minority White control in that nation. He also was initially receptive to the détente efforts of the Republic of South Africa. As the tide of battle in nearby Angola turned

and the Soviet–Cuba–backed faction came into power, Kaunda's attitude visibly changed to one of tacit support for the Soviet–Cuban adventurism in central Africa, but if—as he recently expressed during a ·visit to Washington—the United States can take a more forceful role in the problems of southern Africa (in other words, in the Republic of South Africa) his views could change.

There was a historic meeting in a large mobile home astride the border between South Africa and Botswana in 1982 between President Kaunda and President Botha of the Republic of South Africa. Although the leaders declared the talks were "constructive," as is well known, this usually means nothing was agreed upon. Kaunda spent four days in Washington in late March 1983. He indicated that he strongly supported the presence of Cuban troops in neighboring Angola under "present circumstances" and called on the U.S. to create conditions to permit them to leave. His implication was that the United States must "force" South African troops to withdraw from Angola (see Angola and Namibia). Kaunda quietly urged the U.S. not to over–react to African criticism, and pointed out that Black Africa also criticized the Soviet Union.

Kaunda responded with enthusiasm to the election of President de Klerk in South Africa in 1989, and met with him shortly before he took office. He strongly urged negotiations without preconditions between the *ANC* and the government of South Africa.

In order to receive desperately needed funds from the International Monetary Fund and the World Bank, austerity programs were instituted in the 1980's which were unpopular and failed to improve economic conditions. Zambia broke with the IMF in May 1987 and decreed that only 10% of its export earnings would be used to repay and service external debt. Of course this led to a freeze on outside assistance at a time when the country was again gripped by drought.

Principally because of a tribal custom widely prevalent in Zambia, the nation is gripped with an epidemic of the AIDS disease. When a husband or wife dies, it is mandatory that the survivor be cleansed by having relations with an in–law. The disease affects both sexes equally; it is estimated that 23% of the population tests positive for HIV antibodies, an indicator of the disease. Even the president's son died of the disease, which has its highest rate among skilled, vitally needed workers and personnel.

Kaunda allowed the *African National Congress* (see South Africa) to set up its headquarters in Lusaka. Predictably, this led to raids by South African commandos in 1985 and 1986; in spite of widespread criticism, President Botha of South Africa

said the raids would be repeated if necessary, indicating they were directed against terrorists.

Unopposed, President Kaunda was re-elected to a sixth five–year term in late 1988. Voting turnout was substantially lower than in prior elections, indicating increasing dissatisfaction with the government. This was further evidenced by the arrest on suspicion of an alleged *coup* of nine prominent persons.

The year 1990 was filled with political and economic change. A *UNIP* spring conference endorsed the single–party system. But in June, an announced increase in the price of cornmeal from $2.80 to $6.70 provoked riots and an attempted *coup*, the latter of which was unsuccessful. In September the party announced a referendum as to whether a multi–party system would be allowed. Bowing to intense dissatisfaction, President Kaunda announced multi–party elections would be allowed.

Thus, on October 31, 1991, Zambians voted to decide the fate of one of Africa's most senior statesmen in the first multi–party elections in 23 years.

The campaign during 1991 leading up to the elections of October was hard–fought. Kaunda's references to his opponents were insulting. He was accused of being out of touch with the people and failing to stem the tide of economic events which had produced an annual inflation rate of 400%. Frederick Chiluba, his opponent, a labor leader and head of the *Movement for Multi–Party Democracy (MMD)*, also stressed the need to eliminate almost universal corruption and theft in the government.

Kaunda, a senior African statesman who had been in power for 27 years, was soundly defeated. Chiluba's party gained 125 of the 150 legislative seats. His accomplishments have included a reduction in Zambia's external debt from more than $8

President Frederick Chiluba

billion to $6 billion through negotiation and stabilizing the economy so that inflation now is lower than 100% annually. The Chiluba government has been plagued by accusations of corruption and resignations for the same reason. Voters thought they would have a change from the Kaunda style, but have become apathetic—only 10% turned out for regional and local elections in 1993. An alleged attempted *coup* was supposed to have involved Kaunda, but it more probably was an attempt by the entrenched bureaucracy to eliminate those in authority and thus prevent them from examining closely any matters related to continuing corruption in government.

Culture: The territory of Zambia contains some of the most interesting ethnic groups of all Africa. The people are conservative and closely knit within their communities—the majority are Christian, particularly in the more densely populated South and West, but many in the rural section of the North retain their traditional beliefs.

Art and music occupy a prominent place in the lives of the Zambians and are actively promoted by the government. A large radio station in metropolitan Lusaka broadcasts traditional music, not only to Zambia, but to the rest of the world.

Lusaka, the capital (Livingstone was the capital until 1935), is a modern, urban center of education, entertainment and commerce.

Economy: Many experts once predicted that Zambia would be Africa's brightest success story. The economy can be summed up in one word: copper. It has one quarter of the world's known reserves and has been the second largest producer after Chilean nationalization of copper production in 1971. Exports were valued at about $1 billion in the early 1970's, but in 1975–1978 prices began to fall, creating a financial crisis in the country. A trade surplus was replaced with an external debt which by 1988 was more than $5.5 billion.

The government had to impose strict economic controls in order to receive credit from the International Monetary Fund in 1983, but these were suspended in 1987 when things could hardly be squeezed any tighter. As a result of further decreases in the prices of copper in 1973–1988, the price descended from $1.40 per pound to $1.00 in 1988; this amounts to 20¢ a pound in 1973 dollars. Although Zaïre's copper production has come to a halt, Chile is developing mines steadily to satisfy world demand. It actually costs *more* to mine the ore than it can be sold for in Zambia, but foreign exchange is desperately needed. The copper and cobalt deposits will be depleted by 2005 at the present rate of production.

This potential breadbasket, due to inefficient agriculture on small farms, became a food importer except in years of plentiful rain; prices have steadily risen. A top–heavy government bureaucracy has helped thousands, but it has done almost nothing for the average Zambian. Small farms must be incorporated into large, mechanized units. But to do so would create a upheaval that might not be socially acceptable.

The only way out of the copper predicament, is to diversify from the one–commodity economy. But adverse conditions during the 1980's made this impossible. Something cannot be made from nothing. In 1984 Zambia had to import 10 million gallons of diesel fuel from South Africa for lack of foreign exchange. The railway to Dar es Salaam was shut down for a period and now is in extremely poor condition due to tropical conditions. Almost three–quarters of the farm tractors are inoperative—no spare parts or fuel. Electrical power is spotty in the capital city. The Kwacha was severely devalued in the last three years. Its value was set on a weekly auction market according to the availability of foreign exchange, but this was discontinued in 1987 in favor of a government–fixed price. Inflation and population growth without accompanying agricultural expansion contributed to a lowering of actual income during the 1980s by 40%.

The Future: Kaunda, now 70, has resurfaced as a politician and probably has the backing of South Africa's *ANC*. But his own party has disapproved of his ambition to be elected president in October 1996. The people are fragmented and discouraged; their per capita income is *down* 35% from two decades ago. Hobbled by bureaucratic corruption, no end is in sight to the decline of this nation.

Early morning in Lusaka

The Republic of Zimbabwe

The ancient ruins which gave their name to the nation

Area: 391.090 sq. km. = 151,000 sq. mi. (slightly larger than Montana).

Population: 10.8 million (estimated).

Capital City: Harare (Pop. 883,000, estimated).

Climate: Hot and humid in the southern Limpopo and Sabi River regions; temperate in the central and northern highlands. A rainy season normally lasts from October to April and there is a dry season from May to September. Drought conditions prevailed from 1981 to 1984.

Neighboring Countries: Zambia (North); Namibia (South–West Africa, West); Botswana (Southwest); Republic of South Africa (South); Mozambique (East).

Official Language: English.

Other Principal Tongues: A number of Bantu dialects of the Shona people, Sindebele, dialects of Bavenda groups closely related to the Tswana of Botswana.

Ethnic Background: Bantu, primarily Shona (71%); Ndebele (16%); other (12%); White (1%).

Principal Religions: Christianity combined with traditional tribal beliefs (51%), Christianity (24%), traditional tribal beliefs (24%), Islam. Figures are approximate.

Chief Commercial Products: Tobacco, light manufactured goods, gold, cotton, asbestos, chrome ore, nickel.

Annual Per Capita Income: About U.S. $700.

Currency: Zimbabwean Dollar.

Former Colonial Status: Administered by the British South Africa Company (1889–1923); Autonomous state within the British Commonwealth (1923–1965); unilateral independence as *Rhodesia* (1965–1980), recognized independence (1980).

Chief of State: Robert Mugabe, President.

Independence Date: April 18, 1980.

National Flag: Seven horizontal stripes (top to bottom) of green, gold, red, black, red, gold, green. A white triangle at the staff contains a red star in which is centered the gold Zimbabwean bird.

Zimbabwe is hot and humid in the southern river basin areas. Cluttered forests of hardwood predominate in these lowlands, with both teak and mahogany towering above the scrub vegetation that

155

is the breeding ground of the tsetse fly, carrier of dreaded sleeping sickness.

In the central areas the altitude rises in a series of fertile plateaus, with corresponding modification of the tropical climate. During the winter, the land sometimes gives off enough heat at night to allow the intrusion of a thin frost by dawn. The land that is not forested by tall trees, growing in a less densely vegetated woodland, is under cultivation.

Victoria Falls, located on the Zambezi River above the Kariba Lake is one of the greatest sights of Africa—they are more than twice as high as Niagara Falls and have a width of about one mile. The sparkling waters of the lake, the largest man–made body of water in the world, stretch narrowly to the northeast, held back by the 420–foot–high walls of the Kariba Dam that provides electric power to both Zimbabwe and Zambia.

History: There were successive waves of Bantu migration into Zimbabwe which may have started as early as about the 4th century A.D. The Zimbabwe ruins, the only pre–European remnant of architecture found below the Sahara in Africa, is attributed to people known as the Monoma, and are dated sometime between the 6th and 13th centuries, A.D. The Mashonas settled at an unknown time in the region; the Zulu and Barotse passed through during their migration to the south, and the Ndebele eventually came to dominate both the Shonas and the region. For details of earlier history, see Historical Background and *The British in Africa.*

Much has been written about the unilateral declaration of independence in 1965 by the government controlled by the White minority led by Ian Douglas Smith. In reality, the White government was granted independence by the British in 1923. Following a referendum limited to Whites, Rhodesia became an autonomous member of the British Commonwealth. Although the British reserved authority in the areas of foreign relations and military defense, that authority was never in fact exercised. A parliament of White British settlers was chosen; African people could not, with little exception, pass the educational tests required to gain voting rights.

White control was further solidified in 1931 with the passage of the Land Apportionment Act. About 150,000 settlers were given roughly one–half of the choicest land and 3 million Africans were relegated to the remainder. During the post–World War II period there was substantial additional migration of Whites into the region, so that by the late 1970's half of the 230,000 Whites were immigrants to Zimbabwe.

Rhodesia was joined with what are now Zambia and Malawi into the Federation of Rhodesia and Nyasaland in 1953—a loosely–knit combination conceived principally for the promotion of free trade between the three. In keeping with the growth of nationalism among the African people during the 1950's, substantial movements arose in all three colonies; the White minority in Rhodesia successfully suppressed the movement until 1980.

With British approval, the Rhodesians amended their constitution in 1961 to provide for two rolls of voters. The "A" role was in reality composed only of White voters and the "B" role consisted of about 40,000 Black Africans out of 4 million; they were educated sufficiently to pass the required test. The nationalist movements in Malawi (then Nyasaland) and Zambia (then Northern Rhodesia) vigorously opposed this system and succeeded in convincing the British that the federation should be dissolved and that both should receive independence under African majority rule; this was carried out in 1963–1964.

Negotiations for Rhodesian independence between the British and the Whites broke down in 1965 and Ian Smith, the Rhodesian Prime Minister, declared Rhodesia to be an independent nation ruled by the White minority. From that time, the Rhodesian regime and the British negotiated, sometimes with fervor, sometimes with disillusionment, but never with genuine success in reaching a final solution. The Smith regime seldom dealt with the British in good faith.

The Black African nations sponsored UN resolutions condemning White rule in Rhodesia with regularity, one of which forbade any member nation to trade with Rhodesia. This posed a hardship not only on Rhodesia, but on other nations, including the U.S. and West Germany, since Rhodesia is one of the very few sources (outside the U.S.S.R.) of chrome ore, vital to the manufacture of hard steel. Rather than have the U.S. buy Soviet chrome ore (at a very high price), the Congress of the U.S. allowed resumption of import of lower–priced Rhodesian chrome ore in 1971, infuriating the Black African nations.

Minor acts of rebellion took place between 1965 and 1972, originating in neighboring Zambia. The African name for Rhodesia was and is *Zimbabwe.* Stiff resistance to the White government centered around two groups: Joshua Nkomo's *Zimbabwe African People's Union* (*ZAPU*) and Robert Mugabe's *Zimbabwe African National Union* (*ZANU*). Both movements were originally based in Lusaka, Zambia, but since that nation's independence, *ZANU* operated from Mozambique. A third organization, this one operating openly within Rhodesia— also concerned itself with the future relationship of White and Black people in the

government: the *United African National Council* led by Bishop Abel Muzorewa of the American United Methodist Church.

Prime Minister Smith, anxious to deal with moderate elements, began a series of talks with Bishop Muzorewa and two other Black leaders, Chief Jeremiah Chirau and the Rev. Ndabaningi Sithole. Both Britain and the U.S. urged that *ZAPU* and *ZANU* leaders be included in the talks, but this plea was ignored.

Smith announced in 1978 that the three Black leaders had worked out a formula which would turn the government over to Black rule by the end of the year. The four men formed an executive council; each key government position would have one Black and one White minister.

Mugabe and Nkomo scoffed at the internal settlement, branding the Black leaders as "Uncle Toms." Even when total amnesty was offered to the estimated 8,000–*Patriotic Front* (an uneasy union between *ZAPU* and *ZANU*), the leaders of the guerrilla forces rejected it and vowed to continue fighting until victory was won. The target date for independence was not met due to lack of agreement on the inclusion or exclusion of the *Patriotic Front Guerrillas*, who, through intimidation and murder, tried to sabotage elections.

In a referendum held in early 1979, White voters approved a new constitution which would grant majority rule, but which also would protect White interests by allotting them (4% of the electorate) 28 out of the 100 seats in forthcoming parliamentary election for a "transition period" of up to 10 years. In the general elections held in April 1979, approximately 2.9 million (64%) cast their ballots—possibly for that elusive thing called "peace" to end strife which had become virtually continuous. It came as no surprise that Bishop Abel Muzorewa's *United African National Council* won 51 of the 72 seats allotted to Black candidates, assuring that the Bishop would become Prime Minister. Smith, who initially had promised to stay out of the government, won one of the White seats, making it probable that he would hold a cabinet post. Sithole initially describing the campaign and elections as completely fair, protested "irregularities" when his party won only 12 seats.

Prime Minister–elect Muzorewa quickly called upon the United States to lift economic sanctions against his country and made it clear that aid would be accepted from other sources, if necessary. The newly–elected government decided the nation should be called *Zimbabwe–Rhodesia.* The new parliament met for the first time in May 1979. but Sithole's 12 members boycotted the session and refused two cabinet positions. Things *were* changing—but not fast enough.

Warfare continued because of the absence of the *Patriotic Front* in the government. Reluctantly, Britain decided to turn its back on Muzorewa and try to initiate a government which would include all elements. A conference began in September 1979 with *Bishop* Muzorewa (the guerrilla leaders did not recognize his official position), Joshua Nkomo and Robert Mugabe. Week after endless week of bickering ensued, punctuated by threats of the guerrilla leaders to walk out. Within Zimbabwe (*Rhodesia* was dropped in August 1979) there was continuous fighting—an average of 100 lives were lost each day.

The draft constitution reduced White representation to 20 seats in the parliament. The guerrilla leaders literally out-talked the opposition until virtually any scheme of government would have been accepted. Muzorewa reluctantly accepted the British plan and when it became apparent that no further concessions would be granted to the *Patriotic Front*, Nkomo and Mugabe gave in. The parliament dissolved itself and Zimbabwe temporarily came under British control until elections could be held and a new government installed. By January 14, 1980, with promises of amnesty and a cease–fire, 21,370 guerrillas entered 39 cease–fire centers. Politicking for the elections began with a roar and became louder. Everyone was talking unity, but at the same time they were busy verbally attacking others. Mugabe's ZANU announced it would field candidates for every district possible; his organization consisted primarily of the more numerous Shona people. Nkomo's support was been primarily among the Ndebele people of the South.

Violence did not end. A grenade was thrown at Mugabe's house in early February 1980 and a few days later explosives discharged on a road just after his car had passed during a campaign swing. Ian Smith surprisingly endorsed Nkomo (because of his hatred of the radical, marxist Mugabe). With a keen sense of humor and folksy manner, Nkomo openly courted Mugabe's followers; the latter looked more like a conservatively–dressed school teacher than the radical that he actually was.

As the February 27th elections approached, tensions increased. The British sent in 500 representatives, including police, to man the polling places; they fanned out over the country in an effort to guarantee free elections. There was a heavy turnout throughout the country. Although Mugabe was confident of victory, he was surprised by the extent to which he succeeded. His guerrilla forces were quite conspicuous around polling places and people who rebelled at taking their instructions on how to vote were shot. ZANU captured 57 of the 80 Black seats in the parliament; Nkomo's ZAPU was successful in 20 contests. Bishop Muzorewa was sent to a humiliating defeat with only three victories. The White minority was badly frightened at the prospect of having marxist Robert Mugabe as Prime Minister, but he hurriedly assured them they would be treated as all other Zimbabweans; he even hinted there would be Whites in his cabinet. Peter Walls, commander of the Rhodesian security forces which had killed thousands of guerrillas, was appointed to preside over the integration of the guerrilla forces and the military. With representatives of 100 nations on hand, Zimbabwe achieved recognized independence on April 18, 1980.

Except for the disruption caused by several strikes, the first weeks of Mugabe's administration promised a good future for Zimbabwe. Nkomo was given the high–ranking position of Home Affairs Minister, giving him charge over the 53 administrative districts as well as tribal lands. Two Whites were appointed to the cabinet. Stable relations with foreign nations were established. Victory at the polls, however, was not enough for Mugabe. He decided within a short time to eliminate future competition. In late 1980 the arrest of nine senior ZAPU officials was ordered—the first ''detainees'' of the Black government, who also had been imprisoned by the Smith regime.

All White–owned newspapers were taken over by the government in early 1981 on the ground that they were too White–oriented and did not carry enough news about Africa. The post–election relative calm was decisively broken in early 1981, starting with a beer–hall brawl in Bulawayo, Zimbabwe's second–largest city. Mugabe men in the national army exchanged heated insults with former guerrillas loyal to Nkomo. Fighting broke out and grew into open warfare between the two groups; gunfire could be heard in all parts of the city and fires burned out of control. Several hundred were reported killed.

Nkomo had been demoted in the cabinet and in 1982 he was fired after government troops supposedly discovered caches of arms and munitions. Mugabe charged that Nkomo was trying to take over the government. By this time two other factors destined to change Zimbabwe were underway. Drought conditions commenced in 1981 and continued. The effect of a White exodus which had been increasing since 1979 became apparent, particularly in the farmlands. The departures came in spite of strict measures prohibiting removal of wealth from the country—the Whites simply forfeited that for which they had worked. Corn pro-

Harare

Courtesy: CALTEX Petroleum Corporation

duction dropped sharply from 2 million tons in 1981 to 620,000 tons by 1983; the principal cause was principally three successive years of scorching drought (1982, 1983, 1984), which gripped Matabeland. Zimbabwe rapidly became a food importer instead of exporter following independence. Departure of White farmers and breakdown of machinery compounded the problem. But a return of the rains in 1985 resulted in a crop of 1.6 million tons. The drought did virtually wipe out cattle production, which, exported to Europe, since has resumed.

The government conducted sweeping raids throughout Matebeleland after 1981. This southwest area was the principal source of Nkomo's support. Nkomo was arrested in March 1983 at the Bulawayo airport as he was about to board a flight enroute to an international conference in Czechoslovakia; he was detained for eight hours without reason. Upon his release, he promptly fled first to Botswana and later to London.

The government placed a strict curfew on the Ndebele people and withheld vital food shipments to the area, arousing international anger over what was regarded as an attempt to starve people into obedience. Nkomo, who returned in mid–1983, denounced the measures. Villagers told of executions and torture. The government, needless to say, denied all such allegations. But by April 1984 food restrictions could no longer be justified. Thirty thousand tons of corn was authorized for the region one day after the government signed a food transfer agreement with the U.S., which pledged $11 million in aid. There still were reports of torture and executions in Matabeleland in 1986.

Since assuming a political role, Robert Mugabe intended that Zimbabwe would be a one–party nation, and openly stated he was determined to make ZANU "a truly Marxist–Leninist party to ensure the charting of an irreversible social course and create a socialist society." When asked what socialism is, a minister of the government said it's very simple: "In Zimbabwe, socialism means what's mine is mine, but what's yours we share."

Systematic, continued persecution, including crude torture, of members of ZAPU in particular and Matabeles in general in 1983–1984 had a predictable result in 1985 elections. Although ZANU won no seats in the region, its victory in all other parts of the nation was overwhelming. Mugabe was infuriated when the White voters returned Ian Smith to office as a member of the 20–seat delegation reserved for Whites. Ominously, Mugabe pronounced that the Whites "had not repented in any way," and promised to abolish the constitutional guarantee of White seats in parliament. This was done in early 1987.

President Mugabe

Nkomo, apparently realizing (at the age of 68) that further resistance was useless and would only result in further suffering in Matabeleland, threw in the towel in March 1986 and announced a merger of ZANU and ZAPU. U.S. assistance, the most generous in Africa except for Egypt, dwindled sharply after 1980. After Mugabe solidified his power, Zimbabwe started voting in the UN in a solid pattern adverse to U.S. interests, causing substantial irritation in Washington.

At a celebration of U.S. Independence Day on July 4, 1986 in Harare, for reasons only known to him, Mugabe dispatched a very minor government official who proceeded to lambast the United States. Former President Jimmy Carter, who was present, walked out on the speaker, together with all American officials. Shortly thereafter, all aid to Zimbabwe was suspended by the U.S. It was restored in 1988 in greatly reduced amounts.

South Africa has erected a concrete–electric wire fence closing the border with Zimbabwe. President Mugabe had announced intentions to become a leader in the imposition of sanctions against its southern neighbor. He appointed a task force to explore the possible effects of retaliation by South Africa, which proceeded at a snail's pace and never completed its work. In making the threat, the president overlooked the fact that an average of 200,000 tons of grain was exported annually to South Africa in exchange for tractors and other farm equipment. Talk of sanctions were unrealistic in view of the fact that South African railways are the most feasible way to transport Zimbabwean exports.

The International Monetary Fund has been extremely reluctant to furnish grants to Zimbabwe due to Mugabe's inept meddling with the economy and the high level of corruption among his cronies. Foreign investment has been limited by Zimbabwean insistence on preventing profits from leaving the country and use of a series of ever–changing schemes to accomplish that goal.

Mediocre rains in 1985–6 and severe drought in the following year and again in 1991–3 sharply lowered crop production and made Zimbabwe an importer of food. When the latter struck, Marxist rhetoric in Zimbabwe was heard much less. A scheme of Mugabe's late wife to make the nation one–party was rejected repeatedly in 1991.

About 100,000 White people remained after independence—the families of some 4,500 farmers who efficiently have farmed the most fertile one–third of the nation's farmland, the earnings of which provided desperately needed foreign exchange with machine–grown crops during years of good rainfall.

With the expiration of the basic independence treaty in 1990, Mugabe & Co. embarked on a well–meant but hazardous scheme of land redistribution:

110,000 poor Blacks would be resettled on 15 million acres of White land "purchased" by the government with Zimbabwean dollars for about 1/20 of its true value. The ensuing drought postponed the plan, but it was renewed in 1993 with the announcement that 70 farms averaging 67,000 acres each would be divided under the plan, a total of almost a half million acres.

The plan in theory would have put tens of thousands of unemployed to work, but inefficiently and unprofitably. The loss in potential export earnings will be at least a thousand times the value of their labor. A firestorm of protest arose in 1993, both internally from the White farmers and internationally, from the IMF and creditor nations and sources, which infuriated Mugabe to the point of irrationality. He threatened to seize the farms and expel the farmers without compensation, denounced his foreign critics as "racial bigots" and said Zimbabwe would refuse "filthy" money from abroad.

The untold part of the story is that since 1980 the top echelon of *ZANU* has been enriching itself immensely by the expropriation of desirable lands with utterly no thought of the poor people in Zimbabwe. This is widely known and resented in Zimbabwe and Mugabe knows this. The first farm of 3,000 acres was appropriated in 1993; it was intended for 33 Black farmers. But in March 1994 it was leased (for a pittance) to a favorite in the government. The explanation: "he had an application on file" and he met the right criteria. Mugabe was personally charged with a "betrayal of confidence" by White farmers.

The Mugabe government realizes that the planned redistribution of land would be an economic disaster for Zimbabwe. To avert this, a commission has been created to study *which* land *might* be redistributed. The process will take years—decades—if it happens at all.

There even has been scattered talk of how perhaps a return of Ian Smith to power would result in the prosperity of years past.

A 1990 constitution provided for six–year terms for the president and members of the single–chamber legislature. The opposition was weak and divided in elections held in early April 1995, enabling *ZANU* to capture 118 legislative seats. The remainder of the legislature consists of 10 traditional chiefs and 20 appointees selected by Mugabe. One accurate observer commented that in Zimbabwe Whites own the economy and Blacks own the political system.

Culture: The White and African populations lived apart for decades; independence has not changed this. Black workers provided labor on White plantations as well as in urban homes and stores.

Harare, Umtali, Gweru and Bulawayo were all modern, thriving cities possessing almost all conveniences of European or American urban areas, but have been in decline since 1980. There is no legal discrimination in the cities—the races mix in public places, but somewhat uncomfortably. The countryside has been a different scene, particularly in the north, where fortified villages became more and more commonplace as the former government attempted to limit contact between the guerrillas and the people. Rural violence has been seen in all parts of Zimbabwe since independence, particularly in Matabeleland.

A large number of primary, secondary and technical schools have provided training for Black Zimbabweans; the literacy rate exceeds 80%; this is the highest of any African nation.

The majority of people combine their traditional tribal beliefs with Christianity (Protestant). The remaining White people are primarily Anglican and Presbyterian, and there is an active Catholic Church in which the Bishops openly oppose terrorist measures of the current government.

As some White farmers have departed rather than face possible violence, squatters have moved onto the large plantations they owned. In order to prevent this, the government has been manning them with militia and soldiers. Reports that the White farmers have been returning have been overstated.

AIDS is raging throughout Zimbabwe; about 25% of the sexually active population is infected, as well as an equal number of children under five. More than half of

The recently discovered stone carving of the *Zimbabwe Bird*.
Courtesy: CALTEX Petroleum Corp.

the 50,000 military has the disease. Worst of all, rural myths and urban legends hold that having sex with a virgin *cures* the disease. Current projections are that one-third of youngsters will be orphans by 2010 or before.

Five tall, modern buildings now dominate the skyline of Harare. Owned by international business interests, they have been constructed since 1990 and symbolize White predominance in the economy.

Economy: Traditionally Zimbabwe has gained its chief income from agricultural exports. This has changed; mineral resources are now the main export. Corn is the main staple of the people and production dropped to about 35% of pre–independence levels, due to a combination of drought and farms which consume more than they produce.

The government consistently spends more than it takes in despite an effort by the International Monetary Fund to institute reforms. Loan agreements from that body were suspended in 1984.

Foreign investment was extremely limited during the years of the Smith regime and is now virtually nonexistant because of a regime which in practice, although not officially, is marxist–socialist.

The willingness of about 4,500 White commercial farm families to remain is doubtful, particularly in the two provinces inhabited by Ndebele people. The market for agricultural products is now government–controlled. Corruption in government, in spite of stringent measures, has reached near–crisis levels. Added to overspending by the government, this contributes to an annual inflation rate of about 20%.

Due to the extremely successful education program put into effect in 1980, skilled workers are now in a state of oversupply—there is a 50% unemployment rate among high school graduates. College graduates also face a bleak future. About 280,000 graduate from high school each year, but there are only about 12,000 jobs. This may prove to be the undoing of the Mugabe regime.

The Future: Loosening of government press controls in early 1995 were probably the result of Mugabe's feeling that his control is and remains firm in Zimbabwe. The two major threats are drought and the spread of *AIDS*. As in other parts of the world, communism has become irrelevant.

EAST AFRICAN ISLAND NATIONS
The Democratic Republic of Madagascar

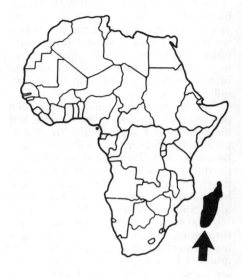

Area: 595,000 sq. km. = 229,730 sq. mi. (somewhat smaller than Texas).

Population: 12.2 million (estimated).

Capital City: Antananarivo (Pop. 1.2 million, estimated. Pronounced Tah–nah–nah–*reev*).

Climate: Interior–warm and rainy (November–April); cool and dry (May–October); the southern portion of the island is semi–arid. The coastal areas are uniformly hotter than the inland altitudes. The east coast has a heavy, almost year–around rainfall brought by Indian Ocean trade winds and monsoons.

Neighboring Countries: The closest neighbor of this island republic is Mozambique, 300 miles west on the African mainland.

Official Language: Malagasy and French.

Other Principal Tongues: Malagasy is universally understood and spoken by the people, although there are several dialects, particularly in the coastal areas.

Ethnic Background: There are 18 ethnic groups, predominantly Malaysian–Indonesian–Polynesian in origin; the principal one is the Merina. Coastal tribes include the Betsimisaraka and Tsimihety. Other smaller groupings are of African origin. There are small communities of French, Indian and Chinese.

Principal Religions: Christianity (about 41%); traditional tribal beliefs with overtones of ancestor worship, Islam.

Chief Commercial Products: Coffee, vanilla, sisal, sugar, tobacco and cloves.

Annual Per Capita Income: About U.S. $250.

Currency: Malagasy Franc (no longer tied to the French Franc).

Former Colonial Status: French Protectorate (1894–1960).

Independence Date: June 26, 1960.

Chief of State: Dr. Albert Zafy, President.

Head of Government: Francisque Ravony, Prime Minister.

National Flag: A vertical stripe of white closest to the pole with two horizontal stripes of red and green.

The Democratic Republic of Madagascar, the fourth–largest island of the world situated in the Indian Ocean off the southeastern part of Africa is a land of contrast throughout its 990–mile length.

The west coast, facing the Mozambique Channel, is a low, tropically wet and dry region, particularly in the extreme South. A series of broad plateaus rise from the coast to increasing heights of 2,300 to 4,500 feet. More abundant rainfall occurs here, and the altitude tempers the otherwise hot climate. Almost daily rains fall during the summer; the weather from May to October is cooler when temperatures in the higher altitudes drop as low as the freezing point. Several mountain ranges rise above this plateauland—Mount Tsaratanana majestically looms to a height of 9,450 feet.

The eastern shore is a narrow strip between the sea and the steep sides of the mountains. Washed by the warm waters of the Indian Ocean, and visited by the trade winds and monsoons, this coastal strip is almost uniformly hot and humid, with an annual rainfall exceeding 110 inches.

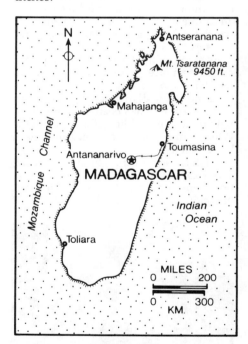

History: The Indonesian, Arab and African heritage of the people of Madagascar gives some indication of its early history. From the time of the Christian era, there were successive waves of immigration to the island by people from what are now Indonesia and Malaysia. For early and colonial history, see Historical Background and *The French in Africa.*

Philibert Tsiranana (*Feel*–eh–bear Tsear–ah–*nah*; the last vowel in Malagasy names is not pronounced), a moderate, was president after independence. His *Social Democratic Party* won 104 out of 107 seats in the House of Deputies in 1965 and 1970 as well as all of the 54 elective seats in the Senate; there were an additional 18 appointed Senators. The *Congress Party* received the remaining House seats; it was prominent in several city governments.

Although in failing health, the elderly Tsiranana dealt swiftly with an uprising in April 1971 in the southern area, accusing Maoist revolutionaries with responsibility for the strife. Although he was reelected in 1972, immediate protests ensued. Student unrest and widespread civil strife resulted in a decree of martial law. The powers of government were given to the military and the legislature was abolished. However, the military regime came under increasing criticism directed principally against radical economic measures intended to lessen and ultimately eliminate dependence on France. After the Chief of Staff was assassinated in early 1975, the Military Directory selected Lt. Commander Didier Ratsiraka (*Deed*–year Rot–*see*–rakh) as President of the Supreme Council of the Revolution.

A new constitution was approved in 1975 by 94% of the voters and the Democratic Republic of Madagascar was proclaimed. Ratsiraka assumed the presidency for his first seven–year term, and for a second term in 1983. All political expression was through a five–party coalition, the *National Front for the Defense of the Revolution.* In the 1983 elections, the president had only nominal opposition, which was outlawed. When the president announced postponement of 1987 elections until November 1989, three of the opposition parties split from the coalition; there is a fourth opposition faction in France.

Madagascar took a sharp swerve to the left under Ratsiraka—government control over the economy soared from 14% to more than 75%, with nationalization of banks and industries. He gave his cronies and favorites control over various sectors of the economy in a manner similar to that which occurred in Haiti prior to the ouster of the Duvalier regime. Multiple and repeated loans from the International Monetary Fund and a host of other sources since 1980 have meant the difference between survival and chaos for the island. But in 1986 there was an abrupt change. Realizing that no foreign investment would be available so long as rigid, state–controlled socialism prevailed, all laws were changed to create a free market economy and moves were made away from the Soviet Union and east bloc nations.

In particular the rice market was taken from government control—this is the staple diet grain of the people. Import limits have been set to encourage a renewal of local production. (Things had gotten so bad that the poor of the cities were *selling* small children they were unable to feed.) Hunger and famine were widespread in 1987 and were followed by riots against Asiatic mercantile establishments together with a six month strike at the largest university. Conditions have been slowly improving in spite of devastating hurricanes which have lambasted the island, lowering crop production even further.

The president was reelected to a seven–year term in March 1989 after he advanced the elections from November. Although politicking was intense, all parties were within an umbrella organization. About half the electorate voted. Thousands of protestors within a coalition of 16 opposition parties jammed the streets of the capital for most of June 1991 calling for political reform, and especially the resignation of Ratsiraka and the scrapping of the socialist constitution.

Under external and internal pressure, Madagascar selected an interim government which included opposition members; it governed until elections were held in late 1992 and 1993. The contest was generally fair, with scattered violence. Although about one–third of the ballots were marred, the result was the sound repudiation of Ratsiraka's seventeen–year rule, and marxism–socialism.

Dr. Albert Zafy, a surgeon by profession and leader of *Forces Vivre* ("Living Forces"), a collection of 11 political parties, won by a margin of two to one. His coalition group has 78 of the 138 seats in the National Assembly; Ratsiraka's coalition came in a distant fourth in the contest. The current government consists overwhelmingly of persons of Merina heritage. Political infighting and shifting alliances forced the prime minister to appoint a new cabinet in mid–1994.

Culture: The diversity in the heritage of the people of this great island is modified by the fact that all speak or understand the highly developed language called Malagasy and an estimated 53% are

President Albert Zafy

literate. It has some distinctively oriental features, derived from ancient Indonesia and Malaysia; there is a great deal of literature and poetry of a distinctive style.

The dances of the people give further insight into their ethnic background. The Merina dances are usually accompanied by song and an instrument made from bamboo strings in a manner derived from the far east. The Sakalava dances include hand–clapping by the audience in a characteristically African style. Other dances are measured by the rhythm of drum and whistle, a style which also comes from the continent.

Although about 41% of the people are Christian, most have joined traditional beliefs with ancestor worship of Hindu origin—a religious combination of east and west. The people are nominally divided into tribes, but the real basis of social life is the family unit. The capital of Antananarivo is located on the site of the old capital city of the Merina Kingdom in the high plateau region. Its population of about one million consists largely of Merina people. The coastal ports of Toumasina, Mahajanga, Toliara and Antseranana are

Preparing cotton for shipment, Mahajanga　　　　WORLD BANK Photo

populated mainly by Malagasy Christians, with communities of Chinese and Indian merchants.

Education has been thorough for the most part; elementary and secondary schools provide education for almost 1 million students, and regional university centers have increased student enrollment from 5,000 in 1972 to about 80,000 today.

Economy: Madagascar's economy, like that of many of its mainland neighbors, has been in utter anarchy. About 90% of the work force is engaged in agriculture. Madagascar was a rice *exporting* nation, but has had to import 200,000 tons in recent years. This has been directly attributable to widespread nationalization, which did nothing to spur production.

Madagascar is still using rice varieties that are outdated and low–yielding. Economic growth has, even in good years, been very slow due to almost total dependence of the island on world prices paid for its crop exports.

France remains the principal trading partner of the island and has provided an annual grant which is modestly supplemented by the United States. Most of this money is intended for education of farmers into the use of more modern machinery to replace traditional methods of agriculture.

The beginnings of industry have come to Madagascar in the form of an oil refinery (temporarily shut down by a devastating cyclone), a paper mill and two automobile assembly plants, as well as electronic facilities.

Relatively large amounts of foreign aid have been necessary to keep Madagascar from chaos, which caused the foreign debt to rise to a level impossible to repay (U.S. $3 billion). France, Germany and the U.S. have forgiven over a billion dollars of this in exchange for conservation measures including preservation of endangered species, particularly lemurs. Forests have been 80% destroyed by slash and burn agriculture, creating serious land erosion problems.

The years of experimentation with socialism postponed progress in Madagascar for a generation; the per capita income is comparatively low. Severe drought in 1991–3 caused great suffering and is recurring in 1995.

The Future: Foreign investment is desperately needed. Since the government appears stable, it may be able to attract this urgent source which can induce economic progress. A careful understanding of the island and its people, however, is advisable before any commitment is made.

The Republic of Mauritius

Area: 1,856 sq. km. = 717 sq. mi., excluding Rodrigues (40 sq. mi.) and other small islands (45 sq. mi.)—slightly larger than Kauai, one of the Hawaiian Islands).

Population: 1.2 million (estimated).

Capital City: Port Louis (Pop. 281,000, estimated).

Climate: Tropically hot and humid, with slightly cooler temperatures in the highlands of Mauritius which rise as high as 2,500 feet.

Neighboring Countries: Mauritius is located 550 miles east of Madagascar; Rodrigues is 350 miles northeast of Mauritius.

Official Language: English.

Other Principal Tongues: Creole (a French dialect), French, Hindu, Urdu, Chinese.

Ethnic Background: Hindu Indian (54%); Islamic Indian (14%); Creole, a group of African and African–European descent (25%); European descent, Chinese and other (7%). Figures are approximate.

Principal Religions: Hinduism (54%), Islam (15%); Christianity (26%), other (5%). Figures are approximate.

Chief Commercial Products: Light manufactured products, sugar, tourism, tea, coffee.

Per Capita Annual Income: About U.S. $2,800.

Currency: Mauritius Rupee.

Former Colonial Status: French possession (1715–1810); British possession (1810–1968).

Independence Date: March 12, 1968.

Chief of State: Cassam Uteem, President.

Head of Government: Aneerood Jugnauth, Prime Minister.

National Flag: Red, blue, gold and green horizontal stripes.

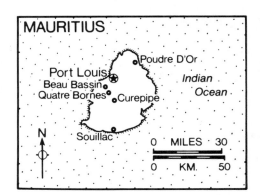

The land mass that is now the island of Mauritius is the result of volcanic activity that occurred thousands of years ago. The craggy, hardened lava, covered with fine ash and silt was in turn covered with a carpet of green vegetation, growing swiftly in the tropical sun. The island is a series of plateaus and interesting variations caused by small streams, waterfalls, crevices and coastal indentations. The island of Rodrigues is a smaller version of Mauritius.

History: The Dutch arrived at this island, uninhabited by man prior to the time, in 1598, naming it after a prince of Holland. They remained for a century and started sugar production at the time the last clumsy dodo birds walked upon the island. Concluding that the island offered no profit, they withdrew, and the French arrived in 1715. The small group of settlers was augmented by African slaves, who worked the sugar plantations that came to dominate the island.

There was some intermarriage between the French and the Africans resulting in the evolution of a stable group of people now known as Creoles, the upper class of which remain pure White in ancestry. The British seized the island during the Napoleonic wars in 1810. Slavery had been abolished and a program of importing large numbers of people from India to perform the strenuous labor on the plantations commenced. When the Suez Canal opened in 1869, the island of Mauritius quickly became one of the earth's forgotten places; it formerly had been a port of call for ships going to and from the Middle and Far East.

Following World War II, the world-wide surge of nationalism gradually entered Mauritius, particularly among those of Indian descent who had risen in numbers to be a majority of the population. When Great Britain announced the withdrawal "east of the Suez" in 1966, Mauritius was intended to be a part of this plan. Ethnic diversity was the biggest problem—the Indian majority favored independence, but the Creole people were opposed.

In order to placate the Creoles, a complicated plan was devised to apportion the seats of the legislature among the ethnic groups, and elections were held. The result was that the Hindu Indians were able to command a majority; the Creoles a minority and the Islamic Indians were unable to elect a single representative.

Since independence, Mauritius has been walking a tightrope. It must appear to support the Black African nations' views, and at the same time refrain from antagonizing White–ruled South Africa, which purchases a large portion of its food exports.

For about 41 years until 1982, Sir Seewoosagur Ramgoolam and his *Labor Party* dominated the political scene. The party was challenged in June 1982 elections by a French Mauritian, Paul Berenger, and the vote was so split along party and ethnic lines that a coalition government emerged headed by Aneerood Jugnauth, which included Berenger as Finance Minister. A second collapse in the government in mid–1983 led to a second election. Jugnauth, realizing that he had to effectively compete with opponents, organized the *Mauritian Socialist Movement, (MSM)*, which won over Berenger's *Mauritian Militant Movement*. Elections in 1987 led to a repeat of this victory of the coalition. These elections did show one thing: a political party in Mauritius can never be judged by its name. Staunchly capitalist, Mauritius is now the world's number three exporter of manufactured woolens. Numbers of Hong Kong garment manufacturers are relocating to Mauritius in view of the uncertainties when mainland China attains sovereignty over that territory. Export of manufactured textiles has been growing at the rate of 25% annually for the last decade. In spite of its extremely dense population, Mauritius actually faces a labor shortage. Establishment of offshore, international (or money laundering) banks, whichever name you prefer, is now underway. Unfortunately, this may be associated with growing illicit drug trafficking, which Jugnauth blamed for two attempts on his life in 1988 and 1989.

Active promotion of tourism and facilities of vacationers has paid handsome dividends. Mauritius rates among the top locales in the world for "getting away from it all."

Elections in September 1991 saw an overwhelming victory for Jugnauth's coalition government, and in October the Prime Minister announced that Mauritius would break ties with the British crown. It became a republic within the Commonwealth on March 12, 1992. The office of governor–general became president, elected for a five–year term by a simple majority of the legislature.

Culture: With a population density of more than 1,200 per square mile, Mauritius is overcrowded. The various ethnic groups have very little to do with each other. Education, formerly limited, now is widespread and there is a relatively high literacy rate of 60%.

The Creoles have evolved into a social class which tends to exclude Asians. Sixteen newspapers on the tiny island are frequently harsh critics of the government.

Economy: Light manufacturing at last has replaced sugar, produced at a cost higher than the price for which it is sold, as the main source of external income. Rice must be imported, since it cannot be grown, but a program is underway to convert sugar areas to corn production; the only problem with this is the cyclones which all too often smash the island—there have been years when even the sugar crop has been all but wiped out. The improved international airport has boosted tourism by those wishing to stay in this paradise; this also is a favorite port of call for cruise ships.

The Future: Minor political reshuffling in anticipation of 1996 elections is occurring. The prime minister can and may call them at any time. The population will exceed 2 million by 2015. The immediate future of this prosperous island nation is bright.

Prime Minister Jugnauth

EASTERN AFRICA

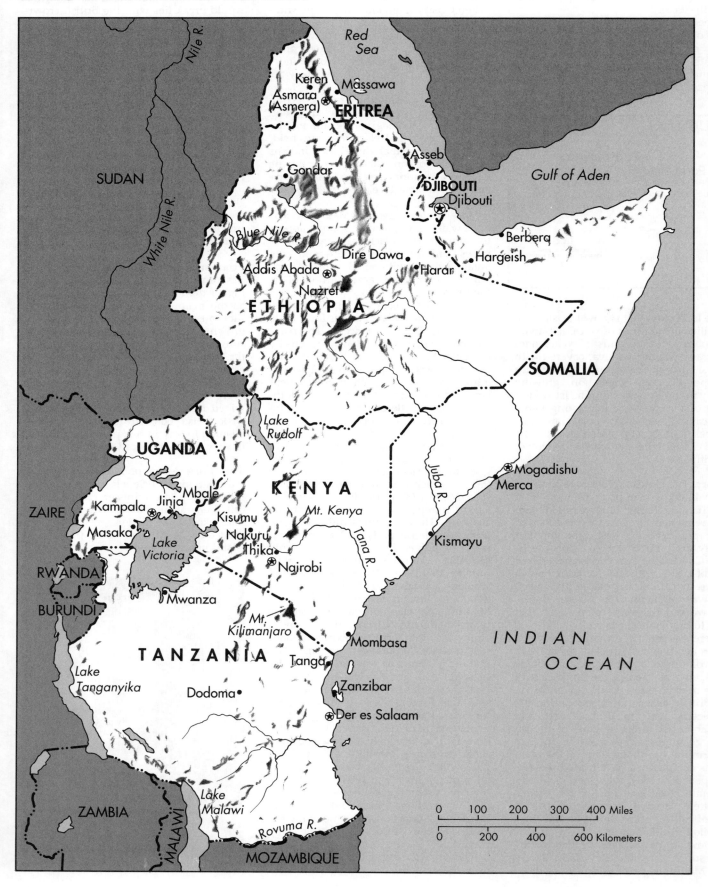

164

The Republic of Djibouti

Area: 23,000 sq. km = 9,000 sq. mi. (slightly larger than Massachusetts).

Population: 550,000 (estimated).

Capital City: Djibouti (Pop. 205,000, estimated; pronounced Gee–boo–tee).

Climate: Hot and arid.

Neighboring Countries: Ethiopia (North, West, South); Somali Republic (Southeast).

Official Language: Arabic, French.

Other Principal Tongues: Somali, Afar (Danakil), Arabic.

Ethnic Background: Somali (47%), Afar (37%), European, Ethiopian, Arab.

Principal Religions: Islam (92%), Christian (8%).

Chief Commercial Products: Livestock and hides. Substantial revenues have traditionally come from commerce to and from Ethiopia via the Addis Ababa–Djibouti railroad; during the last decade traffic has been periodically interrupted by warfare and guerrilla activity.

Annual Per Capita Income: About U.S. $1,270.

Currency: Djibouti Franc.

Former Colonial Status: French Territory (1896–1977).

Independence Date: June 27, 1977.

Chief of State: Hassan Gouled Aptidon, President.

National Flag: A white triangle upon which is centered a red star (at the staff) inserted into two broad horizontal stripes of dark blue and green.

The Republic of Djibouti is a tiny, sun–blistered pocket of land strategically located at the entrance to the Red Sea. The only reason for its separate existence as a colony was the deep, natural harbor at the city of Djibouti, through which Ethiopian exports and imports traveled overland since the beginning of the century. The desert country of the interior is parched and bleak, an irregular landscape seen infrequently by other than the nomadic herdsmen who pass through. It has been said that this area is even too hot for the devil.

History: The Republic of Djibouti was undoubtedly a focal point of African–Asian migration and travel for centuries. For details of early and colonial history, see Historical Background and *The French in Africa.*

France, after granting all of its remaining African colonies independence in 1960 did not concern itself with this remaining African territory until 1966. The late French President Charles de Gaulle visited late in that year, and was greeted by noisy demonstrations on the part of the Issa people of Somali ancestry. A plan was announced whereby a referendum would be held in 1967. The voting rolls were restricted because France feared that thousands of nomadic Somalis might show up at the polls; all persons had to have proof that they had been residents of the colony.

This favored the Afars, a people of Ethiopian derivation found mostly in the city of Djibouti. The Ethiopian government favored continued French control in order to insure access to Djibouti; the Somali Republic favored independence and even more— it wished to incorporate the territory, then known as French Somaliland, into its Republic.

The official result of the referendum favored continued French control. The Issa leaders immediately boycotted the initial meetings of the territorial government and the Afar members passed a resolution that the colony be renamed *The Territory of the Afars.* This was modified in Paris to "The French Territory of the Afars and Issas."

President Hassan Gouled Aptidon

Pressures for independence continued to mount during the ensuing years. All nations involved (France, Ethiopia and the Somali Republic) eventually agreed that there should be independence, but no one was able to come up with a formula agreeable to the inhabitants of the territory.

Violence erupted in the territory on several occasions in 1975–1976, including the kidnapping of a school bus full of French children and the killing of militant partisans. Ali Aref Bourhan, President of the Governing Council since 1967 and leader of the *National Union for Independence,* an Afar, lost his majority in the Assembly because of the turbulence.

In a referendum held in May 1977 the people overwhelmingly and peacefully voted for independence, which was granted. An assembly consisting of 33 Issas, 30 Afars and 2 Arabs was chosen from a single list. Elections since then have resulted in a continuation of Issa domination.

Defense has remained the responsibility of France; about 4,000 troops are maintained, principally to safeguard the important port facilities.

The president was re–elected in 1981 and 1986 by majorities of over 90%; this was reduced to 60% in 1993 when opposition parties and candidates were allowed to run. His opponents claimed the latest contest was "the object of massive fraud and riddled with serious incidents."

Fighting of varied intensity with a rural, Afar–led rebel group *(Front for the Restoration of Unity and Democracy— FRUD)* has continued since late 1991 in spite of efforts by President Gouled to include a number of Afars in his cabinet and notwithstanding repeated French attempts at mediation. Divisions within *FRUD* during 1994 further dimmed the possibility for an end to hostilities.

Culture: The city of Djibouti is distinctly French in atmosphere; about 24,000 Europeans live in the capital, including the French military force and dependents. Fearful of violence after independence, some of the former European residents departed. Djibouti is a very clean city, but it, like other African cities, is surrounded by squalid shanties on its fringes. In the interior, the people live in the uncontrolled solitude which they prefer.

Economy: Traditionally a fueling station for ships of every nation plying the Suez route to India and East Asia, Djibouti suffered greatly when the canal was closed from 1967–1975, but there since has been renewed commercial activity. Commerce has not regained its previous levels since Ethiopia attempted to divert foreign trade through its (pre–Eritrea) port of Assab, just north of Djibouti, on the Red Sea. Traditional exports, such as coffee from Ethiopia and locally produced hides are now minimal due to drought conditions. Without an annual subsidy from France, in amounts of $2 to $7 million, Djibouti would go bankrupt.

Development of deep water harbor facilities, Intelsat and Arabsat stations, will increase the strategic importance of this tiny nation.

Ethiopian refugees have severely burdened the county. In April 1989 more rainfall drenched the country in three days than it usually receives in a year; severe flooding resulted, requiring extensive foreign aid.

The Future: The transition to plural politics was relatively smooth in Djibouti. The end result, however, pits tribe against tribe—Afars and Issas.

The State of Eritrea

Downtown Asmara

Photo by Veronica Rentmeesters

Area: 93,679 sq. km. = 40,800 sq. mi. (larger than Maine).

Population: 3.6 million (estimated).

Capital City: Asmara (Pop. 400,000, estimated).

Climate: Generally dry, moderate to chilly in the central highlands; hot and dry in the desert regions, hot and humid along the coastline.

Neighboring Countries: Sudan (North and East); Ethiopia (South); Djibouti (Southeast).

Official Language: None.

Other Principal Tongues: There are nine local languages which are the same as the groups speaking them except for To Bedawi (Hadareb) and Arabic (Rashaida). Arabic and English are often used on official letterheads; Trigrinya is prevalent in the southern areas.

Ethnic Background: Cushitic, divided into nine major groups: Afar, Bilen, Hadareb, Kunama, Nara, Rashaida, Saho, Tigre, Tigrayan.

Principal Religions: Islam, Christianity, both overlaid with traditional beliefs.

Chief Commercial Products: Hides and leather products, beer.

Annual Per Capita Income: About U.S. $100.

Currency: Birr.

Former Colonial Status: Italian colony (1890–1941); British trusteeship (1941–1952); absorbed by Ethiopia 1962–1991 (defeat of Ethiopian forces), referen-

dum in April 1993 resulted in total independence.

Independence Date: May 24, 1991.

Chief of State: Isaias Afwerki, President (April 1993).

National Flag: A red triangle at the pole divides a green field at the top, from a blue one at the bottom. A gold olive branch appears on the red triangle close to the pole.

Geological evidence indicates that Eritrea was a relatively flat plateau of green trees and grass prior to the arrival of

modern mankind. At an known time, massive earthquakes caused the land to change into a terrain of sharp peaks accentuated by smoldering, active volcanoes which spewed their lava freely. Although the volcanoes are now dead, the peaks remain, often rising to more than 14,000 feet, with a craggy appearance caused by lava rock formations. If the land were lower in altitude, it would be arid and closely resemble that of Sudan to the west. Instead, except for the coastal areas, the climate is moderate, with frost appearing above 11,000 feet. Variation in temperature from noon to midnight may be as much as 60 degrees.

Eritrea is semi–arid at best, and rainfall is irregular. This, combined with the rugged terrain which dominates all but the coast along the Red Sea, makes the land somewhat unhospitable and generally incapable of producing field crops. Rainfall amounts in a given year depend upon variations in the generally west to east prevailing winds. If the currents aloft are from southwest to northeast, moisture capable of generating rainfall arrives from central Africa's vast rain forest area. But if the prevailing pattern is from the northwest to the southeast, the hot winds of the Sahara and sub–Sahara, hot and dry, arrive and roast any crops that were planted.

Although almost 80% of the people are engaged in agriculture and animal husbandry, they provide Eritreans with only 70% of the calories necessary to reasonably survive. This borderline existence means starvation in years of drought; one out of every five children born does not live until its fifth birthday.

History: By Biblical tradition, the people of the horn of Africa, including Eritreans, are descendants of of the tribe of Ham, one of whose children was Cush, hence the description *Cushite*. The general appearance of the people supports this idea; they are generally Indo–European (Middle Eastern), possessing no negroid characteristics, although they have a darker complexion than Caucasians.

Nothing is known of the early Christian era history of this region. The Coptic Christian Church established outposts in Ethiopia and Eritrea in the 4th century, and Islam arrived most probably as a result of continued contact with Arabs by the first part of the 8th century. Today, the people are almost evenly divided between Christianity and Islam. Eritreans continued to live a life of unrecorded, localized independence until overtaken by the swirl of events in the late 19th century associated with Italian efforts at colonization and the efforts of Menelik II, King of Ethiopia, to assemble what became modern Ethiopia. For details of early history, see *Historical Background,* pp. 15, 35.

The Italian conquest of Eritrea and later of Ethiopia effectively created a separate identity for each although they were similar to each other. After the Italians were expelled in 1941, the British assumed control over the territory. Under pressure from the British and Ethiopia, the UN adopted a plan for the federation of Ethiopia and Eritrea in 1950; this was intended to preserve Eritrean autonomy. But Ethiopia's Haile Selassie announced a union of the two in 1952.

The UN plan was based on the assumption that the people of both areas were similar and would therefore have no objection. But a basic difference had already been the cause of a half century of conflict between the two in varying intensity. The monarchy of Ethiopia was completely entwined with the Ethiopian Coptic Church and the two institutions were conservative and stifling. The predominant leadership of Eritrea was Muslim and resented domination by Addis Ababa, which regarded the people of the North as impoverished country cousins.

As might have been expected, the forces of the Cold War chose up sides in the conflict in the early 1950s. The *Eritrean Liberation Front (ELF)* increasingly used weapons provided by the Soviets and the Chinese, and the conservative Ethiopian monarchy received massive aid and military materiel from the U.S. The armed rebellion gradually escalated into a steady warfare by the 1970s. The *ELF* was joined by the predominantly Coptic *Ethiopian People's Liberation Front (EPLF).* Both groups were marxist.

Anti–monarchy posters posters began to appear in Ethiopia and the aging Emperor Haile Selassie gradually lost his grip. The military decreed the end of his rule in 1974, but because of internal bickering, didn't take over until 1977. The military regime quickly became communist and sought Soviet aid, presenting the latter with a genuine problem: it was on both sides of an ongoing conflict between Eritrean guerrillas and the Ethiopian army. It chose what had become its Ethiopian client whereupon the rebels sought and received assistance from a wide spectrum of Islamic nations of the Middle East.

The strife continued at irregular levels, worsened by massive periodic droughts with neither side "winning." But the rebels effectively controlled Eritrea. Their fortunes improved when their struggle against the government was joined by the *Tigray People's Liberation Front (TPLF).* By 1991, Addis Ababa was threatened by the Eritrean rebels and five other factions loosely joined into a federation. The communist regime was toppled in May, leaving Ethiopia ungoverned.

A provisional government was formed in Eritrea which brought order out of chaos slowly; Eritrea functioned as an autonomous region of Ethiopia until 1993. A UN–sponsored referendum was held in April 1993 with a single question: should Eritrea be independent. The answer was a resounding "Yes!" (99.8%). A month later the formal declaration of independence was issued and elections were held. Issaias Afewerki, who had been prominent in the leadership of the *EPLF* (into which the *ELF* had merged) became the first president.

President Isaias Afwerki

Immense problems are faced by the president and the appointed State Council through which he governs. Locusts and *too much* rain ruined about 80% of the 1993 harvest, resulting in an international appeal for aid.

The *EPLF* renamed itself the *People's Front for Democracy and Justice (PFDJ)* in early 1994 and became the only political party, although others are not prohibited. The final draft of a constitution is now being prepared. A provisional government is now functioning which includes the National Assembly of 75 members.

Eritrea claimed late in 1994 that fundamentalists were trying to overthrow the government, with the backing of Sudanese troops massed at their mutual border. This accusation has not been verified.

Culture: Most of the people live in rural isolation in this mountainous land, tilling the uneven land with techniques which prevailed two centuries ago in the rest of the world. There is one major road and one railroad and thus little communication between nine major ethnic groups.

Islamic traditions predominate in most areas, but the people are otherwise quite similar. The major factor that led this nation to independence was the stifling nature of the Coptic Christian Church and resentment of the monarchy and military control in Addis Ababa. The literacy rate is moderately high (55%) and Arabic and English are favored as second languages among the educated and commonly used in commerce.

Just as religious beliefs are divided between Islam and Coptic Christian, the names of the people are half Arabic–based and half Amharic (Ethiopian).

Economy: Thirty years of rebellion and civil war, punctuated by periodic severe drought and rarer flood conditions, have limited the economy so severely it can only be termed dependent. Eritrea will depend on international aid and assistance for a decade and even a generation before it can economically enter the 20th century. By the time this happens, the 21st century will have arrived.

Light industries which developed, principally in the seaport city of Massawa during the Italian and British colonial era became inoperative during the 30–year struggle for independence. Potential natural resources with commercial value include gold, copper, potash and iron ore. The government appears to be stable and capable of making Eritrea an attractive possibility for foreign investment.

The Future: The provisional government will continue in office until 1998. The people of this new, poor nation have a unity of purpose, a rare asset on the African continent.

The People's Democratic Republic of Ethiopia

Drought in an already parched land

Area: 1,178,450 sq. km = 455,000 sq. mi. (larger than Texas and New Mexico).

Population: 42 million (census) to 54 million (estimate).

Capital City Addis Ababa (Pop. 1.5 million, estimated. Pronounced *Odd*–is *Ahb*–aba).

Climate: Hot in the lowlands, cool and invigorating in the plateau highland. There are normally two wet seasons (June–September and February–April).

Neighboring Countries: Kenya (Southwest); The Sudan (West); Somali Republic, Djibouti (East, Southeast).

Official Languages: Amharic, English.

Other Principal Tongues: Galigna, Tigregna, Somali, Arabic (Eritrea).

Ethnic Background: Semitic, Hamitic and a mixture of the two: Cushite. Principal ethnic groups are Oromo (41%), Amhara and Tigrean (31%), other smaller groups (28%).

Principal Religions: Ethiopian Orthodox (Coptic) Christianity (75%), Islam (10%), traditional tribal beliefs.

Chief Commercial Products: Coffee, hides and skins, spices and aromatics.

Annual Per Capita Income: It is doubtful that this exceeds U.S. $100.

Currency: Birr.

Former Colonial Status: Ethiopia has never been a colony in its history of almost 4,500 years. It was briefly occupied by the Italians (1936–1941).

National Holiday: National Revolution Day, September 12 (1974).

Chief of State: Meles Zenawi, Interim President (Since June 1, 1991).

National Flag: Three horizontal stripes of green, yellow and red.

168

Many centuries before the advent of modern mankind, Ethiopia was a relatively flat land of green grass and trees. Severe earthquakes occurred, causing fiery volcanos to push skyward, spewing molten lava throughout the land.

Today, Ethiopia is a land of sharp mountains rising to more than 15,000 feet. Their rough appearance is produced by volcanic rock formations. The Rift depression enters the country in the Southeast, and the majestic peaks on either side of the gorge march in parallel formation towards the Red Sea. Slightly above Addis Ababa, the mountains separate and those on the left hand proceed north to the Red Sea at Asmara in Eritrea; the right hand peaks extend towards the Somali Republic.

The rugged terrain is one of the most isolated in the world. Surrounded by desert and arid land on all sides, the mountains rise so swiftly that they are almost impenetrable. The Blue Nile, originating from the cool waters of Lake Tana, flows through a gorge more magnificent that the Grand Canyon of Arizona. This river channel, more than a mile deep and 20 miles across, is surrounded by slopes of deep green vegetation.

There are three semi–arid regions in Ethiopia: in the southeast portion, enclosed by the Somali Republic; in the northwest bordering Eritrea and the Sudan. These areas have been hard hit by the drought which has continued since 1981.

The climate of the highland plateaus and mountains is temperate and invigorating. Frost occurs regularly above 11,000 feet, where the daily range in temperature may span as much as 80° from noon to midnight.

History: For details of earlier periods, see Historical Background and *The Italians in Africa*.

Haile Selassie became emperor in 1930 and within one year promulgated the first constitution which provided for a two–chamber legislature. In reality, he retained absolute power over the affairs of Ethiopia. A short time later, the Italians mounted their invasion of the country.

Following the return of the emperor in 1941 and during the postwar period, increasing emphasis was placed on modernization of what had been a very backward nation. The constitution was amended in 1955, providing for a Chamber of Deputies of 251 members elected by universal suffrage to four–year terms of office. The Senate was composed of 125 members selected by the emperor from among distinguished Ethiopians to serve for six years.

The Crown Council, a traditional institution, included Crown Prince Asfa Woosen and the Archbishop of the Coptic Church, which had separated from the Egyptian Coptics, as well as other dignitaries drawn from the ruling class; it assisted in forming basic policy and was convened at the call of the monarch.

Further constitutional reform in 1966 gave the Prime Minister the right to select his own cabinet, subject to the approval of the Emperor. Eritrea was joined with Ethiopia in 1962 after a popular referendum, but the *Eritrean Liberation Front*, a band of Islamic guerrillas, continued sporadic battles which escalated into an armed rebellion in 1970 and has continued since that time. The rebels, estimated to then number 1,500 to 2,000, were equipped with Soviet and Chinese weapons.

Ethiopia, financed by substantial periodic grants from the U.S. and considered in the post–World War II period to be trouble–free, was conservative and ruled by a clan of wealthy landowners. The beginning of the end of this was in the 1970's when a series of natural and man–made disasters occurred. Drought gripped the nation in 1972; rising prices and unemployment, accompanied by hordes of refugees in the cities from the parched countryside provoked a widespread strike. The military, reacting to high prices, *demanded* higher salaries and started a limited military rebellion. Em-peror Haile Selassie, aged and shaken, granted a partial increase. Riots caused by lack of land reform occurred in the southern provinces; peasants demanded and seized productive plantation land owned by absentee landlords.

By 1974, anti–monarchy posters and pronouncements became commonplace. In September, the military summoned the old ruler and read him a decree ending his rule.

Ethiopia was gripped by anarchy by 1975. The revolution in Eritrea had sharply escalated and had wide popular support—the Moslem *ELF* was joined by the Coptic *Ethiopian People's Liberation Front (EPLF)*. Both were openly Marxist. Members of the old upper class were summarily executed. The military leadership constantly bickered among itself; the threat of a *coup* was continuous. The death of aging Haile Selassie of natural causes was announced. It soon was revealed that he was smothered with a pillow by an assassin sent by the Marxists; documents uncovered in 1995 indicate that he was actually strangled while in bed.

Finally, Lt. Col. Mengistu Haile Mariam took office in February 1977 as President of the Provisional Military Administrative Council. Seeking *any* explanation for all of Ethiopia's continuing difficul-

Former Emperor Haile Selassie at his desk

169

ties, he and his leftist supporters decided to blame any and all troubles on the United States.

Sensing the weakened state of Ethiopia, the Somali Republic unleashed a band of rebels (and later regular army troops) to seize the Ogaden Desert region of its neighbor—most of the people of the Ogaden are ethnic Somalis. By mid–1977 they penetrated as far as Diredawa. The Soviets stepped in and began to send massive quantities of arms and technical personnel to Ethiopia. This, however, placed the USSR in the embarrassing position of being patron and supporter of *both* sides of a war in which neither had any interest in compromise. This was brief; the Somalis ejected the Soviets from their nation.

The war was short. Following shipment of arms from the Soviets there came wave upon wave of Cuban troops—flown from Angola—to support the fledgling communist regime. By early 1978 the Somalis had been routed in disarray back across their border. Although Ethiopia warned Somalia against further guerrilla activity in the Ogaden, it continued unabated.

In the midst of chaos, the government made minimal efforts to improve the lot of the people through social reforms, especially in education, health and land distribution. It claimed the literacy rate was raised from 7% to 25%, but a more realistic figure is 15%. Nationalization of land went forward rapidly, and peasants no longer had to provide half or more of their crops to the upper–class landlords as rent. As might have been expected, the nationalization of large farms and plantations, traditional sources of external income for Ethiopia, resulted in sharply reduced revenues.

At the urging of the Soviets, efforts were started in 1981 to form a communist party—a difficult task for a nation with no tradition of political activity and where the king represented the authority of the state. In late 1984 the plunge was taken and the *Workers Party of Ethiopia (WPE)* was born, complete with a hammer and sickle flag. It was and is actually a small body of about 60,000 people, several thousand of whom were sent to the Soviet Union or East Germany for intensive training. The Politburo and Central Committee came to be completely dominated by the military.

Widespread starvation and disease in Ethiopia in 1984–1986 was officially blamed on a fierce drought which gripped the nation. Incompetence, mismanagement, corruption, coupled with continuing strife in the northern provinces with the ever–stronger rebel movements were equally, if not more, to blame. The Soviets provided arms to Ethiopia, but food contributions were minimal—the Soviets themselves were

buying 40 million tons of grain from the U.S. to make up for their own shortfall.

Although U.S. aid was initially substantial, it was criticized by the regime as insufficient. It didn't understood that U.S. law forbids aid to any foreign nation which has nationalized American property without making a good–faith effort to pay for it. The government has also grumbled about receiving aid in the form of food and medical supplies instead of dollars which could be played with by it. So, it then insisted that even food assistance be routed through the Ethiopian army. Much of it was diverted into government ''channels'' and blocked from delivery, particularly to the rebellious

Lt. Col. Mengistu Haile Mariam

northern provinces, to the point that an airlift was required. Even worse, while countless tens of thousands were starving to death, the government held a huge celebration on the tenth anniversary of the revolution at a cost estimated to be substantially more than $100 million.

In connection with its efforts against the rebels the government embarked on vast programs of ''resettlement'' and ''villagization.'' The first was intended to resettle people from the often arid north to the rainier southern regions. Illiterate and fearful, the people often fled, both before and after being moved, to Sudan and Somalia. Many were shot—in the back—while fleeing. They then lived in horrible squalor in refugee camps, where more arrivals occurred by the hundreds each week and disease was rampant, sapping what little strength the people had left. The second program was calculated to give the government more con-

trol over the people in rural, inaccessible areas so they couldn't support rebel movements. It also was intended to make the collectivization of agriculture easier. This was initially criticized by observers, who later correctly concluded this is the only lasting solution to frequent famine in this nation.

The government did not hesitate to use foreign aid to lure people into these programs who otherwise would have had nothing to do with them. As usual, with food shortages widespread, children were the first to starve, becoming living skeletons before drawing their last breath. The 17,000 Cubans had to be fed first.

The *Workers Party of Ethiopia WPE)* and Mengistu unveiled a proposed new constitution in 1986. Not surprisingly, it was almost a perfect replica of the Soviet system. This, while its mentor was retreating from communism, Ethiopia was moving toward it. In an attempt to appease rebellious tribes and factions, it provided for ''autonomous'' areas which were meaningless. The party was not popular; it actually was a small band of military elite. There was at least one attempt at a *coup* in 1986 by a dissatisfied faction in the military.

When the new constitution went into effect in 1987, it simply meant that the military had traded uniforms for civilian dress. Corruption, which had been terrible, became rampant. The regime initially allowed foreign humanitarian aid to be delivered to starving people, but announced that its own distribution system was capable of delivering foodstuffs. The opportunity to ''skim'' a portion of the food was avidly desired.

As the 1980s drew to a close, conditions rapidly worsened. The Soviets were rapidly going bankrupt and had little to spare for Ethiopia. Food aid from western countries for Ethiopia was actually being diverted to ships headed for Russia. The Eritrean rebellion escalated; when the rebels captured the seaport of Massawa, the Addis Ababa regime retaliated with aerial attacks, destroying 50,000 tons of grain destined to feed hungry people. Conditions throughout Ethiopia were grim.

Severe drought struck in 1988–9. In a crude attempt to get its hands on vital relief foodstuffs, the Mengistu regime expelled all relief organizations except the United Nations Children's Fund (UNICEF). A *coup* attempt in 1989 by the military resulted in the dismissal of about 20 generals, who were replaced by unskilled party hacks. Their arrival in the field brought all–time low military morale. In 1990, with Soviet aid at an end, Mengistu desperately tried to mend relations with the U.S. and other western nations, but was coldly received.

Six rebels groups started cooperating

The old town of Harar

171

and closed in on Addis Ababa and entered the city in May 1991. The army, consisting principally of raw teenage recruits, had no will to fight against the determined rebels. Mengistu, anticipating the end of his power, dispatched his wife and children to Zimbabwe, where he also was granted asylum when he fled on May 28.

Higher level government figures were told to report for detention; some did and others fled. Lower level bureaucrats were told to go back to work. In mid–June, Meles Zenawi, leader of the *Ethiopian People's Revolutionary Democratic Front EPRDF* indicated that the country was on the road to democracy. As acting president, he made a further statement that still plagues Ethiopia: there should be self–determination for all peoples in Ethiopia, and if Eritrea voted for independence it would be allowed to separate from Ethiopia.

But democracy, particularly multi–party democracy is a foreign concept in Ethiopia. Self–determination is a cherished goal, even though its benefits may be illusory at best. Since 1991, Ethiopia has been governed by a loosely–knit Council of Representatives most known for disagreement on just about everything. Regional coalitions, particularly those in the southern part of the country, 10 parties loosely joined into the *Southern Ethiopian People's Democratic Union (SEPDU)* have chafed under the domination of the Council by *EPRDF* members.

At a Paris conference (March 1993) of opposition "Peace for Ethiopia" a resolution was adopted charging there is no law and order in Ethiopia and declaring that the transitional process is not working. The Council of Representatives countered by suspending five of its members of the *SEPDU*, representing the southern Oromo people.

The statement of the Paris conference is accurate. There is not genuine central authority in Ethiopia. Stated in an over–simplified manner, there is a struggle between the central–northern leadership, principally Tigrayan, and the leaders of the south–southwest groups, chiefly the Oromo people for control of what is left of Ethiopia. Numerous other ingredients are in the boiling political pot. The transitional government, dominated by Tigrayans, shows increasing signs of becoming permanent. The government has shown itself capable of what appears to be a purge: leaders were expelled from the *EPRDF* in mid–1993 "for the good of the people."

Communist leaders are not allowed in the government and soldiers that served under the former regime must undergo re–education before serving.

Hundreds of thousands of Ethiopians who have not already dropped dead from famine face starvation. An estimated 100,000 died in 1994 and 7 million more are in the grip of famine.

Voting for the 547–seat Constituent Assembly, charged with the duty of drafting a constitution, occurred in mid–1994, resulting in a majority for *EPRDF* and ethnic Somali allies. The basic question was whether Ethiopia would be a federation of sovereign states or a unified nation under a central government. The compromise provided both: a central government, and regional autonomy, including the right of secession. Nine states were created in the document, including one large one joining 45 ethnic groups in southern Ethiopia.

Culture: The Ethiopian people (except the youthful, radical students) have traditionally been basically conservative and backward. The Coptic Church is the state church, and although the communist regime tried to downgrade it, that effort was unsuccessful after being met with stiff resistance. About 75% of the people identify with the church and most remain active members. The liturgies and ceremonial practices are very old and quite intricate.

The people range in complexion from quite light to dark, the latter predominating. In the extreme south there are some Negroid characteristics noticeable which are absent in the central and northern region.

Higher education was in English until 1965 when it was changed to Amharic; it now is English. The several colleges were

A young cattle herder drives his charges past a sign indicating 4-wheel drive only on the Diredawa road.

172

An Ethiopian newspaper in the Amharic script

gathered together in 1964 to form the Haile Selassie University which attracted students from all Africa. Standards declined seriously during the years of what was called communism. The people in general were culturally unprepared for the strong dose of marxism–leninism that the regime attempted to impose. Ethiopia was held together by a feudal system in which an elite owned almost all valuable land, passing it from one generation to another. Fields were rented to the poor under the Ethiopian equivalent of share–cropping. With the advent of communism, the elite and their money emigrated swiftly, and the poor left behind adapted to communal ownership of the land very poorly. The "villagization" plan was a failed effort to get them off the land into communes. Those resisting the program were shot dead, most frequently in the back.Lacking any allegiance to a feudal overlord, it was thought the average Ethiopian would look to the communist leadership for authority. Instead, most looked to tribal, regional leaders, a pattern that plagues Ethiopia today.

Ethiopian food is quite varied and includes ingredients found in no other cooking. Immigrants to the U.S. carried recipes with them that are enjoyed by many in fine restaurants.

Television is widely available in the cities, and was used by the communists attempting to spread propaganda. When it works (electrical service is sporadic), programming is primarily re–runs of American and British shows now.

A number of Ethiopian *Falashas*, Ethiopian Jews with a history probably going back to the Old Testament period, practiced a crude form of Judaism and were believed by some to be a "lost tribe" of the ancient Hebrews. They were clandestinely airlifted to Israel, where they encounter racial problems not unlike those of the *Sephardic* (Mediterranean) Jews, who are generally looked down upon by Jews of European descent (*Ashkenazem*).

Economy: Under the Emperor, the Ethiopian economy was a national one, supported by feudal landowners who also served as lower–level tax collectors. This structure was wiped out by the arrival of the military–"communist" government, and was "replaced" by a teeming bureaucracy of incompetents unable to cope with the most ordinary problem. To help combat widespread famine which resulted from the economic downturn, liberals worldwide organized a global semi–rock concert "Live Aid" with its memorable song "We Are the World." The resulting funds were turned over to a government known for its skill of fostering famine and human rights violations at the same level as the *Khmer Rouge* of Cambodia.

A steady stream of foreign humanitarian aid has been no substitute for agricultural production, which has dropped to one–third of its pre–communist level in Ethiopia. When frequent drought is added to the picture, it is a tragic nightmare. The latest drought alarm was in December 1993; massive aid was necessary to avert starvation of more than a million people.

Programs are underway to split up massive state farms which had replaced the plantations of the elite, but they are being split up into economically impossible 2–1/2 acre plots, which only produce enough for those living on the plots a meager amount of food which is cultivated by hand. During years of drought, of course, it produces little or nothing.

Internal squabbling among the factions of the Council of Representatives has prevented any unity of purpose in the government. Until this is achieved, no economic progress will be made. Ethiopia desperately needs foreign agricultural technologists and economists to assist with government planning and introduction of modern techniques of food production.

Ethiopia's concerns over being landlocked following the independence of Eritrea were eased by assurances that its access to the port city of Assab would continue.

The Future: The domination by leaders of the northern–central people of Ethiopia will continue. The "balance of power" is narrow enough to ensure at least ten years of misery for the Ethiopian people. The practical effect of the right of states to secede is an unknown part of the future of Ethiopia. Until the effect of this is apparent, Ethiopia will not be a wise place in which to invest.

Carrying a water jug

173

The Republic of Kenya

Among the world's greatest athletes

Area: 582,750 sq. km = 225,000 sq. mi. (larger than twice the size of Nevada).

Population: 25.3 million (estimated).

Capital City: Nairobi (Pop. 1.5 million, estimated).

Climate: Hot and dry in the area from the Tana River to the north and northeast; hot and dry, but with a short rainy season in the southeast area below the Tana River; temperate and usually moist in the central highlands and southwestern grassy plains, with two wet seasons.

Neighboring Countries: Tanzania (South, Southwest); Uganda (West); Sudan (Northwest); Ethiopia (North); Somali Republic (Northeast).

Official Language:s KiSwahili, English.

Other Principal Tongues: KiSwahili is almost universally spoken. English is widely known and is the educational language. Other dialects include the Bantu tongues of the Kikuyu, Kamba and Maru tribes; the Nilotic dialects which include that of the Luo; Nilo–Hamitic dialects are those of the Nandi, Masai, and Suk groups.

Ethnic Background: Kikuyu, Kamba and Meru (Bantu); Luo (Nilotic); Nandi, Masai and Suk (Nilo–Hamitic); Cushites and Somalis (Hamitic–Semitic).

Principal Religions: Christianity (60%,) Traditional tribal beliefs (24%); Hindu (1%); figures are approximate.

Chief Commercial Products: Tea, coffee, petroleum products, sisal, pyrethrum, meat and dairy products.

Annual Per Capita Income: About U.S. $350.

Currency: Kenya Shilling.

Former Colonial Status: British Protectorate (1895–1963).

Independence Date: December 12, 1963.

Chief of State: Daniel T. arap–Moi, President.

National Flag: Three horizontal stripes of black, red and green; a shield with two crossed spears is in the center.

Lying immediately below the heart of Africa on the east coast, Kenya extends from the Indian Ocean to the lake region of East Africa. North of the winding Tana River, there is an arid countryside which slowly rises to the southern mountains of Ethiopia. The lack of rainfall in this half of the country has produced a semi–desert type of land the same as is found in the Somali Republic.

South of the Tana River, the coastline is hot and oppressively humid—this is the only part of Kenya that is truly tropical. This gives way immediately to a thorn-bush country of gently rising land extending about 175 miles from the coast.

The south central portion of Kenya is a beautiful land of high plateaus stretching between the mountains. Mount Kenya, in this area, reaches a height of 17,040 feet 80 miles north of Nairobi. The Gregory Rift, extending in an almost straight line to the south from Lake Rudolf, is an immense trench almost 3,000 feet lower than the mountains which enclose it.

From the western side of this rift formations, the land slowly descends to the shores of Lake Victoria. The cool climate of the southeastern and south central areas is invigorating—though the Equator divides these regions from northern Kenya, the climate is temperate because of the altitude. These are normally fertile lands; it is frequently possible in many sections to harvest two crops each year. Intermittent drought since 1982 has sharply curtailed production of foodstuffs.

History: Arab traders called on the coast of Kenya for an undetermined time, establishing a community in the 8th century which remains to this day. Portuguese mariners landed in Kenya as early as 1498, seeking a sea route to the Far East. Colonial activity in this area was by the British and Germans; for details of early and colonial history, see Historical Background, *The Germans in Africa* and *The British in Africa*.

Elections conducted in May 1963 resulted in an overwhelming victory for the *Kenya African National Union (KANU)* led by Jomo Kenyatta. Under pressure from this majority, Britain recognized the independence of Kenya; although initially a part of the British Commonwealth, Kenya adopted a republic form of government in 1964.

Elections in 1966 gave an overwhelming majority to *KANU*; the *Kenya People's Union* led by Oginga Odinga, who had been expelled from *KANU*, won only a handful of seats. Internal rivalry in *KANU* after the elections led to a reorganization of the government. Charging Odinga with communist sympathies, Kenyatta jailed him.

Under continuing pressure, particularly from the Luo people, Kenyatta (a Kikuyu) released Odinga (a Luo) and in an effort to placate the opposition, he appointed another Luo as Minister of Finance.

Elections were scheduled for 1969, to be contested by candidates from *KANU* and *KPU*. This plan was abandoned when the finance minister was assassinated in July 1969 by a Kikuyu tribesman; the Luo rioted before and after his funeral, causing severe unrest.

The murder of the cabinet officer was symbolic of increasing tensions between the Kikuyu and the Luo. Although denied and ignored by the government, administration of *Mau Mau* type oaths (see colonial history) had been resumed. Bands of Kikuyu gangs had been attacking Luo people and engaging in other acts of terrorism.

Faced with the threat of serious unrest, Kenyatta threw Odinga back into jail, where he remained for most of the time until Kenyatta's death in August 1978. Things continued rather evenly in Kenya, with Kenyatta exercising vise–like control. *KANU* was the only legal party. But even within it, there was criticism of the aging leader.

Members of *KANU* in parliament spoke openly in Parliament (but never by name—critical remarks always referred and still do to "some people" or "they," etc.). Kenyatta proceeded to arrange the ambush and assassination of one of its most persistent opponents. In spite of a barrage of radio propaganda, the Parliament investigated (to the extent it wasn't blocked or hampered by the police). A report critical of the government was adopted in spite of Kenyatta's disapproval. Some of the dissidents were arrested and expelled from the parliament.

President Kenyatta died suddenly in August 1978 and was immediately succeeded by Vice President Daniel T. arap–Moi (pronounced *moy)* who was duly elected in his own right in November 1979 to a five–year term. In mid–1982 a group of Air Force officers attempted to overthrow the government, blaming worsening economic conditions on the Moi regime. But the base was cleverly infiltrated by loyal government troops claiming to be in sympathy with the *coup* leaders; once inside the base they simply shot the rebels. There was massive looting following the news of the attempted takeover; over 100 people were killed and many hundreds were wounded. Final executions of officers occurred in 1985.

President Moi disbanded the Air Force and closed the University in Nairobi where student supporters of the *coup* were numerous, opening it so the students could complete their year the following April. Odinga remained in prison, finally being released in 1983. His son, Raila Odinga, is now in jail.

Premature elections were called by *KANU* and held in September 1983; Moi was the only candidate for president. There were multiple candidates for the seats in parliament which were hotly contested, and more than 40 deputies were replaced.

Drought and semi–drought conditions since 1982 have plagued Kenya. This, coupled with lingering ethnic distrusts and differences has made governing difficult. The urban Kikuyus of Nairobi criticize Moi for cronyism because of his inclusion of fellow Kalenjin tribesmen within the government.

The border with Tanzania was opened in 1983; tense relations in the past led to the dissolution of the East Africa Union with that country and Uganda. The union furnished important economic and transport services to all three.

Kenya was a one–party nation after independence until 1992. One had to be a member of *KANU* to work for the government. President Moi was at first generally popular in spite of frequent charges of human rights violations. These created an international stir in 1986–8; vitally needed foreign aid was threatened. In addition to potential drought, Kenya must deal with four other major problems. The birth rate (resulting in a population increase of 4% a year) must come down, but this is almost an insurmountable problem.

Second, world coffee stockpiles are accumulating which threaten lower prices. Third, Kenya's famous game parks have fallen onto hard times. They are expensive, overcrowded with tourists and staffed by corrupt political hacks for the most part and their physical condition is declining seriously because of insufficient funding. Ever–present game poaching has seriously depleted the elephant herds that have been a star attraction in the past. A magnificent total of 37,000 of the majestic beasts in 1970 has been reduced to fewer than 5,000; corrupt game wardens and starving poachers armed to the teeth, willing to attack even tourists, are responsible. Ivory is sent to the Far East via Burundi and Middle East Arab na-

Carrying water home

A pride of lions in safari country, Kenya

tions. Fourth, Kenya is politically divided; democracy all but disappeared and has not really returned. The secret ballot was abolished in favor of a "queuing" system where people have to publicly line up according to their political preferences. This led to intimidation and widespread election fraud; in some districts there was only a 20% turnout in 1988, down from the former 90%. The suspicion of coercion of people lingers. Finally, human rights violations continue and are commonplace. When the foreign minister criticized the regime for corruption, he was rewarded with a bullet in the head arranged by a prominent Moi associate and fellow Kalenjin tribesman.

The International Monetary Fund indicated that Kenyans own $2.62 billion in overseas bank accounts. But charges of corruption did not result in efforts toward reform, but rather a crackdown on dissent. Many government critics fled the country. A massive demonstration in Nairobi in late 1991, punctuated with cries of "peace" and "democracy" was met with tear gas and riot batons. The government dismissed the participants as agitators and anarchists.

Racism

U.S. Ambassador Smith Hempstone, one of Moi's most outspoken critics, was the target of charges in late 1991 which he shrugged off, accusing Moi of being guilty of undisguised racism. He reminded Moi that one of the official policies of *KANU* was the idea that the people of Kenya are *so primitive* they must have a single–party system to avert clashes between the country's 40 tribal groups.

Further protest came from international aid agencies—the International Monetary Fund, the World Bank and several creditor nations, all of which cut off money destined for Kenya. This was more than the Moi regime could stand; quietly, provisions for multi–party election in 1992 were made. In order to protect *KANU* and his own tenure, Moi immediately embarked on a course intended to divide (and conquer). Exploitation of every difference possible among the opposition had the desired effect. *KANU* would have been soundly defeated by a united opposition.

They not 'only refused to cooperate, they carefully split among themselves; this included a division with the *Forum for the Restoration of Democracy (FORD)*, which initially had wide suppport that transcended traditional tribal rivalries, including that of the Kikuyu and Luo.

In spite of last minute resignations of several reputable cabinet members, *KANU* rallied and went on to the victory in December 1992. Moi personally campaigned vigorously. For added insurance, his people in the legislature rammed rodded through a constitutional amendment providing that in order to be elected, a presidential candidate would have to win at least 25% of the vote in five of the seven districts. Since he and his Kalenjin tribesmen controlled the western mountain district and other significant areas through political patronage, this virtually assured that none of his three principal opponents stood a chance. Had they united behind one candidate and one issue (down with Moi) they would have won.

The result was Moi, 36%, three princi-

pal opponents (25%, 19.5%, 17.5%—a total of 63%). The election was tainted by widespread violence and intimidation. The election judge, a party hack, was bought off. Notwithstanding the fact that 63% voted against him, he reveled in the "victory." (At the same time, an outdated electoral process in the U.S. produced a president who received 43% of the vote.)

In the legislature, things were more realistic. *KANU* elected 95 delegates to 88 for the opposition. However, riots broke out on the opening day in 1993; Moi simply dissolved the legislature rather than face such vocal opposition, the first in a decade. The International Monetary Fund, infuriated by the printing of special shillings to finance *KANU's* effort in the election, imposed more rigid conditions on future loans, a move that was dismissed by an enraged Moi. But by late 1993–early 1994 differences between Kenya and the Fund, as well as other sources of foreign aid and income, had been resolved; money is now flowing again to this nation.

The group Africa Watch has correctly charged that human rights violations multiplied during and after 1992 as a result of the regime's "deliberate manipulations" by Moi and his "inner circle."

Oginga Odinga had joined in 1991 the opposition coalition *FORD*. Although initially promising, the group split along Luo (Odinga) and Kikuyu (Kenneth Matiba), permitting Moi to easily win the 1992 elections. Odinga died of natural causes in early 1994. Although Smith Hempstone is no longer ambassador, he speaks frequently in opposition to Moi.

Culture: The Kikuyu and Luo tribal customs dominate most of rural Kenya— these are two of the largest and oldest groups in eastern Africa. The Kenyans are for the most part intensely loyal and place great value on an oath or promise, regarded as semi–sacred obligations. They are very industrious and have succeeded in maintaining the high level of agriculture introduced during the colonial period by White farmers after an initial post–independence setback.

Persons of Indian descent live in Nairobi and Mombasa. They control over half the trading and commerce even though they are about 1% of the population. The large cities are modern; luxury hotels in Nairobi have attracted large numbers of tourists, although at very expensive rates for deteriorating accomodations. The invigorating climate, the excitement of the big game hunt either with gun or camera and the wide variety of flora and fauna formerly made this one of the most interesting countries of Africa to visit.

KiSwahili was adopted as the official language of Kenya in 1974, but English, particularly in education, is of equal importance. About 40% of the population is literate.

Tradition in Kenya is that virility of the men in most societies is measured by the number of children they father. Further, the women and children of age do the vast majority of the work in the fields. Men lead a rather leisurely existence, for the most part, gathering in marketplaces to debate and quarrel over little or nothing most of the day. The birthrate of more than 4% is little diminished by international birth control assistance and is resisted vigorously by custom and the Catholic Church. Girls frequently are pregnant at the age of 12, and live only to work unbelievably long hours and bear more children, totally submissive to their husbands.

One unfortunate result of the above is street children—Nairobi has an estimated 30,000 of them. They beg, steal and engage in prostitution to eke out an existence. Efforts to educate and change them have had very little success.

Economy: Having meager mineral resources, the economy of Kenya has traditionally rested on agriculture and tourism. The adverse effects of pre–independence strife have been largely overcome and increasing amounts of light industry are being located in Kenya. The fertile highlands produce coffee and tea which traditionally have dominated exports of Kenya. Both Britain and the U.S. have maintained programs of aid to assist in economic development.

Prior to 1979, contrasted with neighboring countries, Kenya was relatively prosperous—at least for the clique of politicians and businessmen who control the nation's wealth. A world oil "shortage"

A young Masai herdsman

Courtesy: Jon Markham Morrow

with sharply increased prices followed by a world–wide recession shook the economy, followed by drought in 1982. After that year, the fertile central highlands received less than 30% of the usual rainfall and the crops simply dried up. The government issued a plea for 1 million tons of corn. Aid came from external sources, but did not reach the drought–plagued northwest where there was the most need. Government corruption siphoned off far too much of that which was received.

A dramatic reversal occurred in 1985–86 coupled with tumbling oil prices and steeply rising coffee prices, producing a temporarily brighter future for Kenya. But the world surplus of coffee soon defeated this. A time bomb is ticking: by 2000 the 7 million strong labor force (non–government) will double. But at the present rate, only about 3,000 new jobs appear each year.

A heavy external debt of more than $6 billion requires too much of available resources to just make interest payments. Stringent economic belt–tightening required by the IMF has been cast irresponsibly to the winds. The Moi regime perceives the austerity measures of the Fund as a transparent attempt to end its vise-like grip on Kenya. An example of what is considered economically important is found in the *Uhuru* ("Freedom") Park in

Nairobi—it has a 60–story building nearby, replete with a four–story statue of you know who.

The drought has sporadically reappeared since the mid–1980s, taking a heavy toll on the economy. This is one of the last places on earth in which to put investment funds under present conditions. Indeed, if goods are shipped to Kenya, it would be wise to have payment in advance before the ship is unloaded at Mombasa—in hard, foreign currency backed up by foreign bank deposits.

An $87 million+ "international airport" is scheduled to be constructed at Eldoret, in the heart of the homeland of President Moi. Most regard it as an unfunded white elephant.

The Future: Arrogant and overbearing, President arap–Moi is nevertheless the glue that holds Kenya together. Upon his departure from natural or other causes, this country may well become the scene of widespread tribal conflict. The Kalenjin associated with the Moi government, who universally have used bribery and corruption as an adjunct of government will flee Nairobi. "Resettlement of Refugees" will mean continuation of measures intended to block political opposition from the Kikuyu and Luo people.

President Daniel arap–Moi addresses a gathering

The Somali Democratic Republic

The National People's Assembly, Mogadishu

Photo by Ali Abdi Addaue

Area: 637,140 sq. km. = 246,000 sq. mi. (slightly larger than Texas).

Population: 9.2 million (estimated).

Capital City: Mogadishu (Pop. 500,000 +/−).

Climate: Hot, with scarce and irregular rainfall and frequent droughts.

Neighboring Countries: Djibouti (Northwest); Ethiopia (West); Kenya (Southwest).

Official Language: Somali, Arabic.

Other Principal Tongues: Italian, English.

Ethnic Background: Darot (North–Northeast); Hawiya (central area); Rahanwein (South); Ishaak (North Central area); all of the foregoing are collectively referred to as Somali (85%); Bantu derivation (14%).

Principal Religion: Islam (Sunni sect), state religion.

Chief Commercial Products: Livestock, skins and hides, bananas.

Annual Per Capita Income: Negligible.

Currency: Foreign currencies.

Former Colonial Status: The North was a British Protectorate (1897–1960); the South was an Italian Colony (1892–1941); British administration (1941–1949); Italian Trust Territory (1949–1960).

Independence Date: July 1, 1960.

Chief of State: None since late 1991.

National Flag: A five–pointed white star on an azure blue background.

The Somali Republic, the easternmost nation of Africa, covers an area often referred to as the *Horn of Africa;* it has a 1700–mile coastline on the tropical waters of the Gulf of Aden and the Indian Ocean. Although the northern part of the country is hilly, reaching altitudes of 4,000 feet, the larger portion to the south is a flat, semi–arid land which is uni-

formly hot. But for the presence of sporadic rainfall, this land would be as oppressive as the central part of the great Sahara Desert. The endless expanses are covered with large volcanic boulders and stones having a sponge–like appearance, lying on a soil that resembles red dust. During the "dry season" when there is utterly no vegetation, these rocks absorb the heat of midday, which brings their temperature often to more than 150°F. There is no activity to be seen on the land during the daytime of this semi–arid area—both man and beast wait for the cool of the evening to travel and hunt.

Acacia trees, with their roots reaching far into the land to obtain precious water, spread their umbrella–like foliage, shading portions of the otherwise shadeless, vacant countryside. Goats and antelope must stand on their hind legs to reach their precious food from these trees. There are periods of rain which produce a cover of green grass and vegetation punctuated by widely scattered termite mounds which reach heights of 15 feet.

The locusts which invaded Egypt at the time of Joseph and his brethren probably came from Somalia, since this is one of the major breeding grounds of the African locust. The frankincense and myrrh carried to the cradleside of Christ by the three Eastern Kings possibly came from Somalia, where these aromatic woods are found today.

History: Although tradition holds that the ancestors of the Somali people, of Hamitic–Cushitic origins, lived in this region of Africa more than 2,000 years ago, the earliest traces of people date to the 7th century A.D. The Koreishite Kingdom was established at that time by a group of people from nearby Yemen. For details of early and colonial history, see

Historical Background, *The Italians in Africa* and *The British in Africa.*

After World War II the United Nations again divided the territory into two trusteeships—British in the North and Italian in the South, to continue for a period of ten years. Elections were held in British Somaliland in 1960 which resulted in a request for independence so the area could become united with Italian Somaliland, shortly to become a free nation. The two joined on July 1, 1960 to form the Somali Republic.

The constitution provided for a Moslem, native Somali president at least 45 years old; if married, his wife also had to be Somali. He and the National Assembly of 124 members had a six–year term of office.

The *Somali Youth League,* which controlled the nation since independence, won 1967 elections and Dr. Rashid Ali Shermarke became president. Political calm disappeared when he was murdered

in October 1969 by a police officer. Within a few days the army seized control of the Republic, installing Major General Mohamed Siyad Barre as Chairman of the Supreme Revolutionary Council. He was a large, energetic man constantly on guard against the ambitions of younger officers.

The regime took some leftist moves, including nationalization of foreign interests, such as oil–marketing companies. Closer ties were established with the Soviet Union and charges were leveled that the Somalis had allowed the installation of a Soviet refueling and missile station at Berbera—charges vehemently denied, although inspection (to the extent possible) revealed the accuracy of the charges.

By March 1977 there appeared to be a widening gulf between Somalia and the Soviet Union, and the Somalis began to turn to the west. President Siyad Barre had made it clear that anyone who stood in the way of the "unification" of the Somali people was an enemy. The crux of the matter was that Ethiopia's Ogaden Desert region, which juts into Somalia, was largely peopled by ethnic Somalis. At first there were some guerrilla skirmishes in the region, and finally in May 1977, a force of some 5,000 men of the *Western Somali Liberation Front (WSLF)* poured over into the Ogaden. As the weeks wore on, it became clear that the Somali army was standing shoulder–to–shoulder with the *WSLF* guerrillas; the combined military effort penetrated deep into the Ogaden and threatened some of Ethiopia's larger cities. Ethiopians fell back in disarray in the face of the Somali onslaught, but the fighting was intense and the Somali troops were slowed down.

The whole picture changed in a few weeks. In late 1977 the Soviet Union began to airlift military supplies into Ethiopia as well as thousands of technicians. Cuban troops poured into Ethiopia and the tide of warfare completely reversed. An estimated 17,000 Cubans were fighting alongside the Ethiopians.

Somali appeals for western help fell on deaf ears except for non–military aid such as food supplied by the United States. The foreign policy of the U.S. was in disarray; at the same time ex–President Carter was making feeble protests about the Soviet and Cuban assistance to Ethiopia, UN Ambassador Andrew Young of the United States was praising the contribution to that country made by the communists.

By mid–March 1977 the Somalis had been hurled back over their borders and the Ethiopians gave warning that if the government allowed the *WSLF* to continue its guerrilla activities from within Somali borders, Ethiopia would be forced to penetrate into Somalia. By early June 1978, the United States was preparing to send the Somalis arms for strictly defensive purposes.

There were reports in December 1979 that Somalia had offered the United States limited use of the former Soviet naval base at Berbera—hotly denied by the Somali authorities. However, in 1980, the U.S. began reconsidering its ban on military supplies in view of the urgent need for bases in the turbulent Middle East. Support materiel was granted to Somalia—radar, trucks and non–military aircraft. The U.S. did not wish to become embroiled in the ongoing Ogaden dispute.

After 1982 a mounting presence of regular Somali forces was evident in the desert area; refugees, mainly women and children, fled to Ethiopia. As the strife died down slowly, efforts were made in 1984 and afterwards to resettle Somali refugees among the general population. This task was complicated by ongoing drought conditions. Living in tent and shack communities, they have had less than a 50% chance of survival. Continuing and varying relief efforts from a large number of international sources did not provide the results intended.

President Siyad, probably in his late seventies, was seriously injured in an automobile accident in mid–1986. In spite of a slow recovery, he retained his office, naming close associates to handle the day–to–day business of the government. He was reelected in 1986 to another seven–year term.

Siyad was able to negotiate an informal peace in the Ogaden region with Ethiopia's Mengistu. When Somalia relinquished any claim it might have had to the Ogaden, the Somali Isaak people of that region rose in rebellion after they had been forced from the area. As many as 90,000 were killed or wounded in the conflict. The U.S., not understanding the conflict, initially sent guns and ammunition, and later hospitals to treat the wounded. Military aid was ultimately withdrawn in 1988 because of human rights violations.

What had initially been a low–level rebellion degenerated into inter–clan warfare. President Siyad was driven from the presidential palace and fled to Kenya. Although a businessman was technically named interim president, Somalia was gripped by anarchy.

The years after 1987 were poor; there was drought with intermittent flooding causing severe losses of life, particularly in rural areas.

Rendering aid to Somalia's poor and starving in the 1980s and 1990s has been complicated by the general lawlessness. Although inter–clan rivalry was the primary cause of strife, a second was the emergence of groups of uneducated boys and young men who only know how to wield arms. Gathered in small gangs, some of which allied themselves with one

Somali nomads, who let their hair grow until married (left) and have it cut when married.

A Somali newspaper

Xidigta Oktoobar

Waa Wargeys maalin walba ka soo baxa Wasaaradda Warfaafinta iyo Hanuuninta Dadweynaha ee J.D.S.

Waxaana lagu daabacaa W.MQ., Qlimihiisuna waa 10 Sh. So., Tel. 21057 - 21012 - 20865 - S.B. 1178 - Muqdisho

ISNIIN 18ka Jannaayo 1988

Tusaalooyinka Madaxweynaha

Barnaamijka Cusub ee Hawlgalka Xisbiga Hantiwadaagga Kacaanka Soomaaliyeed, ujeeddadiisu waxay tahay la dagaallanka asluubxumida, caddaalad-darrida, sinnaan la'aanta eexda, laaluushka, iyo xatooyada xoolaha Qaranka, meelmarintiisuna ay tahay waajibaad saaran muwaadin kasta.

(Jaalle Siyaad)

Xoghayaha Guud ee XHKS oo ka warramay sida dhibaatooyinka dhaqaale ee dunida ay u saameeyeen waddamada soo koraya oo aynu ka mid nahay

Muqdisho, 17 Jan. (SONNA) — Shirkii Hoggaannada Golaha Dhexe ee XHKS oo uu shir Guddoomiye ka ahaa, Xoghayaha

Guud ee XHKS, Madaxweynaha JDS Jaalle Maxamed Siyaad Barre ayaa shalay lagu qabtay Xarunta Dhexe ee Xisbiga ee magaalada Muqdisho.

Xoghayaha Guud ee XHKS, Jaalle Maxamed Siyaad Barre oo shirkaasi ka hadlay waxa uu ka warra-

Madaxweynaha oo qaabilay Kaaliyaha Xoghayaha Arrimaha Dibedda ee Mareykanka u qaabilsan Arrimaha Afrika

may dhibaatooyinka dhaqaale ee maanta ka jira dunida, gaar ahaan sida arrintaasi ay u saameysay dalalka dunida saddexaad oo JDS ay ka mid tahay, wuxuuna sheegay in wadliqada kellya ee looga gudbi karo duruufaha dhaqaale ay tahay in dhab ahaan loogu jeesto wax soo saar iyo shaqo adag.

Jaalle Siyaad waxa uu caddeeyay in Ummad kasta xawliga horumarkeeda uu

Jaalle Siyaad oo helay dhambaal hambalyo ah

Muqdisho, 17 Jan. (SONNA) — Madaxweynaha JDS, Jaalle Maxamed siyaad Barre waxa uu shalay dhambaal hambalyo ah oo ku saabsan sannadka cusub ka helay Madaxweynaha dalka Faransiiska Mudane Francois Metterand.

Madaxweyne Metterad waxa uu dhambaalkaa uu u soo diray Jaalle Siyaad ku yiri:— "Waxaa farxad weyn ii ah inaan kuu soo diro Madaxweynow, dhambaalkan hambalyada ah oo ku beegan sannadka cusub ee 1988ka, waxaanu kuu rajev-

---

of the clans, they virtually destroyed all possibility of working and living in Somalia. They took what they saw and wanted by force, including desperately needed foodstuffs from abroad, bartered for their necessities.

These young boys and men led a marginal existence which was made just a bit more enjoyable by *qat* a plant with mild narcotic qualities. As conditions deteriorated in the late 1980s, *qat* was increasingly obtained from the Arabian peninsula across the Red Sea. These youths slept until the afternoon, rose and purchased a bunch of leaves and twigs, chewing them avidly and getting high by late in the afternoon. They then rode about in small, appropriated military vehicles with high powered weapons to steal and rob anything or from anyone available lacking protection. Stopping only for irregular meals, this continued until the morning hours, when they collapsed wherever they were for some sleep.

By 1992, fighting was intense; anti–aircraft and machine guns were being used indiscriminately on innocent people. Communications between Mogadishu and the outside world were severed. UN efforts to impose a cease–fire were futile. Attempts to send food and medical supplies to Somalia had little success—they were stolen and sold as fast as they arrived while at the same time the country had become filled with walking skeletons who had but a few days or hours to live.

Conditions were unbelievable by mid–1992. Finally in December "Operation Restore Hope" got underway. President

Bush had offered troops to the UN Secretary General; although the UN was the nominal authority under which the force operated, it was actually from the U.S. (later joined by small numbers of troops from other nations). The scene at Mogadishu was a modern version of the Crimean War of the 19th century, when wealthy nobility gathered atop hill and mountain tops to watch troops slaughter each other on the adjacent plains. But in 1992, television cameras greeted the landing boats full of marines, providing livingroom entertainment worldwide. The marines just gritted their teeth and went about their work and the hoped–for bloodshed did not materialize to a level suitable for continued TV coverage.

It was only with difficulty that indiscriminate gunfire was ended in Mogadishu and later in the interior parts of the country. The world was greeted with TV coverage of incredibly thin, emaciated people, particularly children. Amid sporadic shooting and ambushes, food aid was provided and mass starvation was barely averted. The police force, later named UNISOM–II as technical command of it passed to the UN, had to maintain cover against clan and tribal militias which were, in turn, were fighting among themselves.

Through a process which was unclear, in the spring of 1993 the U.S. decided that Mohammed Farah Aydid (Aydeed) was the chief villain in Somalia. In just about the silliest act in modern history, it asked for and received a UN *warrant* for his arrest. A warrant is a formality of old English law which is utterly useless in this part of the world! Soldiers knocked

on doors asking for Aydid and were told he wasn't there. (He probably laughed as he sat there and witnessed such events!) A more suitable means of apprehending him would have been the quiet payment of a suitable bribe to one of his many competitors.

In the summer and fall, the effort at salvation of Somalia turned very sour. Aydid became a folk hero, denouncing the UN effort as interference in Somalia's internal affairs. But things became too hot for him, so he fled to Kenya and Uganda. The muscles of the people so wasted by starvation gathered strength and starting stoning anything foreign. UN Secretary–General Boutros Boutros-Ghali placed a $25,000 reward for the capture of Aydid. Eighteen U.S. troops on a mission to capture the fugitive were killed; the body of one dragged through the streets lit up television screens in America.

A befuddled Bill Clinton announced in October 1993 the withdrawal of U.S. troops from the UN force by March 1, 1994, a terrible mistake. Announcing intention to retire from the battlefield five months later makes all which occurs after the decision meaningless. The U.S., assuming that only Aydid could govern Somalia, requested *withdrawal* of the warrant for this dubious person. He had returned to Somalia in the spring of 1994 and was given a hero's welcome.

Following the U.S. announcement, almost all other nations contributing troops to UNISOM–II withdrew them. By mid–1994 the militias and youth gangs had resumed operations, and started kidnapping UN relief workers for ransom. The U.S. dispatched almost 4,000 marines to assist withdrawal of UN personnel in early 1995. Amid widespread shouts of "UNISOM get out!" they were successfully evacuated in March. Somalis had completely looted and stripped the buildings from which relief was distributed.

More than 100 "peacekeepers" were killed; 42 U.S. military personnel met the same fate. Millions of Somalis were fed enough to keep them alive until starvation enters the land again. The warlords again reign in ever–shifting patterns.

Culture: The vast majority of Somalis are used to a nomadic existence in this land of little rainfall. This was formerly based on ownership of camels, cattle, sheep and goats. These people do not know national boundaries and frequently were found in Ethiopia, Kenya and Djibouti, and could be identified by their common language known as Somali. Other languages of instruction in schools were Arabic, Italian and English, with the use of the latter steadily growing. The loose–fitting clothing of the people is similar to that found on the Arabian Peninsula.

Mogadishu was a comparatively mod-

180

ern city on the warm Indian Ocean and had substantial European and Arab communities which largely departed more than a decade ago. Indians and Pakistanis were the traditional merchants and traders of the city. Although the climate is generally hot, the city is pleasant during the greater part of the year. It is only during the "Tangambili" periods, when there is no cooling breeze from the sea, that it becomes extremely hot and oppressive.

Mogadishu now is a sullen city with no apparent purpose except being a distribution point for foreign aid. All buildings are pock–marked by gunfire and most are now run down. Even though thousands of weapons have been confiscated, there are replacements which are readily available. It is not a safe place in which to be found wandering about after dark. The presence of troops altered the appearance of the city, but only slightly. There was very little socializing with the native Somali population, which frequently expressed hatred toward the mercenaries, which they were. The Somalis' attitude was actually hatred of Somalia and its wretched inability to reasonably govern itself.

Although the government in the past made a stab at controlling the consumption of qat, it was unsuccessful. This narcotic is too much a part of native Somali life to even think of eradicating it or even coming close to such a goal.

Economy: Before endemic violence became a way of life in Somalia, the

Front and back of the Somali Shilling

economy was accurately termed a dependent one in which nomadic production of cattle was not sufficient to support the people and there was no other wealth or source of external income. Drought conditions for the last 20 years caused severe shortages and hardships. Agriculture is limited by scanty and irregular rainfall, and is restricted to the banks of rivers, coastal regions and a small area in the northern section. Even these portions of the country are visited by frequent droughts.

Aromatic woods, derived from a small forested area, contribute modestly to exports. Larger river plantations produced sugar for local consumption and bananas and corn for export, but they now are idle.

Assistance has come from the United States, Libya, Kuwait and the International Monetary Fund and World Bank. Most of this dried up after 1987 when conditions for further loans by the IMF were rejected. Somalia imposed its own austerity measures which were received with great hostility throughout the nation and probably caused the downfall of President Siyad Barre. Because of violence there is no economy in the usual sense of that word in this woefully poor nation.

The Future: Are the militias armed and dangerous because there is no work in Somalia? Or, is there no work in Somalia because the militias are armed and dangerous? The answer to these questions doesn't matter, because they all result in *anarchy*. Unbridled, indefinite anarchy is the future of Somalia, with acompanying starvation and suffering.

View of Mogadishu and the ocean

181

The United Republic of Tanzania

Mount Kilimanjaro

Area: 939,652 sq. km = 362,800 sq. mi. (includes the islands of Zanzibar and Pemba; as large as Texas and most of New Mexico.

Population: 27.8 million (estimated).

Capital City: Dar es Salaam (Pop. 1.5 million, estimated). Some government offices have been moved to Dodoma which is to be the new capital at an undetermined time.

Climate: Tropically hot and humid in the coastal area, hot and dry in the central plateau and semi–temperate in the highlands where cooler weather prevails as the altitude increases.

Neighboring Countries: Mozambique (Southeast); Malawi, Zambia (Southwest); Zaïre, Burundi, Rwanda (West); Uganda (Northwest); (Kenya (Northeast).

Official Languages: KiSwahili, English.

Other Principal Tongues: Vernacular dialects of 120 ethnic groups, prima-

rily of Bantu origin. KiSwahili is almost universally spoken or understood.

Ethnic Background: Tanzania has 120 distinct ethnic groups. Those of Bantu origin, constituting a great majority, include the Sukuma and Chagga people. A small number of Kikuyu live in the Mt. Kilimanjaro area. A larger group of Nilo–Hamitic origin, the Masai, live in the northern region.

Principal Religions: Mainland: Traditional tribal beliefs (40%), Christianity (30%), Islam; on Zanzibar and Pemba almost all are Islamic.

Chief Commercial Products: Coffee, cotton, sisal, cashew nuts, diamonds, cloves, tobacco, tea, phosphates.

Annual Per Capita Income: About U.S. $120.

Currency: Tanzania Shilling.

Former Colonial Status: German Colony (1885–1917); British Mandate under

the League of Nations and Trusteeship under the United Nations (1919–1961).

Independence Date: December 9, 1961.
Chief of State: Sheikh Ali Hassan Mwinyi, President. (b. 1925).
National Flag: A triangle of green in the upper left corner; a triangle of blue in the lower right–hand corner with a broad band of black between the two. These three colors are separated by narrow yellow bands.

Tanzania is a large, picturesque country lying just south of the Equator, extending between the great lakes of Central Africa and the Indian Ocean, with a 500–mile coastline. A fertile plain of up to 40 miles in width stretches along the coastline; the land slowly rises in the interior to a large central plateau averaging 4,000 feet in altitude. A mountain range of moderate height in the middle of Tanzania extends from north to south.

At the north end of these peaks, Mount Kilimanjaro rises in majestic splendor to the height of 19,340 feet—the tallest peak in Africa, which, though only three degrees south of the Equator, is capped by snow and icy glaciers year around.

Farther to the northwest, immense, fresh water Lake Victoria spreads its sparkling breadth across the semi–arid plain.

A chain of towering mountains extends along the length of the entire western border, sharply descending to Lake Tanganyika which is 2,534 feet deep. This long, narrow body of water was created centuries ago when an immense fault of land descended sharply, creating an earthquake of immeasurable proportions, and forming what is now called the Great Western Rift Valley. The large East African lakes contribute an area of 20,000 square miles of inland water to the area of Tanzania. Abundant rainfall supports dense vegetation in the coastal area, but the central plateau, hot and dry, has an average of 25 inches of rainfall per year.

In the higher elevations, cooler weather prevails and there is more abundant rainfall, produced by the rush of warm air up the high slopes of the mountains. There are many game parks which protect large numbers of elephants, buffalos, lions, giraffes and other native species. A recent aerial survey of the Serengeti National Park revealed that more than one million animals live within its confines.

History: Countless centuries ago, Persian, Arabic, Indian and Portuguese traders called at the coast of Tanzania and engaged in lively trade with the various people. The country had been settled in unknown times by large numbers of Bantus and small groups of Nilotic and Nilo–Hamitic people. For details of early and colonial history, see Historical Background, *The Germans in Africa* and *The British in Africa*.

Former President Nyerere

President Mwinyi

As a result of pre–independence elections in 1960, the *Tanganyika African National Union*, energetically led by Julius Nyerere, was installed in power. Tanganyika received independence on December 9, 1961, and within a year adopted a constitution providing for a Republic form of government. *TANU*, since renamed the *Chama Cha Mapinduzi (CCM)*, is the only political party in Tanzania; the single–chamber National Assembly consists of 120 elected members from the mainland, 24 members selected by the party, up to 32 members of the *Zanzibar Revolutionary Council* and up to 20 other members from Zanzibar appointed by the president in consultation with the President of Zanzibar. The neighboring islands of Zanzibar and Pemba were British Protectorates until they gained independence in 1963; their first government was by the Arab minority which had controlled the islands for decades. The African majority rose in bloody revolt, mercilessly slaughtering virtually all Arabs on the islands. Tanganyika and Zanzibar joined together as Tanzania in 1964 and representatives from Zanzibar joined *TANU* and became members of the National Assembly.

Initially, Zanzibar was totally autonomous. Sheik Abeid A. Karume, a crude leader, regarded the island as his personal property until he was murdered during a poker game. Life on the island was highly regimented. He was succeeded by Aboud Jumbe, who resigned under pressure in 1983 and was succeeded by Sheikh Ali Hassan Mwinyi. Although Zanzibar is nominally part of Tanzania, it is occupied by mainland military forces who are intensely disliked by the islanders.

On the mainland, the British–trained army was disbanded in 1964 and replaced by a citizen's army trained and armed by the Chinese communists. A rigid system of socialist organization has emerged. Banks and other foreign interests were nationalized in Nyerere's program labeled "African Socialism."

President Mwinyi, educated in England, is a devout Muslim born on the mainland who spent most of his life on the island of Zanzibar. He is regarded as honest and hard–working. The Chairman of the *Chama Cha Mapinduzi (Socialist Party)*, successor to *TANU*, was former President Julius Nyerere (Nee–*rare*–uh), a former school teacher who likes to be called *Mwalimu*—"teacher" in KiSwahili. He held office from independence, resigning in 1985. All candidates for the legislature in 1985 elections were members of the state party. Although the party is "supreme" over the mainland and island governments, the island technically remains autonomous. Since the constitution provides that the President and Prime Minister cannot both come from either the mainland or the island, mainlander Joseph Warioba was selected as Prime Minister.

During 1978–1979, Tanzania was involved in the internal struggles of neighboring Uganda (see Uganda).

Tanzania has done an economic U–turn away from socialism with heavy stress on state monopolies. Under these, for instance, growers of cashew nuts received only 22% of their export price, thus had little incentive to increase production. The difference was sucked up by a burgeoning bureaucracy and party officialdom. The ratio now planned is at least 60%–70%. It has been able to settle differences with the International Monetary Fund and is eligible for assistance from that source. Other economic reform measures, intended to establish a market system to replace the "planned" system are now well underway, too numerous to

Serengeti National Park

mention. At the age of 64, Nyerere retired from the party and went to live on his farm next to Lake Tanganyika.

Tanzania adopted a multi–party system in 1992, but political opposition is split into four groups, each of which had to receive permission of the regime to organize. None has a chance under present conditions to oust the ruling party in 1995 elections.

Islamic fundamentalism (which is really just anti–westernism) has made its presence felt, particularly on Zanzibar. The semi–official response was a proposal to establish separate governments for Tanganyika and Zanzibar. Even the retired president opposes the idea of yet another layer of bureaucrats.

Tax evasion became a national pastime in the 1990s, accompanied by rampant corruption in the bloated governmental force. In late 1994 Sweden and Norway threatened to withdraw aid unless these problems were dealt with, resulting in some reform moves which were actually insufficient to make basic corrections. A new Swahili word was invented to describe it which literally means "buying air."

Tanzania, with UN assistance, received innumerable refugees from the strife in neighboring Rwanda and Burundi in 1994–5, but in April 1995 closed its border, possibly in an effort to extract additional money from the UN.

Culture: The numerous tribes of proud Africans have a rich diversity of customs and traditions which contribute to the distinctiveness of Tanzania. The Kikuyus of the North extend into Kenya and are hunters and warriors. The fabled Masai,

one of the best known tribes, actually are few in number—they are highly ornamented cattle herdsmen with a singular custom of living on a diet principally of milk and blood from their cattle. Their main sport is killing lions with their spears in order to obtain material for their elaborate headdresses.

The larger group of Chaggas in the north–central plains around Mt. Kilimanjaro are an advanced, Christian people devoting their lives to business and coffee growing. Another Bantu group, similar to the Chaggas, the Sukuma, are well–educated, industrious people, constituting the largest tribal group in Tanzania.

Modern education is being extensively promoted by the government. Many students from Tanzania are pursuing advanced courses in universities located in Uganda and Europe. A program of adult education is now underway with a goal of eliminating illiteracy; literacy now stands at an admirable rate of about 85%.

KiSwahili is more and more becoming the national language and is credited with instilling a national pride within the country. Whereas most of the other former European colonies still use as their official tongue the language they inherited from them, Tanzania is an exception. The editor of an important newspaper in Dar es Salaam has been having a difficult time finding journalists qualified to *speak* and *write* in English. While KiSwahili has definitely been a major factor in unifying the Tanzanian people, English is still the "international" language, and many Tanzanians are concerned that the country will lose certain economic advantages by slowly "burying" the other official language.

The wealth derived from the export of cloves has enabled Zanzibar to provide many welfare benefits for its citizens; it became in 1974 the first place in Africa to broadcast *color* television. Notwithstanding this, Zanzibar is poverty–stricken. It may be rescued from this by a tourism program conceived by the Aga Khan of India, leader of Zanzibar's Black *Ismaili* Moslems, who has ample funds to transform this into a European tourist's winter haven.

The present capital, Dar–es–Salaam (Haven of Peace), is a majestic city of modern buildings with an incomparably beautiful beach on the warm waters of the Indian Ocean. It also is a crowded city. Merchants and traders from many other cultures have made this busy port city a "melting pot" of people. Two smaller cities, Moshi and Arusha, both lying within the shadow of Mt. Kilimanjaro, are centers of agriculture and commerce. In an effort to "open up" the interior regions of the country, centrally–located Dodoma, with a present population of about 90,000 has been selected as the new capital city. Actual transfer of the functions of government and completion of the building program to make this a reality will probably stretch over a period of ten years because of limited government funds.

The government–controlled *Daily News* is widely circulated on the mainland; publication on Zanzibar is sporadic.

Economy: The agriculturally–based economy is subject to worldwide price fluctuations. Ex–president Nyerere knew next to nothing about economics but insisted on continuous meddling. The results were disastrous. More than one–half of the farm machinery became idle for lack of spare parts. Time after time, projects have started up and then quickly failed for lack of proper operation and maintenance.

Zanzibar produces most of the world's cloves; revenue from this spice provides more than enough funding for the government. On the mainland, farms formerly owned by Europeans were nationalized with little or no compensation in order to transform them into *Ujamaa*—"extended family farms"—Nyerere's name for collective farms. Output declined, creating severe economic problems for Tanzania. A poorly conceived plan to force Africanization of all mercantile enterprises was halted shortly after it began in the face of widespread shortages of consumer goods.

China, using 20,000 militarily trained workers, built a rail line over which Zambia's copper has been shipped through Tanzania's capital. Because of lack of maintenance, the line is now in a state of disrepair. An estimated $100 million is scheduled to be used to rehabilitate the line. The U.S. provided assistance in re-surfacing roads. Although potentially self–sufficient in sugar and salt, Tanzania must import these products; a sugar mill was lost in the Uganda war in 1978 and a salt refinery is rusting because the French were not allowed to show Tanzanians how to operate it properly. Food imports in excess of $100 million a year should be unnecessary, but they are.

Ex–president Nyerere in 1984 ordered that all persons of work capability must carry identification papers showing where they live and work or else face compulsory employment on state farms. Efforts are now underway to denationalize state enterprises. Sisal production had been 220,000 tons in 1970, but diminished to 47,000 tons in 1984. It took Nyerere more than 20 years to discern that many bad mistakes had been made.

The Future: The political institutions created by Nyerere are not capable of dealing with Tanzania's problems. The constitution was amended to provide for the tabling of any impeachment resolution in the legislature. The reason: virtually every measure brought to the floor either had a section moving the impeachment of the president, or one was added. This reflects a high level of dissatisfaction and a low level of judgment of the participants.

Economic gains of 4–10% per year since 1985 sound impressive, but actually are meaningless since the base figure was $75 per capita income. No meaningful foreign investment will be available because of the persistence of Nyerere–style patterns.

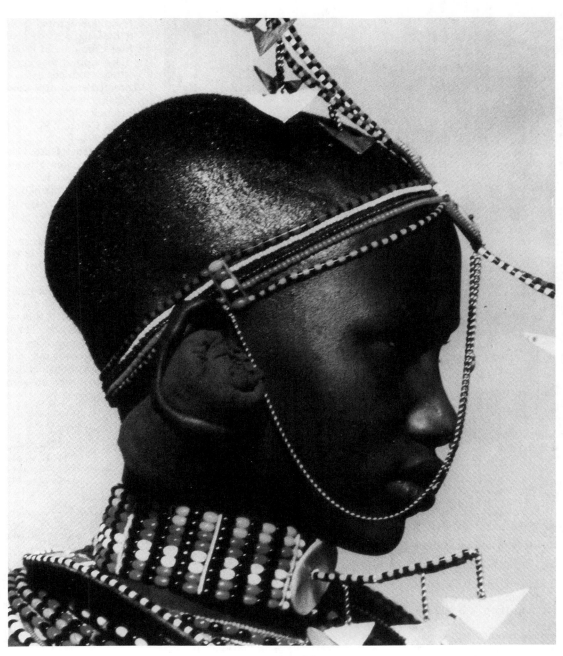

A Masai maiden

The Republic of Uganda

His Majesty Ronald Muwenda Mutebi II, King of Buganda, a traditional ruler of Uganda

been announced to make KiSwahili the official language.

Other Principal Tongues: Luganda, Lusoga, Lutoro, Lunyoro, Ateso, Luo and several other tribal dialects. Luganda and KiSwahili are widely understood and spoken.

Ethnic Background: Bantu majority, including the Baganda, Basoga, Batoro and Banyoro tribes; Nilotic in the Northwest and Southeast, including the Acholi, Lango, Alur and Luo tribes; Nilo–Hamitic in the Northeast, including the Karamajong and Iteso tribes.

Principal Religions: Christianity (60%); Traditional tribal beliefs (30%); Islam (10%); figures are approximate.

Chief Commercial Products: Coffee, cotton, copper, tea, agricultural and livestock products.

Annual Per Capita Income: About U.S. $300.

Currency: Uganda Shilling.

Former Colonial Status: British Protectorate (1894–1962).

Independence Date: October 9, 1962.

Chief of State: Yoweri Museveni. (b. 1941), President.

National Flag: Six bands of black, yellow and red (repeated) with a silver circle in the center enclosing a crested crane.

This fertile expanse of highland lies astride the Equator in central East Africa between the Eastern and Western Rift formations. Uganda, dotted with lakes, and with immense Lake Victoria on the South, lies at an altitude of between 3,000 and 6,000 feet. If this country were at a lower altitude, its climate would be hot, moist and oppressive, but it is quite pleasantly temperate with ample rainfall to support intense cultivation. In the extreme Northeast, the climate is somewhat more dry.

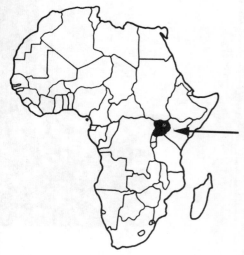

Area: 235,690 sq. km. = 91,080 sq. mi.

Population: 18.6 million (estimated).

Capital City: Kampala (Pop. 1.3 million-,estimated).

Climate: Temperate, though equatorial, because of altitudes averaging 4,500 feet with ample rainfall in most years (except in the semi–arid northwest) interrupted by two short dry seasons.

Neighboring Countries: Rwanda, Tanzania (Southwest); Zaïre (West); The Sudan (North); Kenya (Northeast).

Official Language: English. Plans have

Approximately 15% of the country is covered by fresh water. The Ruwenzori Mountains to the west divide Uganda from Zaïre, having altitudes of almost 17,000 feet. In the southwest, close to Rwanda, the Virunga range of active volcanos reaches skyward. In the East, Mount Elgon rises to a height of 14,000 feet, prominent among its neighbors of the Eastern Rift Mountains.

The Victoria Nile originates from the banks of Lake Victoria, heavily populated with hippopotomi and crocodiles, and flows to Lake Kyoga, an irregularly shaped body of water with large swamps. From there the Nile flows north and west through immense mountains to empty into Lake Albert. The Albert Nile flows northward, leaving Uganda at the Sudanese border to continue its journey of more than 4,000 miles to the Mediterranean Sea.

The great expanse of plains traditionally has been dotted with many farms and plantations, and, as is true in Tanzania to the south, wildlife of many varieties is abundant.

History: It is difficult to trace the migrations of the Bantu people whose descendants live in Uganda today. The last Kabaka (King) of Buganda, claimed to be the 37th member of an uninterrupted line of monarchs. It is not possible to determine the exact time when the Nilotic and Nilo–Hamitic groups came to northern Uganda. The evidence indicates that there was a gradual migration from the Nile Valley in the 10th–13th centuries. For details of early and colonial history, see Historical Background and *The British in Africa*.

The United Kingdom of Uganda was granted internal autonomy on March 1, 1962, becoming fully independent on October 9 of that year. The government

Milton Obote

initially consisted of a federation of the kingdoms of Buganda, Busoga, Butoro and Bunyoro, which retained local autonomy and the rest of the country was governed by the central government. Sir Edward Frederick Mutesa II, Kabaka of Buganda, became the first president and Sir William W. Nadiope, King of Bunyoro, was the first Vice–President. Prime Minister Milton Obote wielded considerable power within the central government. The cabinet was selected by a coalition of Obote's *People's Congress Party* and the *Buganda Kabaka Yekka Party;* the formerly dominant *Democratic Party* was in the minority.

The post independence era, more than 23 years long, was dominated by two figures which reduced Uganda to a grisly shambles, replete with starvation and widespread deaths. Milton Obote was the first (1963–1971, 1980–1985) and the second was a military figure, Idi Amin (1971–1979).

Charging Mutesa with making personal profits from the supply of arms in connection with a rebellion in neighboring Zaïre, Obote dismissed him and seized the government. The hereditary king barely escaped when the army stormed the presidential palace; he lived in exiled poverty until his death in 1969. His remains were ceremoniously returned to Uganda in 1971.

Obote abolished the old constitution and the traditional kingdoms; his *PCP* became the sole party and he veered Uganda sharply toward marxism–socialism. As he appointed more and more of his fellow Lango (also Langi) tribesmen to public offices in what had become an overstuffed bureaucracy, army posts and the judiciary, tensions mounted. The country was proclaimed a republic in order to permanently end the old kingdoms. Finally the army revolted, uniting behind an initially curious leader, Idi Amin.

General Amin, a massive man who had been the Ugandan heavyweight boxing champion between 1951 amd 1960, was popular at the time of his takeover of Uganda. He had an overstuffed ego, however, and wasted no time alienating just about everybody. Underneath his broad, confident smile, he was a brutal, crude, shrewd peasant. All Asians were ordered expelled from Uganda in 1972 without thought to the importance of the vital role they played as merchants and traders.

Amin's mental quirks became widely known and initial admiration quickly turned to fear. Educated Ugandans began to leave the country to escape his whims. He expelled African clergy and missionaries, claiming they were foreign agents, and completely outlawed some Christian denominations such as the Jehovah's Witnesses. Brutality became the

Idi Amin

order of the day by 1974. Secret executions, massacres and torture were among his favorite methods and he personally participated in some of these grisly acts. It was reliably reported that he even ate some body parts of the hapless victims.

Military efforts to oust him failed and the perpetrators were executed on the spot. His spies operated at every level and he became more mentally deranged. The economy all but disappeared by 1978 and the country seethed with unrest. In response to an army insurrection, Amin tried to distract attention from his shortcomings by claiming that Tanzania had invaded Uganda; he "responded" to this fabrication by having his troops invade Tanzania. They captured about 710 square miles before withdrawing.

But President Julius Nyerere of Tanzania used the invasion as an excuse to get rid of Amin. Nyerere had personally granted Obote asylum when he was driven from Uganda. The Tanzanian troops, augmented by Ugandan exiles, mounted a swift invasion. Amin's forces, demoralized by his behavior, crumbled after fierce fighting had claimed the lives of many.

The conquering army entered Kampala in April 1979 and was greeted jubilantly. In the confusion, the dictator escaped and now is living comfortably in Saudi Arabia. In elections swiftly scheduled, it appeared that Obote's *UPC* would lose. But a military figure proclaimed himself sole judge of the elections. He announced Obote the winner and immediately became his vice–president.

There ensued five years of strife, frequently inter–tribal, in which an estimated 1 million fled and 300,000 lost their lives. The end of his tumultous rule in 1985 was an act of his own doing. Obote had again promoted his fellow Lango tribesmen to positions of power, this time as army officers, principally at the expense of Acholis, who were in the military service in large numbers. The result was widespread desertion among the lower ranking officers and enlisted men to the point that Milton Obote & Company had an army consisting of many officers, few of whom were gentle men, and no troops.

Although there was a general rebellion that resulted in the ouster of Obote, it was a revolt that involved traditional tribal and clan rivalries to the extent that general chaos prevailed in Uganda from 1985 until 1987. There was a vacuum of power which in 1986 was gradually filled by the *National Revolutionary Army*, armed by Libya and led by Yoweri Museveni.

Remnants of the army from the Acholi people struggled to gain power for a year before surrendering.

Since 1987 Museveni, who became president, has been making tremendous efforts to put Uganda together again. His "troops" had been teenage boys toting machine guns and high powered weapons. The carnage in Uganda had exacted a terrible toll. Piles of skulls remained at crossroads, reminders of the grisly days since independence. Limited foreign assistance has been received, far less than was needed. Once–prosperous Uganda operated at a level less than 30% of that at the time of independence.

Why did this carnage and precipitous decline in living standards occur? In Uganda's case, it was tribalism. Five major Bantu "kingdoms" and four Nilotic groups from the western highlands, together with a few other groups, were all pitted against each other.

Uganda is now ruled by the *National Revolutionary Movement*, successor to the army of the same name. The legislature is called the *National Revolutionary Council* and consists of 210 members and 68 presidentially–appointed persons. It is broadly based, generally without regard to tribal loyalties. Uganda and Museveni have come under pressure from the International Monetary Fund to establish a multi–party democracy. Non–partisan, non–tribal elections were held in early 1994 for a constituent assembly which will draft a constitution for consideration in a later election.

Museveni believes that because of tribalism, Uganda is not prepared for a multi–party democracy. He is right. It would be better for outside sources and forces to allow Uganda to follow its own path toward a more representative form of government. In Uganda, a workable, democratic government would of necessity mean a coalition dominated by two or more tribes. But because of traditional rivalries, Ugandans do not form coalitions.

Museveni has been transforming Uganda with great difficulty from a living graveyard into the semblance of a nation. A program is aired on television each week to enable those with knowledge of atrocities of the years after independence

to explain them. They are almost always attributed to tribalism, helping the people to understand its futility. His revolutionaries, originally youngsters, have matured although still armed and potentially dangerous.

The government was threatened three times since 1986. The first was by royalists of Bugandan heritage who sought to install Ronald Mutesa, son of the former monarch and a law student in England, in power. The second came from remnants of the Nilotic people who were formerly part of the army. The third was rather unbelievable: about 5,000 followers of Miss Alice Lakwena, an Acholi priestess and witch doctor, calling themselves the "Holy Spirit Battalion," spread on their body an oil which she had concocted. It was supposed to make them bulletproof. After government troops had gunned most of them down, she escaped—presumably to improve the recipe so it will work in the future.

President Museveni

President Museveni was able to reschedule debt repayment on generous terms with European banks and to obtain credits from the International Monetary Fund. The current budget, while generous with the military, is replete with development funds which are badly needed. Shifts in the military indicated efforts to lessen corruption. The *NRC* extended its mandate effective January 1990 for five years; it now has 210 elected members from the various regions of Uganda.

In a gesture made to reward the Bagandans for their support during the 1981–6 war, the government allowed installation of Ronald Mutebi to be installed as the 36th *Kabaka* of Buganda. But the inauguration of a king of Butoro was met with disfavor; clashes were feared because of-

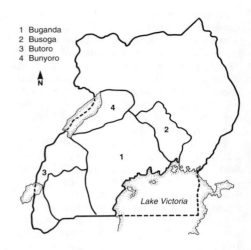

1 Buganda
2 Busoga
3 Butoro
4 Bunyoro

Lake Victoria

border disputes between the two monarchies.

A Constitutional Assembly has been working on a proposed constitution which should be released in the summer of 1995. Saying that the Assembly was taking longer than anticipated, President Museveni postponed elections from early 1995 to December, a move which generated substantial criticism. He also arranged for the document to contain a provision extending the power of the *NRM* for five years, also strongly criticized. The basic problem is whether diversity in Uganda makes it necessary to limit political development, or whether non–democratic rule foments dissent by those who favor multi–party rule.

Another consideration important to Ugandans is economic. After being reduced to the depths of poverty, the economy is working quite well. There is a

A pineaple farm near Jinja
Courtesy: Dr. Robert J. Kowalczyk

definite reluctance on the part of a probable majority of Ugandans to take any measure which could undermine economic improvement.

Culture: The Ugandan people traditionally are an industrious, intelligent and lively folk. Their distinctive local customs, including elaborate dances which are in reality drama, pertain to legends of old. Though traditionally organized into kingdoms, there is little class distinction among the people within tribal divisions, and there has been no antipathy between Europeans and African Ugandans. Although a great majority lead a rural life centered on agriculture, they are not provincial in the least. Literacy was high—more than 50%, but due to the uncertainties since independence, a more realistic figure now would be about 15%.

Drums, traditionally a widely used communication system, are used to spread news rapidly to remote areas. Urban life is centered in the capital of Kampala, 16 miles north of sparkling Lake Victoria, the site of government. Built on seven hills, this formerly busy, modern city now shows the scars of years of strife, but is slowly rebuilding.

Makerere College, officially called the University College of East Africa, is also recovering slowly from the wounds of inter–necine strife. It is chronically short of funds. Founded in 1922, its graduates have in the past assumed important positions in the governments of many African nations.

AIDS has made a dramatic appearance in Uganda, where 10% to 15% of the population is believed to be infected by the virus. Nevertheless, the use of contraceptives for safe sex is almost unheard of; Pope John Paul II preached the desirability of abstinence during a recent visit, advice which was poorly received.

Economy: Coffee and cotton constituted 95% of the value of exports in the pre–independence era and were the basis of a thriving agricultural economy. Following World War II, the government used wealth produced from these crops to expand cultivation of sugar, tea and tobacco. Livestock production is limited by the ever–present tsetse fly.

Uganda is now receiving foreign aid in amounts above that which has been requested. More important, private investment is arriving almost daily to a businessman's paradise. One Israeli investor got government approval for his business venture in three weeks. He commented that in Israel the same permission would have taken two to three years. The stability which Museveni has brought to Uganda is a very large factor in attracting foreign investment.

Indian businessmen, driven from Uganda, are now welcomed back. The currency has stabilized and inflation is a modest 5%. There is a definite potential here for a booming tourist trade based on resort and luxury hotels.

The Future: Privatization of state industries is well underway and will lead to even higher levels of economic improvement. Wages are low—$65 a month for untrained workers, but are actually comparatively high. Opposition to Museveni is so splintered he no doubt will win elections. The ultimate question is whether he will step down after serving five more years, or suddenly become indispensable.

School children singing songs of welcome to visitors   Courtesy: Dr. Robert J. Kowalczyk

SOUTH SAHARA AFRICA

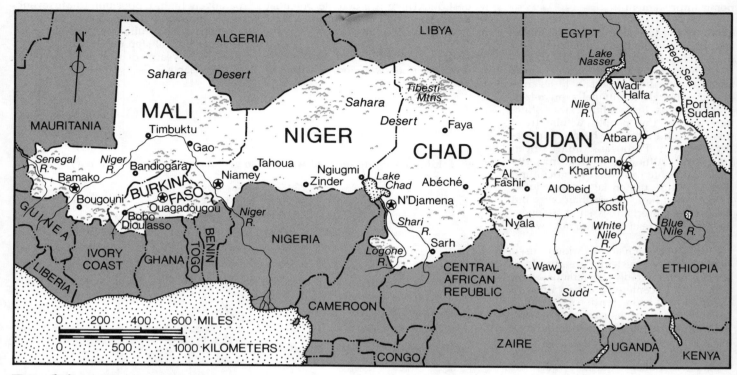

Burkina Faso (Formerly Upper Volta)

Area: 274,540 sq. km. = 106,000 sq. mi. (slightly larger than Colorado).

Population: 9.6 million (estimated).

Capital City: Ouagadougou (Pop. 580,000, estimated. Pronounced Wah–gah–*doo*–goo).

Climate: Cooler and drier (November–March); warm and dry (March–May; warm with usually ample rainfall (June–October).

Neighboring Countries: Mali (West and North); Niger (East); Benin (Southeast); Togo, Ghana, Côte d'Ivoire (South).

Official Language: French.

Other Principal Tongues: Mossi, Gourounsi, Bobo, Lobi, Mande and several other sub–dialects.

Ethnic Background: Mossi (Central area); Gourounsi (South–central area); Bobo (Southwest); Lobi (Southeast); Mande (East); Hausa (urban dwellers); Peulh, or Fulani and Tuareg (semi–nomads of the North).

Principal Religion: Traditional tribal beliefs.

Chief Commercial Products: Cattle, cotton, peanuts.

Annual Per Capita Income: About U.S. $300.

Currency: CFR Franc (no longer tied to the French franc).

Former Colonial Status: French Colony (1896–1932); part of Ivory Coast, Niger and French Soudan (1932–1957); French Overseas Territory (1958–1960).

Independence Date: August 5, 1960.

Chief of State: Col. Blaise Compaore, President.

National Flag: Three horizontal stripes running in equal length from top to bottom—black, white and red.

This country of gently rolling hills, north of the hot, steamy equatorial zone, with an average altitude of 800 feet, has a comparatively pleasant climate. The tall grass of the plains and the green forest grow rapidly during the usual wet season from May to November in years of normal rainfall. Almost daily rains are usually short thunderstorms—the rest of the day during these months is warm and sunny.

Toward the end of November, the rains become less frequent and finally almost cease altogether. The grasses of the plains which have risen to heights of six feet turn brown, waiting to be consumed by localized brush fires.

A drier area is found in the North and Northwest, which is a transition zone between the plains and the hot Sahara further north. It is from this great desert that the *harmattan* (the hot wind of the dry season) comes, covering the whole country. The rivers of Burkina Faso, the Black, Red and White Voltas, and the tributaries of the Niger in the East—are not navigable. Travel to and from land– locked Burkina Faso is principally over the railway from

Ouagadougou through Bobo–Dioulasso to Abidjan in Côte d'Ivoire.

History: More than 800 years ago, great numbers of conquering horsemen, the Mossi, penetrated a small region in the southeast of Burkina Faso, subduing the passive farmers of the plateau. They established a feudalistic system based on collective leadership.

The Mende and Bobo, related groups, have been in this country for countless centuries. Legend does not indicate the time of origin of the several other groups of Burkina Faso.

Although the Mossi became peaceful farmers through the centuries, they were able to forcefully defeat efforts of the Islamic people of the North to conquer them and convert them to Islam. The Arab Berbers, however, presented a continuing threat. For details of early and colonial history, see Historical Background and *The French in Africa,*

A treaty was signed in 1960 granting what was then Upper Volta independence from France. A new constitution was adopted, taking effect in that year. Upper Volta was governed by a president elected for a five–year term, and a 75–member National Assembly, both elected by universal suffrage. The constitution provided for a separate judiciary. Maurice Yameago's *Volta Democratic Union* captured all the seats of the Assembly and he became the first president. Although quite popular, a combination of corruption and adverse economic conditions, including high unemployment led to his downfall. Col. Sangoulé Lamizana assumed charge; Yameago was tried and imprisoned in 1969, but was released in 1971.

Col. Lamizana was a burly, imposing figure with tribal scars on his cheeks. A devout Moslem, he made a pilgrimage to the city of Mecca. He appeared to be making progress toward restoring civilian rule, but in 1970 a constitution was adopted providing that he serve for a transition period of four years; thereafter the president would be elected.

However, the National Assembly functioned until 1974, when Lamizana had it dissolved; he appointed himself to the additional positions of Prime Minister and Army Chief of Staff, declaring that Upper Volta would be a one–party nation. Upper Voltans voted in late 1977 overwhelmingly to return to civilian rule—and for political parties to be allowed to resume their activities. But by some strange quirk of Upper Voltan politics, a military man was elected to a seven–year term of office: General Lamizana.

During the next two years Upper Volta plunged to economic depths. Corruption was rampant in the government and little effort was made to relieve the suffering of the peasant majority or in overcoming the continuing effects of drought. Opposition parties were squeezed out of existence. But a powerful labor movement remained, and during late 1980, teachers, government workers and employees in private industry caused a series of paralyzing strikes. Lamizana tried to reassure the groups, but made no promises. The military looked on with increasing alarm as the government floundered and the nation seemed headed for civil war. In late 1980 the President was placed under house arrest.

The leader of the bloodless *coup* was

World Bank Photo

Lamizana's former foreign minister, Colonel Saye Zerbo, who was immediately proclaimed President of the Military Committee for Reformation and National Progress—and, of course, chief of state. Zerbo sternly warned the 60,000–strong work force that there was no money for salary increases, all political activity was banned and the government would not tolerate any further strikes.

The principal goal of the new government was to rout out corruption and to try to set the country back on its economic feet, but it made almost no headway; in late 1982 other officers staged a *coup* which toppled Zerbo's government.

A Provisional People's Salvation Council was formed, which accused Zerbo of betraying the people and using his government as an instrument of terror. The new president, Col. Jean–Baptiste Ouedraogo had planned elections for November 1984, but in August 1983 Capt. Thomas Sankara led yet another *coup* and became President of the National Council for the Revolution.

Unrest continued and anti–government plots boiled. An alleged attempted *coup* by military elements occurred in 1984; Sankara meant business—seven of the participants were tried and executed within a month. When school teachers

President Blaise Compaore

struck, 1,400 were fired. Corruption trials resulted in the acquittal of Lamizana, but Col. Zerbo received a sentence of 8 years in jail and was directed to repay some $150,000 in embezzled funds to the government.

In August 1984, the name of the country was changed in an interesting way to *Burkina Faso*. The words are common to 50 dialects and consist of the Mossi word meaning "land of honest men" (Burkina) and the Dioula word meaning "democratic and republican" (Faso).

Tensions with Mali over a 90–mile mineral–rich strip known as Agacher reached the boiling point in late 1985. A truce between the two sides was negotiated by Nigeria and Libya after 30 days of fighting. The dispute had political overtones; it was ultimately resolved by the World Court.

The Sankara government was relatively honest and efficient; his only mistake was getting involved in the conflict with Mali. Salary decreases were accepted by the civil servants and the military in order that social service levels to the poor could be raised. But when it appeared that trade unions were attempting to dominate the government, a boyhood friend, Blaise Campaore, and senior member of the government led a *coup* in which Sankara and eight others were quickly executed and buried. The dead president was supposed to be plotting against Campaore and other government officials; Sankara was described on the state radio after the move as a "madman."

President Campaore has established a more moderate government than his predecessor. Jailed union leaders were freed and traditional chiefs were granted wider powers. The paramount chief of the Mossi was allowed to hold court at his Ouagadougou palace for the first time in several years. The main problems are jealousies within the *National Council for the Revolution*. There were attempted

coups in September and December 1989, both of which involved personnel directly under Campaore.

When potential opponents boycotted elections held in late 1991, Campaore was voted in for another term of office under a new constitution which allowed opposition parties. In May 1992 his *Organization for Popular Democracy–Labor Movement (ODP–MT)* gained an absolute majority in the 107–member National Assembly.

With effective monetary and fiscal controls, Burkina was able to maintain a satisfactory performance on its external debt in 1993, for which is received praise from the International Monetary Fund. But this caused domestic unrest because of raised prices and lowered salaries for civil servants in early 1994. The upheaval of the CFA franc caused hoarding and instability in 1993–4.

Culture: Foreign cultural influences have not penetrated Burkina Faso. The lives of the people center around old tribal systems; the Mossi group themselves around five leaders, one of whom is paramount. The Bobo and Mende are family–centered, worshiping several Gods, with a supreme God called *Wuro*. There are colorful ceremonies to initiate young men into the family held by firelight at night, during which an ancient dialect is spoken.

Beautiful handcrafted articles adorn the homes of Burkina Faso. The arts of spinning, dying and weaving and how to melt gold dust to create inimitable jewelry were learned centuries ago. The two largest cities, Ouagadougou and Bobo–Dioulasso are acquiring modern architecture; both are colorful market centers for the people of Burkina Faso.

Economy: The economy of Burkina Faso is one of the most limited in Africa. The largest resource traditionally has been cattle—more than 5 million were exported annually. However, the drought has wiped out 90% of the herds and there has been widespread hunger and starvation as a result. Almost two–thirds of the government's $200 million budget is financed by foreign aid, and virtually all of it is taken up by maintaining the civil service and the army. During years of plentiful rainfall, $100 million has been earned from the export of meat, cotton, peanuts and about $70 million comes from the thousands of workers (15% of the work force) who live and work in prosperous Côte d'Ivoire to the south. This has diminished, however, as the drought has invaded that nation. Overall per capita income is about $150.

The Future: Having almost the same high percentage of agricultural workers (85%) as there were a generation ago, this country will not emerge from abject poverty for years.

A market scene at Po

World Bank Photo

The Republic of Chad

On the Chadian desert

Courtesy: Embassy of Chad

Area: 1,284,640 sq. km. = 496,000 sq. mi. (the size of Texas, New Mexico and Arizona).

Population: 6 million (estimated).

Capital City: N'Djamena (Pop. 370,000 estimated).

Climate: Dry desert in the North varies from 10° to 122°F.; the central and southern areas are warm with increasing rainfall and humidity in the South, where there is a six–month dry season; Chad has been gripped by drought and the advancing Sahara Desert.

Neighboring Countries: Cameroon (Southwest); Niger and Nigeria (West); Libya (North); The Sudan (East); Central African Republic (Southeast and South).

Official Languages: French and Arabic.

Other Principal Tongues: Sara (a Bantu language) and 24 other local languages.

Ethnic Background: There are nine Moslem–Arabic groups in the northern and central areas and three Bantu and Sudanic groups in the southern region.

Principal Religions: Traditional tribal beliefs (45%), Islam (45%), Christian (10%); figures are approximate.

Chief Commercial Products: Cotton, livestock, animal products.

Annual Per Capital Income: About U.S. $230.

Currency: CFA franc (no longer tied to the French franc).

Former Colonial Status: French Colony (1910–1960).

Independence Date: August 11, 1960.

Chief of State: Idriss Déby, President.

National Flag: Three vertical stripes of blue, gold and red.

Landlocked Chad, more than 1,500 miles from any seaport, lies almost in the center of Africa and is one of the true transitional nations between the desert to the north and the fertile southern area of the continent. For centuries it has been the crossroads of traders going back and forth between the Sahara–Mediterranean Sea region and the tropical areas of West Africa.

Although Chad resembles a shallow basin in which Lake Chad, a former inland sea, occupies the "drain" position to the west, topographically it has three distinct regions. The Chadian Sahara in the North is a land of dry desert sand dunes gently rising to a height of 12,000 feet above sea level in the Tibesti Mountains. Only 1.2% of the population of Chad inhabits this area, mostly tribal nomads. The endless expanse of desert, scorching by day, sinks to below freezing levels at night.

The central portion is a semi–arid land of great treeless plains; this section traditionally has received just enough rainfall to support cattle raising, but is now in the throes of a devastating drought. The green southern area, with more ample rainfall, supports 45% of the country's population, who engage in cotton cultivation.

Lake Chad, fed by the Shari and Logone Rivers in the southwest corner of the nation, has been called a "crowned prairie" by some because of its tangles of grass and reeds that normally cover the surface and its surrounding marshlands. The area of this immense lake has been diminished by the drought which has gripped central Africa.

History: Not very much is known of the early history of the Chad area. Various Semitic tribes and kingdoms were successively established during the western Dark Ages, including the powerful Oueddai Empire. This was a hunting ground for the early slave traders who transported their human cargo to Egypt and the East. For details of early and colonial history, see Historical Background and *The French in Africa.*

At the time of independence, the constitution established a unicameral legislature composed of 75 delegates elected by direct, universal suffrage. There were from the beginning problems of mutual trust and cooperation between the essentially Arabic people of the North and the Sudanic–Bantu people of the South. The legislature was immediately dominated by the *Chadian Progressive Party* of President Tombalbaye, a southerner. There was a period of strife in 1963 which resulted in elimination of most opposition parties. Elections in 1969 further strengthened the position of the party

and the president, who was reelected to a seven–year term.

Tombalbaye accused the French of trying to unseat him in July 1973, fuming about the presence of French troops in Chad which he had hitherto welcomed. The Chadian leader of a "dump Tombalbaye" movement was shot dead in Paris in 1973; Tombalbaye denied any involvement in the affair. The following day the President announced several changes. The party was renamed *National Movement for Cultural and Social Revolution*, the use of Christian forenames was abolished as was the use of French names for streets and places except for Avenue Charles de Gaulle in Fort Lamy (renamed N'Djamena).

Increasing dissatisfaction arising out of drought conditions, coupled with the jailing of a number of the military in 1973 led to changes in Chad in 1975. President Tombalbaye was killed and the army installed General Félix Malloum, its leader, who had been under house arrest since 1973. The country has been in turmoil ever since.

In 1976, the former leader of the northern–based rebellion of the Toubou tribesmen, Hissene Habré (pronounced Ah–*bray*), split with the group over Libya's claim to a large, uranium–rich portion of northern Chad. He was succeeded by the chief of this strict Islamic group, Goukouni Oueddei (Weh–*day*). Habré eventually joined forces with the central government, and in August 1978 General Malloum was proclaimed President and

Habré became Prime Minister. The latter was given the task of seeking national unity after years of fighting between the Moslem north and non–Islamic south; sporadic fighting had occurred, occasionally accelerating into furious combat.

Rebellion and civil war broke out in N'Djamena in early 1979 and there was almost continuous fighting for five weeks. Tribal massacres occurred in the southern and central parts of Chad, with from five to eight thousand Moslems killed—in retaliation for similar human slaughter of non–Moslems in the central and northern areas.

Rumors flew that all non–Moslems would be forced to convert to Islam. During this period Habré and Oueddei somewhat reconciled their differences. In early 1979, both Malloum and Habré resigned their offices and handed over governmental authority to a provisional state council in an effort to finally end the bloodshed. Malloum was promptly replaced by Oueddei as *President* of the State Council.

Even though eleven rival groups signed an agreement in Lagos, Nigeria to form yet *another* provisional government, Oueddei was once again named president. The agreement called for an immediate ceasefire. But this was quickly forgotten. The situation eventually evolved into one where both Oueddei and Habré had their own private armies. Fighting ebbed and flowed in N'Djamena and throughout the country.

All French troops were asked to leave

A native healer

the country in May 1980; most Europeans went with them and the U.S. Embassy was closed. The streets of N'Djamena became a no–man's land. When Libya offered military help to Oueddei's beleagured forces in December, the President accepted, believing that his troops were no match for those of Habré's in the see–saw desert war. Habré's rebels, in turn, could not compete with well–equipped Libyans and faded into eastern Chad to await a better opportunity to seize power.

Oueddei at first welcomed the Libyans—even though that northern neighbor had in 1976 annexed a 60–mile-wide strip of Chad, renaming it "southern Libya." But when in January 1981 Libya announced a *merger* with Chad, the President knew things were out of control. Great pressure on Libya to withdraw was brought by other African governments and in late 1981, Oueddei asked them to leave. Seven thousand troops left for Libya and Habré saw his chance. Within a few days his forces had seized a large part of the country and he was on his way to an easy victory over Oueddei's 11–faction coalition, which actually had never coalesced. An OAU peace–keeping force moved quickly into Chad and easily checked the rebel advance, driving Habré back to eastern Chad.

Life in N'Djamena temporarily returned to a semblance of order; the U.S. Embassy reopened in early 1982. But in mid–1982 Habré's forces swept out of eastern Chad and, amid bitter fighting, seized N'Djamena. The OAU troops remained neutral, Oueddei escaped to Cameroon and Hissene Habré declared himself chief of state. The OAU troops withdrew by the end of June.

The Libyans returned to the assistance of Oueddei and, in response, French and Zaïrean troops came to the aid of Habré. Fighting was sporadic after early 1984. Diplomatic efforts all but totally failed because of the factionalism which gripped Chad. Southern Chadian rebels suspected of sympathizing with Oueddei were badly mistreated until they accepted an amnesty offered by Habré in early 1986.

When Libyan forces reentered Chad in substantial numbers, building an airfield at Ouadi (Wadi) Doum in the northern desert, the French returned, with aircraft. The airfield was hit, and N'Djamena was bombed by a Libyan plane the next day, February 17th. Then came the surprise: Oueddei announced his resignation as head of the rebels. Libya placed him under arrest in Tripoli, where he was wounded in violence during a clash between his bodyguard and Libyan soldiers. He declared his solidarity with Habré.

This left Libya's Qadhafi, the sponsor of a revolution, without a leader. Most of the Chadian rebels had simply deserted

the cause. With French assistance, Chadian forces struck the Libyan force in northern Chad, devastating it. Libyans left about $1 billion in Soviet armaments, including tactical weapons. In response to a decree by the International Court of Justice, Libya ceded the strip to Chad on May 31, 1994.

Although there were relatively free elections in 1990, since then Chad continued to be torn by incessant quarreling, several attempted *coups* and invasions from Sudan and Nigeria, which gave rise to the need for a French force in excess of 1,000, stationed in the capital city. The *Patriotic Salvation Movement (MPS)* of Idriss Deby controlled little more than the capital.

As many as 21 opposition parties, legal and illegal, mainly based on sheer tribalism, was the source of continued disturbances. Sixteen of them united in 1992, but the president created a *National Reconciliation Confrence* in 1993 and has successfully included all but a few revolutionaries in the central government.

Elections were supposed to have been held in April 1995. But the political atmosphere was so clouded they were postponed (as has frequently happened throughout Africa) to enable the present government to put itself in a winning position. A referendum on a new constitution will be held in November, followed by presidential elections in January 1996. Legislative elections will then take place in April.

Culture: Except for the regions along the rivers and close to the Chad southern frontier, the country is thinly populated by Sudanic–Moslem people who have historically been independent of the central government.

Early rock carvings and paintings in caves of the Tibesti Mountains attest to an unknown civilization located in the area thousands of years ago during the stone age. Limitations on transportation have not permitted exposure of people to outside cultural influences.

Economy: Cotton and livestock have traditionally dominated the Chadian economy for years; 95% of the people live raising crops and cattle. Modern meat packing plants brought livestock production into the money economy during the last decade, but drought conditions have limited production to the extent that there is a domestic shortage of animals. Countless thousands of animals have died and starvation is abroad in the land to the same extent as in Ethiopia. Refugees are flooding into neighboring nations, even from the normally productive south. Lake Chad has been reduced to one–third is usual size and fish production, once prolific, is now very limited. What was lake has now

President Idriss Déby

turned into crusty clay or mucky marshland. A program of international relief is providing insufficient assistance.

Continued drought has brought untold suffering to all but the southernmost portion of the country.

The Future: The election outcome will depend on how many (if any) of the many small parties oppose the government by uniting. The chances of defeating Idriss Déby will, however, be very small.

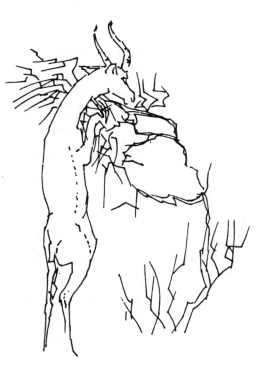

The Republic of Mali

The Great Mosque of Niomo, Niomo, Mali

Area: 1,204,350 sq. km. = 545,190 sq. mi. (more than four times the size of Nevada).

Population: 10 million (estimated).

Capital City: Bamako (Pop. 400,000, estimated).

Climate: Hot and dry in the northern two thirds of the country; increasing rainfall and more temperate in the southern third. Two short rainy seasons have watered the South, but high temperatures cause rapid evaporation.

Neighboring Countries: Senegal (Southwest); Mauritania (North, Northwest); Algeria (Northeast); Niger (East, Southeast); Burkina Faso, Ivory Coast, Guinea (South).

Official Language: French.

Other Principal Tongues: Mandingo (Hamitic) dialects, including Bambara, Malinke, Bozo, Somono, Dogon, Sonraig. Other Hamitic dialects include those of the Mossi, Bobo and Tukuler people. In the North, a community of Moors and Tuaregs speak Berber dialects. Peulhs (Fulani), of Sudanic origin, have their own distinctive language.

Ethnic Background: Mandingo (Hamitic) with many subgroups; Moor and Tuareg (Berber); Peulh (Fulani), Sudanic.

Principal Religions: Islam (90%) Traditional tribal beliefs (9%); Christianity (1%); figures are approximate.

Chief Commercial Products: Livestock, peanuts, dried fish, cotton, skins.

Annual Per Capita Income: About U.S. $340.

Currency: CFA franc. (no longer tied to the French franc).

Former Colonial Status: Part of French West Africa (1890–1960).

Independence Date: September 22, 1960.

Chief of State: Alpha Oumar Konare, President (elected April 1992).

National Flag: Three vertical stripes of green, yellow and red.

Northern Mali is a flat, dry stretch of land which is part of the Sahara Desert. This empty land, inhabited by descendants of the Berber tribes, who live a nomadic, pastoral life, has virtually no rain. The otherwise flat terrain is broken occasionally by rocky hills. The country becomes more hospitable to the south of fabled Timbuktu, which lies along an ancient caravan route of Arab merchants. The Niger River, lifeblood of Mali, flows in an irregular pattern through lakes from Timbuktu to Bamako, the capital city.

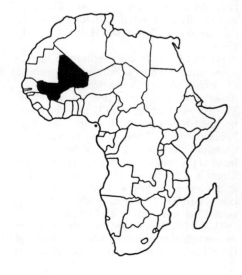

196

Independence Day festivities in Bamako

This is the farmland of Mali. In a manner similar to the Nile River, the Niger overflows its banks each year, flooding the surrounding crop lands, rendering them fertile. Most of the people of the country are gathered in this section surrounding the river, which is navigable from mid–June to mid–December. The river abounds in many varieties of fish.

The country becomes slightly more temperate south of the Niger, receiving greater rainfall in average years. This section is part of the so–called Guinea Savanna, a brush and low tree belt stretching from the Atlantic coast 3,000 miles inland to the east. It is principally in this region that the wild life of Mali is abundant, including giraffes, elephants and other species.

History: The known history of the Republic of Mali dates back to the 11th century when a powerful Islamic king succeeded in establishing his authority over the area about the same time William the Conqueror invaded Saxon England. For details of early and colonial history, see Historical Background and *The French in Africa*.

Known as French Soudan, Mali became part of the *French Community* in 1958, with almost complete internal autonomy. With French permission, Soudan and Senegal joined in 1959 to form the Mali Federation, but this was dissolved in 1960 when Senegal withdrew. After achieving independence in 1960, the government headed by Modibo Keita withdrew from

the *French Community* which had evolved into a post–independence economic union of former French colonies in association with France.

Keita, announcing that Mali was a socialist nation, sought assistance from the Soviet Union and later from communist China. Russian aircraft and weapons were received, and the Chinese sent technical assistance and limited financial aid. The result was a gradual decline in the limited economy of Mali during the ensu-

ing years which was obscured by government propaganda and continuing small amounts of communist–bloc assistance. The government, ruled by the *Soudanese Union Party*, which also controlled the press, labor unions and state youth organizations, gradually splintered into two groups. One favored a total commitment to the economic power of the Soviets and Chinese, whereas the other saw advantages in moving toward economic cooperation with the former French colonies and with France itself.

By 1967 it appeared that President Keita had been convinced by the pro–French faction and moves were undertaken to accomplish the result desired by that group. The economy was totally disorganized and the government was bankrupt. Keita instituted a program of austerity and devalued the Mali Franc to half of its former value. This had the effect of halving the income of the small segment of Malians who were in the wage economy.

Unrest resulted; Keita dissolved the Political Bureau of the state party because "it ceased to enjoy the confidence of the people." The real reason was probably stiff opposition to Keita by pro–communist officials in government. It later was evident that the real threat was not from the political leftists, but from the conservative factions of the army of Mali.

A group of young army officers seized control in a move unopposed even by the president's personal guard; Keita was imprisoned on unspecified charges in a remote area of the Sahara Desert. The officers formed the *National Liberation Committee* which ultimately was headed by Lieutenant (later, General) Moussa Traoré; a pro–Mali, pro–western course

Sheep sale in rural Mali

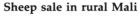

197

was adopted which has attracted foreign assistance and capital.

Events since 1968 have been calm. A trial of 25 officers accused of desiring to restore Keita to power occurred in 1969, and in late 1970 the country's twelve trade unions were dissolved. They had demanded freedom of the press, release of political prisoners, freedom of assembly and expression and the right to strike, declaring they were a political organization. The government refused to tolerate such demands.

Elections were held in June 1979—there are four year terms for the 82 members of the National Assembly and the President. Since the *Democratic Union of the Malian People* was the only party, President Traoré has been ceremoniously sworn in to succeeding terms of office. The elections in mid–1988 resulted in a respectable turnout of 88% of the electorate and returned the ruling party and president to office.

The President was trying very hard to forge a feeling of unity among the people and to give them a wider voice in government, but to the majority, government

President Alpha Oumar Konare

government and party. With a nudge from the International Monetary Fund, a program of privatization (sale of state–controlled commercial monopolies) is now underway. It is hoped that if these enterprises are privately controlled there will be less opportunity for official corruption. This may work if the personnel from the government are not a part of the package. In February–March 1991 there was considerable agitation against Traoré's regime. About 150 people were killed by government forces before he was ultimately ousted from office and arrested on March 26, 1991. During the strife there was widespread looting. The

avowed purpose of the revolutionaries was to rid the government of military rule and install multi–party democracy.

The ousted president was succeeded in office by young Lt. Col. Amadou Tourmani Touré, head of the National Reconciliation Council, who promised democratic reforms. One year later he kept his promise. By electing 47–year–old opposition leader Alpha Oumar Konare to the presidency, Mali emerged as the third African country—after Benin and Zambia—to bridge the transition from a one–party state to a multi–party democracy. However, having had the chance to vote in a free election for the first time in the country's history, only 20% of the people did so.

In spite of a 1992 accord with the northern Tuaregs to end their sporadic rebellion, it has continued at a low level and still persists. A reshuffling of the cabinet in late 1994 was no more than an effort by the president to remind all politicians of who is in charge.

Culture: The traditions of more than 80% of the people are derived from the darker ethnic groups of western Africa. Though of African Negro descent, these people are, almost without exception, Islamic, and have adopted many customs of the Arabs. The costumes of the people are colorful—in addition to using brilliant prints, patchwork effects are popular.

Ninety per cent of the people are rural, agricultural folk. In the northern dry re-

Former President Traoré

seems to be an unnecessary nuisance. Border disputes with Algeria and Niger were resolved peacefully. A border clash with Burkina Faso in 1984–5 had political overtones, centering nominally on the location of the borderline between the two countries. It was settled by the World Court, which gave each about half of the disputed territory.

Corruption and inefficiency among government servants, a tradition in Mali, was the target of President Traoré during his last two years. But he was careful not to attack *too much* graft lest he be swept from office by Mali's elite within the

Market Scene in Bamako

gions, the descendants of the Berbers remain quite aloof from the culture of the southwestern people. These nomads include the picturesque Tuaregs, who resist all efforts to intrude upon either their lands or their traditions.

Bamako, the large capital city, has stately white buildings of Moorish architecture framed by gently waving palm trees. The other highly populated centers of Bougouni, Bandiogara and Gao are devoted principally to the local marketing of farm crops and livestock raised nearby. The government has made strides in education since independence; literacy has risen from a mere 8% to more than 33%.

Much of Lassiné Minta's lifetime career as a master stonemason has been devoted to the transformation of a small local mosque into a monument of Islam—the Great Mosque in Niomo. Commissioned by a Committee of Elders, and assisted by his sons with the support of the entire community, the structure is elegantly beautiful. He received the 1983 Aga Khan Award for Architecture at a ceremony in Turkey that year.

Economy: On the economic front, Mali's immediate prospects are miserable. One of the world's poorest countries, it had a socialist–type system—26 companies were state–run, with only three or four operating at a profit; the others built up enormous debts and owe the government large amounts in back taxes. Just the salaries of the employees and government civil servants eat up more than 70% of the country's annual budget, which has grown enormously. Drastic slashes had to be made in 1993 to satisfy the World Bank. Having to wait months for their pay, government workers are not enthusiastic ones.

Subsistence agriculture is normally possible in the southern regions, and although Mali has some of the best farmland of any of the Sahelian countries, nurtured by two major river systems—the Senegal and the Niger—farmers are simply not paid enough by the government for their yields to make working hard very worthwhile. Instead, there is more of a "I'll produce just enough to feed my family" attitude.

The traditional cash export has been peanuts, purchased mainly by France, and livestock raising became a steady source of income; the animals were exported on the hoof to Ghana and Côte d'Ivoire at the start of the dry season in October of each year. The drought which has been underway since 1972 has reduced cattle herds by more than 15 million animals. Harsher drought since 1983 has made it necessary to obtain more than 400,000 tons of grain a year from external sources—principally international aid.

A rural literacy class in Mali

The government recently asked foreign oil companies to do some exploration, but this thus far has been without success. Drought conditions in 1987–8 have caused many of the nomadic people to drift toward the Niger River. Massive swarms of locusts were added to Mali's problems in the same period. An agreement for the future import of Algerian natural gas is intended to lower the demand for wood as fuel, and thus try to halt the invasion of the desert through continued tree growth.

The Future: Algeria has offered aid in ending the strife with the Tuaregs, but is very busy with its own problems. The devaluation of the CFA Franc caused substantial economic difficulty in Mali which continues, partially alleviated by IMF assistance.

199

The Republic of Niger (pronounced Nee–*zhair*)

Children at a primitive well

Photo by Ken Brown

There is an orange globe in the middle of the white stripe.

The Republic of Niger covers an immense area in north central Africa. It is one of the most thinly populated nations of the continent. A huge plateau, the country is desolate but diversified, sometimes rocky and sometimes sandy, furrowed in many places by fossilized beds of ancient Sahara rivers. Hot and dry, it is pockmarked with small basins in the southern area which briefly turn into ponds during the "winter."

A narrow belt of territory in the south stretches along the entire width of the country and is the only fertile region. This area of trees and shrubs, interspersed with cultivated land supported by irrigation or wells, gives way quickly to a transition zone where the trees become smaller, and the lack of moisture supports only sporadic grazing by nomads' animals. In the northern two–thirds of the territory, the shifting sands of the hot desert render human life impossible except in the region of uranium mines, and only sparse, rudimentary animal life is found.

Little more than 2% of the land area is under cultivation, most of which is gathered around the 185–mile–long portion of the Niger River within the country's boundaries. The river floods from June to September, helping to provide moisture for the surrounding vegetation. The climate is exceedingly hot and dry during eight months of the year.

History: An empire was established in Niger by the Songhai people in the 7th century. Not much is known of the life of the people in the centuries of the Dark Ages. The Toubous conquered the Songhais at an unknown time and they were

Area: 1,266,510 sq. km = 489,000 sq. mi. (three times the size of California).

Population: 8.2 million (estimated).

Capital City: Niamey (Pop. 508,000, estimated).

Climate: Hot and dry desert in the North; semi–arid and warm in the South with a wet season from June to September producing 9 to 30 inches of rainfall in normal years.

Neighboring Countries: Burkina Faso (Southwest); Mali (West); Algeria (Northwest); Libya (North); Chad (East); Nigeria and Benin (South).

Official Language: French.

Other Principal Tongues: Hausa (widely used for trade), Djerma, Buduma, Tuareg, Toubou, Fulani.

Ethnic Background: Hausa, Djerma, Songhai (West African Negro); Tuareg, Toubou, Tamachek (Berber–Arab), Fulani, or Peulh (Hamitic–West African Negro).

Principal Religions: Islam. There is a small number of Christians.

Chief Commercial Products: Uranium, peanuts, livestock, hides, skins.

Per Capita Annual Income: About U.S. $340.

Currency: CFA franc (no longer tied to the French franc)

Former Colonial Status: French Colony (1921–1960).

Independence Date: August 3, 1960.

Chief of State: Mahamane Ousmane, President, elected in March 1993 in the first free elections since independence.

National Flag: Three horizontal stripes of orange, white and emerald green.

200

succeeded by the Djermas in the 17th century, who migrated from the north in large numbers. At the same time, the Hausas were asserting their power in the West and the semi–arid section, while the Tuaregs were moving into their confederations in the lonely north. For details of early and colonial history, see Historical Background and *The French in Africa.*

Niger was a member of the *French Community* from 1958 to 1960, but with the proclamation of independence it withdrew from that organization.

Under the first post–independence constitution, the president held office for a term of five years and was elected by universal suffrage. The National Assembly of 60 members, elected in the same manner, sat for five years. The government could be ousted and the Assembly dissolved either by a motion of censure requiring a two–thirds majority or a vote of *no confidence* by a simple majority.

After independence, the largest political party, led by Diori Hamani, dominated the government of Niger; the *Niger Progressive Party* held all seats of the National Assembly. Its membership was composed chiefly of persons of moderate outlook.

Niger was especially hard–hit by the drought which began in late 1972 and has continued since then. This, together with the usual African pressures for change, led to a bloodless *coup* which ended the 14–year rule of Diori Hamani in 1974. The slender head of the army, Seyni Kountché seized the government and installed himself as president of a twelve-man military council in 1974. There were at least three attempted *coups*. Frequent cabinet changes followed by executions reflected the restive state of Niger politics. Opposition groups formed, merged, split and disappeared. When President Kountché died in Paris of AIDS in late 1987, his cousin, Col. Ali Saibou, became chief of state.

President Saibou grudgingly agreed to a new constitution; it was promulgated after he was elected president in 1989. It was approved in 1992, greatly curtailing the power of the military and mandating elections which were held in 1993 after being postponed three times. A 43–year–old economist, Mahamane Ousmane won a majority, but could not reign in the chaotic political climate of Niger.

He appointed Abdoulaye Souley as Prime Minister in late 1994 but the truculent National Assembly rejected the choice. The president made the appointment again, and when it was rejected for the second time, elections were set, as mandated by law, for December 31, 1994. The result: a joint coalition government. President Ousmane's *Niger Party for Democracy and Socialism (PNDS)*, a coalition, came in second (40 seats) to the opposition *National Movement for a Development Society (MNSD),* also a coalition, (43 seats).

Ousmane remains president, the prime minister is Adamou Hama of the *MNSD* and assorted coalition members hold posts in the cabinet.

The Tuareg unrest in the North continues. These people just want to be left alone—clan leaders are quite enough for them.

Culture: The traditions and customs of Niger are derived principally from the ethnic groups of West African Negro origin with an admixture of Sudanic and Hamitic blood. The Hausa, Songhai and Djerma people wear colorful, long–flowing costumes and the women ornament themselves with intricately fashioned jewelry. Most of the people live in a rural life centered around the family unit.

The nomadic Fulani (Peulh), Tuaregs and Toubous lead a somewhat lonely existence tending their flocks in the shrinking semi–arid regions of the country, but millions of their animals have perished in the drought during the last decade.

There are a number of story–telling bards and troubadors called *Griots,* who travel the country telling the legends and history of the people with skills often derived from the training of their fathers, grandfathers and remote ancestors.

Niamey, located on the fertile banks of the Niger River, is the center of commerce and trade as well as the seat of government. The National Museum, towering above the river, endeavors to present the traditions, customs, art and folklore of Niger in a natural setting.

Economy: Ninety–five per cent of the people have derived their income from agriculture and stock raising in the past. The peanut crop is raised in the narrow fertile belt of land adjoining Nigeria. There have been as many as 10 million cattle, sheep and goats, which supported expanded meat–packing and refrigeration facilities; transport of meat by air was replacing long cattle drives. The last decade of drought destroyed all but about one million animals and brought conditions of starvation to the countryside.

The military government was for a period successful in achieving the goal of making Niger self–sufficient in food production. In 1980, Niger produced 1.7 million tons of grain—200,000 tons more than needed for internal consumption. But drought conditions since 1983 made the import of almost a half million tons of cereal grain each year necessary.

A good harvest in 1985–7 gave some relief, but 1988 production again fell because of lowered rainfall. Uranium exports formerly provided a stable, steady source of income, but falling world prices have lowered income from this source. The president issued an urgent call for 250,000 tons of grain to avert starvation.

The government has a tight rein on the budget, constantly auditing its accounts. However, an undetermined amount of unreported trade hampers this effort and makes it difficult to calculate actual productivity.

Drought and increased fuel prices since 1980 were partially offset by the discovery of commercial uranium deposits. Niger became the world's fifth largest exporter of refined uranium ore. But with the end of the Cold War, prices have been steadily falling and this resource has proved in recent years to be not as dependable as it had been.

France and the U.S. are the two principal benefactors of this poor nation. Niger received a postponement on the repayment of foreign debt in 1969 and in 1994 France simply wrote off $60 million.

The Future: In years of reasonable rainfall, Niger will be able to hold its own. The military will remain in the background so long as it is satisfied that a civilian administration without corruption is possible.

President Mahamane Ousmane

The Republic of the Sudan

The Nile River at Khartoum

Busy street in downtown Khartoum

Area: 2,504,530 sq. km = 967,000 sq. mi. (An area as large as the U.S. east of the Mississippi joined by Louisiana, Arkansas and Missouri).

Population: 27.7 million (estimated).

Capital City: Khartoum (Pop. 7.7 million, estimated, including the city of Omdurman and surrounding areas filled with squatter camps).

Climate: The northern half is arid desert, the middle and southern areas are temperate and semi–arid; the southwest is hot with a six month rainy season.

Neighboring Countries: Zaïre and Central African Republic (Southwest); Chad (West); Libya (Northwest); Kenya and Uganda (Southeast).

Official Language: Arabic.

Other Principal Tongues: Local Arabic dialects, English, dialects of the southern Nilotic people, dialects of the Hamitic and Semitic people close to Ethiopia and the Red Sea, Bantu dialects in the southern provinces.

Ethnic Background: Sudanic Arabs, in a multitude of combinations, including Kababish, Kawahla, Ja'alin and Baggara (45%), traces of older ethnic groups, including Nubian (Berbinne), Fur, Ingessana and others (3%); southern Sudan is peopled with Sudanic, Nilotic and Nilo–Hamitic groups, including the Dinka, Nuer, Azande, Shilluk, Bari, Lutuka, often divided into local sub–groups; there are small Bantu groups in the southernmost area; all of these non–Arabic groups total about (52%).

Principal Religions: Traditional tribal beliefs (55%), Islam (45%); figures are approximate. Most sources overestimate the ratio of practicing Islamic people compared with the remainder of the population.

Chief Commercial Products: Cotton, gum arabic, livestock.

Annual Per Capital Income: No reliable figure available; projected to be less than U.S. $150.

Currency: Sudanese Pound (foundering, not traded internationally).

Former Colonial Status: Egyptian (1821–1885); British–Egyptian (1899–1956).

Independence Date: January 1, 1956.

Chief of State: Brig. Gen. Omar Hassan Ahmed el–Bashir, Chairman of the Revolutionary Council (b. 1947).

National Flag: Three horizontal stripes of red, white and black with a green triangle at the pole.

Sudan is the largest nation of Africa, covering an area of almost one million square miles. The vast Sahara Desert lies in the northern sector and is succeeded by a semi–arid plains country in the region near Khartoum, the capital city. This gently rolling territory is succeeded in the south by tropical plains land with more abundant rainfall; in the extreme south, the land becomes choked by dense jungle growth. The historic Nile River, the longest in the world, virtually divides the country and is the main route of north–south communication and travel between the Mediterranean Sea and the lower part of the African continent. The river has two points of origin— the waters of Lake Victoria flow into a portion known as the Victoria Nile. After a short distance, the river becomes lost in the Sudd swamp region of southern Sudan, which covers an immense area of land. The stream emerges again to flow northward through central Sudan. The Blue Nile originates to the east near Lake Tana in the mountains of Ethiopia. The two rivers join at Khartoum to form the main Nile, which, as it proceeds through northern Sudan, has a slight downward slope, interrupted periodically by rough cataracts. As it nears Wadi Halfa on the

Egyptian border, the Nile shapes itself into an almost perfect "S" curve. Were it not for the predominantly muddy waters of this river, much of Sudan and Egypt would be empty and desolate.

High mountains rise in the extreme east of Sudan, close to the Ethiopian border and along the Red Sea coast. Other mountains are found to the west on the Chad border, and in the South.

History: The ancient history of Sudan, one of the oldest civilizations in the world, revolves around the Pharaohs of Egypt and the Nubian people in central Sudan. Gigantic formations of stone in the Nile area to the north furnished the material from which many of the picturesque temples and burial grounds of ancient Egypt were carved and built. For a period, the Egyptian Pharaohs reigned from Khartoum, the present capital. At the beginning of the Christian era, Sudan split into a collection of small, independent states. There were some conversions of people to Christianity in the 6th century, but much of the country remained pagan until there was a widespread adoption of Islam, primarily in the North, at the end of the 13th century. For details of early and colonial history, see Historical Background and *The British in Africa*.

Col. Jaafar Mohammed al Nimeri

Following independence in 1956, a coalition government consisting of the *Umma Party* and the *People's Democratic Party* gained control of the government, remaining in power until deposed by a military *coup* in 1958. Political parties were banned and the Sudan was ruled until 1965 by a Supreme Council of the Armed Forces.

Political activity resumed in northern and central Sudan in 1964; elections were held in 1965 to select a Constituent Assembly that was to draft a new constitution. The Assembly gradually evolved into the government of Sudan, never completing work on the constitution. Political life was turbulent, involving principally the *Democratic Unionist Party* and the *Umma Party*. This latter group, extremely conservative, was split into two sub–groups led by two men with the magic name *Mahdi*. A variety of coalitions were entered into, but in April 1969 it appeared that the two leaders of the *Umma Party*, who had patched up their differences, might gain control.

In a swift move, the army intervened. Colonel Jaafar Mohammed al Nimeri was named head of state, and all political organizations, including the huge communist party, were ordered disbanded. For a year, things were turbulent—there was about one plot per month against the government. Continued opposition from the Mahdis, gathered on an island near Omdurman across the river from Khartoum, resulted in an air attack followed by government forces overrunning the fortress. The followers who escaped, known as the *Ansar Sect*, fled to Ethiopia

A truck meets a camel caravan on a bridge over the Blue Nile in the Sudan

203

where they have been living as refugees supported by the UN and the Ethiopian regime in recent years. However, in mid–1974, Sayed Ahmed al Mahdi was permitted to return to Sudan.

Nimeri was elected president in 1971 by a vote of 98%; he was the only candidate. An elected People's Council, formed in late 1972, drafted a constitution for Sudan which was adopted in 1973. The first elections under its provisions were held in 1974; of the 250 members of the Assembly, 125 were elected from the single party, the *Sudanese Socialist Union*. At least two candidates ran for each seat. The remaining 125 members of the Assembly were selected by women's, youth and village associations, the army, trade unions, "capitalists," "intellectuals," civil servants and the president. This tentative move towards representative government gradually disappeared, and for several years, all decision making was by Nimeri and his associates. This development was coupled with immensely growing economic problems and a constant revolt of people living in the three southern provinces, Equatoria, Upper Nile and Bhar al Ghazal.

Support for the rebellion came from ethnic Sudanese living in exile in Uganda, and most recently, from Libya and Ethiopia. A settlement reached in 1972 with the *Anyanya* ("snake poison") rebels appeared to be permanent.

The Khartoum government offered minimal concessions in the form of limited local self–control, without success. The principal obstacles to settlement of differences are the discovery of significant oil deposits in the southern provinces and Nimeri's attempt to impose Islamic law on the southern provinces from Khartoum, a measure feared and despised by the non–Moslems of the South. Coupled with this has been resistance of southern army units to rotation with troops from the North for obvious reasons.

Relations between Sudan and the U.S. have been erratic. Severed in 1967 as a result of Sudanese support of Egypt in its battle with Israel, ties were reestablished in 1972.

Nimeri was plagued by numerous attempted real and imaginary *coups*, supposedly sponsored by Libya's erratic leader, Moamer al Gadhafi, who Nimeri despised (the feeling was mutual). Nimeri expelled Russian diplomats in 1977 and supported the Somali Republic in its effort to claim territory from Ethiopia, which had by that time become a client state of the Russians.

Student riots in the following years had a distinctly anti–American tone. Although the U.S. has provided considerable assistance, not all of it benefited the average Sudanese because of governmental corruption. In response to de-

mands from the International Monetary Fund in 1981, Nimeri devalued the Sudanese Pound and sharply reduced food and other subsidies for students and others.

The government issued a proclamation in September 1983 that henceforth Islamic law *(Sharia)* would be strictly enforced throughout the country. This angered and frightened the non–Moslem and Moslem people alike. When the Ansar Moslem leader, Dr. Sadiq al-Mahdi, announced his opposition, he was imprisoned for a year (1983–1984). His brother–in–law, Hassan Abdullah al–Turabi, a lawyer educated in England and France, drafted the

Dr. Sadiq al-Mahdi

Sharia law. The *Republican Brothers* movement urged a "modern interpretation" of Islam. Initially sentenced to be hanged, after their 76–year–old leader went to the gallows, they were released when they confessed to "deviation."

Under *Sharia*, a person found guilty of armed robbery must have his right hand and left foot chopped off as an example to all. Amnesty International reported 58 public amputations in six months, including 12 "cross limb" ones. Consumption of alcoholic beverages was strictly forbidden. Drinking had been common in the north and fairly widespread in the south. The government is said to have dumped more than $10 million worth of liquor into the Nile (presumably no swimming was allowed on the occasion), but Scotch whiskey became available on the black market for anyone willing to pay hundreds of dollars for a bottle.

Nimeri gathered three Islamic *mullahs* (holy men) to advise him on economic matters and three Moslem lawyers to

consult with on legal matters. After 1983 the economy descended into utter chaos. Long lines were and are encountered even for the most basic commodities and frequently the shelves of stores are bare. The external debt grew to more than $10.5 billion, and Sudan was not able to pay the interest as it became due. It had no foreign credit—all materials were delivered on a cash in advance basis.

The United States withheld all but humanitarian aid. Refugees from the Ethiopian drought and starvation poured in daily; they numbered more than a half million, crowding into squalid camps and the teeming cities. Appeals for international assistance have not resulted in fulfillment of long–term needs.

The *Republican Brotherhood* plotted a *coup* and there were mass arrests. Rampant strikes and riots occurred. While Nimeri was abroad, the military acted, seizing power. All laws enacted by the previous regime were repealed, although Islamic law was nominally retained. This retention of *Sharia* fueled the fires of revolt in the south—the Dinkas, led by Col. John Garang, formed the *Sudan People's Liberation Army* and another tribal group, the *Anyanya II* also emerged.

The military promised elections in early 1986; they were held in April and the result was a victory for center–rightists who formed a coalition with Dr. Sadiq al–Mahdi, great–grandson of the founder of the *Ansar* sect of Islam, who became Prime Minister, leading the *Umma Party*. More than 30 parties fielded candidates for a National People's Assembly, which was supposed to draft a new constitution. Garang's revolutionaries prevented any voting in the southern provinces.

The Islamization of Sudan initially continued under al–Mahdi; he would have been cast aside if he did otherwise. It is direct violation of understandings reached between the Moslems and the Christians in 1974; the latter insist that Sudan must become a secular state. Close ties with Libya, established by the prior military regime, have been maintained, severely straining relations with the U.S., which again discontinued all asssistance. Since the Sudan is in financial default, the International Monetary Fund refused further loans.

In the midst of this chaos, al–Mahdi attempted to eliminate large parts of *Sharia* which roused the ire of moderate elements; coupled with a quarrel between the *Umma Party* and the *Democratic Unionist Party* with which it ruled in a coalition, the government collapsed in August 1987. The Moslem Brotherhood joined in the *National Islamic Front* led by Hassan Tourabi. The military was faring poorly in the southern civil war and was incapable of retaining consistent control of anything but the larger cities.

There are Sudanese refugees in Ethiopia, Kenya, Uganda and Zaïre. There are Ethiopian refugees in the Sudan (as well as Ugandans fleeing their country). The ultimate and unfavorable condition that has resulted is a lack of interest in the Sudan by any major power until the confusion and killing ends. Humanitarian aid from outside sources is difficult, since it has become popular to take those distributing vitally needed commodities as refugees. The present problems facing the government are summed up as follows:

Religion: Hassan Tourabi and the *National Islamic Front* drafted an even stricter version of *Sharia* under which an armed robber is sentenced to crucifixion and the penalty for converting from Islam to Christianity is death. Arabic newspapers demanded that it be adopted. This led to even more determination on the part of the southern revolutionaries. When submitted to the National People's Assembly (where it was opposed by moderate Moslems) it died a quiet death in committee. The *NIF* is now doing its best to undermine the government. Efforts to "water down" *Sharia* have met with strong condemnation.

Drought: The southern region was stricken by extreme drought in 1987–8. Food production was all but impossible, particularly when coupled with the ongoing strife.

Floods: The worst floods in the 20th century struck Khartoum–Omdurman and the "suburbs" in 1988, leaving more than 2 million homeless in addition to acute shortages of food. Most of these were people from the South living in squatter camps.

Unions: Every time the government tries to remove subsidies for basic commodities, strong labor unions call a massive strike, forcing restoration of the funds or other forms of subsidy. Stated otherwise, Sudan for years has been consuming more than it produces.

Corruption: The legislature was paralyzed and the bureaucracy was and is incredibly corrupt and inefficient. Even the transport of humanitarian aid to areas in dire need of it requires the payment of suitable bribes and has been plagued by unimaginable mismanagement.

Sadiq al–Mahdi was forced to govern by coalition, which never worked in Sudan. Continued civil war in the South and his own inability to make basic decisions doomed his efforts. One half million starved to death in 1988–9 and about 200,000 per year in the period which followed.

The rebellion follows a decades-old pattern: during the dry season government troops advance into the South and seize the important towns and villages while the rebels control the countryside. During the wet season, when everything turns to mud, and the whole *Sudd* (swamp) region of which the South is made up resembles the U.S. Everglades, the army is driven northward by the rebels. Every time the towns and villages change hands, there is a terrible loss of life and destruction. Refugees flee to the countryside, seeking non–existent relief camps. When the government occupies a town, Garang's forces have prevented relief supplies from getting through.

About 2–1/2 million refugees from the southern strife squatted in and around the capital city; another million fled to

In the south, a dugout canoe glides silently by

AP/Wide World Photo

205

Gen. Omar Hassan al-Bashir

Ethiopia and Uganda. With virtually all of Sudan in a frenzy, a group of middle-level army officers staged a *coup* in mid-1989, ousting and imprisoning Mahdi (thereby infuriating the Moslem fundamentalists). Colonel (now general) Omar Hassan al-Bashir emerged as leader of the *Revolutionary Council*. Except for hu-

manitarian measures, all U.S. aid to Sudan was cut off, since it is forbidden by law when a military *coup* ousts an elected government.

Bashir has done nothing to stop the backward slide of Sudan which has reentered the 19th century. The southern conflict continues unabated and Sudan has gone deeper in debt to the point where it is now over its head and in a state of economic chaos.

With world events swirling elsewhere in the past 5 years, Sudan has largely been forgotten. UN relief efforts in the form of tons of food and medical supplies have not been sufficient to put more than a slight dent in the human misery there. The *Revolutionary Council* dissolved itself in late 1993 and ceded power to rule by decree to Bashir until elections, supposedly multi-party, a measure that was no more than window dressing.

The U.S. has classified Sudan as a terrorist state, exporting violent Islamic fundamentalism. The IMF revoked Sudan's membership after it defaulted on $1.2 billion owed to that institution. But in the fall of 1994 the Organization of Petroleum Exporting Countries decided to grant Sudan sizable loans. They were just enough to avert immediate threatened disaster, but had a ulterior purpose: to encourage Sudan to hope for more loans and, in order to obtain them, to refrain from exporting Islamic fundamentalism (i.e. terrorism) to OPEC nations.

The basic aim of Bashir was made clear in early 1995 when the University of Khartoum decreed that all coeds must clothe themselves in a "decent" dress style: covering the body and the head to avoid expulsion.

The Black Christian and animist people of the South continue to suffer horribly in a conflict which appears will go on indefinitely. In addition to a million dead, there are three million refugees dying rapidly in Sudan, Ethiopia, Uganda Kenya, Zaire, Central African Republic and Chad.

It must be pondered why Moslem women are directed to so completely clothe themselves in such generally hot climates. Was it because Muhammad himself was titillated by women more scantily clad? Or was it necessary to draw the attention of men to Allah by diverting it from the beauty of females?

In his later life, in the Satanic verses, he (or someone) allegedly wrote of three voluptuous Goddesses, indicating a feeling of tedium with one God, Allah. The author has read three translations of the Quran (Koran), each with subtle differences. Perhaps it is bold to even pose such questions; an answer to them, if there be such, is not apparent).

A Sudanese village on the Nile

AP/Wide World Photo

206

Culture: The people of Sudan have gathered in many distinct groups, speaking approximately 200 identifiable languages and dialects. The majority of the people in the North are Moslems, but their number is equaled by non–Moslems. Customs almost identical to those of the Arabian peninsula prevail in the North; the people in the equatorial jungle area have cultures very similar to the groups of Zaïre, Uganda and Kenya—rural life centered around family and tribal grouping. They are largely occupied in agriculture, in contrast to the rural, nomadic herdsmen in the drier North.

There are several large cities; Khartoum, the busy capital, Omdurman, across the Nile River and Port Sudan on the Red Sea combine modern architecture and shantytowns where people struggle for each day's food.

A large number of schools provide primary education in the North, exclusively in the Islamic tradition. All Christian missions providing education in the South are closed because of the overwhelming exposure of their staffs to lethal danger. A generation has literally been lost in this respect.

Economy: The predominantly agricultural economy of Sudan centers around the production of long–fiber cotton, famed the world over for its exceptionally soft quality, and gum arabic, picked from the wild acacia trees, of which Sudan processes 80% of the world's supply. Little more than 5% of the land is under cultivation, though there is potential for cultivation of one–third with appropriate agricultural and irrigation techniques. The vast, semi–arid region has supported herds of cattle, sheep, goats and camels, which once numbered in excess of 24 million. The African drought which has affected so many nations on the continent has not left Sudan untouched. The desert is expanding southward and eastward, eliminating even marginal grazing land. Cultivation techniques, including deforestation, have had a dreadful effect on the middle regions of Sudan in the last 25 years. This has assisted the desert to spread.

Financial assistance from Saudi Arabia and a slowdown in nationalization resulted in a small degree of improvement, but the future will not brighten under the present regime. With an external debt of more than $13 billion and having failed to even pay the interest

Picking cotton in Butri

World Bank photo

since 1987, Sudan will not receive vitally needed foreign assistance or consideration. This is definitely just about the worst place in the world in which to invest *anything*.

The Future: Until Islamic fundamentalism is at least muted, or preferably nations. This modern version of fanaticism is actually a form of blatant anti–westernism, coupled with greed. It will result in the continued isolation of Sudan, and freeze it into the 19th century. It will take decades to overcome its adverse effects.

NORTH AFRICA

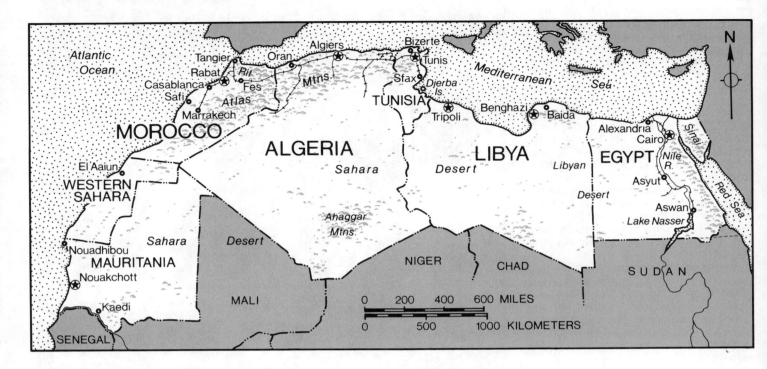

The Democratic and Popular Republic of Algeria

Area: 2,460,500 sq. km. = 950,000 sq. mi. (Almost as large as the U.S. east of the Mississippi River).

Population: 27 million (estimated).

Capital City: Algiers (Pop. 4.2 million, estimated).

Climate: In the coastal region, temperate Mediterranean weather prevails. Inland, it is temperate and cooler in the high altitudes of the mountains. South, in the Sahara Desert, it is hot and dry—90°F.–170°F.

Neighboring Countries: Morocco (Northwest); Tunisia and Libya (East); Niger (Southeast); Mali, Mauritania (Southwest).

Official Language: Arabic.

Other Principal Tongues: French, Berber dialects.

Ethnic Background: Arab–Berber–European.

Principal Religions: Islam.

Chief Commercial Products: Petroleum, natural and liquified gas (98%), Cereals, citrus fruits, vegetables, tobacco, dates, figs, olives, wine.

Annual Per Capita Income: About U.S. $1,800.

Currency: Algerian Dinar.

Former Colonial Status: French Colony (1831–1870); integral part of France (1870–1962).

National Day: Revolution Day, November 1st.

Chief of State: Lamine Zeroual, Interim President.

National Flag: Two vertical stripes, green and white, with a red crescent enclosing a five–pointed star in the center.

Algeria existed as a seat of civilization long before recorded history. Its ports and commerce were the lifeblood of early times. The dazzling white city of Algiers, founded about 1,000 years ago, is a cosmopolitan crossroads of the East and West, climbing the Atlas Mountains from the blue Mediterranean. South of the fertile coastal regions and the mountainous areas stretches the vast Sahara Desert, where caravans similar to those of prehistoric days still cross the parched wastelands. Gleaming modern highways now lead to green oases and oil fields. Atomic science has invaded the silence of the desert.

Algeria has a 620–mile coastline on the Mediterranean. Two Atlas Mountain chains cross the country horizontally, dividing Algeria into three geographic zones: the northern Mediterranean zone, the high arid plateau between the ranges and the Sahara. The northern zone, known as the *Tell*, is a sun–bathed coastal area where vineyards, orange, fig and olive trees flourish in the valleys and hillsides. The high plateau is primarily the home of grazing herds of goats, sheep and camels. South of the Sahara, the immense Ahaggar Mountains are the territory of the Tuaregs, a Berber group with singular customs—the men, not the women, are veiled. Although this is a land of extremes, the most heavily populated areas have a pleasant climate.

History: Some of the first traces of human culture are to be found in the mountain range of the southern Sahara, including neolithic frescoes and carvings. The people who have lived the longest in Algeria are the Berbers, thought to be descendants of ancient Numidians who lived during Roman Empire times. For details of early and colonial history, see

208

Historical Background and *The French in Africa*.

After a bitter eight–year struggle against Arab nationalists from 1954 to 1962, France granted independence to Algeria four months after a cease–fire had been negotiated. More than one million French citizens and other European residents left the country.

Ahmed Ben Bella, a prominent member of the *National Liberation Front (FLN)* which had led the fight for independence, headed the new government. Although leftist and socialist, he quickly outlawed the communist party and shortly thereafter was elected president. A wide range of reforms was undertaken, including the redistribution of land—drastic changes in a country which had only recently been shaken by the departure of skilled Europeans. Closer ties were established with the European communist–bloc nations.

Constant bickering within the *FLN* led to the quiet removal of Ben Bella in 1965. He was placed under house arrest, but was never charged nor tried for any crime. In July 1979 he was placed under reduced restriction, provided with a villa, and was even allowed to receive visitors—but prohibited from making political statements or meeting with the press.

Colonel Houari Boumedienne was installed as chief of state with widespread support of the party leadership. The National Assembly was dissolved and the constitution suspended. Boumedienne, the former defense minister, established a 26–man Revolutionary Council to assist in governing the nation. He continued in power with the assistance of tight security measures which were able to successfully resist a 1967 attempt to oust him, and in 1968 a plot to assassinate him. Widespread changes in the army took place in 1969 and 182 political prisoners were tried by a hand–picked military court.

Starting in 1967, the Algerian government began the process of building new political institutions, beginning with communal assemblies and then provincial assemblies. A new constitution was finally adopted in late 1976 which was openly Marxist in tone; President Boumedienne was reelected with a 99% majority. A new National Assembly was elected in 1977. The 261 members were selected from a list of 783 candidates, all *FLN* members who had gained party approval. The new assembly includes several women and numerous young people. The farmers and lower class workers were not as successful in their campaigns as were teachers and government personnel.

One of the problems which created tension between Algeria and Morocco was the status of the former Spanish Sahara—see *Western Sahara*. in the section on Morocco. However, with increased successes of Morocco in dealing with the rebel movement (or "independence movement" if you prefer), Algerian enthusiasm for the insurgents waned.

President Boumedienne died in late December 1978, the victim of a rare blood disease from which he had been suffering for several months. In early 1979 elections were held in which there was but one candidate: Colonel Chadli Bendjedid, former commander of the military district in western Algeria and informal coordinater of defense during Boumedienne's illness. He also became Secretary General of the *FLN*, the two positions interwoven in the one–party governmental structure. The president appeared to be somewhat more moderate than his predecessor, yet he stated that he would continue to uphold the traditional goals of the Algerian revolution—the usual ones . . . improve the social and economic conditions of the nation.

In early 1980 Algeria was shaken by riots led by Moslem fundamentalists who sacked hotels, cafes and restaurants where alcohol—a violation of Islamic teachings—was served. Algeria has always been one of the most secular nations of the Arab world, keeping religion *strictly* out of government, but the successful Islamic revolution in Iran has sparked a wave of "back to the basic teachings of the holy Koran" atmosphere in the country. The rioters also attacked several "pleasure houses" provided for Algerian troops stationed near the border with Tunisia. Alcohol and sin *had* to go if Moslem standards were to be held high.

President Chadli felt the riots were inspired by outsiders—and he may well have been referring to Libyan President Gadhafi. Some blamed Marxist–inspired students at the University of Algiers. If true, it was a curious alliance—Marxists who *deny* religion banding together with Moslems who place religion before all.

A serious problem occurred when there was a strike by about a quarter of the 70,000 students at the University. The group spoke only Arabic. This presented a problem in a country where French had been the predominant language of government and commerce, especially in higher–paying positions. This remnant of colonialism remained in spite of efforts to "arabize" society, which included the appointment of 600 young Arabic–trained judges.

President Chadli was elected to a third five–year term in 1989. But in a decade, Algeria had changed drastically, and at last painfully reflected years of foolish spending by the *FLN*, and fluctuations of world oil prices. The external debt was impossibly high—$28 billion—and required 80% of export earning to pay principal and interest on it. Algeria's population had changed dramatically in a generation. Literacy had more than doubled from 25% to 57%, agricultural workers had declined from 57% to 14% and service employment had increased from 26% to more than 75%.

The leadership of the *FLN* had squandered oil royalties in "window–dressing" spending on visible projects that sustained its popularity (at least on the surface) but *failed to invest for the future*. Business loans to sound, job–producing enterprises should have been the first priority, but weren't. Widespread corruption in the government added insult to injury. By the 1990s the unemployment rate of skilled people exceeded 30%. Young people faced with this bleak picture had been raised with the expectation of creature comforts associated with western life, and had rejected Islamic laws that banned alcohol and bikini bathing suits. With their dreams shattered, they felt that they had one of two alternatives: emigrate, or adopt Islamic fundamentalism. The first choice was not available.

Islamic fundamentalism offered an alternative to the *FLN*, and *any* alternative would be better, they reasoned, without thinking. What they did not and do not realize is that they were being used by ruthless manipulators who cared not one whit for their future. The message of Islamic fundamentalists throughout North Africa and the Middle East is quite simple: anti–westernism. And the fundamentalist leaders seek not religious purity—they seek the treasury of Algeria, for themselves, not for Algerians.

The president, in response to external and internal pressures, legalized political parties in 1989 and the first to register was the *Islamic Salvation Front (FIS)*. It had already been at work, clandestinely exploiting discontent among young people. As the movement gathered steam, President Chadli declared very firmly, "all attempts to return Islam to the era of charlatism (sic) and myths, or to use it an an instrument of demagogy (sic) and political opportunism" would be rejected. But that is exactly what has been and is now happening in Algeria.

But they weren't. In the first round of multi–party elections since independence in late 1991, the *FIS* won, but didn't receive a majority. Rather that hold a second round in which the Islamists would undoubtedly have won, the military, supported by hundreds of thousands of marchers in Algiers, cancelled the contest; President Chadli resigned. A five–member High State Council was formed and the *Islamic Salvation Front* was banned, its leaders were arrested and a 60–member National Consultative Council was proclaimed to advise the government during a projected proclaimed 12–month state of emergency. Murders, assassinations and massacres became common; modern weaponry was widely available and used.

The temporary president, Mohamed Boudiaf, hero of the war of independence, was shot in the back within three weeks by an assassin. Ali Kafi assumed the position. *FIS* locals, which had gained control of 60% of Algeria's municipalities, were booted out of office. About 7,000 fundamentalists were detained by the end of 1992; a few were released. Trials by secret courts became common, with no right of appeal. The age of criminal responsibility was lowered to 16 and six newspapers were shut down for publishing articles "against national interest." The *FIS* leadership was sentenced to 12 years confinement (instead of life, as asked for by the government).

Terror and subversion continued after 1992 in ever–increasing quantity and violence on both sides. Central authority all but evaporated, and violence by the fundamentalists was increasingly directed against innocent foreigners of every description (devils!). Many nations have curtailed diplomatic representation. A weary military chose Brig. Gen. Lamine Zeroual as president in early 1994 to replace Ali Kafi.

President Liamine Zeroual

Efforts at negotiation have been futile. The Islamic would–be owners of the Algerian treasury (they don't deserve the name fundamentalist) are split into almost 100 factions, a figure which illustrates their greed and lack of religious devotion.

Even the military spends more than is taken in. The $26 billion external debt required 59% of export revenues for payment of the principal and interest. The remainder of the oil revenue is spent on "entitlement" social programs and the bureaucracy; nothing is left for investment.

The U.S. State Department now considers the installation of an Islamic "fundamentalist" government in Algeria inevitable and is preparing for such an eventuality. Should this occur, it could lead to a disruption of the country when the government announces the seizure of all oil production facilities.

Internal and external pressures in 1994 led the military to announce that elections would be held by December 1995, perhaps sooner. The *FIS* and other groups immediately began calling for negotiations to end the strife—negotiations on matters previously deemed non–negotiable. Why? They realized that if their violence continued, they would go down to defeat at the polls, particularly considering their internal division. The U.S. urged that there be negotiations with the "moderate" *FIS*. The problem is that *FIS* has never been moderate.

The army leadership convened a meeting for a national dialogue of eight parties in early 1994, but refused to invite the *FIS* to send representatives. The result of the conference was inconclusive.

In March the armed forces swept Islamic militant strongholds, killing about 3,000 and virtually eliminating the radical *Armed Islamic Group*. Continued violence is likely because of poor discipline among the rebel ranks. The recipe for avoiding a victory of the fundamentalists in Algeria is obvious: 1. Make sure all 100+ fundamentalist groups are registered and on the ballot. 2. Persuade the eight principal political parties to unite into a coalition with an inspiring name to be listed on the ballot by warning of the possibility of fundamentalist unity at the polls. 3. Register as many women as possible. 4. Run TV coverage of little girls mercilessly murdered by fundamentalists because their heads were not covered as they went to school, etc. 5. Run TV material showing improvements of women's rights in the last two decades. 6. Make sure all balloting is secret and enact a law making election intimidation a crime with severe, painful punishment (fundamentalists generally do not fear death).

It must be remembered that the fundamentalists are spurred on by Sudan and Iran. The problem will not disappear if the rebels lose elections or are simply barred from competing.

Culture: Arab and Berber cultural patterns have almost completely replaced those centering on European traditions existing prior to independence, at least on the surface. Education has developed rapidly; government figures indicate there are more than 2 million in schools from primary to high school, in contrast to less than 1/4 million Arab students prior to independence. College and university education is widely available;

there are more than 150,000 enrolled in such studies at present.

The country's libraries hold priceless manuscripts in Arabic, Turkish and Berber, many of which are masterpieces of the arts of calligraphy, binding and illumination. Although independence from France was achieved, there remains a strong French influence among the people, expressed by European–style clothing found in the cities; this is now, however, being replaced by some with more traditional Arab garb as part of a "back to Islam" movement that has the approval of the government.

In spite of this, American television shows have taken on a fascination for vast numbers of Algerians—*Dallas*, for example, is almost a cult. Sadly, most Algerians know next to nothing about Americans and these super–rich seem to be "typical." According to one source, Moslem prelates decry *Dallas* and all the evils it stands for— yet they all seem to know what happened in the last episode.

Interesting changes are taking place in Algeria. Once a stridently militant, left–leaning nation, wealth has given Algerians a taste of the "good life" to which their oil and gas wealth has entitled them. President Chadli paid a state visit to France, a step which most Algerians felt might take another decade to accomplish due to lingering bitterness over the long struggle for independence. Among the prime topics of discussion was relaxation of visa requirements so that more Algerians can travel to France.

Not surprisingly, the legislature passed a controversial measure giving women fuller rights. Although males may still have more than one wife, number one must approve of any second female before there can be a marriage. A woman may divorce her husband for immoral conduct after a leave of absence of more than a year. These measures are virtually alien to Arab nations.

Economy: Algeria suffered from the departure of more than 1 million skilled Europeans following independence, and after eight years of devastating warfare. Agriculture, formerly the mainstay of the economy based on mechanized plantations, now is largely on collectives supposedly owned by the people, but actually controlled by the state.

Oil production started in 1957 at Hassi Messouad and Ejelek; it was quickly expanded through pipelines, refineries and additional wells made possible by investment of foreign oil companies. Following the Arab–Israeli conflict in 1967, Boumedienne announced that Algeria owned 51% of the foreign oil companies' holdings. Compensation for this seizure was paid by assessing the companies with large amounts of back taxes. The French, faced with an oil shortage in the 1970's, had to settle ownership disputes with Algeria on less than favorable terms. Recent agreements provided for additional French exploration for petroleum; Algeria will own 51% of any discovery. Oil production had reached the level of 60 million metric tons per year before production quotas were imposed by OPEC. Algeria joined with other Arab nations, Nigeria and Venezuela in the Organization of Petroleum Exporting countries (OPEC). The purpose of this group has been to obtain the highest prices and royalties possible for petroleum, a purpose which was dramatically fulfilled in late 1973 and early 1974 because of increased worldwide demands for energy resources. Natural gas exports, including those to the U.S. and other nations, were initially substantial. The gas is liquified to a temperature of –260°F. which greatly reduces its volume. Transported in huge tankers, the gas produced substantial income. This income diminished, however, since 1983 principally because of Norwegian development of offshore gas fields.

The years 1984 and 1985 were hard on oil producing nations. Increased production by non–OPEC nations, principally in the North Sea, produced an oversupply of oil, driving the price down. There were further price decreases in 1986—to as low as $10 a barrel. Some rebound in 1987–8 was of assistance. Most oil–producing OPEC nations have borrowed heavily against expected revenues; it is becoming increasingly difficult to enforce quotas, particularly in places such as Nigeria.

France agreed in early 1982 to buy a quarter of its gas supplies from Algeria at a price well above the current world market to help that country's industrial development. It is said to be about 20% more than paid to the Soviet Union in a similar deal. This marked a new phase of cooperation just 20 years after Algerian independence. Algeria, in turn, agreed to purchase $1.88 billion worth of material from France, including a half million Renault trucks at a time when the state–owned firm's heavy vehicle division was in serious trouble.

Economic relations with the U. S. have been good. Major agricultural development projects are underway in which U.S. technology is expected to play a major part. Algeria, under the French, was self–sufficient in food. Programs have been underway to recreate this pleasant condition.

The government's confidence was shown when in the summer of 1983, with almost no notice, shantytown dwellers around Algiers and some other coastal cities were forced into army trucks and hauled back to their birthplaces in the interior. Their "houses" were bulldozed; estimates are that from 200,000 to 1 million

Algiers' *Casbah,* **the native section of the capital**

AP/Wide World Photo

211

A workman with wire for new railway signal lines

people were relocated. (Had this occurred in South Africa, world outrage would have been overwhelming).

In August 1974 a project was undertaken to protect the fertile land of Algeria from the mighty sands of the Sahara Desert: a 30–mile–wide belt of trees began to be planted from east to west across the country; most of the work was done by young men during their service of two years in the military. This enormous job has almost been completed and stretches 1,000 miles across the nation, varying from 200 to 300 miles back from the coast near the edge of the plateau region.

The political crisis of 1991–2 has had a devastating effect on Algeria's economy. It had been growing at a robust 5% a year, but now is in a downslide of 5%–7%.

This is presenting immense problems with payments on external debt ($26 billion) and balance of trade deficits. It must be remembered that oil revenues actually decreased in the latter half of the 1980s. This, and a population growth rate which only recently declined to 2.5% annually from 3.7%, created instability in the economy's foundation to the extent that the political crisis and strife have been exaggerated.

The Future: If any semblance of order is to be brought to Algeria, it will only occur if two things are accomplished. First, there must be a radical restructuring of external debt and a balance of trade. A surplus of at least $4 billion annually must be pumped into the

economy in the form of job–producing business loans free of government corruption and influence. Second, there must be widespread use of radio and television to re–educate the young radicals and wean them away from the Islamic fundamentalists. In the latter effort, the fundamentalists must clearly be shown for what they are: would–be thieves, and in particular, thieves of Algerian popular will. Further, the re–education process must reveal the years of irresponsibility of the *FLN* and show clearly what went wrong. But the army leadership is all either active or former members of the *FLN*. Its name should be changed to the "New" *FLN*.

The fact that the Islamists did not command a majority of votes in the first round

212

The Sahara's ever-shifting sand dunes hide a tiny fresh-water oasis

In the Valley of the Kings . . . the Pharaohs gaze into Eternity

Photo: Jon Markham Morrow

The Arab Republic of Egypt

Commuters at rush hour in Cairo

WORLD BANK Photo by Ray Witlin

Area: 1,000,258 sq. km. = 386,200 sq. mi. (The size of Texas and New Mexico).

Population: 58 million (estimated).

Capital City: Cairo (Pop. 14 million, estimated, including numerous suburbs).

Climate: Dry, semi–tropical and hot. Temperatures are lower in the north during winter.

Neighboring Countries: Libya (West); Israel (Northeast); The Sudan (South).

Official Language: Arabic.

Other Principal Tongues: English, French.

Ethnic Background: Hamitic, Semitic (Arab); Sudanic (Nubian), Greek, Italian, Syro–Lebanese.

Principal Religions: Islam (94%); Coptic Orthodox Christianity (6%).

Chief Commercial Products: Petroleum, cotton, textiles, rice, cement, iron, steel.

Annual Per Capita Income: About U.S. $700.

Currency: Egyptian Pound.

Former Colonial Status: British Protectorate (1914–1922); British exercised domination in various forms over Egypt from 1882 to 1952.

Independence Date: July 23, 1952.

Chief of State: Hosni Mubarak, President.

National Flag: Three horizontal stripes of red, white and black.

Strategically occupying the northeast corner of Africa, the land route between Africa and Asia, and commanding the sea route between the Mediterranean and Indian Ocean via the Suez Canal, Egypt is a rainless expanse of desert. The habitable portion of this country has historically been only about 4% of its area. The remainder, within the great Sahara Desert, is a hot, endless landscape of sand dunes dotted with occasional green oases. It is not difficult for the inexperienced traveler to become lost in the sands of the desert since there are utterly no landmarks. The nomads have no trouble finding their way along the routes through the desert which have existed for centuries. Irrigation projects are slowly transforming the desert wasteland into fertile ground in areas close to the Nile River.

The people of Egypt are gathered on the banks of the Nile with a population density of more than 2,000 people per square mile. The Nile is the lifeblood of Egypt, providing water for irrigation and (in former years) fertile silt for the farmlands. With the exception of Mt. Sinai located on the peninsula named for it, there are few other mountains in Egypt.

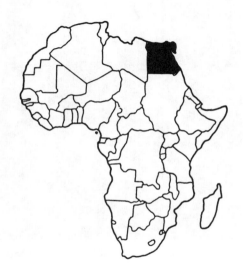

215

History: Egypt is the oldest cohesive nation in the world, its history dating back to before 3,000 B.C. For details of early and colonial history, see Historical Background and *The British in Africa*.

By the end of World War II in which Egypt was neutral, restiveness of the lower classes rose to feverish heights. The people were governed and exploited by King Farouk and a number of wealthy landowners *(Pashas)* who controlled almost all the wealth and spent long periods of their time in Europe.

A huge mob revolted and seized Cairo in early 1952; in the succeeding months, a *junta* of military officers assumed control of the nation and in mid–1952 ousted King Farouk and his court of followers. The succeeding years were ones of strife and turmoil because of continuing friction with the newly–founded Israeli state in nearby Palestine. Egypt found itself in the difficult position of being the front offensive/defensive line against a group deeply hated by Arabs because of their seizure of land from Palestinians.

The United States refused in 1956 to finance a high dam at Aswan on the Nile River. Egypt nationalized the Suez Canal with the intent of using income from that source to build the dam. British, French

and Israeli forces invaded, withdrawing only under intense pressure from the U.S. and the Soviet Union. Ultimately, Egypt signed an agreement to compensate the shareholders of the Canal Company.

There was a brief period of union with Syria from 1958 to 1961 which created the name United Arab Republic; Syria withdrew and Egypt later reverted to its old name.

Gamal Abd–al Nasser (Nasir) completely dominated the Egyptian government after the ouster of the King; he dissolved two parliaments and ruled through a tightly–controlled *Arab Socialist Union* which was the only political organization permitted. Nasser's desire for power, not only within Egypt, but in the whole Middle East, caused him to make several mistakes. After nationalization of the Suez Canal, he announced as a gesture of support for Arabs displaced from Palestine by Israel that no shipping either to or from Israel would be permitted through the waterway. Israeli shipping to and from the Indian Ocean was then diverted through the Gulf of Aqaba and the port city of Eilat; Mediterranean ports served as terminals for vessels from Europe and the Western Hemisphere. This arrangement prevailed for a decade, but in 1967, pressured by other Arab nations, Nasser decided to change things.

Announcing sympathy for the Syrian government which was loudly protesting *possible* aggression on the part of Israel, in 1967 Nasser demanded withdrawal of UN forces located along armistice demarcation lines with Israel, supposedly to enable Egypt to assist Syria (if necessary).

View of Cairo from the Mohammed Ali Mosque

Photo: Jon Markham Morrow

Dhows **catching the Nile's breezes**

Photo: Wayne C. Thompson

Mild–mannered Secretary General U Thant of the UN ordered the immediate withdrawal of the forces without consulting the Security Council or the General Assembly. Nasser's forces quickly occupied the heights of Sharm–al–Sheikh, a strategic overlook commanding the entrance to the Gulf of Aqaba. It was announced that all shipping to or from Israel was barred from the Gulf. *Al Ahram*, the semi–official newspaper of Cairo, published an editorial gleefully declaring that Israel had no choice but to fight if it wished to have access to the Red Sea.

Seizing the offensive, Israel made a three–pronged attack against Egypt, Syria and Jordan in mid–1967, bombing Iraqi airfields to eliminate air assistance from that country. The initial surprise assault on Egypt was by air from the *west*, catching almost all Egyptian aircraft (supplied by the Soviets) on the ground. In the ensuing five days of battle, the Arab forces were completely routed. A UN–imposed cease–fire established an uneasy peace, which continued in effect until the fighting gradually escalated in 1970–1971, requiring another informal cease–fire agreement. In order to replace $5 billion in lost arms, the USSR supplied almost $7 billion in equipment to Egypt after 1967.

Nasser continually threatened a war to regain occupied territory. Trial of the 1967 military leadership of Egypt for incompetence resulted in sentences of 10 to 15 years, which were protested as being too lenient. Most of those still in prison were quietly released in 1974. Unrest continued in 1968 and at one point Cairo was torn by riots.

Nasser died unexpectedly in 1970 from a reported heart attack; Egypt and the Arab world were plunged into mourning. There was a dramatic funeral for the fallen leader.

Anwar Sadat, installed as Vice–President in 1969 and elected president by a vote of 70% in 1970 was supposed to be a weak figurehead, but things turned out otherwise. He quickly ousted his rivals and made frequent and dramatic threats to "invade" and "crush" Israel, but until 1973 took no actual move in that direction. This delay was the basis of criticism, which was dealt with by cabinet changes, party expulsions and threats. When the Soviets leveled criticism at the quality of the Egyptian military prowess, Sadat decreed the ouster of all Soviet military advisors in 1972, charging that the fault lay with the Soviet failure to furnish enough modern weaponry to enable Egypt to conquer Israel. The reasons for the move were threefold—(1) to satisfy anti–Soviet feeling among conservative

Anwar Sadat

Egyptians and the leadership of Saudi Arabia with which a closer alliance was being promoted; (2) to move toward closer relations with the United States (which did not respond); and (3) to fight a war without the close observation and direction of the Soviets, who would take credit for any successes in battle.

Israeli control in the Sinai peninsula after the 1967 war tightened; there were Israeli settlements, and oil wells appeared. In an effort to wrest the occupied area from Israel, Egypt and Syria launched a two–front attack with the military and financial support of other Arab states and the USSR. The move, made during the Jewish religious festival of *Yom Kippur*, in October 1973, took Israel completely off guard and it appeared that Egypt might well be successful during the initial days of the conflict. Israel responded by first driving the Syrians back to within shell range of their capital city of Damascus, then turned to the Egyptian front. After the largest tank battle in history, the Israelis made daring crossings of the Suez Canal, launching a "pincer" attack which threatened to surround the Egyptians. Within hours the tide of battle had shifted and Cairo itself was threatened.

In such a situation, a cease–fire was arranged with U.S. mediation. The U.S. literally strong–armed the Israelis into giving up all territory west of the canal and enough territory in the Sinai Peninsula to salvage Sadat's reputation. Additional Sinai territory, including the Abu Rudeis oil field, was ceded to Egypt in late 1976. The Suez Canal, closed since the 1967 strife, was in operation by mid–1975 with U.S. assistance.

Although progress toward some basic settlement of the Egyptian–Israeli conflict was supposed to take place in 1974, because of Israeli stubbornness, the parties were as far apart in 1977 as they ever had been, particularly after election of a conservative, militant and expansionist government in Israel. Although the Soviets rearmed Egypt and Syria, in 1977 Soviet–Egyptian relations were at an all–time low, with Cairo newspapers and *Pravda* exchanging insults. Egypt shifted away from Soviet support to contributions from Arab oil states (principally Saudi Arabia) and from the United States. During the period 1957–1977 the Soviets had poured more than $20 billion into Egypt with nothing to show for their investment.

Elections in late 1976 resulted in an overwhelming victory for Sadat's *Arab Socialist Party* (280 out of 342 seats). The elections for the People's Assembly were genuinely free. By–elections and appointed members filled the remaining seats.

Following thirty years of strife, Sadat undertook the most controversial move

President Sadat speaks before the Israeli *Knesset*   AP/Wide World Photo

of his career: he flew to Jerusalem to address a session of the Israeli Knesset. The Israelis were stunned and excited at this "breakthrough." Sadat delivered an impassioned plea for a just and lasting peace, but he held fast to the position that Israel must withdraw from occupied Arab territory and must grant Palestinians "their rights." Israeli Prime Minister Begin countered with the Israeli position: we are willing to negotiate, but your price is too high. He insisted that Israel must have "defensible borders."

After much "shuttle diplomacy," a peace treaty between Egypt and Israel was signed at The White House on March 26, 1979. When each nation was assured it would be protected from surprise attack, placement of their respective troops and a UN peace–keeping contingent, the treaty boiled down to these key points: (1) Israel agreed to withdraw all its armed forces and civilians from the Sinai Peninsula within a period of three years; (2) Egypt guaranteed passage of Israeli ships and cargoes through the Suez Canal; (3) both nations pledged full diplomatic, cultural and economic relations and (4) there would be a free movement of people and goods between the two countries. There was some extremely vague language about some sort of autonomy for the Gaza Strip and the West Bank of the Jordan River, both of which remain yet to be accomplished.

Many Arabs feel that the two occupied areas should come into being as a Palestinian State, but Israel insists that to create a political entity, up to the present a hostile one, right in the heart of the Jewish state would be like inviting the fox into the chicken coop.

The various phases of the peace treaty

took effect in orderly fashion, although there were many rocky shoals to be avoided, but the outcry among the conservative, Islamic fundamentalists was deafening from the moment the treaty was signed. Banners began to appear proclaiming "True believers do not take Christians and Jews as friends," an accusation directed precisely against Sadat. Then the blow came.

While reviewing a military parade in late 1981, Sadat was fatally gunned down by rebel soldiers who were members of *Al Jihad* ("Holy War!"). Eight days after the slaying and one day after a overwhelming nationwide referendum, Vice-President Hosni Mubarak took the oath as Egypt's fourth president, pledging to continue the policies of the fallen leader.

There emerged two fundamental views of Sadat. Both are valid, and hotly disputed. Some view him as a man who concluded that the Egyptians had been used by the Arab world three times to fight the Palestinians' battles against the Israelis and who decided that Egypt must get out at any price. It is pointed out that King Hussein threw the Palestinians out of Jordan, they were a plague in Lebanon and had, in the eyes of many, become lazy, professional refugees. (This does not include present residents of the West Bank). This view holds that the settlement reached was the best which Egypt, plagued by a host of problems, could hope for.

The second view is less kind. Militant, conservative Arabs believe Sadat was an ignorant, lower middle–class traitor to Islam, willing to deal with the despised Jews. He is considered the betrayer of helpless Palestinians whose land was stolen from them.

President Hosni Mubarak

The validity of these schools of thought will be revealed in time. One observation should be made, however. *Not one* of the Arab nations so critical of Sadat invited Palestinian refugees to relocate within its territory. (Many ethnic Palestinians are gainfully employed throughout the Middle East, however.)

Egypt's president is a stocky former bomber pilot with a style totally different from that of Sadat. Hosni Mubarak is plain–spoken, quiet and practical. He has conferred with a wide range of advisors, experts and even opposition leaders before taking any important action. He immediately was faced with a boycott of Egypt by Arab nations other than the Sudan. But by 1985 he largely placated the would–be enemies of Egypt and relationships were informally resumed. In 1987 it became official—Egypt was again accepted as a member of the Arab League.

The president had tried to reconcile the many factions within Egypt—Moslems, Christians, the political elite, professionals, leftists, and even the *Moslem Brotherhood*, the arch foe of Sadat during his final years. Multitudes of political prisoners have been freed, but until 1990, many were retained without being charged. Moslem extremists, including those of *Al Jihad*, are not tolerated; more than 2,000 have been imprisoned and about 200 were convicted. President Mubarak visited Washington in 1982 and succeeded in obtaining a substantial aid package, both financial and military, over which Egypt has a large degree of control. He unsuccessfully tried to pressure Washington into derailing Israel's attempted colonization of the West Bank territory.

Mubarak decreed the legality of political parties and guaranteed them freedom of the press. Elections were held in 1984. Somewhat less than half of the 12.4 million registered voters cast ballots, but gave an overwhelming vote of confidence to Mubarak's *National Democratic Party*, which won 73% of the total seats in the People's Assembly—391 out of 448 which were contested. The *New Wafd Party* won 15.1% and a total of 57 seats.

The years 1984–86 were not kind to the president, however, No matter what was been done, one or more factions hotly opposed it. Food price increases led to widespread riots. The conservative Moslems continued to snipe at Mubarak. When he released the Coptic Pope from desert exile imposed by Sadat and within a few days attended a midnight mass at which the president urged peace between the two groups, the Moslem Brotherhood denounced Mubarak as an infidel.

With an external debt of about $25 billion, economic conditions in Egypt declined sharply in the mid–1980s. Foreign credit, principally from Arab nations, had been refused because of what was perceived to be Mubarak's conciliatory attitude toward the Israelis. In the latter part of the decade, foreign assistance again became available. U.S. aid and assistance has been steady, about $3 billion per year.

The basic problems of the late 1980s substantially remain: falling oil revenues, lowered receipts fram canal revenues and smaller remittances from Egyptians living outside of their country. Widespread subsidies for just about everything and everyone are costly, and have been steadily opposed by the International Monetary Fund which desires a structured, organized welfare system for the truly needy.

Tourism, traditionally a reliable source of income, slumped in 1983–5 because of terrorism, but rebounded, doubling from 1987 to 1991 and producing $3 billion a year. But a resurgence of terrorism in 1992–3 decreased this by almost 50%. Currency reforms of the 1980s greatly reduced the traditional black market influence in Egypt.

April 1987 elections resulted in an outstanding victory for the *National Democratic Party*, successor to the *Arab Socialist Party*. The Moslem Brotherhood, although officially banned in the 1950s by Nasser, reemerged by entering into an

Suez Canal

219

His Holiness Pope Shenuda III of the Egyptian Coptic Church, a prelate who also enjoys an occasional Coca-Cola
Photo: Wayne C. Thompson

alliance with the *Liberal Party* and the *Socialist Labor Party*. This combination became the official opposition. The government had allowed the Brotherhood to resume operations to counter the rigidly fundamentalist *Islamic Jihad*, emanating from Iran and responsible for the assassination of Sadat.

Elections in late 1990 resulted in an equally impressive victory by President Mubarak and his party (348 out of 444 elected seats) in the National Assembly. The president's periodic attempts to mediate the lingering impasse between Israel and the Palestinians over the West Bank have met with little success because of (1) Israeli rigidity reflecting the desires of its citizens and (2) Mubarak's unwillingness to alienate Arab nations by seeming to be too conciliatory.

By 1990 Egypt's external debt had risen to $50 billion. When it pledged 20,000 troops to assist in the assault on Iraq in 1991, half of this was forgiven, and more than $7 billion was made available by the Gulf Cooperation Council consisting of oil–producing Arab nations. But the tensions associated with the Gulf war just about dropped the bottom out of the tourism industry.

The intensity of Islamic fundamentalist action rose dramatically in 1992 and has been a matter of paramount importance since then. With support from Iran and Sudan, it has sought, in the name of Islam, to oust the Mubarak government from power because of Egypt's reputation as a secular rather than a religious state. Violence and terrorism, allegedly to enforce the will of Allah on earth, became more and more frequent, and has been directed particularly against tourists. Severe counter–measures taken by the government, including trial by military courts, gave rise to international criticism for human rights violations.

Although there are several fundamen-

talist groups, *Al–Jihad* is the principal organization behind fundamentalist violence. It has had a unit in New York City, under the guidance of fugitive Sheikh Abdul Rahman, which bombed the World Trade Center in 1992 and conspired to commit similar acts elsewhere. Several have been convicted and sentenced.

Terrorist attacks steadily escalated in 1993–5, including execution–style slayings of security force personnel. After brief trials by military courts, several dozen terrorists were publicly hanged without appeal. Attempts on the lives of prominent government officials have been made.

The situation has been complicated by scholars and sheikhs at Al Azhar University in Cairo who have become increasingly vocal about modern Islam. Anwar Sadat had encouraged increased importance of Islam in Egypt as a counter to communism. The faculty is now eager to issue *fatwas* (decrees) on how either Allah or Mohammad would feel on contempo-

Hon. Boutros Boutros–Ghali

rary as well as traditional matters. The equivalent would be a U.S. with only a few universities, with the faculty of the leading one making pronouncements on what Jesus would say about affirmative action, industrial waste, auto emission standards and gun control. These intellectual leaders usually take positions almost identical to the tenets of the Islamic fundamentalists.

The military, 430,000 strong, is in sympathy with the efforts of the Mubarak government to control (and preferably eliminate) the fundamentalists. The self–serving nature of the fundamentalists is evident when the amounts of foreign aid from the U.S. and other western nations in the last 15+ years is considered.

Amounts equivalent to this are not available from Arab states, and would totally disappear if Egypt should come under control of the fundamentalists. It should be remembered that historically, the only stable theocracies have been based upon a single faith expressed in a unified fashion. Both Christianity and Islam believers are split into so many divisions, subdivisions and sects that involving either of those two general categories in government would be an invitation to disaster. But repudiation of either of the two traditions can also lead to calamity.

As stated elsewhere in this book, Islamic fundamentalism is basically no more than anti–westernism being used by very crafty people as a means of getting hold of a nation's treasury. It has no genuine relation to Islam itself.

Egypt was honored in 1992 when Boutros Boutros–Ghali took office for a five–year term as Secretary General of the United Nations. He has proved to be assertive and often controversial, in contrast to his predecessors.

Culture: The backbone of Egyptian society traditionally has been the peasant. Largely immovable, remaining in the area of their ancestors, they are energetic and fatalistic. An age–old class system is now virtually extinct, replaced by a large measure of individual pride among the people. Formerly termed *Fellahin* (plowmen), in recent years these peasants, densely packed along the Nile, are engaging in increasingly modern methods of farming, although beans and dark bread are still the staple food for millions.

Illiteracy, once widespread, has been substantially reduced; 44% are literate in Arabic or another language. In the upper Nile region there are a large number of Nubian–descended people with a culture derived from ancient traditions and customs. A small number of Bedouin nomads live in black tents in the desert. There are an estimated five million Christians in Egypt, members of the Coptic Church established in the days of the Apostles. Tens of thousands of college and university students periodically cause disturbances in the large cities for the usual reasons.

Cairo, the capital, with its suburbs, contains more than 14 million people— the largest city in Africa. There are programs of modernization underway in this metropolis. Tall industrial and commercial building now raise their shoulders to heights exceeding the towers of the many old and beautiful mosques.

The treasures of ancient Egyptian civilizations are displayed in many museums in Egypt and throughout the world.

A major discovery was made near Cairo in 1979—the ruins of ancient Iyon, a 3,000–year–old site once the capital of world culture and home to Plato, Moses and Joseph! By early 1980, the palaces of Cleopatra and Marc Antony were said to have been found in the murky waters of Alexandria's harbors. Modern scientific techniques are unearthing ancient treasures. Fortunately, no antiquities were found during the six years when the Cairo subway was being dug. Now operating, it carries more than 800,000 per day, running from Helwan, south of Cairo, to the center of the city; it is Africa's first subway. Additional trackage has been planned with French technical assistance.

The price of modernization in this ancient nation is costly insofar as its heritage is concerned. In spite of valiant repair efforts, ancient temples and artifacts are being eaten by acid rain and pollution. The Aswan High Dam has permitted widespread agricultural irrigation, which has raised the ground water level underneath many structures. The result is a seepage upward by a "wicking" process which is rotting stone put in place thousands of years ago by the pharaohs.

Economy: Prior to 1967, the government was having a moderate degree of success in diversifying the one–crop economy (cotton); oil production and light industry were started. To make up for lost revenues caused by the closing of the Suez Canal, Saudi Arabia and Libya contributed substantial sums and the Soviet Union provided tremendous loans to purchase military equipment.

The Aswan High Dam was dedicated in early 1971 and is capable of supplying water for the farming of an additional 30% of the land. Land reclamation is now a major project, but in the past has met with only partial success. Further, there is only a fraction of the former quantities of fertile silt below the dam, making it necessary to purchase fertilizer to grow crops. Water patterns close to the Mediterranean have changed, eroding the land and altering fishing activities. The High Dam was refurbished with U.S.–built generators which increased its generating capacity by 10%, about a third of Egypt's electricity. It was lower than normal due to falling river volume associated with the African drought of the 1980s. In spite of greater areas of land being available for cultivation as a result of the dam, Egypt still imports half of its food.

The *Sumed* pipeline from the Red Sea to the Mediterranean is now open, making it possible to ship oil to Europe via supertankers which are too large for the canal.

Peace with Israel is beginning to make dramatic changes in Egypt, although the new prosperity has not yet filtered down to the mass of people. The United States has been pouring about $3 billion annually to strengthen friendship with Egypt;

this does not include military assistance, intended to replace Soviet equipment which is outdated. Some critics in the U.S. feel that Egypt is over–armed, but in spite of·this, an agreement for Egyptian manufacture of the heavy Abrams tank of America is underway, some of which have been added to Egypt's armaments.

Industry is still 90% government–owned, but free enterprise is beginning to flourish and become increasingly attractive to Egyptians. Fifty–seven television stations operate in Egypt, two of them government–run, but a new third station is now offering "real entertainment"—a welcome change for the viewer who for years has had little more than news programs and old movies.

A tunnel is being constructed under the Suez Canal which will be open to international traffic, and the Egyptian–Israeli border is now open (but still somewhat restricted) to auto traffic. There is now commercial air service between the two nations.

A big oil field in Egypt's western desert was discovered in 1982, conceivably containing as much as 30 billion barrels— enough to supply the nation's needs for 18 years. The new wells went into production in 1984. Energetic exploration efforts, in cooperation with foreign investors, are now underway at about fourteen different locations within Egypt.

An October 1992 earthquake in the Cairo vicinity caused widespread damage to lower class housing, placing the government under severe pressure to locate living quarters for more than 100,000 families. Many Arab nations pledged assistance as a result of the disaster. The items now at the top of the agenda are (1) privatization of state–owned, corrupt and inefficient monopolies and (2) elimination of subsidies on basic commodities, principally foodstuffs, since Egyptians are now generally well–fed.

An enlarged subway in Cairo is scheduled for completion in 1997; two German–made boring machines, the *Hatshepsut* and the *Nefertiti* will bring modern transport to this most ancient nation. Egypt shows signs of prosperity amid poverty. It is not rich, but is progressing toward that goal.

The Future: Military and financial subsidies from the U.S. will continue. Egyptians generally do not favor Islamic fundamentalism, but are willing to turn to anything perceived capable of improving their lives economically. An energetic program of re–education of the people as suggested in the section on Algeria would be useful in controlling the Islamists, the leaders of which have their personal enrichment foremost in mind. Egypt will maintain a proper, but distant, posture on matters of controversy in Israel/Palestine.

Students stroll on the grounds of the American University, Cairo

Photo: Wayne C. Thompson

Socialist People's Libyan Arab Jamahiriya

Marketplace in Benghazi

Area: 1,758,610 sq. km = 680,000 sq. mi. (about the size of Alaska plus Arizona).

Population: 5.1 million (estimated).

Capital Cities: Tripoli (Pop. 1.2 million, estimated) and Benghazi (Pop. 750,000, estimated), co–capitals; Baida is the administrative center; moves are now underway to transfer the administrative sector to Al Jofor.

Climate: Mediterranean, with summer and winter in a narrow 50–mile–wide band along the coast; semi–arid in the region adjoining the coastal belt, arid and hot in the remainder within the Sahara Desert.

Neighboring Countries: Algeria and Tunisia (West); Egypt (East); The Sudan (Southeast); Chad and Niger (South).

Official Language: Arabic

Other Principal Tongues: Berber dialects, English, Italian.

Ethnic Background: Arab, Berber and a mixture of the two.

Principal Religion: Islam, the State Religion.

Chief Commercial Products: Petroleum, processed foods, textiles.

Annual Per Capita Income: About U.S. $7,100.

Currency: Libyan Dinar.

Former Colonial Status: Turkish Colony (1553–1911); Italian Colony (1911–1943) British–French jurisdiction (1943–1951).

Independence Date: December 24, 1951.

Chief of State: Col. Moamer al–Qadhafi "Leader of the Revolution."

National Flag: A plain green field.

Libya covers a vast area of central North Africa, most of which lies within the blistering Sahara Desert. The coastal area is fertile and populous—in reality it is a series of oases in an otherwise dry countryside. Further inland, mountains rise in plateaus to heights of up to 3,000 feet. There is irregular rainfall in the region due to the perpetual struggle between the moist winds of the Mediterranean and the dry, hot air of the desert.

A short distance inland, rainfall becomes increasingly light. Sudden showers, when they occur, fill otherwise dry river beds to overflowing, sweeping valuable topsoil to the sea. Temperatures in the winter often go below freezing, but they may rise quickly to as high as 80°F. in January because of the *Ghibli*, a hot, arid wind from the desert.

The low mountains, with scattered scrub vegetation, provide forage for the Barbary sheep which need little water to survive. The sands of the Sahara take charge about 50 miles from the sea, where temperatures may soar as high as 137°F. in the shade. In the extreme South, the land rises abruptly to heights of 10,000 feet and more in the majestic and remote Tibesti Mountains.

History: Since unknown times Libya was subject to foreign rule. As early as 1000 B.C. Phoenician traders established themselves along the coastline, founding what later became the city of Cyrene. Three coastal cities to the west were given the name *Tripolitania*, or *three cities*, by the Romans—Sabratha, Leptis Magna and Oea. The first two are now ruins. Oea became Tripoli. Ruins of the empire structures are intermingled throughout Libya with those of earlier temples and buildings dating back to 1000 B.C. In Tripoli, Marcus

Aurelius constructed a great arch as a monument to Roman power.

After the fall of the Roman Empire, Libya was successively invaded and ruled by Vandals, Byzantines and Greeks. A massive Arab invasion from the East subdued the people in the 8th century, bringing Islam to the native Berber people. For details of early and colonial history, see Historical Background and *The Italians in Africa*.

By the turn of the 20th century, Libya had been historically divided into three provinces—Cyrenaica, Tripolitania and Fezzan. At the close of World War II, the allied powers, the United States, France, Great Britain and the Soviet Union could not agree on the future of Libya. Italy had renounced all rights to the colony under the terms of the peace treaty it signed in 1947. The provinces of Cyrenaica and Tripolitania were under British control and the French administered Fezzan.

At about the same time that the so-called "Big Four" submitted the question of Libya to the UN for a decision, the British recognized Emir El Sayyid Muhammad al–Mahdi el–Senussi as the head of state in Cyrenaica; he took the name King Idris. A grandson of the founder of the *Senussi* sect of Islam, he set up a government and proclaimed independence of all Libya. The UN debated for many months, and then in 1949 passed a resolution providing for Libyan independence by 1951. The National Constituent Assembly met and passed a resolution proclaiming Idris to be King of Libya; a constitution was prepared which came into effect with the formal declaration of independence in 1951.

Initially a loose federation under the monarch, a new constitution was adopted in 1963 which provided for a central government and merged the provinces. The Kingdom had a two–chamber legislature; the Senate was ap- pointed by the King and the Chamber of Deputies was elected by the people. There were no political parties.

Because of the failure of Idris to ally Libya firmly enough with the Arab cause against Israel, a group of army officers, headed by 1st Lt. Moamer al–Qadhafi deposed the King in September 1969. Ironically, the King, because of illness, was prepared to announce his abdication the next day. He died in Cairo in 1983.

The government was placed in the hands of a revolutionary council and radical changes were undertaken—U.S. military bases were closed and 25,000 Italians either left or were expelled, many of them leaving their property, including $25 million in bank deposits, to be confiscated.

From that point Qadhafi became the darling of any hysterical revolutionary who came down the road. He yearned for Arab unity, and he has spent his years in power financing various revolutionary movements throughout the world, but especially in Africa and the Middle East, using Libya's immense oil–produced bankroll. He attempted to persuade the leaders and people of virtually every Arab nation to enter into a union with Libya—with Syria, Tunisia and even with tiny Malta. Failure to achieve a single union has led to frustration which he has expressed in statements denouncing the leadership of states unwilling to join the ranks of Arab unity.

King Idris I on his 75th birthday, 1965

Egypt's *El Ahram*, that nation's semi-official newspaper, reporting alleged Libyan involvement in a terrorist attack on Egypt's military college, accused Qadhafi of being a "maniac and mere highwayman, even though he may own the gold of Midas." His frequent visits at European mental institutions are a very poorly kept "secret."

The restless Qadhafi convened a General People's Congress in late 1976; it met again in 1977. The Revolutionary Council was dissolved and an organization took its place called the "Secretariat." There have been numerous attempts on Qadhafi's life, but he has been able to survive by keeping his movements and whereabouts secret. The latest have been in 1984–1985 by conservative army elements who see power slipping into the erratic hands of "People's Congresses" and the "General Secretariat."

In 1976 Qadhafi annexed a sixty–mile-wide strip of northern Chad based on an unratified 1935 agreement between Italy and France. It is reported to be rich in uranium ore. He did not waste the opportunity to become involved in what had been a sporadic civil war in Chad, supporting rebel troops against the central government, probably with the ambition of seizing even more of that nation. The battles subsided after Chadian troops, with French assistance, routed the Libyans, capturing about $1 billion of Soviet–manufactured military materiel. This occurred in 1987 while Qadhafi was moping in seclusion after American air raids on Libya.

Although during his years in power he frequently denounced the Soviet Union, actually he was not unfriendly with that nation, even though he did not always see eye to eye with it; he denied repeated requests for port facilities along Libya's 1100–mile coastline. The Soviets sold Libya billions of dollars in military equipment during the 1970s and 1980s—in fact more weaponry than it had troops to use and pilots to fly. The hard, western cash Libya used to pay for this materiel was badly needed by its supplier. Qadhahi made friendly visits to several of the former Soviet client states in Eastern Europe.

The relationship between Libya and the United States has been a strange one. Libya has needed food and technical experts from the U.S. and America has, until imports were halted, been a major importer of Libyan oil. In spite of this, in 1979 Libyan mobs swept down on the U.S. Embassy and sacked it; diplomatic personnel, forewarned, had left the building safely. Relations between the two countries came to a standstill while the U.S. insisted that Libya take full responsibility for the attack. The Libyans (Qadhafi), however, called it a "spontaneous demonstration by *students*".

Early in 1981 Qadhafi appeared to be making efforts to mend fences with the U.S., but these gestures came too late. By May the Reagan administration asked Libyan diplomats to leave the country because of that nation's continued support of terrorist activities—the U.S. Embassy has been closed since May 1980 after what officials had described as constant harassment.

The verbal offensive against the United States escalated in 1981 when two U.S. fighters shot down two Libyan jets over the Gulf of Sidra in what Libya regards as its territorial waters. The U.S. responded that the incident was caused by an unprovoked attack on U.S. jets, but Qadhafi raged that the U.S. was the aggressor. But then, in a strange turnabout, he admitted that the Libyan planes had fired first. Relations continued to descend; in late 1981 the U.S. ordered all Americans (most of the 1,500 connected with the oil industry) to leave Libya. Although travel restrictions to Libya were established by the U.S. government, Libya has followed a policy of allowing technicians to enter without proper passports and visas; about 1,500 remain.

The Reagan administration, exasperated by Qadhafi's erratic actions, ordered all oil imports from Libya cut off. Although this amounted to about 3% of Libyan exports, it has hurt because of

Moamer al–Qadhafi

production cuts ordered by the Organization of Petroleum Exporting Countries (OPEC) and falling world prices for oil.

Qadhafi instituted his own version of a "back to Islam" movement which is distorted and subject to change without notice. He does not use the title of president; he prefers "leader of the revolution." He decreed that Libya has no central government, just a series of "Basic People's Congresses" the decisions of which are carried out by layer upon layer of committees and a General Secretariat. He made military training under the congresses mandatory for girls as well as boys in secondary schools, in spite of the Islamic tradition which seeks to *shelter* women. This program, as well as the formation of a "People's Army" containing school and university students, made conservative elements of the military very apprehensive. There have been countless attempts on Qadhafi's life.

The fact is that the vast majority of Libyans are not at all revolutionary in their feelings, yet they are led by a wild and erratic one. This nation, with few people, has 3,000 tanks—nearly one–quarter of those possessed by the U.S. It also has about the same number of Soviet "advisors." The total bill for weaponry has exceeded $ 12 billion.

There has been trouble abroad, particularly in European cities. In mid–1984 70 masked demonstrators gathered outside the Libyan Embassy in London chanting anti–Qadhafi slogans. A sniper inside the building sprayed machine–gun fire on the crowd, killing a British policewoman and wounding 11 student demonstrators. After a stand–off of several days, the Libyans were allowed passage out of England and the British Embassy officials in Tripoli returned to London; relations were severed.

Perhaps the classic exposé of Qadhafi's terrorism occurred in Egypt in late 1984. A team of British and Maltese assassins were given the task of murdering Abdel Hamid Bakoush, an exiled Libyan opposition leader who had been Prime Minister under King Idris. Imprisoned, he escaped in 1977 and fled to Egypt. Egyptian security forces became aware of the plot and "joined" the assassins; the Egyptians faked a photograph of the Libyan lying in a pool of blood and issued a press release announcing the murder. The Libyan radio triumphantly announced that "the sentence of execution" on the target, who had "sold his conscience to the enemies of the Arab nations" had been accomplished by a "revolutionary force" thereby carrying out "the resolution of the Basic People's Congresses" which had formed internal and external committees to "liquidate the enemies of the revolution" (He is alive and well). Egypt's Mubarak announced his secret police had uncovered several other plots involving persons in Britain, France, West Germany and India.

Another maneuver of Qadhafi has observers puzzled: he formed an "alliance" with the late Khomeini of Iran, an *Imam* of the Shi'a sect of Islam. Traditionally the Senussi and Shi'a have been hostile toward each other.

In 1984–1986, terrorism, both within Libya and in foreign nations was primarily directed at Libyan dissidents living in exile and randomly selected foreign targets. By late 1985, President Reagan urged all Americans living illegally in the country to leave Libya and again forbade the issuance of travel visas to that country. About 1,500 had remained behind because of high pay associated with the oil industry; others were admitted without a visa to circumvent the President's order. In early March 1986, Qadhafi made an ominous pronouncement: threats of the U.S. against Libya "turned us into terrorists and [gave] us legitimacy to be so and to act as terrorists." The U.S. then sent a naval task force into the Gulf of Sidra past what Qadhafi had labeled "the line of death," sinking two Libyan patrol boats and conducting air raids against Libyan radar and missile installations on the mainland. Shortly thereafter a bomb ripped a discotheque in West Berlin, killing two U.S. servicemen; irrefutable evidence indicated Libya to be responsible.

With European nations perspiring nervously, President Reagan in April 1986 ordered an air strike against Libya, conducted from bases in England because France would not allow the U.S. aircraft to fly over its territory. A sea route via the Mediterranean was therefore necessary. Among the hits made was Qadhafi's residence. American spokesmen curtly stated "We didn't know he was home." He was, and the attack visibly shook him. When he finally appeared on television about five weeks later, he was at times incoherent—listeners could not understand his Arabic. He appeared to be heavily sedated.

For the next 18 months Qadhafi was continuously on the move, fearful of losing his power, his life or his mind. He alternately wept and uncontrollably raged against what he considered the unreasonable enmity of others, particularly former President Reagan. His popularity sank to an all–time low when basic commodities disappeared from markets because of lowered oil prices which prevailed during this period. But starting in 1988 he emerged and erratically embarked on a course to show that he was a reasonable and rational person. His popularity at home soared with the return of basic goods for the people as oil prices rose, ultimately to $20 per barrel.

Terrorist activity emanating from Libya appeared to be abandoned, but was not in reality. It simply became clandestine rather than open. At the urging of North African leaders, in 1989 Qadhafi piously announced to reporters that he was discontinuing all support of terrorist (but not "freedom fighting") groups.

Libya's external debt, largely due to "white elephant" projects upon which oil revenues were squandered, had reached $5 billion and Qadhafi sought to again curry favor in Europe and the Arab world. His administrators were able to temporarily shore up the debt problem, but his attempt to return to more balanced relations was greeted with profound silence. He did join with the leaders of the *Mahgreb* traditional region of Africa, consisting of Libya, Tunisia, Algeria, Morocco and Mauritania to organize a loose union which had little substance. In addition, they urged Qadhafi to renounce terrorism, pledge not to threaten Israel with chemical warfare, discontinue his inflammatory speeches and mend fences with the U.S. He has done none of this consistently.

In particular, he purchased all materials for a chemical weapons factory from two West German concerns. At first, both he and Chancellor Kohl vigorously denied that the factory produced anything but medicines. He offered the press a tour of the facility; when the invitation was accepted, reporters were loaded in buses and driven to the front door of the facility at Rabta, 50 miles southwest of Tripoli—and back to Tripoli. Both Presidents Reagan and Bush indicated the factory would be destroyed if it commenced production, and on January 5, 1989 U.S. aircraft shot down two Libyan MIG fighter planes reported to be taking aggressive actions over the Mediterranean. Libyans, terrified of another American attack, lined up at gas stations and stockpiled food. Kohl later quietly retracted his denial and West Germany ceased supplying the facility.

Intensive investigation revealed that two Libyan agents committed the planting of a bomb aboard Pan Am Flight 103 which detonated above the town of Lockerbie, Scotland; 270 people were killed. For months in 1991–2 demands were made by the U.S., Britain and France for their extradition from Libya. But Qadhafi insisted they had nothing to do with the act of terrorism and refused to relinquish them.

A petition was made to the UN Security Council, which, after compromise, adopted Resolution 731 calling for appropriate action against Libya because of its refusal. Faced with threatened sanctions or even a possible military attack, Libya promised cooperation, but delivered none. It even went to the World Court in March 1992, attempting to halt a campaign of "illegal and arbitrary blackmail" by those seeking custody of the two suspects.

But reliable sources indicated that the two agents had disappeared from Tripoli in February. This placed Libya in the ridiculous posture of in effect saying "They didn't do it. If you don't believe that, they're not home." U.N. sanctions were expanded in 1993 to include everything but oil and gas (needed by Italy, France and other European nations). Then Libya announced that *perhaps* a trial of the two suspects in the Hague, Netherlands, *might* be acceptable. The latest edition of this farce came in the form of a "documentary film" which purported to show that the airline bombing was (1) financed by Iran, (2) Syrian backed, (3) carried out by the Syrian *Ahmed Jibral's* Palestinian–based *Popular Front for the Liberation of Palestine* (4) using a bomb planted inside the baggage of a Lebanese, (5) working for the U.S. CIA and Drug Enforcement Agency (6) at Frankfort, Germany airport and, (7) "western intelligence" had advance knowledge of the whole thing before it happened, but (8) because of clumsiness failed to prevent the explosion aboard the plane.(!) The film was quietly withdrawn from the London Film Festival of 1994.

Culture: The Islamic Libyans tend to be basically conservative in their outlook. The lodges of the Islamic Senussi brotherhood have been the traditional centers of art, religious philosophy and learning, but they are gradually giving way to a system of public education based on more modern concepts and "Qadhafi ideology." Compulsory, free education greatly reduced a pre–1951 illiteracy rate of 90% to less than 50%. High schools and technical colleges emphasize the development of practical skills calculated to contribute to the growth of the economy.

The cities of Tripoli and Benghazi are beautiful combinations of round, arched Arab architecture and modern skyscrapers, interspersed with the classic ruins of past civilizations and the towers of gleam-

ing mosques. Several modern supermarkets have taken their place alongside the traditional open–air markets, and many of the comforts of European and American living are available—if you can afford them.

Economy: Prior to 1959 the economy of Libya was almost nonexistent. The export of oil, started in 1961, grew by leaps and bounds to levels of 180 million tons per year by 1973. Libya, together with other Arab nations, joined the Organization of Petroleum Exporting Countries (OPEC), a group having the primary purpose of driving up the international price for oil. The effort has been initially successful in view of increasing demands for oil production and received a tremendous boost in 1973 when a brief boycott of oil exports was instituted as a gesture of support for Egypt in its battle against Israel. During the boycott, Libya shipped considerable quantities of petroleum to nations against which the measure was directed, including the U.S. (done, of course, quietly and indirectly).

Libya, as might be expected, nationalized all foreign oil interests, principally those of British Petroleum, Texaco and Shell. Britain boycotted Libyan oil, which caused retaliation in the form of a withdrawal of Libyan funds from British banks and a deposit of them in Swiss banks. The oil–consuming nations were initially defenseless against any measure taken by Libya because of their continuing need for petroleum. This has changed as production from North Sea deposits have increased steadily.

Qadhafi and Libya have not hesitated to profit at the expense of those who least could afford it—other African nations, almost all of whom have huge external debt loads because of moneys paid to fatten Libya's (and other Arab nations) coffers. Starvation faces up to 150 million people on the continent who have no money to buy food. The 1986 decline in oil prices lowered Libya's income. The response to this has been public advocation of a return to a "market" economy—capitalism—by the government.

Among the many impractical projects dreamed up by Qadhafi is the "Great Man–Made River," a large concrete pipe being laid from distant desert oases to cities and farmlands along the coast. The cost: $25 billion. Food could be purchased from abroad for a small fraction of that amount versus sums required to operate and maintain the water pipeline.

As of 1995, it appears that Qadhafi is again playing around with another German chemical weapons plant, this time near Tarhuna. It is possible that companies from several western European nations are involved in the effort.

The Future: The significance of tensions between the No. 2 man in Libya, Abdel Salem Jalloud, and Qadhafi are not clear. Three devaluations of the currency in 1992–4 indicate that sanctions have been having the intended effect, at least partially. A sensitive issue is whether the embargo against Libya includes flights of its aircraft carrying pilgrims on their *hajj* to the holy city of Mecca.

Tripoli in the shimmering heat of midday

The Islamic Republic of Mauritania

Crane operator at a mining site near Nouadhibou

Area: 1,085,210 sq. km. = 419,000 sq. mi. (One and one–half times the size of Texas).

Population: 2.2 million (estimated).

Capital City: Nouakchott (Pop. 735,000, estimated).

Climate: Hot and arid; drought conditions have existed for the last decade.

Neighboring Countries: Senegal (Southwest); Western Sahara (Northwest); Algeria (Northeast); Mali (East and Southeast).

Official Language: Arabic.

Other Principal Tongues: French (widely used in commerce).

Ethnic Background: Moorish (Arab–Berber, about 85%); Sudanic African including Tukuler, Sarakole, Peulh (Fulani) and Wolof.

Principal Religions: Islam.

Chief Commercial Products: Fish, lobster, iron ore, copper, cattle, dates.

Annual Per Capita Income: About U.S. $600.

Currency: Ouguiya.

Former Colonial Status: French Colony (1920–1960).

Independence Date: November 28, 1960.

Chief of State: Maouya Ould Sidi Ahmed Taya, President.

National Flag: A crescent and gold star on a green background.

Mauritania lies on the upper west coast of Africa, almost wholly within the immense Sahara Desert. The northern two–thirds of the country is totally flat and stony, with virtually no rain.

Thunderstorms occasionally intrude and brief but heavy rainfall collects into streams and rivers within a few minutes. Two hours after the end of the storm, there is no sign of moisture. In some places, the water descends to great depths, supporting a few green oases which stand out in the otherwise vacant countryside.

A narrow band of semi–arid land stretches from west to east in the southern region of the country. Its rainfall of about four inches per year supports low, sparse scrub vegetation. The most heavily populated area of the country lies along the Senegal River. The rich soil ia periodically flooded during normal years by the river which, when added to the rainfall of 10 to 25 inches, permits cultivation and cattle raising.

History: The first inhabitants of Mauritania were of West African Negro heritage. Thinly scattered throughout the immense country, these people who were not carried off into slavery were pushed to the south by a Berber invasion in the 11th century. The few Negroid people who remained adopted the Islam faith of their conquerors. For details of early and colonial history, see Historical Background and *The French in Africa*.

Mauritania achieved full independence in 1960; the government adopted the presidential system, replacing the original parliamentary form.

The president was elected for a five–year term by all citizens. The first presidential elections were held in 1961; those which took place in 1966 resulted in a second term for President Moktar Ould Daddah, who was also returned to office in 1971 and 1976. The unicameral National Assembly of forty members was also elected by universal suffrage.

The *People's Party* was dominant after 1959, holding all seats in the National Assembly. It was formally created by a union of all political groups in 1961.

Relations with Morocco and Algeria were quite close—the three nations desired to jointly share the 10 billion tons of phosphate in former Spanish Sahara. However, in a flurry of diplomatic and guerrilla activity, Spain, weary of trying to appease internal and external opinion over its continued possession of a colony on the African continent, decided to surrender Spanish Sahara to literally anyone. Mauritania joined with Morocco to exclude Algeria from the desert wasteland. The end result was a *de facto* partition of the former Spanish colony, with Mauritania receiving a portion in the south and Morocco receiving a larger northern area. In proceedings before various international bodies, some parties insisted that the land was *terra nullius*—it belonged to no one, probably the most accurate analysis if there were not such immense phosphate deposits.

France pledged to help Mauritania against attacking *Polisario* guerrillas supported by Algeria in its effort to obtain some or all of the wealth. These guerrillas established the *Saharan Arab Democratic Republic* in the former colony of Spanish Sahara. Air strikes were frequently made from bases near Dakar, Senegal.

Without warning, a military *coup* toppled the Ould Daddah government in mid–1978. There had been growing dissatisfaction with the fragile state of the economy, badly drained by a staggering military budget which had increased army strength in two years from 1,500 to 15,000 men. *Polisario* attacks on the railroad which shipped iron ore to Nouadhibou caused up to two month delays in the export of iron ore which accounted for over 70% of the nation's exports.

In 1979 Mauritania officially ended its role in the desert war over the southern half of Western Sahara. Drained financially by its costly struggle with *Polisario* guerrillas, it renounced all claims to the territory. It recognized the Saharan Arab Democratic Republic in 1983.

Morocco, left alone to fight the guerrillas, labeled the peace agreement "shameful" and further stated that Mauritania was nothing but an artificial creation by former colonial powers. Morocco then proclaimed the southern sector of Western Sahara to be its 37th province. If Mauritania had been able to continue with Morocco, it would have eventually ended up with part of the territory in all probability. (see Morocco–Western Sahara).

While former president Mohammed Haidalla was out of the country in December 1984, the government was seized in a bloodless *coup* by Col. Maouya Ould Sidi Ahmed Taya to halt the growth of "personal power" and to "reestablish the state's credibility." Actually the reason was economic—Mauritania was badly in need of outside assistance and loans which had been unavailable.

President Taya was able to sell fishing rights previously reserved to Portugal and France to all EC nations. Fish harvesting has replaced iron ore as the largest export of the country, made possible by the rich offshore waters. Based on an improving economy, Mauritania was able to persuade European banks to reschedule its external debt of $1.7 billion on quite favorable terms.

Internal dissention occurred with the tightening of Islamic *sharia* laws within Mauritania. A ban on alcohol was particularly resented by the non–Islamic people (about 20% of the population), most of whom are seasonal workers from Senegal. They published pamphlets accusing the Moslem majority of "Islamic apartheid."

The administration of President Taya initially governed because of the backing of the military. In 1991 a new constitution was promulgated which provided for multiple political parties; this was intended to end the monopoly of the former *Peoples Party*. The *Social Democratic Repulican Party (PRDS)* which registered was in reality the successor to the *People's Party*. In 1992 elections, the opposition was divided into four principal groups and many minor ones. As a result, Taya, an ex–military figure, received 63% of the vote. The losers charged that there was wholesale fraud in the contest, which was charitably termed "enormous difficulties" by foreign observers.

The government rejected a call for postponement of March legislative elections and, as a result, the opposition boycotted the contest. Of the 79 seats in the National Assembly, the *PRDS* won 67. Only 38% of eligible voters cast ballots in the presidential contest; the figure in the legislative contest was 33%.

Successes of the *PRDS* in 1993 local elections (about 80%) indicated its continuing popularity; charges of voting irregularities reflected a high degree of inter–clan rivalry. Lingering tensions exist between Arabic–speakers and Blacks of the South, most of whom fled to Senegal in the 1980s.

The government cracked down on a local Islamic fundamentalist movement, the *Hasim* in late 1994; it has support from Tunisia and Sudan and is now well–controlled.

Culture: The Moorish people of Mauritania are primarily of Berber origin, with some mixture of Arab and Negro blood. The pure Arabic strains are characteristic in descendants of the aggressive *Beni Hassan*, who have traditionally exercised great power. In spite of this, there is no class distinction dividing the people of the country.

The Islamic traditions are passed along through the *Marabout* tribes, a group of holy men and priests who have a well–organized brotherhood. The dress of the people resembles that of North Africa—long, flowing white robes, with white headdresses.

The city of Nouakchott has been constructed since 1960, growing swiftly with modern architecture. It is now surrounded by countless shacks and shanties of refugees from the arid countryside who have flocked to the city for help. Originally having a population of 5,000 people, it now has more than 700,000. Nouadhibou (formerly Port Etienne) is a modern busy city of more than 40,000 with comfortable hotels and an attractive beach . . . all surrounded by a host of hungry people.

Economy: The vast majority of Mauritanians have led a semi–nomadic existence based on the production of cattle, sheep and goats. The farming economy is situated in the Senegal River region and the southern, normally less arid portion of the country. Drought has gripped the nation for more than a decade and the Sahara is advancing into formerly fertile lands at the rate of four miles per year. Cattle production, adversely affected by the dry conditions has declined as tens of thousands of beasts died for lack of food and water.

Grain production was 90,000 tons in the late 1960's; it declined to 40,000 tons by the late 1970's, to 20,000 tons in 1982 and 12,000 tons in 1983.

Active fishing produces more than 100,000 tons of fish per year, some of which is processed in Mauritania for export.

Export of iron ore remains important. Immense deposits were discovered in the late 1950's in the northwest region around Fort Gouraud. Facilities for enriching the ore have been undertaken. Extensive copper deposits were found not far from the Atlantic Ocean in the early 1950's; a copper refining mill produces 10,000 tons of copper and 1,700 pounds of gold annually, but falling world prices (except for gold) have seriously affected the value of these resources.

Improved rainfall in 1986 resulted in production of 40% of the nation's needs in foodstuffs—the maximum possible because of the encroaching desert. Imports of 100,000 tons of cereals together with powdered milk and butter were necessary, however, to make up the difference. With assistance from the International Monetary Fund, managment has been above average.

The Future: Increased fishing activities by EC countries and Russia have made this industry more productive than iron ore export. Nevertheless, Mauritania will not be an economically viable nation—its needs consistently exceed production.

President Maouya Ould Sidi Ahmed Taya

The Kingdom of Morocco

Casablanca: fisherman unloading a fresh catch

Courtesy: Mr. & Mrs. Schuyler Lowe

Area: 458,730 sq. km. = 200,320 sq. mi. (larger than California; does not include Western Sahara, now actually a part of Morocco).

Population: 26.2 million (estimated).

Capital City: Rabat (Pop. 955,000, estimated).

Climate: Semi–tropical and moist along the coastline and inland for 125 miles. Cool, with frost and snow in the high altitudes of the Atlas Mountains. A hot, semi–arid plateau on the south side of the Atlas Mountains quickly gives way to the Sahara Desert. The dry season of the coastal regions is from April to October.

Neighboring Countries: Algeria (East, Southeast); Mauritania (South); Morocco claims the entire territory of Western Sahara, formerly Spanish Sahara, most of which it occupies.

Official Language: Arabic.

Other Principal Tongues: Berber, French, Spanish.

Ethnic Background: Berber, Arab, Semitic Jew (37,000), European (about 135,000, many more during tourist season).

Principal Religions: Islam (State religion), Christianity, Judaism.

Chief Commercial Products: Phosphates, iron ore, fish, manganese ore, foodstuffs, wine, textiles, tourism, manufactured goods.

Annual Per Capita Income: About U.S. $1,200.

Currency: Dirham.

Former Colonial Status: French Protectorate (1912–1956).

Independence Date: March 2, 1956.

Chief of State: Hassan II, King (b. 1929).

Head of Government: Mohammed Karim Larmani, Prime Minister.

National Flag: A five–pointed star in green outline on a red background.

Situated on the northwest corner of Africa, Morocco is the closest nation of Africa to the European continent, separated from Spain by the Strait of Gibraltar. The country has three distinct geographical areas: the coastal belt, the high Atlas Mountains and the semi–arid plateaus close to them and, finally the Sahara Desert. The coastal region is fertile, with a gentle climate and ample rainfall; intense cultivation of the land is possible. White beaches along the seacoast stretch for almost 1700 miles along the Atlantic Ocean and the Mediterranean Sea. The Rif Mountains are located close to the Mediterranean, forming a crescent of land 6,000 feet high. The view of these mountains from the sea, with the sandy beaches at their base, is one of the most beautiful in Africa.

One hundred miles inland, the Middle Atlas Mountains rise sharply, descend slightly and are succeeded by the High Atlas which reach a height of 13,000 feet. The Atlas, stretching almost the entire width of Morocco, form a natural barrier between the fertile coast and the dry Sahara Desert. Temperatures are cool in

the highlands and bitterly cold in the winter. They are often snow–capped in the summer, permitting skiing at the same time bathers relax in the sun along the coast.

History: Many centuries before the birth of Christ, the Phoenicians had established trading posts in what is now Morocco and settled numerous people in the land. From the 1st century B.C. until the 5th century A.D. Morocco was a Roman province, providing foodstuffs for the people of the Empire.

Under the overwhelming influence of a strong Moroccan King and an indepen-

dence party, France relinquished its protectorate and Morocco became independent in 1956. The government of Mohamed V first exercised absolute powers which were modified by a royal charter proclaimed on May 8, 1958 establishing a constitutional monarchy.

King Hassan II became the ruler of Morocco upon the death of his father in 1961. He promptly drafted a new constitution providing for a government including a Parliament to be approved by a popular vote in 1962. Elections were held in 1963 and the National Assembly began to function. Political bickering and opposition to the King led to suspension of the legislature and revision of the constitution in 1965 by the King. Leftist leader Mehdi Ben Barka was exiled and the King initially ruled through an appointed cabinet of 25 members, but added an appointed Premier in 1967.

Political parties became loosely–knit factions that seldom functioned with unity. A new constitution was promulgated in 1970 which allowed the resumption of political activity, but only on a limited basis. The plan was endorsed by the *Popular Movement*, an organization with rural support closely associated with the monarchy. The leftist *National Union of Popular Forces* joined with the extremely conservative *Istiqlal* (independence) *Party* to form a "National Front" opposed to the constitution and both announced they would boycott future elections.

Hassan appears to have led a charmed life since assuming office. There were attempts to murder him in 1971 and 1972 by the military. When he tried to give political parties and the legislature more power in 1972, extremists on the right and left caused so much trouble that he wound up dissolving the Chamber of Representatives and having numerous opponents arrested, tried and executed. Promised elections were frequently postponed in the ensuing years, but were finally held in 1977 in two stages. The people voted first, and then the various local government councils cast their ballots. The result was a Chamber of Representatives with 141 Independents (actually, supporters of the King), 49 *Istiqlal* members, 44 from the *Popular Movement* and 30 from several small organizations.

The latest 1984 elections saw 270 members of five parties generally supporting the King elected and 36 "opposition" members. Many observers believe this whole process to be but a facade of democracy.

During the last several years, King Hassan has systematically eliminated remaining opposition to his government. When food price increases were announced in January 1984, serious rioting resulted, followed by a partial roll–back by the government. However, promoters of the rioting were tried in May–August

King Hassan II

1984, and more than 150 people, including students and Moslem fundamentalists, received stiff sentences. At almost the same time, Hassan granted amnesty to 252 people who had been in prison since the late 1960's and early 1970's; 102 additional prisoners had their remaining sentences reduced by royal decree. Substantial questions concerning human rights violations within Morocco have been raised by foreign observer bodies. Sporadic rioting has occurred since 1984 over the rising cost of living.

Morocco has an external debt of more than $22 billion; although there are some bright spots in the economy, population growth pressures keep the nation basically off balance. The International Monetary Fund withdrew support until most subsidies on basic commodities were withdrawn, a move that was not popular among the people. Credit was restored in 1988. Substantial numbers of state monopolies are now being sold, with suitable guarantees being offered to foreign investors.

One–third of the people live at a "minimal poverty level," meaning that if lucky, they have one meal a day. The perception of the future among young people is so low that many try to escape across the Strait of Gibraltar to Europe; several drowned persons attempting to do so wash onto the beaches of Spain and Morocco each month.

Hassan wisely dispatched a force of 1,300 men to the Persian Gulf area during the 1990–1 conflict. Although sharply criticized within Morocco, this died down when the final results of the contest became known.

Instead of holding elections as mandated, King Hassan proposed a new constitution in 1992 and held a referendum in September to seek its approval by the people. The move was denounced as being meaningless by the weakened opposition, but when the votes were tallied,

97% of eligible voters cast a ballot and of those, 99% favored the proposed new constitution. Elections, postponed from late 1992 but held in mid–1993 reconfirmed wide support for the center–right coalition which supports King Hassan.

Islamic fundamentalism has fared poorly in Morocco, due to the ecclesiastical authority of Hassan, who claims as head of the Alouite Dynasty to be a direct descendant of the Prophet. He commands the titles *Imam* (Teacher), *Amir al–Mu'minin* (Commander of the Faithful) and *Khalifat Allah Fi'lArd* (Allah's Deputy on Earth).

Western Sahara

Western Sahara, formerly known by the names of its two former subdivisions, Saguia el–Hamra and Rio de Oro, is totally within one of the most oppressive parts of the immense Sahara Desert. A narrow band along the coast receives torrential thunderstorms wafted inland by the steady trade winds. The only thing that remains after the rain is more erosion—the water either spills into the short rivers emptying silt into the Atlantic Ocean or is quickly swallowed up by the scorched land that has a thirst which cannot be quenched.

This thinly populated desert region became a Spanish colony because no other nation wanted it during the rush of European claims to African territory at the close of the 19th century. For details of earlier and colonial history, see Historical Background and *The Spanish in Africa*.

The territory, then known as Spanish Sahara, came under Moroccan–Mauritanian domination as a result of a series of diplomatic and military actions after the Spanish left in 1975. The Spanish had been principally occupied with administration of the colony and with the extraction of phosphate deposits which are located in the desert and transported to the sea by a conveyor belt.

Morocco, Algeria and Mauritania had joined together in the early 1970's to bring anti–colonial pressure upon Spain to relinquish the territory. Spain dragged its feet as long as possible, mining the phosphate resources. When guerrilla activity commenced in 1974 and resulted in sabotage of the conveyor belt in 1975, Spain, led by an aging Franco who died in late 1975, decided to surrender the territory. The question, of course, was to *who* or *what* it should be relinquished. Cooperation between Morocco and Mauritania continued, but Algeria, sensing that it would receive little or nothing, went its separate way. There was a flurry of diplomatic activity in 1975 in which the head of state, the foreign minister and/or diplomatic personnel of all three were constantly on the move.

The Algerians supported the *Polisario*, a

name which was derived from *Popular Front for the Liberation of Saguia el–Hamra* and *Rio de Oro*, an organization which demanded "independence" for the whole territory.

Morocco, then backed by Mauritania, insisted that Spain should "return" the western Sahara to its "homeland" rather than setting up an independent nation under *Polisario*, which it claimed was a gang of mercenaries that didn't represent the nomadic people who wandered in and through the region. The UN had decided earlier that Spain should determine the wishes of "the people." That resolution was readopted with a further statement that the people should have a right to self–determination.

Seizing the initiative, King Hassan announced a "green march" of Moroccans into Spanish Sahara. Spain nominally resisted the move and Algeria, needless to say, was furious. Some 200,000 civilians crossed the border from Morocco and penetrated six miles into the territory. A visit by soon–to–be King Juan Carlos of Spain convinced the Spanish that action could no longer be postponed. A tripartite agreement was reached in Madrid whereby Spain would withdraw from Spanish Sahara and transfer administration to Morocco and Mauritania. The UN, although it had agreed to an Algerian resolution for self–determination, also adopted a resolution recognizing the Morocco–Mauritanian interim administration. The organization thus in effect favored both sides of the issue. The matter came before the Organization of African Unity after the *Polisario* proclaimed the existence of the *Saharan Democratic Arab Republic,* which was immediately recognized by Algeria and later by other African nations as the only legitimate government. The OAU initially ducked the issue, resolving that member states could do as they wished in recognizing such government as they saw fit.

Moroccan and Mauritanian troops quickly solidified their position in Western Sahara, while Algeria supported *Polisario* sabotage and violence.

Polisario operated from bases in Algeria, principally Tindouf (to which Morocco had made a claim). When not wandering elsewhere, perhaps as many as 50,000 *Sahrawis* were in refugee camps in western Algeria.

It initially appeared that Morocco and Mauritania were in firm control, but guerrilla activities of *Polisario* posed substantial problems for both nations. Incursions into Mauritania itself posed a threat to the capital city. Spanish Sahara, divided in a manner which gave Morocco two–thirds of the land and all of the phosphate deposits, was a battlefield with no clear lines of control.

Mauritania, a poor nation with an all but non–existent military capability,

folded in August 1978. The guerrillas, supported by Algerian oil money were just too much to overcome. When it recognized the *Polisario* as the legitimate government of Western Sahara, King Hassan branded it a "traitor" and proclaimed southern Western Sahara to be the 37th province *of Morocco.*

For the last several years *Polisario* has broadcast glowing tales of its military successes on Radio Algiers. When it *really* had one in 1987, listeners yawned with disinterest: they had heard it too often. The most important aspect of the limited conflict is that *Polisario* is not recognized by any Islamic nation except Algeria, and it is disregarded by all major world powers. It is only a creature of the "Third World" nations.

Hassan exercised some brilliant diplomacy in 1983–1984, which coupled with energetic Moroccan military action, all but finally ended the question of Western Sahara. Libya's Gadhafi, a fanatic willing to support *any* guerrilla movement, had joined Algeria in supporting the *Polisario.* Hassan visited President Chadli of Algeria and concluded an agreement relinquishing any claim Morocco may have had to an area near Tindouf. Algerian troops then intervened to prevent *Libyan* military assistance to the *Polisario.*

Morocco successfully established borders increasing its control over Western Sahara, particularly the phosphate–rich regions. Knowing of Gadhafi's obsession with the elusive idea of Arab unity, Hassan offered him an agreement of union in 1984. The terms of the agreement were vague and left much up to future negotiations. But the 12th article contained crucial language: "any aggression against one of the countries will be regarded as aggression against the other." Further, Article 11 demands "absolute respect" for the sovereignty of both countries. Since Morocco claims Western Sahara is an integral part of Morocco, under the treaty terms, Libyan aid to *Polisario* had to cease. The only other announced provider of support to the *Polisario* was Burk-

ina Faso, which in its own right is so poor it desperately needs aid.

In a last–ditch attempt, Algeria invited observers to see "the people" of Western Sahara at Tindouf in 1985. They conveniently were divided into three camps, with signs to indicate *which part* of Western Sahara they allegedly had been born or had lived in. The truth is that in this part of the world few people are natives of *anywhere.* Nomads, they were always "on the road" in a landscape which had no roads. When *Polisario* was seated at the OAU, Morocco walked out as did its sympathizers.

Apparently realizing that OAU recognition would not advance its cause, the *Polisario* leadership agreed to indirect talks with Morocco in 1986, but they came to nothing.

Morocco now controls all but the easternmost small portion, which is walled by a ten–foot–high "berm" intended to keep the native *Sahrawi* "rebels" out. They are accused of being mercenaries, which until recently, was correct. King Hassan and former president Chadli of Algeria reached some sort of understanding in 1987 the nature of which was unclear.

Since that time the rebel activity has been irregular. Most are sheltered in camps near Tindouf, Algeria. As Algeria was threatened by Islamic fundamentalists, widespread unrest, violence, and fell on hard economic times, its support for the cause waned sharply in 1992. In order to solidify his position in Western Sahara, King Hassan ordered that the territory be included in the Moroccan national referendum of September 1992. This meant that the multitude of Moroccan settlers in the territory were treated as resident Moroccan citizens.

A UN–sponsored referendum was postponed from 1992 to 1993, then to 1994 and again to 1995 because of constant haggling over *who* is a voter. Western Sahara does not exist in reality, only in the minds of some 70 "third world" nations that rushed to recognize it as a

King Hassan holding Court

The Hotel Rif in Tangier

nation. The latest postponement suggests that the hunt for voters will go on indefinitely, and probably in vain.

Culture: Moorish culture is not limited to the territory of its seat in Morocco. Magnificent Moorish architecture exists in most of North Africa and in many parts of Spain today. The flamenco dancers of Spain perform to plaintive and energetic melodies of Semitic origin punctuated by characteristic Arab handclapping.

Traditional Moorish–Moroccan dress is quite distinctive—the hood *djellabah* reaches from the shoulders to the ground; white or saffron goat leather encloses the foot; an ornately carved dagger and an embroidered leather satchel are slung over the hips, and a white turban is wound around the heads of the men. In the cities, western dress is becoming almost universal. Some women in rural areas continue to wear a veil, but this practice has largely disappeared in the cities.

Although progress has been made in education, there still remains a shortage of buildings and teachers. A tiny upper-class minority attends private schools where they are taught in French at a level comparable to that found in Europe. Literacy among the people as a whole is less than 30%.

Casablanca, Morocco's main commercial center, is a microcosm of the problems of the Third World nations—overpopulation, unemployment, under-nourishment and underschooling, particularly of the young, are rampant. In mid–1981 rioting erupted in the city and there was an orgy of stoning, looting and burning touched off by rising food costs. Almost half of the city's population is under 15! Hordes of idle children and teenagers swarm in the streets—with nothing to do and little hope for the future.

Economy: Almost 42% of the people derive their living from the soil, producing Morocco's grain, citrus fruits, vegetables and bean crops. Because of a high population density, however, there are periodic food shortages. Most of Morocco's trade is with France, which has agreed to continue assistance notwithstanding the nationalization of farmlands owned by French living in Morocco. At the time of independence, land which had been appropriated by the French was nationalized, but the 1974 move was directed toward land which had been purchased and paid for. After negotiations, the government agreed to pay a fraction of the worth of the seized lands to the French government, which distributed it, together with funds added by it to the displaced persons. The number of French people in Morocco steeply declined because of this measure, but is now increasing again.

The government has been actively promoting the establishment of small industries with some success. Mineral production now centers around phosphate, principally from the western Sahara region, as well as iron and manganese ores. Tourism is energetically promoted and adds heavily to the economy. Although quality has in the past been uneven, some international "mainline" resort hotels are building lush facilities in selected spots. Privatization of resort facilities has been underway since 1992.

Agriculture is increasingly mechanized, permitting export of large quantities of produce and citrus to Europe each year. Privatization of agriculture and other enterprises has attracted more than $2 billion in foreign investment since 1992. The stability of the government and the astuteness of Hassan indicate a positive economic future for Morocco.

Great emphasis is now being placed on harvesting the riches of the sea. Several fishing boats are now operating and more were ordered. These went into service and by 1991 were producing catches worth more than one billion dollars.

The Future: Political dissent will be tolerated within limits in Morocco under the slightly less rigid government provided for in the new constitution. But the result of criticizing the king *too* directly or without cautious civility, will continue to result in imprisonment. Unemployed youths are attracted to small cells of Islamic fundamentalists, but they are rigidly controlled by the king and his Interior Minister, Driss Hasri.

The Republic of Tunisia

A group of men discuss the day's events at the harbor of Sousse

Area: 164,206 sq. km. = 63,431 sq. mi. (slightly larger than Florida).

Population: 8.6 million (estimated).

Capital City: Tunis (Pop. 1.6 million, estimated).

Climate: Warm, Mediterranean in the northern and central parts; hot and dry in the semi–Sahara south–southwest.

Neighboring Countries: Algeria (West); Libya (East, southeast).

Official Language: Arabic.

Other Principal Tongues: French is widely used, particularly in commerce.

Ethnic Background: Arab–Berber.

Principal Religions: Islam (State religion).

Chief Commercial Products: Oil (40%), textiles, phosphate, olive oil, citrus fruit.

Annual Per Capita Income: About U.S. $2,000.

Currency: Dinar.

Former Colonial Status: French Protectorate (1881–1956).

Independence Date: July 20, 1956.

Chief of State: Zine Abidine Ben Ali, President.

National Flag: A white disk bearing a red crescent and a five–pointed star centered on a red background.

Tunisia, the smallest country of North Africa, lies almost in the center of the Mediterranean Sea coastline, with a seashore almost 1,000 miles long. The coastal belt, with an average of 50 miles in width, is the site of farmland. The coastline extends horizontally for 140 miles in the North and then proceeds irregularly southward for a lineal distance of 300 miles. There are three large gulf areas of gentle warm waters which carve semi–circles. The coastal strip is succeeded by a gently rolling tableland with an average altitude of 1,600 feet—an area of grass and forestland. This, in turn, is followed by the semi–desert to the south–southwest where there is little rainfall, and shallow salt lakes. Though this sparsely settled territory is within the desert, it is not quite as bleak and hot as the central Sahara.

History: The early history of Tunisia includes the presence of almost every powerful empire of old. An early settlement of Phoenicians developed in the 6th century B.C. Ruins of the city of Carthage as it existed in the days of Hannibal lie today a short distance north of Tunis. Elephants undoubtedly were present in this northern area at the time Hannibal used them

232

in his famed offensive against the Roman Empire. For details of early and colonial history, see Historical Background and *The French in Africa*.

France recognized Tunisian independence on July 20, 1956. The old monarchy was abolished in 1957 when the Constituent Assembly established a republic, naming Habib Bourguiba president. Following adoption of a Constitution, the first elections were held in 1959 in which there was only small opposition to the *New Constitution Party* of President Bourguiba.

The single–chamber Assembly is elected for terms of five years. There is a separate judiciary patterned on that of France. Elections since independence have uniformly resulted in overwhelming victories for the *New Constitution Party* and Bourguiba. Although aging, the President was elected to a third term in October 1969 and in late 1974 he was proclaimed president for life.

Close ties have been maintained with France after some tension caused by a delay in the withdrawal of French forces. The lands of French farmers were nationalized in 1965 and an attempt was made to organize them into collectives. This, coupled with a 1969 drought, had a highly damaging effect on the economy.

During 1970–71, when Bourguiba was suffering from a liver ailment, there were increasing pressures for constitutional reform. The basic issue was whether the National Assembly should have the power to vote a censure of an administration when dissatisfied on a particular issue. Bourguiba, somewhat recovered, wisely resisted the move, arguing that such a system was bound to result in a new government several times a year. Fully recovered in 1974, he presided over a party congress which "erased" the memory of the 1971 reform movement.

Libya's Qadhafi made energetic and sometimes hysterical moves to persuade Tunisia to unite with Libya in 1973. It was approved "in principle" by Bourguiba, who undoubtedly thought such a move would take years and years. Qadhafi did not understand what "in principle" meant and demanded immediate action; the whole idea died a quick death— Bourguiba was the undertaker. There remains nominal cooperation between the two nations, which have roller–coaster relations.

An open split between the government and trade unions occurred in 1977; they had been consistent supporters of the president. The government held a hard line, putting down strikes and refusing to negotiate with the strikers. Tunisia has been plagued since independence by widespread unemployment (20%–30%), low wages and an uneven distribution of income; these conditions have sparked many clashes. The *Destour Socialist Party (DSP)* of which President Bourguiba was chairman, continued a tough policy by making many arrests and removing from the cabinet ministers who felt the government should assume a more moderate position.

A general strike in 1978 lasted 24 hours; a state of emergency was declared and there was rioting in Tunis and some of the larger cities. Other strikes and riots occurred since that time, usually after announcement of increases in food costs; the latest was in early 1984.

As in other North African nations, there is a rising tide of Moslem fundamentalism. Zealots want to oust the "old men" governments and replace them with "Islamic" administrations patterned after that of the late Khomeini of Iran. The Tunisian constitution recognizes Islam as the state religion, but this has always been a tolerant and open society. Bourguiba, however, did many things to make the Moslem fanatics angry. He permitted wives to institute divorce proceedings against their husbands and encouraged women to enter all trades and professions. He also westernized the court system by abolishing most of the powers of the Moslem religious courts and rabbinical tribunals by turning their functions over to the civil courts. All distinctions between religious and public schools were abolished. He even went further in 1984, and included two women in his cabinet after a reorganization. The fundamentalists see these moves as cutting the tap roots of the Islamic traditions.

Some 3,000–4,000 Islamic fundamentalists were arrested by the government from 1981 until the departure of Bourguiba, who refused to allow them to function as a political party; stiff prison sentences were substituted for death penalties. The straw that broke the camel's back came in June 1981 when the "brotherhood," as they call themselves, made a raid on a summer vacation beach resort where Europeans in sometimes scanty

Relief from the desert heat in a cool oasis

233

President Bourguiba

attire lived "the good life;" the resort was all but destroyed. This was a terrible blow to Tunisia's profitable tourist industry and marked the beginning of the crackdown on the zealots.

Bourguiba, uneasy of the fundamentalist movement, legalized the formerly outlawed *Tunisian Communist Party* in 1981. This is a small, but vocal group of intellectuals. Renewed pledges of cooperation with Libya in 1982 were calculated to eliminate terrorist attacks from that nation.

The government engaged in an uneasy balancing act. In order to maintain foreign credit, sources had to be raised by elimination of subsidies for the most basic of foodstuffs such as wheat. This practically guaranteed domestic riots. Tunisia has been suffering an incurable problem: too many people living on too little suitable land. The poorest regions of the country in the south–southwest suffer the most from the grip of poverty, and in 1988 severe drought.

Former President Bourguiba remained quite popular in spite of advancing years. When a dispute erupted over succession to the presidency in 1984 he quickly settled it. The Prime Minister (who wielded considerable power) would immediately become president and name a successor prime minister.

Tunisia was literally caught in the middle when Israeli aircraft bombed Palestinian Liberation Organization headquarters which had been set up in the country when the PLO was ousted from Lebanon. The U.S. took the unusual position of condoning the attack as a legitimate response to terrorism while at the same time it sent condolences to President Bourguiba.

Intrigue at the presidential palace rose

to all–time highs, centering around the ouster of Bourguiba's second wife, Wassila, an influential member of Tunis society, and the installation of Bourguiba's niece as "first lady." When his son protested the proposed divorce, he lost his job as presidential advisor. One observer compared the daily scene to installations of "Dynasty." Persons in political favor were determined by whether their picture appeared as part of the entourage of Bourguiba's guests during his daily, well–publicized walk.

Basic cabinet changes were made in 1986—Prime Minister Mohamed Mzali was discharged because he was too liberal concerning dissidents of the far right and left and because of deteriorating economic conditions associated principally with declining oil prices.

After thirty years in power, Habib Bourguiba, suffering from Parkinson's Disease, became visibly senile—he could not remember things he had done the previous day and started taking irrational actions. His persecution of Islamic fundamentalists, whose number had been swollen by migration to the cities from rural areas, reached an intolerable level. Acting swiftly, former Prime Minister Zine Abidine Ben Ali declared Bourguiba incapable of carrying out his office and removed him on November 7, 1987, thus becoming president of Tunisia. The move had widespread support from all elements and factions within Tunisian society. Among his first moves, the new president commuted the sentences of

several hundred Islamic fundamentalists and suggested he would dissolve the parliament and hold elections earlier than the scheduled date in 1991. He had scheduled them for November 1989.

President Ben Ali

When it appeared that he and his party were well ahead of any competitor, President Ben Ali advanced the contest to April 1989. His judgment was correct— the *Democratic Constitutional Rally (RCD)*, the new name of Bourguiba's party, won more than 80% of the vote and all 141 seats in the National Assembly. Although the president officially welcomes political competition, he has firmly insisted that no political party shall be based on religion.

By late 1991 the Islamic fundamentalists had again bloomed and seriously threatened a tourist industry which was

A stone carver

234

reaching new heights of prosperity. The government, acting through the military in 1992, brought 171 members and leaders of the outlawed *Nahda* group before the Tunis military court. Thirty–five received life sentences, 142 received sentences of 3 to 20 years and four were acquitted. A splinter group of *Nahda*, the *Commandos of Sacrifice*, were dealt equally severe sentences. Emphasizing its intolerance of the Islamists, the government arrested women clad in traditional garb indicating their support of the "back to Islam" movement.

The president was reelected in March 1994 by a margin of 99.9% of the vote. Opposition was freely permitted (but not by Islamic fundamentalists) but won only 19 seats in the National Assembly; Ben Ali's *RCD* won 144.

As a result of [firm] [harsh] treatment (take your choice), the Islamic fundamentalists have been quite muted since 1992 unlike those in nearby Algeria. This has been necessary to preserve the vital tourist industry.

Culture: The people of Tunisia are well–educated, modern and of predominantly Arab outlook (albeit with strong European overtones). European customs have intruded into the lives of the people. French is widely spoken; the literacy rate exceeds 60%. Mosques are open to non–Moslems. The government maintains a cabinet post devoted to cultural affairs which fosters development of all forms of art and music, including a school of art and a classical music college. Another cabinet post is for the promotion of women's rights. A substantial part of the national budget is devoted to universal education. Fine collections of artifacts dating from the 6th century B.C., Roman mosaics, Arabic and Oriental manuscripts and elaborate jewelry and pottery are maintained at several museums.

In the arid, thinly populated south–southwest, a group of desert Bedouins live in black tents, raising herds of sheep and goats under a system of semi–nomadic grazing. These distinctive people have preserved the customs of their ancestors, and live today much in the same manner as they did in centuries past.

The two large port cities of Tunis and Bizerte, both located on the waters of the blue Mediterranean, contain small communities of many Europeans in addition to the urban Arab inhabitants. The handsome buildings of gleaming modern design are interrupted by the tall columns of ancient mosques from which the people are summoned to prayer each day. A unique community of Jewish people has lived on the island of Djerba in the southern part for a period of 1965 years. Tunisia somewhat hesitatingly agreed to allow the Palestinian Liberation Organization to locate within its borders after it offi-

The medina in Kairouan

cially, but not actually, departed from Lebanon in 1983.

Economy: Historically a granary of the Mediterranean, Tunisia's main export now is oil. Falling prices have not helped the overburdened economy. The country is now having difficulty in feeding its own population, even with efficient farming.

Phosphate rock, mined in the Gafsa district, is also a major export, but world prices for this fertilizer ingredient also have been falling. Refineries are being constructed to use recently discovered additional oil deposits for local consumption. Light industry, based on the processing of olive oil, fruit juices, canned fish and dates are located predominantly in urban areas. Intricately fashioned handcrafted articles, also from the cities, are treasured throughout the world.

In the past the U.S. has been a large financial contributor to the nation's aid programs, but this has been tapering off with Tunisia's comparative prosperity (more than $1,000 per capita income annually) compared to that of other nations in greater need. Foreign investment from Germany, France and the Arab na-

tions has gone into new industrial and agricultural projects to help in the problem of Tunisia's chronic unemployment among school graduates and dropouts. Anyone working more than two days a week is considered employed.

Since border tensions were eased in 1988, Libyans have been flocking to Tunisian markets that have an abundance of consumer good which cannot be bought in Libya. Currency exchange rates have made this extremely profitable—gross receipts now total well in excess of $1 billion annually—and there is no indication this trade will decrease. The Libyans are also able to enjoy some delights unavailable at home: extra–marital sex and alcohol.

The economy has been growing at a steady 4–5% annually for the last decade. Tunisia has ready access to all forms of international credit and investment.

The Future: Elections will be held in neighboring Algeria by the end of 1995. Should that country come under the control of Islamic fundamentalists, a cloud will be cast over Tunisia's present, prosperous future.

The Indian Ocean Commission
Founded in 1982, consisting of Madagascar, Mauritius, Sao Tomé and Príncipe and most recently, the Comoros, exists in name only.

THE REPUBLIC OF CAPE VERDE *(Vair*–day)

Land area and terrain: 4,040 sq. km. = 1,559 sq. mi. Ten rather mountainous islands about 400 miles off the coast of Senegal.
Population: 405,000 (estimated).
Capital City: Praia (on São Tiago island, Pop. 83,000, estimated).
Chief Commercial Products: Salt, fish, bananas.
Independence date from Portugal: July 5, 1975.
Chief of State: Antonio Mascarenhas (1990, Mas–car–*en*–has), President.

Portuguese speaking and overwhelmingly Roman Catholic, widespread demonstrations occurred when abortion was legalized in 1987. It again is a stopover point for New York–South Africa flights, which generate vitally needed revenue. Privatization of state enterprises and reduction of bureaucracy are the current programs underway in order to shore up a sagging economy.

THE DEMOCRATIC REPUBLIC OF SAO TOME AND PRINCIPE
(Sow Toe–*may* and *Preen*–see–pay)

Land area and terrain: 964 sq. km. = 372 sq. mi. São Tomé is 275 miles off the coast of Gabon; Príncipe is 125 miles off (mainland Equatorial Guinea). The islands are hilly, with good areas for farmland.
Population: 130,000 (estimated).
Capital City: São Tomé (on São Tomé island, Pop. 11,000, estimated).
Chief Commercial Products: Cacao, coffee, palm oil, bananas.
Independence date from Portugal: July 12, 1975.
Chief of State: Miguel Trovoada, President. (1990)

This small nation maintains close relations with Portugal; France pays 15 million francs a year for EC fishing rights in the island areas. The marxist–oriented sole party, the *Social Democratic Party* (Movement for the Liberation of São Tomé and Principe) remained in power from 1975 until the first multi–party elections were held in 1991. After a brief interim, it was returned to power (by coalition) in late 1994.

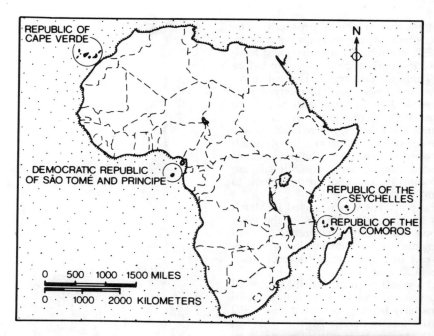

THE FEDERAL ISLAMIC REPUBLIC OF THE COMOROS

Land area and terrain: 2,170 sq. km. = 838 sq. mi. The Comoro *group* consists of four mountainous islands lying between Tanzania and the northern coast of Madagascar: Grand Comore, Anjouan, Moheli and Mayotte. The latter, with a substantial Christian minority, opposed joining the other three and, although claimed by the Republic, remains a dependency of France.
Population: 505,000 (estimated).
Capital City: Moroni (on Grand Comore, Pop. 32,000, estimated).
Chief Commercial Products: Vanilla, oils for perfumes, cloves.
Independence date from France: December 31, 1975 (declared unilaterally).
Chief of State: Said Mohammed Djohar, President.

Located close to Mozambique, this island nation has avoided involvement in the struggles which have gripped that mainland country. The president, former head of the Supreme Court, took office when his precessor was assassinated in late 1989. He was confirmed by 1990 elections. Moves toward democracy during 1991–3 were extremely rough. "Opposition" was clustered in no less than 22 parties. November 1992 elections did not occur until December 1993, at which time the president's coalition received a majority in the Federal Assembly. There were claims of election irregularities which were valid.

President René of The Seychelles

THE REPUBLIC OF THE SEYCHELLES
(Say–shells)

Land area and terrain: 100 sq. mi., about 1,000 miles off the east coast of Kenya in the Indian Ocean, consisting of some 92 islands, half of which are mountainous and very scenic. The others are little more than coral atolls.
Population: 75,000 (projected).
Capital City: Victoria (on Mahè, pronounced Mah–*hay*, pop. 21,000, estimated).
Chief Commercial Products: Coconut products, cinnamon, vanilla. European tourism is a very important source of income.
Independence date from Britain: January 29, 1976.
Chief of State: France Albert René, President, reelected to a final four–year term in mid–1989.

This very small nation flirted with communism after independence, but not seriously. Tourism from Europe is the basis for rapid resort hotel expansion. A new constitution, followed by elections in 1993 resulted in a stable government with the president's party holding a majority of legislative seats.

Selected Bibliography of Key English Language Sources

General

Adedeji, Adebayo, and Timothy M. Shaw, eds. *Economic Crisis in Africa: African Perspectives on Development Problems and Potentials.* Boulder, CO: L. Rienner, Publishers, 1985.

Bender, Gerald J. *African Crisis Areas and U.S. Foreign Policy.* Berkeley, CA: Univ. of California Press, 1985.

Birmingham, David, and Phyllis M. Martin, eds. *History of Central Africa.* London & New York: Longman, 1983. 2 vols. (Excellent maps; covers Cameroon to Zimbabwe.)

Boahen, A. Adu. *African Perspectives on Colonialism.* Baltimore, MD. Johns Hopkins University Press, 1987.

Carter, Gwendolyn and Patrick O'Meara, eds. *African Independence: The First Twenty –Five Years.* Bloomington, IN: Indiana University Press, 1985.

Chabel, Patrick, ed. *Political Domination in Africa: Reflections on the Limits of Power.* Cambridge, Cambridgeshire & New York: Cambridge University Press, 1986.

Chazan, Naomi and Timothy M. Shaw, eds. *Coping with Africa's Food Crisis.* Boulder, CO: L. Rienner, Publishers, 1988.

Chazan, Naomi, et al, eds. *Politics and Society in Contemporary Africa.* Boulder, CO: L. Rienner, Publishers, 1988.

Decalo, Samuel. *Psychoses of Power: African Personal Dictatorships.* Boulder, CO: Westview Press, 1989.

DeLancey, Mark W., ed. *Aspects of International Relations in Africa.* Bloomington, IN: African Studies Program, Indiana University, 1979.

DeLancey, Mark W., ed. *Handbook of Political Science Research on Sub-Saharan Africa: Trends from the 1960s to the 1990s.* Westport, CN: Greenwood Press, 1992.

Duignon, Peter and Robert H. Jackson, eds. *Politics and Government in African States, 1960–1985.* Stanford, CA: Hoover Institution Press, 1986.

Duignon, Peter and L.H. Gann. *The United States and Africa: A History.* Standord, CA: Hoover Institution Press, 1984.

El–Ayouti, Yassin and William I. Zartman. *The OAU After Twenty Years.* New York: Praeger, 1984.

Gifford, Prosser and Wm. Roger Louis, eds. *The Transfer of Power in Africa: Decolonization, 1960–1980.* New Haven, CT: Yale University Press, 1988. (The second of 2 vols; an extremely important resource totaling 1305 pages, combined).

Glantz, M. H., ed. *Desertification: Environmental Degradation in and Around Arid Lands.* Boulder: Westview Press, 1977.

Harrison, Lawrence E. *Underdevelopment is a State of Mind.* Lanham, MD: Center for International Affairs, Harvard University and University Press of America, 1985.

Jackson, Robert H. *Personal Rule in Black Africa.* Univ. of California Press, 1982.

July, Robert W. *A History of the African People.* New York: Scribners, 1980.

Kennedy, Dane Keith. *Islands of White: Settler Society and Culture in Kenya and Southern Rhodesia, 1890–1939.* Durham, NC: Duke University Press, 1987.

Lamb, David. *The Africans.* New York: Random House, 1982.

Liebenow, J. Gus. *African Politics: Crises and Challenges.* Bloomington, IN: Indiana University Press, 1986.

Miller, Norman and Richard Rockwell, eds. *AIDS in Africa: The Social and Policy Impact.* Lewiston: Edwin Mellen Press, 1988.

Nyang'oro, Julius E., and Timothy M. Shaw, eds. *Corporatism in Africa: Comparative Analysis and Practice.* Boulder, CO: Westview Press, 1989.

Onwuka, Ralph I. and Timothy M. Shaw, eds. *Africa in World Politics: Into the 1900s.* New York, NY: St. Martins Press, 1989.

Ottaway, David and Marina Ottaway. *Afrocommunism.* New York, NY: Africana Publishing Co., 1983.

Pakenham, Thomas. *The Scramble for Africa.* New York: Avon Books, 1992.

Putholm, Christian P. *The Theory and Practice of African Politics.* Englewood Cliffs, NJ: Prentice–Hall, 1979.

Rothchild, Donald and Naomi Chazan, eds. *The Precarious Balance: State and Society in Africa.* Boulder. CO: Westview Press, 1988.

Shavit, David. *The United States in Africa: A Historical Dictionary.* New York, NY: Greenwood Press, 1989.

Shaw, Timothy M. and Olajide Aluko, eds. *The Political Economy of African Foreign Policy: Comparative Analysis.* New York, NY: St. Martin's Press, 1984.

Shaw, Timothy M. *Towards a Political Economy for Africa: The Diaelectics of Dependence.* New York, NY: St. Martin's Press, 1985.

Sithole, Ndabiningi. *The Secret of American Success: Africa's Great Hope.* Washington DC: Gazaland Publishers, 1988 (A leader of Zimbabwe's independence movement takes a look at U.S. achievements as a model for Africans.)

Ungar, Sanford J. *Africa: The People and Politics of an Emerging Continent.* New York: Simon and Schuster, 1986.

Wilkins, Gregory L. *African Influence in the United Nations, 1967–1975: The Politics and Techniques of Gaining Compliance to UN Principles and Resolutions.* Lanham, MD: University Press of America, 1981.

Young, Crawford. *Ideology and Development in Africa.* New Haven, CT: Yale University Press, 1982.

Zartman, William I. *Conflict in the Sahara.* Washington, DC: Middle East Institute, 1979.

Coastal West Africa

Chabal, Patrick. *Amilcar Cabral: Revolutionary Leadership and People's War.* Cambridge, Cambridgeshire & New York: Cambridge University Press, 1983.

Clarke, Peter B. *West Africa and Islam: A Study of Religious Development from the 8th to the 20th Century.* London: E. Arnold, 1982.

Davidson, Basil. *No Fist is Big Enough to Hide the Sky: Liberation of Guine and Cape Verde. Aspects of an African Revolution.* London: Zed, 1981 (With a forward by Amilcar Cabral; preface by Aristides Pereira).

Decalo, Samuel. *Historical Dictionary of Benin.* 2nd ed. Metuchen, NJ: Scarecrow Press, 1987.

Decalo, Samuel. *Historical Dictionary of Togo.* 2nd ed. Metuchen, NJ: Scarecrow Press, 1987.

Deveneaux, Gustav H. K. *Power Politics in Sierra Leone.* Ibadan, Nigeria: African Universities Press, 1982.

Gailey, Harry A. *Historical Dictionary of The Gambia.* 2nd ed. Metuchen, NJ: Scarecrow Press, 1987.

Gellar, Sheldon. *Senegal—An African Nation Between Islam and the West.* Boulder, CO: Westview Press, 1982.

Harrell–Bond, Barbara E. and Sarah Forer. *Guinea–Bissau.* Hanover, NH: American Universities Field Staff, 1981.

Hart, Keith. *The Political Economy of West African Agriculture.* Cambridge and New York: Cambridge University Press, 1982

Law, Robin. *The Horse in West African History: the Role of the Horse in the Societies of Pre–Colonial West Africa.* Oxford & New York: Published for the International African Institute by the Oxford University Press, 1980.

Liebenow, J. Gus. *Liberia: The Quest for Democracy.* Bloomington, IN: Indiana University Press, 1987.

Lobban, Richard and Marilyn Halter. *Historical Dictionary of the Republic of Cape Verde.* 2nd ed. Metuchen, NJ: Scarecrow Press, 1988.

Lobban, Richard and Joshua Forrest. *Historical Dictionary of the Republic of Guinea–Bissau.* 2nd ed. Metuchen, NJ: Scarecrow Press, 1988.·

Lubeck, Paul M., ed. *The African Bourgeoisie: Capitalist Development in Nigeria, Kenya, and the Ivory Coast.* Boulder, CO: L. Rienner, 1987.

Mundt, Robert J. *Historical Dictionary of the Ivory Coast (Côte d'Ivoire).* Metuchen, NJ: Scarecrow Press, 1987.

Nelson, Harold D., ed. *Liberia, a Country Study.* 3rd ed. Washington D.C.: Foreign Area Studies, the American University, 1985 (sold by U.S. Supt. of Documents).

Onyemelukwe, J.O.C. and M.O. Filani. *Economic Geography of West Africa*. London & New York, NY: Longman, 1983.

Onyemelukwe, J.O.C. *Industrialization in West Africa*. New York, NY: St. Martin's Press, 1984.

O'Toole, Thomas. *Historical Dictionary of Guinea (Republic of Guinea/Conakry)*. 2nd ed. Metuchen, NJ: Scarecrow Press, 1987.

Pellow, Deborah and Naomi Chazan. *Ghana: Coping with Uncertainty*. Boulder, CO: Westview Press, 1986.

Ray, Donald Iain. *Ghana: Politics, Economics and Society*. Boulder, CO: L. Rienner, Publishers, 1986.

Roberts, George O. *The Anguish of Third World Independence: The Sierra Leone Experience*. Washington, DC: Univ. Press of America, 1982.

Central West Africa

DeLancey, Mark W. *Historical Dictionary of the Republic of Cameroon*. Metuchen, NJ, Scarecrow Press, 1990.

Diamond, Larry Jay. *Class, Ethnicity and Democracy in Nigeria: The Failure of the First Republic*. Syracuse, NY: Syracuse University Press, 1988.

Fegley, Randall. *Equatorial Guinea: An African Tragedy*. NY, P. Lang, 1989.

Kalck, Pierre. *Historical Dictionary of the Central African Republic*. 2nd ed. Translated by Thomas O'Toole. Metuchen, NJ, Scarecrow Press, 1992.

Kirk–Greene, Anthony Hamilton Millard and Douglas Rimmer. *Nigeria Since 1970*. New York, NY: Africana Publ Co., 1981.

Lubeck, Paul M. *The African Bourgeoisis* . . . (see Coastal West Africa).

Lubeck, Paul M. *Islam and Urban Labor in Northern Nigeria: The Making of a Muslim Working Class*. Cambridge Univ. Press, 1986.

O'Toole, Thomas. *The Central African Republic: The Continent's Hidden Heart*. Boulder, CO: Westview Press, 1986.

Oyewole, A. *Historical Dictionary of Nigeria*. Metuchen, NJ: Scarecrow Press, 1987.

Schiavo–Campo, Salvatore, et al, eds. *The Tortoise Walk: Public Policy and Private Activity in the Economic Development of Cameroon*. Washington, DC: U.S. Agency for International Development, 1983 (AID Evaluation Special Study No. 10).

Shaw, Timothy M. and Olajide Aluko, eds. *Nigerian Foreign Policy: Alternative Perceptions and Projections*. New York, NY: St. Martin's Press, 1983.

Zartman, I. William, ed. *The Political Economy of Nigeria*. New York: Praeger, 1983.

Equatorial West Africa

Aicardi de Saint–Paul, Marc. *Gabon: The Development of a Nation*. Translated by A., F., and T. Palmer. NY, Routledge, 1989.

Angola, an Introductory Economic Review. Washington, DC, World Bank, 1991.

Bobb, F. Scott. *Historical Dictionary of Zaïre*. Metuchen, NJ: Scarecrow Press, 1988.

Denny, L.M. *Sao Tome and Principe*. [Second of two titles bound with J. Torp. *Mozambique*. See under **Southern Africa**.]

Hodges, Tony. *Sao Tomé and Principe: From Plantation Colony to Microstate*. Boulder, CO: Westview Press, 1988.

MacGaffey, Janet. *Entrepreneurs and Parasites: The Struggle for Indigenous Capitalism in Zaire*. Cambridge Univ. Press, 1987.

Thompson, Virginia McLean and Richard Adloff. *Historical Dictionary of the People's Republic of the Congo*. 2nd ed. Metuchen, NJ: Scarecrow Press, 1984.

Young, Crawford and Thomas Turner. *The Rise and Decline of the Zaïrian State*. Madison, WI: University of Wisconsin Press, 1985.

Southern Africa

Akenson, Donald Harman. *God's Peoples: Covenant and Land in South Africa, Israel, and Ulster*. Cornell Univ. Press, 1992.

Andersson, Hilary. *Mozambique: A War Against the People*. New York St, Martin's Press, 1992.

Barber, James P., Jesmond Blumenfeld and Christopher R. Hall. *The West and South Africa*. London: Royal Institute of International Affairs; London & Boston: Routledge and Kegan Paul, 1982

Bardill, John E. *Lesotho: Dilemmas of Dependence in Southern Africa*. Boulder, CO: Westview Press, 1983.

Blumenthal, Jesmond, ed. *South Africa in Crisis*. London & New York: Croom Helm for the Royal Institute of International Affairs, 1987.

Booth, Alan R. *Swaziland: Tradition and Change in a Southern African Kingdom*. Boulder, CO: Westview Press, 1983.

Brewer, John D. *After Soweto: An Unfinished Journey*. New York, NY: Clarendon Press, 1986.

Burdette, Marcia M. *Zambia: Between Two Worlds*. Boulder, CO: Westview Press, 1988.

Caute, David. *Under the Skin: The Death of White Rhodesia*. Northwestern Univ. Press, 1983.

Cell, John W. *The Highest State of White Supremacy: the Origins of Segregation in South Africa and the American South*. Cambridge, Cambridgeshire & New York, NY: Cambridge University Press, 1982.

Colclough, Christopher. *The Political Economy of Botswana: A Study of Growth and Distribution*. Oxford Univ. Press, 1980.

Davis, Stephen M. *Apartheid's Rebels: Inside South Africa's Hidden War*. New Haven, CT: Yale University Press, 1987.

Ellis, Stephen. *Comrades against Apartheid: The ANC & the South African Communist Party in Exile*. Indiana Univ. Press, 1992.

Frederikse, Julie. *The Unbreakable Thread: Non–racialism in South Africa*. Indiana Univ. Press, 1990.

Gann, Lewis H. and Thomas H. Henriksen. *The Struggle for Zimbabwe: Battle in the Bush*. New York, NY: Praeger, 1981.

Grundy, Kenneth W. *Soldiers Without Politics: Blacks in the South African Armed Forces*. Univ. of California Press, 1983.

Grundy, Kenneth W. *South Africa: Domestic Crisis and Global Challenge*. Boulder, Westview Press, 1991.

Harris, Betty J. *The Political Economy of the Southern African Periphery: Cottage Industries, Factories, and Female Wage Labour in Swaziland Compared*. New York: St. Martin's Press, 1993.

Hartland–Thunberg, Penelope. *Botswana: an African Growth Economy*. Boulder, CO: Westview Press, 1978.

Holland, Heidi. *The Struggle: A History of the African National Congress*, NY, G. Braziller, 1990.

Horowitz, Donald L. *A Democratic South Africa?: Constitutional Engineering in a Divided Society*. Berkeley, CA: Univ. of California Press, 1991.

Isaacman, Allen F. *Mozambique: From Colonialism to Revolution, 1900–1982*. Boulder: Westview Press, 1983.

Johns, Sheridan, ed. *Mandela, Tambo, and the African National Congress: The Struggle against Apartheid, 1948–1990: A Documentary Survey*. Oxford Univ. Press, 1991.

Johnson, Phyllis. *Apartheid Terrorism: The Destabilization Report*. Indiana Univ. Press, 1989.

Kaplan, Irving, ed. *Zambia, a Country Study*. 3rd ed. Washington, DC: Foreign Area Studies, American University, 1979 (sold by the U.S. Supt. of Documents).

Keller, Edmond J., ed. *South Africa in Southern Africa: Domestic Change and International Conflict*. Boulder, L. Rienner, 1989.

Kelly, Michael J. *Education in a Declining Economy: The Case of Zambia, 1975–1985*. Washington, D.C., World Bank, 1991.

Kempton, Daniel R. *Soviet Strategy toward Southern Africa: The National Liberation Movement Connection*. NY, Praeger, 1989.

Kitchen, Helen, ed. *South Africa in Transition to What?* New York, NY: Praeger: Washington, D.C.: Published with the Center for Strategic and International Studies, 1988.

Kuper, Hilda. *The Swazi: A South African Kingdom*. 2nd ed. NY, Holt, Rinehart, & Winston, 1986.

Lamar, Howard and Leonard Thompson, eds. *The Frontier in History: North America and Southern Africa Compared*. New Haven, CT: Yale University Press, 1981.

Legum, Colin. *The Battlefronts of Southern Africa*. New York: Africana Pub. Co., 1988.

Meer, Fatima. *Higher than Hope: The Authorized Biography of Nelson Mandela*. NY, Harper & Row, 1990.

Mermelstein, David, ed. *The Anti-Apartheid Reader: The Struggle Against White Racist Rule in South Africa*. New York, Grove Press, 1987.

Nelson, Harold D., ed. *Mozambique: a Country Study*. 3rd ed. Washington, DC: Foreign Area Studies, American University, 1985 (sold by the U.S. Supt. of Documents).

Neuhaus, Richard John. *Dispensations: The Future of South Africa as South Africans See It*. Grand Rapids, MI: W.B. Eerdmans Pub. Co. 1986.

Norval, Morgan. *Inside the ANC: The Evolution of a Terrorist Organization*. Washington, DC, Selous Foundation, 1990.

Parson, Jack. *Botswana: Liberal Democracy and the Labor Reserve in Southern Africa*. Boulder, CO: Westview Press, 1984.

Parson, Jack, ed. *Succession to High Office in Botswana: Three Case Studies*. Athens, OH: Ohio Univ. Center for International Studies, 1990.

Pottier, Johan. *Migrants No More: Settlement and Survival in Mambwe Villages, Zambia*. Indiana Univ. Press, 1988.

Soggot, David. *Namibia: The Violent Heritage*. NY, St. Martin's Press, 1986.

Staunton, Irene, ed. *Mothers of the Revolution: The War Experiences of Thirty Zimbabwean Women*. Indiana Univ. Press, 1991.

Stoneman, Colin. *Zimbabwe: Politics, Economics, and Society*. NY, Pinter Publishers, 1989.

Tambo, Oliver. *Preparing for Power: Oliver Tambo Speaks*. Compiled by Adelaide Tambo. NY, G. Braziller, 1988.

Torp, Jens Erik. *Mozambique*. NY, Pinter Publishers, 1989. [also contains L. Denny. *São Tomé and Príncipe*. See under Equatorial West Africa].

Vail, Leroy and Landeg White. *Capitalism and Colonialism in Mozambique: a Study of Quelimane District*. Minneapolis, MN: University of Minnesota Press, 1980.

Van Zyl Slabbert, Frederik. *The Last White Parliament: The Struggle for South Africa by the Leader of the White Opposition*. New York, NY: St. Martin's Press, 1987.

Wilson, Monica and Leonard Thompson, eds. *The Oxford History of South Africa*. New York, NY: Oxford University Press, 1969–1971, 2 vols.

Wiseman, Henry. *From Rhodesia to Zimbabwe: The Politics of Transition*. New York: Pergamon Press, 1981.

Periodicals
National Media Limited (40 Heerengracht, Capetown, South Africa) *Focus on South Africa*. A collection of press articles and short essays published by the government which is reasonably objective.

M*Com PR Consultancy (P.O. Box 220, Paardekraal 1752, Republic of South Africa) *Focus on South Africa*. A collection of press articles and short essays which is informative and objective. 6 mos. $43. U.S., 1 yr. $65. U.S. Highly recommended.

Argus Publications (P.O. Box 15643, 78 Queen Victoria Street, Vlaeburg, 8018, South Africa) *Leadership*. This handsome periodical has not hesitated to publish articles constructively critical of the government and leadership of all contesting factions in South Africa, particularly insofar as they involve race relations. In-depth interviews provide much insight on contemporary issues.

Videotape
Zulu. This 1964 British epic is now available as a videotape. Narrated by the late Sir Richard Burton, starring Jack Hawkins, it depicts British efforts to defend missionary stations in South Africa during the colonial era. With about half of it devoted to vivid battle scenes, it is exciting and generally historically accurate, although overplayed.

East African Island Nations
Bunge, Frederica M., ed. *Indian Ocean: Five Island Countries*. (Area Handbook Series) Washington, DC, 1983. Sold by Supt. of Documents. Chapters on Madagascar, Mauritius, Comoros, and Seychelles.

Covell, Maureen. *Madagascar: Politics, Economics, and Society*. NY, F. Pinter, 1987.

Franda, Marcus F. *The Seychelles: Unquiet Islands*. Boulder, CO: Westview Press, 1982.

Huntington, Richard. *Gender and Social Structure in Madagascar*. Bloomington, IN: Indiana University Press, 1988.

Kottak, Conrad Phillip, ed. *Madagascar: Society and History*. Durham, NC: Carolina Academic Press, 1986.

Newitt, M.D.D. *The Comoro Islands: Struggle Against Dependency in the Indian Ocean*. Boulder, CO: Westview Press, 1984

Ostheimer, John M., ed. *The Politics of the Western Indian Ocean Islands*. New York, NY: Praeger, 1975.

Eastern Africa
Abeda Tesfagiorgis. *A Painful Season & A Stubborn Hope: The Odyssey of an Eritrean Mother*. Trenton, NJ: Red Sea Press, 1992.

Clapham, Christopher S. *Transformation and Continuity in Revolutionary Ethiopia*. Cambridge Univ. Press, 1988.

Coulson, Andrew. *Tanzania: A Political Economy*. Oxford Univ. Press, 1982.

Hazelwood, Arthur. *Education, Work, and Pay in East Africa*. Oxford Univ. Press, 1989.

Hodd, Michael, ed. *Tanzania after Nyerere*. NY, Pinter Publishers, 1988.

Iliffe, John A. *A Modern History of Tanganyika*. Cambridge & New York, NY; Cambridge University Press, 1979.

Jorgensen, Jan Jelmert. *Uganda: A Modern History*. New York: St. Martin's Press, 1981.

Keller, Edmond J. *Revolutionary Ethiopia: From Empire to People's Republic*. Indiana Univ. Press, 1988.

Laitin, David D. *Somalia: Nation in Search of a State*. Boulder, CO: Westview Press, 1987.

Lewis, I.M. *A Modern History of Somalia: Nation and State in the Horn of Africa*. Rev. ed. Boulder, CO: Westview Press, 1988.

Lubeck, Paul M. *The African Bourgeoisis* . . . (see Coastal West Africa).

Miller, Norman N. *Kenya: The Quest for Prosperity*. Boulder, CO: Westview Press, 1984.

Mirza, Sarah, ed. *Three Swahili Women: Life Histories from Mombasa, Kenya*. Indiana Univ. Press, 1989.

Nelson, Harold D. and Irving Kaplan, eds. *Ethiopia, a Country Study* 3rd ed. Washington, DC: Foreign Area Studies, the American University, 1981 (sold by the U.S. Supt. of Documents).

Nelson, Harold D. ed. *Kenya, a Country Study*. 3rd ed. Washington, DC: Foreign Area Studies, The American University, 1984 (sold by the U.S. Supt. of Documents).

Saint Veran, Robert and Robert Tholomier. *Djibouti: Pawn of the Horn of Africa*. An abridged tranlation and postscript by Virginia Thompson and Richard Adloff. Metuchen, NJ: Scarecrow Press, 1981.

Smith, George Ivan. *Ghosts of Kampala*. New York, NY: St. Martin's Press, 1980.

Wubneh, Mulaty and Yohannis Abate. *Ethiopia: Transition and Development in the Horn of Africa*. Boulder, CO: Westview Press, 1988.

Yeager, Rodger. *Tanzania: An African Experiment*. 2nd ed. Boulder, CO: Westview Press, 1989.

South Sahara Africa
Decalo, Samuel. *Historical Dictionary of Chad*. 2nd ed. Metuchen, NJ: Scarecrow Press, 1987.

Decalo, Samuel. *Historical Dictionary of Niger*. 2nd ed. Metuchen, NJ: Scarecrow Press, 1989.

Deng, Francis Mading and Prosser Gifford, eds. *The Search for Peace and Unity in the Sudan*. Washington, DC: Wilson Center Press, Lanham MD, 1987.

Eprile, Cecil. *War and Peace in the Sudan, 1955–1972*. Newton Abbott, Devon, North Pomfret, VT: Davis & Charles, 1974.

Fuglestad, Finn. *A History of Niger, 1850–1960*. Cambridge Univ. Press, 1983.

Imperato, Pascal James. *Historical Dictionary of Mali*. 2nd ed. Metuchen, NJ: Scarecrow Press, 1986.

Niblock, Tim. *Class and Power in Sudan: The Dynamics of Sudanese Politics, 1898–1985*. Albany, NY: State University of New York Press, 1987.

Porch, Douglas. *The Conquest of the Sahara*. New York: Knopf, 1984.

Thompson, Virginia McLean. *Conflict in Chad*. Berkeley, CA: Institute of International Studies, University of California, 1981.

North Africa

Abun–Nasir, Jamil M. *A History of the Maghrib*. 2nd ed. Cambridge & New York, NY: Cambridge University Press, 1975.

Allan, John Anthony. *Libya: The Experience of Oil*. Boulder: Westview Press, 1981.

Baker, Raymond William. *Egypt's Uncertain Revolution Under Nasser and Sadat*. Cambridge, MA: Harvard University Press, 1978 (a study of their influence on Egyptian society).

Bearman, Jonathan *Qadhafi's Libya*. (With a forward by Claudia Wright. London and Atlantic Highlands, NJ: Zed Books, 1986 (argues that Libya is socially revolutionary, but is not a socialist society, pinpointing the weaknesses and contradictions in the transformation).

Bennoune, Mahfoud. *The Making of Contemporary Algeria, 1830–1987*. Cambridge University Press, 1988.

Cambridge Encyclopedia of the Middle East and North Africa. Cambridge University Press, 1988.

Cooley, John K. *Libyan Sandstorm*. New York: Holt, Rinehart & Winston, 1982 (a journalists observations at the scene).

Damis, John James. *Conflict in Northwest Africa: The Western Sahara Dispute*. Stanford, CA: Hoover Institution Press, 1983 (points out that Greater Morocco, including Western Sahara, constitutes a national, historical, geographic and social entity under the spiritual authority of the King).

Davis, John. *Libyan Politics: Tribe and Revolution: An Account of the Zuwaya and their Government*. Univ. of California Press, 1988.

Deeb, Marius. *Libya since the Revolution: Aspects of Social and Political Development*. New York: Praeger, 1982.

Drysdale, Alasdair. *The Middle East and North Africa: A Political Geography*. New York: Oxford University Press, 1985.

Farnie, D.A. *East and West of Suez: The Suez Canal in History*. Oxford: Clarendon Press, 1969 (a comprehensive study).

Girgis, Monir S. *Mediterranean Africa*. Lanham, MD: University Press of America, 1987.

Goldschmidt, Arthur. *Modern Egypt: The Formation of a Nation–State*. Boulder, CO: Westview Press, 1988.

Heggoy, Alf Andrew. *Insurgency and Counterinsurgency in Algeria*. Bloomington, IN: Indiana University Press, 1972 (argues that the French won the military struggle but the *FLN* influenced the minds of the French and won the political struggle).

Hinnebusch, Raymond A., Jr. *Egyptian Politics Under Sadat: The Post–Populist Development of an Authoritarian–Modernizing State*. Cambridge, Cambridgeshire & New York, NY: Cambridge University Press, 1985.

Hirst, David and Irene Benson. *Sadat*. London: Faber & Faber, 1981 (a study of Sadat's early years).

Hodges, Tony, *Western Sahara: The Roots of a Desert War*. Westport, CT: L. Hill, 1983.

Hutchinson, Martha Crenshaw. *Revolutionary Terrorism: The FLN in Algeria, 1954–1962*. Stanford, CA: Stanford University, 1978 (attempts to avoid making a moral judgment for or against terrorism and to analyze the impact of the use of terror in the Algerian struggle for independence).

Ismael, Tareq Y. *The Communist Movement in Egypt, 1920–1988*. Syracuse, NY: Syracuse Univ. Press, 1990.

Keenan, Jeremy. *The Tuareg: People of Ahaggar*. New York, NY: St. Martin's Press, 1977 (the social and economic structure of the people of southeastern Algeria, their resistance to change and their integration into post–independence Algeria).

Lawless, Richard, ed. *North Africa: Contemporary Politics and Economic Development*. New York: St. Martin's Press, 1984.

Lemarchand, Rene, ed. *The Green and the Black: Qadhafi's Politics in Africa*. Indiana Univ. Press, 1988.

Long, David E., ed. *The Government and Politics of the Middle East and North Africa*. 2nd ed. Boulder, CO: Westview Press, 1986.

McDermott, Anthony. *Egypt from Nasser to Mubarak: A Flawed Revolution*. NY, Croom Helm, 1988.

Metz, Helen Chapin, ed. *Libya, a Country Study*. 4th ed. Washington, DC: Federal Research Division, Library of Congress, 1988. (For sale by the U.S. Supt. of Documents).

Nelson, Harold D., ed. *Algeria, a Country Study*. 4th ed. 1986; *Morocco, a Country Study*. 5th ed. 1985; *Tunisia, a Country Study*. 3rd ed. 1986, Washington, DC: From American University's Foreign Area Studies (all of these are sold by the U.S. Supt. of Documents).

Norris, H.T. *The Arab Conquest of the Western Sahara. Studies of the historical events, religious beliefs and social customs which made the remotest Sahara a part of the Arab World*. Burnt Mill, Harlow, Essex: Longman; Beirut, Lebanon: Librarie du Liban, 1986 (places the migrations of the 14th through the 17th centuries in the context of Spanish expansion and the rise of warrior clans which Arabized themselves to achieve social status, a process still taking place).

Norris, H.T. *The Tuaregs: Their Islamic Legacy and Its Diffusion in the Sahel*. Warminster: Aris & Phillips, 1975.

Nyrop, Richard F., ed. *Egypt, a Country Study*. Washington, DC: Foreign Area Studies, the American University, 1983 (sold by the U.S. Supt. of Documents).

Piscatori, James P., ed. *Islam in the Political Process*. Cambridge Univ. Press, 1983. (contains chapter on Algeria).

Reich, Bernard, ed. *Political Leaders of the Contemporary Middle East and North Africa: A Biographical Dictionary*. New York: Greenwood Press, 1990.

Rosen, Lawrence. *Bargaining for Reality: The Construction of Social Relations in a Muslim Community*. Chicago, IL: University of Chicago Press, 1984 (a study of the social life of the Moroccan city of Sefrou).

Simon, Reeve S., ed. *The Middle East and North Africa: Essays in Honor of J. C. Hurewitz*. New York: Middle East Institute, Columbia University, 1990.

Talbott, John E. *The War Without a Name: France in Algeria, 1954–1962*. New York, NY: Knopf. Distributed by Random House, 1980 (a study of the Algerian War from the French points of view, both pro and con).

Thompson, Virginia McLean and Richard Adloff. *The Western Saharans: Background to Conflict*. London: Croom Helm; Totowa, NJ: Barnes & Noble Books, 1980.

Vatikiotis, Panayiotis J. *The History of Egypt*. 3rd ed, Baltimore, MD: Johns Hopkins University Press, 1986 (places particular emphasis on recent years).

Vatikiotis, Panayiotis J. *Nasser and His Generation*. New York, NY: St. Martin's Press, 1978.

Waterbury, John. *The Egypt of Nasser and Sadat: The Political Economy of Two Regimes*. Princeton Univ. Press, 1983.

Wright, John L. *Libya, a Modern History*. Baltimore, MD: Johns Hopkins University Press, 1982.

Zartman, I. William, ed. *The Political Economy of Morocco*. NY, Praeger, 1987.

Zartman, I. William, ed. *Tunisia: The Political Economy of Reform*. Boulder, L. Rienner, 1991.